Visual culture: the reader

Visual Culture: The Reader

This Reader provides some of the set readings for a 16-week module (D850 *The Image and Visual Culture*) which is offered by The Open University Masters in Social Sciences Programme.

The Open University Masters in Social Sciences

The MA Programme enables students to select from a range of modules to create a programme to suit their own professional or personal development. Students can choose from a range of social science modules to obtain an MA in Social Sciences, or may specialize in a particular subject area. D850 *The Image and Visual Culture* is one of the modules leading to an MA in Cultural and Media Studies.

At present there are three study lines leading to:

an MA in Cultural and Media Studies
an MA in Environmental Policy and Society
an MA in Psychological Research Methods.

Other study lines being planned include an MSc in Psychology and an MA in Social Policy/MA in Social Policy and Criminology.

OU Supported Learning

The Open University's unique, supported open ('distance') learning Masters Programme in Social Sciences is designed to introduce the concepts, approaches, theories and techniques associated with a number of academic areas of study. The MA in Social Sciences programme provides great flexibility. Students study in their own environments, in their own time, anywhere in the European Union. They receive specially prepared course materials, benefit from structured tutorial support throughout all the coursework and assessment assignments, and have the chance to work with other students.

How to apply

If you would like to register for this programme, or simply find out more information, please write for the Masters in Social Sciences prospectus to the Course Reservations Centre, PO Box 724, The Open University, Walton Hall, Milton Keynes, MK7 6ZW, UK (Telephone +44 (0) 1908 653232).

Visual culture: the reader

edited by
Jessica Evans
and Stuart Hall

visual culture

SAGE Publications
London • Thousand Oaks • New Delhi

in association with The Open University

SAGE Publications Ltd
6 Bonhill Street
London EC2A 4PU

SAGE Publications Inc.
2455 Teller Road
Thousand Oaks, California 91320

SAGE Publications India Pvt Ltd
32, M-Block Market
Greater Kailash – I
New Delhi 110 048

British Library Cataloguing in Publication data

A catalogue record for this book is available
from the British Library

ISBN 0 7619 6247 6
ISBN 0 7619 6248 4 (pbk)

Library of Congress catalog record available

Text and cover design: Barker/Hilsdon
Typeset by Mayhew Typesetting, Rhayader, Powys
Printed in Great Britain by The Cromwell Press Ltd,
Trowbridge, Wiltshire

Contents

Notes on contributors

Louis Althusser (1918–1990) was a French Marxist philosopher known for his theoretical reformulations of classic Marxism. His memoirs were published after his suicide as *The Future Lasts a Long Time* (1993). His publications include *Lenin and Philosophy and Other Essays* (1972), *Reading Capital* (1975), *For Marx* (1977), *Philosophy and the Spontaneous Philosophy of the Scientists* (1989).

Roland Barthes (1915–1980) studied French literature and classics at the University of Paris. He was Directeur d'Études at the École Pratique des Hautes Études where he taught a course on the sociology of signs, symbols and collective representations. His books include *S/Z, Elements of Semiology* (1964), *The Fashion System* (1967), *Mythologies* (1967), *Writing Degree Zero* (1967), *A Lover's Discourse* (1979), *Image, Music Text* (1977).

Walter Benjamin (1892–1940) was a German-Jewish writer whose wide-ranging work in poetry and literature, Marxism and cultural commentary was only recognized years after his death. He was never a member of the Frankfurt School but had debates and disagreements with some of their central members. His works translated into English are mostly collections of essays, and they include: *Illuminations* (1969, ed. H. Arendt), *Charles Baudelaire* (1977), *Understanding Brecht* (1977), *One-way Street and Other Writings* (1979), *Moscow Diary* (1986).

Homi Bhabha is Professor of Art History and of English in the Department of Art History at the University of Chicago. He researches in the areas of colonial and post-colonial theory, cosmopolitanism, nineteenth and twentieth century British and other English language literatures. His publications include *Nation and Narration* (1990), *The Location of Culture* (1994), and, with Pier Luigi Tazzi, *Anish Kapoor* (1998).

Pierre Bourdieu is Professor of Sociology at the Collège de France and Director of Studies at the École des Hautes Études en Sciences Sociales. A sociologist whose work is strongly rooted in anthropology, he has published numerous influential books and essays in the fields of the sociology of education, leisure, consumption and culture. His publications include *Photography: A Middlebrow Art* (1965), *Outline of a Theory of Practice* (1977), *Homo Academicus* (1988), *The Logic of Practice* (1990), *Language and Symbolic Power* (1991), *The Rules of Art* (1992), *The Field of Cultural Production* (1993).

Norman Bryson is Professor of Fine Arts at Harvard University and previously Director of English Studies at King's College, Cambridge. He was educated at Cambridge, the University of California at Berkeley, and the Courtauld Institute, London. His publications include *Vision and Painting* (1983), *Word and Image: French painting of the Ancien Regime* (1983) *Looking at the Overlooked: Four Essays on Still Life Painting* (1990). He co-edited *Visual Culture: Images of Interpretation* (1994).

Victor Burgin is an artist and writer. He teaches semiotic and psychoanalytic theory of images in the History of Consciousness Program at the University of California, Santa Cruz. His books include the edited collection *Thinking Photography* (1982), *Between* (1986), *The End of Art Theory: Criticism and Postmodernity* (1986), *In/Different Spaces: Place and Memory in Visual Culture* (1986), *Passages* (1991). His catalogues include *Some Cities* (1996).

Elizabeth Cowie is Senior Lecturer in Film Studies in the School of Arts and Image Studies at Kent University and one of the founding editors, in 1978, of the feminist theory journal *M/F*. She has published *Representing the Woman: Cinema and Psychoanalysis* (1997) and edited, with Parveen Adams, *The Woman in Question: M/F* (1990).

Douglas Crimp an art critic and AIDS activist currently teaches gay and lesbian studies at Sarah Lawrence College, US. He was co-editor of *October* for thirteen years and his collection of essays on art and photography, *On the Museum's Ruins*, was published in 1993. He co-wrote, with Adam Rolston, *AIDS Demo Graphics* (1990), and edited *AIDS: Cultural Analysis/Cultural Activism* (1988).

Guy Debord (1932–1994) was a key member of the Situationist International, established in 1957, and contributor to its journal *Internationale Situationniste* until its demise in 1969. Some of his writings can be found in the *Situationist International Anthology* (1981). His book *Society of the Spectacle* (1967) provided the more sober theoretical foundation for the movement, drawing from the work of Marx, Hegel, and Lukacs, in contrast to SI member Raul Vaneigem's more passionate and anecdotal *The Revolution of Everyday Life*, published in the same year. It has been said that the ideas of Baudrillard, and, to a lesser extent Lyotard, can be directly attributed to Debord – an observation which is born out by

Debord's *Comments on the Society of the Spectacle*, first published in France in 1988.

Mary Ann Doane is Professor of Modern Culture and Media at Brown University, Rhode Island. She is the author of *The Desire to Desire: the Woman's Film of the 1940s* (1987) and co-editor of *Revision: Essays in Feminist Film Criticism* (1984), *Femme Fatales: Feminism, Film Theory, Psychoanalysis* (1991).

Richard Dyer is Professor of Film Studies in the Department of Film and Television Studies at Warwick University. His many publications include *The Matter of Images: Essays on Representation* (1993), *The Silent Screen* (1997), *Stars* (1998, second edition), and *White* (1997).

Jessica Evans is Lecturer in Cultural and Media Studies in the Sociology Discipline at the Open University. She has published on photography and visual culture, and is currently researching in psychoanalysis and its relations with popular culture. She is editor of *The Camerawork Essays* (1997).

Franz Fanon (1925–1961) was born in the French colony of Martinique, leaving to join the Free French in the Second World War. He remained in France after the war to study essays and plays and while there wrote his most influential statement of anti-colonial revolutionary thought, *Black Skin, White Masks* (1952). In 1953, Fanon became Head of the Psychiatry Department at the Blida-Joinville Hospital in Algeria, during which time the war for Algerian independence broke out. He resigned his post with the French government to work for the Algerian cause. He continued to work openly with the Algerian independence movement from both Tunisia and Ghana but developed leukaemia. He completed his final indictment of the colonial condition *The Wretched of the Earth* (1961), which was published by Jean-Paul Sartre in the year of his death.

Otto Fenichel (d. circa 1970), worked as a psychoanalyst in Germany in the 1930s, but in the Nazi period was exiled to Oslo and later moved to the USA. A Freudian, he wrote three carefully reasoned papers in 1935 complicating Freud's thesis of the development of the girl through the Oedipal phase and the need to shift her love to the father. He was also a Marxist and with Wilhelm Reich, from whose work he later distanced himself, wrote a paper entitled 'Psychoanalysis and dialectical materialism' and followed this up with is own 'The drive to amass wealth' (1938), amongst others. His papers are collected in the two volume *The Collected Papers of Otto Fenichel* (1954, eds H. Fenichel and D. Rapaport).

Michel Foucault (1926–1984) social scientist, philosopher and historian of ideas, was Professor of History and Systems of Thought at the Collège de France. One of the most celebrated and intellectually controversial intellectuals of the twentieth century, he wrote frequently for French newspapers and reviews, and edited *Critique*. His many books include: *History of Sexuality, Madness and Civilisation* (1961), *The Order of Things* (1966), *The Archaeology of Knowledge* (1969), *The Birth of the Clinic* (1973), *Discipline and Punish* (1975). His collections of interviews and essays include *Language, Counter-Memory, Practice* (1977, ed. D. Bouchard) and *Power and Knowledge* (1980, ed. C. Gordon).

Sigmund Freud (1856–1939) lived and worked in Vienna, and died in Hampstead London in 1939. Trained as a neuropathologist, Freud invented psychoanalysis as a technique of free association whereby through a relationship between patient and the analyst and by means of the latter's interpretation, both a cure and an understanding of human nature could be achieved. He attempted to develop a scientific approach to the understanding of the human mind, proposing structures of mind and of development based on the concepts of repression and the unconscious, sexual drives and sexual difference. The foundation of his metapsychology was his clinical work, and he wrote numerous case studies and essays on the techniques of psychotherapy. His most important papers are generally considered to be *The Interpretation of Dreams* (1900) and *Three Essays on Sexuality* (1905). His ideas are continually examined critically but have entered into the language and he remains one of the most influential figures of the twentieth century.

Jane Gaines is Associate Professor of Literature and English, and directs the Film and Video Program at Duke University, US. Her interests are film, television theory, feminist theory, critical legal studies and cultural studies. Her recent work is in African and African-American literature and film melodrama. She has published *Contested Culture: The Image, the Voice and the Law* (1991) and is now working on a book on early cinema entitled *Other/Race/Desire*.

Dick Hebdige is Dean of the School of Critical Studies at the California Institute of Arts. From 1984–92 he was Reader in Communications at the Department of Media and Communications, Goldsmiths College, London. He has written extensively on popular culture, contemporary art and design, and anthropology of consumption and media and critical theory. He has published *Subculture: The Meaning of Style* (1979), *Cut 'n' Mix: Culture, Identity and Carribean Music* (1987), and *Hiding in the Light: On Images and Things* (1988), as well as numerous catalogue essays on contemporary art.

Rosalind Krauss is co-editor and co-founder of the journal *October* and a Professor of Art History at Hunter College in New York. Her numerous publications in critical art theory include *The Originality of the Avant-Garde and Other Modernist Myths* (1986), *The Optical Unconscious* (1994), *The Picasso Papers* (1998). She also co-edited, with Jane Livingstone, *L'Amour Fou: Women and Surrealism* (1986), and with Annette Michelson, *October: The Second Decade 1986–1996* (1998).

Kobena Mercer is a writer, critic and lecturer. He has published *Welcome to the Jungle: New Positions in Black Cultural Studies* (1994), *Self-Evident* (1995) and *Mirage: Enigmas of Race, Difference and Desire* (1996) and written essays in the field of art and photographic criticism.

Laura Mulvey is a film-maker, critic, and feminist cultural theorist. She is Director of the MA in Cinema and Television Studies at the British Film Institute/Birkbeck College, London. She has published *Visual and Other Pleasures* (1989) and *Fetishism and Curiosity* (1996) and the BFI Film Classic *Citizen Kane*.

Mary-Louise Pratt is Professor in the Department of Spanish and Portugese, and of Comparative Literature, at Stanford University, California. Her publications include *Imperial Eyes* (1992) *Profane Passions, Politics and Culture in the Americas* (co-authored with J. Franco 1999), *Towards a Speech Art Theory of Literary Discourse* (1977) and *Amor Brujo: Images and Culture of Love in the Andes*, co-authored with Louis Millones (1990).

Jacqueline Rose is Professor of English at Queen Mary and Westfield College, University of London. She is well known for her work on female sexuality and Lacanian theory. She is author of *Sexuality in the Field of Vision* (1986), *The Case of Peter Pan: Or, the Impossibility of Children's Fiction* (1992), *Why War? Psychoanalysis and the Return to Melanie Klein* (1993) and *States of Fantasy: The Clarendon Lectures in English Literature* (1996). She co-edited, with Juliet Mitchell, *Feminine Sexuality – Jacques Lacan and the École Freudienne* (1982).

Susan Sontag is a prolific critic in the fields of art, photography and literary criticism and critical cultural theory. She is also a writer of short stories, plays and novels. Amongst her publications are *On Photography* (1977), *Against Interpretation* (1978), *Aids and its Metaphors* (1988) and *Illness as Metaphor* (1988). Collections of her key essays in cultural criticism are published as *A Susan Sontag Reader* (1982) and *Under the Sign of Saturn* (1991). She is also the editor of *A Barthes Reader* (1983).

Allan Sekula is a photographic artist and photographic theorist and historian. He is Director of the photography programme at the California Institute of the Arts. His many essays on photography and catalogues of his own work include *Photography Against the Grains: Essays and Photo Works 1973–1983* (1984), *Geography Lesson: Canadian Notes* (1997), and with Benjamin H.D. Bucholh, *Fish Story* (1995).

Kaja Silverman is author of *The Subject of Semiotics* (1983), *The Acoustic Mirror: The Female Voice in Psychoanalysis and Cinema* (1988), *Male Subjectivity at the Margins* (1992) and *The Threshold of the Visible World* (1995).

Don Slater is Lecturer in Sociology at Goldsmiths College, University of London. His research focuses on theories of consumer culture, economic sociology and photography. Publications include *Consumer Culture and Modernity* (1997).

Abigail Solomon-Godeau is a photographic theorist and art historian. She has published extensively in journals such as *Afterimage, Art in America, Camera Obscura, October*, the *Print Collector's Newsletter*, and *Screen*. A book of her collected essays, *Photography at the Dock*, was published in 1991. Since then she has published *Mistaken Identities* (1993) and *Male Trouble: A Crisis in Representation* (1997).

Jackie Stacey lectures in women's studies and film Studies in the Sociology Department at Lancaster University, UK. She has published work on Hollywood stars and women audiences and her latest work is on cultural and feminist approaches to illness. Her publications include *Teratologies: A Cultural Study of Cancer* (1997), and, with Annette Kuhn, *Screen Histories: A Screen Reader* (1998).

John Tagg is Professor of Art History at the State University of New York at Binghampton. Previously, he lectured on art theory, art history and history of photography at the Goldsmiths College, University of London, Leeds University and the Polytechnic of Central London. He is the author of *The Burden of Representation: Essays on Photographies and Histories* (1988), *Grounds of Dispute: Art History, Cultural Politics, and the Discursive Field* (1992) and the editor of *The Cultural Politics of 'Postmodernism'* (1989).

Simon Watney is director of the Red Hot Aids Charitable Trust in London, which distributes funds internationally for HIV/AIDS prevention and education. He was previously Senior Lecturer in Photographic Theory at the Polytechnic of Central London (now University of Westminster) and has published widely in photographic, art and cultural theory. His *Policing Desire: Pornography, Aids and the Media* (1987), is now in its third edition; he is also co-editor of *Photography/Politics Two* (1986).

Acknowledgements

The majority of the articles and extracts that make up the chapters in this volume have been abbreviated as appropriate to the overall theme and purpose of this collection. Original illustrations and footnotes have been included where the editors consider them useful for reference and, in the case of illustrations, where we have been able to obtain them. Some of the older readings use terminology – such as extensive use of 'he' or 'negro' – that are unacceptable in current usage. However, we have not made any alterations as we believe it is important that the readings are read as historical documents. The editors are grateful to both the authors and original publishers for permission to publish their writings. We hope that the use of their work in a new setting will both extend their familiarity and use, and form a valuable starting point for students of the image in the wider context of visual culture.

The authors and publishers wish to thank the following for permission to use copyright material.

Texts

Chapter 1: Macmillan Ltd, UK and Yale University Press, USA for Chapter 1, 'The natural attitude' in *Vision and Painting,* Norman Bryson, 1983.

Chapter 2: Harper Collins Publishers (UK) and Farrar, Straus & Giroux, Inc. (USA) for 'Rhetoric of the image' from *Image, Music , Text.* Roland Barthes, 1977.

Chapter 3: Rivers Oram Press for Victor Burgin, 'Art, commonsense and photography' from *The Camerawork Essays,* edited by Jessica Evans, 1997.

Chapter 4: Jonathan Cape for Roland Barthes (1973) 'Myth today' from *Mythologies.*

Chapter 5: Penguin UK for Michel Foucault (1977) 'Panopticism' *Discipline and Punish.* (Allen Lane 1977, first published as *Surveiller et punir: Naissance de la Prison* by Editions Gallimard, 1975). Translation © Alan Sheridan, 1977.

Chapter 6: Harcourt Brace & Company and Harvard University Press for extracts from Walter Benjamin (1968) 'The work of art in the age of mechanical reproduction' in *Illuminations.*

Chapter 7: Penguin UK for 'The image world' from *On Photography*. (Allen Lane, 1978) © Susan Sontag 1973, 1974, 1977.

Chapter 8: Black and Red (USA) for Guy Debord (1983) extracts from *Society of Spectacle*.

Chapter 9: Comedia/Routledge for 'The bottom line on planet one: squaring up to *The Face*' in *Hiding in the Light*, Dick Hebdige, 1988.

Chapter 10: Comedia/Routledge for Simon Watney (1986) 'On the institution of photography' in P. Holland, J. Spence and S. Watney (eds), *Photography/Politics:Two*.

Chapter 11: Blackwell Publishers (UK) and Stanford University Press (USA) for extracts from Pierre Bourdieu (1990) *Photography : A Middlebrow Art*. Translated by Shaun Whiteside. English translation © 1990 Polity Press, Cambridge in association with Basil Blackwell, Oxford.

Chapter 12: Comedia/Routledge for Allan Sekula (1983) 'Reading an archive' in P. Holland, J. Spence and S. Watney (eds), *Photography/Politics: Two*.

Chapter 13: MIT Press (Cambridge, MA) for Rosalind Krauss (1989) 'Photography's discursive spaces' in *The Contest of Meaning: Critical Histories of Photography*, edited by R. Boston.

Chapter 14: MIT Press (Cambridge, MA) for Douglas Crimp (1993) 'The Museum's old, the library's new subject' from *On The Museum's Ruins*.

Chapter 15: The John Logie Baird Centre, Glasgow for Abigail Soloman-Godeau (1987) 'Living with contradicitons :critical practices in the age of supply-side aesthetics' *Screen* , 28 (3): 2–23.

Chapter 16: Macmillan Ltd for John Tagg (1987) 'A means of surveillance' (Chapter 2) and 'Evidence, truth and order' (Chapter 3) from *The Burden of Representation*.

Chapter 17: Addison Wesley Longman for Jessica Evans (1998) 'Feeble monsters: "making up" Disabled People' in A. Briggs and P. Cobley (eds), *The Media: An Introduction*.

Chapter 18: Blackwell Publishers, Oxford and St. Martin's Press, New York for Don Slater (1985) 'Marketing mass photography' in H. Davies and P. Walton (eds), *Language, Image, Media*.

Chapter 19: Verso for Louis Althusser (1994) 'Ideology and ideological state apparatuses' from Slavojzizek (ed.), *Lenin and Philosophy and Other Essays*.

Chapter 20: Random House for Sigmund Freud (1977) 'Fetishism' in *On Sexuality, Collected Works*. © Copyrights, the Institute of Psychoanalysis and Hogarth Press for permission to quote from THE STANDARD EDITION OF THE COMPLETE WORKS OF SIGMUND FREUD, translated and edited by James Strachey.

Chapter 21: W. W. Norton , New York for Otto Fenichel (1954) 'The scoptophilic instinct and identification' in Hanna Fenichel and David Rappaport (eds), *The Collected Papers of Otto Fenichel, Second Series*.

Chapter 22: Oxford University Press Inc., New York for 'The subject' from *The Subject of Semiotics*, Kaja Silverman, 1983.

Chapter 23: Macmillan Press Ltd for 'Fantasia' from *Representing the Woman*. Elizabeth Cowie, 1997.

Chapter 24: The John Logie Baird Centre, Glasgow for Homi Bhabha (1983) 'The other question – the stereotype and colonial discourse', *Screen*, 24 (6): 18–36.

Chapter 25: The John Logie Baird Centre Glasgow for Laura Mulvey (1975) 'Visual pleasure and narrative cinema', *Screen,* 16 (3): 6–18.

Chapter 26: Jackie Stacey and The Woman's Press Ltd for Jackie Stacey (1988) 'Desperately seeking difference' in Lorraine Gamman and Margaret Marshment (eds), *The Female Gaze.*

Chapter 27: The John Logie Baird Centre, Glasgow for Jane Gaines (1988) 'White privilege and looking relations-race and gender in feminist film theory', *Screen*, 29 (4): 12–27.

Chapter 28: Verso for Jaqueline Rose (1986) extracts from *Sexuality in the Field of Vision.*

Chapter 29: Grove/Atlantic, Inc. (USA) for Franz Fanon (1967) 'The fact of blackness', from *Black Skin, White Masks.* Translated by Charles Lam Markmann.

Chapter 30: Routledge for Mary Louise Pratt (1992) 'Humboldt and the reinvention of America' from *Imperial Eyes.* London, Routledge.

Chapter 31: Routledge for Kobena Mercer (1994) 'Reading racial fetishism' from *Welcome to the Jungle.* London, Routledge.

Chapter 32: Routledge for Mary Ann Doane (1991) 'Dark continents' from *Femmes Fatales.* London, Routledge.

Chapter 33: The John Logie Baird Centre, Glasgow for Richard Dyer (1988) 'White', *Screen*, 29 (4): 44–65.

Illustrations

Archivi Alinari (Florence, Italy) for Figure 1.1 *The Family of Vunnerius Keramus* (Civico Museo dell'eta' cristiana), Figure 1.2 *Cimabue Madonna and Child Enthroned with Angels and Prophets* (Alinari Collection) and Figure 1.3: Giotto *Madonna and Child Enthroned with Saints and Angels* (Alinari Collection).

Panzani Freres for Figure 2.1, Panzani advertisement

The Estate of Diane Arbus c/o Pelosi & Wolf, LLP (USA) for *Identical Twins, Roselle, NJ, 1966.* © 1971 The Estate of Diane Arbus, LLC.

The Advertising Archives, London for Figure 3.6, *Martini advertisement.*

Hachette Filipacchi Associes for Figure 4.1, *Paris Match* front cover no.326.

Practical Photography for Figure 10.1 *front cover*, Figure 10.2 *inside spread*, both from November 1998 issue. Figure 10.3 *inside spread* from December 1994 issue.

University College of Cape Breton for Figures 12.2, 12.3, 12.4, 12.5 and 12.6 from *Miming Photographs and Other Pictures: A Selection from the Negative Archives of Shedden Studio.*

The Museum of Modern Art, New York for Figure 13.3, Eugene Atget *Verrieres, coin Pittoresque,* 1922. Abbott-Levy Collection. Copyright © 1998, The Museum of Modern Art and for Figure 13.4, Eugene Atget *Sceaux, coin Pittoresque,* 1922. Abbott-Levy Collection. Copyright © 1998, The Museum of Modern Art.

Louise Lawler, New York for Figure 14.1, Ed Ruscha, *Twenty-Six Gasoline Stations*, Texas, 1962 and for Figure 14.2, Ed Ruscha, *Twenty-Six Gasoline Stations*. Mobil Williams, 1962.

Mary Boone Gallery for Figure 15.1, Sherrie Levine, *Untitled After Walker Evans:2*, 1981.

Figure 15.2 courtesy of Marvin Heiferman, Frank Majore, *Cocktails*, 1983.

Metro Pictures, New York for Figure 15.4, Laurie Simmons, *Aztec Crevice*, 1984 and for Figure 15.5, Cindy Sherman, *Untitled* (film still), 1979.

Barbara Gladstone Gallery for Figure 15.6 Richard Prince, 1980–84 *Untitled (Cowboy)*.

John Weber Gallery, New York for Figure 15.7 Hans Haacke, *MetroMobiltan*, 1985.

The Public Record Office, London for Figure 16.1, Unknown photographer 1873, *Wandsworth Prison Records*.

The Royal Society of Medicine, London for Figure 16.2, print from the Diamond Collection.

Stockport Central Library, Stockport Borough Council for Figure 16.3, Unknown photographer 1865, *Stockport Ragged and Industrial School*.

Barnardos Film Archive for Figure 16.4 from Thomas Barnes and Roderick Johnstone, 1874–1883 *Personal History of a Child at Dr Barnado's Home*.

Cambridgeshire Constabluary for Figure 16.5, Unknown photographer 1872, *Huntingdon County Gaol Records* (from original deposited at the County Record Office in Huntingdon.

The Mansell Collection for Figure 16.6, John Thompson *The Crawlers* from Street Life in London 1877–78 and Figure 16.7, Thomas Annan (1867) *Close No.11 Bridgegate* from 'Photographs of Old Streets etc. The Mitchell Library, Glasgow (Glasgow City Council).

Konica UK Limited for Figure 18.1 advertisement titled 'The mini series you don't want to miss' in *Practical Photography* December 1994.

James P Graham, London for Figure 18.2, photograph accompanying Canon ES advertisement, 'Leave others to their snaps while you take a photograph'.

The Ronald Grant Archive , London for Figure 27.1, '*Photographer Sean's aggressive treatment of model Tracey in 'Mahogany'*.

Art and Commerce Inc, New York for Figure 31.1, Robert Mapplethorpe, *Jimmy Freeman*, 1982; Figure 31.2 Robert Mapplethorpe, *Roedel Washington*, 1986; Figure 31.3 Robert Mapplethorpe, *Derrik Cross*, 1983 and Figure 31.4 Robert Mapplethorpe, *Thomas*, 1986. Mapplethorpe Photography © The Estate of Robert Mapplethorpe/A+C Anthology.

Every effort has been made to trace all the copyright holders, but if any have been overlooked, or if any additional information can be given, the publishers will be pleased to make the necessary amendments at the first opportunity.

Jessica Evans and Stuart Hall

Certain themes imbued with visual metaphors and terminologies of looking and seeing have become the staple diet of cultural and media studies: the society of the spectacle and the simulacrum; the politics of representation; the male gaze and the possibility of a female gaze; the 'mirror stage'; fetishism and voyeurism; the reproduction of the image; the 'other' as the projection of racialized discourse. It may thus appear contentious to claim, as we do, that 'visual culture' has been somewhat overlooked in the rapid expansion of cultural and media studies throughout the past decade and a half. Contentious because, after all, the work of Barthes, Benjamin, Lacan and Foucault, with their clearly visual concerns – not to mention a host of others – forms the canonical foundations upon which much cultural and media studies rest.

Moreover, the mechanically or electronically reproduced image is the semantic and technical unit of the modern mass media and at the heart of post-war popular culture. However, while this is acknowledged widely within the discipline of media and cultural studies, normally via ritual reference to the seminal work of Walter Benjamin, the visual image or photograph seems only of interest as the origin, as the technological dawn, of a great process of development in which, in an era of mass communication and the commodification of information, messages can be transmitted in principle to a plurality of recipients and audiences.

In fact, the neglect of specifically visual culture is understandable, logical even, and for a number of reasons. First, we can consider matters of epistemology. The revolution across much of the social and human sciences, characterized by what is variously termed the 'linguistic turn' or, we would prefer, more broadly, the 'cultural turn', has led to an emphasis upon social practices and relations as signifying practices – practices which organize and constitute social actions and involve/assume interpretative, meaning-making persons. In the field of image studies, then, we cannot turn back to the pre-semiotic assumptions of reflectionism; we cannot any longer think of social experience as existing in a pre-linguistic realm, abstracted from the signifying systems which in fact structure it. Furthermore, as is well known in terms of the *raison d'être* of cultural studies as a discipline in its own right, this approach has permitted a reach into the cultural practices of the everyday – such as the popular practices of photography, hitherto dismissed for their trite and highly restricted iconography. None the less, there is a sense that the privileging of the linguistic model in the study of representation has led to the assumption that visual artefacts are fundamentally the same, and function in just the same way, as any other cultural text. Accordingly, the specific rhetoric, genres, institutional contexts and uses of visual imagery can become lost in the more global identification of cultural trends and their epic narratives of transformations of consciousness in the rubric of 'postmodern culture'. As the art historian Carol Armstrong has put it, 'Within this model paintings and such are to be viewed not as particularized things made for particular historical uses, but as exchanges circulating in some great, boundless, and often curiously ahistorical economy of images, subjects, and other representations. That within the increasingly cyberspace model of visual studies, ''text'' is the mother-model for utterances, performances, fashionings, and sign collections of all kinds is not unrelated to this disembodiment of the cultural object' (Armstrong in 'Visual Culture Questionnaire', 1996: 27).

Secondly, there are matters of a substantive kind here, connected with the nature of the objects one studies. It is quite clear, for example, that 'photography' is not a unified practice, but a medium utterly diverse in its functions, a medium 'whose status as a technology varies with the power relations which invest it' (Tagg, this volume, p. 246). It is hard to think of one institution in society that does not use reproduced images. Market research surveys suggest that just under three-quarters of the adult population own a camera. 'Family' occasions are frequently cited as one of the principle reasons for camera ownership (see the discussion in *Cultural Trends*, 1990: 43–45). It therefore makes no sense to consider the 'meaning of photography' without considering the ways in which the meanings and uses of photography are regulated by the formats and institutions of production, distribution and consumption (be they magazines or newspapers, the advertising and publicity industries, camera manufacturers – or other socially organized relations such as the family). However, under the alibi of 'visual culture' one can easily 'slip' into an analysis of these contexts alone. It is here that the notion of discourse is central. In its emphasis upon the integral relations of meaning and use, it rescues us from the solely textual concerns of a semiotic analysis, but also allows us to check the slide into older 'productionist' models which provide a limiting view of practices of meaning and cultural construction, seeing them only as manifestations of determining and logically prior events at the level of the economic (see Watney, Chapter 10). One cannot understand, for example, the practices of the amateur snapshot photographer, nor account for the severely restricted 'style' of the images he or she typically produces, without also considering how this practice intersects with the camera and film manufacturing industry, with the developing and processing companies, with the relationships in modern societies between work and leisure, with definitions, idealizations and activities of family life, and, not least, with localized and historically specific gendered conceptions of the identity, beliefs and skills of the photographer (see Porter, 1989/90; Holland and Spence, 1991; Watney and Slater, Chapters 10 and 18 in this volume).

As we have indicated, cultural studies rests on the achievements of semiotics as a whole and stakes its distinctiveness upon the analysis of the symbolic, classificatory and, in short, meaning-making practices that are at the heart of all cultural production and consumption. Any study of the image conducted under the impact of cultural studies is indebted to semiotics. Part I, 'Cultures of the Visual', then, begins with some classic statements of the semiotic position, the readings dealing in particular with the still perplexing issue of the sameness and difference of written and verbal language to the visual image. Their underlying preoccupation is with the extent to which we can conceive of images as a 'language'.

However, the scrupulously pure project of the structuralist moment of semiotics, which conceives of language as a system of signs immanent to a single or bounded group of texts and studied independently of history or the particular utterances of human subjects, needs to be both augmented and qualified. Accordingly, our ensuing selection of readings, though rooted in the basic assumptions of classical semiotics, seeks in various ways to develop and complicate its insights and conclusions. The selections in Section B of Part I depart from the model established by semiotics; thus, they are not concerned with the 'meaning' of any image or corpus of images but with a culture in which reproducibility provides the conditions of existence of any particular meaning. Other readings in this section are underwritten by the assumption that the sensibilities of modern societies are shaped through cultural technologies – such as modern penal architecture and the camera – which reinvent the relations between seeing and knowing as mutually constitutive.

Part II, 'Regulating Photographic Meanings', goes on to consider the particular historical, institutional and archival conditions which both enable and contrain and, in short, regulate photographic meaning. The readings in Section C represent some key statements of the methodological approaches to the study of photography, constituted by the problem of how to account for photographic 'style', and how best to trace the relationships of 'determination' between those institutions which facilitate the production of photographs and those bodies of beliefs and values which inform the 'look' and meaning of photographs and the practices which centre upon them. Some readings employ a discursive approach to photography, evoking Foucault's notion of the archive, that is, 'the system that governs the appearances of statements as unique events' (Foucault, 1972: 129). Those in Section D centre explicitly on a range of institutional contexts for the production, collection and display or 'consumption' of photographs – from the collecting practices of the museum to the use of photographs as documentary 'records' for surveillance and publicity and the camera marketers' creation of amateur photography.

Part III, 'Looking and Subjectivity', relativizes semiotics by shifting the emphasis away from the texts of representation to the question of the subject who is at the centre of meaning, but for whom meaning very often works below the threshold of consciousness. Here, our selection indicates that meaning is constituted not in the visual sign itself as a self-sufficient entity, nor exclusively in the sociological positions and identities of the audience, but in the articulation between viewer and viewed, between the power of the image to signify and the viewer's capacity to interpret meaning. The selections in Part III expand further the problem of how to conceptualize 'visual culture' and the visual field first posed in Part I, which is in fact the dominant theme of the whole volume. For when referring to visual culture, we imply the existence of particular structures for the gaze, for seeing and for the excitement, desire, voyeurism or fear in looking; visual culture always provides a physical and psychical place for individual spectators to inhabit. Part III thus adds a range of theoretical approaches and conceptualizations to those selected earlier, which serve to bring into focus the crucial but neglected field of the cultural practices of looking and seeing and the paradigmatic relationship which organizes this area of enquiry – that between the capacity of the image to signify and the subjective capacities of the subject to take and produce meaning.

How best to think of the various components of visual culture? The image, which stands at the centre-point of contemporary visual culture, presents itself as a simple, singular, substantive entity – a sort of 'fact' or punctuation point (punctum), as Roland Barthes once called it, in its own right, whose capacity to index or reference things, people, places and events in the 'real' world appears palpable, irreducible and unquestionable. In fact, as W. J. T. Mitchell reminds us in his essay. 'The Pictorial Turn', despite the all-pervasive image-making which characterizes our world, 'we still do not know exactly what pictures are, what their relation to language is, how they operate on observers and on the world, how their history is to be understood, and what is to be done with or about them' (Mitchell, 1994: 13). The picture, he goes on to argue, is 'a complex interplay between visuality, apparatus, institutions, bodies and figurality' (1994: 16). Each of these indicates a complex set of practices which lie behind and make possible the image and its capacity to convey meaning, each of which requires its own conceptualization. 'Visuality' refers to the visual register in which the image and visual meaning operate. The 'apparatus' refers to the means or 'media' by which images are produced and circulated, which are increasingly sophisticated and complex in our world of electronic reproduction, video and cybernetic technology. The 'institutions' refer to the organized social relations of image-making and circulation, which today are often large scale and corporate in structure, global in their scale of operations. 'Bodies' reminds us not only of one of the image's privileged subjects, but of the presence of the viewer, spectator, observer, as the necessary 'other' in the circuits of visual meaning, which make meaning possible, and whose conduct images regulate. 'Figurality' reminds us of the image's privileged position in relation to representing or 'figuring' the world to us in pictorial form. However, one cannot 'read off' any one of these individual 'moments' from another since they are not in a relationship of causal or sequential determination; nor do they only have external relations to each other. Rather, we would prefer to think about the orbit of the image according to the theoretical model of articulation, in which a number of distinct elements interact, in a moment of temporary unity, leading to 'variable and contingent outcomes' (see du Gay et al., 1997).

We have expressed above our concern with how the study of visual images is subsumed under often unsubstantiated and metaphysical claims about contemporary cultural developments, operating under the banner of 'postmodern', 'simulation', and even, more recently, 'prosthetic' culture. For instance, Benjamin's writings on the 'dream worlds' and phantasmagoria resulting from the proliferation of industrialized objects in the arcades and department stores of the late nineteenth-century modern city (see Buck Morss, 1989) – themselves building upon Marx's work on commodity fetishism and the reification of appearance – seems to have been recycled one time too many. To the extent that this is the case, it seems likely that, for many, the notion of 'visual culture', too, is grandiloquent, even fallacious. In part, this is due to the fact that it denotes an area of nascent study whose objects and modes of analysis are not yet consistently or clearly delineated, nor whose territory is established. None the less, we should explain here the definition of visual culture, if somewhat unrefined, that is both assumed and deployed in this Reader. The dissemination of the term 'visual culture' is generally attributed to Svetlana Alpers, who in 1972, was also the first to use the term 'new art history' in print. She writes recently that:

> When, some years back, I put it that I was not studying the history of Dutch painting, but painting as part of Dutch visual culture, I intended something specific. It was to focus on notions about vision (the mechanism of the eye), on image-making devices (the microscope, the camera obscura), and on visual skills (map making, but also experimenting) as cultural resources related to the practice of painting. (Alpers, 1996: 26)

As she goes on to elucidate, her specific orientation arose from the nature of her subject for she was dealing with a culture in which visual skills were definitive: 'a culture in which images, as distinguished from texts, were central to the representation (in the sense of the formulation of knowledge) or the world' (1996: 26).

In a similar way, W. J. T. Mitchell speaks of how the study of the visual field is transformed by the 'realization that spectatorship (the look, the gaze, the practices of observation, surveillance, visual pleasure) may be as deep a problem as various forms of reading (decipherment, decoding, interpretation, etc.) and that visual experience or visual literacy may not be fully explicable on the model of textuality' (Mitchell, 1994: 16). One way of thinking of 'visual culture', then, is in terms of particular and historically specific combinations of meanings and subjects – 'scopic regimes' whose histories remain to be written. Mitchell's description is useful in that it encourages us to hold back from deploying textual methods in a universalizing manner. In our extract (chapters) from *Discipline and Punish* (1977), for example, Foucault does not conceptualize the panopticon as a primarily textual device; rather, he considers it as a spatially organized technology in which power is exerted through the capacity to 'survey'; it is designed to achieve quite specific effects in the conduct of both prisoners and warders. In the modern prison, then – along with the factory, the hospital and the school – is manifested a new disciplinary regime based less on spectacular uses of force than on the training and reform of individuals through continuous surveillance and documentation. Foucault's often visual accounts of events and his use of paintings throughout much of his work does not arise from a concern with what things are made to look like in representation, but with how things came to be considered appropriate for codification as visual 'data'; how knowledge could be founded upon 'sight', how things were shown to knowledge and power.

In 1996, the editors of the North American art and cultural theory journal *October* devoted an important special issue, including the results of a questionnaire to well-known art theorists, to the vicissitudes of the concept of 'visual culture' as it has emerged as a discrete study area in the university sector over the past ten years or so. (It must, however, be acknowledged that in the UK, particularly in the former polytechnic sector, the cultural study of the image has been a staple part of pioneering photography and art history degrees since the late 1970s.) They were concerned with the location of visual culture studies in relation to the traditions of humanities disciplines such as art history, and claimed that 'the interdisciplinary project of visual culture is no longer organized on the model of history (as were the disciplines of art history, architectural history, film theory etc.) but on the model of anthropology' (*October*, 1996: 25). In an article in the same issue, Hal Foster asks whether, although conceding that the concept of visual culture 'totalizes prematurely', 'visual culture [might] rely upon techniques of information to transform a wide range of mediums into a system of image-text, a database of digital terms, an archive without museums' (1996: 97). He counterposes this to the technique of art history, which typically 'relied upon techniques of reproduction to abstract a wide range of objects into a system of style . . . (e.g. open versus closed composition, linear versus painterly technique) (1996: 97). What is noteworthy for Foster in the displacement of art history by visual culture is the dual shift from art to visual, and history to culture.

We can see that this new conception of visual culture cuts across specific media and the teleological narratives of the individual disciplines constructed around them. To a great extent, this view underpins the project of this Reader. We are also guided by Benjamin's observation that, in the future, 'the caption [will become] the most important part of the shot' (1972: 25). Benjamin's call for a citizenry which has acquired a critical facility with visual and verbal communication and his prediction of the increasing inter-dependency of word and image were a matter of urgency when the German National Socialists advanced a synergetic use of every available mass medium – but are surely of pressing relevance today. However, the differences between language and the visual remain significant and require further attention; that is, the different cultural technologies and industries built upon them, their characteristic forms and rhetorical devices, and the ways in which they are put to work, disseminated and made sense of by readers and viewers. In an important sense, a study of, say, the meaning of 'Hollywood', a contemporary lifestyle magazine, the advertising industry or an episode of the Jerry Springer Show would be incomplete were we to limit ourselves to the analysis of words, or interpreted images as if they only functioned as artefacts to be read rather than as sights and often exhibitionist performances to be looked at. A culture which is pervaded at all levels by a host of cultural technologies designed to disseminate viewing and looking practices through primarily visually mediated forms provides a challenge for those seeking, as do our contributors to this Reader, to trace the ways in which 'the image' is invariably articulated within the picturing sensibilities of a wider 'visual culture'.

References

Alpers, Svetlana (1996) 'Visual Culture Questionnaire', in *October*, 77 (summer).
Benjamin, Walter (1972) 'A short history of photography', in *Screen* 13, 1 (spring).
Buck Morss, Susan (1989) *The Dialectics of Seeing: Walter Benjamin and the Arcades Project*. Cambridge, MA: MIT Press.
Cultural Trends (1990) 8, London: Policy Studies Institute.
Foster, Hal (1996) 'The archive without museums', in *October*, 77 (summer) pp. 97–119.
Foucault, Michel (1972) *The Archaeology of Knowledge*. London: Tavistock.
Foucault, Michel (1977) *Discipline and Punish*. London: Penguin.
du Gay, Paul; Hall, Stuart; Janes, Linda; Mackay, Hugh and Negus, Keith (1997) *Doing Cultural Studies: the Story of the Sony Walkman*. London: Sage/Open University.
Holland, Patricia and Spence, Jo (eds) (1991) *Family Snaps: the Meanings of Domestic Photography*. London: Virago.
Mitchell, W. J. T. (1994) 'The pictorial turn', in *Picture Theory*. Chicago and London: University of Chicago Press.
'Visual Culture Questionnaire' (1996) in *October*, 77 (summer) (includes contributions from Svetlana Alpers, Carol Armstrong, W. J. T. Mitchell and Martin Jay among others).
Porter, Gaby (1989/90) 'Trade and industry', in *Ten.8*, 35 (winter) pp. 45–48.
Rajchman, John (1988) 'Foucault's Art of Seeing', *October*, 44 (spring) pp. 88–119.
Tagg, John (1987) *The Burden of Representation*. London: Macmillan (extracted in chapter 16 of this volume).

Cultures of the visual

Theories of the image, from ancient Greece and the Renaissance, through the period of Romanticism, to modernist painting, have been dominated, almost unchallenged, by the idea of the purely visual. Modernist painting has, for example, sought to create nothing more than the 'pure' self-referential image – abstract, non-verbal, free of representation, reference and narrative – although this interpretation of modernist works was fortified by the elaborate verbal discourses of modernist art theory. The presupposition that the visual is a terrain of perception and experience untainted by precepts, concepts and language, has most often been buttressed by the idea of mimesis, characterized variously as the 'reflectionist' or 'picture theory of language' or the 'essential copy' (see Mitchell, 1994; Hall, 1997; Bryson, Chapter 1 in this volume).

For instance, Norman Bryson argues in 'The Natural Attitude' that, in the historicist narratives upon which art history's early disciplinary rationale was founded, successive schools of painting move steadily towards a goal of the perfect reproduction of reality, shedding their predecessor's formulaic or inhibited approach along the way, guided by the assumption of the 'Universal Visual Experience'. In fact, Richard Rorty (1979) has characterized the whole tradition of Western epistemology as equating knowledge with representations which are judged according to their adequacy as 'reflections' of an external reality. It is precisely the reflectionist attitude, in which the image is considered to act as a transparent 'relay' to a singular originary presence which is imagined to lie behind it, that Saussure's semiological linguistics defied. It is the project of semiotics, and the vicissitudes of its application to the visual image, that forms the subject of our selections in Section A. The central questions posed by these readings is: what is the identity of an image, what relations does it have with what is considered to be 'other' than itself (such as 'reality'), and how, and to what extent, do images function like a language?

Saussure inverted the common-sense reflectionist understanding of the relationship between words and things (Saussure, 1974). Common sense tells us that the words we use are mere naming devices which allocate to each object a discrete word. Quite the reverse is true, according to semiotics. Language is a series of 'negative' values, each sign not so much expressing a meaning as marking a divergence of meaning between itself and other signs within the collective symbolic system of language (*la langue*). It is not just that the sign's relationship to its referent is arbitrary, so that dog operating in English is *hund* operating in German – a commonplace interpretation that governs much commentary in this area. It is that arbitrariness lies within the sign itself; in this way, a given phonetic substance – the signifier – is sliced from the range of the sound possibilities of speech, simultaneously articulating a conceptual cut, setting up a signified, or ideational, unit. Nor is it the case that each language has an arbitrary sound/image (signifier) for a concept in universal existence (the signified 'dog') but that the system of distinctions is entirely specific to each social institution of language (*la langue*). An underlying code or set of distinctions between dead/living, cooked/raw operate in English, then, to distinguish between the signifiers mutton and sheep, whereas the French signifier *mouton* cuts out only one conceptual unit. It is not the case that there is pure, positive content, which is then 'clothed in the form of a signifier'. In this way semiotics unsettles hallowed divisions between 'form' and 'content' operative in those branches of the sociology of culture and art history which have not reconstructed these categories via the 'linguistic turn' (see Burgin, Chapter 3).

It is important to avoid the literal application of structural linguistics to the visual image. Still images do not function according to *la langue* of written language, to use Saussurian terminology; that is, they do not obey the precise grammatical construction, the underlying rule system, of written language. There is no verb, nor an obvious 'subject', nor a grammar of tense. Metz's observations still stand, that a still image is not in itself 'a discrete unit' (Metz, 1974: 26). It 'yields to the receiver a quantity of indefinite information, like statements but unlike words' (1974: 26). Thus, a photograph of a woman is less the equivalent simply of 'woman' than it is a series of disconnected descriptions: 'an older woman, seen in the distance, wearing a green coat, watching the traffic as she crosses the road' (see Burgin, 1982b). Nor do pictures have tense – one only has to think through the problems of constructing a set of pictures of a gun so that it can say 'This was a gun', or 'This will be the gun of the future', or 'This gun was used by the Soviet army in 1944' to realize that it cannot be done with any precision. Moreover, as Barthes says in 'Rhetoric of the Image' (Chapter 2) the conjunction of 'spatial immediacy' and 'temporal anteriority' that is peculiar to the photograph makes for its illogical sense as both 'here-now' and 'there-then'.

This is what Barthes meant by the photograph as a 'message without a code'. It seems to present us with an object as a *fait accompli*, as if this object is implacably there, independent of a viewing subject, since the photograph represents first of all a world whose components have to be literally identified: 'all that is needed is the knowledge bound up with our perception', which is a matter of 'almost anthropological knowledge' (p. 36). This is the level of knowledge that we require in order to determine what the image appears to 'show', rather what it 'tells' – the area of connotation. The idea that the photograph does not have a code is derived from the capacity of photography as a medium to operate as what Charles Peirce, the American pragmatist philosopher, termed an indexical sign. While Saussure argued that linguistics could serve as a model for semiotics because in the case of language and arbitrary and conventional nature of the sign is especially clear, Peirce was concerned that non-linguistic signs may be less arbitrary; his extension of the analysis of the sign into the triad of sign, icon and index was an attempt to think about the relationship between signs and referents, an approach explicitly outlawed in Saussure's model in which it is only the conventional relationship between signifier and signified that is relevant. Thus, in the same way that a knock at the door is an indexical sign of someone's presence, or a weathercock is an index of the direction of the wind, the photograph, unlike a drawing or computer-generated image, is thus physically or causally linked to its referent, being the result of an optical redistribution of light rays emanating from an object on to light-sensitive materials. It is precisely the indexical nature of photography which, for positivists, makes the photograph slavishly hold to the full material presence of the object, so that it posits nothing beyond what is presented to it as 'the idolater of that-which-is' (Slater, 1997: 99). It is the power of this aspect of the image which Barthes, for one, was loathe to forsake, even as he embraced structuralist linguistics, and it accounted for his wish, derived from the trauma of his mother's death, that the photograph could make present what has been so lost (Barthes, 1982).

However, it is indexicality which paradoxically also makes for the widely acknowledged polysemic ambiguity of the still visual image, a characteristic about which Barthes writes in 'Rhetoric of the Image' where he first deploys the terms 'anchorage' and 'relay' to discuss the function of text and captions for the meaning of the image. For, although the photograph's indexicality guarantees the sense that it represents a lapse in time (Barthes' 'having-been-there'), any individual photograph is at the same time freed of any moorings in sequential temporality (as is so well revealed when contact sheets are shown) since it transforms a fraction of a second into an enduring moment. A photograph is thus epistemologically complex, making available a multitude of deductive logics. Thus, to use a well-known example, a photograph taken at the moment at which Margaret Thatcher's hand, during a process of waving at Conservative party members, is positioned in a pose which mimics the Nazi salute, can be said to be both 'true' and 'false' simultaneously. It is the denotative power of the image – its apparent power to merely 'show' – that, as Barthes explains in 'Myth Today' (Chapter 4), provides the evidential alibi for its connotation, in this case, that Thatcher has fascist sympathies. In *Mythologies* (1973), Barthes expands upon the idea of denotation and connotation – drawn from the work of the Danish linguist Louis Hjelmslev – by turning Saussure's analysis of the system of language into a study of myth. Myth is, for Barthes, located in the relations between the two orders of signification, for it is the denotation that allows the connotation to be innocently consumed. Barthes' classic exemplification of this is the young black soldier saluting the French flag on the front cover of *Paris-March* at the time of the Algerian war of independence (see Chapter 4). He demonstrates how this paradigmatic selection of a black soldier, instead of a white soldier – metonymically standing in for the army, and by extension the French nation – supports a 'myth' conducive to the French government of the time that 'there is no better answer to the detractors of an alleged colonialism than the zeal shown by this Negro in serving his so-called oppressors' (p. 54).

Burgin puts the position as regards images-as-a-language succinctly: 'there is no "language" of photography, no single signifying system (as opposed to technical apparatus) upon which all photographs depend (in the sense in which all forms of spoken and written language in English ultimately depend upon the English language') (Burgin, 1982a: 143). Even the iconic sign, long considered to be the least assimilable into semiotic analysis, has proved to be just as arbitrary and non-continuous as the conventional sign, since it reproduces some of the basic mechanisms of everyday perception, themselves 'coded' according to economic principles (see Eco, 1982). And as we have seen, 'the indexical nature of the photograph . . . is therefore highly complex, irreversible, and can guarantee nothing at the level of meaning' (Tagg, 1988: 3). So, as Victor Burgin has argued most persuasively, there is a heterogeneous complex of codes upon which photography may draw – only a few of which are peculiar to photography (i.e. various meanings built around 'blur', and 'focus', and some of the pictorial elements of newer genres such as family snaps) – and therefore most of which are not (e.g. codes of lighting may be drawn from painting or film, codes of body gesture). Moreover, as is noted by Burgin (1982a, b), Barthes ('Rhetoric of the Image', Chapter 2) and Benjamin (1972), photographs are often literally traversed by language, since most images have words attached in the form of captions of surrounding text or superimposed. But even a photograph that is not juxtaposed with writing is normally constituted by codes identifiable as belonging to a particular genre; moreover, photographs often employ classical rhetorical language and the literary figures of metaphor, simile and metonymy, as are most often apparent in the persuasive discourses of advertising. It is precisely in the formal devices of photographic construction that the workings of ideology reside. This is the subject of Victor Burgin's 'Art, Common Sense and Photography' (Chapter 3) which is informed by Barthes' argument that the function of myth is to naturalize and construct as inevitable that which is created within particular social relations and is therefore historical.

The enquiries of Section B do not arise out of attention to any particular image or group of images, nor with the particular conditions of their production, distribution and spectatorship. Rather, the concern of these readings is with the way in which we think and talk about the idea of imaging, seeing and picturing. In Foucault's *Discipline and Punish* (1977), which constitutes Chapter 5, this concern is not expressed via reference to 'representation' but to the various effects and outcomes of modern techniques, in this case, penal architecture, designed to create a physical distance between seer and seen in order to manage the conduct of a criminal population. 'Panopticism' indicates Foucault's genealogical interest in tracing the conditions of emergence of the visual as the ground of knowledge: how it could become possible that the visual could be construed as an object for power/knowledge. A persistent theme of Foucault's historical accounts is the invention of institutional arrangements at the end of the eighteenth century, at the threshold of an age recognizable as our modernity, in which looking and the gaze became central to the production of knowledge and the regulation of subjects. In *Discipline and Punish* he traces the shift from a regime of punishment centred on the public spectacle of physical torture, symbolic of the body of the king, to the creation of self-monitoring subjects in the reforming ethos of the modern prison, of which the panopticon, with its induction of the inmate into a 'state of conscious and permanent visibility' (p. 65), is the paradigmatic example. As Foucault points out, although the panopticon appears to be 'merely the solution of a technical problem . . . through it a whole type of society emerges' (p. 69).

For the purposes of the arguments in the chapters of this section, it is worth noting that Foucault sharply distinguishes his methodological and historical approach from those of other contemporary French writers of an anti-ocular persuasion, such as Debord (Chapter 8). Thus, the 'whole type of society' to which he refers is one in which it is now the relations between people *qua* individuals and the state that is to be regulated but in a form which is the 'exact reverse of the spectacle' (p. 69). This is because Foucault does not operate with a functionalist or Marxian view of 'society' as an integrated whole in which the social is supported and 'glued' together by the production, through ideological images, of a generalized form of consent. Rather, Foucault's historically sensitive analysis points to the 'material operations of power' involved in the production of subjects at the most routine and concrete levels of social interaction. The defining feature of modern forms of power is that they are disciplinary, involving often unwritten protocols for conduct and the regulation of habitual norms and manners specific to the domains they develop and which, furthermore, are not to be 'explained' as deriving from a more fundamental source in the economic relations of a society or a monolithic state. So, for Foucault, the situationist's 'spectacle' simply rehearses the still dominant juridical discourse of political theory in which it is the king and later, for liberal theorists, the state which are individualized, made known in written accounts and visual representations, and thus marked as the height of visibility; whereas the modern period is characterized by the ever-increasing disciplinary attention paid to the particular case, to the observation, comparison and classification of separate individuals, which is, in short, a 'reversal of the political axis of individualisation' in which power becomes more anonymous, exercised by 'surveillance rather than ceremonies' (Foucault, 1977: 192–3).

The other readings in this section focus on how images separate the viewer from the viewed by a discontinuity in the relations between time and space. They can be understood as representing various frameworks for conceptualizing a society whose material culture appears to be dominated by an environment of reproduced images, with all that this implies for our capacities to know and to experience. They thus consider the consumption of the conglomerate sum of images comprising the public and private spheres. It should be observed here that consumption is mostly understood phenomenologically, as imputed to people's experience – who are normally considered as a homogeneous mass – rather than as the subject of an empirical investigation into the responses and interpretations of actual viewers and spectators.

We only have to cast our minds back to the extraordinary global response in September 1997 to Princess Diana's death to realize the power of images to personify the public sphere through the mass distribution of the image of persons, such as Diana, who come to be seen as the embodiment, the fabric of the public sphere. We need not here delve into the various possible interpretations of the ostensible 'grieving' surrounding her death. However, for our present purposes it can be surmised that the capacity for a significant number of people to have felt a huge loss at the death of someone they did not really know, however voraciously they read about and looked at her, was a function of her existence for them as primarily an image, an image which was, it seems, endlessly (mis)taken as a part-object of the real Diana. Her image, in iconophilic mode, was loved for being the bearer of the presence of that which it represents. It is precisely because of her presence as an image that this grief could, one or so years on, prove to be short-lived and superficial, incomparable to the grief felt for a person one has really known. In fact, the 'grief' expressed at her death is muted by the afterlife she has as a key character in the public sphere. Her death now appears to be a small puncture in the continuous reproduction of her image.

It is instructive to think about the proliferation of images as part of a key characteristic of modern social organization, that is, as described by Anthony Giddens, 'the precise coordination of the actions of many human beings physically absent from each other – not constrained by the mediation of place' (1990: 17). Modernity is characterized by a process Giddens calls 'disembedding': the 'lifting out of social relations from local contexts' and their "recombination" across infinite tracts of time/space' (1990: 18). The contribution of photography (whether mechanical silver-based or in its newer electronic form – the distinction is not important for the purposes of the argument) to this process cannot be underestimated – as has been noted, Roland Barthes makes much of the abyss between the moment of the making of the picture and that of its viewing. This is precisely what Walter Benjamin felt was positive – against Adorno and other members of the Frankfurt School – about the impact of mechanical reproduction upon the viewing conditions for art, expressed in his 1936 essay, 'The Work of Art in the Age of Mechanical Reproduction' (Chapter 6). He reminds us that the art object has its origins in ritual and was initially used as a devotional object. The cult object rendered present that which was absent, namely the deity or spirit, but it also partook of the latter's absence or inapproachability, rendering it 'distant', 'however close it may be' (p. 75). But, through the substitution of a 'unique existence' for a plurality of copies and the discursive recasting of the object into situations and contexts beyond the reach of original, the techniques of reproduction detach the art object from its traditional domain. The production of meaning can then be understood as contingent and collective. Where the modernist category of art as autonomous and auratic assumes ideas of uniqueness, eternal value, distance and the single creative producer, the post-auratic conditions inaugurated by reproducibility anticipate democratic and 'mass' modes of perception, involving intertextual combinations of text and image, recontextualized imagery and montage – all intimately connected to what Benjamin rather ambiguously refers to as the 'mass movements' (1968: 241). Benjamin's technological determinism, his disregard for the social relations and institutions which shape the use and meaning of technologies, has been attacked from many quarters but none the less foreshadowed the work of McLuhan and Baudrillard.

W. J. T. Mitchell reminds us that the fear of the image, the sense of the image as a powerful, potentially destructive thing, and the anxieties which its potential power awakens, are not only considerable but as old as image-making itself (1994: 15). In the Bible, God forbade the making of graven images of Himself lest the worship of what today we would call His 'simulacrum' would substitute for true worship. And, ever since, the questions of representations of the divine have constituted troubled and contested terrain in many religious and traditional societies with their fetishism, idolatry and totemism. There is, for example, the long-established anthropomorphic fear that the image made by the ethnographer will 'steal' the essence of the individual or tribe. However, an iconomanic and psychically primitive attitude to picture is not confined to the 'pre-modern' or non-modern world. Magical thinking pervades *our* treatment of pictures – although we may 'know' that the pictures we study are only flat, two-dimensional objects marked with colours and shapes, we frequently talk and act as if they had consciousness, desire or agency. We might know that a photograph of our mother is not our mother but – to use Freud's insight about the conflict between knowledge and belief – this is disavowed, to the extent that we may still be reluctant to destroy or discard it. The living image – the statue that moves and the eyes that follow one around a room – remain popular ideas. Images – from paintings to advertisements – are the subject of physical assault. In modern times, there is a fear that images will overwhelm us, partly because they are both extremely immediate in their impact and powerful in the meanings and feelings they convey, yet their precise meaning and reference remain somewhat unfixed. They float or hover within the purview of the image, without our being able quite to offer an interpretation of how this power works on us which fully explains and in so doing exhausts its potentiality – its *potentia*. Contemporary British and American society, in the best traditions of iconoclastic thinking, is thus mired in 'moral' debates assuming an excessive capacity of some types of image to deceive or corrupt, taking as their basic assumption the idea that the image has immanent, causal capacities. Of course, the discourse of the iconoclast is often self-excepting, imputing to others a seduction by the image to which they themselves are immune, having attained the learned and educated response of critical detachment.

On the anti-capitalist left, as has been investigated so well in the work of W. J. T. Mitchell (1986), the analysis of ideology is constituted by a discourse of suspicion about images. Mitchell notes that etymologically 'idea' comes from the Greek verb 'to see', thus helping to explain the long-lasting association of ideas with mental images. The Marxist theory of ideology is rooted in the assumption of a close link between images and idolatry, the famous 'mind as reflection' and camera obscura metaphors suggesting a set of fake notions and images ('phantoms', 'echoes', 'inversions' or reified appearances) that distort apprehension of 'real', existing social relations (see Williams, 1977). Much of the intellectual work which sought to 'decode' advertising from the late 1970s onwards (Williamson, Haug, and more recently Jhally), though often buttressed by the insights of post-structuralism, represents a continuation of Marx's critique of commodity fetishism. The central plank of this theory is that there has been a rupture in capitalist society between the way things appear (what is visible) and their real or actual, underlying and structural meanings (what remains hidden). Fetishism of commodities consists of things seeming to have value inherent in them, and this occurs because the commodity form alone connects producing units in market society, i.e. via exchange value, when in fact, according to Marxian analysis, value is produced by the labour power of workers in definite social relations of production. Hence, 'a definite social relation between men . . . assumes, in their eyes, the fantastic form of a relation between things' (Marx, 1976: 165). In this passage, Marx finds an analogy between the fetishism of commodities whose social character is repressed, 'mist-enveloped', and the optics of perception: 'In the same way the light from an object is perceived by us not as the subjective excitation of our optic nerve, but as the objective form of something outside the eye itself' (1976: 165).

Mitchell makes the important point that, when it comes to his use of image metaphors, Marx's materialism is not easily separable from the tradition Marx dedicated himself to overturning: the idealism of Western philosophy (1986: 187). If, for Marx, ideology is a method for separating true ideas from false ones by determining which ideas have a true connection with external reality (Mitchell, 1986: 165), then, in the idealist tradition, images are but a poor representation of universal ideas. Both of these, in Derrida's terms, are wedded to a 'metaphysics of presence' in which representation is judged in terms of its success or failure to reconstitute the missing 'presence' thought to be the originary source, the original 'content' of the empirical form of the representation so that, in the words of Jonathan Culler, 'everything would be itself' (Culler, 1985: 132; see also Burgin, 1982b: 54–5).

One can thus place Marx in a much broader tradition – from Plato to Brecht, though fatally undermined in the work of Baudrillard – in which representations are fundamentally to be mistrusted, or at least accused of being severely limited to the appearance of the world. In the metaphysical Platonic tradition, which is precisely the target of semiotics, the 'idea' is to be understood as something quite different from imagery or pictures. Ideas are stable concepts, 'suprasensible ideas', independent of the words used to describe them, or the sensible impression that provides a mere 'likeness' (the *eidolon*). Thus this specific actual chair I sit on is a copy of the Idea of chair, a representation of it (for Plato, a mere 'copy') which exists at one remove. Plato famously condemned painting as an illusion produced by fictitious simulations, and banned it from his utopian state in

The Republic. His complaint about the mimetic arts was not so much that they are illusory or deceptive but that they are not suitable vehicles for providing us with knowledge. This attitude continued for many centuries as a deep-seated prejudice in Western philosophy against images as mimetic or as 'likenesses'; they are considered too close to their objects to embody the intellectual preconceptions characteristic of language and thought – they are mere 'shadows'. The metaphors of the shadow and the cave run right through Susan Sontag's book *On Photography*, from which Chapter 7 is taken. Her intellectual mentors here are the Frankfurt School: photography typifies a world in which experience is converted into the pseudo-reality of an image, jeopardizing face-to-face interaction. Her book opens with the statement: 'Humankind lingers unregenerately in Plato's cave, still revelling, its age-old habit, in mere images of the truth' (Sontag, 1977: 3). The remedy, expressed at the end of the chapter we have selected here, is a conservationist rationing of images produced and consumed. For the difference between Plato's misgivings about the image, at a time of artisanal production, and Sontag's, who places her study in the context of a consumer culture, is that now images turn reality into a shadow: 'they are more real than anyone could have supposed' (p. 93). In our extract (Chapter 8) from the classic situationist text of 1967 *Society of the Spectacle* (1977) one can see how Guy Debord regards the 'spectacle' as a totalized condition in which production and consumption are indivisible. As Jonathan Crary (1989: 97) notes, this was the first time that the definite article had been placed before 'spectacle', suggesting such a single and seamless eclipse of every part of society – a standpoint which predated Baudrillard by a good decade.

Of note in Sontag and Debord's work is the particular use of the term 'consumption' typical of a position that has been termed the 'production of consumption' or 'culture industry' approach, after the Frankfurt School (see du Gay et al., 1997). Consumption is seen negatively, as following the predetermined paths set out for it by production. Thus consumption is a simple expression of the intentions of the producers, its activities reduced to the metaphors of 'using up' or 'burning up' a product (which could be an object or an image such as an advert) whose meanings are already determined, rather than, as in more recent analyses, being a productive moment in its own right, in which consumers or viewers also contribute their own meanings through the ways in which they put artefacts and images to use. Moreover, the production of consumption approach tends to think about the population in terms of the homogeneous 'masses', which are always, as Raymond Williams (1958: 289) succinctly puts it, a formula for 'the others, whom we don't know and can't know'. Dick Hebdige, in 'The Bottom Line on Planet One' (Chapter 9), is careful to depart from productionism. His article is selected chiefly for the historical conjuncture that informs it: published originally in 1985 (in *Ten.8*, no. 19), this was at a time when *The Face* was still a novelty, having completed six years, along with Margaret Thatcher's administration, and when interest in the work of Jean Baudrillard was at a peak. Hebdige's task is to account for the relativist lifeworld of *The Face* by contrasting it with the profane 'realism' of *Ten.8*, a now sadly defunct journal central to the development of critical photographic theory in the UK. Rather than assuming a nebulous 'mass' audience, he seeks to understand *The Face* as having achieved an elective affinity with the sensibilities of a generation not moulded by the culture of the post-war welfare state settlement, and in so doing sees it in Raymond Williams' terms as a documentary record of its time. Accordingly, he distances himself from the nihilism of Baudrillard by showing an ambivalence towards the epistemological status of 'Planet Two's seductive pleasures, toying with what the 'bottom line' of a 'Planet One'-style critique might be – from 'outside' as it were. And that, one might suppose, is the 'bottom line' of the iconoclast's worldview, in its attempt to rid us of a love of the image or representation and return to a more authentic identity with the world.

References

Barthes, Roland (1973) *Mythologies*. London: Paladin.

Barthes, Roland (1977) 'The photographic message', in *Image–Music–Text*, trans. S. Heath. New York: Hill and Wang.

Barthes, Roland (1982) *Camera Lucida: Reflections on Photography*. London: Jonathan Cape.

Benjamin, Walter, (1968, first pub. 1936) 'The work of art in the age of mechanical reproduction', in Hannah Arendt (ed.), *Illuminations*. New York: Schocken Books.

Benjamin, Walter (1972, first pub. 1931) 'A short history of photography', *Screen* (spring); reprinted in David Mellor (ed.), *Germany: the New Photography 1927–33*. London: Arts Council of Great Britain, 1978.

Burgin, Victor (1982a) 'Looking at photographs', in V. Burgin (ed.), *Thinking Photography*. London: Macmillan.

Burgin, Victor (1982b) 'Photographic practice and art theory', in V. Burgin (ed.), *Thinking Photography*. London: Macmillan.

Crary, Jonathan (1989) 'Spectacle, attention, counter-memory', *October*, 50 (fall) pp. 97–107).

Culler, Jonathan (1985) *Structuralist Poetics*. London: Routledge and Kegan Paul.

Eco, Umberto (1982) 'Critique of the image', in V. Burgin (ed.), *Thinking Photography*. London: Macmillan.

Foucault, Michel (1977) *Discipline and Punish*. London: Penguin.

du Gay, Paul; Hall, Stuart; Janes, Linda; Mackay, Hugh and Negus, Keith (1997) *Doing Cultural Studies: the Story of the Sony Walkman*. London: Sage/Open University.

Giddens, Anthony (1990) *Modernity and Self-Identity*. Cambridge: Polity Press.

Hall, Stuart (ed.) (1997) *Representation: Cultural Representations and Signifying Practices*. London: Sage/Open University.

Marx, Karl (1976) *Capital, Volume 1*, trans. Ben Foulkes. Harmondsworth: Pengin Books.

Metz, Christian (1974) *Film Language: a Semiotics of the Cinema*. Oxford: Oxford University Press.

Mitchell, W.J.T. (1986) *Iconology*. Chicago: University of Chicago Press.

Mitchell, W.J.T. (1994) 'The pictorial turn', in *Picture Theory*. Chicago: University of Chicago Press.

Peirce, Charles S. (1931–58) 'The icon, index and symbol', in Charles Hartshorne and Paul Weiss (eds), *Collected Works*, 8 vols. Cambridge, MA: Harvard University Press.

Rorty, Richard (1979) *Philosophy and the Mirror of Nature*. Princeton, NJ: Princeton University Press.

de Saussure, Ferdinand (1974) *Course in General Linguistics*. London: Fontana.

Slater, Don (1977) 'The object of photography', in J. Evans (ed.), *The Camerawork Essays*. London: Rivers Oram.

Sontag, Susan (1977) *On Photography*. Harmondsworth: Penguin.

Tagg, John (1988) *The Burden of Representation*. London: Macmillan.

Williams, Raymond (1977) 'From reflection to mediation', in *Marxism and Literature*. Oxford: Oxford University Press.

Williams, Raymond (1958) *Culture and Society 1780–1950*. Harmondsworth: Pelican.

A

Rhetorics of the image

The natural attitude   **Norman Bryson**

It is hard to imagine a more revealing story about painting in the West than this, from Pliny:

> The contemporaries and rivals of Zeuxis were Timanthes, Androcydes, Eupompus, Parrhasius. This last, it is recorded, entered into a competition with Zeuxis. Zeuxis produced a picture of grapes so dexterously represented that birds began to fly down to eat from the painted vine. Whereupon Parrhasius designed so lifelike a picture of a curtain that Zeuxis, proud of the verdict of the birds, requested that the curtain should now be drawn back and the picture displayed. When he realised his mistake, with a modesty that did him honour, he yielded up the palm, saying that whereas he had managed to deceive only birds, Parrhasius had deceived an artist.[1]

The enduring relevance of Pliny's anecdote is remarkable: indeed, unless art history finds the strength to modify itself as a discipline, the anecdote will continue to sum up the essence of working assumptions still largely unquestioned. The Plinian tradition is a long one. When the Italian humanists came to describe the evolution of painting in their own epoch, it was to the *Natural History* that they turned, updating Pliny by substituting the names of contemporary painters for those of antiquity. Painting is once again thought of as a rivalry between technicians for the production of a replica so perfect that art will take the palm from nature. That the goal of the painter is to outstrip his competitors was already enshrined in Dante:

This chapter is taken from Norman Bryson, *Vision and Painting* (London, Macmillan, 1983), pp. 1–12.

> Credette Cimabue ne la pinture
> tener lo campo, e ora ha Giotto il grido,
> sí che la fama di colui è scura.[2]

Once, Cimabue was thought to hold the field
In painting; now it is Giotto's turn;
The other's fame lies buried in the dust.

To the humanists, the recent rivalry vividly recalls antiquity. Villani, in the history of painting he includes in his encyclopedic *De Origine Civitatis Florentiae*, models his account of Giotto's surpassing of Cimabue directly on Plinian precedent:

> First among the painters was John, whose surname was Cimabue, who summoned back with skill and talent the decayed art of painting, wantonly straying from the likeness of nature as this was, since for many centuries previously Greek and Latin painting had been subject to the ministration of but clumsy skills . . . After John, the road to new things lying open, Giotto – who is not only by virtue of his great fame to be compared with the ancient painters, but is even to be preferred to them for skill and talent – restored painting to its former worth and great reputation.[3]

It was Apollodorus who first gave his figures the appearance of reality (Pliny: *hic primus species instituit*): so in the modern age Cimabue summoned back the art of painting and restored it by his skill and talent to the stature it had known in antiquity. It was through the gate opened by Apollodorus (Pliny: *ab hoc artis fores apertas*) that Zeuxis entered, so excelling his predecessor in skilful replication that even the birds were deceived: in just this way, Giotto entered the road opened by Cimabue (*strata iam in novis via*) and cast his predecessor's memory into eclipse, as Dante observes.[4] Vasari expands the Plinian tale and multiplies its *dramatis personae* into a whole saga of triumph and obsolescence, beginning with the obligatory references to Cimabue and Giotto and culminating in Michelangelo, hero, genius, saint.

In the nineteenth century, as positivism takes hold of the discussion of art, this innocent tale will no longer suffice: scholarship, and the market, demand an analysis that will do justice to work seen more and more in terms of formal technique. Yet no sooner has Morelli expounded the principles of morphological analysis that will enable an exact science of attribution to develop, than Berenson pulls the Morellian technology back into the service of the Plinian account: just as it was Cimabue who first questioned the bi-dimensionality of the Byzantine image, so it was Giotto who set Renaissance painting firmly on the road to discovery of tactile values.[5] Even more recently, when Francastel stands before one of the most firmly imprinted of Renaissance images, Masaccio's *Tribute Money*, it is still in terms of the ancient formula that he portrays his reaction.

> Placed at the edge of the space and of the fresco, his calves tense, his bearing insolent, this magnificent *sabreur* bears no relation to the figures of gothic cathedrals: he is drawn from universal visual experience. He does not owe his

imposing presence to the weight and volume of robes: his tunic moulds itself on his body. Henceforth man will be defined not by the rules of narrative, but by an immediate physical apprehension. The goal of representation will be appearance, and no longer meaning.[6]

What Francastel voices here is not only the view of the illustrious ancestors, but of received opinion: the generally held, vague, common-sense conception of the image as the resurrection of Life. Life does not mean, Life is; and the degree to which the image, aspiring to a realm of pure Being, is mixed with meaning, with narrative, with discourse, is the degree to which it has been adulterated, sophisticated, as one 'sophisticates' wine. In its perfect state, painting approaches a point where it sheds everything that interferes with its reduplicative mission; what painting depicts is what everyone with two eyes in his head already knows: 'universal visual experience'.

The ancient tale, repeated across the generations from Pliny to Francastel, might seem capable of engendering a historical discipline. Its emphasis is, after all, on change, and the rapidity of change, within the evolution of the image. Apollodorus appears: Zeuxis outstrips him. Cimabue appears: Giotto surpasses him. Painting is seen as a constant mutation within history. Yet although the study of mutations may possess a historically changing object of enquiry, morphology by itself is not art history: indeed, history is the dimension it exactly negates. The ancient tale sees painting as faced with a task of enormous magnitude: it is to depict everything – gods, men, beasts, things; 'groves, woods, forests, hills, fish-pools, conduits, and drains, riverets, with their banks, and whatsoever a man would wish to see'.[7] The problem lies in the task – its performance, its infinity of possible subject matter, its manual difficulty – but not in the means by which the task is to be performed.[8] Painting itself has no problematic. The difficulties confronted by the painter are executive and concern the fidelity of his registration of the world before him. The world painting is to resurrect exists *out there*, already, in the plenitude of its Being; and all the image is required to do is to approximate as closely as possible the appearances of that plenary origin. Painting corresponds here closely to what Husserl describes as the 'natural attitude'.

> I find ever present and confronting me a single spatio-temporal reality of which I myself am a part, as do all other men found in it and who relate to it in the same way. This 'reality', as the word already indicates, I find existing out there and I receive it just as it presents itself to me as something existing out there [*als daseiende vor und nehme sie, wie sie sich mir gibt, auch als daseiende hin*]. 'The' world as reality is always there: at most it is here and there 'other' than I supposed it and should it be necessary to exclude this or that under the title 'figment of the imagination', 'hallucination', etc., I exclude it from this world which in the attitude of the general thesis is always the world existing out there. It is the aim of the *sciences issuing from the natural attitude* to attain a knowledge of the world more comprehensive, more reliable, and in every respect more perfect than that offered by the

information received by experience, and to resolve all the problems of scientific knowledge that offer themselves upon its ground.[9]

Husserl's remarks concerning how the sciences developed out of the natural attitude invite direct application to painting, at least as theorised in the account that stretches back in time from Francastel to Pliny. The world is pictured as unchanging in its foundation, however much its local appearance may modify through history; history is conceived here as an affair of the surface, and, so to speak, skin-deep. It will be inevitable, therefore, that painting, whose function it is to attend to the surface and to record in minute detail its local manifestations, will give the impression of constant change at the level of content: costume, architecture, and the immediate physical neighbourhood around the human body, are in continual flux, and painting will record that flux with devoted attention. There will be no immediate question, however, that the reality painting records belongs to any category other than that of nature: it is as the natural that the substratum underlying superficial cultural rearrangement is apprehended.

Figure 1.1

The Family of Vunnerius Keramus (Civico Museo dell'Eta Cristiana, Brescia)

The major term suppressed by the natural attitude is that of history; and the first objection that must be raised against the Plinian account is that the real ought to be understood not as a transcendent and immutable given, but as a production brought about by human activity working within specific cultural constraints. Cultural production and reproduction concern not only the shifting cosmetic surface, but the underlying foundation which any given society proposes and assumes as its Reality. While the image of a Roman family such as that of Vunnerius Keramus (Figure 1.1) seems to state the timelessness of the human body, and would appear to confine the province of change to the limited margin of costume, the historical reality to which the figures in the image belong is precisely that which the image brackets out. The power of the image in this way to evoke an ahistorical sense of human reality, and in particular a sense of the culturally transcendent status of the body, is extreme. Under certain conditions, such as those exemplified by the Keramus portrait, the image seems to have sublimed the historical dimension altogether.

Within the natural attitude, which is that of Pliny, Villani, Vasari, Berenson, and Francastel, the image is thought of as self-effacing in the representation or reduplication of things. The goal towards which it moves is the perfect replication of a reality found existing 'out there' already, and all its effort is consumed in the elimination of those obstacles which impede the reproduction of that prior reality: the intransigence of the physical medium; inadequacy of manual technique; the inertia of formulae that impede, through their rigidity, accuracy of registration. The history of the image is accordingly written in negative terms. Each 'advance' consists of the removal of a further obstacle between painting and the Essential Copy: which final state is known in advance, through the prefiguration of Universal Visual Experience.

The painter, in this project, is passive before experience and his existence can be described as an arc extending between two, and only two, points: the retina, and the brush. A binary epistemology defines the world as anterior and masterful, and the painter's function before it as the secondary instrument of its stenographic transcription. His work is carried out in a social void: society may provide him with subject-matter, but his relation to that subject-matter is essentially optical. In so far as the task he is to perform involves any other human agents, the involvement is not with other members of the society but with other painters, whose existence is reduced to the same narrow and optical scope. Moreover, the interaction between the individual painter and the community of painters is once again negative: his aim is to outstrip them, to shed their formulaic legacy, to break whatever limited bond exists between that community and himself, as Zeuxis outstripped Apollodorus, and as Giotto discarded and rendered obsolete the work of Cimabue.

The domain to which painting is said to belong is that of *perception*. The painter who perceives the world insensitively or inaccurately falls below the standards of his craft; he will be unable to advance towards the Essential Copy. Advance is known to have taken place when the viewer is able to detect the reproduction of an item from Universal Visual Experience that has not before appeared in the image. There will be no doubt concerning the presence of such an advance: everyone will see it in the same way; since each human being universally experiences the same visual field, consensus will be absolute. All men are agreed that Giotto's registration of the visual field is subtler, more attentive, and in every way superior to that of Cimabue (Figures 1.2 and 1.3).

Such consensus is matched by a definition of style as personal deviation. The struggle towards perfection is recognised as long and arduous: the Essential Copy, if it were ever achieved, would possess no stylistic features, since the simulacrum would at last have purged away all traces of the productive process. The natural attitude has no way to legitimate style except by way of the limited tolerance it extends to inevitable human weakness. With a ruthless optimism that never fails it, the natural attitude turns all its attention towards the Essential Copy, or at least towards the niche where eventually it will be installed. The modes of failure to achieve the desired and perfect replication are therefore of no more interest to it than are random and extinct mutations to the evolutionary process. Style is a concept that is juridically absent from the scene.

Figure 1.2

Cimabue, *Madonna and Child Enthroned with Angels and Prophets* (Uffizi, Florence; photograph: Mansell Collection)

Idiosyncrasies of the palette, habitual deformations of the figures, the characteristic signature of brushwork, these reflexes that spring from the body and from the past history of the painter are therefore consigned to an underside of the official ideology.[10] Style, serving no apparent purpose within the project of transcription, except here and there to impede its progress, is given no clear argument with which to justify its existence. Lacking in purpose, and the result of no clear intention, it appears as an inert and functionless deposit encrusting the apparatus of communication. Indifferent to the exalted mission with which the image has been entrusted, style emanates from the residue of the body which its optical theorisation had thought to exclude; what had been pictured as an ideal arc extending from retina to brush is discovered to cross another zone, and almost a separate organism, whose secrets, habits, and obsessions distort perception's impersonal luminosity. The Morellian method, with its focus on the telltale details of drapery, hands, and hair, is entirely forensic: style *betrays* itself, in the manner of crime. And the agency with an active interest in such detective-work will be a market hungry for precise attribution in order to maximise the worth of the authentic commodity, and to introduce into its transactions the stability of standard measurement.

Apart from the tax of style that must be paid to human fallibility, the dominant aim of the image, in the natural attitude, is thought of as the communication of perception from a source replete in perceptual material (the painter) to a site of reception eager for perceptual satisfaction (the viewer). Setting aside the informational 'noise' caused by style, by the resistance of the medium, and by the vicissitudes of material decay, the communication of the image is ideally pure and involves only these termini: transmitter and receiver. The rest of the social formation is omitted. The family of Vunnerius Keramus looks much as a comparable family in Rome might look today: the visual essence has been captured.

The global outlook of the natural attitude amounts, then, to a commitment to these five principles:

Figure 1.3

Giotto, *Madonna and Child Enthroned with Saints and Angels* (Uffizi, Florence; photograph: Mansell Collection)

1 *Absence of the dimension of history.* The production of the image is a steady-state process where variation in the image is accounted for either in terms of changing emphases on different aspects of the anterior and unchanging reality, or in terms of fluctuation in the executive competence of the painter. History has a place in the account, but only as a superficially changing spectacle whose alteration does not affect the underlying and immutable substrate. The basic visual field remains the same across the generations, and corresponds to the fixed nature of the optical body. Visual experience being universal and transhistorical, it is therefore given to every viewer to judge, along a sliding scale, how closely a particular image approximates the truth of perception. The scale itself is outside historical process. No one has ever doubted and no one ever will doubt that Zeuxis outstripped Apollodorus, or that Giotto's *Madonna Enthroned* marks an objective advance over Cimabue's version of the same subject.

2 *Dualism.* Between the world of mind and the world of extension there is a barrier: the retinal membrane. On the outside, a pre-existent and plenary reality, flooded with light, surrounds the self on all sides; within, a reflection of that luminous scene is apprehended by a passive and specular consciousness. The self is not responsible for constructing the content of its consciousness: it can do nothing to stem or modify the incoming stream of information stimuli; the visual field it experiences is there by virtue of anatomical and neurological structures that lie beyond its influence. From the material and muscular body, continuous with physical reality and capable of performance within physical reality, a reduced and simplified body is abstracted. In its classical and Albertian formulation, this body of perception is monocular, a single eye removed from the rest of the body and suspended in diagrammatic space.[11] Having no direct access to experience of spatial depth, the visual field before it is already two-dimensional, is already a screen or canvas. The suspended eye witnesses but does not interpret. It has no need to process the stimuli as these arrive, since they possess an intelligibility fully formed and theirs by virtue of the inherent intelligibility of the outer world. The barrier is not, therefore, in any sense opaque, nor does it perform tasks of scansion or censorship on the incoming data: it is a limpid and window-like transparency, without qualities. Once the image comes to recreate the passive translucence of the retinal interval, the Essential Copy will be achieved.

3   *The centrality of perception.* The natural attitude is unable easily to account for images that depart from universal visual experience except in negative terms: the painter has misperceived the optical truth, or has been unable, through lack of skill, or through excess of 'style', to match optical truth on canvas. The appearance on canvas of a wholly imaginary object which nevertheless cannot be characterised as the result of misperception or of executive incompetence is explained either as the combination of disparate segments of the visual field into a new synthesis, or as a personal 'vision' manifesting within the consciousness of the painter and repeated on canvas in the same manner as any other content of consciousness. In all these cases, departure from optical truth is recuperated by restating the departure again as perception, perception that has undergone only minor modification: the project of the painter is still the transmission of the content of his visual field, whether actual (the scene before him) or imaginary (a scene manifesting in consciousness but not in perception). The material to be transmitted exists prior to the work of transmission: it stands before the painter fully formed, before the descent into material transcription begins.

4   *Style as limitation.* The Essential Copy would be immediately and entirely consumed by the viewer's gaze. The same gaze applied to an image that falls short of perfect replication consumes as much of the image as corresponds to universal vision, but will then discover a residue indicating the degree of the image's failure, and running counter to its whole purpose. Where success consists in the perfect preservation of the original precept, style indicates its decay: where communication in its ideal form follows a single direction from transmitter to receiver, style *lacks destination*: where the visual field is the shared property of all, style indicates a withdrawal into privacy and solitude. Style attests to the existence of a physiology that is not at all the decorous and abstract outline sketched in the diagrams of perceptual psychology, but a carnal structure that cannot be subsumed into the official project. If the success of an image and its degree of approximation to universal vision is characterised by the speed of its consumption by the viewing gaze, style is something dense, non-flammable, inert. Ontogenetically, the individual painter is unable to

subdue the inclinations and habits of creatural clay; phylogenetically, a generation of painters is unable to see and to overcome the dead weight of inherited formulae.

5   *The model of communication.* The content of the image is alleged to antedate its physical exteriorisation. The present case is posited as the echo or repetition, more or less distorted, of a prior instance for whose existence, nevertheless, there is no evidence; or rather, the present instance is itself viewed evidentially, as product and proof of an earlier and more perfect incarnation. The location of the earlier image is a metal space within the psyche of the painter. The present image does what it can to transport intact the event within that space into the corresponding mental space in the consciousness of the viewer. A physical entity – the material image – is required if the interchange between non-physical mental spaces is to take place: yet in so far as the material image interposes its own physicality between the communicating fields, it constitutes an impediment to their union. Success can occur only when the image manages to minimise or to conceal its independent material existence.

My aim in this book is the analysis of painting from a perspective very much opposed to that of the Natural Attitude, a perspective that is, or attempts to be, fully materialist. Where it falls short of that aim, on its own terms it fails, and the degree of its failure is for the reader to judge. The topics on which the book touches could be discussed at far greater length, and in choosing to limit discussion to its present brevity, I hope I am not subjecting my reader to undue strain. In reading the text, he or she may well sense a difficulty of topology or affiliation which I myself have been unable to resolve. Where the discussion stands in relation to the work of Gombrich, Wittgenstein, and Saussure, is clear, at least to me. Where it stands in relation to the work of N. Y. Marr and V. N. Vološinov, and to the Soviet materialist tradition in general, is harder to estimate. The intellectual quality I find most to admire in materialist thinking is its firm grasp of a tangible world. My approach to the subject is historical, and it is materialist; yet my argument finds itself in the end in conflict with Historical Materialism. Throughout the writing of this book, I have felt the difficulty of mapping the political implications of its intellectual position on any right-to-left spectrum. It is quite possible that all I understand by 'materialism' is clear-sightedness.

Notes

1   Pliny, *Natural History*, book xxxv, 64–6.
2   Daite, *Purgatorio*, XI, 94–6.
3   *Philippi Villani Liber de civitatis Florentiae famosis civibus*, ed. G. C. Galletti (Florence, 1847); text here taken from Vatican MS Barb. lat. 2610 (circa 1395); cited in M. Baxandall, *Giotto and the Orators* (Oxford, Clarendon Press, 1971), pp. 70, 146–7. See also L. Venturi, 'La critica d'arte alle fine del Trecento (Filippo Villani e

Cennino Cennini)', *L'Arte*, 28 (1925), pp. 233–44; M. Meiss, *Painting in Florence and Siena after the Black Death* (Princeton, NJ, Princeton University Press, 1951), p. 69; and E. Panofsky, *Renaissance and Renascences in Western Art* (Stockholm, Almqvist and Wiksell, 1960), pp. 14–19.

4   Baxandall, *Giotto and the Orators*, pp. 76–8.

5   G. Morelli, *Die Werke italienischer Meister in den Galerien von München, Dresden und Berlin* (Leipzig, Seeman, 1880). On Berenson's debt to Morelli, see M. Secrest, *Being Bernard Berenson* (London, Weidenfeld and Nicolson, 1980), pp. 90–2; and E. Samuels, *Bernard Berenson: the Making of a Connoisseur* (Cambridge, MA and London, Harvard University Press, 1979), pp. 97–105.

6   P. Francastel, *Le figure et le lieu* (Paris, 1967), pp. 234–5.

7   For the full inventory, see Pliny's account of the work of Ludius in *Natural History*, book XXXVI; perhaps at its best in Philemon Holland's translation (reprinted by Southern Illinois University Press; New York, McGraw-Hill, 1962), pp. 421–2.

8   The strategy of the realist project with regard to painting here closely resembles its strategy with regard to textual practice: see S. Heath, *The Nouveau Roman* (London, Elek, 1972), pp. 15–43; R. Barthes, *S/Z* (Paris, Editions du Seuil, 1970); and G. Genette, *Figures II* (Paris, Editions du Seuil, 1969), pp. 73–5.

9   Husserl; cited in Heath, *The Nouveau Roman*, p. 13.

10   Cf. R. Barthes, *Le degré zéro de l'écriture* (Paris, Editions de Seuil, 2nd edn, 1972), pp. 11–17.

11   See Alberti, *De pictura*, book I, 5–20, ed. C. Grayson (London, Phaidon, 1972), pp. 39–57. The archetypal form of the monocular diagram derives, however, from the notebooks of Leonardo.

Rhetoric of the image   **Roland Barthes**

According to an ancient etymology, the word *image* should be linked to the root *imitari*. Thus we find ourselves immediately at the heart of the most important problem facing the semiology of images: can analogical representation (the 'copy') produce true systems of signs and not merely simple agglutinations of symbols? It is possible to conceive of an analogical 'code' (as opposed to a digital one)? We know that linguists refuse the status of language to all communication by analogy – from the 'language' of bees to the 'language' of gesture – the moment such communications are not doubly articulated, are not founded on a combinatory system of digital units as phonemes are. Nor are linguists the only ones to be suspicious as to the linguistic nature of the image; general opinion too has a vague conception of the image as an area of resistance to meaning – this in the name of a certain mythical idea of Life: the image is re-presentation, which is to say ultimately resurrection, and, as we know, the intelligible is reputed antipathetic to lived experience. Thus from both sides the image is felt to be weak in respect of meaning: there are those who think that the image is an extremely rudimentary system in comparison with language and those who think that signification cannot exhaust the image's ineffable richness. Now even – and above all if – the image is in a certain manner the *limit* of meaning, it permits the consideration of a veritable ontology of the process of signification. How does meaning get into the image? Where does it end? And if it ends, what is there *beyond*? Such are the questions that I wish to raise by submitting the image to a spectral analysis of the messages it may contain. We will start by making it considerably easier for ourselves: we will only study the advertising image. Why? Because in advertising the signification of the image is undoubtedly intentional; the signifieds of the advertising message are formed *a priori* by certain attributes of the product and these signifieds have to be transmitted as clearly

This chapter, originally published in 1964, is taken from *Image, Music, Text*, edited by S. Heath (New York, Hill and Wang, 1977).

as possible. If the image contains signs, we can be sure that in advertising these signs are full, formed with a view to the optimum reading: the advertising image is *frank*, or at least emphatic.

The three messages

Here we have a Panzani advertisement (Figure 2.1): some packets of pasta, a tin, a sachet, some tomatoes, onions, peppers, a mushroom, all emerging from a half-open string bag, in yellows and greens on a red background.[1] Let us try to 'skim off' the different messages it contains.

The image immediately yields a first message whose substance is linguistic; its supports are the caption, which is marginal, and the labels, these being inserted into the natural disposition of the scene '*en abyme*'. The code from which this message has been taken is none other than that of the French language; the only knowledge required to decipher it is a knowledge of writing and French. In fact, this message can itself be further broken down, for the sign *Panzani* gives not simply the name of the firm but also, by its assonance, an additional signified, that of 'Italianicity'. The linguistic message is thus twofold (at least in this particular image): denotational and connotational. Since, however, we have here only a single typical sign,[2] namely that of articulated (written) language, it will be counted as one message.

Putting aside the linguistic message, we are left with the pure image (even if the labels are part of it, anecdotally). This image straightaway provides a series of discontinuous signs. First (the order is unimportant as these signs are not linear), the idea that what we have in the scene represented is a return from the market. A signified which itself implies two euphoric values: that of the freshness of the products and that of the essentially domestic preparation for which they are destined. Its signifier is the half-open bag which lets the provisions spill out over the table, 'unpacked'. To read this first sign requires only a knowledge which is in some sort implanted as part of the habits of a very widespread culture where 'shopping around for oneself' is opposed to the hasty stocking up (preserves, refrigerators) of a more 'mechanical' civilization. A second sign is more or less equally evident; its signifier is the bringing together of the tomato, the pepper and the tricoloured hues (yellow, green, red) of the poster; its signified is Italy or rather *Italianicity*. This sign stands in a relation of redundancy with the connoted sign of the linguistic message (the Italian assonance of the name *Panzani*) and the knowledge it draws upon is already more particular; it is a specifically 'French' knowledge (an Italian would barely perceive the connotation of the name, no more probably than he would the 'Italianicity' of tomato and pepper), based on a familiarity with certain tourist stereotypes. Continuing to explore the image (which is not to say that it is not entirely clear at the first glance), there is no difficulty in discovering at least two other signs: in the first, the serried collection of different objects transmits the idea of a total culinary service, on the one hand as though Panzani furnished everything necessary for a carefully balanced dish and, on the other, as though the concentrate in the tin were equivalent to the natural produce surrounding it; in the other sign, the composition of the image, evoking the memory of innumerable alimentary paintings, sends us to an aesthetic signified: the *'nature morte'* or, as it is better expressed in other languages, the 'still life';[3] the knowledge on which this sign depends is heavily cultural. It might be suggested that, in addition to these four signs, there is a further information pointer, that which tells us that this is an advertisement and which arises both from the place of the image in the magazine and from the emphasis of the labels (not to mention the caption). This last information, however, is co-extensive with the scene; it eludes signification insofar as the advertising nature of the image is essentially functional: to utter something is not necessarily to declare *I am speaking*, except in a deliberately reflexive system such as literature.

Thus there are four signs for this image and we will assume that they form a coherent whole (for they are all discontinuous), require a generally cultural knowledge, and refer back to signifieds each of which is global (for example, *Italianicity*), imbued with euphoric values. After the linguistic message, then, we can see a second, iconic message. Is that the end? If all these signs are removed from the image, we are still left with a certain informational matter; deprived of all knowledge, I continue to 'read' the image, to 'understand' that it assembles in a common space a number of identifiable (nameable) objects, not merely shapes and colours. The signifieds of this third message are constituted by the real objects in the scene, the signifiers by these same objects photographed, for, given that the relation between thing signified and image signifying in analogical representation is not 'arbitrary' (as it is in language), it is no longer necessary to dose the relay with a third term in the guise of the psychic image of the object. What defines the third message is precisely that the relation between signified and signifier is quasi-tautological; no doubt the photograph involves a certain arrangement of the scene (framing, reduction, flattening) but this transition is not a *transformation* (in the way a coding can be); we have here a loss of the equivalence characteristic of true sign systems and a statement of quasi-identity. In other words, the sign of this message is not drawn from an institutional stock, is not coded, and we are brought up against the paradox (to which we will return) of a *message without a code*. This peculiarity can be seen again at the level of the knowledge invested in the reading of the message; in order to 'read' this last (or first) level of the image, all that is needed is the knowledge bound up with our perception. That knowledge is not nil, for we need to know what an image is (children only learn this at about the age of four) and what a tomato, a string bag, a packet of pasta are, but it is a matter of an almost anthropological knowledge. This message corresponds, as it were, to the letter of the image and we can agree to call it the literal message, as opposed to the previous symbolic message.

If our reading is satisfactory, the photograph analysed offers us three messages: a linguistic message, a coded iconic message, and a non-coded iconic message. The linguistic message can be readily separated from the other two, but since the latter share the same (iconic) substance, to what extent have we the right to separate them? It is certain that the distinction between the two iconic messages is not made spontaneously in ordinary reading: the viewer of the image receives *at one and the same time* the perceptual message and the cultural message, and it will be seen later that this confusion in reading corresponds to the function of the mass image (our concern here). The distinction, however, has an operational validity, analogous to that which allows the distinction in the linguistic sign of a signifier and a signified (even thought in reality no one is able to separate the 'word' from its meaning except by recourse to the metalanguage of a definition). If the distinction permits us to describe the structure of the image in a simple and coherent fashion and if this description paves the way for an explanation of the role of the image in society, we will take it to be justified. The task now is thus to reconsider each type of message so as to explore it in its generality, without losing sight of our aim of under-standing the overall structure of the image, the final inter-relationship of the three messages. Given that what is in question is not a 'naïve' analysis but a structural description,[4] the order of the messages will be modified a little by the inversion of the cultural message and the literal message; of the two iconic messages, the first is in some sort imprinted on the second: the literal message appears as the *support* of the 'symbolic' message. Hence, knowing that a system which takes over the signs of another system in order to make them its signifiers is a system of connotation,[5] we may say immediately that the literal image is *denoted* and the symbolic image *connoted*. Successively, then, we shall look at the linguistic message, the denoted image, and the connoted image. [*Editor's note*: Barthes goes on to discuss the connoted aspect of the image but our extract concerns itself only with the complexity of the denoted message.]

The linguistic message

Is the linguistic message constant? Is there always textual matter in, under, or around the image? In order to find images given without words, it is doubtless necessary to go back to partially illiterate societies, to a sort of pictographic state of the image. From the moment of the appearance of the book, the linking of text and image is frequent, though it seems to have been little studied from a structural point of view. What is the signifying structure of 'illustration'? Does the image duplicate certain of the informations given in the text by a phenomenon of redundancy or does the text add a fresh information to the image? [. . .] Today, at the level of mass communications, it appears that the linguistic message is indeed present in every image: as title, caption, accompanying press article, film dialogue, comic strip balloon. Which shows that it is not very accurate to talk of a civilization of the image – we are still, and more than ever, a civilization of writing,[6] writing and speech continuing to be the full terms of the informational structure. In fact, it is simply the presence of the linguistic message that counts, for neither its position nor its length seems to be pertinent (a long text may only comprise a single global signified, thanks to connotation, and it is this signified which is put in relation with the image). What are the functions of the linguistic message with regard to the (twofold) iconic message? There appear to be two: *anchorage* and *relay*.

As will be seen more clearly in a moment, all images are polysemous; they imply, underlying their signifiers, a 'floating chain' of signifieds, the reader able to choose some and ignore others. Polysemy poses a question of meaning and this question always comes through as a dysfunction, even if this dysfunction is recuperated by society as a tragic (silent, God provides no possibility of choosing between signs) or a poetic (the panic 'shudder of meaning' of the Ancient Greeks) game; in the cinema itself, traumatic images are bound up with an uncertainty (an anxiety) concerning the meaning of objects or attitudes. Hence in every society various techniques are developed intended to *fix* the floating chain of signifieds in such a way as to counter the terror of uncertain signs; the linguistic message is one of these techniques. At the level of the literal message, the text replies – in a more or less direct, more or less partial manner – to the question: *what is it?* The text helps to identify purely and simply the elements of the scene and the scene itself; it is a matter of a denoted description of the image (a description which is often incomplete) or, in Hjelmslev's terminology, of an *operation* (as opposed to connotation).[7] The denominative function corresponds exactly to an *anchorage* of all the possible (denoted) meanings of the object by recourse to a nomenclature. Shown a plateful of something (in an *Amieux* advertisement), I may hesitate in identifying the forms and masses; the caption ('*rice and tuna fish with mushrooms*') helps me to choose *the correct level of perception*, permits me to focus not simply my gaze but also my understanding. When it comes to the 'symbolic message', the linguistic message no longer guides identification but interpretation, constituting a kind of vice which holds the connoted meanings from proliferating, whether towards excessively individual regions (it limits, that is to say, the projective power of the image) or towards dysphoric values. An advertisement (for *d'Arcy* preserves) shows a few fruits scattered around a ladder; the caption ('*as if from your own garden*') banishes one possible signified (parsimony, the paucity of the harvest) because of its unpleasantness and orientates the reading towards a more flattering signified (the natural and personal character of fruit from a private garden); it acts here as a counter-taboo, combatting the disagreeable myth of the artificial usually associated with preserves. Of course, elsewhere than in advertising, the anchorage may be ideological and indeed this is its principal function; the text *directs* the reader through the signifieds of the image, causing him to avoid some and receive others; by means of an often subtle *dispatching*, it remote-controls him towards a meaning chosen in advance. In all these cases of anchorage, language clearly has a function of elucidation, but this elucidation is selective, a metalanguage applied not to the totality of the iconic message but only to certain of its signs. The text is indeed the creator's (and hence society's) right of inspection over the image; anchorage is a control, bearing a responsibility – in the face of the projective power of pictures – for the use of the message. With respect to the liberty of the signifieds of the image, the text has thus a *repressive* value and we can see that it is at this level that the morality and ideology of a society are above all invested.

Anchorage is the most frequent function of the linguistic message and is commonly found in press photographs and advertisements. The function of relay is less common (at least as far as the fixed image is concerned); it can be seen particularly in cartoons and comic strips. Here text (most often a snatch of dialogue) and image stand in a complementary relationship; the words, in the same way as the images, are fragments of a more general syntagm and the unity of the message is realized at a higher level, that of the story, the anecdote, the diegesis (which is ample confirmation that the diegesis must be treated as an autonomous system).[8] While rare in the fixed image, this relay-text becomes very important in film, where dialogue functions not simply as elucidation but really does advance the action by setting out, in the sequence of messages, meanings that are not to be found in the image itself. Obviously, the two functions of the linguistic message can co-exist in the one iconic whole, but the dominance of the one or the other is of consequence for the general economy of a work. When the text has the diegetic value of relay, the information is more costly, requiring as it does the learning of a digital code (the system of language); when it has a substitute value (anchorage, control), it is the image which detains the informational charge and, the image being analogical, the information is then 'lazier': in certain comic strips intended for 'quick' reading the diegesis is confided above all to the text, the image gathering the attributive informations of a paradigmatic order (the stereotyped status of the characters); the costly message and the discursive message are made to coincide so that the hurried reader may be spared the boredom of verbal 'descriptions', which are entrusted to the image, that is to say to a less 'laborious' system.

The denoted image

We have seen that in the image properly speaking, the distinction between the literal message and the symbolic message is operational; we never encounter (at least in advertising) a literal image in a pure state. Even if a totally 'naïve' image were to be achieved, it would immediately join the sign of naïvety and be completed by a third – symbolic – message. Thus the characteristics of the literal message cannot be substantial but only relational. It is first of all, so to speak, a message by eviction, constituted by what is left in the image when the signs of connotation are mentally deleted (it would not be possible actually to remove them for they can impregnate the whole of the image, as in the case of the 'still life composition'). This evictive state naturally corresponds to a plenitude of virtualities: it is an absence of meaning full of all the meanings. Then again (and there is no contradiction with what has just been said), it is a sufficient message, since it has at least one meaning at the level of the identification of the scene represented; the letter of the image corresponds in short to the first degree of intelligibility (below which the reader would perceive only lines, forms, and colours), but this intelligibility remains virtual by reason of its very poverty, for everyone from a real society always disposes of a knowledge superior to the merely anthropological and perceives more than just the letter. Since it is both evictive and sufficient, it will be understood that from an aesthetic point of view the denoted image can appear as a kind of Edenic state of the image; cleared utopianically of its connotations, the image would become radically objective, or, in the last analysis, innocent.

This utopian character of denotation is considerably reinforced by the paradox already mentioned, that the photograph (in its literal state), by virtue of its absolutely analogical nature, seems to constitute a message without a code. Here, however, structural analysis must differentiate, for of all the kinds of image only the photograph is able to transmit the (literal) information without forming it by means of discontinuous signs and rules of transformation. The photograph, message without a code, must thus be opposed to the drawing which, even when denoted, is a coded message. The coded nature of the drawing can be seen at three levels. First, to reproduce an object or a scene in a drawing requires a set of *rule-governed* transpositions; there is no essential nature of the pictorial copy and the codes of transposition are historical (notably those concerning perspective). Secondly, the operation of the drawing (the coding) immediately necessitates a certain division between the significant and the insignificant: the drawing does not reproduce *everything* (often it reproduces very little), without its ceasing, however, to be a strong message; whereas the photograph, although it can choose its subject, its point of view and its angle, cannot intervene *within* the object (except by trick effects). In other words, the denotation of the drawing is less pure than that of the photograph, for there is no drawing without style. Finally, like all codes, the drawing demands an apprenticeship (Saussure attributed a great importance to this semiological fact). Does the coding of the denoted message have consequences for the connoted message? It is certain that the coding of the literal prepares and facilitates connotation since it at once establishes a certain discontinuity in the image: the 'execution' of a drawing itself constitutes a connotation. But at the same time, insofar as the drawing displays its coding, the relationship between the two messages is profoundly modified: it is no longer the relationship between a nature and a culture (as with the photograph) but that between two cultures; the 'ethic' of the drawing is not the same as that of the photograph.

In the photograph – at least at the level of the literal message – the relationship of signifieds to signifiers is not one of 'transformation' but of 'recording', and the absence of a code clearly reinforces the myth of photographic 'naturalness': the scene *is there*, captured mechanically, not humanly (the mechanical is here a guarantee of objectivity). Man's interventions in the photograph (framing, distance, lighting, focus, speed) all effectively belong to the plane of connotation; it is as though in the beginning (even if utopian) there were a brute photograph (frontal and clear) on which man would then lay out, with the aid of various techniques, the signs drawn from a cultural code. Only the opposition of the cultural code and the natural non-code can, it seems, account for the specific character of the photograph and allow the assessment of the anthropological revolution it represents in man's history. The type of consciousness the photograph involves is indeed truly unprecedented, since it establishes not a consciousness of the *being-there* of the thing (which any copy could provoke) but an awareness of its *having-been-there*. What we have is a new space–time category: spatial immediacy and temporal anteriority, the photograph being an illogical conjunction between the *here-now* and the *there-then*. [. . .]

At all events, the denoted image, to the extent to which it does not imply any code (the case with the advertising photograph), plays a special role in the general structure of the iconic message which we can begin to define (returning to this question after discussion of the third message); the denoted image naturalizes the symbolic message, it innocents the semantic artifice of connotation, which is extremely dense, especially in advertising. Although the *Panzani* poster is full of 'symbols', there nonetheless remains in the photograph, insofar as the literal message is sufficient, a kind of natural *being-there* of objects: nature seems spontaneously to produce the scene represented. [. . .] This is without doubt an important historical paradox: the more technology develops the diffusion of information (and notably of images), the more it provides the means of masking the constructed meaning under the appearance of the given meaning. [. . .]

Notes

1   The *description* of the photograph is given here with prudence, for it already constitutes a metalanguage. The reader is asked to refer to the reproduction.

2   By *typical sign* is meant the sign of a system insofar as it is adequately defined by its substance: the verbal sign, the iconic sign, the gestural sign are so many typical signs.

3   In French, the expression *nature morte* refers to the original presence of funereal objects, such as a skull, in certain pictures.

4   'Naïve' analysis is an enumeration of elements; structural description aims to grasp the relation of these elements by virtue of the principle of the solidarity holding between the terms of a structure: if one term changes, so also do the others.

5   Cf. R. Barthes, 'Eléments de sémiologie', *Communications* 4 (1964), p. 130 (trans. *Elements of Semiology*, London, 1967; New York, 1968, pp. 89–92).

6   Images without words can certainly be found in certain cartoons, but by way of a paradox; the absence of words always covers an enigmatic intention.

7   Barthes, 'Eléments de sémiologie', pp. 131–2 (trans. pp. 90–4).

8   Cf. Claude Bremond, 'Le message narratif', *Communications*, 4 (1964).

3

Art, common sense and photography   **Victor Burgin**

The main thrust of photographic criticism these days is towards the consideration of photography as Art. *Camerawork*, on the other hand, has raised the issue of photography as an instrument of ideology. Many people believe that these two approaches are incompatible. Art is thought to have nothing to do with politics, 'political' art is thought to be irretrievably compromised as Art. But the two may not be quite as mutually exclusive as these people like to think.

Work with an obvious ideological slant is often condemned as 'manipulative'; that is to say, first, that the photographer manipulates what comes over in the image; second, that as a result his or her audience's beliefs about the world are manipulated. Not much is known about how the media influence opinions, although we can be fairly sure that people aren't simply led by the nose by photographs. Whatever the case, both charges can be similarly answered: manipulation is of the essence of photography; *photography would not exist without it.*

In photography, certain physical materials are technically handled so that meanings are produced. Photographers are people who manipulate the physical means of production of photography: cameras, film, lighting, objects, people. Using the productive capabilities of photography to reproduce the world as an object of aesthetic contemplation, and nothing else, is no less 'manipulative' than is any other use of photography: to turn away is an act, to turn away from situations of immediate social relevance is a political act, and to perform such acts in every working moment adds up to a political policy.

The only imaginable non-political being is a totally self-sufficient hermit. The photographer who has chosen to live in a society and enjoy its benefits, even though he also chooses to put on blinkers when he squints into a viewfinder, is willy-nilly an actor in a political situation. So how is it

This chapter, originally published in 1976, is taken from *The Camerawork Essays*, edited by J. Evans (London, Rivers Oram Press, 1997), pp. 74–85.

that so many people can genuinely believe that they lead a-political lives and that it is others – 'militants' and 'extremists' – who 'have' ideology, not themselves? We must first say what we mean by 'ideology'.

When we look at the day-to-day life of a distant culture – behaviour, customs, dress, diet – we are immediately struck by its strangeness: why do they do that? Why do they eat those? What does it all mean? Few such questions trouble us as we pursue our own lives in our own culture, and if they were asked, they would probably get short shrift. Why does a man generally let a female stranger precede him when he is going into a shop, but not when he is boarding a bus? Why do men hang ties around their necks when they wear a shirt, but not when they wear a roll-neck jumper? The questions appear silly, the answers obvious: this is ideology as 'world-view', a common-sense understanding of 'the way things are' which is unquestioningly 'taken for granted'.

What we do ourselves seems so natural to us that we even cease to notice what we do. 'Habitualisation', said the critic Viktor Shklovsky, 'devours work, clothes, furniture, one's wife and the fear of war.' Through habitualisation, working men and women accept lives of tedium, or even misery, as their natural lot, while others accept the social cost of their own greed as being just as unavoidable. The media by which we are informed characteristically reinforce such attitudes: 'Unemployment is expected to rise next month. More rain is expected in the south-west' – both facts appear equally to belong to the natural order of things, acts of God against which there can be no insurance.

The sort of habitualisation which leads millions to collude in their own repression, and which allows the rich and privileged to continue to act selfishly 'in all good faith', Marx called 'false consciousness'. For example, in order that the institutions of the state should continue to serve the interests of a ruling oligarchy, it is necessary that most people should continue to believe that such institutions serve everyone equally. Or again, the belief common to both those who own the means of production and those who do productive work that labour may fairly be bought for wages is a mystification which conceals the fact that, as the value of a commodity depends on the labour invested in it, the owner is appropriating as profit what belongs by right to the labourer: profits are unpaid wages. The idea of false-consciousness is another important aspect of the meaning of the term 'ideology'.

The politically 'Left' photographer wants to help correct society's false picture of its actual conditions of existence, to raise such questions as: why this practice? What does it mean? What interests does it serve? Such a photographer wants to help people become conscious of the forces which shape their day-to-day lives; to realise that the social order is not a natural order and thus beyond all change, but is made by people and can be changed by them. The political dissident photographer, however, is involved in an apparent paradox, that of seeking to penetrate appearances with an instrument designed specifically to record appearances and appearances alone.

Bertolt Brecht found the camera a politically deficient instrument: a photograph of a factory, he pointed out, tells us nothing of the economic forces governing the lives of those who work in it. Roland Barthes made a similar point when he reviewed *The Family of Man* exhibition: of course babies are born and nursed by their mothers all around the world, but photographs of them tell us nothing of the child's life expectancy or of the likelihood that its mother might have died giving birth.[1]

Such writers, notably including Walter Benjamin, have concluded that as language itself is the instrument best adapted to making a politically specific statement, then the photograph can only serve the text. But, although the premise here is correct, the conclusion does not necessarily follow from it. In his essay 'The Great Family of Man', Barthes condemns the failure of photography to make a political statement, yet in this same essay he condemns the exhibition precisely for making such a (mystificatory) political statement.

A photograph of a baby at the breast of a woman in a private nursing home in Switzerland may be placed alongside a photograph of a similarly composed mother and child group in a village in rural India. Assuming that there are no obvious signs of deprivation on the one hand, or of privilege on the other, the two images together will pronounce: 'Mothers and their babies are the same everywhere.' Such a smugly reassuring message was indeed communicated by *The Family of Man* exhibition. The caption, the title of the exhibition, served mainly to underline what had already been said. In this case, the texts served the photographs.

Here, an ideological content is produced by a formal device. The message, 'the condition of motherhood is the same all over the world', would not have been conveyed so readily by either of the photographs alone. Only the juxtaposition of the two creates such a content, in such clarity and with all the immediacy of an observed natural truth. The message is ideological not simply because it is wrong in what it says – simply to be mistaken is not necessarily to be in a state of false consciousness – it is ideological because it misrepresents the actual material condition of the world *in the service of specific vested interests.*

Because we have separate words for 'form' and 'content', we are easily misled into believing that they stand for totally distinct areas of experience. But there is no content without a form, and no form which does not shape a content. In that they have both been misled by a picture of the world given to us by language, 'artists' and 'activists' alike tend to inhabit the same aesthetic ideology. Artists believe that they can present a totally content-free world of pure forms. Activists believe in the autonomous power of 'the truth' which will impose itself regardless of formal considerations. It will pay us, if we are concerned with what photographers 'say', to examine the devices which enable photography to say things, devices so familiar to us they may pass unnoticed.

Popular photography magazines periodically carry articles advising their readers to look for 'contrast'. Such articles generally begin with a directive to look for contrasts of light and dark tones, rough and smooth textures, and then move from form-orientated to content-oriented oppositions such as young/old, happy/sad, etc. Such contrasts are indeed part of the stock-in-trade of the professional – take, for example, the picture Victory and Defeat in Figure 3.1.

Most active photographers are aware of the phenomenon of the 'third effect': two images side by side tend to generate meanings not produced by either image on its own. This effect may be produced by bringing together two physically distinct prints (from two separate negatives), or by juxtaposing two distinct elements within a single frame. In the latter case, the juxtaposition may be brought about by chance (happy coincidence) or by design; if by design, then either 'natural' means (casting, posing, etc.) or 'technical' means (darkroom manipulation, collage, etc.) may be used.

For example, take the picture of George V on Derby Day in Figure 3.2: in this image, we believe that the contrast of rich and poor is made on the basis of a coincidence – the photographer just happened to be there – but it is equally possible, although perhaps less likely, that the two main elements of the image were assembled in the darkroom from separate negatives. Or, again, it is not beyond possibility that the situation depicted was 'set up' for the camera – for example, the photographer could have directed a suitably cast and dressed person to run up to the coach at a predetermined spot. Further to all this, the contradiction of rich and poor could have been communicated by juxtaposing two separate photographs, taken at different times and places from one another.

Of the above possibilities, we would probably conclude that the picture we have here is in actuality the most effective. The photojournalistic 'snap' has an authority which other forms of picture-making lack; it presents itself as factual evidence of an actual state of affairs. In photojournalism, a particular moment may somehow come to signify a general truth. This 'somehow' is generally considered to be unaccountable except in terms of such things as 'luck', 'talent' or a combination of the two. Certainly the photographer of George V was lucky, and he may very well have been 'talented' (whatever that means), but while the picture before us may have depended on luck for its existence, it does not depend upon luck or talent for its meaning – its meaning is something we can account for.

All communication takes place on the basis of signs, most predominantly on the basis of visible and audible signs. To say that one person has communicated with another is to say that each of them has understood how to use and interpret the signs which made up the message between them. If you speak to me in Greek, I have no problem hearing the noises you are making, but if I do not 'know Greek' in common with you, then I cannot understand what you are saying.

The photograph is a sign or, more correctly speaking, a complex of signs, used to communicate a message. If you show me a photograph of a pile of stones then, at an immediate level, my eye receives visual noise just as my ear received verbal noise when you spoke to me in Greek. We can suppose that I have seen photographs since I was a child and so have no problem interpreting these irregular patches of light and dark tones as representing stones. (When African bushmen were first shown photographs, they had to be taught to read them.) But what beyond this? If I go on to remark that the photograph depicts a temple, that the temple is ruined, and that it is Greek, then I am relying upon knowledge that is no longer 'natural', 'purely visual'; I am relying upon knowledge that is cultural, verbally transmitted and, in the final analysis, ideological (I might think 'cradle of civilisation' or 'damned Greeks' according to when and where I happened to be born).

Most photographers are aware of using some sort of system of effects in their work, but such systematisation as may be achieved is generally believed to concern only the purely formal – the 'visual'. Content, it is believed, is just there in the world, and therefore in the picture, whether lined up with the frame or composed on the diagonal. But once we reject the idea of photography as a purely visual language, understood equally by everybody everywhere, then we may begin to consider the possibility that content, too, may be produced as deliberately as one may plan the formal composition of the photograph.

To return, then, to contrast. All contrasts are juxtapositions, but not all juxtapositions are contrasts. The *Derby Day* and *Boxing* pictures are based upon a contrast: that is to say, a dissimilarity of contents (rich/poor, victory/defeat). The well-known Diane Arbus picture of identical twins, on the other hand (Figure 3.3), is based upon a similarity of both form and content. The fashion picture (Figure 3.4) is based upon a juxtaposition of similar forms which have dissimilar contents (e.g., animate/inanimate).

Looked at more closely, the photographer's stock-in-trade of 'contrast' may be seen to consist of a number of distinct communicative devices, devices which nevertheless seem to evolve upon the common basis of the various relationships into which two or more visual elements may enter. The nub of such a system is formed by relationships of similarity and dissimilarity of form and of content, with additional manipulations in the form of substitutions and permutations of elements. The working out of such a system in its entirety is one of the tasks which might be undertaken within a 'semiotic' study of photography.

Semiotics, or semiology, is the science which studies signs. We recognise that some photographers are more successful communicators than others. The semiotician is interested in the reasons for their success or failure – not, of course, in terms of the photographer's personal history, but in terms of the photographic sign itself. The semiotician works from the assumption that wherever we recognize 'mastery' of an art, we also implicitly acknowledge the existence of some system which has been mastered – whether the 'master' is consciously aware of the system or not.

In the early days of 'structuralist' semiology (Roland Barthes's *Elements of Semiology* first appeared in France in 1964) exclusive attention was paid to the analogy between 'natural' language (the phenomenon of speech and writing) and visual 'language'. It had long been common for people to speak loosely of 'the language of . . .' this or that activity, including, of course, 'the language of photography', but it was not until the

1960s that any systematic investigation of forms of communication outside of natural language was conducted from the standpoint of linguistic science.

There were two main reasons for approaching visual communication through linguistics: first, language is the most elaborate and comprehensive form of communication ever evolved, and it seemed at least a reasonable working hypothesis to assume that other forms of human communication might have evolved along basically similar limes; second, modern structural linguistics was itself a sufficiently established science to provide the necessary ready-made theoretical models of communication to start the new science of semiology on its way.

One aspect of natural language use which was found to have a particular bearing on the topic of visual communicative devices is rhetoric. Simply speaking, rhetoric is the artful use of language in order to persuade. In rhetoric, language draws attention to itself in order to attract and retain the attention of the listener or reader – form is manipulated to engage interest in the contents.

Rhetoric first evolved in the Classical period, and one of the difficulties in studying rhetoric today is that the ancient terms are still in use to

Figure 3.4

Fashion picture
(source unknown)

label its 'figures': terms such as *antanaclasis, chiasmus, synechdoche,* etc. However, the meaning of most of these terms becomes clear once examples are provided. In *antanaclasis,* a single word is repeated with different senses, e.g. 'Learn a craft in your youth so that in your old age you can earn your living without craft'; in *chiasmus,* words are repeated but inverted in their order in the course of a single sentence, e.g. 'You should eat to live, not live to eat'; in *synechdoche,* a word is used in a sense of which its usual sense is only a part, e.g. 'Give me your heart' (when the entire body is being sought).

Advertising is the most obvious place we might expect to find rhetorical figures (of which there are literally hundreds). In the first place, there is no doubt that someone is setting out deliberately to persuade; in the second place, there is little doubt that everything in the advertisement has been most carefully placed for maximum effect. Commercial publicity, obviously, endorses and perpetuates the commodity values central to our capitalist ideology. On the Left, the prevailing view of advertising tends to be simply one of disapproval. From one point of view in 'classic' semiology, however, the structure of advertising may be disengaged from its contents: the rhetorical structures of advertising are 'indifferent' to the emotional and ideological value of the contents they handle; much as, for example, an arithmetical structure like two plus two equals four 'doesn't care' whether we are adding up taxicabs or tomatoes. In this view, therefore, there is no reason why, once the devices of advertising have been isolated by semiotic analysis, they may not be 're-cycled' in counter-ideological message-making. Another opinion to be derived from semiotics argues against this, but there is insufficient space here to discuss the apparent contradiction.

The rhetorical analysis of advertising may be conducted along three main 'planes': the image plane; the plane of the text (headline, caption, body-copy); and the plane of the text/image bond. For example, an image which showed a bottle of milk as big as a house would present a figure of *hyperbole* (overstatement). If we then added the headline 'Pour Some More, Mum', the text would be based in rhyme, and we would have established a figure of *litotes* (understatement) in the relationship of the text to the image. Let's take some further, actual examples: figure 3.5 is a visual *hyperbole* much like our hypothetical example except that in this case the exaggeration is doubly charged through sexual allusion; figure 3.6 is an example of *chiasmus* in the plane of the text; figure 3.7 presents a paradox in the text/image plane, and may be worth considering in some more detail. The image in this example draws upon the iconography of poverty – the bath in a zinc tub, the squalid 'back yard', the washing on a line (as opposed to in a spin-dryer). These remarks suffice to show that this is 'poverty' in the definition of a particular culture at a particular historical

Figure 3.5 (top)

*Champagne
advertisement
(source unknown)*

Figure 3.6

*Martini
advertisement
(The Advertising
Archives)*

juncture – the same assembly of signs might connote relative affluence in a 'third world' context. The striped T-shirt is associated in the British mind with the iconography of France and the sea, its connotation of 'St Tropez-ness' establishes a figure of *irony* within the image.

It is likely that the people in the photograph will have been chosen for their – in Barthes's expression – 'canonic generality'; that is to say, each individual represents his or her own 'type', each individual stands for a class of individuals. In rhetoric the figure of *antonamasia* is the one in which the particular stands for the general. Nearly all advertising images contain this figure. Thus, the woman in our example represents all economically disadvantaged mothers (there is no evidence in the picture which proves she is the mother of these children, but the very wide use of images of the family dictates that she represent one). The scene depicted here should cause no offence to either the poor or the comfortably off: there are no torn clothes or matted hair, the children are being washed and (imminently) fed; this is a 'poor but honest' milieu.

The remarks I have made so far concern what is actually to be observed in the image; more observations could be added along these lines. Beyond what is to be seen in the image, however, there are many stories to be *construed* from what is seen. This photograph could serve equally well to illustrate a variety of stories. For example: 'one-parent families'; 'health in the home'; 'domestic life in industrial towns', and so on. The photographic image can carry a large number of different meanings. It is 'polysemic'. Generally, the polysemy of the image is controlled by its juxtaposition with a verbal text.

Roland Barthes has identified two different functions which the verbal message can adopt in relation to the image; these he calls *anchorage* and *relay*.[2] The text adopts a function of anchorage when, from a multiplicity of connotations offered by the image, it selects some and thereby implicitly rejects the others. Thus, in a cigarette advertisement, the contradictory connotations 'cigarettes give pleasure' and 'cigarettes give cancer' are selectively handled in such a caption as 'cool as a mountain stream', a simile which endorses the suggestion of pleasure while rejecting that of unwholesomeness.

In relay, the image and the linguistic text are in a relationship of complementarity: the linguistic message explains, develops, expands the

Figure 3.7

Advert for
Psychology Today
(source unknown)

significance of the image. Figure 3.8 is a particularly clear and simple example of relay. In our previous example, the caption is in a relationship of relay to the image. 'It's all in the mind' is not amongst the connotations we might expect to be summoned by the image alone. It is not therefore 'anchored' from amongst the connotations already available. The rhetorical structure of the text/image relation in this case is that of *paradox*. The dominating connotation of the image may be labelled (but not contained) by the linguistic term 'poverty'. Substituting this term for the image gives us the statement: 'Poverty, it's all in the mind.' However, we know the poverty depicted in the image to be a material poverty, hence the paradox, and hence the effect gained by the juxtaposition of such a caption with such an image.

The semiotician Jacques Durand made these remarks in the course of his 1970 study of rhetoric in advertising:

The myth of 'inspiration', of 'the idea', reigns supreme in the creation of advertising at the present time. In reality, however, the most original ideas, the most audacious advertisements, appear as transpositions of rhetorical figures which have been indexed over the course of numerous centuries. This is explained in that rhetoric is in sum a repertory of the various ways in which we can be 'original'. It is probable then that the creative process could be enriched and made easier if the creators would take account consciously of a system which they use intuitively.[3]

Typical of the nineteenth-century Romantic aesthetic attitudes which prevail in present-day writings on photography is the notion that there are unique essences within things and people which are ordinarily concealed from us but which artistic genius can reveal. This is an idea which photographers had handed down to them from the 'Fine Art' they originally sought to emulate. [. . .] Largely, this idea is a projection of the market relations which characterise our commodity society – the concept of 'genius' guarantees the investment value of the product; the concept of transcendental 'essences' protects the product against practical interrogation.

Brecht took the view that what essences there are behind appearances are to be reached through investigation rather than through intuition. Photography has tended to treat us to an interminable rhetoric of 'humanity – its joys, its sorrows'. The material forces which cause such

Figure 3.8

Jeans advertisement
(source unknown)

emotions and, further, shape our entire lives, may be described. It remains to be seen whether photography will become effective in showing them. What is certain is that if it is to do so, we need to treat the photographic image as an occasion for skepticism and questioning – not as a source of hypnosis.

Notes

1   'The great family of man', in R. Barthes, *Mythologies* (London, Paladin, 1973).
2   See R. Barthes, 'Rhetoric of the image', in *Image–Music–Text* (New York, Hill and Wang, 1977), pp. 32–51 [extracted in Chapter 2 of this volume].
3   Jacques Durand, 'Rhétorique et image publicitaire', *Communication*, 15 (1970).

4

Myth today **Roland Barthes**

What is a myth, today? I shall give at the outset a first, very simple answer, which is perfectly consistent with etymology: *myth is a type of speech*.[1]

Myth is a type of speech

Of course, it is not *any* type: language needs special conditions in order to become myth: we shall see them in a minute. But what must be firmly established at the start is that myth is a system of communication, that it is a message. This allows one to perceive that myth cannot possibly be an object, a concept, or an idea; it is a mode of signification, a form. Later, we shall have to assign to this form historical limits, conditions of use, and reintroduce society into it: we must nevertheless first describe it as a form.

It can be seen that to purport to discriminate among mythical objects according to their substance would be entirely illusory: since myth is a type of speech, everything can be a myth provided it is conveyed by a discourse. Myth is not defined by the object of its message, but by the way in which it utters this message: there are formal limits to myth, there are no 'substantial' ones. Everything, then, can be a myth? Yes, I believe this, for the universe is infinitely fertile in suggestions. Every object in the world can pass from a closed, silent existence to an oral state, open to appropriation by society, for there is no law, whether natural or not, which forbids talking about things. A tree is a tree. Yes, of course. But a tree as expressed by Minou Drouet is no longer quite a tree, it is a tree which is decorated, adapted to a certain type of consumption, laden with literary self-indulgence, revolt, images, in short with a type of social *usage* which is added to pure matter.

This chapter is taken from Roland Barthes, *Mythologies* (1973), pp. 109–143.

Naturally, everything is not expressed at the same time: some objects become the prey of mythical speech for a while, then they disappear; others take their place and attain the status of myth. Are there objects which are *inevitably* a source of suggestiveness, as Baudelaire suggested about Woman? Certainly not: one can conceive of very ancient myths, but there are no eternal ones; for it is human history which converts reality into speech, and it alone rules the life and the death of mythical language. Ancient or not, mythology can only have an historical foundation, for myth is a type of speech chosen by history: it cannot possibly evolve from the 'nature' of things.

[. . .]

Let me therefore restate that any semiology postulates a relation between two terms, a signifier and a signified. This relation concerns objects which belong to different categories, and this is why it is not one of equality but one of equivalence. We must here be on our guard for despite common parlance which simply says that the signifier *expresses* the signified, we are dealing, in any semiological system, not with two, but with three different terms. For what we grasp is not at all one term after the other, but the correlation which unites them: there are, therefore, the signifier, the signified and the sign, which is the associative total of the first two terms. Take a bunch of roses: I use it to *signify* my passion. Do we have here, then, only a signifier and a signified, the roses and my passion? Not even that: to put it accurately, there are here only 'passionified' roses. But on the plane of analysis, we do have three terms; for these roses weighted with passion perfectly and correctly allow themselves to be decomposed into roses and passion: the former and the latter existed before uniting and forming this third object, which is the sign. It is as true to say that on the plane of experience I cannot dissociate the roses from the message they carry, as to say that on the plane of analysis I cannot confuse the roses as signifier and the roses as sign: the signifier is empty, the sign is full, it is a meaning. Or take a black pebble: I can make it signify in several ways, it is a mere signifier; but if I weight it with a definite signified (a death sentence, for instance, in an anonymous vote), it will become a sign. Naturally, there are between the signifier, the signified and the sign, functional implications (such as that of the part to the whole) which are so close that to analyse them may seem futile; but we shall see in a moment that this distinction has a capital importance for the study of myth as semiological schema.

Naturally these three terms are purely formal, and different contents can be given to them. Here are a few examples: for Saussure, who worked on a particular but methodologically exemplary semiological system – the language or *langue* – the signified is the concept, the signifier is the acoustic image (which is mental) and the relation between concept and image is the sign (the word, for instance), which is a concrete entity.[2] For Freud, as is well known, the human psyche is a stratification of tokens or representatives. One term (I refrain from giving it any precedence) is constituted by the manifest meaning of behaviour, another, by its latent or real meaning (it is, for instance, the substratum of the dream); as for the third term, it is here also a correlation of the first two: it is the dream itself in its totality, the parapraxis (a mistake in speech or behaviour) or the neurosis, conceived as compromises, as economies effected thanks to the joining of a form (the first term) and an intentional function (the second term). We can see here how necessary it is to distinguish the sign from the signifier: a dream, to Freud, is no more its manifest datum than its latent content: it is the functional union of these two terms. [. . .]

In myth, we find again the tri-dimensional pattern which I have just described: the signifier, the signified and the sign. But myth is a peculiar system, in that it is constructed from a semiological chain which existed before it: it *is a second-order semiological system*. That which is a sign (namely the associative total of a concept and an image) in the first system, becomes a mere signifier in the second. We must here recall that the materials of mythical speech (the language itself, photography, painting, posters, rituals, objects, etc.), however different at the start, are reduced to a pure signifying function as soon as they are caught by myth. Myth sees in them only the same raw material; their unity is that they all come down to the status of a mere language. Whether it deals with alphabetical or pictorial writing, myth wants to see in them only a sum of signs, a global sign, the final term of a first semiological chain. And it is precisely this final term which will become the first term of the greater system which it builds and of which it is only a part. Everything happens as if myth shifted the formal system of the first significations sideways. As this lateral shift is essential for the analysis of myth, I shall represent it in the following way, it being understood, of course, that the spatialization of the pattern is here only a metaphor:

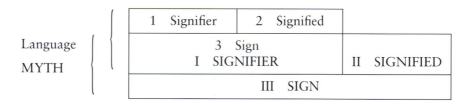

It can be seen that in myth there are two semiological systems, one of which is staggered in relation to the other: a linguistic system, the language (or the modes of representation which are assimilated to it), which I shall call the *language-object*, because it is the language which myth gets hold of in order to build its own system; and myth itself, which I shall call *meta-language*, because it is a second language, *in which* one speaks about the first. When he reflects on a metalanguage, the semiologist no longer needs to ask himself questions about the composition of the language-object, he no longer has to take into account the details of the linguistic schema; he will only need to know its total term, or global sign, and only inasmuch as this term lends itself to myth. This is why the semiologist is entitled to treat in the same way writing and pictures: what he retains from them is the fact that they are both *signs*, that they both reach the threshold of myth endowed with the same signifying function, that they constitute, one just as much as the other, a language-object.

It is now time to give one or two examples of mythical speech. I shall borrow the first from an observation by Valéry.[3] I am a pupil in the second form in a French *lycée*. I open my Latin grammar, and I read a sentence, borrowed from Aesop or Phaedrus: *quia ego nominor leo*. I stop and think. There is something ambiguous about this statement: on the one hand, the words in it do have a simple meaning: *because my name is lion*. And on the other hand, the sentence is evidently there in order to signify something else to me. Inasmuch as it is addressed to me, a pupil in the second form, it tells me clearly: I am a grammatical example meant to illustrate the rule about the agreement of the predicate. I am even forced to realize that the sentence in no way *signifies* its meaning to me, that it tries very little to tell me something about the lion and what sort of name he has; its true and fundamental signification is to impose itself on me as the presence of a certain agreement of the predicate. I conclude that I am faced with a particular, greater, semiological system, since it is co-extensive with the language: there is, indeed, a signifier, but this signifier is itself formed by a sum of signs, it is in itself a first semiological system (*my name is lion*). Thereafter, the formal pattern is correctly unfolded: there is a signified (*I am a grammatical example*) and there is a global signification, which is none other than the correlation of the signifier and the signified; for neither the naming of the lion nor the grammatical example is given separately.

And here is now another example see Figure 4.1: I am at the barber's, and a copy of *Paris-Match* is offered to me. On the cover, a young Negro in a French uniform is saluting, with his eyes uplifted, probably fixed on a fold of the tricolour. All this is the *meaning* of the picture. But, whether naïvely or not, I see very well what it signifies to me: that France is a great Empire, that all her sons, without any colour discrimination, faithfully serve under her flag, and that there is no better answer to the detractors of an alleged colonialism than the zeal shown by this Negro in serving his so-called oppressors. I am therefore again faced with a greater semiological system: there is a signifier, itself already formed with a previous system (*a black soldier is giving the French salute*); there is a signified (it is here a purposeful mixture of Frenchness and militariness); finally, there is a presence of the signified through the signifier.

Before tackling the analysis of each term of the mythical system, one must agree on terminology. We now know that the signifier can be looked at, in myth, from two points of view: as the final term of the linguistic system, or as the first term of the mythical system. We therefore need two names. On the plane of language, that is, as the final term of the first system, I shall call the signifier: *meaning* (*my name is lion, a Negro is giving the French salute*); on the plane of myth, I shall call it: *form*. In the case of the signified, no ambiguity is possible: we shall retain the name *concept*. The third term is the correlation of the first two: in the linguistic system, it is the *sign*; but it is not possible to use this word again without ambiguity, since in myth (and this is the chief peculiarity of the latter), the signifier is already formed by the *signs* of the language. I shall call the third

Figure 4.1

*Paris-Match, no. 326
1955 (© IZIS)*
PARIS MATCH

N° 326

LE NAUFRAGE DE RIVA-BELLA

•

Les enquêteurs recherchent les responsabilités et revivent par la photo les dix minutes d'horreur de

LA TRAGEDIE DU MANS

term of myth the *signification*. This word is here all the better justified since myth has in fact a double function: it points out and it notifies, it makes us understand something and it imposes it on us.

The form and the concept

The signifier of myth presents itself in an ambiguous way: it is at the same time meaning and form, full on one side and empty on the other. As meaning, the signifier already postulates a reading, I grasp it through my eyes, it has a sensory reality (unlike the linguistic signifier, which is purely mental), there is a richness in it: the naming of the lion, the Negro's salute are credible wholes, they have at their disposal a sufficient rationality. As a total of linguistic signs, the meaning of the myth has its own value, it belongs to a history, that of the lion or that of the Negro: in the meaning, a signification is already built, and could very well be self-sufficient if myth did not take hold of it and did not turn it suddenly into an empty, parasitical form. The meaning is *already* complete, it postulates a kind of knowledge, a past, a memory, a comparative order of facts, ideas, decisions.

When it becomes form, the meaning leaves its contingency behind; it empties itself, it becomes impoverished, history evaporates, only the letter remains. There is here a paradoxical permutation in the reading operations, an abnormal regression from meaning to form, from the linguistic sign to the mythical signifier. If one encloses *quia ego nominor leo* in a purely linguistic system, the clause finds again there a fullness, a richness, a history: I am an animal, a lion, I live in a certain country, I have just been hunting, they would have me share my prey with a heifer, a cow and a goat; but being the stronger, I award myself all the shares for various reasons, the last of which is quite simply that *my name is lion*. But as the form of the myth, the clause hardly retains anything of this long story. The meaning contained a whole system of values: a history, a geography, a morality, a zoology, a Literature. The form has put all this richness at a distance: its newly acquired penury calls for a signification to fill it. The story of the lion must recede a great deal in order to make room for the grammatical example, one must put the biography of the Negro in parentheses if one wants to free the picture, and prepare it to receive its signified.

But the essential point in all this is that the form does not suppress the meaning, it only impoverishes it, it puts it at a distance, it holds it at one's disposal. One believes that the meaning is going to die, but it is a death with reprieve; the meaning loses its value, but keeps its life, from which the form of the myth will draw its nourishment. The meaning will be for the form like an instantaneous reserve of history, a tamed richness, which it is possible to call and dismiss in a sort of rapid alternation: the form must constantly be able to be rooted again in the meaning and to get there what nature it needs for its nutriment; above all, it must be able to hide there. It is this constant game of hide-and-seek between the meaning and the form which defines myth. The form of myth is not a symbol: the Negro who salutes is not the symbol of the French Empire: he has too much presence, he appears as a rich, fully experienced, spontaneous, innocent, *indisputable* image. But at the same time this presence is tamed, put at a distance, made almost transparent; it recedes a little, it becomes the accomplice of a concept which comes to it fully armed, French imperiality: once made use of, it becomes artificial.

Let us now look at the signified: this history which drains out of the form will be wholly absorbed by the concept. As for the latter, it is determined, it is at once historical and intentional; it is the motivation which causes the myth to be uttered. Grammatical exemplarity, French imperiality, are the very drives behind the myth. The concept reconstitutes a chain of causes and effects, motives and intentions. Unlike the form, the concept is in no way abstract: it is filled with a situation. Through the concept, it is a whole new history which is implanted in the myth. Into the naming of the lion, first drained of its contingency, the grammatical example will attract my whole existence: Time, which caused me to be born at a certain period when Latin grammar is taught; History, which sets me apart, through a whole mechanism of social segregation, from the children who do not learn Latin; paedagogic tradition, which caused this example to be chosen from Aesop or Phaedrus; my own linguistic habits, which see the agreement of the predicate as a fact worthy of notice and illustration. The same goes for the Negro-giving-the-salute: as form, its meaning is shallow, isolated, impoverished; as the concept of French imperiality, here it is again tied to the totality of the world: to the general History of France, to its colonial adventures, to its present difficulties. Truth to tell, what is invested in the concept is less reality than a certain knowledge of reality; in passing from the meaning to the form, the image loses some knowledge: the better to receive the knowledge in the concept. [. . .]

What must always be remembered is that myth is a double system; there occurs in it a sort of ubiquity: its point of departure is constituted by the arrival of a meaning. To keep a spatial metaphor, the approximative character of which I have already stressed, I shall say that the signification of the myth is constituted by a sort of constantly moving turnstile which presents alternately the meaning of the signifier and its form, a language-object and a metalanguage, a purely signifying and a purely imagining consciousness. This alternation is, so to speak, gathered up in the concept, which uses it like an ambiguous signifier, at once intellective and imaginary, arbitrary and natural.

I do not wish to prejudge the moral implications of such a mechanism, but I shall not exceed the limits of an objective analysis if I point out that the ubiquity of the signifier in myth exactly reproduces the physique of the *alibi* (which is, as one realizes, a spatial term): in the alibi too, there is a place which is full and one which is empty, linked by a relation of negative identity ('I am not where you think I am; I am where you think I am not'). But the ordinary alibi (for the police, for instance) has an end; reality stops the turnstile revolving at a certain point. Myth is a *value*, truth is no guarantee for it; nothing prevents it from being a perpetual alibi: it is enough that its signifier has two sides for it always to have an 'elsewhere' at its disposal. The meaning is always there to *present* the form; the form is always there to *outdistance* the meaning. And there never is any contradiction, conflict, or split between the meaning and the form: they are never at the same place. In the same way, if I am in a car and I look at the scenery through the window, I can at will focus on the scenery or on the window-pane. At one moment I grasp the presence of the glass and the distance of the landscape; at another, on the contrary, the transparence of the glass and the depth of the landscape; but the result of this alternation is constant: the glass is at once present and empty to me, and the landscape unreal and full. The same thing occurs in the mythical signifier: its form is empty but present, its meaning absent but full. To wonder at this contradiction I must voluntarily interrupt this turnstile of form and meaning, I must focus on each separately, and apply to myth a static method of deciphering, in short, I must go against its own dynamics: to sum up, I must pass from the state of reader to that of mythologist.

And it is again this duplicity of the signifier which determines the characters of the signification. We now know that myth is a type of speech defined by its intention (*I am a grammatical example*) much more than by its literal sense (*my name is lion*); and that in spite of this, its intention is somehow frozen, purified, eternalized, *made absent* by this literal sense. (*The French Empire? It's just a fact: look at this good Negro who salutes like one of our own boys.*) This constituent ambiguity of mythical speech has two consequences for the signification, which henceforth appears both like a notification and like a statement of fact. [. . .]

Myth is depoliticized speech

And this is where we come back to myth. Semiology has taught us that myth has the task of giving an historical intention a natural justification, and making contingency appear eternal. Now this process is exactly that of bourgeois ideology. If our society is objectively the privileged field of mythical significations, it is because formally myth is the most appropriate instrument for the ideological inversion which defines this society: at all the levels of human communication, myth operates the inversion of *anti-physis* into *pseudo-physis*.

What the world supplies to myth is an historical reality, defined, even if this goes back quite a while, by the way in which men have produced or used it; and what myth gives in return is a *natural* image of this reality. And just as bourgeois ideology is defined by the abandonment of the name 'bourgeois', myth is constituted by the loss of the historical quality of things: in it, things lose the memory that they once were made. The world enters language as a dialectical relation between activities, between human actions; it comes out of myth as a harmonious display of essences. A conjuring trick has taken place; it has turned reality inside out, it has emptied it of history and has filled it with nature, it has removed from things their human meaning so as to make them signify a human insignificance. The function of myth is to empty reality: it is, literally, a ceaseless flowing out, a haemorrhage, or perhaps an evaporation, in short a perceptible absence.

It is now possible to complete the semiological definition of myth in a bourgeois society: *myth is depoliticized speech*. One must naturally understand *political* in its deeper meaning, as describing the whole of human relations in their real, social structure, in their power of making the world; one must above all give an active value to the prefix *de-*: here it represents an operational movement, it permanently embodies a defaulting. In the case of the soldier-Negro, for instance, what is got rid of is certainly not French imperiality (on the contrary, since what must be actualized is its presence); it is the contingent, historical, in one word: *fabricated*, quality of colonialism. Myth does not deny things, on the contrary, its function is to talk about them; simply, it purifies them, it makes them innocent, it gives them a natural and eternal justification, it gives them a clarity which is not that of an explanation but that of a statement of fact. If I *state the fact* of French imperiality without explaining it, I am very near to finding that it is natural and *goes without saying*: I am reassured. In passing from history to nature, myth acts economically: it abolishes the complexity of human acts, it gives them the simplicity of essences, it does away with all dialectics, with any going back beyond what is immediately visible, it organizes a world which is without contradictions because it is without depth, a world wide open and wallowing in the evident, it establishes a blissful clarity: things appear to mean something by themselves. [. . .]

Notes

1   Innumerable other meanings of the word 'myth' can be cited against this. But I have tried to define things, not words.
2   The notion of *word* is one of the most controversial in linguistics. I keep it here for the sake of simplicity.
3   *Tel Quel* [French Journal], II, p. 191.

B

Techniques of the visible

Panopticism   **Michel Foucault**

The following, according to an order published at the end of the seventeenth century, were the measures to be taken when the plague appeared in a town.[1] First, a strict spatial partitioning: the closing of the town and its outlying districts, a prohibition to leave the town on pain of death, the killing of all stray animals; the division of the town into distinct quarters, each governed by an intendant. Each street is placed under the authority of a syndic, who keeps it under surveillance; if he leaves the street, he will be condemned to death. On the appointed day, everyone is ordered to stay indoors: it is forbidden to leave on pain of death. The syndic himself comes to lock the door of each house from the outside; he takes the key with him and hands it over to the intendant of the quarter; the intendant keeps it until the end of the quarantine. [. . .]

This surveillance is based on a system of permanent registration: reports from the syndics to the intendants, from the intendants to the magistrates or mayor. At the beginning of the 'lock up', the role of each of the inhabitants present in the town is laid down, one by one; this document bears 'the name, age, sex of everyone, notwithstanding his conditions': a copy is sent to the intendant of the quarter, another to the office of the town hall, another to enable the syndic to make his daily roll call. Everything that may be observed during the course of the visits – deaths, illnesses, complaints, irregularities – is noted down and transmitted to the intendants and magistrates. The magistrates have complete control over medical treatment; they have appointed a physician in charge; no other practitioner may treat, no apothecary prepare medicine, no confessor visit a sick person without having received from him a written note 'to prevent anyone from concealing and dealing with those sick of the contagion, unknown to the magistrates'. The registration of the pathological must be constantly centralized. The relation of each individual to his disease and to

This chapter is taken from Michel Foucault, *Discipline and Punish* (London, Penguin, 1977), pp. 195–228. Reproduced by permission of Penguin Books Ltd.

his death passes through the representatives of power, the registration they make of it, the decisions they take on it. [. . .]

The plague is met by order; its function is to sort out every possible confusion: that of the disease, which is transmitted when bodies are mixed together; that of the evil, which is increased when fear and death overcome prohibitions. It lays down for each individual his place, his body, his disease and his death, his well-being, by means of an omnipresent and omniscient power that subdivides itself in a regular, uninterrupted way even to the ultimate determination of the individual, of what characterizes him, of what belongs to him, of what happens to him. Against the plague, which is a mixture, discipline brings into play its power, which is one of analysis. A whole literary fiction of the festival grew up around the plague: suspended laws, lifted prohibitions, the frenzy of passing time, bodies mingling together without respect, individuals unmasked, abandoning their statutory identity and the figure under which they had been recognized, allowing a quite different truth to appear. But there was also a political dream of the plague, which was exactly its reverse: not the collective festival, but strict divisions; not laws transgressed, but the penetration of regulation into even the smallest details of everyday life through the mediation of the complete hierarchy that assured the capillary functioning of power; not masks that were put on and taken off, but the assignment to each individual of his 'true' name, his 'true' place, his 'true' body, his 'true' disease. The plague as a form, at once real and imaginary, of disorder had as its medical and political correlative discipline. [. . .]

If it is true that the leper gave rise to rituals of exclusion, which to a certain extent provided the model for and general form of the great Confinement, then the plague gave rise to disciplinary projects. Rather than the massive, binary division between one set of people and another, it called for multiple separations, individualizing distributions, an organization in depth of surveillance and control, as intensification and ramification of power. The leper was caught up in a practice of rejection, of exile-enclosure; he was left to his doom in a mass among which it was useless to differentiate; those sick of the plague were caught up in a meticulous tactical partitioning in which individual differentiations were the constricting effects of a power that multiplied, articulated and subdivided itself; the great confinement on the one hand; the correct training on the other. The leper and his separation; the plague and its segmentations. The first is marked; the second analysed and distributed. The exile of the leper and the arrest of the plague do not bring with them the same political dream. The first is that of a pure community, the second that of a disciplined society. Two ways of exercising power over men, of controlling their relations, of separating out their dangerous mixtures. The plague-stricken town, traversed throughout with hierarchy, surveillance, observation, writing; the town immobilized by the functioning of an extensive power that bears in a distinct way over all individual bodies – this is the utopia of the perfectly governed city. The plague (envisaged as a possibility at least) is the trial in the course of which one may define ideally the exercise of disciplinary power. In order to make rights and laws function according to pure theory, the jurists place themselves in imagination in the state of nature; in order to see perfect disciplines functioning, rulers dreamt of the state of plague. Underlying disciplinary projects the image of the plague stands for all forms of confusion and disorder; just as the image of the leper, cut off from all human contact, underlies projects of exclusion.

They are different projects, then, but not incompatible ones. We see them coming slowly together, and it is the peculiarity of the nineteenth century that it applied to the space of exclusion of which the leper was the symbolic inhabitant (beggars, vagabonds, madmen and the disorderly formed the real population) the technique of power proper to disciplinary partitioning. Treat 'lepers' as 'plague victims', project the subtle segmentations of discipline onto the confused space of internment, combine it with the methods of analytical distribution proper to power, individualize the excluded, but use procedures of individualization to mark exclusion – this is what was operated regularly by disciplinary power from the beginning of the nineteenth century in the psychiatric asylum, the penitentiary, the reformatory, the approved school and, to some extent, the hospital. Generally speaking, all the authorities exercising individual control function according to a double mode; that of binary division and branding (mad/sane; dangerous/harmless; normal/abnormal); and that of coercive assignment, of differential distribution (who he is; where he must be; how he is to be characterized; how he is to be recognized; how a constant surveillance is to be exercised over him in an individual way, etc.). On the one hand, the lepers are treated as plague victims; the tactics of individualizing disciplines are imposed on the excluded; and, on the other hand, the universality of disciplinary controls makes it possible to brand the 'leper' and to bring into play against him the dualistic mechanisms of exclusion. The constant division between the normal and the abnormal, to which every individual is subjected, brings us back to our own time, by applying the binary branding and exile of the leper to quite different objects; the existence of a whole set of techniques and institutions for measuring, supervising and correcting the abnormal brings into play the disciplinary mechanisms to which the fear of the plague gave rise. All the mechanisms of power which, even today, are disposed around the abnormal individual, to brand him and to alter him, are composed of those two forms from which they distantly derive.

Bentham's *Panopticon* is the architectural figure of this composition (see figure 5.1). We know the principle on which it was based: at the periphery, an annular building; at the centre, a tower; this tower is pierced with wide windows that open onto the inner side of the ring; the peripheric building is divided into cells, each of which extends the whole width of the building; they have two windows, one on the inside, corresponding to the windows of the tower; the other, on the outside, allows the light to cross the cell from one end to the other. All that is needed, then, is to place a supervisor in a central tower and to shut up in each cell a madman, a patient, a condemned man, a worker or a schoolboy. By the effect of backlighting, one can observe from the tower, standing out precisely against the light, the small captive shadows in the cells of the periphery. They are like so many

Figure 5.1

N. Harou-Romain:
Plan for a
penitentiary, 1840: a
prisoner, in his cell,
kneeling at prayer
before the central
inspection tower
(From N.P. Project de
Penitencier, 1840)

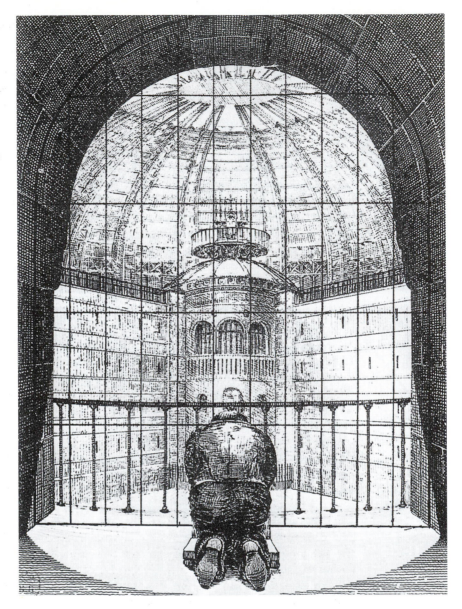

cages, so many small theatres, in which each actor is alone, perfectly individualized and constantly visible. The panoptic mechanism arranges spatial unities that make it possible to see constantly and to recognize immediately. In short, it reverses the principle of the dungeon; or rather of its three functions – to enclose, to deprive of light and to hide – it preserves only the first and eliminates the other two. Full lighting and the eye of a supervisor capture better than darkness, which ultimately protected. Visibility is a trap.

To begin with, this made it possible – as a negative effect – to avoid those compact, swarming, howling masses that were to be found in places of confinement, those painted by Goya or described by Howard. Each individual, in his place, is securely confined to a cell from which he is seen from the front by the supervisor; but the side walls prevent him from coming into contact with his companions. He is seen, but he does not see; he is the object of information, never a subject in communication. The arrangement of his room, opposite the central tower, imposes on him an axial visibility; but the divisions of the ring, those separated cells, imply a lateral invisibility. And this invisibility is a guarantee of order. If the inmates are convicts, there is no danger of a plot, an attempt at collective escape, the planning of new crimes for the future, bad reciprocal influences; if they are patients, there is no danger of contagion; if they are madmen there is no risk of their committing violence upon one another; if they are schoolchildren, there is no copying, no noise, no chatter, no waste of time; if they are workers, there are no disorders, no theft, no coalitions, none of those distractions that slow down the rate of work, make it less perfect or cause accidents. The crowd, a compact mass, a locus of multiple exchanges, individualities merging together, a collective effect, is abolished and replaced by a collection of separated individualities. From the point of view of the guardian, it is replaced by a multiplicity that can be numbered and supervised; from the point of view of the inmates, by a sequestered and observed solitude.[2]

Hence the major effect of the Panopticon: to induce in the inmate a state of conscious and permanent visibility that assures the automatic functioning of power. So to arrange things that the surveillance is permanent in its effects, even if it is discontinuous in its action; that the perfection of power should tend to render its actual exercise unnecessary; that this architectural apparatus should be a machine for creating and sustaining a power relation independent of the person who exercises it; in short, that the inmates should be caught up in a power situation of which they are themselves the bearers. To achieve this, it is at once too much and too little that the prisoner should be constantly observed by an inspector: too little, for what matters is that he knows himself to be observed; too much, because he has no need in fact of being so. In view of this, Bentham laid down the principle that power should be visible and unverifiable. Visible: the inmate will constantly have before his eyes the tall outline of the central tower from which he is spied upon. Unverifiable: the inmate must never know whether he is being looked at at any one moment; but he must be sure that he may always be so. In order to make the presence or absence of the inspector unverifiable, so that the prisoners, in their cells, cannot even see a shadow, Bentham envisaged not only venetian blinds on the windows of the central observation hall, but, on the inside, partitions that intersected the hall at right angles and, in order to pass from one quarter to the other, not doors but zig-zag openings; for the slightest noise, a gleam of light, a brightness in a half-opened door would betray the presence of the guardian. The Panopticon is a machine for dissociating the see/being seen dyad: in the peripheric ring, one is totally seen, without ever seeing; in the central tower, one sees everything without ever being seen.

It is an important mechanism, for it automatizes and disindividualizes power. Power has its principle not so much in a person as in a certain concerted distribution of bodies, surfaces, lights, gazes; in an arrangement whose internal mechanisms produce the relation in which individuals are caught up. The ceremonies, the rituals, the marks by which the sovereign's surplus power was manifested are useless. There is a machinery that assures dissymmetry, disequilibrium, difference. Consequently, it does not matter who exercises power. Any individual, taken almost at random, can operate the machine: in the absence of the director, his family, his friends, his visitors, even his servants.[3] Similarly, it does not matter what motive animates him: the curiosity of the indiscreet, the malice of a child, the thirst for knowledge of a philosopher who wishes to visit this museum of human nature, or the perversity of those who take pleasure in spying and punishing. The more numerous those anonymous and temporary observers are, the greater the risk for the inmate of being surprised and the greater his anxious awareness of being observed. The Panopticon is a marvellous machine which, whatever use one may wish to put it to, produces homogeneous effects of power.

A real subjection is born mechanically from a fictitious relation. So it is not necessary to use force to constrain the convict to good behaviour, the madman to calm, the worker to work, the schoolboy to application, the patient to the observation of the regulations. Bentham was surprised that panoptic institutions could be so light: there were no more bars, no more chains, no more heavy locks; all that was needed was that the separations should be clear and the openings well arranged. The heaviness of the old 'houses of security', with their fortress-like architecture, could be replaced by the simple, economic geometry of a 'house of certainty'. The efficiency of power, its constraining force have, in a sense, passed over to the other side – to the side of its surface of application. He who is subjected to a field of visibility, and who knows it, assumes responsibility for the constraints of power; he makes them play spontaneously upon himself; he inscribes in himself the power relation in which he simultaneously plays both roles; he becomes the principle of his own subjection. By this very fact, the external power may throw off its physical weight; it tends to the non-corporal; and, the more it approaches this limit, the more constant, profound and permanent are its effects: it is a perpetual victory that avoids any physical confrontation and which is always decided in advance.

[. . .] [T]he Panopticon also does the work of a naturalist. It makes it possible to draw up differences: among patients, to observe the symptoms of each individual, without the proximity of beds, the circulation of miasmas, the effects of contagion confusing the clinical tables; among schoolchildren, it makes it possible to observe performances (without there being any imitation or copying), to map aptitudes, to assess characters, to draw up rigorous classifications and, in relation to normal development, to distinguish 'laziness and stubbornness' from 'incurable imbecility'; among workers, it makes it possible to note the aptitudes of each worker, compare the time he takes to perform a task, and if they are paid by the day, to calculate their wages.[4]

So much for the question of observation. But the Panopticon was also a laboratory; it could be used as a machine to carry out experiments, to alter behaviour, to train or correct individuals. To experiment with medicines and monitor their effects. To try out different punishments on prisoners, according to their crimes and character, and to seek the most effective ones. To teach different techniques simultaneously to the workers, to decide which is the best. To try out pedagogical experiments – and in particular to take up once again the well-debated problem of secluded education, by using orphans. One would see what would happen when, in their sixteenth or eighteenth year, they were presented with other boys or girls; one could verify whether, as Helvetius thought, anyone could learn anything; one would follow 'the genealogy of every observable idea'; one could bring up different children according to different systems of thought, making certain children believe that two and two do not make four or that the moon is a cheese, then put them together when they are twenty or twenty-five years old; one would then have discussions that would be worth a great deal more than the sermons or lectures on which so much money is spent; one would have at least an opportunity of making discoveries in the domain of metaphysics. The Panopticon is a privileged place for experiments on men, and for analysing with complete certainty the transformations that may be obtained from them. The Panopticon may even provide an apparatus for supervising its own mechanisms. In this central tower, the director may spy on all the employees that he has under his orders: nurses, doctors, foremen, teachers, warders; he will be able to judge them continuously, alter their behaviour, impose upon them the methods he thinks best; and it will even be possible to observe the director himself. An inspector arriving unexpectedly at the centre of the Panopticon will be able to judge at a glance, without anything being concealed from him, how the entire establishment is functioning. [. . .]

The plague-stricken town, the panoptic establishment – the differences are important. They mark, at a distance of a century and a half, the transformations of the disciplinary programme. In the first case, there is an exceptional situation: against an extraordinary evil, power is mobilized; it makes itself everywhere present and visible; it invents new mechanisms; it separates, it immobilizes, it partitions; it constructs for a time what is both a counter-city and the perfect society; it imposes an ideal functioning, but one that is reduced, in the final analysis, like the evil that it combats, to a simple dualism of life and death: that which moves brings death, and one kills that which moves. The Panopticon, on the other hand, must be understood as a generalizable model of functioning; a way of defining power relations in terms of the everyday life of men. No doubt Bentham presents it as a particular institution, closed in upon itself. Utopias, perfectly closed in upon themselves, are common enough. As opposed to the ruined prisons, littered with mechanisms of torture, to be seen in Piranese's engravings, the Panopticon presents a cruel, ingenious cage. The fact that it should have given rise, even in our own time, to so many variations, projected or realized, is evidence of the imaginary intensity that it has possessed for almost two hundred years. But the Panopticon must not be understood as a dream building: it is the diagram of a mechanism of power reduced to its ideal form; its functioning, abstracted from any obstacle, resistance or friction, must be represented as a pure architectural and optical system: it is in fact a figure of political technology that may and must be detached from any specific use.

It is polyvalent in its applications; it serves to reform prisoners, but also to treat patients, to instruct schoolchildren, to confine the insane, to supervise workers, to put beggars and idlers to work. It is a type of location of bodies in space, of distribution of individuals in relation to one another, of hierarchical organization, of disposition of centres and channels of power, of definition of the instruments and modes of intervention of power, which can be implemented in hospitals, workshops, schools, prisons. [. . .]

In each of its applications, it makes it possible to perfect the exercise of power. It does this in several ways: because it can reduce the number of those who exercise it, while increasing the number of those on whom it is exercised. Because it is possible to intervene at any moment and because the constant pressure acts even before the offences, mistakes or crimes have been committed. Because, in these conditions, its strength is that it never intervenes, it is exercised spontaneously and without noise, it constitutes a mechanism whose effects follow from one another. Because, without any physical instrument other than architecture and geometry, it acts directly on individuals; it gives 'power of mind over mind'. The panoptic schema makes any apparatus of power more intense: it assures its economy (in material, in personnel, in time); it assures its efficacity by its preventative character, its continuous functioning and its automatic mechanisms. It is a way of obtaining from power 'in hitherto unexampled quantity', 'a great and new instrument of government . . . its great excellence consists in the great strength it is capable of giving to *any* institution it may be thought proper to apply it to.'[5]

[. . .]

How is power to be strengthened in such a way that, far from impeding progress, far from weighting upon it with its rules and regulations, it actually facilitates such progress? What intensificator of power will be able at the same time to be a multiplicator of production? How will power, by increasing its forces, be able to increase those of society instead of confiscating them or impeding them? The Panopticon's solution to this problem is that the productive increase of power can be assured only if, on the one hand, it can be exercised continuously in the very foundations of society, in the subtlest possible way, and if, on the other hand, it functions outside these sudden, violent, discontinuous forms that are bound up with the exercise of sovereignty. The body of the king, with its strange material and physical presence, with the force that he himself deploys or transmits to some few others, is at the opposite extreme of this new physics of power represented by panopticism; the domain of panopticism is, on the contrary, that whole lower region, that region of irregular bodies, with their details, their multiple movements, their heterogeneous forces, their spatial relations; what are required are mechanisms that analyse distributions, gaps, series, combinations, and which use instruments that render visible, record, differentiate and compare: a physics of a relational and multiple power, which has its maximum intensity not in the person of the king, but in the bodies that can be individualized by these relations. At the theoretical level, Bentham defines another way of analysing the social body and the power relations that traverse it; in terms of practice, he defines a procedure of subordination of bodies and forces that must increase the utility of power while dispensing with the need for the prince. Panopticism is the general principle of a new 'political anatomy' whose object and end are not the relations of sovereignty but the relations of discipline.

The celebrated, transparent, circular cage, with its high tower, powerful and knowing, may have been for Bentham a project of a perfect disciplinary institution; but he also set out to show how one may 'unlock' the disciplines and get them to function in a diffused, multiple, polyvalent way throughout the whole social body. These disciplines, which the classical age had elaborated in specific, relatively enclosed places – barracks, schools, workshops – and whose total implementation had been imagined only at the limited and temporary scale of a plague-stricken town, Bentham dreamt of transforming into a network of mechanisms that would be everywhere and always alert, running through society without interruption in space or in time. The panoptic arrangement provides the formula for this generalization. It programmes, at the level of an elementary and easily transferable mechanism, the basic functioning of a society penetrated through and through with disciplinary mechanisms.

[. . .]

A few years after Bentham, Julius gave this society its birth certificate.[6] Speaking of the panoptic principle, he said that there was much more there than architectural ingenuity: it was an event in the 'history of the human mind'. In appearance, it is merely the solution of a technical problem; but, through it, a whole type of society emerges. Antiquity had been a civilization of spectacle. 'To render accessible to a multitude of men the inspection of a small number of objects': this was the problem to which the architecture of temples, theatres and circuses responded. With spectacle, there was a predominance of public life, the intensity of festivals, sensual proximity. In these rituals in which blood flowed, society found new vigour and formed for a moment a single great body. The modern age poses the opposite problem: 'To procure for a small number, or even for a single individual, the instantaneous view of a great multitude.' In a society in which the principal elements are no longer the community and public life, but, on the one hand, private individuals and, on the other, the state, relations can be regulated only in a form that is the exact reverse of the spectacle: 'It was to the modern age, to the ever-growing influence of the state, to its ever more profound intervention in all the details and all the relations of social life, that was reserved the task of increasing and perfecting its guarantees, by using and directing towards that great aim the building and distribution of buildings intended to observe a great multitude of men at the same time.'

Julius saw as a fulfilled historical process that which Bentham had described as a technical programme. Our society is one not of spectacle, but of surveillance; under the surface of images, one invests bodies in depth;

behind the great abstraction of exchange, there continues the meticulous, concrete training of useful forces; the circuits of communication are the supports of an accumulation and a centralization of knowledge; the play of signs defines the anchorages of power; it is not that the beautiful totality of the individual is amputated, repressed, altered by our social order, it is rather that the individual is carefully fabricated in it, according to a whole technique of forces and bodies. We are much less Greeks than we believe. We are neither in the amphitheatre, nor on the stage, but in the panoptic machine, invested by its effects of power, which we bring to ourselves since we are part of its mechanism. The importance, in historical mythology, of the Napoleonic character probably derives from the fact that it is at the point of junction of the monarchical, ritual exercise of sovereignty and the hierarchical, permanent exercise of indefinite discipline. He is the individual who looms over everything with a single gaze which no detail, however minute, can escape. [. . .] At the moment of its full blossoming, the disciplinary society still assumes with the Emperor the old aspect of the power of spectacle. As a monarch who is at one and the same time a usurper of the ancient throne and the organizer of the new state, he combined into a single symbolic, ultimate figure the whole of the long process by which the pomp of sovereignty, the necessarily spectacular manifestations of power, were extinguished one by one in the daily exercise of surveillance, in a panopticism in which the vigilance of intersecting gazes was soon to render useless both the eagle and the sun.

[. . .]

What is now imposed on penal justice as its point of application, its 'useful' object, will no longer be the body of the guilty man set up against the body of the king; nor will it be the juridical subject of an ideal contract; it will be the disciplinary individual. The extreme point of penal justice under the Ancien Régime was the infinite segmentation of the body of the regicide: a manifestation of the strongest power over the body of the greatest criminal, whose total destruction made the crime explode into its truth. The ideal point of penality today would be an indefinite discipline: an interrogation without end, an investigation that would be extended without limit to a meticulous and ever more analytical observation, a judgement that would at the same time be the constitution of a file that was never closed, the calculated leniency of a penalty that would be interlaced with the ruthless curiosity of an examination, a procedure that would be at the same time the permanent measure of a gap in relation to an inaccessible norm and the asymptotic movement that strives to meet in infinity. The public execution was the logical culmination of a procedure governed by the Inquisition. The practice of placing individuals under 'observation' is a natural extension of a justice imbued with disciplinary methods and examination procedures. Is it surprising that the cellular prison, with its regular chronologies, forced labour, its authorities of surveillance and registration, its experts in normality, who continue and multiply the functions of the judge, should have become the modern instrument of penality? Is it surprising that prisons resemble factories, schools, barracks, hospitals, which all resemble prisons?

Notes

1 Archives militaires de Vincennes, A 1,516 91 sc. Pièce. This regulation is broadly similar to a whole series of others that date from the same period and earlier.
2 J. Bentham, *Works*, ed. Bowring (1843), iv, pp. 60–4.
3 Ibid., p. 45.
4 Ibid., pp. 60–4.
5 Ibid., p. 66.
6 N. H. Julius, *Leçons sur les prisons*, I (1831, Fr. trans) pp. 384–6.

The work of art in the age of mechanical reproduction
Walter Benjamin

[. . .]

I

In principle a work of art has always been reproducible. Man-made artifacts could always be imitated by men. Replicas were made by pupils in
practice of their craft, by masters for diffusing their works, and, finally, by
third parties in the pursuit of gain. Mechanical reproduction of a work of
art, however, represents something new. Historically, it advanced intermittently and in leaps at long intervals, but with accelerated intensity. The
Greeks knew only two procedures of technically reproducing works of art:
founding and stamping. Bronzes, terra cottas, and coins were the only art
works which they could produce in quantity. All others were unique and
could not be mechanically reproduced. With the woodcut graphic art
became mechanically reproducible for the first time, long before script
became reproducible by print. The enormous changes which printing, the
mechanical reproduction of writing, has brought about in literature are a
familiar story. However, within the phenomenon which we are here
examining from the perspective of world history, print is merely a special,
though particularly important, case. During the Middle Ages engraving
and etching were added to the woodcut; at the beginning of the nineteenth
century lithography made its appearance.

    With lithography the technique of reproduction reached an essentially
new stage. This much more direct process was distinguished by the tracing of
the design on a stone rather than its incision on a block of wood or its
etching on a copperplate and permitted graphic art for the first time to put its
products on the market, not only in large numbers as hitherto, but also in

This chapter,
originally published in
1936, is taken from
Illuminations, edited
by Hannah Arendt
(New York, Schocken
Books, 1968),
pp. 217–242.

daily changing forms. Lithography enabled graphic art to illustrate everyday life, and it began to keep pace with printing. But only a few decades after its invention, lithography was surpassed by photography. For the first time in the process of pictorial reproduction, photography freed the hand of the most important artistic functions which henceforth devolved only upon the eye looking into a lens. Since the eye perceives more swiftly than the hand can draw, the process of pictorial reproduction was accelerated so enormously that it could keep pace with speech. A film operator shooting a scene in the studio captures the images at the speed of an actor's speech. Just as lithography virtually implied the illustrated newspaper, so did photography foreshadow the sound film. The technical reproduction of sound was tackled at the end of the last century. These convergent endeavors made predictable a situation which Paul Valéry pointed up in this sentence: 'Just as water, gas, and electricity are brought into our houses from far off to satisfy our needs in response to a minimal effort, so we shall be supplied with visual or auditory images, which will appear and disappear at a simple movement of the hand, hardly more than a sign.'[1] Around 1900 technical reproduction had reached a standard that not only permitted it to reproduce all transmitted works of art and thus to cause the most profound change in their impact upon the public; it also had captured a place of its own among the artistic processes. For the study of this standard nothing is more revealing than the nature of the repercussions that these two different manifestations – the reproduction of works of art and the art of the film – have had on art in its traditional form.

II

Even the most perfect reproduction of a work of art is lacking in one element: its presence in time and space, its unique existence at the place where it happens to be. This unique existence of the work of art determined the history to which it was subject throughout the time of its existence. This includes the changes which it may have suffered in physical condition over the years as well as the various changes in its ownership. The traces of the first can be revealed only by chemical or physical analyses which it is impossible to perform on a reproduction; changes of ownership are subject to a tradition which must be traced from the situation of the original.

The presence of the original is the prerequisite to the concept of authenticity. Chemical analyses of the patina of a bronze can help to establish this, as does the proof that a given manuscript of the Middle Ages stems from an archive of the fifteenth century. The whole sphere of authenticity is outside technical – and, of course, not only technical – reproducibility.[2] Confronted with its manual reproduction, which was usually branded as a forgery, the original preserved all its authority; not so vis à vis technical reproduction. The reason is twofold. First, process reproduction is more independent of the original than manual reproduction. For example, in photography, process reproduction can bring out those aspects of the original that are unattainable to the naked eye yet accessible to the lens, which is adjustable and chooses its angle at will. And photographic reproduction, with the aid of certain processes, such as enlargement or slow motion, can capture images which escape natural vision. Secondly, technical reproduction can put the copy of the original into situations which would be out of reach for the original itself. Above all, it enables the original to meet the beholder halfway, be it in the form of a photograph or a phonograph record. The cathedral leaves its locale to be received in the studio of a lover of art; the choral production, performed in an auditorium or in the open air, resounds in the drawing room.

The situations into which the product of mechanical reproduction can be brought may not touch the actual work of art, yet the quality of its presence is always depreciated. This holds not only for the art work but also, for instance, for a landscape which passes in review before the spectator in a movie. In the case of the art object, a more sensitive nucleus – namely, its authenticity – is interfered with whereas no natural object is vulnerable on that score. The authenticity of a thing is the essence of all that is transmissible from its beginning, ranging from its substantive duration to its testimony to the history which it has experienced. Since the historical testimony rests on the authenticity, the former, too, is jeopardized by reproduction when substantive duration ceases to matter. And what is really jeopardized when the historical testimony is affected is the authority of the object.

One might subsume the eliminated element in the term 'aura' and go on to say: that which withers in the age of mechanical reproduction is the aura of the work of art. This is a symptomatic process whose significance points beyond the realm of art. One might generalize by saying: the technique of reproduction detaches the reproduced object from the domain of tradition. By making many reproductions it substitutes a plurality of copies for a unique existence. And in permitting the reproduction to meet the beholder or listener in his own particular situation, it reactivates the object reproduced. These two processes lead to a tremendous shattering of tradition which is the obverse of the contemporary crisis and renewal of mankind. Both processes are intimately connected with the contemporary mass movements. Their most powerful agent is the film. Its social significance, particularly in its most positive form, is inconceivable without its destructive, cathartic aspect, that is, the liquidation of the traditional value of the cultural heritage. This phenomenon is most palpable in the great historical films. It extends to ever new positions. In 1927 Abel Gance exclaimed enthusiastically: 'Shakespeare, Rembrandt, Beethoven will make films . . . all legends, all mythologies and all myths, all founders of religion, and the very religions . . . await their exposed resurrection, and the heroes crowd each other at the gate.'[3] Presumably without intending it, he issued an invitation to a far-reaching liquidation.

III

During long periods of history, the mode of human sense perception changes with humanity's entire mode of existence. The manner in which human sense perception is organized, the medium in which it is accomplished, is determined not only by nature but by historical circumstances as well. The fifth century, with its great shifts of population, saw the birth of the late Roman art industry and the Vienna Genesis, and there developed not only an art different from that of antiquity but also a new kind of perception. The scholars of the Viennese school, Riegl and Wickhoff, who resisted the weight of classical tradition under which these later art forms had been buried, were the first to draw conclusions from them concerning the organization of perception at the time. However far-reaching their insight, these scholars limited themselves to showing the significant, formal hallmark which characterized perception in late Roman times. They did not attempt – and, perhaps, saw no way – to show the social transformations expressed by these changes of perception. The conditions for an analogous insight are more favourable in the present. And if changes in the medium of contemporary perception can be comprehended as decay of the aura, it is possible to show its social causes.

The concept of aura which was proposed above with reference to historical objects may usefully be illustrated with reference to the aura of natural ones. We define the aura of the latter as the unique phenomenon of a distance, however close it may be. If, while resting on a summer afternoon, you follow with your eyes a mountain range on the horizon or a branch which casts its shadow over you, you experience the aura of those mountains, of that branch. This image makes it easy to comprehend the social bases of the contemporary decay of the aura. It rests on two circumstances, both of which are related to the increasing significance of the masses in contemporary life. Namely, the desire of contemporary masses to bring things 'closer' spatially and humanly, which is just as ardent as their bent toward overcoming the uniqueness of every reality by accepting its reproduction. Every day the urge grows stronger to get hold of an object at very close range by way of its likeness, its reproduction. Unmistakably, reproduction as offered by picture magazines and newsreels differs from the image seen by the unarmed eye. Uniqueness and permanence are as closely linked in the latter as are transitoriness and reproducibility in the former. To pry an object from its shell, to destroy its aura, is the mark of a perception whose 'sense of the universal equality of things' has increased to such a degree that it extracts it even from a unique object by means of reproduction. Thus is manifested in the field of perception what in the theoretical sphere is noticeable in the increasing importance of statistics. The adjustment of reality to the masses and of the masses to reality is a process of unlimited scope, as much for thinking as for perception.

IV

The uniqueness of a work of art is inseparable from its being imbedded in the fabric of tradition. This tradition itself is thoroughly alive and extremely changeable. An ancient statue of Venus, for example, stood in a different traditional context with the Greeks, who made it an object of veneration, than with the clerics of the Middle Ages, who viewed it as an ominous idol. Both of them, however, were equally confronted with its uniqueness, that is, its aura. Originally the contextual integration of art in tradition found its expression in the cult. We know that the earliest art works originated in the service of a ritual – first the magical, then the religious kind. It is significant that the existence of the work of art with reference to its aura is never entirely separated from its ritual function.[4] In other words, the unique value of the 'authentic' work of art has its basis in ritual, the location of its original use value. This ritualistic basis, however remote, is still recognizable as secularized ritual even in the most profane forms of the cult of beauty.[5] The secular cult of beauty, developed during the Renaissance and prevailing for three centuries, clearly showed that ritualistic basis in its decline and the first deep crisis which befell it. With the advent of the first truly revolutionary means of reproduction, photography, simultaneously with the rise of socialism, art sensed the approaching crisis which has become evident a century later. At the time, art reacted with the doctrine of *l'art pour l'art*, that is, with a theology of art. This gave rise to what might be called a negative theology in the form of the idea of 'pure' art, which not only denied any social function of art but also any categorizing by subject matter. (In poetry, Mallarmé was the first to take this position.)

An analysis of art in the age of mechanical reproduction must do justice to these relationships, for they lead us to an all-important insight: for the first time in world history, mechanical reproduction emancipates the work of art from its parasitical dependence on ritual. To an ever greater degree the work of art reproduced becomes the work of art designed for reproducibility.[6] From a photographic negative, for example, one can make any number of prints; to ask for the 'authentic' print makes no sense. But the instant the criterion of authenticity ceases to be applicable to artistic production, the total function of art is reversed. Instead of being based on ritual, it begins to be based on another practice – politics.

V

Works of art are received and valued on different planes. Two polar types stand out: with one, the accent is on the cult value; with the other, on the exhibition value of the work. Artistic production begins with ceremonial objects destined to serve in a cult. One may assume that what mattered was their existence, not their being on view. The elk portrayed by the man of the Stone Age on the walls of his cave was an instrument of magic. He did expose it to his fellow men, but in the main it was meant for the spirits. Today the cult value would seem to demand that the work of art remain hidden. Certain statues of gods are accessible only to the priest in the cella; certain Madonnas remain covered nearly all year round; certain sculptures on medieval cathedrals are invisible to the spectator on ground level. With the emancipation of the various art practices from ritual go increasing opportunities for the exhibition of their products. It is easier to exhibit a portrait bust that can be sent here and there than to exhibit the statue of a divinity that has its fixed place in the interior of a temple. The same holds for the painting as against the mosaic or fresco that preceded it. And even though the public presentability of a mass originally may have been just as great as that of a symphony, the latter originated at the moment when its public presentability promised to surpass that of the mass.

With the different methods of technical reproduction of a work of art, its fitness for exhibition increased to such an extent that the quantitative shift between its two poles turned into a qualitative transformation of its nature. This is comparable to the situation of the work of art in prehistoric times when, by the absolute emphasis on its cult value, it was, first and foremost, an instrument of magic. Only later did it come to be recognized as a work of art. In the same way today, by the absolute emphasis on its exhibition value the work of art becomes a creation with entirely new functions, among which the one we are conscious of, the artistic function, later may be recognized as incidental. This much is certain: today photography and the film are the most serviceable exemplifications of this new function.

[. . .]

XIII

The characteristics of the film lie not only in the manner in which man presents himself to mechanical equipment but also in the manner in which, by means of this apparatus, man can represent his environment. A glance at occupational psychology illustrates the testing capacity of the equipment. Psychoanalysis illustrates it in a different perspective. The film has enriched our field of perception with methods which can be illustrated by those of Freudian theory. Fifty years ago, a slip of the tongue passed more or less unnoticed. Only exceptionally may such a slip have revealed dimensions of depth in a conversation which had seemed to be taking its course on the surface. Since the *Psychopathology of Everyday Life* things have changed. This book isolated and made analyzable things which had heretofore floated along unnoticed in the broad stream of perception. For the entire spectrum of optical, and now also acoustical, perception the film has brought about a similar deepening of apperception. It is only an obverse of this fact that behavior items shown in a movie can be analyzed much more precisely and from more points of view than those presented on paintings or on the stage. As compared with painting, filmed behavior lends itself more readily to analysis because of its incomparably more precise statements of the situation. In comparison with the stage scene, the filmed behavior item lends itself more readily to analysis because it can be isolated more easily. This circumstance derives its chief importance from its tendency to promote the mutual penetration of art and science. Actually, of a screened behavior item which is neatly brought out in a certain situation, like a muscle of a body, it is difficult to say which is more fascinating, its artistic value or its value for science. To demonstrate the identity of the artistic and scientific uses of photography which heretofore usually were separated will be one of the revolutionary functions of the film.

By close-ups of the things around us, by focusing on hidden details of familiar objects, by exploring commonplace milieu under the ingenious guidance of the camera, the film, on the one hand, extends our comprehension of the necessities which rule our lives; on the other hand, it manages to assure us of an immense and unexpected field of action. Our taverns and our metropolitan streets, our offices and furnished rooms, our railroad stations and our factories appeared to have us locked up hopelessly. Then came the film and burst this prison-world asunder by the dynamite of the tenth of a second, so that now, in the midst of its far-flung ruins and debris, we calmly and adventurously go traveling. With the close-up, space expands; with slow motion, movement is extended. The enlargement of a snap-shot does not simply render more precise what in any case was visible, though unclear: it reveals entirely new structural formations of the subject. So, too, slow motion not only presents familiar qualities of movement but reveals in them entirely unknown ones 'which, far from looking like retarded rapid movements, give the effect of singularly gliding, floating, supernatural motions'.[7] Evidently a different nature opens itself to the camera than opens to the naked eye – if only because an unconsciously penetrated space is substituted for a space consciously explored by man. Even if one has a general knowledge of the way people walk, one knows nothing of a person's posture during the fractional second of a stride. The act of reaching for a lighter or a spoon is familiar routine, yet we hardly know what really goes on between hand and metal, not to mention how this fluctuates with our moods. Here the camera intervenes with the resources of its lowerings and liftings, its interruptions and isolations, its extensions and accelerations, its enlargements and reductions. The camera introduces us to unconscious optics as does psychoanalysis to unconscious impulses. [. . .]

Notes

1   Paul Valéry, 'The conquest of ubiquity', in *Aesthetics*, trans. Ralph Manheim (New York, Pantheon, 1964), p. 226.

2   Precisely because authenticity is not reproducible, the intensive penetration of certain (mechanical) processes of reproduction was instrumental in differentiating and grading authenticity. To develop such differentiations was an important function of the trade in works of art. [. . .] To be sure, at the time of its origin a medieval picture of the Madonna could not yet be said to be 'authentic'. It became 'authentic' only during the succeeding centuries and perhaps most strikingly so during the last one.

3   Abel Grace, 'Le temps de l'image est venu', *L'Art cinématographique*, 2 (1927), pp. 94ff.

4   The definition of the aura as a 'unique phenomenon of a distance however close it may be' represents nothing but the formulation of the cult value of the work of art in categories of space and time perception. Distance is the opposite of closeness. The essentially distant object is the unapproachable one. Unapproachability is indeed a major quality of the cult image. True to its nature, it remains 'distant, however close it

may be'. The closeness which one may gain from its subject matter does not impair the distance which it retains in its appearance.

5   To the extent to which the cult value of the painting is secularized the ideas of its fundamental uniqueness lose distinctness. In the imagination of the beholder the uniqueness of the phenomena which hold sway in the cult image is more and more displaced by the empirical uniqueness of the creator or of his creative achievement. To be sure, never completely so; the concept of authenticity always transcends mere genuineness. (This is particularly apparent in the collector who always retains some traces of the fetishist and who, by owning the work of art, shares in its ritual power.) Nevertheless, the function of the concept of authenticity remains determinate in the evaluation of art; with the secularization of art, authenticity displaces the cult value of the work.

6   In the case of films, mechanical reproduction is not, as with literature and painting, an external condition for mass distribution. Mechanical reproduction is inherent in the very technique of film production. This technique not only permits in the most direct way but virtually causes mass distribution. It enforces distribution because the production of a film is so expensive that an individual who, for instance, might afford to buy a painting no longer can afford to buy a film. In 1927 it was calculated that a major film, in order to pay its way, had to reach an audience of nine million.

7   Rudolf Arnheim, *Film als Kunst*, Berlin, 1932, pp. 138.

7

The image-world   **Susan Sontag**

Reality has always been interpreted through the reports given by images; and philosophers since Plato have tried to loosen our dependence on images by evoking the standard of an image-free way of apprehending the real. But when, in the mid-nineteenth century, the standard finally seemed attainable, the retreat of old religious and political illusions before the advance of humanistic and scientific thinking did not – as anticipated – create mass defections to the real. On the contrary, the new age of unbelief strengthened the allegiance to images. The credence that could no longer be given to realities understood *in the form of* images was now being given to realities understood *to be* images, illusions. In the preface to the second edition (1843) of *The Essence of Christianity*, Feuerbach observes about 'our era' that it 'prefers the image to the thing, the copy to the original, the representation to the reality, appearance to being' – while being aware of doing just that. And his premonitory complaint has been transformed in the twentieth century into a widely agreed-on diagnosis: that a society becomes 'modern' when one of its chief activities is producing and consuming images, when images that have extraordinary powers to determine our demands upon reality and are themselves coveted substitutes for firsthand experience become indispensable to the health of the economy, the stability of the polity, and the pursuit of private happiness.

Feuerbach's words – he is writing a few years after the invention of the camera – seem, more specifically, a presentiment of the impact of photography. For the images that have virtually unlimited authority in a modern society are mainly photographic images; and the scope of that authority stems from the properties peculiar to images taken by cameras.

Such images are indeed able to usurp reality because first of all a photograph is not only an image (as a painting is an image), an interpretation of the real; it is also a trace, something directly stenciled off the real,

This chapter is taken from Susan Sontag, *On Photography* (Harmondsworth, Penguin, 1978), pp. 153–180. Reproduced by permission of Penguin Books Ltd.

like a footprint or a death mask. While a painting, even one that meets photographic standards of resemblance, is never more than the stating of an interpretation, a photograph is never less than the registering of an emanation (light waves reflected by objects) – a material vestige of its subject in a way that no painting can be. [. . .]

Most contemporary expressions of concern that an image-world is replacing the real one continue to echo, as Feuerbach did, the Platonic depreciation of the image: true insofar as it resembles something real, sham because it is no more than a resemblance. But this venerable naïve realism is somewhat beside the point in the era of photographic images, for its blunt contrast between the image ('copy') and the thing depicted (the 'original') – which Plato repeatedly illustrates with the example of a painting – does not fit a photograph in so simple a way. Neither does the contrast help in understanding image-making at its origins, when it was a practical, magical activity, a means of appropriating or gaining power over something. The further back we go in history, as E. H. Gombrich has observed, the less sharp is the distinction between images and real things; in primitive societies, the thing and its image were simply two different, that is, physically distinct, manifestations of the same energy or spirit. Hence, the supposed efficacy of images in propitiating and gaining control over powerful presences. Those powers, those presences were present in *them*.

For defenders of the real from Plato to Feuerbach to equate image with mere appearance – that is, to presume that the image is absolutely distinct from the object depicted – is part of that process of desacralization which separates us irrevocably from the world of sacred times and places in which an image was taken to participate in the reality of the object depicted. What defines the originality of photography is that, at the very moment in the long, increasingly secular history of painting when secularism is entirely triumphant, it revives – in wholly secular terms – something like the primitive status of images. Our irrepressible feeling that the photographic process is something magical has a genuine basis. No one takes an easel painting to be in any sense co-substantial with its subject; it only represents or refers. But a photograph is not only like its subject, a homage to the subject. It is part of, an extension of that subject; and a potent means of acquiring it, of gaining control over it.

Photography is acquisition in several forms. In its simplest form, we have in a photograph surrogate possession of a cherished person or thing, a possession which gives photographs some of the character of unique objects. Through photographs, we also have a consumer's relation to events, both to events which are part of our experience and to those which are not – a distinction between types of experience that such habit-forming consumership blurs. A third form of acquisition is that, through image-making and image-duplicating machines, we can acquire something as information (rather than experience). Indeed, the importance of photographic images as the medium through which more and more events enter our experience is, finally, only a by-product of their effectiveness in furnishing knowledge dissociated from and independent of experience.

This is the most inclusive form of photographic acquisition. Through being photographed, something becomes part of a system of information, fitted into schemes of classification and storage which range from the crudely chronological order of snapshot sequences pasted in family albums to the dogged accumulations and meticulous filing needed for photography's uses in weather forecasting, astronomy, microbiology, geology, police work, medical training and diagnosis, military reconnaissance, and art history. Photographs do more than redefine the stuff of ordinary experience (people, things, events, whatever we see – albeit differently, often inattentively – with natural vision) and add vast amounts of material that we never see at all. Reality as such is redefined – as an item for exhibition, as a record for scrutiny, as a target for surveillance. The photographic exploration and duplication of the world fragments continuities and feeds the pieces into an interminable dossier, thereby providing possibilities of control that could not even be dreamed of under the earlier system of recording information: writing.

That photographic recording is always, potentially, a means of control was already recognized when such powers were in their infancy. In 1850, Delacroix noted in his *Journal* the success of some 'experiments in photography' being made at Cambridge, where astronomers were photographing the sun and the moon and had managed to obtain a pinhead-size impression of the star Vega. He added the following 'curious' observation:

> Since the light of the star which was daguerreotyped took twenty years to traverse the space separating it from the earth, the ray which was fixed on the plate had consequently left the celestial sphere a long time before Daguerre had discovered the process by means of which we have just gained control of this light.

Leaving behind such puny notions of control as Delacroix's, photography's progress has made ever more literal the senses in which a photograph gives control over the thing photographed. The technology that has already minimized the extent to which the distance separating photographer from subject affects the precision and magnitude of the image; provided ways to photograph things which are unimaginably small as well as those, like stars, which are unimaginably far; rendered picture-taking independent of light itself (infra-red photography) and freed the picture-object from its confinement to two dimensions (holography); shrunk the interval between sighting the picture and holding it in one's hands (from the first Kodak, when it took weeks for a developed roll of film to be returned to the amateur photographer, to the Polaroid, which ejects the image in a few seconds); not only got images to move (cinema) but achieved their simultaneous recording and transmission (video) – this technology has made photography an incomparable tool for deciphering behavior, predicting it, and interfering with it.

Photography has powers that no other image-system has ever enjoyed because, unlike the earlier ones, it is *not* dependent on an image maker. However carefully the photographer intervenes in setting up and guiding the image-making process, the process itself remains an optical–chemical (or electronic) one, the workings of which are automatic, the machinery for which will inevitably be modified to provide still more detailed and, therefore, more useful maps of the real. The mechanical genesis of these images, and the literalness of the powers they confer, amounts to a new relationship between image and reality. And if photography could also be said to restore the most primitive relationship – the partial identity of image and object – the potency of the image is now experienced in a very different way. The primitive notion of the efficacy of images presumes that images possess the qualities of real things, but our inclination is to attribute to real things the qualities of an image.

As everyone knows, primitive people fear that the camera will rob them of some part of their being. In the memoir he published in 1900, at the end of a very long life, Nadar reports that Balzac had a similar 'vague dread' of being photographed. His explanation, according to Nadar, was that

> every body in its natural state was made up of a series of ghostly images superimposed in layers to infinity, wrapped in infinitesimal films . . . Man never having been able to create, that is to make something material from an apparition, from something impalpable, or to make from nothing, an object – each Daguerreian operation was therefore going to lay hold of, detach, and use up one of the layers of the body on which it focused.

It seems fitting for Balzac to have had this particular brand of trepidation: 'Was Balzac's fear of the Daguerreotype real or feigned?' Nadar asks. 'It was real . . .' – since the procedure of photography is a materializing, so to speak, of what is most original in his procedure as a novelist. The Balzacian operation was to magnify tiny details, as in a photographic enlargement, to juxtapose incongruous traits or items, as in a photographic layout: made expressive in this way, any one thing can be connected with everything else. For Balzac, the spirit of an entire milieu could be disclosed by a single material detail, however paltry or arbitrary-seeming. The whole of a life may be summed up in a momentary appearance.[1] And a change in appearances is a change in the person, for he refused to posit any 'real' person ensconced behind these appearances. Balzac's fanciful theory, expressed to Nadar, that a body is composed of an infinite series of 'ghostly images', eerily parallels the supposedly realistic theory expressed in his novels, that a person is an aggregate of appearances, appearances which can be made to yield, by proper focusing, infinite layers of significance. To view reality as an endless set of situations which mirror each other, to extract analogies from the most dissimilar things, is to anticipate the characteristic form of perception stimulated by photographic images. Reality itself has started to be understood as a kind of writing, which has to be decoded – even as photographed images were themselves first compared to writing. (Niepce's name for the process whereby the image appears on the plate was 'heliography', sunwriting; Fox Talbot called the camera 'the pencil of nature'.)

The problem with Feuerbach's contrast of 'original' with 'copy' is its static definitions of reality and image. It assumes that what is real persists, unchanged and intact, while only images have changed: shored up by the most tenuous claims to credibility, they have somehow become more seductive. But the notions of image and reality are complementary. When the notion of reality changes, so does that of the image, and vice versa. 'Our era' does not prefer images to real things out of perversity but partly in response to the ways in which the notion of what is real has been progressively complicated and weakened, one of the early ways being the criticism of reality as façade which arose among the enlightened middle classes in the last century. (This was of course the very opposite of the effect intended.) To reduce large parts of what has hitherto been regarded as real to mere fantasy, as Feuerbach did when he called religion 'the dream of the human mind' and dismissed theological ideas as psychological projections; or to inflate the random and trivial details of everyday life into ciphers of hidden historical and psychological forces, as Balzac did in his encyclopedia of social reality in novel form – these are themselves ways of experiencing reality as a set of appearances, an image.

Few people in this society share the primitive dread of cameras that comes from thinking of the photograph as a material part of themselves. But some trace of the magic remains: for example, in our reluctance to tear up or throw away the photograph of a loved one, especially of someone dead or far away. To do so is a ruthless gesture of rejection. In *Jude the Obscure* it is Jude's discovery that Arabella has sold the maple frame with the photograph of himself in it which he gave her on their wedding day that signifies to Jude 'the utter death of every sentiment in his wife' and is 'the conclusive little stroke to demolish all sentiment in him'. But the true modern primitivism is not to regard the image as a real thing; photographic images are hardly that real. Instead, reality has come to seem more and more like what we are shown by cameras. It is common now for people to insist about their experience of a violent event in which they were caught up – a plane crash, a shoot-out, a terrorist bombing – that 'it seemed like a movie.' This is said, other descriptions seeming insufficient, in order to explain how real it was. While many people in non-industrialized countries still feel apprehensive when being photographed, divining it to be some kind to trespass, an act of disrespect, a sublimated looting of the personality or the culture, people in industrialized countries seek to have their photographs taken – feel that they are images, and are made real by photographs.

A steadily more complex sense of the real creates its own compensatory fervors and simplifications, the most addictive of which is picture-taking. It is as if photographers, responding to an increasingly depleted sense of reality, were looking for a transfusion – traveling to new experiences, refreshing the old ones. Their ubiquitous activities amount to the most radical, and the safest, version of mobility. The urge to have new experiences is translated into the urge to take photographs: experience seeking a crisis-proof form.

As the taking of photographs seems almost obligatory to those who travel about, the passionate collecting of them has special appeal for those confined – either by choice, incapacity or coercion – to indoor space.

Photograph collections can be used to make a substitute world, keyed to exalting or consoling or tantalizing images. A photograph can be the starting point of a romance (Hardy's Jude had already fallen in love with Sue Bridehead's photograph before he met her), but it is more common for the erotic relation to be not only created by but understood as limited to the photographs. In Cocteau's *Les Enfants Terribles*, the narcissistic brother and sister share their bedroom, their 'secret room', with images of boxers, movie stars and murderers. Isolating themselves in their lair to live out their private legend, the two adolescents put up these photographs, a private pantheon. [. . .] For stay-at-homes, prisoners and the self-imprisoned, to live among the photographs of glamorous strangers is a sentimental response to isolation and an insolent challenge to it.

J. G. Ballard's novel *Crash* (1973) describes a more specialized collecting of photographs in the service of sexual obsession: photographs of car accidents which the narrator's friend Vaughan collects while preparing to stage his own death in a car crash. The acting out of his erotic vision of car death is anticipated and the fantasy itself further eroticized by the repeated perusal of these photographs. At one end of the spectrum, photographs are objective data; at the other end, they are items of psychological science fiction. [. . .]

Photographs are a way of imprisoning reality, understood as recalcitrant, inaccessible; of making it stand still. Or they enlarge a reality that is felt to be shrunk, hollowed out, perishable, remote. One can't possess reality, one can possess (and be possessed by) images – as, according to Proust, most ambitious of voluntary prisoners, one can't possess the present but one can possess the past. Nothing could be more unlike the self-sacrificial travail of an artist like Proust than the effortlessness of picture-taking, which must be the sole activity resulting in accredited works of art in which a single movement, a touch of the finger, produces a complete work. While the Proustian labors presuppose that reality is distant, photography implies instant access to the real. But the results of this practice of instant access are another way of creating distance. To possess the world in the form of images is, precisely, to reexperience the unreality and remoteness of the real.

The strategy of Proust's realism presumes distance from what is normally experienced as real, the present, in order to reanimate what is usually available only in a remote and shadowy form, the past – which is where the present becomes in his sense real, that is, something that can be possessed. In this effort photographs were of no help. Whenever Proust mentions photographs, he does so disparagingly: as a synonym for a shallow, too exclusively visual, merely voluntary relation to the past, whose yield is insignificant compared with the deep discoveries to be made by responding to cues given by all the senses – the technique he called 'involuntary memory'. One can't imagine the Overture to *Swann's Way* ending with the narrator's coming across a snapshot of the parish church at Combray and the savoring of *that* visual crumb, instead of the taste of the humble madeleine dipped in tea, making an entire part of his past spring into view. But this is not because a photograph cannot evoke memories (it can, depending on the quality of the viewer rather than of the photograph) but because of what Proust makes clear about his own demands upon imaginative recall, that it be not just extensive and accurate but give the texture and essence of things. And by considering photographs only so far as he could use them, as an instrument of memory, Proust somewhat misconstrues what photographs are: not so much an instrument of memory as an invention of it or a replacement.

It is not reality that photographs make immediately accessible, but images. For example, now all adults can know exactly how they and their parents and grandparents looked as children – a knowledge not available to anyone before the invention of cameras, not even to that tiny minority among whom it was customary to commission paintings of their children. Most of these portraits were less informative than any snapshot. And even the very wealthy usually owned just one portrait of themselves or any of their forebears as children, that is, an image of one moment of childhood, whereas it is common to have many photographs of oneself, the camera offering the possibility of possessing a complete record, at all ages. The point of the standard portraits in the bourgeois household of the eighteenth and nineteenth centuries was to confirm an ideal of the sitter (proclaiming social standing, embellishing personal appearance); given this purpose, it is clear why their owners did not feel the need to have more than one. What the photograph record confirms is, more modestly, simply that the subject exists; therefore, one can never have too many.

The fear that a subject's uniqueness was leveled by being photographed was never so frequently expressed as in the 1850s, the years when portrait photography gave the first example of how cameras could create instant fashions and durable industries. In Melville's *Pierre*, published at the start of the decade, the hero, another fevered champion of voluntary isolation,

> considered with what infinite readiness now, the most faithful portrait of any one could be taken by the Daguerreotype, whereas in former times a faithful portrait was only within the power of the moneyed, or mental aristocrats of the earth. How natural then the inference, that instead of, as in old times, immortalizing a genius, a portrait now only *dayalized* a dunce. Besides, when every body has his portrait published, true distinction lies in not having yours published at all.

But if photographs demean, paintings distort in the opposite way: they make grandiose. Melville's intuition is that all forms of portraiture in the business civilization are compromised; at least, so it appears to Pierre, a paragon of alienated sensibility. Just as a photograph is too little in a mass society, a painting is too much. The nature of a painting, Pierre observes, makes it 'better entitled to reverence than the man; inasmuch as nothing belittling can be imagined concerning the portrait, whereas many unavoidably belittling things can be fancied as touching the man.' Even if such ironies can be considered to have been dissolved by the completeness of photography's triumph, the main difference between a painting and a photograph in the matter of portraiture still holds. Paintings invariably sum up; photographs usually do not. Photographic images are pieces of evidence in an ongoing biography or history. And one photograph, unlike one painting, implies that there will be others.

'Ever – the Human Document to keep the present and the future in touch with the past', said Lewis Hine. But what photography supplies is not only a record of the past but a new way of dealing with the present, as the effects of the countless billions of contemporary photograph-documents attest. While old photographs fill out our mental image of the past, the photographs being taken now transform what is present into a mental image, like the past. Cameras establish an inferential relation to the present (reality is known by its traces), provide an instantly retroactive view of experience. Photographs give mock forms of possession: of the past, the present, even the future. In Nabokov's *Invitation to a Beheading* (1938), the prisoner Cincinnatus is shown the 'photohoroscope' of a child cast by the sinister M'sieur Pierre: an album of photographs of little Emmie as an infant, then a small child, then pre-pubescent, as she is now, then – by retouching and using photographs of her mother – of Emmie the adolescent, the bride, the thirty-year-old, concluding with a photograph at age forty, Emmie on her deathbed. A 'parody of the work of time' is what Nabokov calls this exemplary artifact; it is also a parody of the work of photography.

Photography, which has so many narcissistic uses, is also a powerful instrument for depersonalizing our relation to the world; and the two uses are complementary. Like a pair of binoculars with no right or wrong end, the camera makes exotic things near, intimate; and familiar things small, abstract, strange, much farther away. It offers, in one easy, habit-forming activity, both participation and alienation in our own lives and those of others – allowing us to participate, while confirming alienation. War and photography now seem inseparable, and plane crashes and other horrific accidents always attract people with cameras. A society which makes it normative to aspire never to experience privation, failure, misery, pain, dread disease, and in which death itself is regarded not as natural and inevitable but as a cruel, unmerited disaster, creates a tremendous curiosity about these events – a curiosity that is partly satisfied through picture-taking. The feeling of being exempt from calamity stimulates interest in looking at painful pictures, and looking at them suggests and strengthens the feeling that one is exempt. Partly it is because one is 'here', not 'there', and partly it is the character of inevitability that all events acquire when they are transmuted into images. In the real world, something *is* happening and no one knows what is *going* to happen. In the image-world, it *has* happened, and it *will* forever happen in that way.

Knowing a great deal about what is in the world (art, catastrophe, the beauties of nature) through photographic images, people are frequently disappointed, surprised, unmoved when they see the real thing. For photographic images tend to subtract feeling from something we experience at first hand and the feelings they do arouse are, largely, not those we have in real life. Often something disturbs us more in photographed form than it does when we actually experience it. In a hospital in Shanghai in 1973, watching a factory worker with advanced ulcers have nine-tenths of his stomach removed under acupuncture anesthesia, I managed to follow the three-hour procedure (the first operation I'd even observed) without queasiness, never once feeling the need to look away. In a movie theater in Paris a year later, the less gory operation in Antonioni's China documentary *Chung Kuo* made me flinch at the first cut of the scalpel and avert my eyes several times during the sequence. One is vulnerable to disturbing events in the form of photographic images in a way that one is not to the real thing. That vulnerability is part of the distinctive passivity of someone who is a spectator twice over, spectator of events already shaped, first by the participants and second by the image maker. For the real operation I had to get scrubbed, don a surgical gown, then stand alongside the busy surgeons and nurses with my roles to play: inhibited adult, well-mannered guest, respectful witness. The movie operation precludes not only this modest participation but whatever is active in spectatorship. In the operating room, I am the one who changes focus, who makes the close-ups and the medium shots. In the theater, Antonioni has already chosen what parts of the operation I can watch; the camera looks for me – and obliges me to look, leaving as my only option not to look. Further, the movie condenses something that takes hours to a few minutes, leaving only interesting parts presented in an interesting way, that is, with the intent to stir or shock. The dramatic is dramatized, by the didactics of layout and montage. We turn the page in a photo-magazine, a new sequence starts in a movie, making a contrast that is sharper than the contrast between successive events in real time.

Nothing could be more instructive about the meaning of photography for us – as, among other things, a method of hyping up the real – than the attacks on Antonioni's film in the Chinese press in early 1974. They make a negative catalogue of all the devices of modern photography, still and film.[2] While for us photography is intimately connected with discontinuous ways of seeing (the point is precisely to see the whole by means of a part – an arresting detail, a striking way of cropping), in China it is connected only with continuity. Not only are there proper subjects for the camera, those which are positive, inspirational (exemplary activities, smiling people, bright weather), and orderly, but there are proper ways of photographing, which derive from notions about the moral order of space that preclude the very idea of photographic seeing. Thus, Antonioni was reproached for photographing things that were old, or old-fashioned – 'he sought out and took dilapidated walls and blackboard newspapers discarded long ago'; paying 'no attention to big and small tractors working in the fields, [he] chose only a donkey pulling a stone roller' – and for showing undecorous moments – 'he disgustingly filmed people blowing their noses and going to the latrine' – and undisciplined movement – 'instead of taking shots of pupils in the classroom in our factory-run primary school, he filmed the children running out of the classroom after a class.' And he was accused of denigrating the right subjects by his way of photographing them: by using 'dim and dreary colors' and hiding people in 'dark shadows'; by treating the same subject with a variety of shots –

'there are sometimes long-shots, sometimes close-ups, sometimes from the front, and sometimes from behind' – that is, for not showing things from the point of view of a single, ideally placed observer; by using high and low angles – 'The camera was intentionally turned on this magnificent modern bridge from very bad angles in order to make it appear crooked and tottering'; and by not taking enough full shots – 'He racked his brain to get such close-ups in an attempt to distort the people's image and uglify their spiritual outlook.'

Besides the mass-produced photographic iconography of revered leaders, revolutionary kitsch, and cultural treasures, one often sees photographs of a private sort in China. Many people possess pictures of their loved ones, tacked to the wall or stuck under the glass on top of the dresser or office desk. A large number of these are the sort of snapshots taken here at family gatherings and on trips; but none is a candid photograph, not even of the kind that the most unsophisticated camera user in this society finds normal – a baby crawling on the floor, someone in mid-gesture. Sports photographs show the team as a group, or only the most stylized balletic moments of play: generally, what people do with the camera is assemble for it, then line up in a row or two. There is no interest in catching a subject in movement. This is, one supposes, partly because of certain old conventions of decorum in conduct and imagery. And it is the characteristic visual taste of those at the first stage of camera culture, when the image is defined as something that can be stolen from its owner; thus, Antonioni was reproached for 'forcibly taking shots against people's wishes', like 'a thief'. Possession of a camera does not license intrusion, as it does in this society whether people like it or not. (The good manners of a camera culture dictate that one is supposed to pretend not to notice when one is being photographed by a stranger in a public place as long as the photographer stays at a discreet distance – that is, one is supposed neither to forbid the picture-taking nor to start posing.) Unlike here, where we pose where we can and yield when we must, in China taking pictures is always a ritual; it always involves posing and, necessarily, consent. Someone who 'deliberately stalked people who were unaware of his intention to film them' was depriving people and things of their right to pose, in order to look their best.

Antonioni devoted nearly all of the sequence in *Chung Kuo* about Peking's Tien An Men Square, the country's foremost goal of political pilgrimage, to the pilgrims waiting to be photographed. The interest to Antonioni of showing Chinese performing that elementary rite, having a trip documented by the camera, is evident: the photograph and being photographed are favorite contemporary subjects for the camera. To his critics, the desire of visitors to Tien An Men Square for a photograph souvenir

> is a reflection of their deep revolutionary feelings. But with bad intentions, Antonioni, instead of showing this reality, took shots only of people's clothing, movement, and expressions: here, someone's ruffled hair; there, people peering, their eyes dazzled by the sun; one moment, their sleeves; another, their trousers.

The Chinese resist the photographic dismemberment of reality. Close-ups are not used. Even the postcards of antiquities and works of art sold in museums do not show part of something; the object is always photographed straight on, centred, evenly lit, and in its entirety.

We find the Chinese naïve for not perceiving the beauty of the cracked peeling door, the picturesqueness of disorder, the force of the old angle and the significant detail, the poetry of the turned back. We have a modern notion of embellishment – beauty is not inherent in anything; it is to be found, by another way of seeing – as well as a wider notion of meaning, which photography's many uses illustrate and powerfully reinforce. The more numerous the variations of something, the richer its possibilities of meaning: thus, more is said with photographs in the West than in China today. Apart from whatever is true about *Chung Kuo* as an item of ideological merchandise (and the Chinese are not wrong in finding the film condescending), Antonioni's images simply mean *more* than any images the Chinese release of themselves. The Chinese don't want photographs to mean very much or to be very interesting. They do not want to see the world from an unusual angle, to discover new subjects. Photographs are supposed to display what has already been described. Photography for us is a double-edged instrument for producing clichés (the French word that means both trite expression and photographic negative) and for serving up 'fresh' views. For the Chinese authorities, there are only clichés – which they consider not to be clichés but 'correct' views.

In China today, only two realities are acknowledged. We see reality as hopelessly and interestingly plural. In China, what is defined as an issue for debate is one about which there are 'two lines', a right one and a wrong one. Our society proposes a spectrum of discontinuous choices and perceptions. Theirs is constructed around a single, ideal observer; and photographs contribute their bit to the Great Monologue. For us, there are dispersed, interchangeable 'points of view'; photography is a polylogue. The current Chinese ideology defines reality as a historical process structured by recurrent dualisms with clearly outlined, morally colored meanings; the past, for the most part, is simply judged as bad. For us, there are historical processes with awesomely complex and sometimes contradictory meanings; and arts which draw much of their value from our consciousness of time as history, like photography. (This is why the passing of time adds to the aesthetic value of photographs, and the scars of time make objects more rather than less enticing to photographers.) With the idea of history, we certify our interest in knowing the greatest number of things. The only use the Chinese are allowed to make of their history is didactic: their interest in history is narrow, moralistic, deforming, uncurious. Hence, photography in our sense has no place in their society.

The limits placed on photography in China only reflect the character of their society, a society unified by an ideology of stark, unremitting conflict. Our unlimited use of photographic images not only reflects but gives shape to this society, one unified by the denial of conflict. Our very notion of the world – the capitalist twentieth century's 'one world' – is like a photographic overview. The world is 'one' not because it is united but because a tour of its diverse contents does not reveal conflict but only an even more astounding diversity. This spurious unity of the world is effected by translating its contents into images. Images are always compatible, or can be made compatible, even when the realities they depict are not.

Photography does not simply reproduce the real, it recycles it – a key procedure of a modern society. In the form of photographic images, things and events are put to new uses, assigned new meanings, which go beyond the distinctions between the beautiful and the ugly, the true and the false, the useful and the useless, good taste and bad. Photography is one of the chief means for producing that quality ascribed to things and situations which erases these distinctions: 'the interesting'. What makes something interesting is that it can be seen to be like, or analogous to, something else. There is an art and there are fashions of seeing things in order to make them interesting; and to supply this art, these fashions, there is a steady recycling of the artifacts and tastes of the past. Clichés, recycled, become meta-clichés. The photographic recycling makes clichés out of unique objects, distinctive and vivid artifacts out of clichés. Images of real things are interlayered with images of images. The Chinese circumscribe the uses of photography so that there are no layers or strata of images, and all images reinforce and reiterate each other.[3] We make of photography a means by which, precisely, anything can be said, any purpose served. What in reality is discrete, images join. In the form of a photograph the explosion of an A-bomb can be used to advertise a safe.

To us, the difference between the photographer as an individual eye and the photographer as an objective recorder seems fundamental, the difference often regarded, mistakenly, as separating photography as art from photography as document. But both are logical extensions of what photography means: note-taking on, potentially, everything in the world, from every possible angle. The same Nadar who took the most authoritative celebrity portraits of his time and did the first photo-interviews was also the first photographer to take aerial views; and when he performed 'the Daguerreian operation' on Paris from a balloon in 1855 he immediately grasped the future benefit of photography to warmakers.

Two attitudes underlie this presumption that anything in the world is material for the camera. One finds that there is beauty or at least interest in everything, seen with an acute enough eye. (And the aestheticizing of reality that makes everything, anything, available to the camera is what also permits the co-opting of any photograph, even one of an utterly practical sort, as art.) The other treats everything as the object of some present or future use, as matter for estimates, decisions and predictions. According to one attitude, there is nothing that should not be *seen*; according to the other, there is nothing that should not be *recorded*. Cameras implement an aesthetic view of reality by being a machine-toy that extends to everyone the possibility of making disinterested judgments about importance, interest, beauty. ('*That* would make a good picture.') Cameras implement the instrumental view of reality by gathering information that enables us to make a more accurate and much quicker response to whatever is going on. The response may of course be either repressive or benevolent: military reconnaissance photographs help snuff out lives, X-rays help save them.

Though these two attitudes, the aesthetic and the instrumental, seem to produce contradictory and even incompatible feelings about people and situations, that is the altogether characteristic contradiction of attitude which members of a society that divorces public from private are expected to share in and live with. And there is perhaps no activity which prepares us so well to live with these contradictory attitudes as does picture-taking, which lends itself so brilliantly to both. On the one hand, cameras arm vision in the service of power – of the state, of industry, of science. On the other hand, cameras make vision expressive in that mythical space known as private life. In China, where no space is left over from politics and moralism for expressions of aesthetic sensibility, only some things are to be photographed and only in certain ways. For us, as we become further detached from politics, there is more and more free space to fill up with exercises of sensibility such as cameras afford. One of the effects of the newer camera technology (video; instant movies) has been to turn even more of what is done with cameras in private to narcissistic uses – that is, to self-surveillance. But such currently popular uses of image-feedback in the bedroom, the therapy session, and the weekend conference seem far less momentous than video's potential as a tool for surveillance in public places. Presumably, the Chinese will eventually make the same instrumental uses of photography that we do, except, perhaps, this one. Our inclination to treat character as equivalent to behavior makes more acceptable a widespread public installation of the mechanized regard from the outside provided by cameras. China's far more repressive standards of order require not only monitoring behavior but changing hearts; there, surveillance is internalized to a degree without precedent, which suggests a more limited future in their society for the camera as a means of surveillance.

China offers the model of one kind of dictatorship, whose master idea is 'the good', in which the most unsparing limits are placed on all forms of expression, including images. The future may offer another kind of dictatorship, whose master idea is 'the interesting', in which images of all sorts, stereotyped and eccentric, proliferate. Something like this is suggested in Nabokov's *Invitation to a Beheading*. Its portrait of a model totalitarian state contains only one, omnipresent art: photography – and the friendly photographer who hovers around the hero's death cell turns out, at the end of the novel, to be the headsman. And there seems no way (short of undergoing a vast historical amnesia, as in China) of limiting the proliferation of photographic images. The only question is whether the function of the image-world created by cameras could be other than it is. The present function is clear enough, if one considers in what contexts photographic images are seen, what dependencies they create, what antagonisms they pacify – that is, what institutions they buttress, whose needs they really serve.

A capitalist society requires a culture based on images. It needs to furnish vast amounts of entertainment in order to stimulate buying and anesthetize the injuries of class, race and sex. And it needs to gather unlimited amounts of information, the better to exploit natural resources, increase productivity, keep order, make war, give jobs to bureaucrats. The camera's twin capacities, to subjectivize reality and to objectify it, ideally serve these needs and strengthen them. Cameras define reality in the two ways essential to the workings of an advanced industrial society: as a spectacle (for masses) and as an object of surveillance (for rulers). The production of images also furnishes a ruling ideology. Social change is replaced by a change in images. The freedom to consume a plurality of images and goods is equated with freedom itself. The narrowing of free political choice to free economic consumption requires the unlimited production and consumption of images.

The final reason for the need to photograph everything lies in the very logic of consumption itself. To consume means to burn, to use up – and, therefore, to need to be replenished. As we make images and consume them, we need still more images; and still more. But images are not a treasure for which the world must be ransacked; they are precisely what is at hand wherever the eye falls. The possession of a camera can inspire something akin to lust. And like all credible forms of lust, it cannot be satisfied: first, because the possibilities of photography are infinite; and, second, because the project is finally self-devouring. The attempts by photographers to bolster up a depleted sense of reality contribute to the depletion. Our oppressive sense of the transience of everything is more acute since cameras gave us the means to 'fix' the fleeting moment. We consume images at an ever faster rate and, as Balzac suspected cameras used up layers of the body, images consume reality. Cameras are the antidote and the disease, a means of appropriating reality and a means of making it obsolete.

The powers of photography have in effect de-Platonized our understanding of reality, making it less and less plausible to reflect upon our experience according to the distinction between images and things, between copies and originals. It suited Plato's derogatory attitude toward images to liken them to shadows – transitory, minimally informative, immaterial, impotent co-presences of the real things which cast them. But the force of photographic images comes from their being material realities in their own right, richly informative deposits left in the wake of whatever emitted them, potent means for turning the tables on reality – for turning *it* into a shadow. Images are more real than anyone could have supposed. And just because they are an unlimited resource, one that cannot be exhausted by consumerist waste, there is all the more reason to apply the conservationist remedy. If there can be a better way for the real world to include the one of images, it will require an ecology not only of real things but of images as well.

Notes

1   I am drawing on the account of Balzac's realism in Erich Auerbach's *Mimesis*. The
     passage that Auerbach describes from the beginning of *Le Père Goriot* (1834) – Balzac

is describing the dining room of the Vauquer pension at seven in the morning and the entry of Madame Vauquer – could hardly be more explicit (or proto-Proustian). 'Her whole person', Balzac writes, 'explains the pension, as the pension implies her person . . . The short-statured woman's blowsy *embonpoint* is the product of the life here, as typhoid is the consequence of the exhalations of a hospital. Her knitted wool petticoat, which is longer than her outer skirt (made of an old dress), and whose wadding is escaping by the gaps in the splitting material, sums up the drawing-room, the dining room, the little garden, announces the cooking and gives an inkling of the boarders. When she is there, the spectacle is complete.'

2   See *A Vicious Motive, Despicable Tricks – a Criticism of Antonioni's Anti-China Film 'China'* (Peking, Foreign Languages Press, 1974), an eighteen-page pamphlet (unsigned) which reproduces an article that appeared in the paper *Renminh Ribao* on 30 January 1974; and 'Repudiating Antonioni's anti-China film', *Peking Review*, 8 (22 February 1974), which supplies abridged versions of three other articles published that month. The aim of these articles is not, of course, to expound a view of photography – their interest on that score is inadvertent – but to construct a model ideological enemy, as in other mass educational campaigns staged during this period. Given this purpose, it was as unnecessary for the tens of millions mobilized in meetings held in schools, factories, army units, and communes around the country to 'criticize Antonioni's anti-China film' to have actually seen *Chung Kuo* as it was for the participants in the 'criticize Lin Piao and Confucius' campaign of 1976 to have read a text of Confucius.

3   The Chinese concern for the reiterative function of images (and of words) inspires the distributing of additional images, photographs that depict scenes in which, clearly, no photographer could have been present; and the continuing use of such photographs suggests how slender is the population's understanding of what photographic images and picture-taking imply. In his book *Chinese Shadows*, Simon Leys gives an example from the 'movement to emulate Lei Feng', a mass campaign of the mid-1960s to inculcate the ideals of Maoist citizenship built around the apotheosis of an Unknown Citizen, a conscript named Lei Feng who died at twenty in a banal accident. Lei Feng Exhibitions organized in the large cities included 'photographic documents, such as "Lei Feng helping an old woman to cross the street", "Lei Feng secretly [sic] doing his comrade's washing", "Lei Feng giving his lunch to a comrade who forgot his lunch box", and so forth', with, apparently, nobody questioning 'the providential presence of a photographer during the various incidents in the life of that humble, hitherto unknown soldier'. In China, what makes an image true is that it is good for people to see it.

Separation perfected   **Guy Debord**

> **But certainly for the present age, which prefers the sign to the thing signified,**
> **the copy to the original, fancy to reality, the appearance to the essence . . .**
> ***illusion* only is *sacred, truth profane*. Nay, sacredness is held to be enhanced in**
> **proportion as truth decreases and illusion increases, so that the highest degree**
> **of illusion comes to be the highest degree of sacredness.**
>
> Feuerbach, Preface to the Second Edition of *The Essence of Christianity*

1

In societies where modern conditions of production prevail, all of life presents itself as an immense accumulation of *spectacles*. Everything that was directly lived has moved away into a representation.

2

The images detached from every aspect of life fuse in a common stream in which the unity of this life can no longer be reestablished. Reality considered *partially* unfolds, in its own general unity, as a pseudo-world *apart*, an object of mere contemplation. The specialization of images of the world is completed in the world of the autonomous image, where the liar has lied to himself. The spectacle in general, as the concrete inversion of life, is the autonomous movement of the non-living.

This chapter, originally published in 1967, is taken from Society of the Spectacle (Michigan, Black and Red, 1977), Chapter 1.

[. . .]

4

The spectacle is not a collection of images, but a social relation among people, mediated by images.

5

The spectacle cannot be understood as an abuse of the world of vision, as a product of the techniques of mass dissemination of images. It is, rather, a *Weltanschauung* which has become actual, materially translated. It is a world vision which has become objectified.

6

The spectacle, grasped in its totality, is both the result and the project of the existing mode of production. It is not a supplement to the real world, an additional decoration. It is the heart of the unrealism of the real society. In all its specific forms, as information or propaganda, as advertisement or direct entertainment consumption, the spectacle is the present *model* of socially dominant life. It is the omnipresent affirmation of the choice *already made* in production and its corollary consumption. The spectacle's form and content are identically the total justification of the existing system's conditions and goals. The spectacle is also the *permanent presence* of this justification, since it occupies the main part of the time lived outside of modern production.

[. . .]

8

One cannot abstractly contrast the spectacle to actual social activity: such a division is itself divided. The spectacle which inverts the real is in fact produced. Lived reality is materially invaded by the contemplation of the spectacle while simultaneously absorbing the spectacular order, giving it positive cohesiveness. Objective reality is present on both sides. Every notion fixed this way has no other basis than its passage into the opposite: reality rises up within the spectacle, and the spectacle is real. This reciprocal alienation is the essence and the support of the existing society.

[. . .]

12

The spectacle presents itself as something enormously positive, indisputable and inaccessible. It says nothing more than 'that which appears is good, that which is good appears.' The attitude which it demands in principle is passive acceptance which in fact it already obtained by its manner of appearing without reply, by its monopoly of appearance.

[. . .]

15

As the indispensable decoration of the objects produced today, as the general exposé of the rationality of the system, as the advanced economic sector which directly shapes a growing multitude of image-objects, the spectacle is the main *production* of present-day society.

16

The spectacle subjugates living men to itself to the extent that the economy has totally subjugated them. It is no more than the economy developing for itself. It is the true reflection of the production of things, and the false objectification of the producers.

[. . .]

18

Where the real world changes into simple images, the simple images become real beings and effective motivations of hypnotic behavior. The spectacle, as a tendency *to make one see* the world by means of various specialized mediations (it can no longer be grasped directly), naturally finds vision to be the privileged human sense which the sense of touch was for other epochs; the most abstract, the most mystifiable sense corresponds to the generalized abstraction of present-day society. But the spectacle is not identifiable with mere gazing, even combined with hearing. It is that which escapes the activity of men, that which escapes reconsideration and correction by their work. It is the opposite of dialogue. Wherever there is independent *representation*, the spectacle reconstitutes itself.

19

The spectacle inherits all the *weaknesses* of the Western philosophical project which undertook to comprehend activity in terms of the categories of *seeing*; furthermore, it is based on the incessant spread of the precise technical rationality which grew out of this thought. The spectacle does not realize philosophy, it philosophizes reality. The concrete life of everyone has been degraded into a *speculative* universe.

20

Philosophy, the power of separate thought and the thought of separate power, could never by itself supersede theology. The spectacle is the material reconstruction of the religious illusion. Spectacular technology has not dispelled the religious clouds where men had placed their own powers detached from themselves; it has only tied them to an earthly base. The most earthly life thus becomes opaque and unbreathable. It no longer projects into the sky but shelters within itself its absolute denial, its fallacious paradise. The spectacle is the technical realization of the exile of human powers into a beyond; it is separation perfected within the interior of man.

[. . .]

24

[. . .] The fetishistic, purely objective appearance of spectacular relations conceals the fact that they are relations among men and classes: a second nature with its fatal laws seems to dominate our environment. But the spectacle is not the necessary product of technical development seen as a *natural* development. The society of the spectacle is on the contrary the form which chooses its own technical content. If the spectacle, taken in the limited sense of 'mass media' which are its most glaring superficial manifestation, seems to invade society as mere equipment, this equipment is in no way neutral but is the very means suited to its total self-movement. If the social needs of the epoch in which such techniques are developed can only be satisfied through their mediation, if the administration of this society and all contact among men can no longer take place except through the intermediary of this power of instantaneous communication, it is because this 'communication' is essentially *unilateral*. The concentration of 'communication' is thus an accumulation, in the hands of the existing system's administration, of the means which allow it to carry on this particular administration. The generalized cleavage of the spectacle is inseparable from the modern *State*, namely from the general form of cleavage within society, the product of the division of social labor and the organ of class domination.

[. . .]

34

The spectacle is *capital* to such a degree of accumulation that it becomes an image.

The bottom line on planet one: squaring up to *The Face*
Dick Hebdige

It was quite self indulgent. I wanted it to be monthly so that you were out of that weekly rut; on glossy paper so that it would look good; and with very few ads – at NME the awful shapes of ads often meant that you couldn't do what you wanted with the design.

(Nick Logan, publisher of *The Face* interviewed in *The Observer Colour Supplement*, January, 1985)

Last autumn Alan Hughes, a former member of the *Ten.8* editorial board came to West Midlands College to give a talk on magazine design to students on a Visual Communications course. During his lecture, Alan asked how many of his audience read *Ten.8*. The response was muted and unenthusiastic. Alan's question prompted the following exchange:

A.H.:   'What's wrong with *Ten.8* then?'

Students: 'It's not like *The Face* . . . It's too political . . . It looks too heavy . . . They've got the ratio of image to text all wrong . . . I don't like the layout . . . It depresses me . . . You never see it anywhere . . . It doesn't relate to anything I know or anything I'm interested in . . . It's too left wing . . . What use is it to someone like me?' (*approximate not verbatim transcriptions*)

This chapter, originally published in 1985, is taken from Dick Hebdige, *Hiding in the Light: On Image and Things* (London, Comedia and Routledge, 1988), pp. 155–176.

Clearly, for many of the students, *The Face* was the epitome of good design. It was the primary exemplar, the Ur Text for magazine construction – the standard against which every other magazine was judged. The position it appeared to occupy in the world view of some of my students recalled – in a disconcertingly upside down kind of way – Northrop Frye's thesis on the centrality of the Bible and of Biblically

Figure 9.1

The Face (front

cover), no. 31,

Nov. 1982

derived archetypes in the West.[1] Frye argues that for the past two thousand years, the Bible has acted as what William Blake called the 'Great Code of Art' in Western culture supplying artists and writers not only with a fertile body of myth and metaphor but also with the fundamental epistemological categories, the basic modes of classification and typology which structure Western thought. In the Bible Frye sees the bones of thinking in the West – the essential framework within which a literate culture has unfolded, understood and named itself.

In the pagan, postmodern world in which some of my students live, *The Face* appears to perform a similar function (figures 9.1 and 9.2). For them, *Ten.8* is the profane text – its subject matter dull, verbose and prolix; its tone earnest and teacherly; its contributions obsessed with arcane genealogies and inflated theoretical concerns (figures 9.3 and 9.4). This judgement probably owes more to the conservative format; to the appearance of the typeface, the solid blocks of print in three columns, and to the lingering commitment to the strict rectangular frame than to any more substantial rapport with the content. I suspect it's not so much that they can't understand it. It's that they think they know what they are going to 'learn' before they encounter it on the printed page and they calculate that the energy expended on the *style* of understanding offered in *Ten.8* in relation to the gain made in 'really useful knowledge' is just not worth the effort (or the cover price).

They are not alone in this if the circulation figures are anything to go by (*Ten.8* 1,500–2,500; *The Face*: 52,000–90,000). *The Face* has, in addition, been feted in publishing circles. In 1983, it was voted Magazine of the Year in the annual Magazine Publishing Awards, and the consistently high standard and originality of its design receive regular accolades in the professional journals. *Design and Art Direction* claimed that 'from a design viewpoint [*The Face*] is probably the most influential magazine of the 1980s' whilst the *Creative Review* singled out the work of Neville Brody, who designs unique 'trademark' typefaces for the magazine for special praise, suggesting that 'every typographer should have a copy'.

Long after the seminar with Alan was over. I found myself asking whether it was possible to trace the essential difference which I imagined dividing *Ten.8* from *The Face* back to a single determining factor. Did it reside in the form or the content, in both or neither, in the size and composition of the readership, in the style or the tone, in the mode of address, in the proportion of available space devoted to advertising, to the type of advertising, the mode of financing, the marketing or distribution or editorial policy? Did it stem from the intrinsic ties that bind the magazines to different institutions (education and the arts for *Ten.8*; the pop and fashion industries for *The Face*)? Or did it derive from some more fundamental ideological or ethical polarity between, say, the carnal pursuit of profit and the disinterested pursuit of knowledge, the private and the public sectors?

This last distinction does not stand up to too close an inspection. It is true that the two magazines emerged under different circumstances as the result of quite different initiatives. The *Ten.8* editorial group, formed in

THE FACE

£1.05 (INC VAT)

AT BOY
ORGE!

Shocker
Face Interview

M!
uns go for it!

OMISED LAND
as in Ethiopia

ER IN HOLLYWOOD
s of Philip Marlowe

TOL IN SUBURBIA
the stars tells all!

ANGE · VIVIENNE WESTWOOD · LUTHER
S · STEPHEN LINARD · HEY! ELASTICA

Figure 9.2

The Face (front cover), no. 42, Oct. 1983

1979, was, and still is financed by an Arts Council grant, whereas the £4,000 which was used, one year later, to launch *The Face* was raised by Nick Logan, former editor of *Smash Hits* and the *New Musical Express* from personal savings and by taking out a second mortgage on his flat. However, if it is tempting to regard *The Face* as the embodiment of entrepreneurial Thatcherite drive, it should also be remembered that in a world dominated by massive publishing oligopolies, both *Ten.8* and *The Face* remain relatively marginal and independent, are staffed by a small team of dedicated people ('The entire permanent staff of *The Face* could be comfortably fitted into the back of a London taxi' (*The Face* no. 61)) and, if press reports are to be taken at face value, both are run on what are, by mainstream publishing standards, shoe-string budgets (though, admittedly, *The Face*'s string stretches a lot further than *Ten.8*'s).

> As idiosyncratic as ever, Logan deliberately keeps the advertising content to a minimum which allows him to do little more than break even ('I wear second hand clothes and eat very cheaply' he explains cheerfully . . .). (*Music Week*)

On the other hand, both magazines could be said to offer their readers quite specific forms of cultural capital: from *The Face* 'street credibility,' 'nous', image and style tips for those operating within the highly competitive *milieux* of fashion, music and design whilst *Ten.8* offers knowledge of debates on the history, theory, politics and practice of photography and supplies educationalists with source material for teaching.

But none of this serves to close the distance between *Ten.8* and *The Face*. The chasm that divides them remains as absolute and as inaccessible to concise description as the gulf that separates one element from another. It goes right to the core of things. It has to be approached from a different angle . . .

War of the worlds

Imagine a galaxy containing two quite different worlds. In the first, the relations of power and knowledge are so ordered that priority and precedence are given to written and spoken language over 'mere (idolatrous)

Figure 9.3

Ten.8 Magazine,

no. 15, 1984

Contents page

TEN·8

QUARTERLY
PHOTOGRAPHIC
JOURNAL
No.15
ISSN 0142 9663

**Address for all
correspondence**
60, Holt Street
Aston
Birmingham B7 4BA
Tel: (021) 551 2351

Co-ordinator
Belinda Whiting

Editorial Group
Derek Bishton, Alan
Hughes, Sue Green, Nick
Hedges, Brian Homer,
Paul Lewis, John Reardon,
John Taylor, Belinda
Whiting.

This issue edited by
John Taylor

Designed by
Brian Homer
Alan Hughes

Production
Alan Hughes
Das Harminder Singh

Typesetting and Printing
The Russell Press Ltd,
Nottingham

Cover photograph
Gloria Chalmers from the
cover of *Wigan Pier
Revisited* by Beatrix
Campbell, published by
Virago Press.

Owned and published by
Ten.8 Ltd
81, Grove Lane,
Handsworth
Birmingham B21 9HE
©Ten.8 1984

Acknowledgement
Ten.8 receives financial
assistance from the Arts
Council of Great Britain

The views expressed
herein are not necessarily
those of the editors

imagery'. A priestly caste of scribes – guardians of the great traditions of
knowledge – determine the rules of rhetoric and grammar, draw the lines
between disciplines, proscribe the form and content of all (legitimate)
discourse and control the flow of knowledge to the people. These priests
and priestesses are served by a subordinate caste of technical operatives
equipped with a rudimentary training in physics and chemistry. The
technician's job consists in the engraving of images to illustrate, verify or
otherwise supplement the texts produced by the scribes.

Figure 9.4

Ten.8 Magazine,

no. 11, 1983

Inside spread

Unemployment and all its associated deprivations are not only getting worse, but new technologies threaten to make the situation permanent.

Behind the empty and pathetic talk of increased leisure opportunities and freedom from repetitive labour, stands the spectre of enforced idleness, wasted resources and the squandering of a whole generation of human potential. This is vandalism on a grand scale. Hidden in a smokescreen of cynical double-talk and pious moralising, the shape of the future is nevertheless clearly discernable. Cuts in social spending, including unemployment benefits, mean that the conditions under which they must endure their enforced idleness will rapidly deteriorate to become an intolerable burden, the consequences of which will be enormous. Society has withdrawn its contract from these young people, can they now be expected to live by its rules? They see no real future for themselves, even the 'right' to earn a living is being replaced by a compulsory dependency on sub-human terms. The sense of aimlessness and pent-up frustrations are reaching critical levels where they will be transformed into an explosive anger, directed against the establishment that has been so careless of their hopes and needs.

TEN·8/14

SIGHTS OF THE STRUGGLE

In 1980, when this survey was completed, nearly two-thirds of all unemployed people in West Newcastle were under the age of 30.

No established channels exist to represent or even acknowledge the interests of those involved, and the failure of the political parties, and even the Trade Unions, to contribute anything other than platitudes to the situation increases the alienation of youth still further. Most of their parents' generation have established attitudes and responses, based on their own experiences of unemployment, which are inappropriate in this unprecedented situation, and this is another factor which increases the alienation of youth even from their own families.

The intractable nature of this problem, intensified as it is by the Thatcher Government's extreme 'Free Market' philosophy, opens up a period of bitter conflict as young people grow more and more frustrated and refuse to accept the

logic of an economic system which deprives them of a productive and meaningful future. If the response of young people is at first confused and angry the responsibility for this lies firmly with those who now wield political power, who have embarked on a strategy of class-warfare, masked by appeals for moderation, law and order, stability and a return to the 'traditional values'.

The labour movement must now face up to a heavy and urgent responsibility as young people turn their minds to a way out of their present impasse. Conservative, narrow and parochial attitudes prevalent today are inadequate. The broad and vital aspirations upon which the Trade Unions and the parties of Labour were founded, and upon which, fundamentally, they still rest, must be restored to their full stature and primacy.

It must never be forgotten that there are barbaric and reactionary forces in our society, which, though having no intrinsic appeal to youth themselves, will not be slow to make political capital from an embittered youth, should the labour movement fail to give their search for new social, economic and political values a positive and sustained direction.

More recently, a progressive faction within the priesthood has granted a provisional autonomy to pictures and has – informally and unofficially – adjusted the working relationship between scribes and engravers. These scribes now endeavour to 'situate' the images produced by the engravers within an explanatory historical or theoretical framework. But despite this modification in the rules, the same old order prevails. This world goes on turning and, as it turns, its single essence is unfolded in time. Each moment – watched, argued over and recorded by the scribes – is a point on a line that links a past which is either known or potentially knowable to a future which is eternally uncertain. Each moment is like a word in a sentence and this sentence is called history.

In the second world – a much larger planet – the hierarchical ranking of word and image has been abolished. Truth – insofar as it exists at all – is first and foremost pictured: embodied in images which have their own power and effects. Looking takes precedence over seeing ('sensing' over 'knowing'). Words are pale ('speculative') facsimiles of an original reality which is directly apprehensible through image. This reality is as thin as the paper it is printed on. There is nothing underneath or behind the image and hence there is no hidden truth to be revealed.

The function of language in this second world is to supplement the image by describing the instant it embodies in order to put the image in play in the here and now – to turn it into a physical resource for other image-makers. It is not the function of language here to explain the origins of the image, its functions or effects, still less its meaning(s) (which, as they are plural, are not worth talking about). In this world, the vertical axis has collapsed and the organisation of sense is horizontal (i.e. this world is a flat world). There are no scribes or priests or engravers here. Instead, knowledge is assembled and dispensed to the public by a motley gang of bricoleurs, ironists, designers, publicists, image consultants, *hommes et femmes fatales*, market researchers, pirates, adventurers, *flâneurs* and dandies.

Roles are flexible and as there are no stable systems, categories or laws beyond the doctrine of the primacy and precedence of the image, there is no higher good to be served outside the winning of the game. The name of this game, which takes the place occupied in the first world by religion and politics, is the Renewal of the Now (a.k.a. Survival): i.e. the conversion of the now into the new. Because images are primary and multiple, there is, in this second world, a plurality of gods, and space and time are discontinuous so that, in a sense, neither time nor space exist: both have been dissolved into an eternal present (the present of the image). Because there is no history, there is no contradiction – just random clashes and equally random conjunctions of semantic particles (images and words).

Sense – insofar as it exists at all – resides at the level of the atom. No larger unities are possible beyond the single image, the isolated statement, the individual body, the individual 'trend'. But this world too, goes on turning. It turns like a kaleidoscope: each month as the cycle is completed, a new, intensely vivid configuration of the same old elements is produced. Each month witnesses a miracle: the new becomes the now.

For the sake of argument, let's call the First World *Ten.8* and the Second World, *The Face*. Imagine a war between these two worlds . . .

Just a magazine

When Jean-Luc Godard in his Dziga-Vertov phase coined his famous maxim 'This is not a just image. This is just an image', he struck a blow for the Second World. In one brief, memorable formula, he managed to do three things:

1   He drove a wedge into the word 'good' so that you had to think twice before you said 'This is a good image' when confronted by a photograph by, say, Weegee or Eugene Smith.

2   He problematised the link between, on the one hand, an abstract commitment to ideal categories like Justice and, on the other, the 'politics of representation'.

3   He made the future safe for *The Face*, the political, ideological and aesthetic roots of which lie as much in the 1960s, in Mod, Pop Art, the myth of the metropolis and Situationism as in Mrs Thatcher's 1980s.

The Face follows directly in Godard's footsteps. It is not a 'just' magazine (in the depths of the recession, it renounces social realism, liberation theology and the moralists' mission to expose and combat social ills and promotes instead consumer aesthetics and multiple style elites). It is just a magazine which claims more or less explicitly that it is out to supersede most prevailing orthodox, 'alternative', scholarly *and* common-sense constructions of the relationship between cultural politics, the image and the 'popular'. It's just a short step, in fact it's hardly a step at all, from Godard and 1968 to 1985 and two Second World veterans like Paul Virilio and Félix Guattari, both of whom were quoted in the Disinformation Special entitled 'The End of Politics' in the fifth anniversary issue of *The Face*: 'Classless society, social justice – no one believes in them any more. We're in the age of micro-narratives, the art of the fragment' (Paul Virilio quoted in *The Face*, no. 61).

To find artful fragments from leading Left Bank theorists like Virilio, Guattari, Meaghan Morris, Andre Gorz and Rudolf Bahro[2] jostling alongside photographic portraits of the 'style-shapers of the late 1980s'; an interview with Bodymap, the clothes designers; a Robert Elms dissection of the Soul Boys; an article by Don Macpherson on contemporary architecture; a hatchet job by Julie Burchill on Amockalyptic posturing; a profile of Morrissey, 'the image-bloated clone-zone of pop' by Nick Kent; a photo-spread on how the latest digital video techniques were used to identify a Japanese poisoner of supermarket goods; and a portrait of the 'Sex Object of the Decade', a transmission electron micrograph of stages in the growth of the AIDS virus; all this is only to be expected in a magazine which sets out to confound all expectations. *The Face* is a magazine which goes out of its way every month to blur the line between politics and parody and pastiche; the street, the stage, the screen; between purity and danger; the mainstream and the 'margins': to flatten out the world.

For flatness is corrosive and infectious. Who, after all, is Paul Virilio anyway? Even the name sounds as if it belongs to a B movie actor, a member of Frankie Goes to Hollywood, a contestant in a body-building competition. I know that 'he' writes books but does such a person actually exist? In the land of the gentrified cut-up, as in the place of dreams, anything imaginable can happen, anything at all. The permutations are unlimited: high/low/fold/popular culture; pop music/opera; street fashion; advertising/*haute couture*; journalism/science fiction/critical theory; advertising/critical theory/*haute couture* . . .

With the sudden loss of gravity, the lines that hold these terms apart waver and collapse. Such combinations are as fragile, as impermanent as the categories of which they are composed; the entire structure is a house made of cards. It's difficult to retain a faith in anything much at all when absolutely *everything* moves with the market. In the words of the old Leiber and Stoller song, recorded in the 1950s by Peggy Lee and re-recorded in the late 1970s in a New Wave version by the New York club queen, Christina:

> Is *that* all there is? Is that *all* there is?
> If that's all there is then let's keep dancing.
> Let's break out the booze,
> Let's have a ball.
> If that's all there is.

To stare into the blank, flat *Face* is to look into a world where your actual presence is unnecessary, where nothing adds up to much *anything* any more, where you live to be alive. Because flatness is the friend of death and death is the greater leveller. That's the bottom line on Planet Two.

Living in the wake of the withering signified

> The public does not want to know what Napoleon III said to William of Prussia. It wants to know whether he wore beige or red trousers and whether he smoked a cigar.
>
> (An Italian newspaper editor quoted by Pope John Paul I
> in D. Yallop, *In God's Name*, 1985)

From 19 April to 18 May, the Photographer's Gallery near Leicester Square in London was occupied by Second World forces. The Bill Brandt room was converted – to quote from the press handout – into a 'walk-in magazine': a three-dimensional version of *The Face*.

The exhibition area was divided into five categories corresponding to the regular sections around which the magazine itself is structured: Intro, Features, Style, Expo and Disinformation. In this way it was possible to 'read' *The Face* with your feet. This is entirely appropriate. Since the first issue in 1980, *The Face* has always been a totally designed environment: an integrated package of graphic, typographic and photographic (dis)information laid out in such a way as to facilitate the restless passage of what Benjamin called the 'distracted gaze' of the urban consumer (of looks, objects, ideas, values). (It may be useful at this point to recall that *everything without exception* in the Second World is a commodity, a potential commodity, or has commodity-aspects.)

The Face is not read so much as wandered through. It is first and foremost a text to be 'cruised' as Barthes – a leading Second World spokesperson in his Tel Quel phase – used to say. The 'reader' is invited to wander through this environment picking up whatever s/he finds attractive, useful or appealing. (Incidentally, use-value and desire – needs and wants – are interchangeable on Planet Two. Scarcity has been banished to another, less fortunate planet called the Third World which exists on the galaxy's [southern] frontier.)

The 'reader' is licensed to use whatever has been appropriated in whatever way and in whatever combination proves most useful and most satisfying. (There can be no 'promiscuity' in a world without monogamy/monotheism/monadic subjects; there can be no 'perversion' in a world without norms.)

Cruising was originally introduced as a post-structuralist strategy for going beyond the 'puritanical' confinement of critical activity to the pursuit and taming (i.e. naming) of the ideological signified.[3] By cruising, the 'reader' can take pleasure in a text without being obliged at the same time to take marriage vows and a mortgage on a house. And this separation of pleasure/use-value from any pledge/commitment to 'love, honour and obey' the diktats of the text constitutes the 'epistemological break' which divides Planet One from Planet Two, and which sets up a field of alternating currents of attraction and repulsion between them.

The difficulties facing anyone who tries to negotiate the gap between these two intrinsically opposed models of what photography and writing on photography are and should be doing can be loosely gauged by contrasting the different positions on photography taken by a First World critic like John Berger and the Second World People of the Post (post-structuralism, post-modernism). For more than a decade, in his work with Jean Mohr, Berger has been seeking to bind the photograph back to its originary context. In a series of books – *A Seventh Man, Pig Earth, Another Way of Telling, On Looking, Their Faces Brief as Photographs* – Berger has, amongst other things, attempted to place the photograph within a web of narratives which are designed to authenticate its substance (i.e. that which is depicted) in order to make the image 'tell' its true story.

On the other hand, and during the same period, the disciples of the Post have been working in the opposite direction. They do not seek to recover or retrieve the truth captured in the image but rather to liberate the signifier from the constraints imposed upon it by the rationalist theology of 'representation'.

To recapitulate an argument which will already be familiar to many readers, this is a theology which assumes a real existing prior to signification which is accessible to analysis and transparent description by 'finished', fully centred human subjects – that is by men and women sufficiently in possession of themselves to 'see through' appearances to the essential truths and ideal forms 'behind' those appearances. By retaining a faith in a beyond and a beneath, the members of the First World are thus seen by Second World critics to be perpetuating submission to an outmoded and disabling metaphysic.

Instead of trying to restore the image to its 'authentic' context, the People of the Post have set out to undermine the validity of the distinction between, for instance, good and bad, legitimate and illegitimate, style and substance, by challenging the authority of any distinction which is not alert to its own partial and provisional status and aware, too, of its own impermanence. This, then, is the project of the Post: to replace the dominant (Platonic) regime of meaning – that is, representation – by a radical anti-system which promotes the articulation of difference as an end in itself. It is sometimes argued that this involves the multiplication of those transitory points from which a divinely underwritten authority can be eroded and questioned.

The diverse factions which gather in the Post identify the centralised source of this oppressive power variously as the Word/the Enlightenment Project/European Rationalism/the Party/the Law of the Father/the Phallus as (absent) guarantor of imaginary coherence. In other words, the project is a multi-faceted attack on the authority/authorship diad which is seen to hover like the ghost of the Father behind all First World discourse guaranteeing truth, hierarchy and the order of things.

There are, amongst Second World forces, bands of anarchists and mystics who believe that all local political objectives should be bracketed within this larger, longer term project. Born again in the demolition of the diad, they form an 'impossible class'[4] refusing all law and demanding a subjectivity without guarantees.

However, the consequences of the assault on representation for *écrivains* and image makers are, on the whole, rather more mundane. First the referent (the world outside the text) disappears. Then the signified, and we are left in a world of radically 'empty' signifiers. No meaning. No classes. No history. Just a ceaseless procession of simulacra.[5]

Released from the old bourgeois obligation to 'speak for' truth and liberty or to 'represent' the oppressed, the Third World, the 'downtrodden masses' or the *marginaux* – (represent in the sense in which a Member of Parliament is supposed to 'represent' her/his constituency) – we are free to serve whatever gods we choose, to celebrate artifice, to construct our selves in fiction and fantasy, to play in the blank, empty spaces of the now.

One of the most currently influential of Second World strategists, Jean Baudrillard, has gone further still, declaring that appearances can no longer be said to mask, conceal, distort or falsify reality.[6] He claims that reality is nothing more than the never knowable sum of all appearances. For Baudrillard, 'reality' flickers. It will not stay still. Tossed about like Rimbaud's 'drunken boat' on a heaving sea of surfaces, we cease to exist as rational *cogitos* capable of standing back and totalising on the basis of our experience.

The implication is that 'we' never did exist like that anyway, that there never was a 'behind' where we could stand and speculate dispassionately on the meaning of it all. Thus the 'I' is nothing more than a fictive entity, an optical illusion, a hologram hanging in the air, created at the flickering point where the laser beams of memory and desire intersect. The subject simply ceases . . . this is the Post Modern Condition and it takes place in the present tense. Rimbaud's *bateau ivre*, in fact, is too ecstatic and too bohemian a metaphor to encapsulate the drift into autism that the Baudrillard scene[7] entails – end of judgement, value, meaning, politics, subject–object oppositions.

A more fitting analogy for what it's like to live through the 'death of the subject' might involve a comparison with the new reproductive technologies. Baudrillard's position on what life on Planet Two is like amounts to this: like the heads on a video recorder, we merely translate audio and visual signals back and forth from one terminus (the tape) to another (the screen). The information that we 'handle' changes with each moment – all human life can pass across those heads – but we never own or store or 'know' or 'see' the material that we process. If we live in the Second World, then our lives get played out of us. Our lives get played out for us, played out in us, but never, ever *by* us. In Baudrillard's anti-system, 'by' is the unspeakable preposition because it suggests that there's still time for human agency, for positive action; still some space for intervention and somewhere left to intervene. But this is an inadmissible possibility in a world where politics – the art of the possible – has ceased to have meaning.

For Baudrillard, standing in the terminal, at the end of the weary European line, the music of the spheres has been replaced by the whirring of tape heads. As far as he is concerned, we are – all of us – merely stations on the endless, mindless journey of the signifier: a journey made by nobody to nowhere . . .

The suggestion that we are living in the wake of the withering signified may well sound like science fiction or intellectual sophistry but there are those who argue that all this is linked to actual changes in production[8] – that the flat earth thesis (what Fredric Jameson calls the 'disappearance of the depth model')[9] finds material support in the post-war shift from an industrial to a 'post-industrial', 'media' or 'consumer' society. These terms have been coined by different writers to signal the perceived move from an industrial economy based on the production of three-dimensional goods by a proletariat that sells its labour power in the market into a new, qualitatively different era of multi-national capital, media conglomerates and computer science where the old base-superstructure division is annulled or up-ended and production in the West becomes progressively dehumanised and 'etherealised' – focused round information-and-image-as-product and automation-as-productive-process.

According to some Post people, the tendency towards acceleration, and innovation, to programmed obsolescence and neophilia which Marx saw characterising societies dominated by the capital mode of production – where, to use his own words, 'all that is solid melts into air'[10] – has been intensified under contemporary 'hypercapitalism'[11] to such an extent that a kind of rupturing has occurred which has 'abstracted' production to a point beyond anything Marx could have imagined possible. New commodities untouched by human hands circulate without any reference to vulgar 'primary needs' in a stratosphere of pure exchange.

In such a world, so the argument goes, not only are signifiers material but a *proper* materialist (e.g. Marx himself were he alive today) would proclaim – even, some suggest, celebrate[12] – the triumph of the signifier. A materialist proper would welcome the coming of the flat, un-bourgeois world: a world without distinction and hierarchy, a society in which – although growing numbers of people are without permanent, paid employment – more and more (of not necessarily the same) people have access to the means of *re*production (television, radio, stereo, hifi, audio and videocassette recorders, cheap and easy-to-use cameras, Xerox machines if not portable 'pirate' radio and television transmitters, recording facilities, synthesisers, drum machines, etc.). A world where although many may be 'trained' and few educated, everyone – to adapt Benjamin again – can be an amateur film, television, radio, record, fashion and photography critic.

Meanwhile, the relations of knowledge and the functions of education are transformed as models of knowledge based on linguistics and cybernetics move in to subvert the epistemological foundations of the humanities, and the university faces a crisis as it is no longer capable of transmitting the appropriate cultural capital to emergent technocratic and bureaucratic elites. The proliferation of commercial laboratories, privately funded research bases, of data banks and information storage systems attached to multi-national companies and government agencies, amplifies this trend so that higher education can no longer be regarded – if it ever was – as the privileged site of research and the sole repository of 'advanced' knowledge.[13]

At the same time, recent refinements in telematics, satellite and cable television threaten to erode national cultural and ideological boundaries as local regulations governing what can and can't be broadcast become increasingly difficult to implement. As the related strands of social and aesthetic utopianism, the notions of the Radical Political Alternative and radicalism in Art,[14] are unravelled and revealed as untenable and obsolescent, advertising takes over where the avant garde left off and the picture of the Post is complete.

According to this scenario absolutely nothing – production, consumption, subjectivity, knowledge, art, the experience of space and time – is what it was even forty years ago. 'Experts' equipped with narrow professional and instrumental competences replace the totalising intellectual with *his* universal categories and high moral tone. 'Weak thought',[15] paradoxology and modest proposals in the arts replace the internally consistent global projections of Marxism and the romantic gestures or grand (architectural) plans of modernism ('we no longer believe in political or historical teleologies, or in the great "actors" and "subjects" of history – the nationstate, the proletariat, the party, the West, etc.'[16] The consumer (for Alvin Toffler, the 'prosumer')[17] replaces the citizen. The pleasure-seeking *bricoleur* replaces the truth-and-justice seeking rational subject of the Enlightenment. The now replaces history. Everywhere becomes absolutely different (doctrine of the diverse v. the dictatorship of the norm). Everywhere – from Abu Dhabi to Aberdeen – becomes more or less the same (first law of the level earth: lack of gravity = end of distinction *or* the whole world watches *Dallas* ergo the whole world is Dallas).

This is where *The Face* fits. This is the world where the ideal reader of *The Face* – stylepreneur, doleocrat, Buffalo Boy or Sloane – educated, street-wise but not institutionalised – is learning how to dance in the dark, how to survive, how to stay on top (on the surface) of things. After all, in 1985 with the public sector, education, the welfare state – all the big, 'safe' institutions – up against the wall, there's nothing good or clever or heroic about going under. When all is said and done, why bother to think 'deeply' when you're not *paid* to think deeply?

Sur *le face*

> *Sur-face:*
> 1   The outside of a body, (any of) the limits that terminate a solid, outward aspect of material or immaterial thing, what is apprehended of something upon a casual view or consideration.
> 2   (geom.) that which has length and breadth but no thickness.
>
> (*The Concise English Dictionary*)

A young man with a hair cut that is strongly marked as 'modern' (i.e. 1940s/1950s short) is framed in a doorway surrounded by mist. He carries a battered suitcase. The collar of his coat is turned up against the cold, night air. He walks towards the camera and into a high-ceilinged building. A customs official in a Russian-style military uniform stops him, indicating that he intends searching the young man's bag. A shot-reverse-shot sequence establishes a tense, expectant mood as eyelines meet; the stylish boy confronts the older-man-in-uniform. One gaze, fearful and defiant, meets another diametrically opposed gaze which is authoritarian and sadistic. The bag is aggressively snapped open and the camera discloses its contents to the viewer: some clothes, a copy of *The Face*. The official tosses the magazine to one side in a gesture redolent of either disgust or mounting anger or a hardening of resolve. The implication is that his initial suspicions are confirmed by the discovery of this 'decadent' journal.

At this, the crucial moment, the official's attention is diverted as a VIP, an older, senior official dressed in a more imposing uniform marches past between a phalanx of severe, grim-faced guards. The customs man, eyes wide with terror, jerks to attention and salutes, indicating with a slight movement of the head that the young man is dismissed. The sequence cuts to the young man, still in his coat, standing in a cramped, poorly furnished room. He opens the case, emptying the contents hurriedly on to a table or bed. The camera sweeps in as his trembling hands close around the forbidden article, the object of desire: a pair of Levi jeans.

The confrontation which provides the dramatic structure for the micro-narrative of this, the latest Levi jeans television and cinema commercial, is the familiar one between, on the one hand, freedom, youth, beauty and the West and, on the other, the cold, old, ugly, grey and unfree East. The commercial quotes visual and thematic elements from the spy thriller genre in order to sell a multiple package: the idea of rebellious-youth-winning-through-against-all-odds; the more general myth of the young Siegfried slaying the dragon of constraint; *The Face*; Levi jeans; the image of the 'self-made man' constructing himself through consumption and thereby embodying the spirit of the West. The articulation of commodity consumption, personal identity and desire which characterises life under hypercapitalism has here been universalised. There is nowhere else to go but to the shops. For in a flat world there is an end, as well, to ideology. The only meaningful political struggle left is between the individual body and the impersonal, life-denying forces of the state (whether nominally capitalist of communist).

However, this is not just another bourgeois myth that can be turned inside out and demystified (and hence deactivated) by the methods proposed by the early Roland Barthes, because the fictional scenario upon which the commercial is based has, in its turn, some foundation in fact. Rumour has it that Levi jeans go for high sums on the Russian black market and, according to issue *no. 61*, 'in Moscow old copies of *The Face* are reported to change hands for upwards of £80.' On a flat world, a commercial becomes a social (if not a socialist) realist text. It documents the real conditions of desire in the East and its claims to 'truth' are not challenged by the fact that the copy of *The Face* used in this ad is not, in a sense, 'real' either. It is, according to issue *61*, just a mock-up, a cover, a ghost of a thing, a skin concealing absent flesh. Thus, on the Second World, a cover can stand in for a whole magazine (the face of *The Face* for the whole *Face*). A magazine can stand in for a pair of jeans and the whole package can stand in for the lack of a 'whole way of life' which on a flat earth is unrealisable anywhere under any system (capitalist or otherwise).

But even the shadow of a shadow has a value and a price: 'The rarest issue of *The Face* consists of only one page – a cover designed at the request of Levis for use in a new television and cinema commercial. There are only four copies in existence' (*The Face* no. 61, May 1985). Rarity guarantees collectability and generates desire which promises an eventual return on the original investment. One day, one of the three copies of the copy that we saw all those years ago on our television screens may be auctioned off at Sotheby's and end up in the V & A, the Tate of the Ghetty Collection . . .

. . . Do you remember John Berger speaking from the heart of the First World in the television version of *Ways of Seeing* in 1974 as he flicked through a copy of *The Sunday Times* colour supplement moving from portraits of starving Bangla Deshi refugees to an advertisement for Badedas bath salts? 'Between these images', he said and goes on saying on film and videotapes in Complementary Studies classes up and down the country, 'there is such a gap, such a fissure that we can only say that the culture that produced these images is insane.' *The Face* is composed precisely on this fissure. It is the place of the nutty conjunction.

In the exhibition there is one panel of selected features from *The Face* presumably displaying the inventive layout and varied content. A photo-documentary account of a teenaged mod revivalist as a scooter rally entitled 'The Resurrection of Chad' is placed alongside photographs of the Nuba of Southern Sudan above a portrait of Malcolm McLaren, inventor of the Sex Pistols, and Duck Rock, a pirate of assorted black and Third World (Burundi, Zulu, New York rap) musical sounds against an article on Japanese fashion and an interview with Andy Warhol.

More facetious (a First World critic might say 'unwarranted' or 'offensive') juxtapositions occur elsewhere. A photograph by Derek Ridgers of the Pentecostal Choir of the First Born Church of the Living God shot outside a church (?) in a field in hallucinatory colour is placed next to a glowering black and white portrait of Genesis P. Orridge and friend of the occult/avant garde group, Psychic TV, after they had just signed a £1,000,000 contract. The malevolent duo are posed in front of a collection of metallic dildoes alongside the original caption. 'Which are the two biggest pricks in this picture?' Insolent laughter is, of course, incompatible with a high moral tone. Where either everything or nothing is significant, everything threatens to become just a laugh and, as one look at television's *The Young Ones* will tell you, *that* kind of laughter is never just or kind . . .

On a flat world, it is difficult to build an argument or to move directly from one point to the next because surfaces can be very slippery. Glissage or sliding is the preferred mode of transport – sliding from a television commercial to the end of ideology, from the Bill Brandt Room to a Picture of the Post, from *The Face* exhibition to *The Face* itself . . .

All statements made inside *The Face*, though necessarily brief are never straightforward. Irony and ambiguity predominate. They frame all reported utterances whether those utterances are reported photographically or in prose. A language is thus constructed without anybody in it (to question, converse or argue with). Where opinions are expressed they occur in hyperbole so that a question is raised about how seriously they're meant to be taken. Thus the impression you gain as you glance through the magazine is that this is less an 'organ of opinion' than a wardrobe full of clothes (garments, ideas, values, arbitrary preferences, i.e. signifiers).

Thus, *The Face* can sometimes be a desert full of silent bodies to be looked at, of voices without body to be listened to, not heard. This is because of the terror of naming.

As the procession of subcultures, taste groups, fashions, anti-fashions, winds its way across the flat plateaux, new terms are coined to describe them: psychobillies, yuppies, casuals, scullies, Young Fogies, Sloane Ranges, the Doleocracy, the Butcheoise – and on a flat earth all terminology is fatal to the object it describes. Once 'developed' as a photographic image and as a sociological and marketing concept, each group fades out of the now (i.e. ceases to exist).

The process is invariable: caption/capture/disappearance (i.e. natural-isation). ('. . . information is, by definition, a short-lived element. As soon as it is transmitted and shared it ceases to be information but has instead become an environmental given').[18] Once named, each group moves from the sublime (absolute now) to the ridiculous (the quaint, the obvious, the familiar). It becomes a special kind of joke. Every photograph an epitaph, every article an obituary. On both sides of the camera and the typewriter, irony and ambiguity act as an armour to protect the wearer (writer/ photographer; person/people written about/photographed) against the corrosive effects of the will to nomination. Being named (identified; categorised) is naff; on Planet Two it is a form of living death. A terrifying sentence is imposed (terrifying for the dandy): exile from the now.

And in the words of Baudelaire who preceded Godard in the Second World as Christ preceded Mohammed; as Hegel did Marx in the First: 'The beauty of the dandy consists above all in his air of reserve, which in turn arises from his unshakable resolve not to feel any emotions.'[19] To live ironically is to live without decideable emotion; to be ambiguous is to refuse to 'come out' (of the now). It is to maintain a delicate and impotent reserve . . .

Figure 9.5 (overleaf) *The Face* (inside spread), no 53, Sep. 1984

. . . The aversion to direct speech is also apparent in the tendency to visual and verbal parody. At the exhibition, Robert Mapplethorpe contributes a self-portrait in which he masquerades as a psychotic, 1950s juvenile delinquent. The staring eyes, the bulging quiff, the erect collar, the flick knife laid against the face, all suggest a mock-heroic sado-masochistic fantasy directed at him 'self'. Here the camera discloses no personal details as the body becomes the blank site of screen for the convocation of purely referential signs: *West Side Story*: doowop, 'New York'-as-generalised-dangerous-place, the 'Puerto Rican type': the banal and flattened forms of homoerotic kitsch . . . Annabella, singer with Bow Wow Wow sitting on the grass in the nude surrounded by the other (clothed) male members of the group glumly contemplates the camera and us in an exact reconstruction of Manet's *Déjeuner sur l'herbe* . . . Marilyn and Boy George stand outside the Carburton Street squat where they once lived, the mundane context and milk bottles in ironic counterpoint to their exotic, camp appearance: Hollywood and *The Mikado* come to *Coronation Street* . . . The high-key lighting, the braces, suits and picture ties, Duke Ellington moustaches and cigarette smoke in a black and white studio shot of Lynx are direct quotations from *film noir* and from 1930s/1940s promotional pics for black American jazz artists.

The past is played and replayed as an amusing range of styles, genres, signifying practices to be combined and recombined at will. The then (and the there) are subsumed in the now. The only history that exists here is the history of the signifier and that is no history at all . . .

. . . I open a copy of *The Face*. The magazine carries its own miniature simulacrum: a glossy five-page supplement commissioned by Swatch, the Swiss watch company which is aiming its product at the young, professional, style and design conscious markets. Like a Russian doll, the hollow *Face* opens to reveal a smaller, even emptier version of itself: *International Free Magazine No 2*. The black and red *Face* logo box is reproduced in the top left-hand corner with the words 'Swatch o'clock' in white sans serif caps across it. The host magazine is mimicked and parodied by its guest. A photograph of a model wearing watch earrings – her face reduced to a cartoon with a few strokes in 'wild style' with a felt tip pen – pouts out above a caption reading 'Art o'clock, look chic but rare'. A double page

JOYSTICK WARS

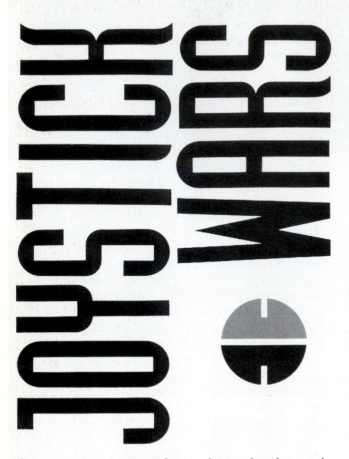

The computer games software house Imagine made Liverpool the capital of a new pop culture. But as with the old pop culture, you're only as good as your last hit. Imagine have had a few misses, and their efforts to create Megagames — pop operas for the home computer — have cost them dearly . . .

Story **Paul Walton** ● Photographs **Daniel Lainé/Actuel**

Kids on Merseyside can now become stars by tapping a keyb rather than plucking a guitar, writing computer games soft instead of hit records for a new kind of high-tech indie label. They' so talented, it's all much more exciting, they all get rich . . . or s story goes in the Sunday papers. But even the new pop busine still business, and Imagine — the runaway success of last year — just gone out of it. What went wrong?

Imagine sold over a million computer games. We spent £80 m on games last year — a tenth of it on Imagine games: cuties lik first hits, *Wacky Waiters*, *Ah Diddums* and *Molar Maul*, blasters as *Zzoom* and *Zip Zap*, tactical games like *Stonkers* and adven like *The Alchemist*. The sign on the wall at their Liverpool head ters reads: **Imagine . . . The Name of the Game.** And for a they were. Their youthful programmers became cult heroes i teenage computer underground.

Success bought Imagine's founders speedy transportation an of friends. "City gents came up from London trying to buy a pie us," said Mark Butler, 24-year-old businessman behind the fir veteran of an industry that, like him, had only just arrived. wasn't "selling any bit of me." Instead, he bought himself a 12 Harris bike *and* an Aston Martin.

But what was it really like in the whizzkid's world? Picture a office with maybe fifty computer terminals scattered anyhow a the carpeted floor, but devoid of the usual filing cabinets, div plants and office paraphernalia. Crouched around the screens t the games are some young kids — a punk, a skin, mostly hippi bikers, few girls or blacks. Belongings are strewn aroun floppy-discs, print-outs, magazines and coffee cups. Program technicians, artists and musicians work around the clock every the week. They enter the 'top secret' site using a plastic securit

Dave Lawson, also in his mid-20s, was the one in creative con this confusion. He is what the teen-mags would call the quiet on "George Harrison look-alike" to his friends. He would rather talk "emerging leisure technologies" than buying cars or being sta Imagine's office earlier this year, he was full of excitement ove next project. "We're producing Megagames next that will mix film and music with computer games to give real entertainment last. Imagine," he exclaimed, unconscious of the pun, "being a get a cartoon character doing what you want it to . . ." At this Butler advised him to "Keep schtum!"

The Megagames, due out by the summer, never appeared. H ambitious, they would have taxed the ingenuity of IBM let Imagine. They were Imagine's 'concept albums' — a quantum le the vernacular art of the home computer game, an art which is its early, unpredictable stages. The hits come and go, and so reputations and the stars.

At the start of last year, Imagine split away from an Merseyside firm, Bug-byte. They were going to expand through to supply ready-to-write games to the publishers Marshall Cave — to accompany a part-work magazine on programming ('You t be a video star!'). But when the games were out on trial kids rej them as boring. Marshall Cavendish asked for their £200,000 b

By May of this year Imagine was in difficulty. They were out public eye — the computer games top ten — for the first time in year. It was the hit single syndrome, the problem of coming up the goods, *again*. They had to move out of their plush HQ. "C were appearing on the walls," it was claimed.

In fact, there were quite a few cracks. The company's in-h design team Studio Sting, which had made Imagine's graphics of the best around, went first. They moved to Manchester ar trying to go it alone. The Megagames turned out to be fraugh bugs. And some of the cracks were so wide that the roof ha fallen in. Imagine was wound up with debts estimated at £30 All but twenty of the original staff have now returned to a predictable Liverpudlian pursuit: trying to find a job. The re staying to complete the Megagames, one way or another, for company being set up by the founders.

"We're really sorry that we had to close down, but we're expe to pick up again soon," said a rueful Butler. "Everyone's worked hard in what was the world's greatest." Together with Dave La and a few other whizzkids, the Imagine team is scraping the together to carry on. They're banking that the Megagames will what else? — a hit. ●

● *This page:* **The boy wonder of computer games, 18-year-old Eugene Evans, at the wheel of his Lotus Esprit. Evans was one of the youngest of Imagine's fifty programmers during their hey-day last year.**

● *Opposite:* **Jeff Minter of Llamasoft, a one-man Northern games factory. Like Dave Lawson at Imagine, Minter has grand dreams for computer games. "I want to develop the ideal game, a game connected by telephone to other players and controlled by a central computer, so they can interact with one another." Unlike Imagine, he has kept the scale of his operation small.**

Figure 9.6

The Face (front cover), no. 29, Sep. 1982

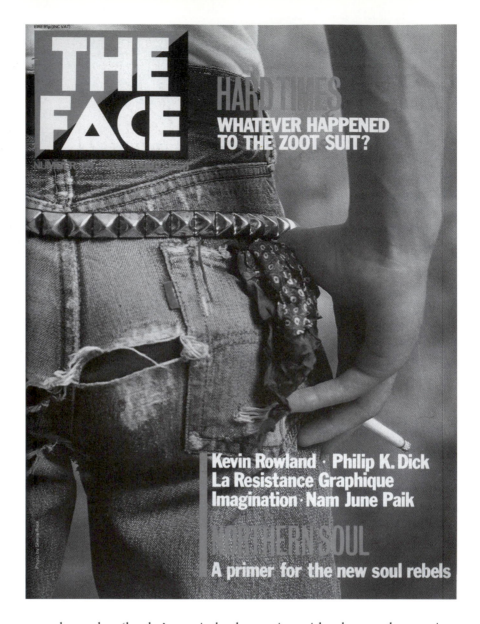

THE
FACE

HARD TIMES
WHATEVER HAPPENED
TO THE ZOOT SUIT?

Kevin Rowland · Philip K. Dick
La Resistance Graphique
Imagination · Nam June Paik

NORTHERN SOUL
A primer for the new soul rebels

spread reveals a 'hunky' man in leather posing with a bow and arrow in a wood. The captions read: 'Homme Swatch. Outdoor, ton corps, ta Swatch'. The 'Swatch' mock-editorial 'explains': '*Parlez vous* Swatch? To look or not to look? That is the question. *Sommaire*. Summer 85: let's go, *l'été*, come on in Swatch, *aujourd'hui la mode o'clock est entrée dans ma tête* . . . etc.' This is a parody of a parody. As the primary objection to advertising on Planet Two is aesthetic rather than ideological – a matter of the signifier and not the signified – potential advertisers can be educated to commission designs compatible with editorial preferences . . .

Advertising – the *eidos* of the marketplace – is pressed into the very pores of *The Face*. For advertisers as for *The Face*, sophists and lawyers, rhetoric is all there is: the seizure of attention, the refinement of technique, the design, promotion, marketing of product (ideas, styles; for lawyers, innocence of guilt depending on who pays). *The Face* habitually employs the rhetoric of advertising: the witty one-liner, the keyword, the aphorism, the extractable (i.e. quotable) image are favoured over more sustained, sequential modes of sense-making. Each line or image quoted in another published context acts like a corporate logo inviting us to recognise its source – the corporation – and to acknowledge the corporation's power.

The urge to compress and condense – to create an absolute homology of form and meaning which cannot be assimilated but can only be copied – is more pronounced in Neville Brody's sometimes barely legible typefaces. It is as if we were witnessing in the various trademark scripts and symbols he devises, a graphic depiction of the power shift from Europe to Japan as the phonetic alphabet takes on before our eyes a more iconic character. The occidental equivalent of Japanese or Chinese script is to be found here in *The Face* in the *semiogram*: a self-enclosed semantic unit – a word, graphic image, photograph, the layout of a page – which cannot be referred to anything outside itself. In the semiogram, *The Face* capitulates symbolically to the empire of signs, robots, computers, miniaturisation and automobiles – to Japan, which has served as the first home of flatness for a long line of Second World orientalists including Roland Barthes, Noel Birch, Chris Marker, David Bowie and, of course, the group Japan. The pages of *The Face*, like a series of masks in an occidental Noh play, act out a farce on the decline of the British Empire. The name of this production: '[I think] I'm going Japanese' . . .

Renouncing the possibility of challenging the game, Baudrillard has formulated a series of what he calls 'decadent' or 'fatal' strategies (where decadence and fatalism are seen as positive virtues). One of these he names 'hyperconformism'. *The Face* is hyperconformist: more commercial than the commercial, more banal than the banal . . .

Behind *The Face*: the bottom line of Planet One

Vietnam was first and foremost a war in representation.

(Jean Luc Godard)

What are Chile, Biafra, the 'boat people', Bologna or Poland to us?

(Jean Baudrillard, *Sur le nihilisme*)

The Tatler: the magazine for the other Boat People.

(Advertising slogan for *The Tatler* accompanying an image of a group of the 'beautiful rich' aboard a yacht.)

Many people of my generation and my parents' generation retain a sentimental attachment – in itself understandable enough – to a particular construction of the 'popular' – a construction which was specific to the period from the inter-war to the immediate post-war years and which found its most profound, its most progressive and mature articulation in the films of Humphrey Jennings and on the pages of *The Picture Post*. We hardly need reminding that that moment has now passed.

The community addressed by and in part formed out of the national-popular discourses of the late 1930s and 1940s – discourses which were focused round notions of fair play, decency, egalitarianism and natural justice now no longer exists as an affective and effective social unit.

Forty years of relative affluence, and regional (if not global) peace; five years of Thatcherite New Realism and go-gettery, of enemies within and without, and of the dream of the property-owning democracy, have gradually worn down and depleted the actual and symbolic materials out of which that earlier construction was made.

At the same time, the popular can no longer be hived off from higher education as its absolute other ('innocent', 'spontaneous', 'untutored') because those same forty years have seen more and more ordinary people gaining some, admittedly restricted (and increasingly endangered) access to secondary, further, higher and continuing education. It is neither useful nor accurate to think about the 'masses' as if they were wrapped in clingfilm against all but the most unsavoury of new ideas.

There have, of course, been positive material advances. To take the most important example, feminist concerns, idioms and issues have become lodged in the very fabric of popular culture even in those areas from television sit-coms to working men's clubs where the implications of feminist critique have been most actively and hysterically resisted. It's also clear that the mass media – whatever other role(s) they may play in social reproduction – have served to democratise, at least to circulate on an unprecedented scale, forms and kinds of knowledge which had previously been the exclusive property of privileged elites.

The Face should be seen as functioning within this transfigured social and ideological field. Whilst I would not suggest that *The Face* is *The Picture Post* of the 1980s. I would go along with the claim asserted in the accompanying notes that *The Face* exhibition 'is about looking at popular social history in the making'. *The Face* has exerted an enormous influence on the look and flavour of many magazines available in newsagents up and down the country and has spawned countless imitations: *I-D*, *Blitz*, *Tomorrow*, *Etcetera*, etc. The repertoire and rhetoric of photographic mannerisms, devices, techniques and styles in the fashion and music press have been fruitfully expanded and the studio has been rediscovered, in a sense re-invented as a fabulous space – a space where every day the incredible becomes the possible. But *The Face*'s impact has gone far beyond the relatively narrow sphere of pop and fashion journalism dictating an approach to the visible world that has become synonymous with what it means for a magazine today to be – at least to look – contemporary. The gentrified cut-up has found its way into the inaptly named *Observer* 'Living' supplement and *The Sunday Times* has followed *The Face* into the continental 30.1 cm × 24.3 cm format.

Amongst its other services, *The Face* provides a set of physical cultural resources that young people can use in order to make some sense and get some pleasure out of growing up in an increasingly daunting and complex environment. It has been instrumental in shaping an emergent structure of feeling, a 1980s sensibility as distinctive in its own way as that of the late 1960s (though how resilient that structure will prove remains to be seen). But in any case, it does no good to consider the readers of *The Face* as victims, culprits, dupes or dopes, as 'kids' or *tabulae rasae* or potential converts. Their world is real already even when the sensibility which *The Face* supports and fosters seems to bear a much closer and more vital relationship to the anomic Picture of the Post that I outlined earlier than it does to the 'social democratic eye' of Hulton's classic photojournal weekly.

The Face reflects, defines and focuses the concerns of a significant minority of style and image conscious people who are not, on the whole, much interested in party politics, authorised versions of the past and outmoded notions of community. The popular and the job of picturing the popular has changed irrevocably out of all recognition even since the 1950s.

It should also be borne in mind that Nick Logan is not Jean Baudrillard and that *The Face* is infinitely better, more popular, significant, influential and socially plugged in than *The Tatler* is or ever could be. It's also clear that the photography, design, and a lot of the writing are, by any standards, good and on occasion attain levels of excellence which are still rare in British pop journalism. And, finally, it is as well to remember that a text is, of course, *not* the world, that no one *has* to live there, that it is not a compulsory purchase, that no one has to pay, that no one has to even pay a visit.

I'm well aware that only a gossip columnist, a fool or an academic could find the time to undertake a close analysis of such self-confessed ephemera or would set aside sufficient energy to go chasing round those circles where, as George Eliot puts it, 'the lack of grave emotion passes for wit'.[20] Yet, despite such reservations, I cannot escape the conviction that something else, something deeper is at stake, not just here in this talk of signifiers, surfaces, post-modernism, but in the broader streams of social life and practice, and in all personal and political struggle, irrespective of where it takes place and irrespective, too, of how these terms and the relations between them get defined.

Something that really matters is at stake in this debate. At the risk of alienating the reader with an analogy already stretched to breaking point, one last battle in the War of the Worlds may help to clarify the issue . . .

. . . I was about to leave *The Face* exhibition feeling vaguely uneasy about the ambivalence of my response when – not for the first time – the beautiful, clear, soulful voice of Chrissie Hynde came drifting across from the video installation in the corner of the room. The promo tapes were on some kind of a loop so that I had heard her sing the same song at least three times as I meandered round the photographs, the layout and typography panels, the cases containing Crolla and Bodymap clothes. As I moved towards the door, that voice rose once more, singing over and over the same agonised refrain: 'It's a bitter line between love and hate . . . .'

And words like 'love' and 'hate' and 'faith' and 'history', 'pain' and 'joy', 'passion' and 'compassion' – the depth words drawn up like ghosts from a different dimension will always come back in the eleventh hour to haunt the Second World and those who try to live there in the now. This is not just pious sentiment. It is, quite simply, in the very nature of the human project that those words and what they stand for will never go away. When they seem lost and forgotten, they can be found again even in – especially in – the most inhospitable, the flattest of environments. John Cowper Powys once wrote:

> We can all love, we can all hate, we can all possess, we can all pity ourselves, we can all condemn ourselves, we can all admire ourselves, we can all be selfish, we can all be unselfish. But below all these things there is something else. There is a deep, strange, inaccountable response within us to the mystery of life and the mystery of death: and this response subsists below grief and pain and misery and disappointment, below all care and all futility.

That something else will still be there when all the noise and the chatter have died away. And it is perhaps significant that the quotation came to me courtesy of one of my students who included it in a deeply moving essay on how the experience of personal loss had transformed his response to photos of his family. He in his turn had found it in an advertisement for a group called The Art of Noise designed by Paul Morley, arch *bricoleur* and publicist, the mastermind at ZTT behind the Frankie Goes to Hollywood phenomenon last year.[21]

Whatever Baudrillard or *The Tatler* or Saatchi and Saatchi, and Swatch have to say about it, I shall go on reminding myself that this earth is round not flat, that there will never be an end to judgement, that the ghosts will go on gathering at the bitter line which separates truth from lies, justice from injustice, Chile, Biafra and all the other avoidable disasters from all of us, whose order is built upon their chaos. And that, I suppose, is the bottom line on Planet One.

Notes

1   Northrop Frye, *The Great Code: the Bible and Literature* (New York, Harcourt Brace Jovanovich, 1981).

2   See, for instance, Paul Virilio and Sylvere Lotringer, *Pure War* (New York, Semio-text(e), Foreign Agents series, 1983); Félix Guattari, *Molecular Revolution, Psychiatry and Politics* (Harmondsworth, Penguin, 1984); Félix Guattari and Gilles Deleuze, *Anti-Oedipus: Capitalism and Schizophrenia* (Minneapolis, University of Minnesota Press, 1983); Meaghan Morris, 'Room 101 or a few worst things in the world', in André Frankovits (ed.), *Seduced and Abandoned: the Baudrillard Scene* (Stonemoss Services, 1984); André Gorz, *Farewell to the Working Class* (Pluto Press, 1983) Rudolf Bahro, *From Red to Green* (London, New Left Books, 1982).

3   See Roland Barthes, *The Pleasure of the Text* (London, Jonathan Cape, 1976). For a more condensed, programmatic manifesto of post-structuralist aims and objectives, see R. Barthes, 'Change the object itself', in S. Heath (ed.), *Image–Music–Text* (Harmondsworth, Penguin, 1977).

4   The phrase the 'impossible class' was originally coined by Nietszche in *The Dawn of the Day*, 1881 (Gordon Press, 1974). The phrase has since been appropriated as a self-description by certain anarchist groups, by situationists, urban Red Indians, radical autonomists, etc. (see for instance, the anarchist pamphlet *Riot not to Work* on the 1981 riots).

5   This is a mutated echo of the title of an article by Jean Baudrillard (see note 6 below): 'The precession of simulacra' in which he postulates that the 'social body' is being mutated by the 'genetic code' of television in such a way that psychotic planar states of drift and fascination emerge to supplant social and psychic space (the space of the subject). In this way, reality is supposedly replaced by a 'hyperreality' (an eventless imaginary). See 'The precession of simulacra', *Art and Text* 11 (spring, 1983).

6   For an excellent introduction, summary and critique of Baudrillard's work, see André Frankovits (ed.), *Seduced and Abandoned: the Baudrillard Scene* (Stonemoss Services, 1984). To retrace Baudrillard's trajectory (for given his flatness it can hardly be a descent) from a semiotic analysis of consumption to flat earth science fiction, see *For a Critique of the Political Economy of the Sign* (Telos, 1981); *The Mirror of Production* (Telos, 1981); *In the Shadow of the Silent Majorities* (New York, Semiotext (e), Foreign Agents Series, 1984); 'The ecstasy of communication', Hal Foster (ed.), *Postmodern Culture* (Pluto Press, 1985). This is the kind of thing that 'happens' in the Baudrillard scene: 'There's no longer any transcendence in the gaze. There's no longer any transcendence of judgement. There's a kind of participation, coagulation, proliferation of messages and signs, etc. . . . And one is no longer in a state to judge, one no longer has the potential to reflect . . . This is fascination. It is a form of ecstasy. Each event is immediately ecstatic and is pushed by the media to a degree of superlative existence. It invades everything' (Baudrillard quoted in Frankovits (ed.) *Seduced and Abandoned*).

7   See Frankovits, *Seduced and Abandoned*.

8   See for instance, Alain Touraine, *The Post-Industrial Society* (Wildwood House, 1974); Gorz, *Farewell to the Working Class*; A. Gorz, *Paths to Paradise* (Pluto, 1985); Daniel Bell, *The Coming Post Industrial Society* (New York, Basic Books, 1973); Alvin Toffler, *The Third Wave* (Bantam, 1981); for post-modernism, see Hal Foster (ed.), *Postmodern Culture*; Jean-François Lyotard, 'Answering the question: what is postmodernism?', in *The Postmodern Condition: a Report on Knowledge* (Manchester University Press, 1984); Fredric Jameson, 'Post modernism or the cultural logic of late capitalism', in *New Left Review*, 146 (1984). For New Left and neo-Marxist critiques of postmodernism, see Perry Anderson, *Considerations on Western Marxism* (New Left Books, 1976).

9   Jameson quoted in Dan Latimer, 'Jameson and postmodernism', in *New Left Review* (November–December 1984).

10   This phrase from *The Communist Manifesto* is taken by Marshall Berman as the title of his book, *All That's Solid Melts into Air* (New York, Simon and Schuster, 1983). The book deals with the dialectics of modernisation – the process of social, demographic, economic and technological change associated with the rise of capitalism – and modernism – the answering innovations in the arts. For a discussion of Berman's account of the 'experience of modernity', see P. Anderson, *Considerations*; M. Berman, 'The signs in the street: a response to Perry Anderson', *New Left Review* 144 (March–April, 1984).

11   This neologism is used by Jean-François Lyotard in 'The sublime and the avant garde', *Art Forum* (April, 1984).

12   See Baudrillard, also Latimer, 'Jameson and postmodernism'. Latimer suggests that Dick Hebdige adopts the celebratory stance in 'In poor taste: notes on pop'. He writes '"We cannot afford," says Jameson, "the comfort of 'absolute moralizing judgements' about post-modernism. We are within it. We are part of it whether we like it or not. To repudiate it is to be reactionary. On the other hand, to celebrate it unequivocally, complacently, is to be Dick Hebdige . . .". Whilst agreeing with Jameson on the facticity of certain aspects of the post-modern condition, the present author would distinguish himself from the 'Dick Hebdige' referred to here.

13   See Jean-François Lyotard, *The Postmodern Condition: a Report on Knowledge*

(Manchester, Manchester University Press, 1984); Edward W. Said, 'Opponents, audiences, constituencies and community', in Foster (ed.) *Postmodern Culture*; Herbert Schiller, *Communication and Cultural Domination* (Pantheon, 1978) and *Who Knows: Information in the Age of the Fortune 400* (Ablex, 1981).

14   See, amongst many others, Herbert Marcuse, *One Dimensional Man* (Beacon Press, 1966); Lyotard, 'The sublime and the avant garde'.

15   The Italian school of 'weak thought' was invoked by Umberto Eco in conversation with Stuart Hall in the opening programme in the series of *Voices* (Channel Four, 1985). 'Weak thought' refers to new, more tentative and flexible styles of reasoning and argumentation developed to avoid the authoritarian and terroristic tendencies within 'classic' (social) scientific theorising.

16   Fredric Jameson, Foreword to Lyotard, *The Postmodern Condition*.

17   Alvin Toffler, *The Third Wave*. Toffler argues that information technology and home computing are rendering 'second wave' (i.e. industrial) patterns of work, leisure, family structure etc. obsolete. Commuting electronically from her/his 'electronic cottage', the prosumer is the new (a)social subject, working, playing, and shopping by computer and thus synthesising in his/her person via her/his terminal the previously separate functions of production and consumption.

18   Lyotard, 'The sublime and the avant garde'.

19   Charles Baudelaire, 'The painter of modern life', in J. Mayne (ed.), *The Painter of Modern Life and Other Essays* (Phaidon Press, 1964).

20   George Eliot, *Daniel Deronda* (1876, Penguin, 1967). This note provides a late opportunity for me to point out that whilst this article is ostensibly about *The Face* and postmodernism, it is also in part an indirect critique of certain aspects of my own work. For instance, *Subculture: the Meaning of Style* (Methuen, 1979), especially the insistence in that book on ambiguity and irony both as subcultural and as critical strategies. This is not a retraction but rather a modification of an earlier position. This note may also explain the subtitle of the present article: 'Squaring up to *The Face*'.

21   The student's essay referred to in the text is 'Paper Ghosts – a Phenomenology of Photography' by Steve Evans.

Regulating photographic meanings

Introduction
Jessica Evans

Our selection in Part II moves away from the formal analysis of meaning construction, and the idea of a society mediated by figural images in general, to that of the regulation and contexts of photographic production and practice. Section C represents a range of theoretical and methodological positions for approaching the medium of photography. The readings in Section D go on to conduct analyses of particular kinds of photographic practices and the institutional arrangements for the production, consumption and regulation of photographic meaning. This introduction contextualizes the readings with some comments on the characteristics of photographs, and on the theoretical problems and issues involved in making an analysis of photography as a medium.

In general, the readings indicate that any investigation into how a delimited corpus of photographs constructs particular views of the world also needs to take account of how key discourses and institutions construct photography itself, furnishing it with the means of legibility and allowing it to mean something to somebody within conditions of use. As John Tagg says, in 'Evidence, Truth and Order' (Chapter 16):

> Histories are not backdrops to set off the performance of images. They are scored into the paltry paper signs, in what they do and do not do, in what they encompass and exclude, in the ways they open on to or resist a repertoire of uses in which they can be meaningful and productive. Photographs are never 'evidence' of history; they are themselves the historical. (p. 247)

The notion of 'use' emphasized here is linked to the preference for thinking in terms of the regulation of meaning through concrete practices rather than the 'determination' of meaning understood in the abstract. On the one hand, determination often implies determinism, a one-way linear model of cause and effect – as is the case with the way in which the relations between economy and culture are conceived in classical Marxism. In this view, cultural artefacts are seen as epiphenomena, as being only externally related to the 'objective conditions' that decide the outcome of the action 'independently of people's wills'. Formulated in this way, the debate tends to focus on the levels of freedom and constraint allowed within the system of social forces being studied. Implicit in the term 'regulation', on the other hand, which can also be understood as a weaker version of 'determination' as already outlined, is the idea that social and cultural forces can be understood as a complex interrelation of limits and pressures (see Williams, 1977 on 'determination'; Hall, 1997 on 'regulation') which are not just targeted negatively on prevention or repression but are understood positively. In the words of Williams: 'Society is not a dead husk that limits social and individual fulfilment . . . it is always also a constitutive process.' He goes on to say that determination of this 'whole kind' is in the 'whole social process itself and nowhere else: not in an abstracted mode of production' (1977: 87).

This has been taken further since Williams, in particular by Stuart Hall and others who have followed the implications of Foucault's objection to the 'repressive hypothesis': thus, it is not a matter of choosing between freedom and constraint, for there are never any circumstances in social life in which regulation does not exist; rather, there are different modes of regulation being applied, each of which reassembles components of law, conventions, moral systems, sets of practices, meanings and values (see Hall, 1997). These arguments bring us back full circle to meaning but in a different way to the more formal and delimited sense of textual meaning as delineated in the semiotic readings of Part I. For if regulation is an active process which incorporates and constitutes people's desires and their sense of motivated participation which, moreover, is not confined to an idea of external 'cause', then cultural norms and differences become essential to the ways in which individuals and social groups conduct their relations. It is not, then, just a case of thinking about how culture is governed by forces outside it, but how culture is a regulatory force in its own right, a mechanism of governance (see Hall, 1997: 233; du Gay, 1997: 287). If we go down this route we consider how cultural forms are normative, specifying how things should be done via conventions and taken-for-granted procedures; how classification systems mark out and legitimate differences between customs and practices, defining the limits of their acceptability (see Chapter 11 by Bourdieu); how categories of persons and identities are produced, often in essentialist or homogeneous manner (such as 'the mentally handicapped' or 'the insane' as discussed in Chapters 16 and 17 by Tagg and Evans on the positivist claims of photographic realism).

One of the well-noted aspects of photography is that it is a medium in which we are all involved, at some point in our lives. Most people in twentieth-century modern culture will at least have had a photograph taken of themselves, and very many will have taken a picture, for it is a medium thoroughly integrated into our activities and identities as members of the family and the school, and as tourists and often as employees or students. The camera is central to one's rites of passage, spliced into those ritualistic events which celebrate the continuity and solidity of family life; for example, births, birthdays, holidays and weddings. Moreover, photography is firmly integrated into the ways in which we all manage our identities and have them managed for us. There can be few who have not attempted to control the image of themselves by constructing their pose for a camera or tearing up the photograph that makes them feel uncomfortable or ugly. Photography is now the second most popular leisure activity in Britain – after gardening – and outstrips DIY (Porter, 1989: 90). Unlike other media, it is used – or at least displayed – within almost every institution in society.

In his introduction to *Photography: a Middlebrow Art*, Pierre Bourdieu says: 'One might say of photography what Hegel said of philosophy: "No other art of science is subjected to this last degree of scorn, to the supposition that we are masters of it without ado"' (1990: 5). Bourdieu comes close here to identifying the main reason why photography remains the least investigated media, under-examined even in the mainstream of cultural studies, when paradoxically photography remains the prevalent form in which visual images intrude upon us, are transmitted and viewed. No doubt this situation is compounded by the elusive feature of photographs: that they are items of material culture which are often not the subject of intentional viewing, unlike television which, although often used for background noise or company, seems more purposefully sought out as something to switch on and engage with. In fact, our very language of reference to highly visual artefacts is still that of reading, which again has the effect of displacing what we actually do with them. So we say we buy *Hello!* or *Marie-Claire* magazine to read it, when in fact we buy it just as much, or more, to look at. Jokes about the *Sun* newspaper in the 1980s were precisely along the lines that 'people buy it to look at the pictures, not to read it' – the denigration here was not just aimed of the 'page three girl' substitute for news stories but the low-status accorded to the visual, in contrast to the written. All this is surely confirmed by the ephemeral nature of the everyday, unexamined use of photographs – which are, unlike other media it seems, consumed and thrown away, just as Sontag saw it.

Unlike the more technically demanding artisanal modes of drawing and painting, photography 'presupposes neither academically communicated culture, nor the apprenticeships and the ''profession'' which confer their value on the cultural consumptions and practices ordinarily held to be the most noble, by withholding them from the man in the street' (Bourdieu, 1990: 5). As Don Slater points out in 'Marketing Mass Photography' (Chapter 18), unlike film, television, radio or the music industry, 'the monopolisation of photography by professionals and the impoverishment of its wider use has not been based on restricting access to the media technology' (p. 290). Like the technology of the pen which anyone can pick up and use, so anyone can 'make' a photograph. The fact that the very means of producing photographic images is not regulated in a legally and economically restricted and centralized manner (in contrast to the institutions of the 'mass' media) is, in part, why photography has therefore often been considered as the medium of democratization. It accounts for the ease with which it appears across public and private domains and the sense that it is a medium we can all take part in, a medium which has no status, class or serious financial barriers to access. That this is so is due largely to the basic division of labour which lies at the heart of mass amateur photography between the camera operator and the process of developing and printing the photograph – a separation which persists today (see Watney, Chapter 10, and Slater, Chapter 18). In the words of George Eastman, whose Kodak box brownie was the first camera to embody this principle, and thus for the first time to industrialize photography to the extent that lower middle-class and working-class people could own and make images of themselves:

> The principle of the Kodak system is the separation of a work that anyone can do in making a photograph, from the work that only an expert can do. We furnish anybody, a man, woman, or child, who has sufficient intelligence to point a box straight and press the button. It can be employed without any preliminary study, without a darkroom, without chemicals. (Kodak advertising copy, 1898)

None the less, we cannot simply assume that the ease with which anyone can, indeed, 'take' their own pictures means that power and its relations have evacuated the sphere of representation. Slater has commented that the paradox which drove him to write his article in the first place was that 'the very means by which the power to represent was democratised also rendered it impotent' (in Evans, 1997: 173). Indeed, the difference between 'taking' and 'making' – so essential to the distinction between the identity of, on the one hand, the snapshooter and, on the other, the serious amateur and especially the art photographer – points to the limits of mass amateur practice. The ethos of the amateur photographer is summed up by Bourdieu, though he does not distinguish here between serious amateur and the snapshooter: 'Nothing is more directly opposed to the ordinary image of artistic creation than the activity of the amateur photographer, who often demands that his camera should perform the greatest possible number of operations for him identifying the degree of sophistication of the apparatus that he uses with its degree of automism' (1990: 6). Jo Spence, John Tagg, Simon Watney, Don Slater and others central to the development of photography theory and history have pointed out that it is in the domain of the most 'ordinary' and private, the most apparently 'everyday' and localized practices of the amateur snapshot photographer that the most stultified and limited repertoire of compositions, subject matter and styles resides. What amateur photography has done, since its inception, has been to associate the private use of the camera with leisure activities in order to affirm the notion of the family as a primary site of consumption.

One of the central operations of power which impinge on photographic practice in order to impoverish its wider use can, to continue Slater's argument, be located in the high-pressure mass marketing of photographic equipment: 'It has been restricted in the course of its very proliferation, through its technical form, through its retailing, through the 'training' of consumers through advertising, the photo press and other publicity organs of the photographic manufacturing industry' (p. 291). Slater has recently admitted one bad prediction made in his article, which was based on one of the reports he used for the research – the death of the 35mm compact camera. He now says this 'not only revived but wiped out the alternative formats in the snapshooting market' (in Evans, 1997: 174). On the other hand, as he says, the invention since the time of the article of the disposable camera is a return, full circle, to the logic of Kodak snapshooting in which technical skill in the making of the picture is removed from the activity of the photographer: 'the camera is merely an adjunct to the film – you buy it preloaded, send it back to base for processing.' Knowledge of photographic process is again reduced to zero and 'constitutes no impediment to film throughput' (1997: 174). Slater has recently made a call for retaining the idea of access as at least a minimal condition for a critical approach to the mass media – since it allows understanding of media products as a structured set of conventions and choices (Slater 1995). But he fears that the arrival of electronics into media products – videos, cameras, computer graphics or games – displaces any need for knowledge about specific media towards the requirement for knowledge about 'programming' in general, so that we may know 'how to choose from pre-set options built into machines and presented to us via the menus' (Slater, 1995: 174–5). Thus, complexity and automation, rather than being opposed principles as they were in 'Marketing Mass Photography', now go together as in the pre-programmed decision pathways of the digital camera: 'The newest Nikon can now behave like an old Kodak or an old Leica, not on the basis of its user's knowledge of photography but their ability to input commands' (Slater, 1995: 175).

There is, moreover, a profoundly important gendered dimension in the construction of the division between the serious amateur and the snapshot photographer which is not brought out in Slater's article (see Porter, 1989/90); serious amateurs are typically male, and aged 25–44. They process and develop their own films, are often members of photography clubs and subscribe to *Amateur Photographer* or *Practical Photography*, magazines which fetishize equipment and impart the aesthetic rules and techniques for a 'good' photograph within a number of limited categories such as 'glamour photography' or 'landscapes'. Photographic self-expression is driven by a culture of aspiration and understood as a process of solving technical challenges through which the amateur may 'make' it as a professional photographer and thus, as Bourdieu sees it, ennoble themselves by attempting to ennoble photography, 'a substitute within their range and grasp for the higher arts' (Bourdieu, 1990: 9). The culture of the snapshooter is entirely different:

in industry terms, it is deeply feminized, and indeed the majority of users are women and from a wider socioeconomic range than the serious amateurs. This constitutes the bread-and-butter 'mass' market for the industry. Products and services for this group are described as 'foolproof' and it is assumed that they have low expectations and few technical competencies – in this way, 'the camera compensates for the lack of skills and confidence of the user.' The photographer's interest in photography is limited to its use as a record of family and leisure activities, which is specified right down to the illustrations on the envelope in which the developing and processing company send back prints (see Porter, 1989/90: 46).

The polysemic nature of the photograph, discussed in the readings of Part I, provides a particular challenge of its own to those wishing to advance the critical study of photography. To the extent that, as is argued in many of the readings in Part II, the meaning of any photograph relies upon the contingencies of its use and its embeddedness within a particular context which puts it to work and enables it to mean something to somebody, photographic meaning seems to be a phenomenon utterly dependent on its 'other', i.e. on what it is not. Accordingly, as was argued in the General Introduction, theoretical attention often seems inclined to slide away, endlessly displaced to the study of that which seems logically prior – to media institutions and organizations, their patterns of ownership, integrating belief systems and values. The critique of this 'productionist' view of cultural artefacts informs, either overtly or implicitly, the readings in Sections C and D. However, their solutions and methods of approach vary.

The fact that photographs exist for such a diversity of purposes means that we should downplay the significance of their common origin in the technology of the camera. The ontological status of photography therefore has little to do with the social forms and uses to which actual photographs are put. This is certainly John Tagg's view, expressed in the extracts from *The Burden of Representation* (1988) which make up Chapter 16:

> What alone unites the diversity of sites in which photography operates is the social formation itself: the specific historical spaces for representation and practice which it constitutes. Photography as such has no identity . . . It is a flickering across a field of institutional spaces. It is this field we must study, not photography as such. (p. 246)

Rosalind Krauss, Douglas Crimp and Allan Sekula adopt this approach in relation to the status of the photograph as an archival object. In particular, they consider the implications of the classifications and recontextualizations of photographs in accordance with the narratives of art history, the values of modernism and, in Sekula's case, with those of commerce. Sekula (Chapter 12) points to the ways in which, once a corpus of photographs is placed in an archive, the 'possibility of meaning is "liberated" from the actual contingencies of use' (p. 183).

Furthermore, although it may appear that photography is only the effect or product of a set of determinations which are logically prior – a view which mitigates against photographic practices deserving attention in their own right – it is important to realize that the institutions of advertising and journalism would not exist as we know them without photography. It is not then a matter of institutions, such as advertising, 'determining' photography, as a neo-Marxist or 'production of culture' critique would have it. Here, Simon Watney's work, 'On the Institutions of Photography' (Chapter 10), is most informative in defining how better to think of the relations of 'determination' of photography. Watney responds to the sociological work of Barbara Rosenblum, an early attempt from a 'labour process' point of view, i.e. stressing the division of labour and levels of automation at the level of production, to delineate the institutional determinants at work in the making of photographic images, in her case, in the areas of fine art photography, photo-journalism and advertising. She went some way to defining photographic style: 'Style consists of predictable combinations of features', but her wider argument is that the technical and social relations at the level of production – how photographs get made – determines their style: 'Style in photography is not exclusively a product of an autonomous set of shared understandings but at least partly determined by social organisation' (Rosenblum, 1978: 423).

Watney critiques what he calls 'sociologistic' approaches to photography (by this he means something similar to what has more recently been termed the 'productionist' approach; see du Gay et al., 1997) and argues that Rosenblum lacks a semiotic grip on the central issue of representation, tending to 'fall back into a latent functionalism, as if the demands of a particular branch of photography such as photojournalism always secure an inflexible uniformity of appearances' (pp. 148–9). He advocates that we respect two moments of analysis that can be taken as analytically separate but 'which interpenetrate with each other in all circumstances of their use'. 'We still need to distinguish between those institutions which facilitate the production of photography in all its forms, and those bodies of beliefs/values/associations which inform and organise the "look" of photographs and their meanings' (p. 145). The photographic artefact, therefore, needs to be understood as both a domain of signifying practice and as a material object regulated by particular institutional conditions.

Bourdieu's answer to the problem of how to reconstruct the relationship between the style of the photograph and the social relations in which it is embedded is slightly different. His sociology of photographic practice is not based on an investigation of the identity of photography as a medium *per se*, for he considers the 'meaning' of photographs only in terms of how their style and composition is judged as appropriate for particular users, who demonstrate certain taken-for-granted expectations arising from their dispositions as members of a class. His ethnographic approach allows him to argue that people's expression of finite and distinctive aesthetic judgements about the genres and compositions of photography manifests the objective constraints – on what is possible to say and imagine – of their place in the social hierarchy. These judgements are the expression of the 'schemes of perception, thought and appreciation common to a whole group' (Bourdieu, 1990: 6), and act as markers of distinction in the hierarchy of legitimated and profane cultural forms. Thus, the 'norms which organize the photographic valuation of the world in terms of the opposition between that which is photographable and that which is not are indissociable from the implicit system of values maintained by a class, profession or artistic coterie' (1990: 6).

Much of photographic theory as it has developed in the British and US contexts has had to struggle and define itself against a view of photography modelled on the teleologies of an unreconstructed art history. Thus the predominant perspective on the history of photography in photographic and art criticism presents us with a story populated by technical innovations and objectively captured truths, buttressed by romantic–aesthetic discourses of self-expression, innovation and creative genius. These values, which dominate most exhibitions and monographs of photography, are anchored in a historicist model of the 'history of photography' akin to the 'history of art' with its succession of art historical movements culminating in the art of our own time; the underlying premise being that an underlying essence of 'photography' is manifested in the unifying discourse of 'the history of photographs'. The main character in this story is the isolated figure of the photo-pioneer, struggling at one and the same time against vague but implacable odds to establish a unique vision of the world, and to impose this on a necessarily abstracted and equally unspecified audience. The basic unit of analysis is the individual photograph, singled out for its excellence or innovative qualities. And common sense, unexamined ideas, typical of photographic and art criticism, categorize photography into 'its' various 'styles' – for example, 'art', 'landscape', 'portraiture' – as if these were self-evident ways of categorizing reality or realizing the aesthetic sensibilities of individual auteurs.

Ian Jeffries (1981), in one of the more self-reflective 'survey' histories of photography, acknowledges that there might be an alternative way of doing 'photographic history', writing in his preface that:

> Photography, a flexible medium, has followed every twist and turn of market and ideological forces since it was developed in the 1840s. It would be possible, and perhaps justifiable, to write a history in which individuals scarcely appear, one in which credit is given to impersonal ideological determinants. Such a history would be centrally concerned with news, advertising and fashion, and would be both fascinating and intricate; it would also be concerned with non-visual matters, opinion forming and social control.
> (Jeffries 1981: 9)

One may here note his caricature of a sociological approach to photography – 'impersonal ideological determinants', 'non-visual matters' – which, he seems to be unaware, precisely begs the question of the doxic regularities by which he defines his object of study. But he does not engage in these methodological questions, nor does he want to pursue, as he would no doubt see it, a utilitarian analysis starting from the functions of the photograph, stating only that he has 'not written such a history'. He claims that he wants to focus instead on the work of the canonical photographers, a category which simply reinforces the humanist individual as self-originated and the source of meaning for the photograph. As Douglas Crimp says in 'The Museum's Old, the Library's New Subject' (Chapter 14), 'if photography was invented in 1839, it was only *discovered* in the 1960s and 1970s'

– discovered, that is, as a discrete and unified entity (see p. 220). His concern is with the repression of the information function of photographs as they come to be reclassified and regrouped within the library as, foremost, photographs and then according to the art function which ascribes authorship and oeuvre. He sees this as a ghettoization of photographs which inhibits their use within other discursive practices. It reflects a culture where the capacity to find 'information' – however problematic this category is – about the world is diminished.

The division between art as expressive creativity and photography as a machine, which so perplexed nineteenth-century advocates and detractors of photography, was resolved in the field of law. As Bernard Edelman has written (1979), regarding the property law of nineteenth-century France, property rights in photography were at first denied on the grounds that the camera did not involve any creative activity by the photographer-subject. As photography seemed a mere mechanical reproduction of reality, the photographer was regarded as a servant of the machine, just an operator, and a plagiarist of nature. In that sense not even the photographer could own the photograph he or she had made, since it could not be considered as the creation of a person, not being invested with the mark of individual creativity. But it was in response to industrial pressure – in the period from 1880 onwards – that photography was reconstrued as a sign of art in order that the photograph might be legally definable as property. For without a legal basis for the ownership of the image being established, the development of a photographic industry would have been impossible: how could mass-reproduced images be bought and sold if no one owned them? In conventional romantic theory, the aesthetic (art) and commerce are constructed as opposing poles, but Edelman's analysis affords a different perspective on the relationship between the two, indicating how the law invented the photographer as a creator, as having put into his work what he owns, his self, so that it thereby became possible for him to own it. However, as John Tagg remarks, the situation was quite different in English law, in which ownership was not based on the principle of creativity. Developing from pressures to protect the book trade, rather than to secure author's rights as such, the 'author' of a photograph was the owner of the material on which the photograph was made at the time it was taken: no creative subject was implied (see Tagg, 1988: 115–16). This remained the case until the 1988 Copyright, Designs and Patents Act when English law allowed the originator, rather than the owner of the film materials, to have rights in the image. These nationally distinct forms of ownership tell us that technology does not in itself have a determining role in the meaning of photography; rather, there are specific cultural and legal definitions and relations which regulate and limit the social use and meaning of technologies.

The division between machine reproduction and the requirement of a creative personality has also been 'resolved', ideologically, in the field of art criticism, by the theory of 'expressive realism'. What has concerned photographic theorists most about photographic criticism is the contradictory admixture of discourses which they embody; that is, expression theory (romanticism) and reflection theory (realism) (see Burgin, 1982: 11). Although they appear to be in absolute opposition to one another, both treat the surface of the picture as if it marked the place of entry to something anterior and more substantial – the mind and perceptions of the artist or the objective nature of the world. As a number of critical theorists have pointed out, a peculiar combination of these approaches is typical of contemporary photographic criticism, resulting in the discourse of 'expressive realism', a sensibility in fact well established by the mid-nineteenth century in Britain (see Abrams, 1953; Belsey, 1980: 8). Art is seen as a joint product of the objective and the projected; a metaphysical parallelism here finds the essences of nature duplicated as ideas in the mind which can then infuse nature with the humanizing thoughts and passions of man (Abrams, 1953: 52). The way round this paradox of art as mimetic and expressive is, in the fundamental conceit of romanticism, to attribute to the artist higher powers of perception that allow her/him to apprehend a reality deeper than mere appearance. Hence the metaphysical rhetoric that plagues artist–photographer's accounts of their own work as well as the monographs, catalogues and exhibitions of fine art photography which respond to the apparent challenge of art produced by a machine: the eye of the photographer-as-seer conjoined with that of the camera lens in a reunification of person and machine; the pre-visualization and pre-conceptualization of the image before the moment of releasing the shutter; the symbolist transcendentalism of the perceptual realm (see Sekula, 1982: 100–3).

It has been argued that there is a general tendency in industrialized capitalist societies for art to lose its social function. As the division of labour becomes more common, along with the commodification of cultural goods and their detachment from religious institutions of patronage, the artist turns into a specialist provider of the aesthetic function (see Burger, 1984). Art institutions in modern society come to promote the artist's product as something special and autonomous and as a continuation of the handicraft mode of production at the same time as mechanization and its associated divisions of labour are being established. In the discourses of art photography – from pictorialism to modernist photography – it is certainly true that technology is redeemed and humanized by suggesting that subjectivity and the machine are readily compatible, appealed to as the place where creative autonomy and full unalienated expression can be realized. Compare our earlier quotation from Kodak's publicity material to this classic statement by Alfred Steiglitz, the inventor of modernist photography gallery practice, writing in contradiction of Benjamin's observations on the effects of mechanical reproducibility: 'Every print I made, even from one negative is a new experience, a new problem. For unless I am unable to vary, to add – I am not interested; there is no mechanicalisation but always photography' (quoted in Newhall, 1964; see also the quote from Ansel Adams in Douglas Crimp's Chapter 14 p. 216). And that brings us to the question implied by many of our readings: to what extent can the category of 'photography', so much under fire here, provide a stable ontological ground for the study of photographic images?

References

Abrams, M.H. (1953) *The Mirror and the Lamp: Romantic Theory and the Critical Tradition*. New York: Norton and Oxford University Press.

Belsey, Catherine (1980) *Critical Practice*. London: Methuen.

Bourdieu, Pierre (1990) *Photography: a Middlebrow Art*. Cambridge: Polity Press.

Burger, Peter (1984) *Theory of the Avant-Garde*. Minneapolis: University of Minnesota Press.

Burgin, Victor (1982) 'Introduction', in V. Burgin (ed.), *Thinking Photography*. London: Macmillan.

Edelman, Bernard (1979) *Ownership of the Image*. London: Routledge and Kegan Paul.

Evans, Jessica (ed.) (1997) *The Camerawork Essays*. London: Rivers Oram Press.

du Gay, Paul (1997) 'Organizing identity: making up people at work', in P. du Gay (ed.), *Production of Culture/Cultures of Production*. London: Sage/Open University.

du Gay, Paul; Hall, Stuart; Janes, Linda; Mackay, Hugh and Negus, Keith (1997) *Doing Cultural Studies: the Story of the Sony Walkman*. London: Sage/Open University.

Hall, Stuart (1997) 'The centrality of culture, in K. Thompson (ed.), *Media and Cultural Regulation*. London: Sage/Open University.

Jeffries, Ian (1981) *Photography: a Concise History*. London: Thames and Hudson.

Newhall, Beaumont (1964) *The History of Photography*. New York: Museum of Modern Art.

Porter, Gaby (1989/90) 'Trade and industry' in *Ten.8*, 35 (winter) pp. 45–48.

Rosenblum, Barbara (1978) 'Style as social process', *American Sociological Review*, 43 (June) pp. 422–438.

Sekula, Allan (1982) 'On the invention of photographic meaning', in V. Burgin (ed.), *Thinking Photography*. London: Macmillan.

Slater, Don (1995) 'Domestic photography and digital culture', in Martin Lister (ed.), *The Photographic Image in Digital Culture*. London: Routledge.

Spence, Jo (1986) *Putting Myself in the Picture*. London: Camden Press.

Spence, Jo (1995) *Cultural Sniping*. London: Routledge.

Tagg, John (1988) *The Burden of Representation*. London: Macmillan.

Williams, Raymond (1977) 'On determination', in *Marxism and Literature*. Oxford: Oxford University Press.

C

Theorizing photography

10

On the institutions of photography   Simon Watney

This chapter is taken
from *Photography/
Politics: Two*, edited
by P. Holland,
J. Spence and
S. Watney (London,
Photography
Workshop/
Comedia, 1986),
pp. 187–197.

The revolution in critical theory which has taken place in Britain since the early 1970s has always been, in effect, a dialogue with Marxism.[1] The entire Cultural Studies Movement (henceforth CSM), which has stimulated so many intellectual and political interventions across the complete range of British education, would have been unthinkable without its initial interrogative attitude to such basic shibboleths of Marxist theory as the supposedly direct determination of a cultural 'superstructure' by an economic 'base'.[2] [. . .]

One of the most fundamental aspects of the British CSM lay in its early mobilisation of the concept of 'cultural production' employed as a strategy to draw attention to the materiality of culture, and to prise away individual areas of practice from local notions of allegedly 'timeless' value, and transcultural significance.[3] Thus, for example, the study of English was redirected beyond the consideration of an ossified canon of 'classic' texts, towards wider issues of writing and reading in all their variant forms and conditions. The economic and political circumstances of literacy and publishing were also taken up, together with issues of class, race and gender, and with them the acknowledgement that literary texts are open to multiple potential readings which cannot be exclusively attributed to aesthetic determinants.[4] In a similar manner the 'new' Art History has looked beyond the Fine Art tradition in order to problematise the category of 'art' itself, and to examine that privileging of oil painting over all other techniques of visual signification which conventional Art History institutionalises and takes for granted in the name of 'connoisseurship'. [. . .]

It remains a basic characteristic of this approach that cultural 'production' is not understood as a single, self-sufficient moment, but rather as a process, inseparable from the full cycle of distribution and consumption, as analysed by Marx.[5] However, certain difficulties have arisen from the immense conceptual weight which the CSM places on the term 'production', as it is levered across from the domain of economics to that of photography, where it is far too abstract to explain the complex interaction and articulation of different sign-systems, such as words and images, with any degree of analytic precision.[6] This strain inevitably arises because of the way in which the British CSM originally hitched the effectively indigenous methods of Marxism to the continental project of semiology (the study of signs). [. . .] This situation did, however, encourage the use of semiology as a means to underwrite the requirement to privilege economic factors in the influential realm of Marxist cultural politics and theory. Thus if photography was re-thought as an 'economy of signs' this still obliged critics to conceive of photographs as if they were commodities like any other. [. . .] In this context we can readily appreciate a growing tension between that current in the CSM which was implacably committed in advance to the disclosure of the economic 'determinations' of culture, and a semiotic imperative to theorise types and areas of signification which were not compatible with such a pre-given agenda.

This situation was exacerbated by the widespread revival of sexual politics in the 1970s, and in particular by the resurgent interest in psychoanalysis as a means to further understanding of the conflicts within individual subjectivity. Available theories of class could not even acknowledge the existence of desire, let alone explain it, as a constitutive force. Marxist cultural theory had traditionally tended to regard cultural production in direct instrumental terms as an agency of class consciousness, supposedly 'true' or 'false'. This Manichaean vision has proved increasingly vulnerable in its refusal (and inability) to offer an account of subjectivity on the side of consumption which is anything like as sophisticated as its explanations of the rest of the process of commodity production. In this respect Marxism offers a social picture of what amounts to an 'empty machine' – empty, that is, because uninhabited by desiring, motivated human beings, who have been theorised away as no more than agents of class struggle. This is not to question the centrality of class conflict in our society. It is, however, to suggest that the ways in which we think of ourselves, and our relations with one another, require more explanation than that offered by the conventional wisdom which insists that class is the central and all-determining factor in the formation of all forms of political and cultural consciousness. Rather, we need to consider how class awareness relates to other areas of individual belief, and to face up to the divisions and conflicts within each of us. This problem has proved to be especially intractable in relation to ongoing debates concerning the *reception* of photographs, which cannot simply be equated with passive and monolithic notions of *consumption*, which are summarily 'explained' and dismissed as a automatic and unified function of class consciousness.

It is from this perspective that we need to consider the study of photography as it is currently practised and, equally importantly, as it might be reconstructed. Unfortunately a clear division has emerged in recent years between loudly proclaimed commitments to 'lived experience', together with the study of institutions, and a semiology-based concern with the analysis of meaning in photographs. In the former case the name of Raymond Williams is frequently invoked, which is regrettable since Williams' work offers an unusually complex and sustained critique of the notion of 'experience' used in this manner as the fount category for all social knowledge, supposedly offering adequate and sufficient meanings directly of and from the 'social'. It is from this same perspective that we are invited, for example, to distinguish between the study of the 'institutional structures and use of a medium',[7] and concerns with the reading and meaning of photographs, as if such approaches were mutually exclusive. What this amounts to is an over-emphasis on the conditions surrounding the production of photography, to the exclusion of equally important considerations of its reception. Such an arbitrary separation cannot help us to understand the uneven, shifting and highly unstable power of the medium. At the same time it is only too often assumed that the notion of an 'institution' is somehow clear, coherent and sacrosanct, with any objections being dismissed in the manner of Dickens' Mr Podsnap, 'clearing the world of its most difficult problems by sweeping them behind him'.

My aim in this paper is precisely to raise some difficult, and at times perhaps unwelcome, problems concerning the study of what we might refer to as the institutions of photography. The more aware we become of the role of context and codes in the establishment of temporarily fixed meanings from the plenitude of potential readings which any photograph may bring into play, the less convincing sounds any hard and fast distinction between 'use' and 'meaning'. Indeed, in semiotic terms we can only conclude that meaning *is* use, as long as the concept of use is not reduced to the terms of political economy, understood as some pre-semiotic level of 'primary' determination. But the crucial terms which we cannot do without in this context are 'ideology' and 'the unconscious', unless of course we are prepared to collapse all the variations of reception into a universal theory of class-determined consumption, magically unified across all differences of age, sexuality, regionalism, race, and *within* classes themselves.

It has been one of the signal achievements of the British CSM to have forced a new awareness of the radical shortcomings of any cultural politics which proposes to resolve inequalities at the levels of the social and the economic via the agency of political culture, without so much as the barest theory of subjectivity or motivation beyond that of class consciousness. The CSM has consistently emphasised how different technologies recruit audiences through the categories and genres by which they narrate and 'make sense' of social experience. This work of ideological consolidation has to be comprehensible to any cultural worker who wishes to work in the opposite direction, against the 'flow'[8] of ideologies, in order to be able to unpick the seams of analogy and contingency which hold together the unstable and fragile ascendancy of the New Right, and which constitute its 'common-sense' right across the field of visual communications, from newspaper cartoons to television commercials. We urgently need, therefore, to understand the many means by which photography punctuates the look of the world into a series of discontinuous signs – photographs –

which are none-the-less endlessly offered as images of totality, merely divided into 'moments'. To treat photographs as no more than 'moments', interrupted from the constant stream of vision, is to ignore the specific ways in which photographic technology works on its objects in order to locate them within the desired arenas of documentary, photo-journalism, and so on. The same object is always open to many potential inflections, just as the same photograph is always able to 'break free' of its moorings within a particular category. The identifiable pin-up used to advertise yesterday's film may become tomorrow's image of the wrongs of patriarchy, the icon of a particular period, a focus for nationalistic nostalgia, or by association with 'stardom' the sign of a new brand of cigarettes. Hence the urgent need to distinguish, as Victor Burgin has put it so clearly, between the representation of politics, and the politics of representation.[9] For if we accept the semiotic *sine qua non* (without which nothing) that photographs do not simply reflect some pre-given 'true' external reality, but rather establish their own psychic reality constituted in the textual interplay of codes and conventions, employing the objects of the material world as *elements* to carry particular meanings, then we cannot expect to be able to harness this approach to an otherwise unreconstructed, non-semiotic sociology. Certainly the study of the ways in which ideologies are anchored in and between distinct regimes of images cannot be developed through mechanical analogies and metaphors from economics. We need to understand the *mobility* of photographic meaning – how photographs draw on fantasy, how their 'logic' may be redirected to new ends, to new audiences, which are not simply 'out there' in the social, ready and waiting for the gauzy veils of false-consciousness to be lifted from their eyes.

Politics concerns institutional change. But not all institutions are as immediately tangible in their presence or their consequences as, for example, the Stock Exchange or one's local Unemployment Office. Whilst photography may engage with the established practices of political struggle, through the use of the camera on demonstrations, at pickets and so on, it should be clear that this does not mean that the resulting images are themselves 'intrinsically' political. They can only become so in relation to other institutions such as Law Courts, Industrial Tribunals, and so on, where they can 'take on' political values. At the same time we have to recognise that such uses run the risk of colluding precisely with dangerous reflection theories concerning the supposed 'nature' of photography itself, as if it were a unified whole, operating in the same way at all times and in all places. Such an approach tends inexorably to marginalise the role of cultural struggle to a series of 'secondary' responses to what are seen as more 'primary' struggles taking place elsewhere in the social formation, and generally identified with the supposed 'point' of production, a notion which is itself incompatible with Marx's own analysis of the full productive cycle, which does not prioritise any one 'moment' inherently above all others. Hence the need to distinguish between *political* struggles taking place in relation to the institutions of employment, the state, education, health-care and so on, and *ideological* struggles taking place across the field of representation – in language and images, and their invariable relations with one another, acknowledged or suppressed. For as Burgin again observes, 'representations . . . cannot simply be tested against the real, as this real is itself constituted, as everyday common sense "reality", *in* representations.'[10] It is therefore of crucial importance to be able to address both the institutions of production *and* reception in such a way that the former is not over-privileged in the misleading name of 'the real', as if ideological and psychological factors which bear down relentlessly on the uses of photography were somehow less substantial or concrete, and thus of secondary importance, if considered at all.

For the purposes of analysis we still need to distinguish, however, between those institutions which facilitate the production of photography in all its forms, and those bodies of beliefs/values/associations which inform and organise the 'look' of photographs and their meanings. Whilst it should be apparent that these two systems interpenetrate with one another in all circumstances of use, it is equally clear that it is not logically helpful to employ the same term 'institution' to such limited, measurable entities as individual corporations or retail chains or processing factories, as well as the larger ideological and psychic forces which are continually reconstituted across the entire domain of photo-practices. Thus, for example, we should not confuse the family, viewed as an institution generating particular types of practice, with the family as an ideological entity, constituted in photography by an identifiable regime of idealising images. In the former sense families are defined and brought into being by clear legal and economic determinants – marriage, patterns of architecture and town-planning, welfare legislation, and so on. The latter sense is a less stable category which only emerges 'in focus', as it were, at the intersection of other ideologies concerning parenting, heterosexuality, age, religion, and so on. Ideologies are not, in this important sense, institutions. The point of this distinction, however, is not to prioritise 'institutions' over 'ideologies' but, rather, to reiterate the point that an exclusively institutional analysis can never adequately come to grips with what photography is, let alone what it might become. Hence the need to consider the role of the sociology of culture by which photographic studies are so deeply informed, since it is there that precisely this type of prioritisation continues to be taken for granted.

The sociology of photography

Sociology emerged as an academic discipline in the late nineteenth century as the 'positive' science of social relations. Taking Darwin's work on evolutionary theory as its basic model, it proceeded to construct its own definitions and categories of knowledge, just as the other newly emergent discipline of anthropology invented, as it claimed to 'discover', a supposedly universal 'science' of Mankind, or as ethnology developed terms which made it possible to think of a 'science' of race, and sexology a 'science' of sexual behaviour. The Social Sciences, as they became known, shared the common assumption that the world is in some fundamental sense a material object governed by empirically deducible laws and structures, which it was (and remains) the task of the social scientist to investigate. Individual schools of sociologists have disagreed violently about the exact nature and significance of these 'laws' and rules, but all agree that 'society' is in some important sense a knowable category, distinct if somehow related to the parallel structures of economics, politics, sexuality, and so on. At the same time, social science also took for granted a model of historical social progress, with the accompanying assumption that all societies develop chronologically and 'improve' according to discernible rules. What constitutes 'improvement' in this picture of things, however, is not necessarily agreed.

Culture has always proved a problem for mainstream sociology, since it is understood both as evidence of social structuration as such, and of the degree of 'progress' which any individual society has achieved. At the same time, the notorious elasticity of the concept of 'culture' itself constantly threatens to overwhelm the weaker abstraction 'society'. It is thus a permanent problem for sociology that its central object of attention – the social – constantly threatens to dissolve away altogether into separate considerations of fashion, eating, customs, language, and so on, which barely permit in their diversity the retention of the larger category of 'the social'. One major holding operation against the total disintegration of 'the social' has involved the study of specific institutions – markets, financing, advertising, householding, and so on. In this manner it remains possible to hold 'culture' and 'society' apart by asking questions of priority, which always presume the fundamental determining power of the latter over the former. The sociology of culture is thus able to domesticate its subject matter by scrutinising it according to its prior categories of knowledge, principally those of class, but also increasingly those of age, gender and race – all of which, needless to say, are regarded as *social* categories, innocent of any psychic coherence or determinations. The sociology of culture has thus come to play a vital role in relation to the main body of sociological enquiry as its most important, and obedient, prop.

Culture also provides evidence of the central subject – and object – of sociological enquiry, 'mankind', discovered through the supposedly universal categories of 'creativity', 'innovation', 'morality', and so on. This humanist figure of Mankind stands at the convergence of the natural and social sciences, their creature, at once determined and determining, revolving in the light of the different 'knowledges' which the different sciences expect and derive from it. And just as the various specialised areas of interest to the sociology of culture tend to fragment the central notion of a unified 'society' which they are expected to bolster, so the various studies of 'man' – his language, sexuality, race, tastes, and so on – tend only to disintegrate the central unified authority of their leading actor. It should, however, be remembered that the origins of photography coincide exactly with the origins of the social sciences, and that it has always been used to guarantee specific notions of 'human' nature. Indeed, there is no other technology which can so easily return to us the impression of ourselves as completely unified, coherent individuals. Which, after all, is largely what it was invented to do. The principal sociological mechanism for stabilising the human figure is the concept of 'role'. Sociology is thus able to overlook variations and conflicts within its social categories by recourse to the concept of role, which has the effect of unifying the divisions at work within subjectivity. The concept of roles also reinforces the central emphasis on institutions, interpreted as those social sites which possess the power to define and enforce all types of role-play.

It is therefore not surprising that the sociology of photography, where it exists as a specific area of critical study, tends to privilege the position of institutions surrounding and organising the various branches of photographic practice which it identifies as 'social' and either role-defined, or role-defining. But how roles might be accepted, negotiated or rejected by subjects, is never theorised. Thus Gisèle Freund, for example, takes it as axiomatic as a socialist that 'a change in social structure influences not only the subject matter but also the techniques artists use in their work.'[11] Thus, in a move familiar within the sociology of culture, the cultural artefact is cut off and abstracted as an object of consideration, and is then submitted to an *a priori* distinction between form and content, with social and economic relations understood as external determining forces on both.

Whilst she is impatient with crude 'copy' theories of photography, Freund none-the-less theorises photography within a critical range which is addressed above all to questions of its 'effects' on social audiences, and the 'intentions' of individual photographers. We are thus offered the familiar continuous history of a technology, and the overall conclusion, which is far from unusual, is that all would be well if only the 'right' people controlled the given institutions of photography, their internal organisation properly democratised, and so on.

John Berger pushes the issue of intentionality much further. For him 'a photograph is a result of the photographer's decision that it is worth recording that this particular event or this particular object has been seen.'[12] All determinations over such decisions are pushed back into the domain of individual 'choice'. What eventually distinguishes 'very memorable photographs and the most banal snapshots' is 'the degree to which the photograph makes the photographer's decision transparent and comprehensible'.[13] Photography, he concludes, 'is the process of rendering observation self-conscious'. However, as far as he is concerned 'there is no transforming in photography', since it 'does not deal in constructs'. Hence his emphasis on intentionality, moments of decision which are uncomplicated in his reading by unconscious motivations. In this manner a social psychology is pushed into place in order to buttress a conventional Marxist sociology of use, and both converge around notions of memory, understood here as a direct means of access to both the 'truth' of the individual, and of his or her society.[14] Yet memory, like intentionality, remains crucially under-theorised in Berger's work, both seemingly giving immediate access to human subjects whose identities are fixed in advance of their lives by clear socio-economic factors, which 'explain' them. Once again we are offered the history of a technology understood to be instrumental to forces of power which reside outside its own domain, and which it relays directly to us in visual terms. Photography thus emerges as an agency for meanings which pass through its 'transparent' space, rather than being constituted by it. Such an approach also leaves the terminal points of photography – production and reception – open to conventional sociological analysis, through the categories which I have described. The image itself is not a problem. It is not even considered, except as 'evidence', in the service of the ostensibly 'neutral' gaze of the social scientist. In this manner the humanist spectre of 'man' as a universal 'social' subject is continually reproduced in the discursive relations between concepts of agency and the analysis of 'institutions'. It should, furthermore, be pointed out that the stress on intentionality which sociology encourages, and which tends to occlude all other considerations of photographic meaning, does so by effectively deflecting attention away from any consideration of the specific rhetoric of photography. This is particularly unfortunate since it is photographic rhetoric – repetition, analogy, irony, and so on – which inflects meaning right across the genres and institutions of photo-practice. It is this same rhetoric which every photographer learns in order to establish meanings of any kind, and in relation to which questions of intentionality are almost entirely irrelevant, since the individual photographer's ability to manipulate rhetoric is almost invariably described in terms of individual 'skill' or 'genius', or thought of simply as evidence of 'professional' competence.

One contemporary sociologist, who has considered the actual look of photographs, is Barbara Rosenblum, whose work proceeds from a central emphasis on questions of style, rather than individual photographers as such. Her work stems from the belief 'that one should understand the social arrangements in which pictures are made in order to understand why they look as they do.'[15] As she points out, 'one sociologically useful way to think about style is that it consists of predictable combinations of features.'[16] Her method involves close consideration of the formal and technical demands made on photographers working in specific institutions, and she proceeds to distinguish general categories of production such as advertising, art photography, and so on, as individual institutions. This approach undoubtedly has the advantage of calling into question the very identity of the photographer from which most commentators proceed. Regarding institutions as a precondition for practice, Rosenblum allows us to think, for example, about the work of a photographer who might free-lance for an advertising agency, teach a few hours in a college, exhibit landscapes in a gallery, and yet at the same time be a full-time member of a co-op selling anonymous 'documentary' images to newspapers. Yet for all its sensitivity to issues of economic gate-keeping, and the various divisions of professionalism which obtain in many sectors of photo-practice, this approach is none-the-less flawed by its inability to proceed beyond generalisations concerning categories of the general 'appropriateness' which govern individual areas of practice. Lacking a semiotic grip on the central issue of representation, Rosenblum tends to fall back into a kind of latent functionalism, as if the demands of a particular branch of production such as photojournalism always secure an inflexible uniformity of appearances. It also makes it difficult to understand the ways in which identifiable styles are constantly employed by institutions other than those from which they originated. For style never stands in a one-to-one relation with individual institutions. It is the rhetoric of photography itself which, in individual contexts, is harnessed to the purposes of very different institutional interests. The 'immediacy' of a half-tone newspaper image may equally well serve the requirements of Fine Art photography, as in the work of Barbara Kruger we can see that the look of advertising may be employed to feminist ends.

Two central problems beset the sociology of photography. Firstly, it is caught inexorably in the grip of descriptive categories of production – documentary, photojournalism, and so on – which interrupt our understanding of how the various discursive formations of photographic practice are articulated. In searching out the institutional 'sources' for these categories they are effectively naturalised, legitimated, and hence reinforced. Secondly, the 'social' emerges as a force working through photographers or subject-matter into photographs. This in turn pre-empts our understanding of the semiotic processes without which we could never produce images at all, or read them. What is missing from the sociological approach is any awareness of the specific power which institutions possess to define and organise the rhetoric of photography. If the categories of production which sociologists identify were indeed entirely independent of one another we should not be able to turn the pages of any magazine without experiencing a total cultural and, for that matter, economic schizophrenia, since we are expected to be able to shift our identifications automatically between the photographically inscribed subject positions of class, gender, sexuality, age, and so on. How we are able to negotiate and inhabit different and frequently incompatible coded identities without obvious confusion is beyond the grasp of sociological enquiry.

In all its many variant forms the sociology of photography assumes the existence of a concrete set of measurable institutions which determine the production, distribution and consumption of photographs, gathered into stylistically unified entities which are held to have particular 'effects' on particular audiences. An immediate problem here lies in the general haziness surrounding what is meant in the first place by an 'institution'. According to Raymond Williams, this 'has become the normal term for any organised element of a society'.[17] It is, however, far from clear that we can identify, for example, advertising as an institution which 'determines' photography, as if the financial and economic organisation of advertising agencies exist independently of, and prior to, the types of photograph which they employ. For without photography the institution itself would not exist in the form with which we are familiar. It is similarly misleading to assume the firm determining priority of 'the Press' on photojournalists, since again photography is a decisive constitutive feature of the modern newspaper. In other words, there would not be institutions of advertising and journalism as we know them without photography. We deceive ourselves if we imagine ourselves in a situation in which 'social' institutions determine the look of photographs in any simple linear kind of one-to-one fashion. For the institutions which control the production of photographs are themselves only possible as the result of photographic technology, with its special capacities to mobilise and connect particular systems of values and beliefs and fantasies. Nor is it clear that we can compare such diverse entities as individual corporations with entire industries. Boots the Chemists is not an institution in the same sense in which marketing might be described as an institution, covering all aspects of photographic commodity sales.

What we do need to understand are the mechanisms whereby specific financing agencies are able to define the sense we make of photographs within their limited sphere of influence, how we are recruited to identify with highly motivated points of view which seem to converge with our own interests. At this point we need to return to what we mean by institutions.

The institutions of photography

From their origins in the nineteenth century the Social Sciences have aimed to extend a 'scientific' understanding of human social conduct modelled on the demystification of the physical world undertaken by the Natural Sciences. Deeply inscribed within the sociological project is a moral ambition to rationally catalogue and distinguish between all that contributes to moral 'order', which is seen as 'healthy', and that which is disintegrative and seen as 'pathological' and corrupt. The hidden agenda of the Social Sciences has therefore always been the intention to 'improve' consciousness in the direction of what is taken as 'rationality'. The sociological quest for social laws pivots around issues of control, cohesion, rules and stability. It is held to be axiomatic that the conditions of our actions explain them, and our motivations. Hence, the emphasis sociologists place on social roles, in which individual subjects are understood as agents of larger social forces. These 'social forces', however, are theorised as if they existed independently of, and prior to, their material formulation in language, images, signs. Thus power is envisaged as a force working on subjects from the outside, since few sociologists recognise the role of signification as 'a constitutive feature of the context of communication itself'.[18] Sociology looks for the presence of the 'social' as an 'influence' on photography, and in turn at the supposed 'effects' of photography on society. This is only possible as long as signification is reduced to a reflective function, and denied a constitutive role in consciousness and actions. It is, however, not surprising, given the dependency of professional sociologists in their actual work on photographs, used as 'evidence' of the very laws and structures which they aim to disclose. Thus, photography is held to contain ideological 'contents' which can be explained by 'economic' or 'social' determinations. In such an approach there is no space for any discussions of desire, or fantasy, or counter-textual meanings, or even metaphor. The photograph is required to *be* that which it is used to signify. Meaning is literalised as power is identified through the image in the social world. The power of photography itself is completely ignored.

Hence the problematic emphasis on institutions which typifies the sociological approach to photography. For sociology depends upon notions of self-evident 'truth' which the semiotics of photography will reveal as an effect of the institutions of sociology themselves. Indeed, the various 'truths' which photography may be made to 'reveal'; derive precisely from the authority of certain privileged institutions to define 'the truth' in the likeness of their own beliefs, values and methodologies, inscribed as it were into the very appearances of the world by the technology of the medium. From small private magazines to huge international corporations, these institutions relate the production and development of the raw materials of photography to the control of its uses, exhibition spaces, reproduction and evaluation. They are present as the conditions under which we invariably produce or look at photographs. It is this range of institutions, both financial and conceptual, which defines our sense of coherent, identifiable styles, as well as our internal sense of what is appropriate to certain types of photography as opposed to others – the conditions of our sophisticated photo-literacy.

Ever since its invention in the early nineteenth century, photography has been a classic example of a capitalist industry – a commodity producing enterprise, massively profitable and highly competitive, strictly controlling its own internal labour relations, speculative, and constantly expanding its market into new areas of potential profitability. It should be remembered that Henry Fox Talbot established the world's first photo-processing factory, in Reading, as early as the 1850s, thus establishing an economic and ideological relation between the suppliers of photography's raw materials – cameras, chemicals, film stock, printing technology, and so on – and their consumers. This relation has guaranteed that photography should continue to be regarded by most people since the 1880s as an essentially passive process of exposing film, of 'taking' photographs, rather than a full act of production.

In this situation we need to be able to distinguish between two separate kinds of photographic marketing operation. On the one hand, as the most cursory glance through any technical magazine will show, there is the professional and 'serious' amateur market (figures 10.1, 10.2, 10.3, see also figure 18.2). This is geared to the production and uses of sophisticated equipment – cameras, lenses, enlargers and darkroom materials which already assume a high level of technical knowledge on the part of the photographer. This market also constructs an idea of the photographer as someone who develops and prints his or her own photographs, with some degree of control over their eventual use. On the other hand, there is the much broader market of 'popular' photography which is heavily dependent on advertising and which is directed towards the selling of much simpler equipment in the form of cameras and film-stock, and assumes that the photographer is someone who does not process his or her own film (figure 10.4, see also figure 18.1). The taking of photographs is thus privileged over and above the subsequent commercial processing operations, which are regarded, if at all, as a kind of unavoidable accident, a regrettable delay in the appearance of the image. The whole weight of attention in this market is to the image, with the profitable and productive domain of processing

Figure 10.1

(opposite) *Practical Photography* (front cover), Nov. 1998

mysteriously suppressed. The Polaroid process is the logical commercial and aesthetic extreme of this particular set of marketing operations.

However, both 'professional' and 'popular' photography are equally dependent on the workings of the multi-national corporations such as Kodak and Fuji, and both are assumed to operate according to similar, if not identical, standards of technical and aesthetic excellence – the immensely powerful notion of what constitutes a 'good' photograph. It is at this point that the economic institutions of photography slide into alignment with the dominant cultural, sexual and ideological systems of society. It is the work of photographic criticism and education to ensure that photography should seem the same for everybody engaged with it, whatever the nature or position of their engagement. In this manner the institutions of photography from the multi-nationals through to the local High Street chemist are harnessed together with the dominant systems of representation prevalent in society, establishing collectively what is understood, without any discussion, as a 'good' family portrait, a 'good' landscape, or a 'good' set of wedding photographs, for example (see figure 10.2). And in this way a 'regime of truth', as Michel Foucault has described it, is established, crossing the divisions between public and private, commercial and non-commercial, at the very point at which it earnestly distinguishes between 'professional' and 'non-professional' identities and evaluative criteria concerning what constitutes 'good' photography.

As photographers and viewers of photographs we stand inescapably in relation both to the institutions of photography and of society as a whole. It is in this context that we have to try to understand the massive ideological operations which guarantee that the endless possibilities of photographic activity are regarded and evaluated against a depressingly narrow set of criteria. And since it is in the market-place of popular photography that the greatest corporate profits are to be made, it is not surprising that so much activity should take place to ensure the continued passivity and obedience of the photographer/consumer in this area. Nor is it surprising that the 'knowledge' of the medium to which the dominant institutions of photography lead us is that of the dominant patriarchal capitalist social order – representing and reproducing the drastically unequal power relations of society within the supposedly neutral categories of photography itself, from photojournalism through to documentary and advertising and 'Fine Art' photography. In this manner photography constructs and reconstructs, as if by nature, all the major divisions within the social formation, between blacks and whites, women and men, adults and children, heterosexuals and gays, always aligning us to specific pre-determined social positions and ranks.

In this context History must be regarded as a fundamental institution in its own right, mobilising official State, corporate and educational institutions to validate a particular range of photo-practices, and lend them the powerful associations of fame, glamour, success – 'historical' significance. The History of Photography in its most common forms may thus be seen as a central aspect of this commercial and conceptual organisation, facilitating the processes of categorisation, evaluation and hence control over vast

FREE BOOK!

PRACTICAL

Photography

TAKING BETTER PICTURES

NOVEMBER 1998 £2.70

US$7.50 BF195

No.1 BRITAIN'S BEST-SELLING PHOTOGRAPHY MAGAZINE

VIEW FROM THE TOP
Earn cash from your landscapes

WIN! WIN! WIN!
Over £10,000 of gear up for grabs

IT IS UNUSUAL
Trick lenses for creative imagery

PICTURES ASSESSED
Expert advice you'll remember

EQUIPMENT SPECIAL
Latest launches tried and tested

MONEY FOR ART's SAKE
How much is a photo worth?

PERFECT PEOPLE

Candid or posed? Real advice for great portraits

numbers of people, separated by enormous physical and political distances, into a shared 'photo-culture'. What is more, this same historical/evaluative account of the medium spills out through school text-books, travel brochures and popularising anthropological texts, to make it seem both inevitable and desirable that some people take photographs, whilst the rest are consigned to positions as the objects of such souvenir-hunting photographic attentions. Thus photography should properly be understood as an invention of the nineteenth century in relation to such other technologies as radio communication, film, and the capitalist press, which permitted ever more speedy and efficient control over the flow of national and international information. The fetishisation of the aesthetic aspects of photography which is so central to the outlook of most photo-critics and historians only bears witness to the general exclusion of all other social aspects of the medium, and its ideological centrality in the modern world. We should, however, note that this aesthetic fetishising, and the relentless emphasis on the 'personality' of individual photographers, could only have taken place given the prior existence of the powerful institutions of the art market, with its ready-made definitions, established in the eighteenth century, both of the 'general public' as an undifferentiated consuming 'mass', and of the artist/photographer as someone somehow outside of this mass, untainted by its values, gazing onto the spectacle of the world, a privileged observer whose observations are supposedly of only 'artistic' significance.

It is abundantly clear that institutions are conceived in the dominant tradition of sociological theory as an interface *between* the 'economic' and the 'cultural'. This view is heavily dependent upon notions and practices of observation which themselves constitute the basis of sociological enquiry, based upon categories which are taken for granted – categories of class, labour, the family, heterosexuality, and so on. In this context photography is usually understood as no more than a convenient means for replicating moments of 'pure' vision, and has therefore become a useful instrument for sociologists – producing and at the same time validating the effects of sociological theory, the beliefs of which may triumphantly be discovered in the moment of photographic immediacy. What we should note is the way in which the 'look' of Social Science is inscribed within the very apparatus of the camera.

In this context we should also note the danger of importing a ready-made theory of class to our understanding of photography. We should learn from the example of those feminists who attempted to theorise women as a class during the early 1970s, attempts which not only failed, but which in turn placed a massive strain on the authority of the concept of class itself, the former key-stone in the Triumphal Arch of Marxist social theory. We need instead to think of class as an iconography, a series of signs in representation which do not simply derive from the inequalities of the social and economic order, the perpetuation of which they none-the-less of course continue to service. In other words, the signification of class values in photography does not merely derive reflectively from 'the real', but is one aspect of a specific politics of representation and knowledge. The former attitude continues to treat photographs either as objects worked

Agfa CT precisa slide film

CT precisa is the latest formulation of Agfa's legendary CT range of high quality slide film. Available process paid in ISO 100 and 200 speeds, it now renders colours even more true to life, and with painstaking exactness. It also offers improved differentiation in tonality, with detail better retained in the shadows and highlights. CT precisa is available from Jessops and other leading photo dealers.

How to arrange groups

"It's important to arrange groups carefully. In this shot I put dad on a little block, with mum and daughter to each side with their legs pointing outwards, and the baby in the front. Basically, what I'm doing is making a triangle – I'm always looking for some way of creating a pleasing shape. You can also go for a circular or a square composition. The last thing you want to do is just stand everybody in a line – you should try to stagger the heads to add interest. For wedding groups we usually take a couple of garden stools. Immediately you've got two different levels, and we may sometimes ask kids to sit on the floor as well. To tie the group together, you then need to get all the expressions the same."

How to shoot 'high key'

"High key portraits, with lots of white in them, are extremely popular – but not that difficult to shoot. Ours is a very simple high-key technique. We've got one light that's pointing down on the white background roll, set to give two stops more exposure than the subject's face. There's a fill light above the camera, and the main light is a 40 inch diameter starfish softbox to the left, both set to give flat, soft lighting. In addition there's a hair light that's coming from above onto the paper in front of the sitter, to fill in any shadows created by the background light.

"Here I asked the girl to go and sit however she felt comfortable on the floor, and this is pretty much the pose she assumed. I just tweaked things slightly by asking her to twist her body round more and move her hands a little.

"One of the problems with high key is that if you sometimes have to sacrifice saturation in the subject to get the background white. But here, thanks to its terrific contrast range, Agfa CTprecisa has produced a really crisp and punchy result"

"I took a series of shots of this young girl using Agfa CT precisa 200 at different exposures, and this one, at ½ stop under, is the one I like best. The colour saturation is absolutely wonderful. In fact I found the film to be surprisingly tolerant of under- and over-exposure. For a slide film, it's extremely forgiving.

"The lighting is very simple: just a softbox to the left and slightly above the subject, together with a reflector bouncing light back up.

"Over the years we've built up a large collection of bits and bobs in the studio, and to add interest to the series we decided to play around with a few props – including the hat shown here.

"These days brown backgrounds are rather passé, and I don't use them very often, but here it seemed to suit the subject matter perfectly.

"People will often ask what to do with their hands – they're very conscious of these things at the end of their arms. My rule is a simple one: if they're not attractive hands I'll hide them, but if they look nice I use them deliberately."

PRACTICAL PHOTOGRAPHER OF THE YEAR 94

LANDSCA

With just two rounds to go, the competition's reaching fever pitch. Who will win the war?

1st place: Lee Davis

"This is a spot I drive past regularly near my home at Tiverton in Devon," Lee told us. "I spotted the hay bales in the field and thought it would be good to photograph early in the morning, so I got up at seven in the morning and took this picture."

He used a tripod-mounted Mamiya 645 Super with a standard 80mm lens using Fujichrome Velvia film stock and an exposure of 1/30 sec at f/16.

WHY IT WON: It was a unanimous decision by the judges for this image which sums up the brief perfectly. The early morning light really makes the picture and it's both well composed and correctly exposed.

2nd place: Adrian Burton

Adrian has been a regular *Practical Photography* reader for a while, but this is the first time he has entered a competition and was suitably chuffed with his success. "It was taken in Scotland near Loch Awe. You have to walk across this railway track to get to the castle there," he told us. "I used my Olympus OM-2N with 28mm lens and red filter. The film was Kodak High Speed Infrared rated at ISO 50 and I used an exposure of 1/60 sec at f/11."

WHY IT WON: Infrared film featured strongly this month and here the bold use of this medium really makes the picture stand out. It's also a dynamic composition with the railway track leading the eye into the picture.

PES

Top 20: Landscapes

Running totals

Picture of the Month

Trevor Buttery

Mont Saint Michel on the border of Brittany and Normandy taken while Trevor was on holiday. The wood in foreground is the remains of an old boat. Taken using a Ricoh XR7 with 24mm lens and an exposure of 1/125 sec at f/11 through a red filter. Printed on Ilford Multigrade III at grade 5.

WHY IT WON: Another high quality infrared image. The composition is excellent and this landcsape has a really ghostly feel.

3rd place: Tim Gartside

Tim's third place this month has made it tight at the top of the leader board and he's chomping at the bit for the final two assignments. "This was taken at Skelwith Bridge in the Lake District and is a nice spot right by the side of the road," Tim told us. "I took a reading from the sky and then bracketed, this shot was taken at f/13 on Fujichrome Velvia using a piece anti-Newton glass to give the soft-focus effect. I used my Mamiya M645 with 35mm lens."

WHY IT WON: A dreamy, almost ethereal picture brought about through subtle filtration. Many filter shots were overdone whereas this is spot on.

THE BEST OF THE REST

Dave Smyth

David Martin

Steve McHale

Nick Despres

Figure 10.3

(previous page)

Practical Photography

(inside spread), Dec.

1994, pp. 52–3

Figure 10.4

Chemist's developing

and processing

packet

(source unknown)

upon by a primary, non-cultural world of class-interests and so on, or as images with behavioural effects. In both cases the question of the subjective is neatly evacuated. Human subjects, according to this picture, are either already fully formed social agents, or else they are *tabulae rasae*, empty vessels, waiting to be filled with alternatively 'improving' or 'corrupting' values. And although these two positions might seem at first sight to be mutually exclusive, they are in fact frequently used in tandem. Where one fails to convince, the other is called upon as an alternative. At the same time, important issues emerge in their interaction. On the one hand, certain areas of consciousness are prioritised, thus partially acknowledging the actual divisions and discontinuities of social and sexual identity, whilst in the latter case identity is regarded as a kind of absence (for those viewed as 'the masses', at any rate), ready to be led, sheep-like, in any direction. However, *neither* recognises or is able to explain the profound unevenness of individual response to still images as such, let alone to single images. Most of these difficulties derive from the tendency to divorce the economic analysis of institutions from the psychic and the ideological, which can only impede our understanding of the power of photography which, after all, is not simply 'another' commodity, to be analysed like margarine or petroleum. And certainly the only too real injuries of class, racial, and sexual differences will not be ameliorated if we slide back into expecting photography to effect change beyond its range of operative competence, in the domains of the directly economic or political, rather than across the territory of representation itself.

Conclusion

The entire significance of the idea of a politics *of* representation is that it refuses to regard cultural practices as merely reflective of, and subservient to, other political struggles taking place in the non-textual. The politics of representation are necessarily much occupied with questions of alignment and identification, with points of view, and perspectives. Such an approach refuses to separate the codes of transmission and reception, or to prioritise between the institutions which govern them. In this way it refuses to concede the priority of the 'economic' which itself emerges as a less than adequate category by which to understand the place and functions of labour or technology in advanced capitalist societies. By the same token, reception is not equated with consumption, as if all consumers are no more than passive social agents, undifferentiated and anonymous. The pressing questions which remain to be answered concern the whole orchestration of image–text relations in different sectors of the photographic industry, in other words who speaks to whom, on whose behalf and in whose interests? How do different branches of photography narrate different fantasies, wish-fulfilments, idealised identities and so on in such a way that conflicts between them rarely emerge into ordinary consciousness? It is obviously important and useful to understand the workings of those commercial enterprises which direct the operations of the giant international companies which 'own' photography. But such (partial) understandings are invariably accompanied by familiar left-humanist assumptions concerning both photographers and audiences, whilst at the same time they fail to uncover the institutional/intellectual network which connects such corporations to museums, galleries, publishing houses, text-books, camera-clubs, and categories of practice. If our major objection to contemporary photography only concerns its capacity for 'truthfulness' then we are merely colluding with the most powerful aspect of photographic culture, namely its association with 'the truth'. It is precisely that association which we need to deny, in all its forms and variations. For behind it there always lurks the old bogey which slips us back from 'mere' representation to the fantasy of 'the real', supposedly spontaneously accessible to all via the magical agency of the camera.

Photographs are no more, and no less, than fragments of ideology, activated by the mechanisms of fantasy and desire within a fragmentary history of images. The commercial institutions of photography are inseparable from the institutions of 'knowledge' and 'truth' upon which photography depends and which it in return validates in the names of 'science', 'art', 'glamour', and so on. We are involved here with an orbiting politics of controlled visibilities, through which our lives are continually being broken down and reconstructed according to local photographic wisdoms, embodied in styles, of 'intelligence', 'femininity', 'youthfulness', 'otherness', and so on. In this situation we should not lament the loss of a unified subjectivity which was itself no more than a species of self-deception and false-consolation. For once we can put aside the picture of particular social groups as *a priori* agents of change, and of a 'unique space in which the political is constituted',[19] we can hopefully become more aware of *new* political forces and struggles and articulations of resistance which are blocked off by the illusion that only certain social sites are suitable (or available) for struggle and contestation.

The pervasive privileging of the economic in contemporary discussions of the institutions of photography diverts our attentions away from the unique capacity of photographs to embody categories of knowledge which are simultaneously productive, in so far as they stimulate, incite and encourage their own continued reproduction, and coercive, in so far as they de-limit the conceptual frame by which 'the visual' is culturally organised. These categories, such as photojournalism, and documentary, are however neither controlled by individual institutions or by style alone. We may think of them as patterns of conformity, *internally* coherent, which do not of course 'reflect' any pre-given 'realities'. Rather, they themselves constitute the cultural grounds from which we variously conceive 'reality' as an apparent stable unity. It is the relatively systematic coherence of this field of photographic signification which is carried over into our assessment of the non-textual world. And it is in relation to these same categories that we experience ourselves as stable, purposive individuals, moving from one area of experience to another, rather than as moving between different parts of ourselves.

It cannot, I think, be sufficiently stressed that there can be no autonomous 'total' theory of photography, since photography itself is not an intrinsically unified object. *We cannot equate any theorisation of the role of the unconscious in our reception of photographs with the traditional aims of the psychology of perception*, let alone with institutional analyses. This is why it is so important to reject any explanation of the 'role' of institutions which maintains the absolute primacy of the 'economic', either as the primary space for political interventions, or as the *a priori* determination of all other social and cultural formations. As Laclau and Mouffe have incisively observed,

> what has been exploded is the idea and the reality itself of a unique space of constitution of the political. What we are witnessing is a politicisation far more radical then any we have known in the past, because it tends to dissolve the distinction between the public and the private, but in terms of a proliferation of radically new and different political spaces. We are confronted with the emergence of a *plurality of subjects*, whose forms of constitution and diversity it is only possible to think if we relinquish the category of 'subject' as a unified and unifying presence.[20]

This relinquishment will doubtless be unacceptable to humanists of the left and the right alike, but it is the indispensable precondition for the emergence of a politics of representation which alone can generate new institutions of photography with attendant 'knowledges', and more serious ways of contemplating and refunctioning the old.

Notes

1 See Stuart Hall, 'Cultural studies: two paradigms', *Media Culture & Society*, 2, 1 (January, 1980).
2 See Sylvia Harvey, 'Ideology: the base and superstructure debate', in T. Dennett and J. Spence (eds), *Photography/Politics: One* (London, Photography Workshop, 1980)
3 See Janet Wolff, *The Social Production of Art*, (London, Macmillan, 1981).
4 See Raymond Williams. 'The writer: commitment and alignment', *Marxism Today*, 24, 3 (June 1980).
5 See K. Marx *Grundrisse*, ed. D. McLellan (London, Paladin, 1973).
6 See Stuart Hall, 'Cultural Studies'.
7 Don Slater, *Marketing Mass Photography: Language Image Media*, eds. H. Davis and P. Walton, (Oxford, Blackwell, 1983).
8 See John Ellis, *Visible Fictions* (London, Routledge and Kegan Paul, 1983).
9 Tony Godfrey, 'Sex text politics: an interview with Victor Burgin', *Black* 7, (1982), p. 26.
10 Victor Burgin, *The Absence of Presence: Conceptualism and Post-Modernism 1965–1972 – When Attitudes Became Form*, (Cambridge, Kettle's Yard, 1984), p. 21.
11 Gisèle Freund, *Photography and Society*, (Gordon Fraser, 1980), p. 3.
12 John Berger, *Understanding a Photograph: Selected Essays* (London, Pelican, 1972), p. 179.
13 Ibid.
14 See John Berger, *Another Way of Telling* (Writers and Readers, 1982).
15 Barbara Rosenblum, Style as social process, *American Sociological Review*, 43 (1978), p. 423.
16 Ibid., p. 424.
17 Raymond Williams, *Keywords* (Flamingo, 1981), p. 169.
18 Anthony Giddens, *Central Problems in Social Theory* (London, Macmillan, 1979), p. 98.
19 Ernesto Laclau and Chantal Mouffe, *Hegemony and Socialist Strategy* (London, Verso, 1985), p. 152.
20 Ibid., p. 181.

11

The social definition of photography
Pierre Bourdieu

Ars simia naturae

If it is legitimate to wonder [. . .] how and why photography is essentially predisposed to serve the social functions which have been very generally conferred upon it, it remains the case that the social uses of photography, presented as a systematic (i.e. coherent and comprehensible) selection from objectively possible uses, define the social meaning of photography at the same time as they are defined by it.

An art which imitates art

Thus it is commonly agreed that photography can be seen as the model of veracity and objectivity: 'Any work of art reflects the personality of its creator,' says the *Encyclopédie française*. 'The photographic plate does not interpret. It records. Its precision and fidelity cannot be questioned.' It is all too easy to show that this social representation is based on the false evidence of prejudices; in fact, photography captures an aspect of reality which is only ever the result of an arbitrary selection, and, consequently, of a transcription; among all the qualities of the object, the only ones retained are the visual qualities which appear for a moment and from one sole viewpoint; these are transcribed in black and white, generally reduced in scale and always projected on to a plane. In other words, photography is a conventional system which expresses space in terms of the laws of perspective (or rather of one perspective) and volumes and colours in terms of variations between black and white. Photography is considered to be a perfectly realistic and objective recording of the visible world because (from its origin) it has been assigned *social uses* that are held to be 'realistic' and 'objective'. And if it has immediately presented itself with all

This chapter, originally published in 1965, is taken from Pierre Bourdieu, *Photography: a Middlebrow Art* (Polity Press, 1990), pp. 73–98.

the appearances of a 'symbolic communication without syntax',[1] in short a 'natural language', this is especially so because the selection which it makes from the visible world is logically perfectly in keeping with the representation of the world which has dominated Europe since the Quattrocento. [. . .] Proust gives a very beautiful illustration of photography's powers to disconcert, of which the common practice is deprived:

> . . . the most recent applications of photography – which huddle at the foot of a cathedral all the houses that so often, from close to, appeared to us to reach almost to the height of the towers, which drill and deploy like a regiment, in file, in extended order, in serried masses, the same monuments, bring together the two columns on the Piazzetta which a moment ago were so far apart, thrust away the adjoining dome of the Salute and in a pale and toneless background manage to include a whole immense horizon within the span of a bridge, in the embrasure of a window, among the leaves of a tree that stands in the foreground and is more vigorous in tone, or frame a single church successively in the arcades of all the others – I can think of nothing that can to so great a degree as a kiss evoke out of what we believed to be a thing with one definite aspect the hundred other things with which it may equally well be, since each is related to a no less legitimate perspective.[2]

[. . .] Is there not as great a distance between these 'magnificent' photographs and ordinary photographs as there is between perspective as a science of the real and perspective as a 'hallucinatory technique'? The ordinary photographer takes the world as he or she sees it, i.e. according to the logic of a vision of the world which borrows its categories and its canons from the arts of the past.[3] Pictures which, making use of real technical possibilities, break even slightly away from the academicism of vision and ordinary photography, are received with surprise. Because that which is visible is only ever that which is legible, subjects in all social milieux always resort to certain systems of reading of which the most common is the system of rules for the reproduction of the real that govern popular photography; [. . .] the omission of the norms of the canonical aesthetic, such as the absence of a foreground or a noticeable background meaningfully linked to the form (for example palm trees to express exoticism), frustrates understanding and appreciation when it does not provoke pure and simple refusal.

[. . .]

Rather than using all the possibilities of photography to invert the conventional order of the visible, which, because it dominates the entire pictorial tradition and consequently an entire perception of the world, has paradoxically ended up by impressing itself with all the appearances of naturalness, ordinary practice subordinates photographic choice to the categories and canons of the traditional vision of the world; it is thus not surprising that photography can appear to be the recording of the world most true to this vision of the world, i.e. the most objective recording.[4] In other words, because the social use of photography makes a selection, from the field of the possible uses of photography, structured according to the categories that organize the ordinary vision of the world, the photographic image can be seen as the precise and objective reproduction of reality. If it is true that 'nature imitates art', it is natural that the imitation of art should appear to be the most natural imitation of nature.

But, at a deeper level, only in the name of a naïve realism can one see as realistic a representation of the real which owes its objective appearance not to its agreement with the very reality of things (since this is only ever conveyed through socially conditioned forms of perception) but rather to conformity with rules which define its syntax within its social use, to the social definition of the objective vision of the world; in conferring upon photography a guarantee of realism, society is merely confirming itself in the tautological certainty that an image of the real which is true to its representation of objectivity is really objective.

'Barbarous taste'

It is doubtless due as much to the social image of the technical object which produces it as to its social use that photography is ordinarily seen as the most perfectly faithful reproduction of the real. In fact 'the mechanical eye' accomplishes the popular representation of objectivity and aesthetic perfection as defined by the criteria of resemblance and legibility because this image is the product of an object; idolaters and detractors of the apparatus most often agree, as M. Gilbert Simondon observes, that the degree of sophistication of an apparatus is proportional to its level of automatism. However, and for the same reason, the photographic act in every way contradicts the popular representation of artistic creation as effort and toil. Can an art without an artist still be an art? It goes without saying that photography does not realize the artistic ideal of the working classes as an ideal of imitation to the same extent as realist painting, the production of reproduction. Many subjects sense and express the difference which in their eyes separates the photographic act from the act of painting; by the very fact that there barely seems to be any photograph that is untakeable, or even one which does not already seem to exist in a virtual state – since all it takes is the simple pressing of a button to liberate the impersonal aptitude by which the camera is defined – the hope is that the photograph will be justified by the object photographed, by the choice made in taking the photograph, or in its eventual use, which rules out the idea of taking a photograph simply in order to take a photograph as either useless, perverse or *bourgeois*: 'It's a waste of film' or 'You have to have film to waste'; 'Some people, I swear, don't know what to do with their time'; 'You'd have to have time on your hands to take things like that'; 'That's *bourgeois* photography.' By contrast, the still life, even if it is unusual, is more readily granted to the painter, because the simple and successful imitation of reality presupposes a difficult art, and thus testifies to mastery.

This gives rise to certain of the contradictions in the attitude towards mechanical reproduction which, by abolishing effort, risks depriving the work of the value which one seeks to confer on it because it satisfies the criteria of the complete work of art. A contradiction that is all the more stark since the work of art, particularly when it is not consecrated, always provokes the fear of being duped; the soundest guarantee against this is the artist's sincerity, a sincerity which is measured according to its effort and the sacrifices it makes. The ambiguous situation of photography within the system of the fine arts could lead, among other things, to this contradiction between the value of the work, which realizes the aesthetic ideal that is still most widespread, and the value of the act that produces it.

But this contradiction, which only becomes apparent in questions (often induced and artificial) about the artistic value of photography, does no more to alter the attachment of the working classes to the photographic image than does the concern, by which aesthetes are haunted, of knowing whether, because of its subordination to a machine, photographic art allows that transfiguration of the object (even if it is ugly or meaningless) by which we are accustomed to recognizing artistic creation. Is the technology that produces the most faithful reproduction not the one most likely to fulfil the expectations of popular naturalism, for which the beautiful picture is only the picture of a beautiful thing, or, but more rarely, a beautiful picture of a beautiful thing? 'Now that's good, it's almost symmetrical. And she's a beautiful woman. A beautiful woman always looks good in a photo.' Thus the Parisian worker echoes the plain-speaking of Hippias the Sophist: 'I shall tell him what beauty is and I'm not likely to be refuted by him! The fact is, Socrates, to be frank, a beautiful woman, that's what beauty is.'

Without a doubt, photography (and colour photography especially) entirely fulfils the aesthetic expectations of the working classes. But must we go so far as to say that popular photographs are the realization of an aesthetic intention or ideal, or, in order to explain it completely, is it enough to mention the constraints and obstacles of technology? It is true that most occasional photographers have access only to instruments which offer a very limited range of possibilities; it is also true that the basic principles of popular technique, communicated by salesmen or other amateurs, particularly consist of prohibitions (not moving, not holding the camera at an angle, not photographing into the light or in bad lighting conditions) which are generally confirmed by experience because of the poor quality of the cameras used and the lack of technical competence. But is it not abundantly clear here that these prohibitions encompass an aesthetic which must be recognized and admitted so that transgression of its imperatives appears as a failure? A different aesthetic might intentionally aim for the blurred or unfocused pictures which the popular aesthetic rejects as clumsy or unsuccessful. If, in the case of popular photography (as was for a long time true for the primitive arts), explanation with reference to technical constraints may be satisfactory at first glance, this is primarily true because the field circumscribed by technical imperatives, that is, the sphere of what may technically be photographed, exceeds the range circumscribed by social imperatives, i.e. the sphere of what must be photographed; in this case the technical and aesthetic quality of a picture defined primarily by its social function can only be a *sine qua non*, without ever arousing interest on its own account.

So everything takes place as if photography were the expression of an implicit aesthetic employing a very strict economy of means, and objectified in a certain type of picture without ever (by its very essence) being perceived as such. In every way the opposite of a pure aesthetic, the popular 'aesthetic' expressed in photographs and in the judgements passed on photographs follows on logically from the social functions conferred upon photography, and from the fact that it is always given a social function.

In its traditional form, this aesthetic strictly identifies aesthetic with social norms, or, perhaps, strictly speaking, recognizes only the norms of propriety and suitability, which in no way excludes the experience and expression of beauty; the making of a gesture or an object in a way that conforms most strictly to the most traditional norms provides the possibility of more or less subtle, more or less successful justifications which permit praise or admiration. Because it presupposes the uniqueness and coherence of a system of norms, such an aesthetic is never better fulfilled than it is in the village community. Thus, for example, the meaning of the pose adopted for the photograph can only be understood with relation to the symbolic system in which it has its place, and which, for the peasant, defines the behaviour and manners suitable for his relations with other people. Photographs ordinarily show people face on, in the centre of the picture, standing up, at a respectful distance, motionless and in a dignified attitude. In fact, to strike a pose is to offer oneself to be captured in a posture which is not and which does not seek to be 'natural'. The same intention is demonstrated in the concern to correct one's posture, to put on one's best clothes, the refusal to be surprised in an ordinary attitude, at everyday work. Striking a pose means respecting oneself and demanding respect.

When one attempts to persuade subjects to keep a 'natural' posture, they become embarrassed, because they do not think themselves worthy of being photographed or, as they say, 'presentable', and the best thing one can hope for is simulated naturalness, the theatrical attitude. [. . .]

And we must avoid bluntly opposing the taste of city-dwellers for 'the natural' to the taste of peasants for the hieratic; this would in effect mean ignoring the fact that concessions to an aesthetic freed from social conventions are always more apparent than real. We might imagine, for example, that holidays favour the production of pictures marked by that casual attitude which they encourage and which is expressive of them. In fact, the 'stage' is most often set up beforehand and if, like painters, many amateur photographers force their models into composed and laborious poses and postures, it is because, here as elsewhere, the 'natural' is a cultural ideal which must be created before it can be captured. Even the surprise picture, the accomplishment of the aesthetic of the natural, obeys cultural models: the ideal is still to be 'naturally' as one wants to appear or as one must appear.

In most group photographs, subjects are shown pressed against one another (always in the centre of the picture), often with their arms around one another. People's eyes converge towards the camera so that the whole picture points to its own absent centre. In photographs of couples, the subjects stand with their arms around each other's waists, in a completely conventional pose. The norms of behaviour which must be maintained before the camera sometimes become apparent, in a positive or negative form. The person who, in a group assembled for a solemn occasion such as a wedding, strikes an unsuitable pose or neglects to look at the camera and pose, provokes disapproval. As they say, 'he isn't there.' The convergence of looks and the arrangement of individuals objectively testifies to the cohesion of the group.

> The expression of this sentiment can be seen in the case of photographs showing families, which have been submitted to different subjects for their judgement: all (except one) prefer a pose which is natural but dignified, and photographs in which people stand upright, motionless and dignified are preferred to photographs 'taken from life'. 'In this one, they're proud; they're out walking . . .' 'In this one they aren't looking straight ahead, they're distracted. The child is leaning on his father.' Another draws the distinction between a pose which is 'stiff (*guindée*)', which would provoke laughter, and one which is 'dignified (*digne*)', and meets with approval. On the other hand, if the picture in which the members of the family seem distracted by one another provokes disapproval, it is because the weak cohesion of the family group is read into it, when it is the group as such that the photograph ought to capture. As one cannot demand that these photographs of strangers should supply what one customarily seeks in them, namely the evocation of familiar faces, memorable places or moments, one demands that they should at least be the representation of a social role, a requirement which would not be asked of one's own photographs since they fulfil it automatically. 'Well, it's a family, I don't like the mum, she looks miles away. She's a bit more of a mum in this one. All the same, though! She's a funny mother, with her dangling arms . . . This picture's horrible. Ah! this one's nice, the children are being polite, mum's giving father her arm. It's a family souvenir.' When we deal with a personal photograph, we know that the mother is a mother and the father a father; in anonymous pictures, the function of the different characters must be clearly symbolized. Mother or father or fiancés, the photograph must show them as such.

It is certainly possible that the spontaneous desire for frontality is linked to the most deep-rooted cultural values. Honour demands that one pose for the photograph as one would stand before a man whom one respects and from whom one expects respect, face on, one's forehead held high and one's head straight.[5] [. . .] The sitter addresses to the viewer an act of reverence, of courtesy, according to conventional rules, and demands that the viewer obey the same conventions and the same norms. He stands face on and demands to be looked at face on and from a distance, this need for reciprocal deference being the essence of frontality.

The portrait accomplishes the objectification of the self-image. Consequently, it is only an extreme form of one's relationship to others.

Thus it is understandable that the taking of photographs always provokes a certain unease, especially among peasants, who are most often condemned to internalize the pejorative image that the members of other groups have of them, and who therefore have a poor relationship to their own bodies. Embarrassed by their bodies, they are unnatural and clumsy in all the occasions which demand that one relax and present one's body as a spectacle, as in dancing and posing before the camera. And it is always as if, by means of obeying the principle of frontality and adopting the most conventional posture, one were seeking as far as possible to control the objectification of one's own image. Axial composition, in accordance with the principle of frontality, provides an impression that is as clearly legible as possible, as if one were seeking to avoid any misunderstanding, even if this were to mean sacrificing 'naturalness'. Looking without being seen, without being seen looking and without being looked at, or candidly, so to speak, and, to an even greater extent, taking photographs in this way, amounts to the theft of the images of other people. Looking at the person who is looking (or who is taking the photograph), correcting one's posture, one presents oneself to be looked at as one seeks to be looked at; one presents one's own image. In short, faced with a look which captures and immobilizes appearances, adopting the most ceremonial bearing means reducing the risk of clumsiness and *gaucherie* and giving others an image of oneself that is affected and pre-defined. Like respect for etiquette, frontality is a means of effecting one's own objectification: offering a regulated image of oneself is a way of imposing the rules of one's own perception.

The conventionality of attitudes towards photography appears to refer to the style of social relations favoured by a society which is both stratified and static and in which family and 'home' are more real than particular individuals, who are primarily defined by their family connections; in which the social rules of behaviour and the moral code are more apparent than the feelings, desires or thoughts of individual subjects; in which social exchanges, strictly regulated by consecrated conventions, are carried out under the constant fear of the judgement of others, under the watchful eye of opinion, ready to condemn in the name of norms which are unquestionable and unquestioned, and always dominated by the need to give the best image of oneself, the image most in keeping with the ideal of dignity and honour.[6] How, under these conditions, could the representation of society be anything other than the representation of a *represented* society?

[. . .]

Unlike the aesthetic of the simple man, unproblematic attachment to one coherent system of norms, the 'popular aesthetic' is defined and manifested (at least partially) in opposition to scholarly aesthetics, even if it is never triumphantly asserted. Reference to legitimate culture is never really excluded, even among manual workers. Unable either to ignore the existence of a scholarly aesthetic which challenges their own aesthetic, or to abandon their socially conditioned inclinations, not to speak of asserting and legitimating them, they escape this contradiction by establishing, sometimes quite explicitly, a dual scale of judgements; they must experience their relationship to aesthetic norms in terms of the logic of dissociation, since they must separate the obligatory practice from the obligatory judgement on that practice: thus, even when they aspire to other photographic genres, at least in intention, they would never dream of condemning the family photograph. This dual set of norms is never so manifest as when it forces a single subject to choose, on his own, between what he does and what he would like to do: 'It's beautiful, but I'd never think of taking it', 'Yes, it's very beautiful, but you'd have to like that sort of thing; it's not for me', formulas which, by their insistent recurrence, demonstrate the tension that affects the 'popular aesthetic' as a 'dominated aesthetic'.

Insofar as it does not encompass the principle of its own systemization, must we see the system of working-class judgements of taste as an aesthetic? It is no accident that, when one sets about reconstructing its logic, the 'popular aesthetic' appears to be the negative opposite of the Kantian aesthetic, and that the popular *ethos* implicitly answers each proposition of the 'Analytic of the Beautiful' with a thesis contradicting it. But manual and clerical workers may take a view completely opposite to that of the philosopher without consequently abandoning the aesthetic qualification of their judgements. One does not photograph simply anything, or, perhaps, not everything is suitable to be photographed; this is the thesis which, implicitly present in all the judgements, provides proof that aesthetic opinions are not simply arbitrary but, like the practice, obey cultural models. 'It's not something you'd take a picture of', 'That's not a photograph' – these judgements, peremptory and clear-cut, often accompanied by scandalized gestures, negatively express something immediately self-evident. The fact that the contravention of a rule may be apparent without the rule being perceived, or, even less, formulated as such, does not rule out the possibility that the key to aesthetic judgement, applied to a particular case, lies in a system of implicit principles and rules which it betrays more than it states.

If sociology – which treats value-systems as so many facts – objectively places practices and works which, like popular photography, might be seen by aesthetes as an anti-aesthetic, under the general heading of aesthetics, it would be a sort of inverse ethnocentricity to see this as the expression of a 'popular aesthetic': in fact, the experiences corresponding to these practices have nothing to do with the pursuit of beauty in and for itself, even though they may be described as analogous, within a different order, to those experiences produced in artists and aesthetes by the contemplation or production of works of art. The judgement of taste analysed by Kant presupposes a different lived experience which, like the popular experience of the beautiful, is socially conditioned or which, at any rate, is never independent of social conditions, those which make possible 'people of taste'.

Kant, in order to apprehend in its pure state the irreducible specificity of aesthetic judgement, strove to distinguish 'that which pleases' from 'that which gratifies' and, more generally, to separate 'disinterestedness', the sole guarantee of the specifically aesthetic quality of contemplation, from the 'interest of the senses' which defines 'the agreeable', and from 'the interest of Reason' which defines 'the Good'. By contrast, working-class people, who expect every image explicitly to fulfil a *function*, if only that of a sign, refer, often explicitly, to norms of morality or agreeableness in all their judgements. Whether praising or blaming, their appreciation refers to a system of norms whose principle is always ethical. Thus, for example, the photograph of a dead soldier may provoke judgements which are only apparently contradictory, i.e. in their individual applications.

'That's not beautiful. I don't like that. On the other hand, I'm a conscientious objector and I'd never take a picture of that.' 'I'm against this photograph from a moral point of view. A subject with no interest for anyone except career soldiers.' 'Well, you see, I did my military service in Algeria, I don't like that, I'm opposed to that.' 'It's a war photograph. I'm a pacifist. I hate that.' 'I don't like pictures like that. There's enough war already.' 'It's a photograph for people who like that kind of thing, and as far as the military and me are concerned, well . . .'

'It could be used to show the horror and uselessness of war.' 'We could use a lot of documents like that to show the horror of war.' 'It's a document, you could use that for propaganda.' (Dead soldier)

These opposing judgements really refer to an aesthetic which makes the signifier completely subordinate to the signified, and which can be better realized in photography than in the other arts. An art of illustration and imagery, photography can be reduced to the project of showing what the photographer chose to show, and with which it becomes, one might say, morally complicit, since it approves of and bears witness to what it shows. And subjects are only reproducing the objective intention of photography when they confer upon what it approves or disapproves a function of approval or disapproval.

This 'functional' aesthetic is necessarily pluralistic and conditional. The judgement of taste necessarily implies a restrictive reference to conditions defined in generic terms, that is in terms of the type of function or the type of intention revealed in the finished photograph.

'It's not bad journalism; taken while it's happening, it'll have been risky enough, but if it was taken afterwards it's of no interest.' 'Brilliant, if it isn't a montage!' 'Fine, if it's to be shown to kids in school.'

The insistence with which subjects recall the limits and conditions of validity of their judgements shows that they are explicitly and determinedly challenging the idea that a photograph may please 'universally'. Discerning, for each photograph, its possible uses and audiences, or more precisely its possible use for each audience, subordinating appreciation to several conditional hypotheses, is a way of understanding, or, rather, of appropriating an impersonal and anonymous photograph, deprived of the obvious function which gives commonplace photography its meaning and value.

The distinguishing principle between that which is photographable and that which is not cannot become independent of the individual imagination: it remains the case that the ordinary photograph, a private

product for private use, has no meaning, value or charm except for a finite group of subjects, mainly those who took it and those who are its objects. If certain public exhibitions of photographs, and particularly colour photographs, are felt to be improper, this is because they are claiming for private objects and privilege of the art object, the right to universal attachment. 'A photograph of a pregnant woman is fine as far as I'm concerned, but no one else is going to like it' (figure 11.1), said one manual worker, finding, through the issue of the rules of propriety, the issue of what is 'showable', that is, for what may claim the right to universal admiration. And it is remarkable that colour photography, which, even more than black-and-white photography, is designed to be shown sometimes obliges photographers to adopt the point of view of others with regard to their own photographs, introducing them through the perspective of human respect to a practice that is more universal in its intentions. Because they are dimly aware that the very fact of showing photographs includes the demand for attachment, photographers may sometimes feel obliged to show only those photographs that could 'interest everyone'.

But the ordinary use of photography almost completely excludes any concern for the universality of the picture that is produced or looked at, and which derives its interest not from what it is in and for itself, but from what it is for one person or for a group of people. This is true to the point where anonymous photographs and personal photographs are subject to two completely different perceptions; invited to give their opinion on the photographs of an unfamiliar family, city-dwellers and even peasants may adopt a purely formal and technical point of view. Having adopted this unfamiliar perspective, they are quite capable of distinguishing natural poses from poses which are false and therefore open to criticism, disagreeable from cheerful dispositions, successes from failures. But it is only because the situation created by the survey is artificial that they isolate, at least partially, the formal or aesthetic aspect of the image. While J. B. and his wife agreed in according their preference to the picture of J. B.'s wife in front of the Eiffel Tower, the picture on which a roadsign is seen coming out of the mother's head is frequently criticized. This is proof that the two images are perceived in quite different ways: in one case, the symbolic tie uniting the person with the object is immediately understood and approved, and therefore necessary, while in the other it is not. [. . .] Because the picture is always judged with reference to the function that it fulfils for the person who looks at it or the function which that viewer thinks it could fulfil for another person, aesthetic judgement most often takes the form of a hypothetical judgement relying explicitly on the recognition of 'genres', whose 'perfection' and range of application are conceptually defined.

Remembering that the paradox of aesthetic judgement lies, for Kant, in the fact that it includes claims to universality without, however, returning to the concept for its formulation, we see that the most common attitude towards the photographs shown is precisely the opposite of this: almost three-quarters of the phrases of appraisal begin with the word 'it', and the judgement provoked by the first reading of the image is almost always generic: 'It's maternal', 'It's human', 'It's a bit risqué'. The effort of recognition is accomplished by classification within a genre or – which amounts to the same thing – the attribution of social use, as the different genres are defined primarily with reference to their use and their users: 'It's a publicity photo', 'It's a pure document', 'It's a laboratory photo', 'It's a competition photo', 'It's a professional photo', 'It's an educational photo', etc. Photographs of nudes are almost always rejected in phrases which reduce them to the stereotype of their social function: 'All right in Pigalle', 'It's the kind of photograph people sell from under their coats.'

Artistic photography escapes this type of categorization only insofar as it is understood as the instrument of a kind of social behaviour: 'That's a competition photo', declare many of the subjects. The confusion provoked by certain pictures reveals a doubt concerning the genre to which they belong, and their attribution to an indifferent genre exempts the viewer from taking a stance on their aesthetic quality. It is from its participation within a genre that each individual photograph derives its purpose and its *raison d'être*. It follows that the hierarchy of preferences expresses the more or less straightforward participation of the photographs shown in more of less consecrated genres [and thus] prohibit[s] entirely unfavourable judgements: 'It goes on', says one worker shown a photograph of a starlet. Certain subjects, as if disarmed by the high frequency of pin-up photographs as a genre, almost apologize for not appreciating them, and refrain from condemning them completely.

It is not surprising that the 'barbarous taste' which bases appreciation on informative, tangible or moral interest most strongly rejects images of the meaningless (*insignificant*), or, which amounts to the same thing in terms of this logic, the meaninglessness of the image.[7] The desire to take a beautiful photograph is insufficient reason for taking a photograph:

> 'It's not a photograph that I would take, personally: it means seeing the photograph as an end in itself and not as a means of expression' (breaking waves). 'That reminds you of nothing, evokes nothing, gives you nothing' (leaf). 'It should give you ideas, that one there doesn't make you think of anything at all.' 'I don't like cubism, unrealistic paintings, Picasso and everything . . . I wonder what made them take this photograph.' (pebbles)

The subordination of the image to a function is such a strong requirement that it would amount to taking some of the ritual character away from the photographic act and depriving the photographed object of its value if one were to introduce the pure intention of aesthetic experiment, capable by definition of being applied to any object, after the manner of theoretical science which, as a particular way of seeing the real, remains, according to

Descartes, essentially identical independent of the nature of the object treated, as the sun remains the same independent of the variety of objects that it illuminates. The taking and contemplation of the family photograph presuppose the suspension of all aesthetic judgement, because the sacred character of the object and the sacralizing relationship between the photographer and the picture are enough unconditionally to justify the existence of a picture which only really seeks to express the glorification of its object, and which realizes its perfection in the perfect fulfilment of that function. Certainly any concern for the aesthetic quality of the picture is more likely to be the exception the more ritualistic the object photographed and, from babies to landscapes, via pets and famous monuments, the likelihood of the suspension of aesthetic concerns continues to diminish without ever quite disappearing. More generally, a photograph, even a figurative one, is rejected when no function can immediately be assigned to it, just as non-figurative paintings are refused when they do not show an identifiable object, that is, when they do not suggest any resemblance to familiar forms. One expects photography to give a narrative symbolism, and as a sign or, more precisely, an *allegory*, unequivocally to express a transcendental meaning and increase the notations which could unambiguously constitute the virtual discourse which it is supposed to bear.

'That would be all right as long as you had a foreground giving you a situation: I'd take that, if there was something to guide you: a balloon, a beach, a parasol.' 'I would have taken a base, a rock so that you could recognize something.' 'I would have taken that from further away so as to have a group, so that you could see what it was.' 'I wouldn't take a picture of water without boats' (breaking waves). 'I can understand how you would photograph flowerbeds, flowers, pretty gardens, but as for this leaf!' 'I would have photographed the whole plant.' (leaf)

When the object photographed is not intrinsically predisposed to be a photographic object and includes nothing which would indisputably merit this promotion, it may sometimes be regretted that the photographic act cannot lend it value by using some technical feat or 'trick', which would reveal the skill involved and thus betray the professionalism and merit of the photographer. But in most cases the judgement applied to the photograph in no way dissociates the object from the picture and the picture from the object, the final criterion of appreciation.

'I might take that if they were pebbles with weird and striking shapes.' 'These pebbles aren't interesting, there's no distinctive sign there unless there's a trick, like enlarged gravel, for example.' 'Yes, if there was some sort of effect, like some water, but like that it's just barren' (pebbles). 'That poor leaf really isn't particularly beautiful!' (leaf)

Of all the intrinsic characteristics of the picture, only colour can suspend the rejection of photographs of trivial things. There is nothing more alien to popular consciousness than the idea that one can and should want to conceive an aesthetic pleasure which, to use Kantian terms, is independent of being agreeable to the senses. Thus, judgement passed on the photographs most strongly rejected because of their uselessness (pebbles, tree-bark, wave) almost always ends up with the reservation that 'in colour, that could be pretty'; and some subjects even manage to make explicit the maxim that governs their attitude when they assert that 'if the colour is good, colour photography is always beautiful.' It is precisely popular taste that Kant is describing when he writes: 'Taste that requires an added element of charm and emotion for its delight, not to speak of adopting this as the measure of its approval, has not yet emerged from barbarism.'[8] In fact, tangible, informative or moral interest is the supreme value of the popular aesthetic.

Refusing the meaningless (*insignificant*) picture (in its twofold sense of being devoid of meaning and devoid of interest) or the picture which is ambiguous and anonymous, actually means refusing photography as an endless finality. The value of a photograph is measured above all by the clarity and the interest of the information that it is capable of communicating as a symbol, or, preferably, as an allegory. The popular reading of photography establishes a transcendent relationship between signifier and signified, meaning being related to form without being completely involved in it. Photography, far from being perceived as signifying itself and nothing else, is always examined as a sign of something that it is not.[9] The *legibility* of the picture itself is a function of the legibility of its intention (or of its function), and the aesthetic judgement to which it gives rise is more favourable the more total the expressive adequacy of the signifier to the signified.[10] However, it includes the expectation of the title or the caption which states the signifying intention and allows one to judge whether the realization is in accordance with the explicit ambition, whether it adequately signifies it or, preferably, illustrates it. The confusion provoked by certain aesthetic experiences is probably basically due to the fact that the subject does not know what its intention is, or even what is intention and what is clumsiness. [. . .]

On the other hand, and although it breaks the rules of the 'popular aesthetic' by amputating the sitter's face, the close-up photograph of an old woman's hands meets with strong appreciation among the peasants because they immediately see it as the allegorical expression of a thesis (figure 11.2): 'Oh, that's easier! The wonderful hands of a good farmer; hands like that have won agricultural prizes hundreds of times. That women has worked in the fields as much as she has in the kitchen; she's certainly tended the vines, looked after the animals: very nice.' What is perceived, understood and appreciated is not the old woman's hands but old age, work and honesty.

A similar process characterizes realist taste: as photographic technology is commonly held to be the technology most capable of providing a faithful and truthful reproduction of reality, the adequacy of the realization to the original proposition plays the same part here as the distance between reproduction and reality, likeness, does in painting. The primary

Figure 11.2

*'Those hands mean
work'* (Russell Lee,
Untitled, *from 'The
Family of Man'
exhibition, 1955)*

form of the judgement of taste
is the appraisal of a disparity
between the realization, the
signifier, and a transcendent
signified, a real idea or model.
While painting encourages a
demand for realism, photography, which always and
automatically appears realistic
and therefore achieves no
special merit by being so,
inclines the viewer to expect
conformity to a formulable
intention.[11] More profoundly,
photography provides an
exceptional opportunity for
the expression of realist taste;

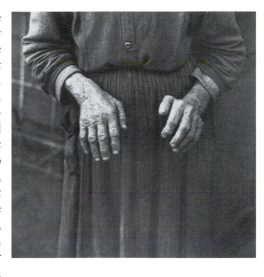

in fact, the moment one questions – because of a distorted image of the
machine – the possibility of the photographic act transfiguring the object
represented, one is forced or enabled to measure the beauty of the
representation against the beauty of the thing represented. What is
shameful about the photograph of a meaningless object is not solely the
fact that it does not refer to anything that precedes or transcends it – any
statement to illustrate, meaning to reconstruct or use to serve – it is also
that one is less willing than ever to admit that this signifier without a
signified only appears meaningless because it is its own signified: once one
takes issue with the true state and merit of the effort of reproduction, the
literal representation of the world becomes a pleonastic treatment of the
world.

Thus, the photographic image ordinarily acknowledged as the most
faithful reproduction of reality perfectly fulfils the expectations of the
popular naturalism that relies on a fundamental attachment to the object
created, naturalist photography, 'the choice that praises', which in many of
its aspects evokes a naturist cult. The picture of a meaningless object is
refused with such force, and the systematic distortion of the given object,
and of the human face in particular, provokes such a feeling of outrage,
because abstracting reinterpretation is seen as a technique of exclusion and
an attempt at mystification, but also and particularly a gratuitous attack on
the thing represented.

Photographs which take too many liberties with the human body provoke
unease or indignation: 'If you're going to take it, you might as well take the
whole thing, mightn't you? The face is missing, it's irritating.' 'It isn't bad,
but I'd like to see the expression on the face.' 'I'd have taken the face as well'
(hands of an old peasant woman). [. . .] The face, and especially the facial
expression, concentrate the expressiveness of the body so that their removal
is felt as a denial of expression. [. . .]

PIERRE BOURDIEU

This is why photographic practice, a ritual of solemnization and consecration of the group and the world, perfectly fulfils the deeper intentions of the 'popular aesthetic', the festive aesthetic, that is, the aesthetic of communication with others and communion with the world.

The hierarchy of legitimacies

'Barbarous taste' is never entirely free of all reference to 'good taste'. It appears, for example, that the inclination of working-class subjects to rely on 'concepts' – of genre or perfection – capable of supplying the norm from which appreciation may be deduced, also expresses the relationship that any culturally disadvantaged group is condemned to have to the legitimate culture from which it is *de facto* excluded; deprived by definition of the implicit and diverse knowledge of the norms of good taste, the working classes always seek objective principles which are the only thing capable, in their eyes, of forming the basis of an adequate judgement, and which can only be acquired by a specific or broad education. The concern with rules or with the rules of the genre, and the hope that judgement in matters of taste (as a 'reflecting judgement') may also become a 'defining judgement', subsuming the particular within the general (rule, principle or law), also ultimately expresses acknowledgement of legitimate culture and the certainty of cultural dispossession. All the same, photography (and the judgements which it provokes) provides an exceptionally favourable opportunity for grasping the logic of the 'popular aesthetic', because it tends – less than fully recognized practices and works – to make one afraid of losing face by revealing one's ignorance of consecrated norms and obligatory opinions.

This is so because, in a given society at a given moment, not all cultural meanings, theatrical presentations, sporting events, recitals of songs, poetry or chamber-music, operettas or operas, are equivalent in dignity and value, and they do not all call for the same approach with the same urgency. In other words, the various systems of expression, from theatre to television, are objectively organized according to a hierarchy independent of individual opinions, which defines *cultural legitimacy* and its gradations. Faced with meanings situated outside the sphere of legitimate culture, consumers feel they have the right to remain pure consumers and judge freely; on the other hand, within the field of consecrated culture, they feel measured according to objective norms, and forced to adopt a dedicated, ceremonial and ritualized attitude. Thus jazz, cinema and photography do not give rise – because they do not claim it with the same urgency – to the attitude of dedication, which is common coin when one is dealing with works of scholarly culture. Some virtuosos, in a bid for legitimation, transfer to these arts models of behaviour that are current in the realm of traditional culture. But in the absence of an institution to teach them methodically and systematically as constituent parts of legitimate culture, most people experience them in quite a different way, as simple consumers. Erudite knowledge of the history of these

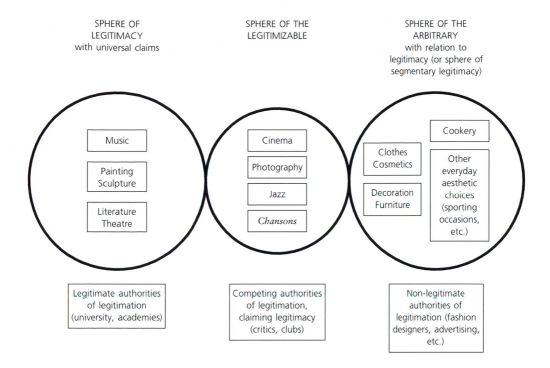

SPHERE OF
LEGITIMACY
with universal claims

SPHERE OF THE
LEGITIMIZABLE

SPHERE OF THE
ARBITRARY
with relation to
legitimacy (or sphere of
segmentary legitimacy)

| Music |
| Painting Sculpture |
| Literature Theatre |

| Cinema |
| Photography |
| Jazz |
| *Chansons* |

| Cookery |
| Clothes Cosmetics |
| Other everyday aesthetic choices (sporting occasions, etc.) |
| Decoration Furniture |

Legitimate authorities
of legitimation
(university, academies)

Competing authorities
of legitimation,
claiming legitimacy
(critics, clubs)

Non-legitimate
authorities of
legitimation (fashion
designers, advertising,
etc.)

Figure 11.3

arts, and familiarity with the technical or theoretical rules that characterize them are only encountered in exceptional cases because people do
not feel as forced as they do in other areas to make the effort to acquire,
preserve and communicate this body of knowledge which is a part of the
obligatory preliminaries and ritualized accompaniments of scholarly
consumption.

One therefore passes gradually from the fully consecrated arts such as
theatre, painting, sculpture, literature and classical music to signifying
systems which are abandoned – at least at first glance – to the arbitrariness
of individual taste, whether they be decoration, cosmetics or cookery
(figure 11.3). The meanings that fall within the sphere of legitimacy all
share the fact that they are organized according to a particular type of
system, developed and inculcated by the school, an institution specifically
responsible for communicating knowledge, organized into a hierarchy,
through a methodical organization of training and practice. It follows that
preferences or skills belonging to the sphere of legitimacy, far from being
randomly distributed, tend towards a hierarchical or methodical organization; systematization clearly operates on a more or less elevated level
according to whether the exercise has been practised for a longer or a
shorter time, and with greater or lesser intensity: and we find that systems
of taste with regard to legitimate works are closely linked to educational
levels.[12] The existence of *consecrated works* and the whole system of rules
defining the sacramental approach presuppose an institution whose
function is not only one of communication and distribution but also one
of legitimation. In fact, jazz and cinema are served by expressive means

which are at least as powerful as more traditional cultural works; there are coteries of professional critics with erudite journals and radio and television discussion platforms at their disposal which, as a sign of their pretension to cultural legitimacy, assume the learned and tedious tone of university criticism, taking on its cult of erudition for erudition's sake, as if, haunted by the issue of their legitimacy, the only thing they could do was to adopt and exaggerate the external signs of statutory authority of the guardians of the monopoly of the cultural legitimacy, the professors: as if their situation of competing for legitimacy and the power of legitimation forced them to express the most divergent or preferably indispensable judgements, and only ever to reach limited groups of amateurs, such as jazz circles and cinema clubs.

The position of photography within the hierarchy of legitimacies, half-way between 'vulgar' practices, apparently abandoned to the anarchy of tastes and noble cultural practices, subject to strict rules, explains as we have seen, the ambiguity of the attitudes which it provokes, particularly among the members of the privileged classes. The effort of some devotees to establish photography as a fully legitimate artistic practice almost always appears foolish and desperate because it can do practically nothing to counteract the social key to photography, which is never recalled so strongly as when one seeks to contradict it. People who wish to break with the rules of ordinary practice, and who refuse to confer upon their activity and its product their accepted meaning and function, are constantly forced to create a substitute (which may not appear as such) for that which is given as an immediate certainty to the devotees of legitimate culture, namely the sense of the cultural legitimacy of the practice and all the supports that go with it, from technical models to aesthetic theories. Unlike a legitimate practice, a practice in the process of legitimation poses and imposes, to those involved in it, the question of its own legitimacy. It is no accident that passionate photographers are always obliged to develop the aesthetic theory of their practice, to justify their existence as photographers by justifying the existence of photography as a true art.

Does this mean that when subjects do not feel measured according to the objective norms of an aesthetic orthodoxy their judgements of taste are abandoned to arbitrariness and deprived of any systematic character? In fact, they are organized according to a type of systematic arrangement which has nothing more to do with individual psychology than that which structures the preferences and knowledge of 'cultivated' people, but which is based precisely upon the *class ethos* – the set of values which, without attaining systematic explanation, tend to organize the 'conduct of life' of a social class. Thus, as we have seen, for the working and middle classes, the aesthetic expressed as much in photographic practice as in judgements on photography, appears as a dimension of the *ethos*, so that the aesthetic of the great mass of photographic works may be legitimately reduced, without being reductive, to the sociology of the groups that produce them, the functions which they assign to them and the meanings which they confer upon them, both explicitly and, more particularly, implicitly.

Notes

1   W. M. Ivins, *Prints and Visual Communication* (Cambridge, MA, MIT Press, 1953), p. 128.

2   Marcel Proust, *Remembrance of Things Past: The Guermantes Way*, trans. Terence Kilmartin, vol. 2 (Harmondsworth, Penguin, 1981) p. 378.

3   Because there is nothing less natural than this selective and conventional representation, photography can still produce, in some subjects, an experience of 'estrangement', even within the familiar universe. An 85-year-old inhabitant of Lesquire showed great astonishment at an old photograph taken from the balcony of a house opposite his own. At first, he could recognize nothing. He turned the photograph around in all directions. He was shown that it was a picture of the town square. 'But where's it taken from?' He passed his finger along the houses. He stopped, and, pointed to the first-floor window of a house, said: 'But that's my house, isn't it?' He recognized the house next door: 'Where's it taken from? Is that the church?' He recognized new details but remained just as confused because he was unable to locate himself.

4   Photographic representations only really appear 'lifelike' and 'objective' because they obey laws of representation which were produced before the media for creating them mechanically existed. Used by painters from the beginning of the sixteenth century [. . .] the camera obscura became very widespread as the ambition to produce 'lifelike' images was reinforced. [. . .] Photography was predisposed to become the standard of 'realism' because it supplied the mechanical means for realizing the *vision of the world invented* several centuries earlier, with perspective.

5   Among the Kabyles, the man of honour is the one who 'looks people in the face (*fait face*)', who looks the others in the face, uncovering his own face (cf. P. Bourdieu, 'The Sentiment of Honour in Kabyle Society', in J. Peristiany (ed.), *Honour and Shame: the Values of Mediterranean Society* (London, Weidenfeld and Nicolson, 1966), pp. 191–241. From a similarity between *sp-ek* (from Latin *specio*) and *sep* (from Sanskrit *sàpati*, to show respect), Émile Benveniste observes that 'notions of "homage" and "looking" are often associated, cf. French *égard* and *regard*, English regard, respect, etc.' (*Origines de la formation des noms en indo-européen*, Paris, Maisonneuve, 1973, p. 157).

6   Philippe Ariès [. . .] establishes a relationship between the transformation of the art of portraiture and the transformation of the structure of the family and the system of related attitudes, noting that there is a progressive movement from paintings in which the members of the family 'pose, in a rather solemn attitude, designed to emphasize the connections that bind them' [. . .] to portraits in which 'the family is captured in an instant, taken from life, at a point in its everyday life' (P. Ariès, *L'enfant et la vie familiale sous l'ancien régime*, pp. 389–90). Thus the different ways of treating the family portrait according to different social classes tend to reproduce, in a synchronic way, the different moments of the history of the portrait.

7   When the image of a meaningless object is accepted, it is because both the fact of its having been taken and the people who took it are held to be meaningless. Thus, peasants can accept that people take photographs of pieces of bark or piles of pebbles, but without attaching the least value to them. If, with a slightly shocked amazement, one accepts this frivolous city-dweller's fancy, it is because, when all is said and done, photography is seen as a meaningless and frivolous activity, which should be left to city-dwellers.

8   I. Kant, *Critique of Judgment*, trans. J. C. Meredith (London, Oxford University Press, 1952), p. 65.

9   This appears to be the popular attitude with regard to all meaning. For example, if classical music or non-figurative painting is found disconcerting, it is because subjects feel incapable of understanding what they *must* mean as signs.

10 Just as much in a rural environment as among the working classes of urban society, the hierarchy of preferences is the result of a compromise between the hierarchy of legibilities and the hierarchy of values. An easily identified photograph, even if it represents a subject that is morally shocking, will be preferred to another, whatever its subject, which is less easily identifiable. [. . .]

11   This means, among other things, that, paradoxically, the most enlightened amateurs and even professionals refuse to base the legitimacy of their creations, as everything would incline them to do, on the exaltation of 'objective chance'. The picture always bears its mechanical origin as a defect, and the most perfect accomplishment is held to be suspicious if it is not legitimated by the statement of an intention.

12   The survey on the museum-going public has revealed the existence of a very close connection between systems of taste with reference to painting and educational level (cf. P. Bourdieu and A. Darbel, *L'amour de l'art, les musées d'art européens et leur public*, Paris, Éditions de Minuit, 1st edn, 1968, 2nd edn, revised with additions, 1969, pp. 93–101).

12

Reading an archive:
photography between labour and capital
Allan Sekula

This chapter is taken from *Photography/ Politics Two*, edited by P. Holland, J. Spence and S. Watney (London, Photography Workshop/Comedia, 1986), pp. 153–161. It was first published as the introduction to a longer, three-part essay entitled 'Photography between Labour and Capital' which appeared in Benjamin H. D. Buchloch and Robert Wilkes (eds), *Mining Photographs and other Pictures: a Selection from the Archives of Shedden Studio, Glace Bay, 1948–1968* (Halifax: Nova Scotia College of Art and Design/ University College of Cape Breton Press, 1983).

Every image of the past that is not recognised by the present as one of its own threatens to disappear irretrievably.

(Walter Benjamin, p. 255)[1]

The invention of photography. For whom? Against whom?

(Jean-Luc Godard and Jean-Pierre Gorin)[2]

Here is yet another book of photographs. All were made in the industrial and coal-mining regions of Cape Breton in the two decades between 1948 and 1968. All were made by one man, a commercial photographer named Leslie Shedden. At first glance, the economics of this work seem simple and common enough: proprietor of the biggest and only successful photographic studio in the town of Glace Bay, Shedden produced pictures on demand for a variety of clients. Thus in the range of his commissions we discover the limits of economic relations in a coal town. His largest single customer was the coal company. And prominent among the less official customers who walked in the door of Shedden Studio were the coal miners and their families. Somewhere in between the company and the workers were local shopkeepers who, like Shedden himself, depended on the miners' income for their own livelihood and who saw photography as a sensible means of local promotion.

Why stress these economic realities at the outset, as if to flaunt the 'crude thinking' often called for by Bertolt Brecht? Surely our understandings of these photographs cannot be reduced to a knowledge of economic conditions. This latter knowledge is necessary but insufficient; we also need to grasp the way in which photography constructs an imaginary world and passes it off as reality. The aim of this essay, then, is to try to understand something of the relationship between photographic culture and economic life. How does photography serve to legitimate and normalise existing power relationships? How does it serve as the voice of authority, while simultaneously claiming to constitute a token of exchange between equal partners? What havens and temporary escapes from the realm of necessity are provided by photographic means? What resistances are encouraged and strengthened? How is historical and social memory preserved, transformed, restricted and obliterated by photographs? What futures are promised; what futures are forgotten? In the broadest sense, these questions concern the ways in which photograph constructs an *imaginary economy*. From a materialist perspective, these are reasonable questions, well worth pursuing. Certainly they would seem to be unavoidable for an archive such as this one, assembled in answer to commercial and industrial demands in a region persistently suffering from economic troubles.[3]

Nonetheless, such questions are easily eclipsed, or simply left unasked. To understand this denial of politics, this depoliticisation of photographic meaning, we need to examine some of the underlying problems of photographic culture. Before we can answer the questions just posed, we need to briefly consider what a photographic archive is, and how it might be interpreted, sampled, or reconstructed in a book. The model of the archive, of the quantitative ensemble of images, is a powerful one in photographic discourse. This model exerts a basic influence on the character of the truths and pleasures experienced in looking at photographs, especially today, when photographic books and exhibitions are being assembled from archives at an unprecedented rate. We might even argue that archival ambitions and procedures are intrinsic to photographic practice.

There are all sorts of photographic archives: commercial archives like Shedden's, corporate archives, government archives, museum archives, historical society archives, amateur archives, family archives, artists' archives, private collectors' archives and so on. Archives are property, either of individuals or institutions, and their ownership may or may not coincide with authorship. One characteristic of photography is that authorship of individual images and the control and ownership of archives do not commonly reside in the same individual. Photographers are detail workers when they are not artists or leisure-time amateurs, and thus it is not unreasonable for the legal theorist Bernard Edelman to label photographers the 'proletarians of creation'.[4] Leslie Shedden, for his part, was a combination artisan and small entrepreneur. He contributed to company and family archives while retaining his own file of negatives. As is common with commercial photographers, he included these negatives in the sale of his studio to a *younger photographer* upon retiring in 1977.

Archives, then, constitute a *territory of images*; the unity of an archive is first and foremost that imposed by ownership. Whether or not the photographs in a particular archive are offered for sale, the general condition of archives involves the subordination of use to the logic of exchange. Thus not only are the pictures in archives often *literally* for sale,

ANNUAL REPORT 1956

Dominion
Coal
Company, Limited

DOSCO CONTINUOUS MINER

Figure 12.1

Dominion Coal
Company annual
report, 1956
(Cape Breton
Development
Corporation Archive,
Glace Bay, Nova
Scotia)

but their meanings are up for grabs. New owners are invited, new interpretations are promised. The purchase of reproduction rights under copyright law is also the purchase of a certain semantic licence. This *semantic availability* of pictures in archives exhibits the same abstract logic as that which characterizes goods in the marketplace.

In an archive, the possibility of meaning is 'liberated' from the actual contingencies of use. But this liberation is also a loss, an *abstraction* from the complexity and richness of use, a loss of context. Thus the specificity of 'original' uses and meanings can be avoided, and even made invisible, when photographs are selected from an archive and reproduced in a book. (In reverse fashion, photographs can be removed from books and entered into archives, with a similar loss of specificity.) So new meanings come to supplant old ones with the archive serving as a kind of 'clearing house' of meaning.

Consider this example: some of the photographs in this book were originally reproduced in the annual reports of the Dominion Steel and Coal Company (figure 12.1), others were carried in miners' wallets or framed on the mantlepieces of working-class homes (figure 12.2). Imagine two different gazes. Imagine the gaze of a stockholder (who may or may not have ever visited a coal mine) thumbing his way to the table of earnings and lingering for a moment on the picture of a mining machine, presumably the concrete source of the abstract wealth being accounted for in those pages. Imagine the gaze of a miner, or of a miner's spouse, child, parent, sibling, lover or friend drifting to a portrait during breaks or odd moments during the working day. Most mine workers would agree that the investments behind these looks – financial on the one hand, emotional on the other – are not compatible. But in an archive, the difference, the *radical antagonism* between these looks is eclipsed. Instead we have two carefully made negatives available for reproduction in a book in which all their similarities and differences could easily be reduced to 'purely visual' concerns. (And even visual differences can be homogenized out of existence when negatives first printed as industrial glossies and others printed on flat paper and tinted by hand are subjected to a uniform standard of printing for reproduction in a book. Thus the difference between a mode of pictorial address which is primarily 'informational' and one which is 'sentimental' is obscured.) In this sense, archives establish a relation of *abstract visual equivalence* between pictures. Within this regime of the sovereign image, the underlying currents of power are hard to detect, except through the shock of montage, when pictures from antagonistic categories are juxtaposed in a polemical and disorienting way.

Conventional wisdom would have it that photographs transmit immutable truths. But although the very notion of photographic reproduction would seem to suggest that very little is lost in translation, it is clear that photographic meaning depends largely on context. Despite the powerful impression of reality (imparted by the mechanical registration of a moment of reflected light according to the rules of normal perspective), photographs, in themselves, are fragmentary and incomplete utterances. Meaning is always directed by layout, captions, text, and site and mode of presentation, as the example given about suggests. Thus, since photographic archives tend to suspend meaning and use, within the archive meaning exists in a state that is both residual and potential. The suggestion of past uses coexists with a plenitude of possibilities. In functional terms, an active archive is like a toolshed, a dormant archive like an abandoned toolshed. (Archives are not like coal mines; meaning is not extracted from nature, but from culture.)

In terms borrowed from linguistics, the archive constitutes the paradigm or iconic system from which photographic 'statements' are constructed. Archival potentials change over time; the keys are appropriated by different disciplines, discourses, 'specialities'. For example, the pictures in photo agency files become available to history when they are no longer useful to topical journalism. Similarly, the new art history of photography at its too prevalent worst rummages through archives of every sort in search of masterpieces to celebrate and sell.

Clearly archives are not neutral; they embody the power inherent in accumulation, collection, and hoarding as well as that power inherent in the command of the lexicon and rules of a language. Within bourgeois culture, the photographic project itself has been identified from the very beginning not only with the dream of a universal language, but also with the establishment of global archives and repositories according to models offered by libraries, encyclopedias, zoological and botanical gardens, museums, police files, and banks.

Figure 12.2

Portrait of five brothers, Glace Bay, 1940–1 (Shedden Studio Archive)

Figure 12.3

*Joy loader operators
posing at the end of
a shift, No. 25
Colliery, Glace Bay,
1954* (Shedden
Studio Archive)

(Reciprocally, photography contributed to the modernization of information flows within most of these institutions.) Any photographic archive, no
matter how small, appeals indirectly to these institutions for its authority.
Not only the truths, but also the pleasures of photographic archives are
linked to those enjoyed in these other sites. As for the truths, their
philosophical basis lies in an aggressive empiricism, bent on achieving a
universal inventory of appearance. Archival projects typically manifest a
compulsive desire for completeness, a faith in an ultimate coherence
imposed by the sheer quantity of acquisitions. In practice, knowledge of
this sort can only be organised according to bureaucratic means. Thus the
archival perspective is closer to that of the capitalist, the professional
positivist, the bureaucrat and the engineer – not to mention the
connoisseur – than it is to that of the working class. Generally speaking,
working-class culture is not built on such high ground.

And so archives are contradictory in character. Within their confines
meaning is liberated from use, and yet at a more general level an empiricist
model of truth prevails. Pictures are atomized, isolated in one way and
homogenized in another. (Alphabet soup comes to mind.) But any archive
that is not a complete mess establishes an order of some sort among its
contents. Normal orders are either taxonomic or diachronic (sequential); in
most archives both methods are used, but at different, often alternating,
levels of organization. Taxonomic orders might be based on sponsorship,
authorship, genre, technique, iconography, subject matter, and so on,
depending on the range of the archive. Diachronic orders follow a
chronology of production or acquisition. Anyone who has sorted or simply
sifted through a box of family snapshots understands the dilemmas (and
perhaps the folly) inherent in these procedures. One is torn between narration and categorization, between chronology and inventory.

What should be recognized here is that photographic books (and exhibitions) frequently cannot help but reproduce these rudimentary ordering schemes, and in so doing implicitly claim a share in both the authority and the illusory neutrality of the archive. Herein lies the 'primitivism'; of still photography in relation to the cinema. Unlike a film, a photographic book or exhibition can almost always be dissolved back into its component parts, back into the archive. The ensemble can seem to be both provisional and artless. Thus, within the dominant culture of photography, we find a chain of dodges and denials: at any stage of photographic production the apparatus of selection and interpretation is liable to render itself invisible (or conversely to celebrate its own workings as a kind of moral crusade or creative magic). Photographer, archivist, editor and curator can all claim, when challenged about their interpretations, to be merely passing along a neutral reflection of an already established state of affairs. Underlying this process of professional denial is a commonsensical empiricism. The photograph reflects reality. The archive accurately catalogues the ensemble of reflections, and so on. Even if one admits – as is common enough nowadays – that the photograph *interprets* reality, it might still follow that the archive accurately catalogues the ensemble of interpretations, and so on again. Songs of the innocence of discovery can be sung at any point. Thus the 'naturalization of the cultural', seen by Roland Barthes as an essential characteristic of photographic discourse, is repeated and reinforced at virtually every level of the cultural apparatus – unless it is interrupted by criticism.[5]

In short, photographic archives by their very structure maintain a hidden connection between knowledge and power. Any discourse that appeals without scepticism to archival standards of truth might well be viewed with suspicion. But what narratives and inventories might be constructed, were we to interpret an archive such as this one in a normal fashion?

I can imagine two different sorts of books being made from Shedden's photographs, or for that matter from any similar archive of functional photographs. On the one hand, we might regard these pictures as 'historical documents'. We might, on the other hand, treat these photographs as 'aesthetic objects'. Two more or less contradictory choices emerge. Are these photographs to be taken as a transparent means to a knowledge – intimate and detailed even if incomplete – of industrial Cape Breton in the post-war decades? Or are we to look at these pictures 'for their own sake', as opaque ends-in-

Figure 12.4

View of the Dosco miner in action, No. 18 Colliery, Glace Bay, 1953 (Shedden Studio Archive)

themselves? This second question has a corollary. Are these pictures products of an unexpected vernacular authorship; is Leslie Shedden a 'discovery' worthy of a minor seat in an expanding pantheon of photographic artists?

Consider the first option. From the first decade of this century, popular histories and especially schoolbook histories have increasingly relied on photographic reproductions. Mass culture and mass education lean heavily on photographic realism, mixing pedagogy and entertainment in an avalanche of images. The look of the past can be retrieved, preserved and disseminated in an unprecedented fashion. But awareness of history as an *interpretation* of the past succumbs to a faith in history as *representation*. The viewer is confronted, not by *historical-writing*, but by the appearance of *history itself*. Photography would seem to gratify the often quoted desire of that 'master of modern historical scholarship', Leopold von Ranke, to 'show what actually happened'.[6] Historical narration becomes a matter of appealing to the silent authority of the archive, of unobtrusively linking incontestable documents in a seamless account. (The very term 'document' entails a notion of legal or official truth, as well as a notion of *proximity to* and verification of an original event.) Historical narratives that rely primarily on photography almost invariably are both positivist and historicist in character. For positivism, the camera provides mechanical and thus 'scientifically' objective evidence or 'data'. Photographs are seen as sources of factual, positive knowledge, and thus are appropriate documents for a history that claims a place among the supposedly objective sciences of human behaviour. For historicism, the archive confirms the existence of a linear progression from past to present, and offers the possibility of an easy and unproblematic retrieval of the past from the transcendent position offered by the present. At their worst, pictorial histories offer an extraordinarily reductive view of historical causality: the First World War 'begins' with a glimpse of an assassination in Sarajevo; the entry of the United States into the Second World War 'begins' with a view of wrecked battleships.

Thus, most visual and pictorial histories reproduce the established patterns of historical thought in bourgeois culture. By doing so in a 'popular' fashion, they extend the hegemony of that culture, while exhibiting a thinly-veiled contempt and disregard for popular literacy. The idea that photography is a 'universal language' contains a persistent element of condescension as well as pedagogical zeal.

The widespread use of photographs as historical illustrations suggests that significant events are those which can be pictured, and thus history takes on the character of *spectacle*.[7] But this pictorial spectacle is a kind of rerun, since it depends on prior spectacles for its supposedly 'raw' material. Since the 1920s, the picture press, along with the apparatuses of corporate public relations, publicity, advertising and government propaganda have contributed to a regularized flow of images: of disasters, wars, revolutions, new products, celebrities, political leaders, official ceremonies, public appearances, and so on. For a historian to use such pictures without remarking on these initial uses is naïve at best, and cynical at worst. What would it mean to construct a pictorial history of postwar coal mining in Cape Breton by using pictures from a company public relations archive

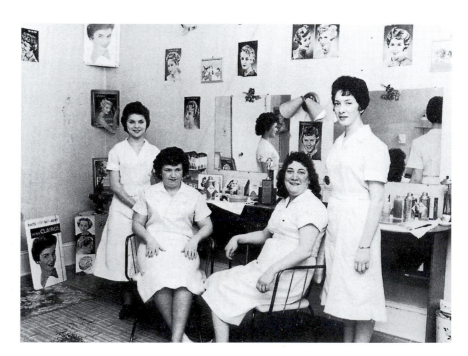

Figure 12.6

Staff at Annie's Beauty Salon, Glace Bay, 1960 (Shedden Studio Archive)

without calling attention to the bias inherent in that source? What present interests might be served by such an oversight?

The viewer of standard pictorial histories loses any ground in the present from which to make critical evaluations. In retrieving a loose succession of fragmentary glimpses of the past, the spectator is flung into a condition of imaginary temporal and geographical mobility. In this dislocated and disoriented state, the only coherence offered is that provided by the constantly shifting position of the camera, which provides the spectator with a kind of powerless omniscience. Thus the spectator comes to identify with the technical apparatus, with the authoritative institution of photography. In the face of this authority, all other forms of telling and remembering begin to fade. But the machine establishes its truth, not by logical argument, but by providing an *experience*. This experience characteristically veers between nostalgia, horror, and an overriding sense of the exoticism of the past, of its irretrievable otherness for the viewer in the present. Ultimately then, when photographs are uncritically presented as historical documents, they are transformed into aesthetic objects. Accordingly, the pretence to historical understanding remains, although that understanding has been replaced by aesthetic experience.[8]

But what of our second option? Suppose we abandoned all pretence to historical explanation, and treated these photographs as artworks of one sort or another. This book would then be an inventory of aesthetic achievement and/or an offering for disinterested aesthetic perusal. The reader may well have been prepared for these likelihoods by the simple fact that this book has been published by a press with a history of exclusive concern with the contemporary vanguard art of the United States and Western Europe (and to a lesser extent, Canada). Further, as I've already suggested, in a more fundamental way the very removal of these photographs from their initial contexts invites aestheticism.

I can imagine two ways of converting these photographs into 'works of art', both a bit absurd, but neither without ample precedent in the current fever to assimilate photography into the discourse and market of the fine arts. The first path follows the traditional logic of romanticism, in its incessant search for aesthetic origins in a coherent and controlling authorial 'voice'. The second path might be labelled 'post-romantic' and privileges the subjectivity of the collector, connoisseur, and viewer over that of any specific author. This latter mode of reception treats photographs as 'found objects'. Both strategies can be found in current photographic discourse; often they are intertwined in a single book, exhibition, magazine or journal article. The former tends to predominate, largely because of the continuing need to validate photography as a fine art, which requires an incessant appeal to the myth of authorship in order to wrest photography away from its reputation as a servile and mechanical medium. Photography needs to be won and rewon repeatedly for the ideology of romanticism to take hold.[9]

The very fact that this book reproduces photographs by a single author might seem to be an implicit concession to a neo-romantic *auteurism*. But it would be difficult to make a credible argument for Shedden's autonomy as a maker of photographs. Like all commercial photographers, his work involved a negotiation between his own craft and the demands and expectations of his clients. Further, the presentation of his work was entirely beyond his control. One might hypothetically argue that Shedden was a hidden artist, producing an original *oeuvre* under unfavourable conditions. ('Originality' is the essential qualifying condition of genuine art under the terms dictated by romanticism. To the extent that photography was regarded as a copyist's medium by romantic art critics in the nineteenth century, it failed to achieve the status of the fine arts.) The problem with auteurism, as with so much else in photographic discourse, lies in its frequent misunderstanding of actual photographic practice. In the wish-fulfilling isolation of the 'author', one loses sight of the social institutions – corporation, school, family – that are speaking by means of the commercial photographer's craft. One can still respect the craft work of the photographer, the skill inherent in work within a set of formal conventions and economic constraints, while refusing to indulge in romantic hyperbole.

The possible 'post-romantic' or 'post-modern' reception of these photographs is perhaps even more disturbing and more likely. To the extent that photography still occupies an uncertain and problematic position within the fine arts, it becomes possible to displace subjectivity, to find refined aesthetic sensibility not in the maker of images, but in the viewer. Photographs such as these then become the objects of a secondary voyeurism, which preys upon, and claims superiority to, a more naïve primary act of looking. The strategy here is akin to that initiated and established by Pop Art in the early nineteen-sixties. The aesthetically informed viewer examines the artifacts of mass or 'popular' culture with a detached, ironic, and even contemptuous air. For Pop Art and its derivatives, the look of the sophisticated viewer is always constructed in relation to the inferior look which preceded it. [. . .]

In general, then, the hidden imperatives of photographic culture drag us in two contradictory directions: towards 'science' and a myth of 'objective truths' on the one hand, and towards 'art' and a cult of 'subjective experience' on the other. This dualism haunts photography, lending a certain goofy inconsistency to most commonplace assertions about the medium. We repeatedly hear the following refrain. Photography is an art. Photography is a science (or at least constitutes a 'scientific' way of seeing). Photography is both an art and a science. In response to these claims, it becomes important to argue that photography is neither art nor science, but is suspended between both the *discourse* of science and that of art, staking its claims to cultural value on both the model of truth upheld by empirical science and the model of pleasure and expressiveness offered by romantic aesthetics. In its own erratic way, photographic discourse has attempted to bridge the extreme philosophical and institutional separation of scientific and artistic practice that has characterized bourgeois society since the late eighteenth century. As a mechanical medium which radically transformed and displaced earlier artisanal and manual modes of visual representation, photography is implicated in a sustained crisis at the very centre of bourgeois culture, a crisis rooted in the emergence of science and technology as seemingly autonomous productive forces. At the heart of this crisis lies the question of the survival and deformation of human creative energies under the impact of mechanization. The institutional promotion of photography as a fine art serves to redeem technology by suggesting that subjectivity and the machine are easily compatible. Especially today, photography contributes to the illusion of a humanized technology, open both to 'democratic' self-expression and to the mysterious workings of genius. In this sense, the camera seems the exemplar of the benign machine, preserving a moment of creative autonomy that is systematically denied in the rest of most people's lives. The one-sided lyricism of this view is apparent when we consider the myriad ways in which photography has served as a tool of industrial and bureaucratic power.[10]

If the position of photography within bourgeois culture is as problematic as I am suggesting here, then we might want to move away from the art-historicist bias that governs most contemporary discussions of the medium. We need to understand how photography works within everyday life in advanced industrial societies: the problem is one of materialist cultural history rather than art history. This is a matter of beginning to figure out how to read the making and reception of ordinary pictures. Leslie Shedden's photographs would seem to allow for an exemplary insight into the diverse and contradictory ways in which photography affects the lives of working people.

Let's begin again by recognizing that we are confronting a curious archive – divided and yet connected elements of an imaginary social mechanism. Pictures that depict fixed moments in an interconnected economy of flows: of coal, money, machines, consumer goods, men, women, children. Pictures that are themselves elements in a unified symbolic economy – a traffic in photographs – a traffic made up of memories, commemorations, celebrations, testimonials, evidence, facts, fantasies. Here are official pictures, matter-of-factly committed to the charting and celebration of progress. A mechanical conveyor replaces a herd of ponies. A mechanical miner replaces ten human miners. A diesel engine replaces a locomotive. Here also are private pictures, personal pictures, family pictures: weddings, graduations, family groups. One is tempted at the outset to distinguish two distinct realisms, the *instrumental realism* of the industrial photograph and the *sentimental realism* of the family photograph. And yet it would seem clear that these are not mutually exclusive categories. Industrial photographs may well be commissioned, executed, displayed, and viewed in a spirit of calculation and rationality. Such pictures seem to offer unambiguous truths, the useful truths of applied science. But a zone of virtually unacknowledged *affects* can also be reached by photographs such as these, touching on an aesthetics of power, mastery, and control. The public *optimism* that suffuses these pictures is merely a respectable, *sentimentally acceptable*, and ideologically necessary substitute for deeper feelings – the cloak for an aesthetics of exploitation. In other words, even the blandest pronouncement in words and pictures from an office of corporate public relations has a subtext marked by threats and fear. (After all, under capitalism everyone's job is on the line.) Similarly, no family photograph succeeds in creating a haven of pure sentiment. This is especially true for people who feel the persistent pressures of economic distress, and for whom even the making of a photograph has to be carefully counted as an expense. Granted, there are moments in which the photograph overcomes separation and loss, therein lies much of the emotional power of photography. Especially in a mining community, the life of the emotions is persistently tied to the instrumental workings underground. More than elsewhere, a photograph can become without warning a tragic memento. [. . .]

Notes

1 Walter Benjamin, 'Theses on the Philosophy of History' (1940) in *Illuminations*, ed. Hannah Arendt, trans. Harry Zohn (New York, 1969), p. 255.

2 Jean-Luc Godard and Jean-Pierre Gorin, *Vent d'Est* (Rome, Paris, Berlin, 1969), filmscript published in Jean-Luc Godard, *Weekend/Wind from the East* (New York, 1972), p. 179.

3 'What is represented in ideology is therefore not the system of the real relations which govern the existence of individuals, but the imaginary relation of those individuals to the real relations in which they live'. Louis Althusser, 'Ideology and ideological state apparatuses' (1969), in *Lenin and Philosophy and Other Essays*, trans. Ben Brewster (New York, 1971), p. 165 [extracted in Chapter 19 of this volume].

4 Bernard Edelman, *Le Droit saisi par la photographie* (Paris, 1973), trans. Elizabeth Kingdom, *Ownership of the Image: Elements for a Marxist Theory of Law* (London, 1979), p. 45.

5 Roland Barthes, 'Rhétorique de l'image', *Communications* 4 (1964), in *Image–Music–Text*, trans. S. Heath (New York, Hill and Wang, 1977), p. 51 [extracted in chapter 2 of this volume].

6 Leopold von Ranke, preface to *Histories of the Latin and Germanic Nations from 1494–1514*, in *The Varieties of History*, ed. Fritz Stern (New York, 1972), p. 57.

7 See Guy Debord, *La Société du spectacle* (Paris, 1967), unauthorized translation, *Society of the Spectacle* (Detroit, 1970, rev. edn, 1977) [extracted in chapter 8 of this volume].

8 Two books counter this prevailing tendency in 'visual history' by directing attention to the power relationships behind the making of pictures: C. Herron, S. Hoffmitz, W. Roberts and R. Storey, *All that our Hands Have Done: a Pictorial History of the Hamilton Workers*, (Oakville, Ontario, 1981); and Sarah Graham-Brown, *Palestinians and their Society 1880–1946* (London, 1980).

9 In the first category are books which discover unsung commercial photographers: e.g., Mike Disfarmer, *Disfarmer: the Heber Springs Portraits*, text by Julia Scully (Danbury, New Hampshire, 1976). In the second category are books which testify to the aesthetic sense of the collector: e.g., Sam Wagstaff, *A Book of Photographs from the Collection of Sam Wagstaff* (New York, 1978).

10 This passage restates an argument made in my essay, 'The traffic in photographs'. *The Art Journal*, 41, 1 (spring 1981), pp. 15–16.

13

Photography's discursive spaces   **Rosalind Krauss**

Let us start with two images, identically titled *Tufa Domes, Pyramid Lake, Nevada*. The first (figure 13.1) is a (recently) celebrated photograph made by Timothy O'Sullivan in 1868 that functions with special insistence within the art-historical construction of nineteenth-century landscape photography. The second (figure 13.2) is a lithographic copy of the first, produced for the publication of Clarence King's *Systematic Geology* in 1878.[1]

    Twentieth-century sensibility welcomes the original O'Sullivan as a model of the mysterious, silent beauty to which landscape photography had access during the early decades of the medium. In the photograph, three bulky masses of rock are seen as if deployed on a kind of abstract, transparent chessboard, marking by their separate positions a retreating trajectory into depth. A fanatical descriptive clarity has bestowed on the bodies of these rocks a hallucinatory wealth of detail, so that each crevice, each granular trace of the original volcanic heat finds its record. Yet the rocks seem unreal and the space dreamlike, the tufa domes appear as if suspended in a luminous ether, unbounded and directionless. The brilliance of this undifferentiated ground, in which water and sky connect in an almost seamless continuum, overpowers the material objects within it, so that if the rocks seem to float, to hover, they do so merely as shape. The luminous ground overmasters their bulk, making them instead the functions of design. The mysterious beauty of the image is in this opulent flattening of its space.

    By comparison, the lithograph is an object of insistent visual banality. Everything mysterious in the photograph has been explained with supplemental, chatty detail. Clouds have been massed in the sky; the far shore of the lake has been given a definitive shape; the surface of the lake has been characterized by little eddies and ripples. And most important for

This chapter, originally published in 1982, is taken from *The Contest of Meaning: Critical Histories of Photography*, edited by R. Boston (Cambridge, MA, MIT Press, 1989), pp. 286–301.

Figure 13.1

Timothy O'Sullivan, Tufa Domes, Pyramid Lake, Nevada, 1868

Figure 13.2

Photolithography after O'Sullivan, Tufa Domes, Pyramid Lake, Nevada (published in King, Systematic Geology, 1875)

the demotion of this image from strange to commonplace, the reflections of the rocks in the water have been carefully recreated, so that gravity and direction are restored to this space formerly awash with the vague luminosity of too rapidly exposed collodion.

But it is clear, of course, that the difference between the two images – the photograph and its translation – is not a function of the inspiration of the photographer and the insipidity of the lithographer. They belong to two separate domains of culture, they assume different expectations in the user of the image, they convey two distinct kinds of knowledge. In a more recent vocabulary, one would say that they operate as representations within two distinct discursive spaces, as members of two different discourses. The lithograph belongs to the discourse of geology and, thus, of empirical science. In order for it to function within this discourse, the ordinary elements of topographical description had to be restored to the image produced by O'Sullivan. The coordinates of a continuous homogeneous space, mapped not so much by perspective as by the cartographic grid, had to be reconstructed in terms of a coherent recession along an intelligible horizontal plane retreating toward a definite horizon. The geological data of the tufa domes had to be grounded, coordinated, mapped. As shapes afloat on a continuous, vertical plane, they would have been useless.[2]

And the photograph? Within what discursive space does it operate?

Aesthetic discourse as it developed in the nineteenth century organized itself increasingly around what could be called the space of exhibition. Whether public museum, official salon, world fair, or private showing, the space of exhibition was constituted in part by the continuous surface of wall – a wall increasingly structured solely for the display of art. The space of exhibition had other features besides the gallery wall. It was also the ground of criticism: on the one hand, the ground of a written response to the works' appearance in that special context; on the other, the implicit ground of choice (of either inclusion or exclusion), with everything excluded from the space of exhibition becoming marginalized with regard to its status as Art. Given its function as the physical vehicle of exhibition, the gallery wall became the signifier of inclusion and, thus, can be seen as constituting in itself a representation of what could be called *exhibitionality*, or that which was developing as the crucial medium of exchange between patrons and artists within the changing structure of art in the nineteenth century. And in the last half of the century, painting – particularly landscape painting – responded with its own corresponding set of depictions. It began to internalize the space of exhibition – the wall – and to represent it.

The transformation of landscape after 1860 into a flattened and compressed experience of space spreading laterally across the surface was extremely rapid. It began with the insistent voiding of perspective, as landscape painting counteracted perspectival recession with a variety of devices, among them sharp value contrast, which had the effect of converting the orthogonal penetration of depth – effected, for example, by a lane of trees – into a diagonal ordering of the surface. No sooner had this compression occurred, constituting within the single easel painting a representation of the very space of exhibition, than other means of composing this representation were employed: serial landscapes, hung in succession, mimed the horizontal extension of the wall, as in Monet's Rouen Cathedral paintings; or landscapes, compressed and horizonless, expanded to become the absolute size of the wall. The synonymy of landscape and wall (the one a representation of the other) of Monet's late water lilies is thus an advanced moment in a series of operations in which aesthetic discourse resolves itself around a representation of the very space that grounds it institutionally.

This constitution of the work of art as a representation of its own space of exhibition is in fact what we know as the history of modernism. It is now fascinating to watch historians of photography assimilating their medium to the logic of that history. For if we ask, once again, within what discursive space does the original O'Sullivan – as I described it at the outset – function, we have to answer: that of the aesthetic discourse. And if we ask what it is a representation *of*, the answer must be that within this space it is constituted as a representation of the plane of exhibition, the surface of the museum, the capacity of the gallery to constitute the objects it selects for inclusion as Art.

But did O'Sullivan in his own day, the 1860s and 1870s, construct his work for the aesthetic discourse and the space of exhibition? Or did he create it for the scientific/topographical discourse that it more or less efficiently serves? Is the interpretation of O'Sullivan's work as a representation of aesthetic values – flatness, graphic design, ambiguity, and, behind these, certain intentions toward aesthetic significations: sublimity, transcendence – not a retrospective construction designed to secure it as Art?[3] And is this projection not illegitimate, the composition of a false history?

This question has a special methodological thrust from the vantage of the present, as a newly organized and energized history of photography is at work constructing an account of the early years of the medium. Central to this account is the photography, most of it topographical, originally undertaken for the purposes of exploration, expedition, and survey. Matted, framed, labeled, these images now enter the space of historical reconstruction through the museum. Decorously isolated on the wall of an exhibition, the objects can be read according to a logic that insists on their representational character within the discursive space of art, in an attempt to 'legitimate' them. The term is Peter Galassi's, and the issue of legitimacy was the focus of the Museum of Modern Art exhibition 'Before Photography', which he organized. In a sentence that was repeated by every reviewer of his argument, Galassi sets up this question of photography's position with respect to the aesthetic discourse. 'The object here is to show that photography was not a bastard left by science on the doorstep of art, but a legitimate child of the Western pictorial tradition.'[4]

The legitimation that follows depends on something far more ambitious than proving that certain nineteenth-century photographers had pretensions to being artists, or theorizing that photographs were as good as, or even superior to, paintings, or showing that photographic societies organized exhibitions on the model of Establishment salons. Legitimations depend on going beyond the presentation of apparent membership in a given family; they demand the demonstration of the internal, generic necessity of such membership. Galassi wants, therefore, to address internal, formal structures rather than external, circumstantial details. To this end he wishes to prove that the perspective so prominent in nineteenth-century outdoor photography – a perspective that tends to flatten, to fragment, to generate ambiguous overlap, to which Galassi gives the name 'analytic', as opposed to the 'synthetic' constructive perspective of the Renaissance – was fully developed by the late eighteenth century within the discipline of painting. The force of this proof, Galassi maintains, will be to rebut the notion that photography is essentially a 'child of technical rather than aesthetic traditions' and an outsider to the internal issues of aesthetic debate and to show, instead, that it is a product of that same spirit of inquiry *within the arts* that welcomed and developed both 'analytic' perspective and an empiricist vision. The radically foreshortened and elliptical sketches by Constable (and even Degas) can then be used as models for a subsequent photographic practice, which in Galassi's presentation turns out overwhelmingly to be that of topography: Samuel Bourne, Felice Beato, Auguste Salzmann, Charles Marville, and, of course, Timothy O'Sullivan.

And the photographs respond as they are bid. The Bourne of a road in Kashmir, in its steep split in values, empties perspective of its spatial significance and reinvests it with a two-dimensional order every bit as powerfully as does a contemporary Monet. The Salzmann, in its fanatical recording of the texture of stone on a wall that fills the frame with a nearly uniform tonal continuum, assimilates its depiction of empirical detail to a representation of the pictorial infrastructure. And the O'Sullivans, with their rock formations engulfed by that passive, blank, collodion sky, flatten into the same hypnotically seen but two-dimensionally experienced order that characterized the *Tufa Domes* of Pyramid Lake. When viewing the evidence on the walls of the museum, we have no doubt that Art has not only been intended but has also been represented – in the flattened, decoratively unifying drawing of 'analytic' perspective.

But here the demonstration runs into difficulty. For Timothy O'Sullivan's photographs were not published in the nineteenth century and their only public distribution was through the medium of stereography. Most of the famous O'Sullivans – the Canyon de Chelly ruins from the Wheeler Expedition, for example – exist as stereographic views, and it was to these that, in O'Sullivan's case, as in William Henry Jackson's, the wider public had access.[5] Thus, if we began with a comparison between two images – the photograph and the lithographic translation – we can continue with a comparison between two cameras: a 9 × 12 plate camera and a camera for stereoscopic views. These two pieces of equipment mark distinct domains of experience.

Stereographic space is perspectival space raised to a higher power. Organized as a kind of tunnel vision, the experience of deep recession is insistent and inescapable. This experience is heightened by the fact that the viewer's own ambient space is masked out by the optical instrument he must hold before his eyes. As he views the image in an ideal isolation, his own surrounds, with their walls and floors, are banished from sight. The apparatus of the stereoscope mechanically focuses all attention on the matter at hand and precludes the visual meandering experienced in the museum gallery as one's eyes wander from picture to picture and to surrounding space. Instead, the refocusing of attention can occur only within the spectator's channel of vision constructed by the optical machine.

The stereographic image appears multilayered, a steep gradient of different planes stretching away from the nearby space into depth. The operation of viewing this space involves scanning the field of the image, moving from its lower left corner, say, to its upper right. That much is like looking at a painting. But the actual experience of this scan is something wholly different. As one moves, visually, through the stereoscopic tunnel from inspecting the nearest ground to attending to an object in the middle distance, one has the sensation of refocusing one's eyes. And then again, into the farthest plane, another effort is made, and felt, to refocus.[6]

These micromuscular efforts are the kinesthetic counterpart to the sheerly optical illusion of the stereograph. They are a kind of enactment, on a very reduced scale, of what happens when a deep channel of space is opened before one. The actual readjustment of the eyes from plane to plane within the stereoscopic field is the representation by one part of the body of what another part of the body (the feet) would do in passing through real space. From this physio-optical traversal of the stereo field derives another difference between it and pictorial space. This difference concerns the dimension of time.

The contemporary accounts of what it was like to look at stereographs all dilate on the length of time spent examining the contents of the image. For Oliver Wendell Holmes Sr, a passionate advocate of stereography, this perusal was the response appropriate to the 'inexhaustible' wealth of detail provided by the image. As he picks his way over this detail in his writing on stereography – in describing, for example, his experience of an E and H. T. Anthony view up Broadway – Holmes enacts for his readers the protracted engagement with the spectacle demanded by stereo viewing. By contrast, paintings do not require (and as they become more modernist, certainly do not support) this temporal dilation of attention, this minute-by-minute examining of every inch of the ground.

When Holmes characterizes this special modality of viewing, where 'the mind feels its way into the very depths of the picture', he has recourse to extreme mental states, like hypnotism, 'half-magnetic effects', and dream. 'At least the shutting out of surrounding objects, and the concentration of the whole attention which is a consequence of this, produced a dream-like exaltation', he writes, 'in which we seem to leave the body behind us and sail sway into one strange scene after another, like disembodied spirits.'[7]

The phenomenology of the stereoscope produces a situation not unlike that of looking at cinema. Both involve the isolation of the viewer with an image from which surrounding interference is masked out. In both, the image transports the viewer optically, while his body remains immobile. In both, the pleasure derives from the experience of the simulacrum: the appearance of reality from which any testing of the real-effect by actually, physically, moving through the scene is denied. And in both, the real-effect of the simulacrum is heightened by a temporal dilation. What has been called the *apparatus* of cinematic process had, then, a certain protohistory in the institution of stereography, just as stereography's own protohistory is to be found in the similarly darkened and isolating but spectacularly illusionistic space of the diorama.[8] And in the case of the stereograph, as was later the case for film, the specific pleasures that seem to be released by that apparatus – the desires that it seems to gratify – accounted for the instantly wild popularity of the instrument.

The diffusion of stereography as a truly mass medium was made possible by mechanized printing techniques. Beginning in the 1850s but continuing almost unabated into the 1880s, the figures for stereo sales are dizzying. As early as 1857 the London Stereoscopic Company had sold five hundred thousand stereoscopes and in 1859 was able to claim a catalogue listing more than a hundred thousand different stereo views.[9]

It is in this very term – *view* – by which the practice of stereoscopy identified its object, that we can locate the particularity of that experience. First of all, *view* speaks to the dramatic insistence of the perspectivally organized depth I have been describing. This was often heightened, or acknowledged, by the makers of stereo views by structuring the image around a vertical marker in fore- or middle ground that works to *center* space, forming a representation within the visual field of the eyes' convergence at a vanishing point. Many of Timothy O'Sullivan's images organize themselves around such a center – the staff of a bare tree trunk, the sheer edge of a rock formation – whose compositional sense derives from the special sensations of the *view*. Given O'Sullivan's tendency to compose around the diagonal recession and centering of the *view*, it is not surprising to find that in his one published account of his work as a Western photographer he consistently speaks of what he makes as 'views' and what he does when making them as 'viewing'. Writing of the expedition to Pyramid Lake, he describes the provisions, 'among which may be mentioned the instruments and chemicals necessary for our photographer to "work up his view"'. Of the Humboldt Sink, he says, 'It was a pretty location to work in, and viewing there was as pleasant work as could be desired.'[10] *View* was the term consistently used in the photographic journals, as it was overwhelmingly the appellation photographers gave to their entries in photographic salons in the 1860s. Thus, even when consciously entering the space of exhibition, they tended to choose *view* rather than *landscape* as their descriptive category.

Further, *view* addresses a notion of authorship in which the natural phenomenon, the point of interest, rises up to confront the viewer, seemingly without the mediation of an individual recorder or artist, leaving 'authorship' of the views to their publishers rather than to the operators (as they were called) who took the pictures. Thus, authorship is characteristically made a function of publication, with copyright held by the various companies, for example, Keystone Views, while the photographers remain anonymous. In this sense the phenomenological character of the view, its exaggerated depth and focus, opens onto a second feature, which is the isolating of the object of that view. Indeed, it is a 'point of interest', a natural wonder, a singular phenomenon that comes to occupy this centering of attention. This experience of the *singular* is, as Barbara Stafford has shown in an examination of singularity as a special category associated with travel accounts beginning in the late eighteenth century, founded on the transfer of authorship from the subjectivity of the artist to the objective manifestations of nature.[11] For this reason, the institution of the view does not claim the imaginative projection of an author so much as the legal protection of property in the form of the copyright.

Finally, *view* registers this singularity, this focal point, as one moment in a complex representation of the world, a kind of complete topographical atlas. For the physical space within which the 'views' were kept was invariably a cabinet in whose drawers were catalogued and stored a whole geographical system. The file cabinet is a different object from the wall or the easel. It holds out the possibility of storing and cross-referencing bits of information and of collating them through the particular grid of a system of knowledge. The elaborate cabinets of stereo views that were part of the furnishing of nineteenth-century middle-class homes as well as of the equipment of public libraries comprise a compound representation of geographic space. The spatiality of the view, its insistent penetration, functions as the sensory model for a more abstract system whose subject also is space. View and land survey are interdetermined and interrelated.

What emerges from this analysis is a system of historically specific requirements that were satisfied by the view and in relation to which *view* formed a coherent discourse. I hope it is apparent that this discourse is disjunct from what aesthetic discourse intends by the term *landscape*. Just as the view's construction of space cannot be assimilated, phenomenologically, to the compressed and fragmented space of what *Before Photography* calls analytic perspective,[12] so the representation formed by the collectivity of these views cannot be likened to the representation organized by the space of exhibition. The one composes an image of geographic order; the other represents the space of an autonomous Art and its idealized, specialized History, which is constituted by aesthetic discourse. The complex collective representations of that quality called style – period style, personal style – are dependent upon the space of exhibition; one could say they are a function of it. Modern art history is in that sense a product of the most rigorously organized nineteenth-century space of exhibition: the museum.[13]

André Malraux has explained to us how the museum, with its succession of (representations of) styles, collectively organizes the master representation of Art. Having updated themselves through the institution of the modern art book, Malraux's museums are now 'without walls', the galleries' contents collectivized by means of photographic reproduction. But this serves only to intensify the reductiveness of the process:

> Thus it is that, thanks to the rather specious unity imposed by the photographic reproduction on a multiplicity of objects, ranging from the statue to the bas-relief, from bas-reliefs to seal-impressions, and from these to the

plaques of the nomads, a 'Babylonian style' seems to emerge as a real entity, not a mere classification – as something resembling, rather the life-story of a great creator. Nothing conveys more vividly and compellingly the notion of a destiny shaping human ends than do the great styles, whose evolutions and transformations seem like long scars that Fate has left, in passing, on the face of the earth.[14]

Having decided that nineteenth-century photography belongs in a museum, having decided that the genres of aesthetic discourse are applicable to it, having decided that the art-historical model will map nicely onto this material, recent scholars of photography have decided (ahead of time) quite a lot. For one thing, they have concluded that given images are *landscapes* (rather than *views*), and they are thus certain about the discourse these images belong to and what they are representations of. For another (but this conclusion is reached simultaneously with the first), they have determined that other fundamental concepts of aesthetic discourse will be applicable to this visual archive. One of these is the concept *artist*, with its correlative notion of sustained and intentional progress to which we give the term *career*. The other is the possibility of coherence and meaning that will unfold through the collective body of work so produced, this constituting the unity of an *oeuvre*. But, it can be argued, these are terms that nineteenth-century topographic photography not only tends not to support but in fact opens to question.

The concept *artist* implies more than the mere fact of authorship; it suggests that one must go through certain steps to earn the right to claim the condition of being an author, the word *artist* being somehow semantically connected with the notion of vocation. Generally, 'vocation' implies an apprenticeship, a juvenilia, a learning of the tradition of one's craft and the gaining of an individuated view of that tradition through a process that includes both success and failure. If this, or at least some part of it, is what is necessarily included in the term *artist*, can we then imagine someone being an artist for just one year? Would this not be a logical (some would say, grammatical) contradiction, like the example adduced by Stanley Cavell in relation to aesthetic judgements, where he repeats Wittgenstein's question: 'Could someone have a feeling of ardent love or hope for the space of one second – *no matter what* preceded or followed this second?'[15]

But this is the case with Auguste Salzmann, whose career as a photographer began in 1853 and was over in less than a year. Little else on the horizon of nineteenth-century photography appeared only to vanish quite so meteorically. But other major figures within this history enter this métier and then leave it in less than a decade. This is true of Roger Fenton, Gustave LeGray, and Henri LeSecq, all of them acknowledged 'masters' of the art. Some of these desertions involved a return to the more traditional arts, others, like Fenton's, meant taking up a totally different field such as the law. What do the span and nature of these engagements with the medium mean for the concept of *career*? Can we study these 'careers' with the same methodological presuppositions, the same assumptions of personal style and its continuity, that we bring to the careers of another sort of artist?[16]

And what of the other great aesthetic unity: *oeuvre*? Once again we encounter practices that seem difficult to bring into conformity with what the term comprises, with its assumptions that the oeuvre is the result of sustained intention and that it is organically related to the effort of its maker: that it is coherent. One practice already mentioned was the imperious assumption of copyright, so that certain oeuvres, like Matthew Brady's and Francis Frith's, are largely a function of the work of their employees. Another practice, related to the nature of photographic commissions, left large bodies of the oeuvre unachieved. An example is the Heliographic Mission of 1851, in which LeSecq, LeGray, Baldus, Bayard, and Mestral (which is to say some of the greatest figures in early photographic history in France) did survey work for the Commission des Monuments Historiques. Their results, some three hundred negatives recording medieval architecture about to be restored, not only were never published or exhibited by the commission but were never even printed. This is analogous to a director shooting a film but never having the footage developed, hence never seeing the rushes. How would the result fit into the oeuvre of this director?[17]

There are other practices, other exhibits, in the archive that also test the applicability of the concept *oeuvre*. One of these is the body of work that is too meager for this notion; the other is the body that is too large. Can we imagine an oeuvre consisting of one work? The history of photography tries to do this with a single photographic effort produced by Auguste Salzmann, a lone volume of archaeological photographs (of great formal beauty), some portion of which are known to have been taken by his assistant.[18] And, at the opposite extreme, can we imagine an oeuvre consisting of ten thousand works?

Eugène Atget's labors produced a vast body of work, which he sold over the years of its production (roughly 1895 to 1927) to various historical collections, such as the Bibliothèque de la Ville de Paris, the Musée de la Ville de Paris (Musée Carnavalet), the Bibliothèque Nationale, the Monuments Historiques, as well as to commercial builders and artists. The assimilation of this work of documentation into a specifically aesthetic discourse began in 1925 with its notice and publication by the surrealists and was followed, in 1929, by its placement within the photographic sensibility of the German New Vision.[19] Thus began the various partial viewings of the ten-thousand piece archive; each view the result of a selection intended to make a given aesthetic or formal point.

The repetitive rhythm of accumulation that interested the *Neue Sachlichkeit* could be found and illustrated within this material, as could the collage sensibility of the surrealists, who were particularly drawn to the Atget shopfronts, which they made famous. Other selections sustain other interpretations of the material. The frequent visual super-impositions of object and agent, as when Atget captures himself as a reflection in the glazed entrance of the café he is photographing, permit a reading of the work as reflexive, picturing its own conditions of making. Other readings of the images are more architectonically formal. They see Atget managing to locate a point around which the complex spatial trajectories of the site will unfold with an especially clarifying symmetry. Most often images of parks and rural scenes are used for such analyses.

But each of these readings is partial, like tiny core samples that are extracted from a vast geological field, each displaying the presence of a different ore. Or like the blind men's elephant. Ten thousand pieces are a lot to collate. Yet, if Atget's work is to be considered art, and he an artist, this collation must be made; we must acknowledge ourselves to be in the presence of an oeuvre. The Museum of Modern Art's four-part exhibition of Atget, assembled under the already loaded title 'Atget and the Art of Photography', moves briskly toward the solution of this problem, always assuming that the model that will serve to ensure the unity for this archive is the concept of an *artist's oeuvre*. For what else could it be?

John Szarkowski, after recognizing that, from the point of view of formal invention, the work is extremely uneven, speculates on why this should be so:

> There are a number of ways to interpret this apparent incoherence. We could assume that it was Atget's goal to make glorious pictures that would delight and thrill us, and that in this ambition he failed as often as not. Or we could assume that he began photographing as a novice and gradually, through the pedagogical device of work, learned to use his peculiar, recalcitrant medium with economy and sureness, so that his work became better and better as he grew older. Or we could point out that he worked both for others and for himself and that the work he did for himself was better, because it served a more demanding master. Or we could say that it was Atget's goal to explain in visual terms an issue of great richness and complexity – the spirit of his own culture – and that in service to this goal he was willing to accept the results of his own best efforts, even when they did not rise above the role of simple records.
>
> I believe that all of these explanations are in some degree true, but the last is especially interesting to us, since it is so foreign to our understanding of artistic ambition. It is not easy for us to be comfortable with the idea that an artist might work as a servant to an idea larger than he. We have been educated to believe, or rather, to assume, that no value transcends the value of the creative individual. A logical corollary of this assumption is that no subject matter except the artist's own sensibility is quite worthy of his best attention.[20]

This inching forward from the normal categories of description of aesthetic production – formal success/formal failure; apprenticeship/maturity; public commission/personal statement – toward a position that he acknowledges as 'foreign to our understanding of artistic ambition', namely, work 'in the service of an issue larger than self-expression', evidently troubles Szarkowski. Just before breaking off this train of thought he meditates on why Atget revisited sites (sometimes after several years) to choose different aspects of, say, a given building to photograph. Szarkowski's answer resolves itself in terms of formal success/formal failure and the categories of artistic maturation that are consistent with the notion of oeuvre.

His own persistence in thinking about the work in relation to this aesthetic model surfaces in his decision to continue to treat it in terms of stylistic evolution: 'The earlier pictures show the tree as complete and discrete, as an object against a ground; as centrally positioned within the frame; as frontally lighted, from behind the photographer's shoulder. The later pictures show the tree radically cut by the frame, asymetrically positioned, and more obviously inflected by the quality of light that falls upon it.'[21] This is what produces the 'elegiac' mood of some of the late work.

But this whole matter of artistic intention and stylistic evolution must be integrated with the 'idea larger than he' that Atget can be thought to have served. If the ten thousand images form Atget's picture of the larger idea, then that idea can inform us of Atget's aesthetic intentions, for there will be a reciprocal relation between the two, one inside, the other outside the artist.

To get hold, simultaneously, of this larger idea and of Atget's elusive intentions in making this vast archive ('It is difficult', Szarkowski writes, 'to name an important artist of the modern period whose life and intention have been so perfectly withheld from us as those of Eugène Atget'), it was long believed to be necessary to decipher the code provided by Atget's negative numbers. Each of the ten thousand plates is numbered. Yet the numbers are not strictly successive; they do not organize the work chronologically; they sometimes double back on each other.[22]

For researchers into the problem of Atget's oeuvre, the numbers were seen as providing the all-important code to the artist's intentions and the work's meaning. Maria Morris Hambourg has finally and most definitively deciphered this code, to find in it the systematization of a catalogue of topographic subjects, divided into five major series and many smaller sub-series and groups.[23] The names given to the various series and groupings (Landscape-Documents, Picturesque Paris, Environs, Old-France) establish as the master, larger idea for the work a collective picture of the spirit of French culture – similar, we could say, to Balzac's undertaking in the *Comédie Humaine*. In relation to this master subject, Atget's vision can be organized around a set of intentions that are socio-aesthetic, so to speak; he becomes photography's great visual anthropologist. The unifying intention of the oeuvre can be understood as a continuing search for the representation of the moment of interface between nature and culture, as in the juxtaposition of the vines growing beside a farmhouse window curtained in a lace representation of schematized leaves (see figure 13.3). But this analysis, interesting and often brilliant as it is, is once again only partial. The desire to represent the paradigm nature/culture can be traced in only a small fraction of the images and then, like the trail of an elusive animal, it dies out, leaving the intentions as mute and mysterious as ever.

What is interesting in this case is that the Museum of Modern Art and Maria Morris Hambourg hold in their hands the solution to this mystery, a key that will not so much unlock the system of Atget's aesthetic intentions as dispel them. And this example seems all the more informative as it demonstrates the resistance of the museological and art-historical disciplines to using that key.

Figure 13.3

Eugène Atget,
Verrières, *coin*
pittoresque, *1922*
(The Museum of
Modern Art, New
York)

The coding system Atget applied to his images derives from the card files of the libraries and topographic collections for which he worked. His subjects are often standardized, dictated by the established categories of survey and historical documentation. The reason many of Atget's street images uncannily resemble the photographs by Marville taken a half-century earlier is that both are functions of the same documentary master plan.[24] A catalogue is not so much an idea as it is a mathesis, a system of organization. It submits not so much to intellectual as to institutional analysis. And it seems clear that Atget's work is the *function* of a catalogue that he had no hand in inventing and for which *authorship* is an irrelevant term.

The normal conditions of authorship that the museum wishes to maintain tend to collapse under this observation, leading us to a rather startling reflection. The museum undertook to crack the code of Atget's negative numbers in order to discover an aesthetic anima. What they found, instead, was a card catalogue.

Figure 13.4

Eugène Atget,
Sceaux, *coin*
pittoresque, 1922
(The Museum of
Modern Art, New
York)

With this in mind we get different answers to various earlier questions, like the problem of why Atget photographed certain subjects piecemeal, the image of a façade separated by months or even years from the view of the same building's doorway or window mullions or wrought-iron work. The answer, it seems, lies less in the conditions of aesthetic success or failure than in the requirements of the catalogue and its categorical spaces.

Subject is the fulcrum in all of this. Are the doorways and the iron-work balconies Atget's subjects, his choices, the manifest expression of him as active *subject*, thinking, willing, intending, creating? Or are they simply (although there is nothing simple in this) *subjects*, the functions of the catalogue, to which Atget himself is *subject*? What possible price of historical clarity are we willing to pay in order to maintain the former interpretation over the latter?

Everything that has been put forward about the need to abandon or at least to submit to a serious critique the aesthetically derived categories of authorship, oeuvre, and genre (as in *landscape*) obviously amounts to an attempt to maintain early photography as an archive and to call for the sort of archaeological examination of this archive that Michel Foucault both theorizes and provides a model for. Describing the analysis to which archaeology submits the archive in order to reveal the conditions of its discursive formations, Foucault writes:

> [They] must not be understood as a set of determinations imposed from the outside on the thought of individuals, or inhabiting it from the inside, in advance as it were; they constitute rather the set of conditions in accordance with which a practice is exercised, in accordance with which that practice gives rise to partially or totally new statements, and in accordance with which it can be modified. [The relations established by archaeology] are not so much limitations imposed on the initiative of subjects as the field in which the initiative is articulated (without however constituting its center), rules that it puts into operation (without it having invented or formulated them), relations that provide it with a support (without it being either their final result or their point of convergence). [Archaeology] is an attempt to reveal discursive practices in their complexity and density; to show that to speak is to do something – something other than to express what one thinks.[25]

Everywhere at present there is an attempt to dismantle the photographic archive – the set of practices, institutions, and relationships to which nineteenth-century photography originally belonged – and to reassemble it within the categories previously constituted by art and its history.[26] It is not hard to conceive of what the inducements for doing so are, but it is more difficult to understand the tolerance for the kind of incoherence it produces.

Notes

1   Clarence King, *Systematic Geology* (1878) is vol. 1 of *Professional Papers of the Engineer Department US Army*, 7 vols and atlas (Washington, DC, US Government Printing Office, 1877–8).

2   The cartographic grid onto which this information is reconstructed has other purposes besides the collation of scientific information. As Alan Trachtenberg argues, the government-sponsored Western surveys were intended to gain access to the mineral resources needed for industrialization. It was an industrial as well as a scientific program that generated this photography, which 'when viewed outside the context of the reports it accompanied seems to perpetuate the landscape tradition.' Trachtenberg continues: 'The photographs represent an essential aspect of the enterprise, a form of record keeping; they contributed to the federal government's policy of supplying fundamental needs of industrialization, needs for reliable data concerning raw materials, and promoted a public willingness to support government policy of conquest, settlement, and exploitation.' Alan Trachtenberg, *The Incorporation of America* (New York, Hill and Wang, 1982), p. 20.

3   The treatment of Western survey photography as continuous with painterly depictions of nature is everywhere in the literature. Barbara Novak, Weston Naef, and Elisabeth Lindquist-Cock are three specialists who see this work as an extension of the landscape sensibilities operative in American nineteenth-century painting, with transcendentalist fervor constantly conditioning the way nature is seen. Thus, the by-now standard

argument about the King/O'Sullivan collaboration is that this visual material amounts to a proof-by-photography of creationism and the presence of God. King, it is argued, resisted both Lyell's geological uniformitarianism and Darwin's evolutionism. A catastrophist, King read the geological records of the Utah and Nevada landscape as a series of acts of creation in which all species were given their permanent shape by a divine creator. [. . .] There is equal support for the opposite argument: King was a serious scientist, who made great efforts to publish as part of the findings of his survey Marsh's paleontological finds, which he knew full well provided one of the important 'missing links' needed to give empirical support to Darwin's theory. [. . .] See Barbara Novak, *Nature and Culture* (New York, Oxford University Press, 1980); Weston Naef, *Era of Exploration* (New York, Metropolitan Museum of Art, 1975); and Elisabeth Lindquist-Cock, *Influence of Photography on American Landscape Painting* (New York, Garland Press, 1977).

4   Peter Galassi, *Before Photography* (New York, The Museum of Modern Art, 1981), p. 12.

5   See the chapter 'Landscape and the published photograph' in Naef, *Era of Exploration*. In 1871 the Government Printing Office published a catalogue of Jackson's work, *Catalogue of Stereoscopic, 6 × 8 and 8 × 10 Photographs by Wm. H. Jackson*.

6   The eye is not actually refocusing. Rather, given the nearness of the image to the eyes and the fixity of the head in relation to it, in order to scan the space of the image a viewer must readjust and recoordinate the two eyeballs from point to point as vision moves over the surface.

7   Oliver Wendell Holmes, 'Sun-painting and sun-sculpture', *Atlantic Monthly*, 8 (July 1861), pp. 14–15. The discussion of the view of Broadway occurs on p. 17. Holmes's other two essays appeared as 'The stereoscope and the stereograph', *Atlantic Monthly*, 3 (June 1859), pp. 738–48; and 'Doings of the sunbeam', *Atlantic Monthly*, 12 (July 1863), pp. 1–15.

8   See, Jean-Louis Baudry, 'The apparatus', *Camera Obscura*, 1 (1976).

9   Edward W. Earle (ed.) *Points of View. The Stereograph in America: a Cultural History* (Rochester, NY, The Visual Studies Workshop Press, 1979), p. 12. In 1856 Robert Hunt in the *Art Journal* reported, 'The stereoscope is now seen in every drawing-room; philosophers talk learnedly upon it, ladies are delighted with its magic representation, and children play with it', ibid., p. 28.

10 'Photographs from the High Rockies', *Harper's Magazine*, 39 (September 1869), pp. 465–75. In this article, *Tufa Domes, Pyramid Lake* finds yet one more place of publication, in a crude translation of the photograph, this time as an illustration to the author's adventure narrative. Thus one more imaginative space is projected onto the blank, collodion screen. This time, in response to the account of the near capsize of the exploration party's boat, the engraver whips the waters into a darkened frenzy and the sky into banks of lowering storm clouds.

11 [. . .] Barbara M. Stafford, 'Towards romantic landscape perception: illustrated travels and the rise of "singularity" as an aesthetic category', *Art Quarterly*, n.s.1 (1977), pp. 108–9.

12 For another discussion of Galassi's argument with relation to the roots of 'analytic perspective' in seventeenth-century optics and the *camera obscura*, see Svetlana Alpers, *The Art of Describing: Dutch Art in the Seventeenth Century* (Chicago, University of Chicago Press, 1983), pp. 243–44, n. 37.

13 Michel Foucault opens a discussion of the museum in 'Fantasia of the library', in *Language, Counter-Memory, Practice*, trans. D. F. Bouchard and S. Simon (Ithaca, Cornell University Press, 1977), pp. 87–109; see also Douglas Crimp, 'On the museum's ruins', *October*, 13 (summer 1980), pp. 41–57.

14 André Malraux, 'Museum without walls', *The Voices of Silence* (Princeton NJ, Princeton University Press, Bollingen Series 24, 1978), p. 46.

15 Stanley Cavell, *Must We Mean What We Say?* (New York, Scribners, 1969), p. 91, n. 9.

16 Students of photography's history are not encouraged to question whether art-historical models might (or might not) apply. The session on the history of photography at the 1982 College Art Association meeting (a session proudly introduced as

the fruits of real scholarly research at last applied to this formerly unsystematically studied field) was a display of what can go wrong. In the paper 'Charles Marville, popular illustrator: origins of a photographic aesthetic', presented by Constance Kane Hungerford, the model of the necessary internal consistency of an oeuvre encouraged the idea that there had to be a stylistic connection between Marville's early practice as engraver and his later work as a photographer. The characterizations of style this promoted with regard to Marville's photographic work (e.g. sharp contrasts of light and dark, hard, crisp contours) were not only hard to see, consistently, but when these did apply they did not distinguish him in any way from his fellows on the Heliographic Mission. For every 'graphic' Marville, it is possible to find an equally graphic LeSecq.

17   An example of this is the nearly four miles of footage shot by Eisenstein in Mexico for his project *Que Viva Mexico*. Sent to California, where it was developed, this footage was never seen by Eisenstein, who was forced to leave the United States immediately upon his return from Mexico. The footage was then cannibalized by two American editors to compose *Thunder over Mexico* and *Time in the Sun*. Neither of these is supposed to be part of Eisenstein's oeuvre. Only a 'shooting chronology' assembled by Jay Leyda in the Museum of Modern Art now exists. Its status in relation to Eisenstein's oeuvre is obviously peculiar. But given Eisenstein's nearly ten years of film-making experience at the time of the shooting (given also the state of the art of cinema in terms of the body of material that existed by 1930 and the extent to which this had been theorized), it is probable that Eisenstein had a more complete sense, from the script and his working conception of the film, of what he had made as a 'work' – even though he never saw it – than the photographers of the Heliographic Mission could have had of theirs. The history of Eisenstein's project is fully documented in Sergei Eisenstein and Upton Sinclair, *The Making and Unmaking of 'Que Viva Mexico'*, eds. Harry M. Geduld and Ronald Gottesman (Bloomington, Indiana University Press, 1970).

18   See Abigail Solomon-Godeau, 'A photographer in Jerusalem, 1955: Auguste Salzmann and his times', *October*, 18 (fall 1981), p. 95. This essay raises some of the issues about the problematic nature of Salzmann's work considered as *oeuvre*.

19   Man Ray arranged for publication of four photographs by Atget in *La Révolution Surréaliste*, three in the June 1926 issue and one in the December 1926 issue. The exhibition 'Film und Foto' (Stuttgart, 1929) included Atget, whose work was also reproduced in *Foto-Auge* (Stuttgart, Wedekind Verlag, 1929).

20   Maria Morris Hambourg and John Szarkowski, *The Work of Atget: Volume 1, Old France* (New York, The Museum of Modern Art; Boston, New York Graphic Society, 1981), pp. 18–19.

21   ibid., p. 21.

22   The first published discussion of this problem characterizes it as follows: 'Atget's numbering system is puzzling. His pictures are not numbered in a simple serial system, but in a confusing manner. In many cases, low-numbered photographs are dated later than high-numbered photographs, and in many cases numbers are duplicated.' See Barbara Michaels, 'An introduction to the dating and organization of Eugène Atget's photographs', *The Art Bulletin*, 41 (September 1979), p. 461.

23   Maria Morris Hambourg, 'Eugène Atget, 1857–1927: the structure of the work', unpublished PhD dissertation, Columbia University, 1980.

24   See *Charles Marville: Photographs of Paris 1852–1878* (New York, The French Institute/Alliance Française, 1981). This contains an essay, 'Charles Marville's old Paris', by Maria Morris Hambourg.

25   Michel Foucault, *The Archaeology of Knowledge*, trans. A, M. Sheridan Smith (New York, Harper and Row, 1976), pp. 208–9.

26   Thus far the work of Allan Sekula has been the one consistent analysis of the history of photography to attack this effort. See Allan Sekula, 'The traffic in photographs', *Art Journal*, 41 (spring 1981), pp. 15–25; and 'The instrumental image: Steichen at war', *Artforum*, 13 (December 1975) [both reprinted in Allan Sekula, *Photography against the Grain*, Halifax, Nova Scotia Press, 1989].

D

Institutions and practices in photography

14

The museum's old, the library's new subject
Douglas Crimp

All the arts are based on the presence of man, only photography derives an advantage from his absence.

(André Bazin, *The Ontology of the Photographic Image*)

This chapter is taken from Douglas Crimp, *On the Museum's Ruins* (Cambridge, MA, MIT Press, 1993), pp. 66–81.

For the fiftieth anniversary of the Museum of Modern Art (MOMA), William S. Lieberman, sole survivor of the museum's founding regime associated with the directorship of Alfred Barr, mounted the exhibition 'Art of the Twenties'. The exhibition's focus was presumably chosen not only to celebrate the decade in which MOMA was born but also because it would necessarily draw on every department of the museum: Film, Photography, Architecture and Design, Drawings, Prints and Illustrated Books, as well as Painting and Sculpture. Indeed, a major impression left by the show was that aesthetic activity in the 1920s was wholly dispersed across the various mediums, that painting and sculpture exercised no hegemony at all. The arts clearly on the ascendant, not only in Paris but more tellingly in Berlin and Moscow, were photography and film, agitprop posters, and other functionally designed objects. With only a few exceptions – Miró, Mondrian, Brancusi – painting and sculpture appear to have been very nearly usurped. Duchamp's *Large Glass* – not, of course, included in the exhibition – may well be the decade's most significant work, and one is hard pressed to define its medium in relation to traditional categories.

'Art in the Twenties' was all the more interesting and appropriate for the museum's anniversary year, coming as it did at the end of another decade in which painting and sculpture had been displaced by other aesthetic options. And yet, if it is possible to assess the 1970s as a time of traditional painting and sculpture's demise, it is equally possible to see it as the decade of an extraordinary resurgence of those modes, just as the 1920s can alternatively be understood as a time of extreme conservative backlash in the arts – when, for example, after the radical achievement of analytic cubism, Picasso returned to traditional representation in his so-called neo-classical period.[1] That radical moves should be accompanied by or cause reaction is not surprising, but the degree to which such reaction is currently embraced, even to the extent of obscuring radical departures, is alarming.

In MOMA's annual report for its jubilee year, the museum's president and director gave less attention to 'Art of the Twenties' than to two of the year's other major events, both of which helped create the first substantial operating surplus in the museum's history. These were the sale, after many legal and public-relations difficulties, of the museum's 'air rights' to a real estate developer for $17,000,000 as the most crucial aspect of the museum's expansion program; and the biggest blockbuster the museum had ever staged, 'Pablo Picasso: A Retrospective', which boasted nearly a thousand artworks and over a million visitors. One other celebratory event was singled out by the museum's top officials as being of particular importance: the exhibition of photographs by Ansel Adams, one of the founding fathers of MOMA's Department of Photography – the first such department in any art museum, as they proudly point out.[2]

The big real estate deal, the blockbuster retrospective of the twentieth century's leading candidate for the title 'artistic genius', the fêting of the best-selling living photographer (a print of Adams's *Moonrise, Hernandez, New Mexico* recently sold for $22,000)[3] – the significance of the conjunction of these events can hardly be lost on anyone forced to cope with the social realities of the current New York art world.[4] In comparison, the importance of 'Art of the Twenties' begins to pale; perhaps the exhibition must after all be seen merely as the swan song of the museum's first era and its curator, who subsequently moved to the Metropolitan Museum.

The notion of art as bound by and deeply engaged in its particular historical moment, as radically departing from the age-old conventions of painting and sculpture, as embracing new technologies for its production – all of this could apparently be swept aside by a notion of art as bound only by the limitations of individual human creativity. Modern art could now be understood as art had seemingly always been understood, as embodied in the masterpieces invented by the master artist: *Picasso* – the man's signature adorned the T-shirts of thousands on the streets of New York that summer, evidence, one supposes, that they had attended the spectacle and were proud to have thus paid homage to a man of genius. But these T-shirt-clad museum goers were themselves part of another spectacle, the spectacle of response. The myths, the clichés, the platitudes, the *idées reçues* about artistic genius – appropriately signified by this *signature* – were never so resoundingly reaffirmed, not only by the mass media, from whom it was to have been expected, but by the museum itself, by curators, dealers, critics, and by artists. The very suggestion that there might be something suspicious, perhaps regressive, about this response was dismissed as misanthropic nay-saying.

A short five year earlier, in a text on contemporary art intended for art-school audiences, I had written that Duchamp had replaced Picasso as the early twentieth-century artist most relevant to contemporary practice.[5] Now, it seems, I'd have to eat those words. In a special 'Picasso Symposium' devoted to responses to the MOMA retrospective, *Art in America* asked various art-world personalities to give their views. Here is that of the recently successful painter Elizabeth Murray: 'Picasso is the avant-garde artist of our time . . . He truly says you can do anything.'[6] Her fellow painter, the former critic Bruce Boice, elaborates on the same point:

> Picasso seems to have had no fear. He just did whatever he wanted to do, and obviously there was a lot he wanted to do . . . For me to speak about what I find so astounding about Picasso is to speak of what is most fundamental to being a painter. Being a painter should be the easiest thing in the world because there are and can be no rules. All you have to do is do whatever you want to do. You can just, and you must, make everything up.[7]

This, then, is the lesson of Picasso. There are no constraints, whether these are construed as conventions, languages, discourses, ideologies, institutions, histories. There is only freedom, the freedom to invent at will, to do whatever you want. Picasso is the avant-garde artist of *our* time because, after so much tedious discussion about history and ideology, about the death of the author, he provides the exhilarating revelation that we are free after all.

This creative freedom fantasized by contemporary artists and confirmed for them by the spectacle of a thousand Picasso inventions is seconded by art historians. A typical response is that of John Richardson, writing in the favored organ of the US literary establishment, the *New York Review of Books*.[8] Calling Picasso 'the most prodigious and versatile artist of all time', Richardson rehearses the biography of artistic genius from its beginnings in the transcendence of the mere child prodigy by 'an energy and a sensibility that are astonishingly mature' through the 'stylistic changes that revolutionized the course of twentieth century art' to the 'poignant' late works, with their 'mixture of self-mockery and megalomania'. Richardson's assessment is perhaps uncharacteristic in only one respect. He claims that 'up to the day of Picasso's death in 1973 the power was never switched off.'

Absolutely characteristic, though, is Richardson's view that Picasso's is a subjective art, that 'the facts of his life have more bearing on Picasso's art than is the case with any other great artist, except perhaps van Gogh.' And so that we don't miss the meaning of any of these great works, Richardson insists that 'every crumb of information should be gathered while there is time. In no other great life are the minutiae of gossip so potentially significant.'[9]

It is, then, as if Duchamp's readymades had never been conceived, as if modernism's most radical developments, including Picasso's own cubist collage, had never taken place, or at least as if their implications could be overlooked and the old myths of art fully revivified. The dead author has been reborn; *he* has returned with his full subjective power restored – as the contemporary artist puts it – to make it all up, to do whatever he wants. Duchamp's readymades had, of course, embodied the proposition that the artist invents nothing, that he or she only uses, manipulates, displaces, reformulates, repositions what history has provided. This is not to divest the artist of the power to intervene in, to alter or expand, discourse, only to dispense with the fiction that that power arises from an autonomous self existing outside history and ideology. The readymades propose that the artist cannot *make*, but can only *take* what is already there.

It is precisely on this distinction – the distinction between making and taking – that the ontological difference between painting and photography is said to rest. The director of MOMA's Department of Photography, John Szarkowski, states it simply enough: 'The invention of photography provided a radically new picture-making process – a process based not on synthesis but on selection. The difference was a basic one. Paintings were *made* . . . but photographs, as the man on the street puts it, were *taken*.'[10] But MOMA's jubilee photographer, Ansel Adams, is uncomfortable with this predatory view of photography. How could the artist Adams wants to call a 'photopoet' be a common thief?

> The common term '*taking* a picture' is more than just an idiom; it is a symbol of exploitation. '*Making* a picture' implies a creative resonance which is essential to profound expression.
>
> My approach to photography is based on my belief in the vigor and values of the world of nature – in the aspects of grandeur and of the minutiae all about us. I believe in growing things, and in the things which have grown and died magnificently. I believe in people and in the simple aspects of human life, and in the relation of man to nature. I believe man must be free, both in spirit and in society, that he must build strength into himself, affirming the 'enormous beauty of the world' and acquiring the confidence to see and to express his vision. And I believe in photography as one means of expressing this affirmation, and of achieving an ultimate happiness and faith.[11]

There is really less contradiction of Szarkowski's position in Adams's Sierra Club humanism, however, than there appears to be. For in both cases there is ultimately a matter of faith in the medium to act as just that, a *medium* of the artist's subjectivity. So, for example, Adams writes,

> A great photograph is a full expression of what one feels about what is being photographed in the deepest sense, and is, thereby, a true expression of what one feels about life in its entirety. And the expression of what one feels should be set forth in terms of simple devotion to the medium – a statement of utmost clarity and perfection possible under the conditions of creation and production.[12]

Compare Szarkowski:

> An artist is a man who seeks new structures in which to order and simplify his sense of the reality of life. For the artist photographer, much of his sense of reality (where the picture starts) and much of his sense of craft or structure (where the picture is completed) are anonymous and untraceable gifts from photography itself.[13]

By construing photography ontologically, as a medium of subjectivity, Adams and Szarkowski contrive a fundamentally modernist position for it, duplicating in nearly every respect theories of modernist autonomy articulated earlier in this century for painting. In so doing, they ignore the plurality of discourses in which photography has participated. Everything that has determined its multiple practice is set aside in favor of *photography itself*. Thus reorganized, photography is readied to be funneled through a new market, ultimately to be housed in the museum.

Several years ago, Julia van Haaften, a librarian in the Art and Architecture Division of the New York Public Library, became interested in photography. As she studied what was then known about this vast subject, she discovered that the library itself owned many books containing vintage photographic prints, especially from the nineteenth century, and she hit on the idea of organizing an exhibition of this material culled from the library's collections. She gathered books illustrated with photographs from throughout the library's many different divisions, books about archeology in the Holy Lands and Central America, about ruined castles in England and Islamic ornament in Spain; illustrated newspapers of Paris and London; books of ethnography and geology; technical and medical manuals.[14] In preparing this exhibition the library realized for the first time that it owned an extraordinarily large and valuable collection of photographs – for the first time, because no one had previously inventoried these materials under the single category of photography. Until then, the photographs had been so thoroughly dispersed throughout the library's extensive resources that it was only through patient research that van Haaften was able to track them down. And furthermore, it was only at the time she installed her exhibition that photography's prices were beginning to sky-rocket. So although books with original plates by Maxime Du Camp or Francis Frith might now be worth a small fortune, ten or fifteen years ago they weren't even worth enough to merit placing them in the library's Rare Books Division.

Julia van Haaften now has a new job. She is director of the New York Public Library's Photographic Collections Documentation Project, an interim step on the way to the creation of a new division to be called Art, Prints, and Photographs, which will consolidate the old Art and Architecture Division with the Prints Division, adding to them photographic materials culled from all other library departments.[15] These materials are thus to be reclassified according to their newly acquired value, the value that is now attached to the 'artists' who made the photographs. Thus, what was once housed in the Jewish Division under the classification 'Jerusalem' will eventually be found in Art, Prints, and Photographs under the classification 'Auguste Salzmann'. What was Egypt will become Beato, or Du Camp, or Frith; Pre-Columbian Middle America will be Désiré Charnay; the American Civil War, Alexander Gardner and Timothy O'Sullivan; the cathedrals of France will be Henri LeSecq; the Swiss Alps, the Bisson Frères; the horse in motion is now Muybridge; the flight of birds, Marey; and the expression of emotions forgets Darwin to become Guillaume Duchenne de Boulogne.

What Julia van Haaften is doing at the New York Public Library is just one example of what is occurring throughout our culture on a massive scale. And thus the list goes on, as urban poverty becomes Jacob Riis and Lewis Hine, portraits *of* Delacroix and Manet become portraits *by* Nadar and Carjat, Dior's New Look becomes Irving Penn, and World War II becomes Robert Capa. For if photography was invented in 1839, it was only *discovered* in the 1960s and 1970s – photography, that is, as an essence, photography *itself*. Szarkowski can again be counted on to put it simply:

> The pictures reproduced in this book [*The Photographer's Eye*] were made over almost a century and a quarter. They were made for various reasons, by men of different concerns and varying talent. They have in fact little in common except their success, and a shared vocabulary: these pictures are unmistakably photographs. The vision they share belongs to no school or aesthetic theory, but to photography itself.[16]

It is in this text that Szarkowski attempts to specify the particulars of 'photographic vision', to define those things that are specific to photography and to no other medium. In other words, Szarkowski's ontology of photography makes photography a *modernist* medium in Clement Greenberg's sense of the term – an art form that can distinguish itself in its essential qualities from all other art forms. And it is according to this view that photography is now being redefined and redistributed. Photography will hereafter be found in departments of photography or divisions of art and photography. Thus ghettoized, it will no longer primarily be *useful* within other discursive practices; it will no longer serve the purposes of information, documentation, evidence, illustration, reportage. The formerly plural field of photography will henceforth be reduced to the single, all-encompassing *aesthetic*. Just as paintings and sculptures acquired a new-found autonomy, relieved of their earlier functions, when they were wrested from the churches and palaces of Europe and consigned to museums in the late eighteenth and early nineteenth centuries, so now photography acquires *its* autonomy as it too enters the museum. But we must recognize that in order for this new aesthetic understanding to occur, other ways of understanding photography must be dismantled and destroyed. Books about Egypt will literally be torn apart in order that photographs by Francis Frith may be framed and placed on the walls of museums. Once there, photographs will never look the same. Whereas we may formerly have looked at Cartier-Bresson's photographs for the information they conveyed about the revolution in China or the Civil War in Spain, we will now look at them for what they tell us about the artist's style of expression.

This consolidation of photography's formerly multiple practices, this formation of a new epistemological construct in order that we may now *see* photography, is only part of a much more complex redistribution of knowledge taking place throughout our culture. This redistribution is associated with the term *postmodernism*, although most people who employ the word have very little idea what, exactly, they're naming or why they even need a new descriptive category. In spite of the currency of its use, *postmodernism* has thus far acquired no agreed-upon meaning at all. For the most part, it is used in only a negative sense, to say that modernism is over. And where it is used in a positive sense, it is used as a catch-all, to characterize anything and everything that is happening in the present. So, for example, Douglas Davis, who uses the term very loosely, and relentlessly, says of it,

> 'Post-modern' is a negative term, failing to name a 'positive' replacement, but this permits pluralism to flourish (in a word, it permits *freedom*, even in the marketplace) . . . 'Post-modern' has a reactionary taint – because 'Modern' has come to be acquainted with 'now' – but the 'Tradition of the New' requires a strong counter-revolution, not one more forward move.[17]

Indeed, counter-revolution, pluralism, the fantasy of artistic freedom – all of these are, for many, synonymous with postmodernism. And they are right to the extent that in conjunction with the end of modernism all kinds of regressive symptoms are appearing. But rather than characterizing these symptoms as postmodernist, I think we should see them as the forms of a retrenched, a petrified, reductive modernism. They are, I think, the morbid symptoms of modernism's demise.

Photography's entrance into the museum on a vast scale, its re-evaluation according to the epistemology of modernism, its new status as an autonomous art – that is what I mean by the symptoms of modernism's demise. For photography is not autonomous, and it is not, in the modernist sense, an art. When modernism was a fully operative paradigm of artistic practice, photography was necessarily seen as too contingent – too constrained by the world that was photographed, too dependent upon the discursive structures in which it was embedded – to achieve the self-reflexive, entirely conventionalized form of modernist art. This is not to say that no photograph could ever be a modernist artwork; the photographs in MOMA's 'Art of the Twenties' show were ample proof that certain photographs could be as self-consciously about photographic language as any modernist painting was about painting's particular conventions. That is why MOMA's photography department was established in the first place. Szarkowski is the inheritor of a department that reflected the modernist aesthetic of Alfred Stieglitz and his followers. But it has taken Szarkowski and *his* followers to bestow retrospectively upon *photography itself* what Stieglitz had thought was achieved by only a very few photographs.[18] For photography to be understood and reorganized in such a way

entails a drastic revision of the paradigm of modernism, and it can happen only because that paradigm has indeed become dysfunctional. Postmodernism may be said to be founded in part on this paradox: it is photography's re-evaluation as a modernist medium that signals the end of modernism. Postmodernism begins when photography comes to pervert modernism.

If this entry of photography into the museum and the library's art division is one means of photography's perversion of modernism – the negative one – then there is another form of that perversion that may be seen as positive, in that it establishes a wholly new and radicalized artistic practice that truly deserves to be called postmodernist. For at a certain moment photography enters the practice of art in such a way that it contaminates the purity of modernism's separate categories, the categories of painting and sculpture. These categories are subsequently divested of their fictive autonomy, their idealism, and thus their power. The first positive instances of this contamination occurred in the early 1960s, when Robert Rauschenberg and Andy Warhol began to silkscreen photographic images onto their canvases. From that moment forward, the guarded autonomy of modernist art was under constant threat from the incursions of the real world that photography readmitted to the purview of art. After over a century of art's imprisonment in the discourse of modernism and the institution of the museum, hermetically sealed off from the rest of culture and society, the art of postmodernism begins to make inroads back into the world. It is photography, in part, that makes this possible, while still guaranteeing against the compromising atavism of traditional realism.

Another story about the library will perhaps illustrate my point: I was once hired to do picture research for an industrial film about the history of transportation, a film that was to be made largely by shooting footage of still photographs; it was my job to find appropriate photographs. Browsing

MOBIL, WILLIAMS

through the stacks of the New York Public Library where books on the general subject of transportation were shelved, I came across the book by Ed Ruscha entitled *Twentysix Gasoline Stations*, first published in 1963 and consisting of photographs of just that: twenty-six gasoline stations (see figures 14.1 and 14.2). I remember thinking how funny it was that the book had been miscatalogued and placed alongside books about automobiles, highways, and so forth. I knew, as the librarians evidently did not, that Ruscha's book was a work of art and therefore belonged in the art division. But now, because of the reconfigurations brought about by postmodernism, I've changed my mind; I now know that Ed Ruscha's books make no sense in relation to the categories of art according to which art books are catalogued in the library, and that that is part of their achievement. The fact that there is nowhere for *Twentysix Gasoline Stations* within the present system of classification is an index of the book's radicalism with respect to established modes of thought.

The problem with the view of postmodernism that refuses to theorize it and thereby confuses it with pluralism is that this view lumps together under the same rubric the symptoms of modernism's demise with what has positively replaced modernism. Such a view has it that the paintings of Elizabeth Murray and Bruce Boice – clearly academic extensions of a petrified modernism – are as much manifestations of postmodernism as Ed Ruscha's books, which are just as clearly replacements of that modernism. For Ruscha's photographic books have escaped the categories through which modernism is understood just as they have escaped the art museum, which arose simultaneously with modernism and came to be its inevitable resting place. Such a pluralist view of postmodernism would be like saying of modernism at its founding moment that it was signaled by both Manet *and* Gérôme (and it is surely another symptom of modernism's demise that revisionist art historians are saying just that), or, better yet, that modernism is both Manet and Disdéri, that hack entrepreneur who made a fortune peddling photographic visiting cards, who is credited with the first extensive commercialization of photography, and whose utterly uninteresting photographs hang, as I write this essay, in the Metropolitan Museum of Art in an exhibition whose title is 'After Daguerre: Masterworks from the Bibliothèque Nationale'.

Notes

1   For a detailed discussion of this between-the-wars reaction in relation to the recent return to representational painting, see Benjamin H. D. Buchloh, 'Figures of authority, ciphers of regression', *October*, 16 (spring 1981), pp. 39–68.

2   *Museum of Modern Art Annual Report 1979–80* (New York, Museum of Modern Art, 1980).

3   As this essay originally went to press in the spring of 1981, a mural-size print of *Moonrise* was sold for over $70,000. Ansel Adams died in 1984.

4   For an important discussion of the relations between real estate development and the art world, see Rosalyn Deutsche and Cara Gendel Ryan, 'The fine art of gentrification', *October*, 31 (winter 1984), pp. 91–111.

5   Douglas Crimp, *Introduction to 1970s Art* (New York, Art Information Distribution, 1975).

6   Lawrence Alloway et al., 'Picasso: a symposium', *Art in America*, 68, 10 (December 1980), p. 19.

7   Ibid., p. 17.

8   John Richardson, 'Your show of shows', *New York Review of Books*, 27, 12 (17 July, 1980), pp. 16–24.

9   For a critique of the prevailing view of Picasso's art as autobiography, see Rosalind Krauss, 'In the name of Picasso', *October*, 16 (spring 1981), pp. 5–22.

10 John Szarkowski, 'Introduction to *The Photographer's Eye*' (1966), in Peninah R. Petruck (ed.), *The Camera Viewed: Writings on Twentieth-Century Photography*, vol. 2 (New York, E. P. Dutton, 1979), p. 203.

11 Ansel Adams, 'A personal credo', *American Annual of Photography*, 58 (1948), p. 16.

12 Ibid., p. 13.

13 Szarkowski, 'Introduction', pp. 211–12.

14 See Julia van Haaften, '"Original sun pictures": a check list of the New York Public Library's holdings of early works illustrated with photographs, 1844–1900', *Bulletin of the New York Public Library*, 80, 3 (spring 1977), pp. 355–415.

15 See Anne M. McGrath, 'Photographic treasures at the NYPL', *AB Bookmans Weekly*, 25 January (1982), pp. 550–60. As of 1982, the photography collection, of which Julia van Haaften is the *curator*, was integrated into what is now called the Miriam and Ira D. Wallach Division of Art, Prints, and Photographs.

16 Szarkowski, 'Introduction', p. 206.

17   Douglas Davis, 'Post-everything', *Art in America*, 68, 2 (February 1980), p. 14. Davis's notion of freedom, like that of Picasso's fans, is the thoroughly mythological one that recognizes no social differences determined by class, ethnicity, race, gender, or sexuality. It is therefore highly telling that when Davis thinks of freedom, the first thing that springs to his mind is 'the marketplace'. Indeed, his notion of freedom appears to be the Reagan-era version of it – as in 'free' enterprise.

18   For a history of MOMA's Department of Photography, see Christopher Phillips, 'The judgment seat of photography', *October*, 22 (fall 1982), pp. 27–63.

15

Living with contradictions:
critical practices in the age of supply-side aesthetics
Abigail Solomon-Godeau

It should have become abundantly clear in recent years that the function of criticism, for the most part, is to serve as a more or less sophisticated public relations or promotional apparatus. This is less a function of the critic's active partisanship (Diderot and Baudelaire, for example, are historically associated with the artists Greuze and Guys, whom they championed as exemplars) than a consequence of the fact that most contemporary art criticism is innocent of its own politics, its own interests, and its own ideology. In fact, the promotional aspect of most art criticism derives from the larger institutional and discursive structures of art. In this respect, the scholarly monograph, the temporary exhibition, the discipline of art history, and last but not least, the museum itself, are essentially celebratory entities. Further – and at the risk of stating the obvious – the institutions and discourses that collectively function to construct the object 'art' are allied to the material determinations of the marketplace, which themselves establish and confirm the commodity status of the work of art.

Within this system, the art critic normally functions as a kind of intermediary between the frenzied pluralism of the marketplace and the sacralized judgment seat that is the museum. Recently, however, even this mediating process has been bypassed; artists such as Julian Schnabel, to take one particularly egregious example, have been propelled from obscurity to the pantheon without a single serious critical text ever having been produced in support of their work. The quantum increase in the scale of the international art market, the unprecedented importance of dealers in creating (or 'managing') reputations and manipulating supply and demand, the emergence of a new class of 'art consultants', and the large-scale entry of corporations into the contemporary art market have all contributed to the effective redundancy of art criticism. Art stars and even 'movements', with waiting lists of eager purchasers in their train, stepped into the

This chapter is taken from *Screen*, vol. 28, no. 3 (1987), pp. 2–23.

spotlight before many art critics knew of their existence.[1] This redundancy of criticism, however, can hardly be understood as a consequence of these developments alone. Rather, the current state of most art criticism represents the final dissolution of what was, in any case, only a fragile bulwark between market forces and their institutional ratification, a highly permeable membrane separating venture capital, so to speak, from blue-chip investment. As a result, art criticism has been forced to cede its illusory belief in the separateness or disinterestedness of critical discourse.

In this essay I am primarily concerned with the condition – and position – of critical practices within art criticism and artmaking in the age of Reagan. In contradistinction to business-as-usual art promotion and the atavistic, cynical, and mindless art production exemplified by pseudoexpressionism, critical practices, by definition, must occupy an oppositional place. But what, we must ask, is that place today? Within the map of the New York art world, where is that place of opposition and what is it in opposition to? Second – and integrally linked to the first set of questions – we must ask what defines a critical practice and permits it to be recognized as such. What, if anything, constitutes the difference between a critical practice and a recognizably political one? If artists as distinct as, for example, David Salle and Sherrie Levine, can both say that their work contributes to a critique of the painterly sign, what common political meanings, if any, ought we attribute to the notion of critical practice? Last – and here is where I am most directly implicated – what is the nature, the terms, even the possibility, of a critical practice in art criticism? Is such a practice not inevitably and inescapably a part of the cultural apparatus it seeks to challenge and contest?

> When I think of it now, I don't think what Julian Schnabel was doing was all that different from what I was trying to do.
>
> Sherrie Levine, *Artnews* (May 1986)

By way of exploring these questions, and in the interest of providing some specificity to the discussion, I want to concentrate primarily on the evolution and development of postmodernist photographic work from the late 1970s to the present, using it as a case history in which to explore the salient issues. This corpus of work, identified with its now fully familiar strategies of appropriation and pastiche, its systematic assault on modernist orthodoxies of immanence, autonomy, presence, originality, and authorship, its engagement with the simulacral, and its interrogation of the problematics of photographic mass media representation may be taken as paradigmatic of the concerns of a critical postmodernism or what Hal Foster has designated as 'oppositional postmodernism'.[2] The qualifier 'critical' is important here, inasmuch as the conceptualization and description of postmodernism in architecture – chronologically anterior – were inflected rather differently.[3] There, it signaled, among other things, a new historicism and/or repudiation of modernist architecture's social and utopian aspirations, and a concomitant theatricalization of architectural form and meaning. In literary studies, the term 'postmodernism' had yet another valency and made its appearance in literary criticism at an even earlier date. Within the visual arts, however, postmodernist photography was identified with a specifically critical stance. Critics such as Benjamin Buchloh, Douglas Crimp, Rosalind Krauss, et al. theorized this aspect of postmodernist photographic work as principally residing in its dismantling of reified, idealist conceptions enshrined in modernist aesthetics – issues devolving on presence, subjectivity, and aura. To the extent that this work was supported and valorized for its subversive potential (particularly with respect to its apparent fulfillment of the Barthesian and Foucauldian prescriptions for the death of the author and, by extension, its subversion of the commodity status of the art object), Sherrie Levine and Richard Prince were perhaps *the* emblematic figures. For myself, as a photography critic writing in opposition to the academicized mausoleum of late-modernist art photography, part of the interest in the work of Vikky Alexander, Victor Burgin, Sarah Charlesworth, Silvia Kolbowski, Barbara Kruger, Louise Lawler, Sherrie Levine, Richard Prince, Cindy Sherman, Laurie Simmons, and Jim Welling (to cite only those I have written about) lay in the way their work directly challenged the pieties and properties with which art photography had carved a space for itself precisely *as* a modernist art form.[4] Further, the feminist import of this work – particularly in the case of Kruger and Levine – represented a theoretically more sophisticated and necessary departure from the essentialism and literalism prevalent in many of the feminist art practices that emerged in the seventies.

In retrospect, Levine's production of the late seventies to the present reveals both the strength and weakness of this variant of critical post-modernism as a counterstrategy to the regnant forms of art production and discourse. The changes in her practice, and the shifts in the way her work has been discursively positioned and received, are themselves testimony to the difficulty and contradiction that attend critical practices that operate squarely within the institutional framework of high-art production.

Levine's work first drew critical notice in the late 1970s, a period in which the triumph of the Right was as much manifest in the cultural sphere as in the political one. As one might well have predicted for a time of intense political reaction, these symptoms of morbidity included the wholesale resurrection of easel painting exemplified by German, Italian, and American pseudoexpressionism, a wholesale retrenchment against the modest gains of minority and feminist artists, a repression (or distortion) of the radical art practices of the preceding decade, a ghastly revival of the mythology of the heroicized (white male) artist, and last, the institutional consolidation and triumphant legitimation of photography as a fully 'auratic', subjectivized, autonomous, fine art.[5]

Against this backdrop, one aspect of Levine's work consisted of directly rephotographing from existing reproductions a series of photographs by several canonized masters of photographic modernism (Edward Weston's nude studies of his son Neil, Eliot Porter's technicolor landscapes, Walker Evans's F.S.A. pictures) and presenting the work as

her own (see figure 15.1). With a dazzling economy of means, Levine's pictures upset the foundation stones (authorship, originality, subjective expression) on which the integrity, value, and supposed autonomy of the work of art are presumed to rest. Moreover, her selection of stolen images was anything but arbitrary; always the work of canonized male photographers, the contents and codes of these purloined images were chosen for their ideological density (the classical nude, the beauty of nature, the poor of the Great Depression) and then subjected to a demystifying scrutiny enabled and mobilized by the very act of (re)placing them within quotation marks. Finally, the strategy of fine-art-photography appropriations had a tactical dimension. For these works were produced in the wake of the so-called photography boom – meaning not simply the cresting of the market for photographic vintage prints, but the wholesale reclassification of all kinds of photography to conform with notions of individual style and authorial presence derived from nineteenth-century connoisseurship.

It goes without saying that Levine's work of this period, considered *as* a critical practice (feminist, deconstructive, and literally transgressive – the Weston and Porter works prompted ominous letters from their estate lawyers), could make its critique visible only within the compass of the art world; the space of exhibition, the market system, art (or photography) theory and criticism. Outside of this specialized site, a Sherrie Levine could just as well be a 'genuine' Edward Weston or a 'genuine' Walker Evans. This, in fact, was one of the arguments made from the Left with the intention of countering the claims for the critical function of work such as Levine's and Prince's (Prince at that period was rephotographing advertising images, excising only the text). The force of this criticism hinged on the work's insularity, its adherence to, or lack of contestation of, the art-world frame, and – more pointedly – its failure to articulate an alternative politics or vision.

In 1982, for example, Martha Rosler wrote an article entitled 'Notes on Quotes' focusing on the inadequacies of appropriation and quotation as a properly *political* strategy:

> What alternative vision is suggested by such work? [She is referring here specifically to Levine.] We are not provided the space within the work to understand how things might be different. We can imagine only a respite outside social life – the alternative is merely Edenic or Utopic. There *is* no social life, no personal relations, no groups, classes, nationalities; there is no production other than the production of images. Yet a critique of ideology necessitates some materialistic grounding if it is to rise above the theological.[6]

Rosler's use of the term 'theological' in this context points to one of the central debates in and around the definition – or evaluation – of critical practice. For Rosler, failure to ground the artwork in 'direct social analysis' reduces its critical gesture to one of 'highlighting' rather than 'engaging with political questions that challenge . . . power relations in society'. Moreover, to the extent that the artwork 'remains locked within the relations of production of its own cultural field', and limited to the terms of a generic rather than specific interrogation of forms of domination, it cannot fulfill an educative, much less transformatory, function.

But 'theological' in its opprobrious sense can cut both ways. It is, in fact, a 'theological' notion of the political – or perhaps one should say a scriptural notion – that has until quite recently effectively occluded issues of gender and subjectivity from the purview of the political. Rosler's objections are to some degree moored in a relatively traditional conception of what constitutes the political in art ('materialistic grounding', 'direct social analysis'). Thus, Rosler's characterization of a purely internal critique of art as ineffective because theological can, from a somewhat different vantage point, be interpreted as a theologized notion of the political. It is, moreover, important to point out that while unambiguously political artists (unambiguous because of their choice of content) are rarely found wanting for their total exclusion of considerations of gender, feminist artists are frequently chastised by Left critics for the inadequacy of *their* political content. Nevertheless, the echoing cry of the women's movement – the personal is political – is but one of the remappings of political terrain that have engendered new ways of thinking the political and new ways of inscribing it in cultural production.

But perhaps even more important, to the extent that art is itself a discursive and institutional site, it surely entails its own critical practices. This has in fact been recently argued as the significance and legacy of the historical avant-garde.[7] For Peter Bürger, the Kantian conception of self-criticism is understood not in Greenberg's sense of a *telos* of purity and essence, but rather as a critical operation performed within and upon the *institution* of art itself. Thus, art movements like dadaism and constructivism and art practices such as collage, photomontage, and the Duchampian readymade are understood to be performing a specifically political function to the extent that they work to actively break down the notion of aesthetic autonomy and to rejoin art and life. Bürger's rigorous account of art *as* an institution in bourgeois culture provides a further justification for considering internal critiques such as Levine's as a genuinely critical practice. Cultural sites and discourses are in theory no less immune to contestation, no less able to furnish an arena for struggle and transformation than any other.[8] This 'in theory' needs to be acknowledged here because the subsequent 'success' of postmodernist photography as a *style* harkens back, as I shall argue, to problems of function, of critical complicity, and the extreme difficulty of maintaining a critical edge within the unstable spaces of internal critique.

In the spring of 1982, I curated an exhibition entitled 'The Stolen Image and its Uses' for an alternative space in upstate New York. Of the five artists included (Alexander, Kolbowski, Kruger, Levine, and Prince), Levine was by far the most controversial and sparked the most hostility. It was, in fact, the very intensity of the outrage her work provoked (nowhere greater than among the ranks of art photographers) that appeared, at the time, to confirm the subversive effects of her particular strategies. But even while such exhibitions or lectures on Levine's works were received outside New York City with indignation, a different kind of appropriation of existing imagery, drawn principally from the mass media, was beginning to be accorded theoretical recognition across a broad range of cultural production. It was less easy to see this kind of appropriation as critically motivated. Fredric Jameson, for example, could in part identify his conception of postmodernism with the strategies of appropriation, quotation, and pastiche.[9] That these strategies could then be said to unify within a single field of discourse the work of Jean-Luc Godard and the work of Brian De Palma constitutes a problem for critical practice. Not only did such an undifferentiated model suppress a crucial consideration of (political and aesthetic) difference, it also implied the impossibility of purposeful cultural opposition within a totalizing system, a position accorded growing intellectual prestige within the art world through the later writings of Jean Baudrillard. Rooted in such a framework, an appropriative strategy such as Levine's (although Jameson does not mention the specific practice of appropriation) could only figure as a synecdochical symptom within a master narrative on postmodernism.

By 1983, plundering the pages of glossy magazines, shooting advertisements from the television set, or 'simulating' photographic tableaux that might have come from either of these media had become as routine an activity in the more sophisticated art schools as slopping paint on canvas. In January of that year the Institute of Contemporary Art in Philadelphia mounted an exhibition entitled 'Image Scavengers'. Included in the exhibition were representatives of the first wave of appropriators and pasticheurs (Kruger, Levine, Prince, Cindy Sherman) and several other artists whose work could be allied to the former only by virtue of their formal devices. Invited to contribute a catalog essay, Douglas Crimp was clearly disturbed at the domestication of what he had himself theorized as the critical potential of photographic appropriation. Under the title 'Appropriating Appropriation', his essay initiated a reconsideration of the adequacy of appropriation as a critical mode. 'If all aspects of the culture use this new operational mode', he wrote, 'then the mode itself cannot articulate a specific reflection upon that culture.'[10] Thus, although appropriative and quotational strategies had now become readily identifiable as a descriptive hallmark of postmodern culture, the terms by which it might once have been understood to be performing a critical function had become increasingly obfuscated and difficult to justify.

By this time, Levine's practice had itself undergone various alterations. In 1982, she had largely abandoned photographic appropriations and was confiscating German expressionist works, either by rephotographing them from book reproductions or by framing the reproductions themselves. In 1983 and 1984, however, she began making handmade watercolor and pencil copies after artbook illustrations, extending her *oeuvre*, so to speak, to include nonexpressionist modern masters such as Malevich and El Lissitzky. Her copies after expressionist drawings, such as Egon Schiele's contorted and angst-ridden nudes, were particularly trenchant comments on the pseudoexpressionist revival; master drawings are, after all, especially privileged for their status as intimate and revealing traces of the artist's unique subjectivity. In 1985, Levine made what might, or might not, be considered a radical departure from her earlier work and began to produce quite beautiful small-scale paintings on wood panels. These were geometrical abstractions – mostly stripes – which, Janus-like, looked backward to late-modernist works or to minimalism and forward to the most recently minted new wave in the art world – neo-geo. Additionally, she accompanied her first exhibition of this new work with unpainted panels of wood in which one or two of the knots had been neatly gilded.

Mutatis mutandis, Levine had become a painter, although I would argue, still a somewhat singular one. Her work, moreover, had passed from the relatively marginalized purview of the *succès d'estime* to a new visibility (and respectability), signaled, for example, by her cover article in the May 1986 *Artnews*. In several of the comments she made to her interviewer, Levine explained her need to distance herself from the kind of critical partisanship that not only had helped establish her reputation, but – more important – had, to a great degree, developed its position and analysis in relation to her work. Levine's professed discomfort with a body of critical writing that positioned her as a critical, indeed an adversarial, presence hinged on two factors. In championing Levine's work as either a poststructuralist exemplum, or a demolition derby on the property relations that subtend the integrity of the art object the (mostly male) critics who had written about her had overlooked, or repressed, the distinctly feminist import of her work.[11] But Levine also took issue with the interpretation of her work that stressed its materialist critique. In this regard, Levine insisted that hers was an aesthetic practice that implied no particular quarrel with the economic determinations of cultural production. Consequently, insofar as her critical supporters had emphasized those aspects of her work that subverted the commodity status of the artwork and demolished those values Walter Benjamin designated as the 'theology of art', Levine began to believe that her activity *as* an artist was itself being repressed: 'I never thought I wasn't making art and I never thought of the art I was making as not a commodity. I never thought that what I was doing was in strict opposition to what else was going on – I believed I was distilling things, bringing out what was being repressed. I did collaborate in a radical reading of my work. And the politics were congenial. But I was tired of no one looking at the work, getting inside the frame. And I was getting tired of being represented by men.'[12]

The repositioning of Levine's work, with respect to both its meaning (now presented as a form of anxious obsequy mourning 'the uneasy death of modernism') and the nature of her activity (commodity making), is disturbing from a number of perspectives. First, it involves its own forms of historical repression. Thus, nowhere in the article was any reference made to Levine's two-year collaboration with the artist Louise Lawler enacted under the title 'A Picture Is No Substitute for Anything'.[13] What is troubling about such an omission is that it parallels – no doubt wholly unintentionally – the institutional and discursive repressions that construct partial and falsified histories of art in the first place and in which the exclusion of women and radical practices is particularly conspicuous. Second, it repressed the active support of women critics, such as myself and Rosalind Krauss. But, more ominously, it traced a move from a position of perceptible cultural resistance to one of accommodation with existing modes of production and an apparent capitulation to the very desires the early work put in question. Whether this move is to be understood strategically (the need to be visible, the need to survive) or developmentally (an internal evolution in the artist's work) is not in itself a useful question. Far more important to consider here are the material and discursive forces that both exceed and bind the individual artist. Whether artists choose to publicly define their positions in opposition to, or in strategic alliance with, dominant modes of cultural production is important only insofar as such definitions may contribute to a collective space of opposition. But, in the absence of a clearly defined oppositional sphere and the extreme rarity of collaborative practice, attempts to clarify the nature of critical practice must focus on the artwork's ability to question, to contest, or to denaturalize the very terms in which it is produced, received, and circulated. What is at stake is thus not an ethics or a moral position but the very possibility of a critical practice within the terms of art discourse. And, as a fundamental condition of possibility, critical practices must constantly address those economic and discursive forces that perpetually threaten to eradicate their critical difference.

Some notion of the juggernaut of these forces can be obtained from a consideration of the parallel fortunes of Levine's earlier photographic appropriations and, indeed, postmodernist photography as a whole. In 1985, for example, three large group exhibitions featuring postmodernist photography were mounted: 'Signs of the Real' at White Columns, 'The Edge of Illusion' at the Burden Gallery, and most grotesque of all, 'In the

Tradition of: Photography' at the Light Gallery. Not the least of the ironies attendant upon the incorporation of postmodernist photography into the now expanded emporium of photography was the nature of the venues themselves: the Burden Gallery was established in January 1985 to function as the display window of *Aperture*, the photographic publication founded by Minor White and customarily consecrated to modernist art photography; the Light Gallery, a veritable cathedral of official art photography, represents the stable of officially canonized modernist masters, living and dead. The appearance of postmodernist photography within the institutional precincts of art photography signaled that whatever difference, much less critique, had been attributed to the work of Levine et al., it had now been fully and seamlessly recuperated under the sign of art photography, an operation that might be characterized as deconstruction in reverse.

How had this happened? The Light Gallery exhibition title – 'In the Tradition of: Photography' – provides one clue, elaborated in an essay that accompanied the show. Postmodernist photography is here understood to be that which follows modernist photography in the same fashion that postimpressionism is thought to follow impressionism. The first of the two epigraphs that introduced the essay was taken from Beaumont Newhall's *History of Photography* – a sentence describing the conservatism of pictorial, i.e., premodernist, art photography (that which preceded the Light Gallery regulars). The second epigraph consisted of two sentences from one of my essays, 'Photography after Art Photography', asserting that the stakes that differentiate the two modes are a function of their position in relation to their institutional spaces. In much the same way that the modernist hagiographer Beaumont Newhall and I were equally useful in framing the thesis that postmodernist photography is part of an evolutionary *telos* having to do only with the internal development of art photography, so too did the gallery space both frame and render equivalent the two practices. This reduction of difference to sameness (a shorthand description for the eventual fate of most, if not all, initially transgressive cultural practices) was emblematically represented by the pairing – side by side – of a Sherrie Levine rephotograph of a Walker Evans and – what else? – a 'real' Walker Evans beneath the exhibition title. That postmodernist photographic work and art photography came to inhabit the same physical site (although with the exception of the Levine/Evans coupling, the two were physically separated in the installation) is of course integrally linked to the nature of commercial space in the first place. In the final analysis, as well as a Marxist analysis, the market is the ultimate legitimizer and leveler. Thus, among the postmodernist work, one could also find excerpts from Martha Rosler's 1977 book project *The Bowery in Two Inadequate Descriptive Systems* (originally published by the Press of the Nova Scotia College of Art and Design). Variously an uncompromising critique of conventional humanist muckraking documentary photography, a text/image artwork, and an examination of the structuring absences and ideological freight of representational systems, *The Bowery* was exhibited at the Light Gallery amid the range of postmodernist photographs and bore a purchase price of $3,500 (purchase of the entire set was required). But what was finally even odder than the effect of going from the part of the gallery in which the Aaron Siskinds, Cartier-Bressons, and Paul Strands hung to the part devoted to the postmodernists was the revelation that postmodernist photography, once theorized as a critical practice, had become a 'look', an attitude, a *style*.

Within this newly constructed stylistic unity, the critical specificity of a Rosler, a Prince, a Levine could be reconstituted only with difficulty (and only with prior knowledge). In large part, and in this particular instance, this was a consequence of the inclusion of a 'second generation' of postmodernist photographers – Frank Majore, Alan Belcher, Stephen Frailey, and so forth – whose relation to the sources and significance of their appropriate strategies (primarily advertising) seemed to be predominantly a function of fascination. Insofar as stupefied or celebratory fascination produces an identification with the image world of commodity culture no different from the mesmerization of any other consumer, the possibility of critique is effectively precluded. Frank Majore's simulations of advertising tableaux employing props such as trimline telephones, champagne glasses, pearls, and busts of Nefertiti all congealed in a lurid bath of fifties-like photographic color are cases in point (see figure 15.2). By reproducing the standard devices of color advertising (with which Majore, as a professional art director, is intimately familiar) and providing enough modification to accentuate their kitschiness and eroticism, Majore succeeds in doing nothing more than reinstating the schlocky glamour of certain kinds of advertising imagery within the institutional space of art. But unlike the strategies of artists such as Duchamp, or Warhol, or Levine, what is precisely *not* called into question is the institutional frame itself. The alacrity with which this now wholly academicized practice was institutionally embraced by 1985 (in that year Majore had three one-person shows at the International Center of Photography, the 303 Gallery, and the Nature Morte gallery) was possible precisely because so little was called into question.

Although this more recent crop of postmodernist artists could only become visible – or saleable – in the wake of the success of their predecessors, the shift from margin to center had multiple determinations. 'Center', however, must be understood in relative terms. The market was and is dominated by painting, and the prices for photographic work, despite the prevalence of strictly limiting editions and employing heroic scale, are intrinsically lower. Nonetheless, the fact remains that in 1980, the work of Levine or Prince was largely unsaleable and quite literally incomprehensible to all but a handful of critics and a not much larger group of other artists. When this situation changed substantially, it was not *primarily* because of the influence of critics or the efforts of dealers. Rather, it was a result of three factors: the self-created impasse of art photography that foreclosed the ability to produce anything new for a market that had been constituted in the previous decade; a vastly expanded market with new types of purchasers; and the assimilation of postmodernist strategies back into the mass culture that had in part engendered

Figure 15.2

Frank Majore,
Cocktails, 1983
(courtesy of Marvin
Heiferman)

There is a genuine unsatisfied desire throughout the world for something new in fashion ... designers have to return to the traditions of great luxury.
Christian Dior

Black and White: Christian Dior Collection, 1949
Color: Christian Dior Jewelry, 1987

Christian Dior

Figure 15.3

Christian Dior
advertisement
(source unknown)

them. This last development may be said to characterize postmodernist photography the third time around, rendering it both comprehensible and desirable and simultaneously signaling its near-total incorporation into those very discourses (advertising, fashion, media) it professed to critique. The current spate of Dior advertisements (figure 15.3), for example, featuring a black-and-white photograph from the fifties on which a contemporary model (photographed in color) has been montaged bears at least a family resemblance to the recent work of Laurie Simmons (figure 15.4). But where Simmons's pictures derived their mildly unsettling effects from a calculated attempt to denaturalize an advertising convention, the reappearance of the same montage tactic in the new Dior campaign marks the completion of a circuit that begins and ends in the boundless creativity of modern advertising.

The cultural loop that can be traced here is itself part of the problematic of critical practice. The more or less rapid domestication and commodification of art practices initially conceived as critical has been recognized as a central issue at least since the time of the Frankfurt School. This means that irrespective of artistic intention or initial effect, critical practices not specifically calibrated to resist recuperation as aesthetic commodities almost immediately succumb to this process. In this respect, the only difference between the fate of postmodernist photography and previous practices is the rapidity of the process and the ease, if not enthusiasm, with which so many of the artists accommodated themselves to it.

As was the case with its pop-art predecessors, the first wave of postmodernist photography pillaged the mass media and advertising for its 'subject', by which I include its thematics, its codes, its emblems. These were then variously repositioned in ways that sought to denaturalize the conventions that encode the ideological and, in so doing, to make those very ideological contents available to scrutiny and contestation. Thus, Cindy Sherman's black-and-white movie stills – always her and never her – aped the look of various film genres to underscore their conventionality, whereas her infinite tabulation of the 'images of women' they generate revealed their status as equally conventionalized signs producing a category (woman) and not a subject (figure 15.5). Additionally, the cherished notion of the artist's presence *in* the work was challenged by the act of literally inscribing the author herself and revealing her to be both fictional and absent.[14] Similarly, Richard Prince's rephotographs of the 'Marlboro Man' advertisements, which he began to produce in the early years of the Reagan administration, pointedly addressed the new conservative agenda and its ritual invocations of a heroic past (figure 15.6). Here, too, the jettisoning of authorial presence was a component of a larger project. By focusing on the image of the cowboy – the individualistic and masculine icon of American mythology – Prince made visible the connections among cultural nostalgia, the mythos of the masculine, and political reaction. Recropping, rephotographing, and recontextualizing the Marlboro men permitted Prince to unpack the menace, aggression, and atavism of such representations and reveal their analogical link to current political rhetoric.

In contrast to practices such as these, work such as Majore's abjures critique, analysis, and intervention on either its purported object – the seductiveness of commodity culture, the hypnotic lure of simulacra – or the material, discursive, and institutional determinations of art practice itself. Not surprisingly, the disappearance of a critical agenda, however construed, has resulted in an apparent collapse of any hard-and-fast

Figure 15.4

Laurie Simmons,

Aztec Crevice, 1984

(courtesy of Metro

Pictures and the

artist)

distinction between art and advertising. In pop art, this willed collapse of the aesthetic into the commercial function carried, at least briefly, a distinctly subversive charge. The erasure of boundaries between high and mass culture, high art and commodity, operated as an astringent bath in which to dissolve the transcendentalist legacy of abstract expressionism. Moreover, the strategic repositioning of the images and objects of mass culture within the gallery and museum reinstated the investigation and analysis of the aesthetic as an ideological function of the institutional structures of art. Postmodernism as style, on the other hand, eliminates any possibility of analysis insofar as it complacently affirms the interchangeability, if not the coidentity, of art production and advertising, accepting this as a given instead of a problem.

Perhaps one of the clearest examples of this celebratory collapse was an exhibition mounted in the fall of 1986 at the International Center of Photographs entitled 'Art and Advertising: Commercial Photography by Artists'.[15] Of the nine artists represented, four came from the ranks of art photography (Sandi Fellman, Barbara Kasten, Robert Mapplethorpe, Victor Schrager), two from the first wave of postmodernist photography (Cindy Sherman and Laurie Simmons), and two from the second (Stephen Frailey and Frank Majore). William Wegman, whose work has encompassed both video and conceptualism, falls clearly into none of these camps. As in the numerous gallery and museum exhibitions organized in the preceding years, the new ecumenism that assembles modernist art photography and postmodernist photography functions to establish a familial harmony, an elision of difference to the profit of all.

Addressing the work of Frailey, Majore, Simmons, and Sherman, the curator Willis Hartshorn had this to say:

> The art of Stephen Frailey, Frank Majore, Laurie Simmons and Cindy Sherman shares a concern for the operations of mass media representation. For these artists to work commercially is to come full circle, from art that appropriates the mass media image, to commercial images that reappropriate the style of their art, However, for the viewer to appreciate this transformation implies a conscious relationship to the material. The viewer must understand the functions that are being compared through these self-referential devices. Otherwise, the juxtapositions that parody the conventions of the mass media will be lost.[16]

Now firmly secured within the precincts of style, postmodernist photography's marriage to commerce seems better likened to a love match than a wedding of convenience. Deconstruction has metamorphosed into appreciation of transformation, whereas the exposure of ideological codes has mellowed into self-referential devices. And insofar as the museum, in the age of Reagan, can institutionally embrace and legitimize both enterprises – art and commerce – Hartshorn is quite right in noting that a full circle has been described. For those for whom this is hardly cause for rejoicing, the history of postmodernist photography is cautionary rather than exemplary.

Figure 15.5
Cindy Sherman,
Untitled film still,
1979 (courtesy of
Metro Pictures)

Figure 15.6
(opposite page)
Richard Prince,
Untitled (Cowboy),
1980–84 (courtesy
Barbara Gladstone
Gallery)

[. . .] [T]hroughout this essay I have chosen to employ the term critical practice in lieu of political practice. That said, the immediate difficulty of definition must still be addressed, and it is made no easier by the fact that a spate of recent practices – so-called simulationism, neo-geo, postmodernist photography in all its avatars – lays claim to the mantle of critical practice. Whether one is to take such claims at face value is another matter. But if we assume that critical practices conceptually assume both an activity and a position, the emphasis needs be placed on discursive and institutional function. In this regard, Walter Benjamin's rhetorical question of 1938 is still germane: 'Rather than ask, "What is the *attitude* of a work to the relations of production of its time?" I should like to ask, "What is its *position* in them?"'[17] The relevance of this question is that it underscores the need for critical practices to establish a contestatory space in which the *form* of utterance or address speaks to otherwise unrecognized, or passively accepted, meanings, values, and beliefs that cultural production normally reproduces and legitimizes. Insofar as contemporary critical practices operate within a society in which, as Victor Burgin observes, 'the market is "behind" nothing, it is *in* everything',[18] the notion of an 'outside' of the commodity system becomes increasingly untenable. This would suggest that the definition or evaluation of a critical practice must be predicated on its ability to sustain critique from within the heart of the system it seeks to put in question.

If we are to grant that a range of postmodernist photographic work that emerged at the end of the 1970s did in fact initially function as a critical practice, it did so very much within these terms. First of all, unlike other contemporaneous critical practices that positioned themselves outside the art world and sought different audiences [. . .] postmodernist photography for the most part operated wholly within the parameters of high-art institutions. As the photographic work of Sherrie Levine clearly demonstrates, the critical specificity of such practice is only operative, can only be mobilized, within a particular context. Its instrumentality, in other words, is a consequence of its engagement with dominant (aesthetic) discourses whose constituent terms (and hidden agendas) are then made visible as prerequisites for analysis and critique. As circumstances change (for example, with the assimilation of appropriation into the culture at large), so too does the position of the artwork alter.

But within the overarching category of immanent critique, it is important to distinguish between those practices that elucidate, engage with, or even contest their institutional frame, and those that suspend or defer their institutional critique in the belief that such critique is already implied within the terms of their focus on the politics of representation. Representation is, after all, itself contextually determined, and the meanings thereby produced and disseminated are inseparable from the discursive structures that contain and enfold them. Consistent with the terms of Peter Bürger's formulation, there is by now a lengthy history of art practices of the former type, ranging from those of the historical avant-garde through more recent production exemplified by Michael Asher, Daniel Buren, Marcel Broodthaers (d. 1976), Hans Haacke (figure 15.7), Louise Lawler,

Figure 15.7

Hans Haacke,

MetroMobiltan, 1985

(courtesy of John

Weber Gallery)

and Christopher Williams. It is, I think, of some significance that the work of these artists has more or less successfully resisted the reduction to stylistics to which postmodernist photography so rapidly succumbed. [. . .]

Notes

1 'Neo-geo', also referred to as 'simulationism', the latest art package to blaze across the art-world firmament, is a good case in point. The artists involved (Ashley Bickerton, Peter Halley, Jeff Koons, Haim Steinbach, Meyer Vaisman – to name only the most prominent) were the subject of massive media promotion from the outset. See, for example, Paul Taylor 'The hot four: get ready for the next art stars', *New York Magazine*, 27 October (1986), pp. 50–6; Eleanor Heartney, 'Simulationism: the hot new cool art', *Artnews*, January (1987), pp. 130–37; Douglas C. McGill 'The Lower East Side's new artists: a garment center of culture makes stars of unknowns', *The New York Times*, 3 June (1986). The media blitz was subsequently ratified by a group exhibition at the Sonnabend Gallery and, on the museological front, by an exhibition at the Institute for Contemporary Art, Boston ('Endgame: Reference and Simulation in Recent Painting and Sculpture', September 25–November 30, 1986) with an accompanying catalog featuring essays by prominent art historians and critics such as Yves-Alain Bois, Thomas Crow, Hal Foster. For a less exalted and intellectualized view of this phenomenon, see 'Mythologies: art and the market', an interview with Jeffrey Deitch, art adviser to Citibank, *Artscribe International* (April/May 1986), pp. 22–6. This interview is of interest because it clearly indicates the determinations and mechanisms in the fabrication and marketing of a new art commodity.

2   See Hal Foster, 'Postmodernism: a preface', in *The Anti-Aesthetic: Essays in Post-modern Culture*, ed. Hal Foster (Port Townsend, Washington: Bay Press, 1983), pp. ix–xvi. [. . .]

3   See Robert Venturi, Denise Scott Brown and Steven Izenor, *Learning from Las Vegas* (Cambridge, MA, MIT Press, 1972), and Charles Jencks, *The Language of Postmodern Architecture* (New York, Rizzoli, 1977).

4   See my 'Winning the game when the rules have been changed: art photography and postmodernism', *Screen*, 25, 6 (November/December 1984), pp. 88–102, and 'Photography after art photography', in *Rethinking Representation*, ed. Bruce Wallis (Boston, David R. Godine, 1986), *Art after Modernism*, pp. 75–87.

5   On the implications and ideology of the revival of pseudoexpressionism, see Benjamin H. D. Buchloh, 'Figures of authority, ciphers of regression', in *October* 10 (spring 1981), pp. 39–68, and 'Documenta 77: a dictionary of received ideas', *October* 22 (fall 1982), pp. 105–26. [. . .]

6   Martha Rosler, 'Notes on quotes', *Wedge* 3 (1982), p. 72.

7   Peter Bürger, *The Theory of the Avant-Garde*, trans. Michael Shaw (Minneapolis, University of Minnesota Press, 1984).

8   The theorization of a localized 'site specificity' for contestatory and oppositional practices is one of the legacies of Louis Althusser and, with a somewhat different inflection, Michel Foucault. See Michel Foucault, 'The political function of the intellectual', *Radical Philosophy* 12 (summer 1977), pp. 12–15, and 'Revolutionary action: "until now"', in *Language, Counter-Memory, Practice: selected Essays and Interviews by Michel Foucault*, ed. Donald F. Bouchard (Ithaca, NY, Cornell University Press, 1977), pp. 218–33.

9   See Fredric Jameson, 'Postmodernism, or the cultural logic of late capitalism', *New Left Review* 146 (July–August 1984), pp. 53–92. An earlier, less developed version of this essay, entitled 'Post-modernism and consumer society', is reprinted in Foster (ed.), *The Anti-Aesthetic*, pp. 111–25.

10   Douglas Crimp, 'Appropriating Appropriation', in *Image Scavengers*, exhibition catalog (University of Pennsylvania, Institute of Contemporary Art, 8 December 1983–30 January 1983), p. 27.

11   Craig Owens, 'The discourse of others: feminists and postmodernism', in Foster (ed.), *The Anti-Aesthetic*, pp. 57–82, is an important exception.

12   Quoted in Gerald Marzorati, 'Art in the (re)making', *Artnews*, 85, 5 (May 1986), p. 97.

13   The activities, events, and objects produced under the rubric of 'A Picture Is No Substitute for Anything' collectively and individually functioned to foreground the mechanisms of cultural production, exhibition, and reception. While the working title implicitly points to – by denying – the fetish status of paintings, the practices themselves (for example, inviting an art public to the studio of Dmitri Merinoff, a recently deceased expressionist painter; the mailing [and exhibition] of gallery announcements; one-night only exhibitions in which Levine and Lawler exhibited and arranged each other's work; the production of embossed matchbooks bearing the legend 'A Picture Is No Substitute for Anything') were constituted as tactical interventions within the structures of art. Inscribing themselves in the mechanisms of publicity, display, and curatorship served to focus attention on the framing conditions of art production, which are thereby revealed to be structurally integral, rather than supplemental, to the field as a whole. See, for example, Andrea Fraser, 'In and out of place', *Art in America* (June 1985), pp. 122–8; Kate Linker, 'Rites of exchange', *Artforum* (November 1986), pp. 99–100. [. . .]

14   This aspect of Sherman's work was of particular importance to critics such as Douglas Crimp. For an interpretation of Sherman's photographs that stresses their feminist critique, see Judith Williamson, 'Images of "Woman"', *Screen*, 24, 6 (November/December 1983), pp. 102–16.

15   Art and advertising: commercial photography by artists', New York International Center of Photography, September 14–November 9, 1986.

16   Willis Hartshorn, gallery handout.

17   Walter Benjamin, 'The author as producer', in Peter Demetz (ed.), *Reflections* (New York, Harcourt, Brace, Jovanovich, 1978), p. 222.

18   [. . .] Victor Burgin, 'The end of art theory', in *The End of Art Theory: Criticism and Postmodernity* (London, Macmillan, 1986), p. 174.

16

Evidence, truth and order: a means of surveillance
John Tagg

Evidence, truth and order:
photographic records and the growth of the state[1]

[. . .] [I]n the last quarter of the nineteenth century, the photographic industries of France, Britain and America, in common with other sectors of the capitalist economy, underwent a second technical revolution which laid the basis for a major transition towards a structure dominated by large-scale corporate monopolies. The development of faster dry plates and flexible film and the mass production of simple and convenient photographic equipment opened up new consumer markets and accelerated the growth of an advanced industrial organisation. At the same time, the invention of means of cheap and unlimited photomechanical reproduction transformed the status and economy of image-making methods as dramatically as had the invention of the paper negative by Fox Talbot half a century earlier. In the context of generally changing patterns of production and consumption, photography was poised for a new phase of expansion into advertising, journalism, and the domestic market. It was also open to a whole range of scientific and technical applications and supplied a ready instrumentation to a number of reformed or emerging medical, legal and municipal apparatuses in which photographs functioned as a means of record and a source of evidence. Understanding the role of photography in the documentary practices of these institutions means retracing the history of a far from self-evident set of beliefs and assertions about the nature and status of the photograph, and of signification generally, which were articulated into a wider range of techniques and procedures for extracting and evaluating 'truth' in discourse. Such techniques were themselves evolved and embodied in institutional practices

This chapter is taken from John Tagg, *The Burden of Representation* (London, Macmillan, 1987), pp. 60–102.

central to the governmental strategy of capitalist states whose consolidation demanded the establishment of a new 'regime of truth' and a new 'regime of sense'. What gave photography its power to evoke a truth was not only the privilege attached to mechanical means in industrial societies, but also its mobilisation within the emerging apparatuses of a new and more penetrating form of the state.

[. . .] The pressing problem locally and generally, was how to train and mobilise a diversified workforce while instilling docility and practices of social obedience within the dangerously large urban concentrations which advanced industrialisation necessitated. The problem was solved by more and more extensive interventions in the daily life of the working class within and without the workplace, through a growing complex of medical, educational, sanitary, and engineering departments which subsumed older institutions and began to take over the work of private and philanthropic agencies. Force was not, of course, absent. Local police forces and the administrative arms of the Poor Law were of central importance to the emerging local state, but even these could not operate by coercion alone. They depended on a more general organisation of consent, on disciplinary techniques and a moral supervision which, at a highly localised and domestic level, secured the complex social relations of domination and subordination on which the reproduction of capital depended. In a tightening knot, the local state pulled together the instrumentalities of repression and surveillance, the scientific claims of social engineering, and the humanistic rhetoric of social reform.

By the closing decades of the century, bourgeois hegemony in the economic, political and cultural spheres seemed beyond all challenge. [. . .] In the course of a profound economic and social transformation, the exercise of power in advanced capitalist societies had been radically restructured. The explicit, dramatic and total power of the absolute monarch had given place to what Michel Foucault has called a diffuse and pervasive 'microphysics of power', operating unremarked in the smallest duties and gestures of everyday life. The seat of this capillary power was a new 'technology': that constellation of institutions – including the hospital, the asylum, the school, the prison, the police force – whose disciplinary methods and techniques of regulated examination produced, trained and positioned a hierarchy of docile social subjects in the form required by the capitalist division of labour for the orderly conduct of social and economic life. At the same time, the power transmitted in the unremitting surveillance of these new, disciplinary institutions generated a new kind of knowledge of the very subjects they produced; a knowledge which, in turn, engendered new effects of power and which was preserved in a proliferating system of documentation – of which photographic records were only a part.

The conditions were in play for a striking rendezvous – the consequences of which we are still living – between a novel form of the state and a new and developing technology of knowledge. A key to this technology from the 1870s on was photography, and it is into the workings of the expanded state complex that we must pursue it, if we are to understand the power that began to accrue to photography in the last quarter of the nineteenth century. It is in the emergence, too, of new institutions of knowledge that we must seek the mechanism which could enable photography to function, in certain contexts, as a kind of proof, even while an ideological contradiction was negotiated so that a burgeoning photographic industry could be divided between the domain of artistic property, whose privilege, resting on copyright protection, was a function of its lack of power, and the scientifico-technical domain, whose power was a function of its renunciation of privilege. What we begin to see is the emergence of a modern photographic economy in which the so-called medium of photography has no meaning outside its historical specifications. What alone unites the diversity of sites in which photography operates is the social formation itself: the specific historical spaces for representation and practice which it constitutes. Photography as such has no identity. Its status as a technology varies with the power relations which invest it. Its nature as a practice depends on the institutions and agents which define it and set it to work. Its function as a mode of cultural production is tied to definite conditions of existence, and its products are meaningful and legible only within the particular currencies they have. Its history has no unity. It is a flickering across a field of institutional spaces. It is this field we must study, not photography as such.

Like the state, the camera is never neutral. The representations it produces are highly coded, and the power it wields is never its own. As a means of record, it arrives on the scene vested with a particular authority to arrest, picture and transform daily life; a power to see and record; a power of surveillance that effects a complete reversal of the political axis of representation which has confused so many labourist historians. This is not the power of the camera but the power of the apparatuses of the local state which deploy it and guarantee the authority of the images it constructs to stand as evidence or register a truth. If, in the last decades of the nineteenth century, the squalid slum displaces the country seat and the 'abnormal' physiognomies of patient and prisoner displace the pedigreed features of the aristocracy, then their presence in representation is no longer a mark of celebration but a burden of subjection. A vast and repetitive archive of images is accumulated in which the smallest deviations may be noted, classified and filed. The format varies hardly at all. There are bodies and spaces. The bodies – workers, vagrants, criminals, patients, the insane, the poor, the colonised races – are taken one by one: isolated in a shallow, contained space; turned full face and subjected to an unreturnable gaze; illuminated, focused, measured, numbered and named; forced to yield to the minutest scrutiny of gestures and features. Each device is the trace of a wordless power, replicated in countless images, whenever the photographer prepares an exposure, in police cell, prison, mission house, hospital, asylum, or school. The spaces, too – uncharted territories, frontier lands, urban ghettos, working-class slums, scenes of crime – are confronted with the same frontality and measured against an ideal space: a clear space, a healthy space, a space of unobstructed lines of sight, open to vision and supervision; a desirable space in which bodies will be changed into disease-free, orderly, docile and disciplined subjects; a space, in Foucault's sense, of a new strategy of power-knowledge. For this is what is at stake in missionary explorations, in urban clearance, sanitary reform and health supervision, in constant, regularised policing – and in the photography which furnished them from the start with so central a technique.

These are the strands of a ravelled history tying photography to the state. They have to do not with the 'externals' of photography, as modernists would have us believe, but with the very conditions which furnish the materials, codes and strategies of photographic images, the terms of their legibility, and the range and limits of their effectiveness. Histories are not backdrops to set off the performance of images. They are scored into the paltry paper signs, in what they do and do not do, in what they encompass and exclude, in the ways they open on to or resist a repertoire of uses in which they can be meaningful and productive. Photographs are never 'evidence' of history; they are themselves the historical. [. . .]

A means of surveillance: the photograph as evidence in law

I

In the decades of the 1880s and the 1890s [. . .] photography underwent a double technical revolution, enabling, on the one hand, the mass production of cheaply printed half-tone blocks and, on the other hand, the mass production of simple and convenient photographic equipment, such as the hand-held Kodak camera. At the very moment when certain professional photographers were seeking, in reaction, to exhibit their status as artists in all kinds of refinement of printing technique, this double revolution stripped the image of what Walter Benjamin called its 'aura' by flooding the market with cheap and disposable photo-mechanical reproductions and by giving untrained masses the means to picture themselves. While aesthetes and pictorial photographers sought to salvage some prestige by preserving superseded techniques and arguing for the autonomy of photography as an art, an unabating technical development ensured the vast expansion of photography in the far from autonomous realms of advertising, of the family as a reconstructed unit of consumption, and of a whole range of scientific, technical, medical, legal and political apparatuses in which photography functioned as a means of record and a source of 'evidence'.

It is into the workings of these institutions that we must pursue photography if we are to understand the *power* that began to accrue to it in the latter half of the nineteenth century. It is in the emergence, too, of new institutions of knowledge that we must seek for the mechanism which could enable photography to function, in certain contexts, as a kind of *proof*, even while an ideological contradiction was negotiated so that photographic practice could be divided between the domain of art, whose privilege is a function of its lack of power, and the scientifico-technical domain, whose power is a function of its renunciation of privilege.

This analysis of power and photography will take us far beyond the boundaries of conventional art history into the institutional spaces of the modern state. Our starting point must be power itself and the attempts that have been made to theorise its functionings. In rough and ready terms, I shall raise two questions: where and how do we find power working; how may this power be opposed and how does it produce its own resistance? Clearly, the answers, however sketchy and provisional, will have definite consequences both for the history and practice of photography. We must know more about power to discover where and how it touches photography. [. . .]

II

Power in the West, Foucault says, is what displays itself most and hides itself best.[2] 'Political life', with its carefully staged debates, provides a little theatre of power – an image – but it is not there that power lies; nor is that how it functions. The relations of power are among the best hidden things in the social body, which may be why they are among the least studied.

On the left, the dominant tradition, following an orthodox and reductive Marxism, has tended to neglect relations of elementary power in its concentration on the determining effectivity of the economy. It has also tended to see power only in the form of state power, wielded in the apparatus of the state, and has thus participated in the very *ideology of power* which conceals its pervasive workings.

[. . .] In the classic texts of Marx and Lenin, too, the state is conceived as an explicitly repressive apparatus, a machine of repression which guarantees the domination and subjection of the working classes by the ruling class. It consists of specialised apparatuses such as the police, the law courts and the prisons, but also the army and, above this ensemble, the head of state, the government and the administration. All these apparatuses execute their functions and intervene according to 'the interests of the ruling class' in a class war conducted by the ruling class and its allies against the dominated working classes. Whatever the value of this description in casting light on all the direct and indirect forms of exploitation and domination [. . .] it also prevents us seeing certain highly pertinent features – features it has become imperative to understand in highly developed modern states. [. . .]

The theoretical development of the classic Marxist view of the state, in keeping with these demands, received new impetus in the analyses of the French Marxist philosopher Louis Althusser, who took up the relatively unsystematised distinction made in the *Prison Notebooks* of the Italian Communist leader, Antonio Gramsci, between the institutions of civil society – the Church, the schools, the trade unions, and so on – and those of the state apparatus proper.[3] Gramsci saw that the state had undergone a crucial change of function in Western bourgeois democracies, so that its real strength could no longer be understood only as the apparatus of government, the politico-juridicial organisation, but demanded attention to the 'private' apparatuses of 'hegemony' or civil society through which the bourgeois class sought to assimilate the entire society to its own cultural and economic level. In his more rigid theoretical framework, Althusser divided the state into two domains or kinds of apparatus: that which functioned primarily and predominantly by 'physical force', and that which functioned primarily and predominantly 'by ideology'. It is the state apparatuses which, principally by force, procure the political conditions for the action of the 'Ideological State Apparatuses' – the educational, religious, family, political, trade-union, communications and 'cultural' apparatuses – which, acting behind a 'shield', largely secure the reproduction of the relations of production. The Ideological State Apparatuses are 'on the side of the repressive State Apparatus', but they must not be confused with it. They are distinct, specialised and 'relatively autonomous' institutions which constitute a plurality [. . .]. 'No class', Althusser says, 'can hold state power over a long period without at the same time exercising its hegemony over and in the State Ideological Apparatuses.'[4]

There is still in Althusser's theoretical amplification something of an idea of power as a privilege to be captured and then exercised; a kind of 'fluid' which may be 'poured' into an apparatus as into a vessel. We shall come on to further difficulties which arise from his attempt to maintain a strict distinction between the State Apparatuses and the Ideological State Apparatuses on the basis of their respective primary functioning by force and ideology. Above all, the anomalies in Althusser's account arise from his conception of preconstituted class identities, in possession of preformed ideologies, which contend for control of the Ideological State Apparatuses which are merely instruments for propounding and enforcing the ruling ideology. Too often, Althusser sees the Ideological State Apparatuses as the *stake*, rather than the *site* of class struggle [. . .]. What he does not show is that it is in the representational practices of these apparatuses themselves that the ideological level is constituted, of necessity including that positionality which constitutes class identity.

This said, a decisive step has been taken towards seeing power – a power still conceived as 'state' power – in more than its repressive functions; towards a total explanation which incorporates those apparently peripheral and independent institutions such as the family, the school and the communications media, in the reproduction of the social relations within which production takes place; and towards the most important realisation that, if these apparatuses function 'by ideology', by interpellating individual subjects in the positions created for them by the socio-technical division of labour, then 'an ideology always exists in an apparatus, and its practice, or practices. This existence is material.[5]

Part of the value of Althusser's account resides, therefore, in the way it opens on an extensive prospect of concrete historical work. It has been the French historian Michel Foucault who has done most to elaborate this materialist analysis in the concrete domain of real history [. . .]. [H]e has studied the genealogy of a cluster of institutions which, born of the profound reorganisation of social relations in European societies in the late eighteenth and early nineteenth centuries, have secreted new and strategically connected discourses about and within them; discourses which themselves function as formidable tools of control and power, producing a new realm of objects both as their targets and as instrumentalities.

It is in the context of the development of such a discursive formation that Foucault has seen the pathologising of the female body, in the eighteenth century, as the object of an immense medical attention; the reconstitution of homosexuality as illness in the new medical and psychiatric analyses of the 1870s; the 'discovery' of 'mental illness' in the workings of the asylum; the generation of delinquency in the new apparatus of the prison and the evolution of the new pseudo-discourses of criminology. All these are products of a determinate range of instruments – the hospital, the asylum, the prison, the school, the barracks – exercising a new range of techniques and acting with precision on their newly constituted and individuated subjects. In his studies of the 'birth' of this constellation of institutions in the eighteenth and nineteenth centuries, Foucault opens up a new territory that is neither violence nor ideology, coercion nor consent; that bears directly and physically upon the body – like the camera's gaze – yet is also a knowledge. This knowledge and this mastery constitute what he calls the political technology of the body: a diffuse and multiform instrumentation which cannot be localised in a particular type of institution or state apparatus but is situated at a different level, that of a 'microphysics' of power, between the great functionings and the bodies themselves, decipherable only in a network of relations in constant tension which go right down into the depths of society.[6]

Power, in this new type of society, has drained deeply into the gestures, actions, discourses and practical knowledge of everyday lives. The body itself is invested by power relations through which it is situated in a certain 'political economy', trained, supervised, tortured if necessary, forced to carry out tasks, to perform ceremonies, to emit signs. Power is exercised in, and not just on, the social body because, since the eighteenth century, power has taken on a 'capillary existence'. The great political upheaval which brought the bourgeoisie to power and established its hegemony across the social order was effected not only in the readjustment of those centralised institutions which constitute the political régime, but in an insistent and insidious modification of the everyday forms of the exercise of power. What this amounted to was the constitution of a new type of régime discovered in the eighteenth century, that is, a scientifico-legal complex impregnated with a new technology of power.

[. . .] What was new in the late eighteenth century was that, by being combined and generalised, the techniques which made up this technology attained a level at which the formation of knowledge and the increase of power regularly reinforced one another in a circular process. [. . .]

III

The development of the police force was integral to this process of change which began in the eighteenth century and effected, in the era of capitalism, a decisive shift from the total power of the monarch to the infinitely small exercise of power necessary to the discipline and productive exploitation of bodies accumulated in large numbers. In order to be effective, this new strategy of power needed an instrument of permanent, exhaustive, omnipresent surveillance, capable of making all visible, as long as it could itself remain invisible. The institution of the police offered just such a means of control which could be present in the very midst of the working population, under the alibi of a criminal threat itself manufactured across a set of new apparatuses ranging from the penitentiary to crime reporting and the crime novel. In England, it was in the latter half of the eighteenth century and the early nineteenth century that pressure grew to replace with a more rigorously organised force the inefficient system of unpaid constables and watchmen which had failed to control crime and disorder in towns swollen by great concentrations of factory workers. [. . .] Manufacturers pressed for greater discipline in work and leisure in the factory towns. Methodists and 'humanitarians' called for order, submissiveness and the suppression of vice. Reformers argued that a more effective preventive police was absolutely necessary to guard over property. From the founding of Henry Fielding's Bow Street Foot and Horse Patrol in London in 1748 till the middle years of the next century, the case was pressed and pressed again for a full-time, uniformed police force.

All kinds of official and semi-official forces grew up in the cities, especially around the ports, canals and navigable rivers where property was at stake. Yet there was still a concerted opposition, and not alone from the radical sections of the populace who always saw the police as an 'engine of oppression'. In 1812, the idea of a centralised force was still seen by one commentator as 'a system of tyranny; an organised army of spies and informers, for the destruction of all public liberty, and the disturbance of all private happiness'.[7] A parliamentary committee of 1818 saw in Jeremy Bentham's proposals for a Ministry of Police 'a plan which would make every servant of every house a spy on the actions of his master, and all classes of society spies on each other'.[8] There was no guarantee that the gaze of surveillance would be fixed in one direction. Merchants and industrialists still feared any powers of inspection which might lead to searches of the houses and premises of those suspected of evading regulations. Older vested interests were also threatened by the new pervasive mechanisms of power. Tories feared an overriding of parochial and chartered rights. Whigs feared an increase in the power of central government. [. . .]

[. . .] Under the Act [of Parliament of 1829], 3,000 blue-uniformed men, in seventeen divisions under a hierarchy of superintendents, inspectors and sergeants, controlled by a commissioner and ultimately responsible to the Home Secretary, were given jurisdiction over the area of a seven-mile radius around Charing Cross. Despite continued agitation for its abolition, the force was bolstered by the appointment of the first special constables in 1831, and systematically extended, first to all urban areas of England and Wales [. . .] and then to the counties and rural areas [. . .]. [A] regular inspectorate was set up to report on the state of efficiency of the widely dispersed constabularies. In this way, the powers and duties of the constable which derived from the ancient common law of England were subsumed but also transformed in the new police constable, who was a member of a disciplined force, subject to strict codes and a hierarchy of inspection and supervision.

[. . .] [I]t was the police which installed the new power–knowledge nexus in the very heart of working-class life, extending the emerging techniques of observation-domination beyond the walls of the new disciplinary and reformatory institutions such as prisons and penitentiaries. This special kind of observation which the police brought to bear had to be accumulated somehow. It began, therefore, to be assembled in a growing series of reports and registers. From the eighteenth and nineteenth centuries onward, an immense police text came increasingly to cover society by means of a complex documentary organisation. But this documentation differed markedly from the traditional methods of judicial or administrative writing. What was registered in it were forms of conduct, attitudes, possibilities, suspicions: a permanent account of individuals' behaviour.

IV

Now is perhaps the moment to turn to the complicity of photography in this spreading network of power. The early years of the development of the photographic process coincided approximately with the period of the introduction of the police service into this country, and for more than a hundred years the two have progressed together. As photographic processes and equipment have been evolved and refined, so have police forces expanded and become more efficient.

The value of photographs for the purposes of identification was realised by the police at a very early stage. Though successful portraiture only became possible with the introduction of faster Petzval lenses and more sensitive Daguerreotype processes by 1841, the police employed civilian photographers from the 1840s onwards. The West Midlands Police Museum has a file of twenty-three ambrotypes of Birmingham prisoners taken by an unknown photographer in the 1850s and 1860s. The poses are simple and plain, but the delicate glass plates are each mounted in an ornamental frame, as if they were destined for the mantelpiece. Other forces possess similarly early records, though it is most likely that at this time the work was carried out by professional photographers who were not yet members of the police force itself. The great growth of specialised police photographers followed the successful development of Sir Edward Henry's system of identification by means of fingerprints, introduced at New Scotland Yard in 1901. It soon became apparent that the only way to record finger impressions found at the scene of criminal activities was to photograph them, and increasing numbers of police photographers were engaged to make best use of the specialised techniques.

Many thousands of identification pictures are now taken each year and the prints filed, together with the prisoner's fingerprints, at the Central Criminal Record Office and at Regional Record Centres. The police in this country have no authority to photograph an accused person who objects, but if necessary an application for a remand in custody enables the prison governor to take the prisoner's photograph under an authority granted by Section 16 of the Prison Act of 1952. Governors of prisons, remand centres, detention centres and Borstal institutes are themselves required by the Criminal Justice Act of 1948 to register and photograph all persons convicted of crime, but these powers go back to 1870 (see figure 16.1). Act 17, Section 3 of the Alien Order Act of 1920 also empowered police officers to order the photographing of any alien. The photographs required, however, were to be full-face, with head uncovered. They did not yet have to follow the standardised format of full-length, full-face and profile, laid down by the Committee of Crime Detection Report of 1938, which endeavoured to improve the quality of prisoners' photographs, going so far as to describe the system of lighting and equipment to be used. What we have in this standardised image is more than a picture of a supposed criminal. It is a portrait of the product of the disciplinary method: the body made object; divided and studied; enclosed in a cellular structure of space whose architecture is the file-index; made docile and forced to yield up its truth; separated and individuated; subjected and made subject. When accumulated, such images amount to a new representation of society.

The use of photography here, as a process which enables accurate records to be made quickly and cheaply, is clearly underpinned by a whole set of assumptions about the reality of the photograph and the real 'in' the photograph which we shall have to examine more closely. For the moment, let us accept that, given this conception of photography, it could be and has been extended to most aspects of police work until, today, almost every photographic process and technique is in use; though the still image may be rapidly overhauled by more accessible video techniques and even the use of holograms. The production of photographs for court evidence is now standard practice. Photographs are used to assist in the control of traffic and in the prosecution of traffic offences; to record evidence of bad driving from mobile police patrol cars; to help assess and apportion blame in fatal accident cases before the coroner's court; to provide accurate records of the scenes of crime and of clues found there; to demonstrate the photo-micrographic analysis of forensic evidence; to present visual evidence to juries in the court room of wounding, injuries or damage; to record and deter offences against property; to identify thieves and other intruders; to detect forgeries and questionable documents and to elucidate the method employed to produce them; to observe unruly behaviour at football matches and other places of assembly; to survey road junctions and public spaces from overlooking buildings, nominally for the purposes of planning traffic flow but also to observe the movements of crowds and

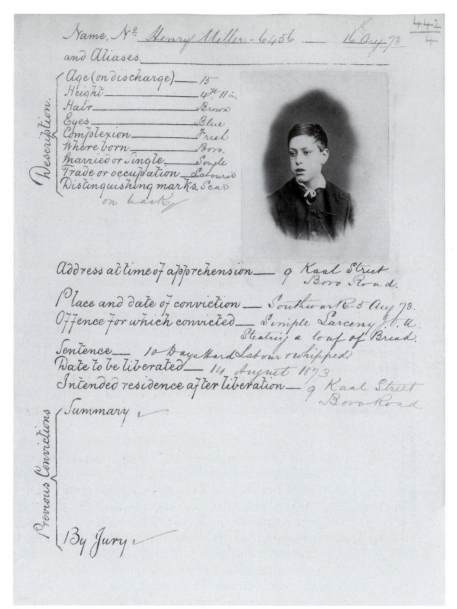

Figure 16.1

Unknown photographer, Wandsworth Prison Records, 1873 (Public Record Office, London, PCOM 2/291)

demonstrations; to catalogue the activities of suspected persons who are under observation; to prove adultery or cohabitation in divorce or social security proceedings. The list is not exhaustive.

However, it is not only the police and the prisons who have found photography such a convenient tool for their new strategies of power. If we examine any of the other institutions whose genealogy Foucault traces, we find photography seated calmly within them. From the mid-nineteenth century on, photography had its role to play in the workings of the factory, the hospital, the asylum, the reformatory and the school, as it did in the army, the family and the press, in the Improvement Trust, the Ordnance Survey and the expeditionary force.

In 1856, Dr Hugh Welch Diamond, founder member of the Royal Photographic Society and resident superintendent of the Female Department of the Surrey County Lunatic Asylum, read a paper to the Royal Society 'On the Application of Photography to the Physiognomic and Mental Phenomena of Insanity'.[9] In it, he expounded his theories on 'the peculiar application of photography to the delineation of insanity', and he illustrated his arguments with photographs he had taken, at his own expense, in the Surrey Asylum (see figure 16.2). Dr Diamond proposed that clinical photography had three important functions in the psychiatric practices of the day. First, it acted as an aid to treatment. Photographic portraits had a value 'in the effect which they produce upon the patient themselves': 'In very many cases they are examined with much pleasure and interest, but more particularly in those which mark the progress and cure of a severe attack of Mental Aberration.'[10] Secondly, these portraits furnished a permanent record for medical guidance and physiognomic analysis:

The Photographer secures with unerring accuracy the external phenomena of each passion, as the really certain indication of internal derangement, and exhibits to the eye the well-known sympathy which exists between the diseased brain and the organs and features of the body . . . The Photographer catches in a moment the permanent cloud, or the passing storm or sunshine of the soul, and thus enables the metaphysician to witness and trace out the connexion between the visible and the invisible in one important branch of his researches into the Philosophy of the human mind.[11]

Central to Diamond's conception of photography as a method of procuring a new kind of knowledge was the idea expressed in *The Lancet* that: 'Photography is so essentially the Art of Truth – and the representative of Truth in Art – that it would seem to be the essential means of reproducing all forms and structures of which science seeks for delineation.'[12] The links of the chain are truth, knowledge, observation, description, representation, record. The value of the camera was extolled because the optical and chemical processes of photography were taken to designate a scientifically exploited but 'natural' mechanism producing 'natural' images whose truth was guaranteed. Photography presented 'a perfect and faithful record, free altogether from the painful caricaturing which so disfigures almost all the published portraits of the insane as to render them nearly valueless either for purposes of art or of science'.[13] It was free, too, from the imprecisions of verbal language:

> The Photographer needs in many cases no aid from any language of his own, but prefers to listen, with the picture before him, to the silent but telling language of nature . . . the picture speaks for itself with the most marked precision and indicates the exact point which has been reached in the scale of unhappiness between the first sensation and its utmost height.[14]

The science of the insane could now go beyond the prosaic descriptions of psychiatrists such as Esquirol or Heinroth:

> Photography, as is evident from the portraits which illustrate this paper, confirms and extends this description, and that to such a degree as warrants the conclusion that the permanent records thus furnished are at once the most concise and the most comprehensive.[15]

What is 'evident' from Diamond's photographs, however, is that their naturalness and concision were the products of a complexly coded intertextuality. As in early police photographs, the props and devices were those of a simple studio, the backgrounds plain, the poses frontal or near frontal, and attention was directed towards the face and hands of the sitter. In conception and organisation, Diamond's picture descended from Philippe Pinel's categorisation of the insane and the earlier typologies of eighteenth-century physiognomy and phrenology. In their pictorial realisation, they drew not only on the conventions of contemporary portraiture but also on the already developed codes of medical and psychiatric illustration found in the line drawings and engravings of works such as J. E. D. Esquirol's *Des Maladies Mentales* of 1838 or the *Physiognomy of Mental Diseases* published in the same year by Sir Alexander Morrison, Diamond's predecessor at the Surrey Asylum. What was remarkable in Diamond's work – for it was not unique, but typified a whole tendency in nineteenth-century photographic practice – was its constitution at the point where discourses of psychiatry, physiognomy, photographic science and aesthetics coincided and overlapped. But the site where they could work together and on each other was a regulated space, a political space, a space in the new institutional order. Here, the knowledge and truth of which photography became the guardian were inseparable from the power and control which they engendered.

The point was not lost on Dr Diamond. His last argument for clinical photography was that it functioned as a means of rapid identification:

> It is well known that the portraits of those who are congregated in prisons for punishment have often times been of much value in recapturing some who have escaped, or in proving with little expense, and with certainty a previous conviction; and similarly the portraits of the insane who are received into Asylums for protection, give to the eye so clear a representation of their case that on their readmission after temporary absence and cure – I have found

the previous portrait of more value in calling to my mind the case and treatment, than any verbal description I may have placed on record.[16]

The methods of the new police force are not far away. Commenting on Diamond's paper, T. N. Brushfield, superintendent of the Chester County Lunatic Asylum, confirmed his view:

> In the case of *criminal* lunatics, it is frequently of great importance that a portrait should be obtained, as many of them being originally of criminal disposition and education, if they do escape from the asylum are doubly dangerous to the community at large, and they may frequently be traced by sending their photographs to the police authorities (into whose hands they are very likely to fall) from some act of depredation they are likely to commit; the photographs would thus cause them to be identified, and secure their safe return to the asylum.[17]

Here, in the tentative photographic practice of Dr Diamond and like-minded superintendents of asylums, is the nexus Foucault describes: the very coincidence of an ever more intimate observation and an ever more subtle control; an ever more refined institutional order and an ever more encompassing discourse; an ever more passive subjection and an ever more dominant benevolent gaze. There are other examples. Henry Hering photographed patients in the Bethlem Hospital in the mid-1850s. In 1860, Charles Le Nègre was ordered to compile a photographic report on the condition of inmates in the Imperial Asylum at Vincennes. Photographs of mentally retarded children were reproduced in *The Mind Unveiled* in 1858. B. A. Morel's *Traité des dégénérescences physiques, intellectuelles et morales de l'espèce humaine et des causes que produisent ses variétés maladises*, published in Paris in 1857, included illustrative photographs taken by Baillarger at the Salpêtrière, where, in the 1880s, Charcot and Richer were to open a Photographic Department to aid their preparation of the *Nouvelle Iconographie de la Salpêtrière*. Whereas, before the invention of photography, clinical records had been confined to spectacular or freakish cases, with the camera, extensive collections and indexes were compiled. The first paper on medical photography had been published in Austria in 1855.[18] The first journal devoted to the subject, the *Internationale medizinisch-photographische Monatschrift* appeared in Leipzig in 1894. It was not a development to be stopped by complaints that the unbridled use of photography in medical practice had gone beyond discretion and ethics.[19]

Such uses of photography were not, however, confined to medicine. In the 1860s, the Stockport Ragged and Industrial School commissioned a local photographer to assemble an album of pictures of each of the teachers and children in the school (see figure 16.3). Similar records were kept in the Greenwich Hospital School. The next decade, the 1870s, saw a great expansion in the use of photographic documentation. The main prisons, such as Wandsworth and Millbank Prisons and Pentonville Penitentiary, set up their own studios employing staff photographers. Local

Figure 16.3

Unknown photographer, Stockport Ragged and Industrial School, c.1865 (Metropolitan Borough of Stockport, Local Studies Library)

Ellen Walton

authorities commissioned photographic surveys of housing and living conditions in working-class areas, and private societies, such as the Society for Photographing Relics of Old London, were founded. Children's Homes and Homes for 'Waifs and Strays' also followed the pattern of development, initially employing local portrait photographers, then taking photographers on to their staff. In May 1874, Thomas John Barnardo opened his first Photographic Department in the 'Home for Destitute Lads' which he had founded at Stepney Causeway in 1871. In its first year, the studio and salaries of photographer and assistant absorbed more than £250 out of an annual budget of £11,571, and photography remained thereafter an important item of expenditure. Between 1874 and 1905, Thomas Barnes and his successor, Roderick Johnstone, produced 55,000 photographs for Barnardo, mostly systematic records of the children as they entered and left the institution. The uses of the photographs were familiar by now:

to obtain and retain an exact likeness of each child and enable them, when it is attached to his history, to trace the child's career.

> To make the recognition easy of boys and girls guilty of criminal acts, such as theft, burglary or arson, and who may, under false pretences, gain admission to our Homes. Many such instances have occurred in which the possession of these photographs has enabled us to communicate with the police, or with former employers, and thus led to the discovery of offenders. By means of these likenesses children absconding from our Homes are often recovered and brought back, and in not a few instances, juveniles who have been stolen from their parents or guardians or were tempted by evil companions to leave home, and at last, after wandering for a while on the streets, found their way to our Institution, have been recognised by parents or friends and finally restored to their care.[20]

Chronological reference albums were kept by the photographers, in which the albumen prints were pasted twelve to a page, with the names and dates of the children written under each photograph. Barnardo himself kept smaller versions, with three photographs to a page, for his own use and to show visitors, parents and police. Photographs were also mounted on personal history sheets on which were filed printed details of each child's background – sometimes including the child's own statement – statistics of colouring, age, height, and subsequent reports and photographs recording the child's progress (see figure 16.4).

Since Barnardo's Homes were neither 'voting charities' nor sponsored by any of the churches, their need for funds was always acute. This induced Barnardo to launch an extensive publicity and advertising campaign which exploited the methods of the successful American revivalist churches. Such methods were controversial. In particular, it was Barnardo's use of photography 'to aid in advocating the claims of our institution' which brought him, in 1877, before a court of arbitration on several accounts of dishonesty and misconduct arising from allegations by the Reverend George Reynolds and the Charity Organisation. Specifically, it was charged that:

> The system of taking, and making capital of, the children's photographs is not only dishonest, but has a tendency to destroy the better feelings of the children . . . He is not satisfied with taking them as they really are, but he tears their clothes, so as to make them appear worse than they really are. They are also taken in purely fictitious positions.[21]

From 1870, Barnardo had commissioned 'before-and-after' photographs, purporting to show the children as they arrived at the Home and then, scrubbed and clean, busy in the workshops. It was one such comparative pairing that the court ruled to have been an 'artistic fiction'. More than eighty such pictures were published, however. Some appeared in pamphlets telling a story of rescue from the iniquities of a previous life and of a happy life in the Home. Others were pasted on to complimentary cards of the

Figure 16.4

Thomas Barnes and
Roderick Johnson,
Personal History of a
Child at Dr Barnardo's
Home, 1874–1883
(The Barnardo
Photographic Archive)

Admitted January 5th, 1876.

Aged 16 Years.

Height, 4-ft. 11-in.

Color of { *Hair, Dark Brown.*
            Eyes, Brown.

Complexion, Dark.

Marks on body—None.

If Vaccinated—Right Arm.

If ever been in a Reformatory or Industrial School ? No.

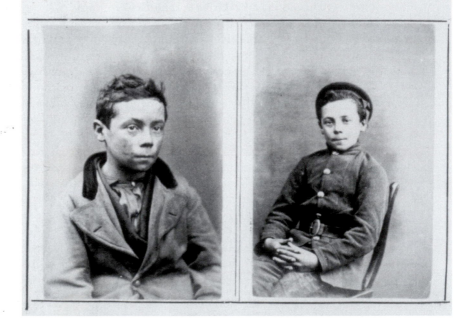

'once a little vagrant – now a little workman' type, which also gave details of the work of the Home and sold in packs of twenty for five shillings or singly for sixpence. To the theme of observation-domination was added that of advertising and the body as commodity.

We have begun to see a repetitive pattern: the body isolated; the narrow space; the subjection to an unreturnable gaze; the scrutiny of gestures, faces and features; the clarity of illumination and sharpness of focus; the names and number boards. These are the traces of power, repeated countless times, whenever the photographer prepared an exposure, in police cell, prison, consultation room, asylum, Home or school (see figure 16.5). Foucault's metaphor for the new social order which was inscribed in these smallest exchanges is that of the 'Panopticon' – Jeremy Bentham's

HUNTINGDON COUNTY GAOL,

5th January 1872

PARTICULARS of Persons convicted of an offence specified in the First Schedule of Habitual Criminals' Act, 1869, and who will be liberated from this Gaol within seven days from date hereof, either on expiration of sentence, or on Licence from Secretary of State.

Name............ *Julia Osgothorpe*
and
Aliases ....

Photograph of Prisoner.

Description when liberated.
- Age (on discharge) *11*
- Height............ *3ft 5*
- Hair............ *L. Brown*
- Eyes............ *Grey*
- Complexion .... *Fresh*
- Where born .... *Nottingham*
- Married or single .... *–*
- Trade or occupation .... *–*
- Any other distinguishing mark......

Address at time of apprehension......... *Grantham*

Whether summarily disposed of or tried by a Jury. *Summarily*

Place and date of conviction .... *Huntingdon 27 Jany 1872*

Offence for which convicted .... *Stealing Bread*

plan for a model institution in which each space and level would be exposed to the view of another, establishing a perpetual chain of observations which culminated in the central tower, itself open to constant public scrutiny.[22] This is the same Jeremy Bentham who advocated a Ministry of Police but, with the development of photography, his utopian structure was to become redundant. Bentham's 'Panopticon' was the culmination and concrete embodiment of a disciplinary technique already elaborated across a range of institutions – barracks, schools, monasteries, reformatories, prisons – in which a temporal-spatial technology, with its enclosed architectural spaces, cellular organisation, minutely graded hierarchical arrangements, and precise divisions of time, was set to work to drill, train, classify and survey bodies in one and the same movement. Foucault took this as a metaphor for that continual process of proliferating local tactics and techniques which operated in society on a micro level, seeking to procure the maximum effect from the minimum effort and manufacturing docile and utilisable bodies. Yet by the end of the nineteenth century, it could be argued, the new will to power, founded on a fateful threefold unity of knowledge, control and utility, could find a new metaphor in the unobtrusive cells of the photographic frame; in its ever more minute division of time and motion; in its ever finer scrutiny of bodies in stringent laboratory conditions. It is a world for which the exhaustive catalogue of bodily movements in Muybridge's images stands as an ominous sign.

V

To reiterate the point, it should be clear that when Foucault examines power he is not just examining a negative force operating through a series of prohibitions. Even where prohibitions can be shown to operate, they do so not only through edicts or laws but in the reality of institutions and practices where they are part of an elaborate economy including all kinds of incitements, manifestations and evaluations – in short, an entire complex, outside which prohibitions cannot be understood. We must cease once and for all to describe the effects of power in negative terms – as exclusion, repression, censorship, concealment, eradication. In fact, power produces. It produces reality. It produces domains of objects, institutions of language, rituals of truth. [. . .]

We might remember, for example, that Marx did not explain the misery of workers, as Proudhon did, as the effect of a concerted theft. He saw that the positive functioning of capitalist production – capitalism's *raison d'être* – was not directed towards starving the workers, but that it could not develop without doing so. Marx replaced a negative, moralistic analysis with a positive one: the analysis of production. So Foucault, in examining the 'birth' of the prison, looks for the possible positive effects of punitive mechanisms rather than their repressive effects alone. He sees the development of penal institutions as a political tactic in a more general field of ways of exercising power. Similarly, in studying the genesis of the asylum, he asks: how did the power exerted in insanity produce psychiatry's 'true' discourse? When he turns to sexuality, he is concerned to discover why it has been the central object of examination, surveillance, avowal and transformation into discourse in Christian societies. [. . .]

Crucial to the development of his thematic has been Foucault's rejection of the idea that knowledge and power are somehow counterposed, antithetical or even separable. [. . .] For Foucault, power produces knowledge. Power and knowledge directly imply one another. The exercise of power itself creates and causes to emerge new objects of knowledge and accumulates new bodies of information. Diffused and entrenched, the exercise of power is perpetually creating knowledge and, conversely, knowledge constantly induces effects of power. [. . .]

Foucault's aim, therefore, is not to write the social history of prohibitions but to trace the political history of the production of 'humanity' as an object of knowledge for a discourse with the status of 'science', the status of 'truth'. As a prerequisite for such a study, he offers us a new set of concepts – a new vocabulary – which must compel us to work over again Gramsci's conception of hegemony and Althusser's conceptions of Ideological State Apparatuses and 'scientific' knowledge. More than this, it must direct our attention to a new and distinct level: that of mechanisms which cannot be reduced to theories, though they overlap them; which cannot be identified with apparatuses or institutions, though they are based on them; and which cannot be derived from moral choices, though they find their justification in morality. These are the modalities according to which power is exercised: the technologies of power.[23]

In analysing these 'technologies', Foucault uncovers a stratum of materials which have so far remained below the threshold of historical visibility. His discoveries have importance both for new and old themes in the history of photography. For example, with the growth of the technology of control and reform, observation and training, a new curiosity arose about the individuals it was intended to transform. It was a curiosity which had been entirely unknown at the beginning of the eighteenth century. In the function of courts at this time, for instance, there had been no need to understand the prisoner or the conditions of the crime. Once guilt had been established, a set of penalties was automatically brought into play that were proportionate and fixed. Yet by the early nineteenth century, In France, Britain and the USA, judges, doctors and criminologists were seeking new techniques to gain a knowledge newly necessary to the administration of power. Prisoners were encouraged to write down their life stories. Dossiers and case histories were compiled. The simple technique of the examination was brought into play, evoking its use on soldiers and children, on the sick and insane. [. . .]

The emergence of the 'documentary' as evidence of an individual 'case' was tied to this development of the examination and a certain disciplinary method, and to that crucial inversion of the political axis of individuation which is integral to surveillance:

> For a long time ordinary individuality – the everyday individuality of everybody – remained below the threshold of description. To be looked at, observed, described in detail, followed from day to day by an uninterrupted writing was a privilege. The chronicle of a man, the account of his life, his historiography, written as he lived out his life formed part of the rituals of his power. The disciplinary methods reversed this relation, lowered the threshold of describable individuality and made of this description a means of control and a method of domination. It is no longer a monument for future memory, but a document for possible use. And this new describability is all the more marked in that the disciplinary framework is a strict one: the child, the patient, the madman, the prisoner, were to become, with increasing ease

from the eighteenth century and according to a curve which is that of the mechanisms of discipline, the object of individual descriptions and bio-graphical accounts. This turning of real lives into writing is no longer a procedure of heroisation; it functions as a procedure of objectification and subjection . . . The examination as the fixing, at once ritual and 'scientific', of individual differences, as the pinning down of each individual in his own particularity . . . clearly indicates the appearance of a new modality of power in which each individual receives as his status his own individuality, and in which he is linked by his status to the features, the measurements, the gaps, the 'marks' that characterise him and make him a 'case'.[24]

It is not only the 'turning of real lives into writing' which is impli-cated in this process, but also the insatiable appropriations of the camera. Whether it is John Thomson in the streets of London (figure 16.6) or Thomas Annan in the slums of Glasgow (figure 16.7); whether it is Dr Diamond among the female inmates of his asylum in Surrey or Arthur Munby among the trousered pit-girls of Wigan; whether it is Jacob Riis among the 'poor', the 'idle' and the 'vicious' of Mulberry Bend or Captain Hooper among the victims of the Madras famine of 1876: what we see is the extension of a 'procedure of objectification and subjection', the transmission of power in the synaptic space of the camera's examination.[25]

Whatever the claims of the traditional evaluations of such photo-graphic 'records', whatever the pretentions of the 'humane' and docu-mentary tradition, we must see them now in relation to the 'small' historical problems with which Foucault concerns himself: problems of the entry of the individual into the field of knowledge, of the entry of the individual description, of the cross-examination and the file. It is in what he calls these 'ignoble' archives that Foucault sees the emergence of that modern play over bodies, gestures and behaviour which is the emergence of the so-called 'science of man' and the constitution of the modern state.[26]

VI

[. . .]

There is a danger that the particular struggles of photographers and other functional intellectuals may become too dispersed and fragmentary. What give such sectional actions a wider significance are their precise positions in that network of constraints which produces truth and which, in turn, induces the regular effects of power. That is to say, what is crucial is their special position in the 'political economy' of truth in our society, to which Foucault has given the name of 'a régime of truth'.[27]

A régime of truth is that circular relation which truth has to the systems of power that produce and sustain it, and to the effects of power which it induces and which redirect it. Such a régime has been not only an effect, but a condition of the formation and development of capitalist societies; to contest it, however, it is not enough to gesture at some 'truth' somehow emancipated from every system of power. Truth itself is already power, bound to the political, economic and institutional régime which produces it. We must forget the claims of a discredited documentary tradition to fight 'for' 'truth' or 'in favour' of 'truth' and see that the battle is one that should be directed at the rules, operative in our society, according to which 'true' and 'false' representations are separated. It is a battle waged against those institutions privileged and empowered in our society to produce and transmit 'true' discourse. It is a battle – going beyond the sectoral and professional interests of photography – around the specific effects of power of this truth and the economic and political role it plays.

The questions which are raised by such a conception of the 'régime of truth' revolve around the conditions of possibility of *struggle* in the particular domain of photography. How is photographic discourse related to those privileged discourses harboured in our society and caused to function as true, and to the institutions which produce them? What are the mechanisms or rules operative in our social formation by which truth and falsehood are to be distinguished and how do they bear on photography? What are the techniques and procedures sanctioned as those which may be used to obtain truth and what particular forms do these take in the techniques and procedures of photography? How is this truth circulated and consumed? Through what channels and institutions does it run? Under the control of what specific powerful apparatuses does it begin to flow? How can it constitute an arena of social confrontation whose object is not the recovery of a pristine 'truth' but the effective displacement of the status of truth and the economic and political role it plays? What would it mean in photography to struggle not for 'correct consciousness' but to change the political, economic and institutional régime of the production of truth, to detach its power from the specific forms of hegemony in which it now operates, and to project the possibility of constructing a new politics of truth?

The territory of the dispute must be clear. You will see that we are thrown back again on that knot of assumptions about the nature of photography which was left to be unravelled in my discussion of police photography. It is the use of the photograph in police work – primarily for its 'value as evidence' – and the insertion of the photograph in legal structures that offer a privileged view of the organisation of the régime of photographic truth in our society, and it is to this that I want to turn.

VII

In a manual of police photography written by a former Detective Chief Inspector of Birmingham City Police, we find the following advice. First, on the level of production:

> A good record should of course be properly exposed, processed and printed. It must be correctly focused and sharp throughout, and all vertical lines of the picture must be upright and should not converge in the print.

Figure 16.6

John Thomson, The Crawlers *from* Street Life in London, 1877–78 (The Mansell Collection)

Figure 16.7
Thomas Annan,
Close No. 11
Bridgegate *from*
Photographs of Old
Closes and Streets of
Glasgow, 1868 (The
Mansell Collection)

A photograph should include everything appertaining to its subject, and relevant to its purpose. If this cannot be done with one picture, then others must be taken in order that the whole subject is covered. Photographs of scenes of crime and other aids to evidence are usually examined in conjunction with a detailed plan to scale, showing the scene and enabling a true picture to be obtained.

Photographs made for the purpose of crime detection or for production in any court proceedings should not be retouched, treated or marked in any way. Exaggerated lighting effects must not be used, and deep shadows or burnt-out highlights could reduce the value, as evidence, of an otherwise good record picture.

Photographs should, where possible, be taken from eye level and this applies to traffic-accident photographs where the views of the drivers concerned may be an important factor.

Prints are usually preferred on the 'soft' side, because detail is more important than print brightness.

The police photographer who has in mind these basic requisites of a good record photograph will standardise his procedure and technique in order that the right type of photograph is produced automatically.[28]

Secondly, on the mode of presentation of the images:

In producing photographs to court, the police photographer must state on oath the time, day and date he took the photographs, and the fact that he processed the negatives himself. He then produces the negatives to show that they have not been retouched or interfered with in any way, and finally produces prints (usually enlarged from the negatives) which are entered as exhibits with the negatives.[29]

If this cannot be done, an affidavit sworn by the technician who processed the film or even the technician in person will have to be produced to prove the chain of possession. Finally, on the status of the photographer as witness to the 'truth':

A qualified police photographer with the necessary experience may be regarded as an expert witness and competent within his own field to express an opinion if asked by the court to do so.

In these and other instances where an opinion is called for, the court places a great deal of reliance on the qualifications and experience of the witness. It follows that every police photographer should take every opportunity to obtain all necessary qualifications by examination and should also gain every possible experience in the specialised fields of photography appertaining to his work. If this is done, his evidence will stand up against any given by some other expert who may be called to rebut his testimony.[30]

Confirmation of these basic conditions and procedures comes from the standard British and American work of reference on photographic evidence by S. G. Ehrlich, a specialist in the preparation of court exhibits, Fellow of the Royal Microscopical Society and member of The American Society of Photographic Scientists and Engineers. Ehrlich is at pains to define the exact requirements of photography as an aid to counsel in civil cases so as to distinguish it from amateur, freelance or photojournalistic practice. But behind his detailed technical discussion lies the notion that:

In addition to understanding the scientific principles of physics, optics and chemistry on which photography depends, the good photographer must have the imagination and creative ability to reproduce scenes on films so that they will convey to the viewer the same information and impressions he would have received had he directly observed the scene.[31]

Later Ehrlich summarises the nature of legal photography thus:

Legal photographs are made for the purpose of ultimate use in a courtroom, or at least to be exhibited to people who are to be informed or persuaded by them. In making photographs for use in litigation, lawyers and photographers should strive for 'legal quality', a term used here to describe photographs having certain characteristics of objectivity and accuracy.

So far as is possible, photographs should show the matter depicted in a neutral, straightforward way. The photographer should be cautioned against producing dramatic effects; any drama in the picture should emanate from the subject matter alone, and not from affected photographic techniques, such as unusual camera angles, printing variations, cropping and the like. Any such attempt to dramatise photographs may result in their exclusion and a consequent suspicion on the part of the jurors that the party offering such photographs cannot be trusted. Therefore, commercial photographers who are not experienced in legal work should be impressed with the importance of a neutral approach when making photographs for courtroom use.

This is not to say that photographers making photographs should dispense with the elements of imagination and artistry, but only that he should strive for accuracy rather than effect. Indeed, advanced techniques, and the use of very specialised and delicate equipment, are often necessary in order to produce photographs that are fair and accurate representations of the matters they depict.

There are courtroom advantages to be gained from using photographs that appear to have been professionally made. Compared with amateur snapshots or home movies, professional photographs have an aura of objectivity and purposefulness, and it is less likely that there will be anything in their appearance to divert the attention of viewers from the matters they depict.

On the other hand, there are instances in which counsel must use photographs of amateurish appearance simply because they are the best, or the only, pictures available. Furthermore, counsel should avoid obtaining photographs that appear too slickly made or too expensive, lest the jurors come to believe that the presentation is being overdone. Legal photographs should be rich in information but not expensive in appearance.[32]

There are disarmingly frank texts, with their recurrent themes of sharpness and frontality, exhaustive description and true representation, the outlawing of exaggerated effects and any overt kind of manipulation, standardised processing and careful presentation, and the expertise and professional status of the photographer. They set these forward, unabashed, as criteria which establish the credentials of the print as a 'good record picture' of 'legal quality' and therefore guarantee its objectivity and accuracy, or even that it presents a scene as it would have been viewed if one had been there. They are unshaken in their belief in the photograph as a direct transcription of the real. The falsifications that can occur – cropping, retouching, interference with the negative – are only perversions of this purity of nature. Behind every distorted or inadequate photograph is a truth which might have been revealed – that 'brute photograph (frontal and clear)' of which Roland Barthes once dreamed.

How are we to explain this configuration of demands and expectations levelled at the photograph? What are we to make of this assertion and qualification of its 'truth'? And how may we bring our explanation closer to our analysis of the field of power relations which constitutes the régime of truth? Recent advances in semiology and the theory of the subject have shown that every text – including the photographic text – is an activity of production of meaning which is carried on within a certain *régime of sense*. It is this régime which gives the productivity of the discourse a certain fixity, dependent on the limits the society in question sets itself, in which the text is produced as natural.

The dominant form of signification in bourgeois society is the *realist* mode, which is fixed and curtailed, which is complicit with the dominant sociolects and repeated across the dominant ideological forms. Realism offers a fixity in which the signifier is treated as if it were identical with a pre-existent signified and in which the reader's role is purely that of consumer. It is this realist mode with which we are confronted when we look at the photograph as evidence. In realism, the process of production of a signified through the action of a signifying chain is not seen. It is the product that is stressed, and production that is repressed. The complex codes or use of language by which realism is constituted appear of no account. All that matters is the illusion; just as in the capitalist market economy, all that matters is the value of the commodity measured against the general medium of exchange – money. Production is entirely elided.[33]

Realist texts are based on a certain, limited plurality of language which is, however, subject to a definite closure: the text is nothing but what it can denote or describe, together with the rhetorical grace with which it does so. It rotates between these two terms in a pre-ordained oscillation: from description to rhetoric; from observation to expression. In this limited movement, it is the business of the language-medium only to 'express' or 'communicate' a pre-established concept. Such is the constriction that signifier and signified appear not only to unite, but the signifier seems to become transparent so that the concept appears to present itself, and the arbitrary sign is naturalised by a spurious identity between reference and referents, between the text and the world.

Realism is a social practice of representation, an overall form of discursive production, a normality which allows a strictly delimited range of variations. It works by the controlled and limited recall of a reservoir of similar 'texts', by a constant repetition, a constant cross-echoing. By such 'silent quotation', a relation is established between the realist 'text' and other 'texts' from which it differs and to which it defers. It is this mutuality which summons up the power of the real: a reality of the intertext beyond which there is no-sense. What lies 'behind' the paper or 'behind' the image is not reality – the referent – but reference: a subtle web of discourse through which realism is enmeshed in a complex fabric of notions, representations, images, attitudes, gestures and modes of action which function as everyday know-how, 'practical ideology', norms within and through which people live their relation to the world. [. . .] It is by the routes it opens to this complex sphere that the realist text trades with that generally received picture of what may be regarded as 'real' or 'realistic' – a picture which is not recognised as such but rather presents itself as, precisely, the Reality. It is a traffic which brings into circulation not a personal and arbitrary 'association of ideas' but a whole hidden corpus of knowledge, a social knowledge, that is called upon through the mechanism of connotation and which gives the encounter with the régime of sense its solidity.

We are not dealing here with a process of signification which is immutable but one that was, in Nietzsche's term, historically 'incorporated' and which is historically changing.[34] Its origins take us back to that same period in which Foucault traced the emergence of a cluster of institutions: the 'disciplinary archipelago'. A crucial part of the attempt of the emergent bourgeoisie to establish its hegemony in the eighteenth and nineteenth centuries was the creation of several institutions of language: in England, for example, the Royal Society with its 'scientific' philosophy of language, as well as the institutions of journalism and literature.[35] It was across such institutions that the realist convention was installed and ceased to be visible as convention, becoming natural – identical with reality. A general evaluation of discourse was established whose absolute value was that of reality itself. The dominant discourse attained this through the creation of an identity between signifier and signified. All other discourses were to be gauged against this measure, according to the varying degree of 'truth' they contained, so that a strict positionality was established whose reference point was the dominant discourse which appeared to have its point of origin in the Real.

[. . .] The documentary mode held in such esteem by certain sections of the left – call it 'real reportage' or what you will – is already implicated in the historically developed techniques of observation-domination and because it remains imprisoned within an historical form of the régime of truth and sense. Both these bind it fundamentally to the very order which it seeks to subvert.

JOHN TAGG

Notes

1   The argument in this [section] is both an introduction to and a highly compressed version of that made at greater length in [Tagg's] chapters which follow. For a closely related study of photography and the labour process, see Allan Sekula, 'Photography between labour and capital', in B. H. D. Buchloh and R. Wilkie (eds), *Mining Photographs and Other Pictures 1948–1968* (Halifax/Cape Breton, Nova Scotia, Nova Scotia College of Art and Design, 1983) [extracted in Chapter 12 of this volume].

2   M. Foucault, 'Power and sex: an interview with Michel Foucault', *Telos*, 32 (summer 1977), p. 157.

3   A. Gramsci, 'State and civil society', in Q. Hoare and G. Nowell-Smith (eds), *Selections from the Prison Notebooks*, (London, Lawrence and Wishart, 1971), p. 210ff.

4   L. Althusser, 'Ideology and ideological state apparatuses (notes towards an investigation)', in *Lenin and Philosophy and Other Essays*, trans. B. Brewster (London, New Left Books, 1971), p. 139 [extracted in Chapter 19 of this volume].

5   Ibid., p. 156.

6   M. Foucault, *Discipline and Punish: The Birth of the Prison*, trans. A. Sheridan (London, Allen Lane, 1977), pp. 26, 213–14; and 'Prison talk: an interview with Michel Foucault', *Radical Philosophy*, 16 (spring 1977), p. 10.

7   J. P. Smith, quoted in E. P. Thompson, *The Making of the English Working Class* (Harmondsworth, Penguin, 1968), p. 89.

8   Ibid., p. 89. See also C. Wegg-Prosser, *The Police and the Law* (London, 1973); and D. Philips, *Crime and Authority in Victorian England: The Black Country 1835–1860* (London, Croom Helm, 1977), ch. 3, 'The old and new police'.

9   H. W. Diamond, 'On the application of photography to the physiognomic and mental phenomena of insanity', in S. L. Gilman (ed.), *The Face of Madness: Hugh W. Diamond and the Origin of Psychiatric Photography* (Secaucus, Brunner-Mazel NJ, 1976), pp. 17–24. The paper was summarised in the *Saturday Review*, 2 (24 May 1856), p. 81; and this summary was reprinted in *The Photographic Journal*, 3 (21 July 1956), pp. 88–9.

10   Diamond, 'Application of photography', p. 21.

11   Ibid., p. 20.

12   The *Lancet*, 22 January 1859, p. 89, quoted in S. L. Gilman, 'Hugh W. Diamond and psychiatric photography', in Gilman (ed.), *The Face of Madness*, p. 5.

13   Diamond, 'Application of photography', p. 24.

14   Ibid., p. 19.

15   Ibid., pp. 20–1.

16   Ibid., pp. 23–4.

17   *The Photographic Journal*, 3 (1857), p. 289, quoted in Gilman (ed.), *The Face of Madness*, p. 9.

18   H. W. Berend, 'Uber die Benützung der Lichtbilder für Heilwissenschaftliche Zwerke', *Wein. med. Wischr*, 5 (1855), p. 291.

19   W. Keiller, *New York Medical Journal*, 59 (1894), p. 788. See also R. Ollerenshaw, 'Medical illustration in the past', in E.F. Linssen (ed.), *Medical Photography in Practice* (London, 1971).

20   Quoted in V. Lloyd and G. Wagner, *The Camera and Dr Barnardo* (Hertford, 1974), p. 14.

21   Ibid., p. 12.

22   On the Panopticon, see Foucault, *Discipline and Punish*, pp. 200–9; and Foucault, 'The eye of power', *Semiotexte*, 3, 2 (1978), pp. 6–19.

23   Foucault, *Discipline and Punish*, pp. 23, 131, 215.

24   Ibid., pp. 191–2.

25   John Thomson, Fellow of the Royal Geographical Society, travelled extensively in the Far East, publishing four volumes of *Illustrations of China and its People* (1873–4). With Adolphe Smith he co-authored *Street Life in London*, which appeared in monthly instalments from February 1877. Thomas Annan photographed in and around Glasgow between 1867 and 1877 for the Glasgow City Improvement Trust, publishing *The Old*

Closes and Streets of Glasgow in 1868 – the first commissioned work of its kind. Arthur Munby recorded details of his encounters with working women from the 1850s on and championed women's right to work at and wear what they wished. He bought and commissioned an extensive collection of photographs of labouring women. Jacob Riis's work as a police reporter in New York led him to take up photography in 1887 to further his personal crusade against slums such as Mulberry Bend. Half-tone reproductions of his photographs illustrated his book, *How the Other Half Lives* (1890). Willoughby Wallace Hooper served with the 4th Regiment of the Madras Light Cavalry from 1858 to 1896 and photographed the victims of the Madras famine of 1876–7.

26   Foucault, *Discipline and Punish*, p. 191.

27   M. Foucault, 'The political function of the intellectual', *Radical Philosophy*, 17 (summer 1977), pp. 13–14, see also *Discipline and Punish*, pp. 27–8.

28   H. Pountney, *Police Photography* (London, 1971), p. 3.

29   Ibid., pp. 3–4.

30   Ibid., pp. 4, 5.

31   S. G. Ehrlich, *Photographic Evidence: the Preparation and Use of Photography in Civil and Criminal Cases* (London, 1967), p. 10.

32   Ibid., pp. 26–7.

33   See the analysis of the structuration of the 'classic' realist text in R. Barthes, *S/Z* (London, Jonathan Cape, 1975); and ch. 4 of R. Coward and J. Ellis, *Language and Materialism: Developments in Semiology and the Theory of the Subject* (London, Routledge, 1977), pp. 45–60.

34   F. Nietzsche, *The Gay Science*, W. Kaufmann (trans.) (New York: Random, 1974, para. 110, pp. 169–71).

35   See Coward and Ellis, p. 47.

Feeble monsters: making up disabled people
Jessica Evans

> **The idea of otherness is complicated, but certain themes are common: the treatment of the other as more like an object, something to be managed and possessed, and as dangerous, wild, threatening. At the same time, the other becomes an entity whose very separateness inspires curiosity, invites inquiring knowledge.**
>
> (L. Jordanova, *Sexual Vision*)

[. . .]

One of the most powerful models of disability, which still dominates professional policy and institutional practices as well as existing at a popular level, has been the medical model. Characteristically, as part of a conservative tradition of political thought, this emphasizes individual loss or incapacities, implying that the impairment is what limits and thus defines the whole person. The focus here is on the failure of the individual to adapt to society as it is, and thus the impairment is regarded as the 'cause' of disability. But increasingly the disabled people's movement and writers in support of it have countered this with a 'social model' which places emphasis on the power of significant groups to define the identity of the 'other' through the lack of provision of accessible environments, lack of provision of sign language, subtitles on television, braille and so on. So while impairment is just one limited fact about a given individual, an individual becomes disabled because of the failure of the social environment to adjust to the needs and aspirations of citizens with impairments (see Barton, 1996). [. . .]

This chapter is taken from *The Media: an Introduction*, edited by A. Briggs and P. Cobley (Harlow, Longman, 1998), pp. 335–353.

Essentialism, disability, sexuality

In his book *Mythologies*, Barthes (1973: 155) points to the way in which ideology in capitalist society 'continuously transforms the products of history into essential types' so that things lose the 'memory that they were once made'. Essentialism is primarily a philosophy of determinism which holds that within each human individual there is some ultimate essence (biological or moral-behavioural) which does not change and which obliges us to behave, as our lives unfold, within more or less predictable limits. My study constitutes a form of ideology-critique; I am interested in the ways in which the production of meaning and cultural value serves to sustain relations of domination and subordination. Essentialism can be regarded as a common strategy of the ideologist who strives to attribute a natural and thus immutable status to what are socially constituted phenomena. In this manner the prejudicial treatment of people with learning difficulties in particular has been justified by asserting the existence of an incurable and innately useless condition. Photographic realism supplies the evidence for this supposed 'truth' of the impaired person. Disabled people are held to be a homogeneous group of people who are more similar to each other than to anyone else through the unifying factor of a shared nature; and therefore, whose situation, behaviour, actions, thoughts and needs are simply expressions of the truth of a deeper biological pathology.

Studies of the representation of disabled people have shown that disabled people are habitually screened out of television fiction and documentary programmes or else occur in a limited number of roles. (For a 'content' analysis of British TV, see Cumberbatch and Negrine, 1992; see also Longmore, 1987; Barnes 1992.) It is as if having a physical or mental impairment is the defining feature of a person to such an extent that it makes a character less than a whole character: it subtracts from personhood and undercuts one's status as a bearer of culture. Writers over many years have used mental and physical impairment or ugliness to signify badness, evil or moral ambivalence in a character – Shakespeare's *Richard III*, Captain Hook in *Peter Pan*, the *Phantom of the Opera*, the Bond villains, *The Hunchback of Notre-Dame*. Where impairment is used as a cipher in this way, it represents the continuation of Judaeo-Christian archaic, pre-scientific and cosmological systems of thought in which biological wholeness is divine, its opposite cast out as legal impurities (see Parkin, 1985). In the medieval period, visibly impaired children were seen as 'changelings' – the devil's substitutes for human children and the product of the mother's involvement with sorcery and witchcraft (see Haffter, 1968). The anthropologist Mary Douglas (1966) has important things to say about how traditional societies view anomaly, which may have a parallel in how contemporary culture 'thinks' people with impairments – as neither human nor animal, neither representing life nor death. (For the pre-Enlightenment treatment of 'disability' in western culture in general, see Ryan and Thomas, 1987.)

Status and authority in images are implicitly associated with an absence of disability. For example, Franklin D. Roosevelt was never seen in a wheelchair although his legs were paralysed. Being President of the USA was felt to be incompatible with being physically damaged – the wheelchair is the ultimate symbol of lack of power. Representations of disability are, however, principally bifurcated by gender. In recent years, for example, the disabled man has been a central character in a number of Hollywood films. The body, its physical aspects and demeanour, are the concrete signifiers which carry associations and concepts of femininity and masculinity. Film-makers rely upon an audience's knowledge of these codes in order to make damage to the body of a character operate as a statement about that character. If masculinity is signified by strength and resolve, independence and will power, then dramatic power can be derived from constructing a narrative around a man who has lost power over his body, for example in the 1990 film *My Left Foot* and *Born on the 4th July*. Judith Williamson, in a review of these films, felt that they were not about disability *per se*. Rather disability was used as a metaphor for the state of mind of the male characters: 'These films are about the hell of dependency for men. And maybe the men have to be in wheelchairs for that dependency to be made vivid' (1990: 26). In the Multiple Sclerosis (MS) Society's campaign 'Tears Lives Apart', posters showed beautiful young bodies being ripped apart by the scourge of MS, a campaign known colloquially by the advertising agency that produced it as 'Beauty and the Beast' (see Hevey, 1992: 43). The series of posters is photographed in and out of focus, pictorialist style; bodies intertwined against a black background with the sculptural drama of Rodin's *The Kiss* (see Hevey, 1992: plate 3). One shows a 30-year-old man being bathed by a sexualized woman – her sleeves rolled up, their heads bowed together. Here, the implication is that disability for men means a loss of (hetero) sexual virility, for where once the woman might have been his girlfriend, the narrative suggests she is now his mother. The text reads 'How does it feel to have a mental age of thirty and a physical age of one?' as if to anchor the meaning of the poster finally in a sense of childlike dependency. The fear portrayed is that physical impairment inevitably means the final triumph of the body over the mind: to be disabled is to be stripped of fundamental human capacities such as thinking, acting, willing and taking responsibility, and being condemned to endlessly re-enact the 'horror' of one's earliest dependency on a woman – as mother.

Representations of disabled women in film have been significantly different. Since the traditional meaning of femininity is often synonymous with dependency and vulnerability, disability cannot be used to pose a threat to women's autonomy. Disability is more commonly therefore used as a sign of women's excessive vulnerability and so blindness is the central signifier in storylines which create a sense of cumulative foreboding, often ending in physical attack (in films such as *Wait Until Dark* (1967) with Audrey Hepburn, *Blind Terror* (1971) with Mia Farrow, and *Blink* (1994) with Madeleine Stowe).

But it is noticeable that, opposed to this, wheelchair-using fictional women characters have been embittered, aggressive, or assertive of their needs (for example, *What Ever Happened to Baby Jane* (1962) with Joan

Crawford and Bette Davis). In these cases my interpretation is that it represents a cultural fear that a physically damaged woman is incompatible with the requirement to be nurturing and caring (i.e. a good and protective mother), and so her assertiveness is a direct threat, portrayed in revenge scenarios and perhaps even destructive of life. Impairment in representation is seemingly transgressive; pointing to the boundaries of taken-for-granted sexual difference and producing transgressive women who are more masculine and tough and conversely making men dependent and vulnerable.

The charitable mind of state

Michel Foucault, the French historian and philosopher, has argued that from the late eighteenth century the biological traits of a population became relevant factors for economic management and state intervention; the body and its health becomes a key bearer of qualities of fertility, sickness and health, strength and weakness, and moral behaviour. A finer and finer 'grid of observation' is placed over the population, in order to create a whole series of 'functional discriminations' between different types of people, such as the wilfully idle and the involuntary unemployed (Foucault, 1980). These categorizations serve as the justificatory framework for the 'career' of a particular individual in the nineteenth-century institutions of the asylum, the medical clinic, workhouse, and prison. The Eugenics Movement, a strong form of applied Social Darwinism, became prominent among the new administrative and professional classes who serviced these institutions; its premise was that the existing social hierarchy resulted from innate differences in the qualities and capacities of individuals [. . .]. Culminating in the exterminations in Nazi Germany, ideologues began to apply the term 'degeneration' to people whose mental and physical defects were thought to be the outcome of hereditary factors. Eugenicists linked idiocy, pauperism, criminals and the sick poor with heredity and argued that the sick must be segregated from the healthy, the poor from the weak in order to protect the 'national stock'. In fact, the first charity to deal specifically with people now referred to as 'learning disabled' was called 'The Royal Commission to Control the Feebleminded', and created by the government in 1908. Its specific aim was to curb the evils of idleness and promiscuity which it was felt were wreaking havoc on the stability of society, and to prevent the so-called feeble-minded from reproducing.[1]

Dr Frederick Treves, the surgeon of Mile End Hospital in London, showed John Merrick ('the Elephant Man') to the London Pathological Society just as police were closing down the Victorian freakshows as an indecent spectacle. In the late nineteenth century we can trace an historical shift from the display of disabled freaks as popular exhibits in circuses, museums, fairs and shows, to that of scientific objects for the production of knowledge and for the purposes of human progress [see Bogdan, 1988]. [. . .]

These are shifts in discursive practice, in the sense that people who have impairments have been the changing objects of thought and investigation. In the nineteenth century, photography had become very important to the formation of new ways of thinking about the relationship between the body, the mind and social relations. The construction of these new kinds of knowledge about the population was executed – within the prison, workhouse, the police force, and psychiatric asylum – through close attention to the visible physiological features by which each individual was measured and compared (see Green, 1984, 1996; Tagg, 1988 and Chapter 16 of this volume). Here the doctrine of physiognomy had pre-eminence as it claimed that a causal relationship existed between the inner pathology of the individual and his or her external, visible characteristics from facial expression to the physical features of the face. Photography, seen as a slave to the visible fact, was perfectly placed to legitimize this 'science' as it promised to show the link between seeing and knowing. However, the postwar charity poster represents the legacy of physiognomic photography but combines it with the mythological narratives of a pre-Enlightenment age of monsters.

Images and publicity published by charitable organizations as part of their fund-raising activities dominate representation in the public sphere. I shall argue that these images undermine disabled people as autonomous human beings with all that that implies – will, purpose and potential. Disabled people become the recipients of others' good will; the charitable ethos *per se* actively structures a mental and social gap between the donor and the disabled recipient. Furthermore, as we shall see, charities invariably reproduce a medical model of disability and undermine the political struggle for citizenship that is being waged by disabled people themselves under the banner of 'rights, not charity'.

During the 1980s the balance between public and private aid for the poor and disadvantaged shifted towards greater reliance on the private charity organizations. Their traditional role of supplementing state provision is being increasingly transformed into one of replacing it, in areas where state support had been withdrawn or decreased. Since the National Lottery was launched (November 1994), on the back of 24-hour television charity 'telethons', the mantra of 'good causes' has helped to drown out any public debate about the privatization of public services and the commercialized regulation of human needs, which are increasingly being cast as private troubles or personal tragedies. It feels like bad faith or just plain cynicism to criticize the whole edifice of a culture increasingly dominated by charity practice and ethos, cast as permeated by unimpeachable motives. As we have seen, there is good reason to be sceptical about the innocence of charities. Jacques Donzolot has written of the way that charitable motivation could 'only be kindled by the fires of extreme misery, by the sight of the spectacular suffering, and then only by the feeling of inflated importance accruing to the giver through the immediate solace his charity brought to the sufferer' (Donzolot, 1977: 45). There is a structurally necessary relationship between the portrayal of disability as a disaster or a tragic loss, and the function of raising money.[2] This means that any critique of representation must also link that critique to the institutional practices and ideologies of charity.

The charity sector is a rapaciously competitive big business (Drake, 1996: 150). Impairment charities go about the business of constructing publicity campaigns in much the same way that any other business markets its product. But the difference is that unlike other companies, charities are advertising products who happen to be people, whose impairment then becomes the 'unique selling proposition' for the charity product. Only disabled persons, constructed as a particular kind of people, are subject to a process of image specialization and as such their image can be constituted as a transaction in the public sphere: an image of a person who has Down's Syndrome, for example, can be magnified a hundred times on a billboard – just because that person has Down's Syndrome.

But charities play down the fact that they are in the business of marketing their wares as this may not be seen as compatible with voluntary giving. Their byline and logo are often discreetly placed at the bottom of the poster. But more importantly, charities seek to differentiate themselves from the whole world of public commercial advertising by adopting different visual conventions for their posters. One common difference is the use of black-and-white naturalist photography, photographs of 'real' disabled people – although some charities have in the last few years begun to introduce colour and to produce more obviously constructed, graphically based posters. Using monochromatic naturalism allows the charity to associate with the tradition of social documentary, itself embedded in a British tradition of philanthropic paternalism, and to distance itself in a protestant fashion from the commercial world of advertising with its promise of instant gratification and its narratives of the pleasure of acquisitiveness.

The marketing success of each charity depends upon it becoming synonymous with a particular impairment, and it is the impairment which the charity constructs as defining that person. Thus, the adherence to the medical model by charities means that the focus for change lies in the individual, who must be rehabilitated, cured or helped to adapt. This is reflected in the ameliorative and compensatory way in which charities choose to spend their income – for example, on specially adapted mini-buses complete with the charity's logo, for the use of designated groups of disabled people (see Drake, 1996). The interests of learning-disabled children and adults are assumed to be represented by Mencap, those children who have Down's Syndrome by the Down's Syndrome Association, those of people with cerebral palsy by SCOPE, those with Multiple Sclerosis by the MS Society, blind people by the RNIB (Royal National Institute for the Blind), and so on. In a report on charity advertising commissioned by the King's Fund, Susan Scott-Parker (1989: 11) says 'As it stands now, charities tend to commission campaigns as though they owned their particular model of disabled person, in much the same way that Ford owns Fiesta cars . . . The aim of the campaign is to raise brand awareness for the charity.' The Multiple Sclerosis Society's 'Tears Lives Apart' rip (the corporate logo of ripped paper) has become the sign by which it and multiple sclerosis have become branded, connected together in the public consciousness. [. . .]

A final point to note here is that, in material terms, the entire relationship between charities, ad. agencies and target audiences is an enclosed 'circuit' which does not depend at all upon the participation of disabled people themselves. They are not clients (the charity is), nor the audience/customer (non-disabled people are targeted as the donors of funds or as potential volunteers), nor the product (which is the charity) (see Scott-Parker, 1989: 13). From the point of view of the advertising agencies, charity accounts enhance their corporate image, allowing them to offset a hard-nosed corporate image with one which is more for the wider social good. For the charities, the agencies offer discounted rates but in practice this means cheaper advertising with often junior staff working on the account and with less time allocated to it. Furthermore, disability-related charities occupy a special niche within the advertising industry and do not usually join the Advertisers' Association or routinely participate in advertising industry events. A national seminar for the advertising industry in 1987 examined 'The Portrayal of People in Advertising' and the only social group left undiscussed was disabled people (by far the largest 'minority' group in the UK estimated at 10–12 per cent of the population). [. . .]

Charity advertisements

An early Mencap poster has a photograph of a young girl ('Nina' in real life) with the words 'Twenty children born on Christmas Day will always have a cross to bear'. A headline on the front cover of *Parents Voice* (the Mencap magazine for its members) in the early 1980s, accompanying a photograph of a smiling baby with Down's Syndrome, read 'Sometimes late is as bad as never'. And on Mencap posters in the late 1980s the following slogans accompanied black-and-white studio portraits of learning-disabled people: 'Joanne can't get better. Her future can'; 'She's different. Her life doesn't have to be'; 'A mental handicap is there for life. So is Mencap' (see Hevey, 1992: plate 5). The charity is bent on informing the public and its own members that the disabled person is inherently damaged goods but that the charity itself is integral to the future of that person. It promises that it can add value to that person's life. 'Mental handicap' is presented as a fixed entity residing in a body from birth, furnishing an individual with predictable limits on life opportunities.

'No Sense, No Feelings?' This headline for a 1985 Mencap poster presents us with the attitude of the prejudiced viewer (indicated by the question mark), which the photograph and the rest of the text are supposed to refute (for illustrations see Evans, 1988: 44). Thus, 'No Sense, No Feelings?' is what the charity is imputing to the prejudiced audience; this is rebutted with 'They may not think as fast but they feel as deeply', representing the authoritative voice of the charity speaking the truth about people with learning disability. But, as we look at the poster, it can only confirm assumptions we might already have about 'mentally handicapped people' as abnormal, inferior, and slaves to their instincts. We are shown a man and a woman with their arms locked together in a heart shape, connoting the wedding or engagement portrait. But although they appear at first to be aspiring to this institution of normal culture, the cumulative effect of the poster is that of a parody of the ideal couple which is apparent when we compare this to the stock conventions of the High Street photographer. The image is a contradictory cohesion of this tradition of honorific portraiture (which continues today in the familial portraits of *Hello!* magazine) with the denigratory tradition of nineteenth-century social scientific portraiture. The latter, taken in the prisons and psychiatric institutions, was a form of physiognomic practice, subjecting the individual to the interrogative gaze of the camera in order to establish evidence of innately degenerate types (see Green, 1984).

Here we look at two models: joined together but otherwise isolated they emerge as if specimens from a black background; they are photographed with a wide-angle lens which when used in close up projects lips, noses and hands forwards into the viewer's space. The use of top lighting from a small source casts deep shadows into their eyes and under their chins and emphasizes the creases in their clothes. The choice of heavy contrast, small source lighting (which throws deep shadows) and the wide angle lens creates the effect used in expressionist or gothic horror films. Moreover, as if to underline this madhouse, the man has a pocketful of combs, implying an obsessional activity – but this is paradoxically offset by both heads of hair being untidy and uncombed. Such is obviously the innate handicapped character: persons who are perhaps mad, certainly very peculiar, who are masquerading as normal by aspiring to the conventions of the honorific portrait and the institution of marriage. The text is similar to the way in which animal lovers seek to defend animal protection – they may not be intelligent (like humans) but they have feelings none the less. Imagine if the text was to be placed against a picture of another social group: it would be denounced as offensively sexist or racist, for example. That a statement such as this can be publicly endorsed by a major organization (one that purports to act in the very interests of disabled people) is an indication of how little power learning-disabled people have. We can also note the use of the charity's corporate logo, 'Little Stephen' as he was called, on the bottom right. Little Stephen, a forlorn and lonely little boy, was abandoned in 1992 after the charity finally capitulated to years of charges from 'People First' advocacy groups and the disability rights movement that it infantilized disabled people. The impact of the poster, from the point of view of the charity, relies upon it being seen as a truthful portrait of 'real' handicapped people – as if they have just walked in off the street. I have been challenged about this in lectures – how do I know they are models? Of course, I do not know for certain, but from the point of view of the politics of representation and the effectiveness of the image, whether they are technically models is besides the point. The point is that these 'models' have been selected and their 'look' has been constructed by making selections from all the various paradigms of the signifying toolkit – clothing, lighting, camera angle, facial expression, etc. What is interesting is that people never question whether in regular 'commercial' advertising models are 'real people' or models! To believe that the models in this and other charity posters are somehow untampered with and authentically 'real' is to fall into the trap of thinking that we can have a direct experience of the truth and then find evidence for it in a photograph. Oscar Wilde might have been right when he said that 'External nature imitates art. The only effects that she can show us are effects that we have already seen through poetry or in paintings' (Gilman, 1982).

In another advert from the mid-1980s Mencap colludes directly with the institutions of medical science: the text says 'On Friday May 6th 1983 these babies were born mentally handicapped' (see Evans, 1988: 46). Below this are laid out geometric and clinical looking rows of medical labels with dates and surnames attached, the kind that newborn babies wear. Then the voice of the charity continues – 'It was an average day'. There is here an ambiguous reference to labelling – the connotations of the medical labels in conjunction with the text which ascribes identity at birth allows the poster to refer at a less conscious level to social labelling and stigmatizing. The advert makes no bones about it – it is a deliberately pessimistic, disparaging attitude to the existence of these babies as if they have absolutely no potential, everything that can be known about them is determined at birth. According to Mencap this is an apparently natural not a social event – 'mental handicap' is established from birth as an entity residing in a body, rather than a matter of social construction and evaluation. This poster invokes fear, implying that there is no protection (except perhaps donating to charity) from the randomness of fate which can deal anyone a dud card – perhaps it could happen to YOU. The dread of bearing monsters is one of the perils of parenthood; the poster demonstrates that the eugenic ideology is alive and well for it is as if certain people already alive should not exist as they threaten our normal existence. It is interesting to note that in western medicine the study of congenital defects is referred to as teratology, a term derived from the Greek word for monster.

Mencap revamped its image dramatically in 1992, although it retained the label 'mental handicap', against the demands of learning-disabled people attending the launch event. The posters it has produced in the 1990s are seemingly different. But as if to show it has learnt from the avalanche of criticisms from both advocacy groups and commentators associated with the disabled people's movement, it departed from the documentary naturalism of previous years. Two of these posters were based on a colour graphic. One of the posters showed a blank easel with the caption 'Life with a mental handicap', underneath which is a tin of paints labelled 'Mencap'. The other had the same captions but displayed an empty canoe on a river, below which is a paddle. The implication here is that the meaning and the life of a learning-disabled person is incomplete and empty without the charity to provide it. He or she is a 'tabula rasa' waiting to be filled up with the beneficence of the charity; the 'career' of the disabled person is a shadow of the organization.

The charitable state of mind: psychoanalysis and disability

Why introduce a psychological dimension to my analysis of images of disabled people? It is my contention that the naturalism employed in charity posters is also a project of constructing a belief on the part of viewers in the illusion of objectivity. To believe in something being real is always also a psychical and emotional investment – there is always some trade-off for the viewer and a motivation at stake: why *should* anyone believe in the reality of the image, and what does it do for them? I should point out that there is a body of psychoanalytical work on visual representations which analyses how advertisements act as a catalyst for unconscious desire in their construction of ideal scenarios of pleasure. There is an incitement of idealizing identificatory processes for the viewing subject. But naturalism or documentary genres, whose codes are recognizably the construction of the non-ideal, gritty 'real' world have usually been exempt from a psychoanalytic form of analysis. The debate has focused on how far the realist image distorts 'reality' or generates consensus for ideological views about the world. But to exclude questions of fantasy and identification with the realist image is partly I suspect a result of collusion with the premise of realism, expressed in the mistaken belief that the realist image *is* somehow less constructed and therefore less susceptible to the operations of unconscious process – and therefore less likely to be distorted by the irrational aspects of subjective life.

In the Middle Ages 'indulgences' were bought by church congregations in order to keep their passage to heaven secure. The mental processes engaged by charitable giving are the same – underneath the masquerade of altruism that pervades charity ethos, the psychic reality is that one gives in order to receive. Charitable giving is both a momentary and psychological transaction, one of social insurance against the prospect of damage to the viewer's own body. Presented, as so often is the case, with an aggressive image of pain or debility, the viewer feels relief (that they are not like that), guilt (for feeling relieved), and hatred (for being made to feel guilt). What I want to argue is that pity and altruism, which is the conscious aspect of reacting to disabled posters, are closely linked to hatred and aggression. Giving to charity is at the same time an act of kindness and an act of rejection, making the giver feel whole and separate; these contradictory values are what makes the treatment of disabled people an arena of conflicting values.

The 'separating devices' of charity posters can be understood as defensive strategies, colluded in by both the charity and intended to be colluded in by the audience. We need to examine the way in which fears about dependency, incompetence and debility are projected on to disabled people, who are then denigrated for what people cannot accept in themselves. Freud used the concept of projection to refer to the operation by which the qualities, feelings and wishes which the subject refuses to recognize or rejects in themselves are expelled from the self and located in another person or thing. Projection, then, is a splitting or a denial of 'bad' parts of the self. A psychoanalyst would argue that strong expressions of hate can be a defence against feelings of love or desire which cannot be acknowledged. For example, those who feel so much fear and hatred towards homosexuality that they will beat up gay men on the streets are driven by an excessive need to disown a feeling of desire toward their own sex which they cannot tolerate. In some of the portrait-based posters that have been discussed, it can be seen that the visible differences of people become exaggerated and/or entirely invented – a sign of the unconscious defences at work. Thus these images construct an object of fear which is at the same time a source of fascination. Viewers and disabled people are, in terms of fantasy, deeply bound together and implicated in each others' characteristics, and these exaggerations and distancing devices commonly used in charity posters (such as the 'They' in the 'No Sense, No Feelings?' poster) are a manifestation of this.

What are the fears of – and the desire to look at – the disabled person about? It is my contention that the infantile characteristics of the unconscious are projected on to disabled people who are seen as childish, dependent and underdeveloped and who are then regarded as 'other' and punished by being excluded from ordinary life. Thus popular images and rhetoric of disabled people abound which confront us with people who are imperfect, helpless, disgusting, shitty, dribbling – a threat to rigid ego boundaries. During the socio-developmental processes of early infancy, a range of strict rules of decorum involving standards of privacy, decency and dignity (for example, in potty training) effect a repression of these taboo activities. These codes are enforced to protect us from the disorder, chaos and dependency that, Freud argued, are characteristic of our experiences in the oedipal and pre-oedipal stages of our development. The posters encourage us to expel that which causes unpleasure to the self simply by representing that expelling as *already complete*. We become literally alienated from (and cannot identify with) the object/person we observe.

The paradox that the disabled person as 'other' is seen as *feeble and fearsome at the same time* never becomes clear to the prejudiced person, and the deeply contradictory nature of the beliefs held simultaneously about the 'other' is something that needs to be confronted. Fantasies of disabled people as dangerously threatening (fearsome) and excessively deserving (feeble) – fantasies we see in charity discourse – are products of a psychological splitting and they complement each other. Just as in the archetypal fairy stories, the witchlike qualities that we dread (will they turn us into a toad?) and the helpless, powerless princess/victim, waiting to be rescued, are two sides of the same coin.

Freud and other psychoanalysts have elaborated on the experiences that all small babies have of being in a state of complete dependency on their mothers. The consequent lack of control over their body can be felt as bewildering or even terrifying. In early development anger against the mother and consequent feelings of guilt about the destructive effects of that anger can lead to a bad body image which is carried forward into adult life as a revulsion against dependency and a flight from dependent relation-ships. This 'badness' can be projected on to others as in the construction of femininity as extreme vulnerability, and particularly on to those who are dependent through disability.

This process is similar to the ways in which old people in our culture are also segregated and treated as people waiting to die. There are very close associations between dependency, illness, dying and death, associations we have already seen operating in the charity adverts which are based on a medical model of disability. It seems that increasingly in our culture there are pressures that encourage a reversion to infantile feelings which have to be madly defended against by the processes of splitting and projection. My point is that defences against dependency can be contained by cultural institutions and social relations or heightened by them, which seems to be the case here.

However, it is important to point out that the disability people's movement can also participate in a manic defence against dependency by not recognizing the limits of the social model.

Conclusion

The relationship between the appearance of the body and the 'state of the mind' is absolutely arbitrary but in the naturalistic media images I have discussed an inevitable relationship is established, so that the whole character of the disabled subject appears to be manifested in the visual appearance of the body. I feel that the charities' obsession with the bodily mark betrays an irrational and even sadistic impulse which goes far beyond their humanist claims to be the defenders of disabled people. I see it as a symbolic violence, but one which is normalized by appearing to be naturally 'of the body'.

The peculiar nature of the 'changing attitudes' charity posters of the 1980s and 1990s lies in the acknowledgement of the existence of prejudice combined with the *exemption of responsibility* for this prejudice. Because for various legal and political reasons charities cannot offer an analysis of the causes of the oppression of disabled people, their publicity images depend on an empiricist visual logic addressing a reformed viewer who can now *see* the disabled person straight and truthfully. In fact it is the whole language of 'seeing them' which is the problem precisely because the oppression and inequality of disabled people is not caused by their bodily impairments but by the social arrangements which allow those impairments to become disabilities.

Charity representation is an aspect of the process whereby, in our society, social issues are continually reduced to being about pathologies inherent in particular individuals. So instead of ensuring that all buildings are accessible for wheelchair users, or that sign language becomes integral to all television programmes, or that learning-disabled people have their needs met in an integrated fashion, millions are poured into finding a 'cure' for congenital forms of disability. The research departments of impairment charities spend a large part of their income on research to remove the source of the impairment, for example, to isolate negative genes. In fact if we look at the spending figures for charities [. . .] their priorities are weighted heavily toward 'cure' rather than 'care'. For example, the Muscular Dystrophy Society spends £2.3 million per year on research, £276,000 on welfare and £286,000 on advertising (see Hevey, 1992: 31).

This fantasy of eradication, a continuation from the eugenic discourse of the Social Darwinists, is based on a denial of the fact that there will always be disabled people and most of us will at some point in our lives be disabled – whether congenitally, or through old age, illness, or accident, and so on. My position is informed here by Ian Craib (1994) who argues that we need to recognize the social and psychical 'importance of disappointment'. He thinks that our culture is dangerously close to denying the inevitability and necessity of suffering and of messy or 'negative' feelings, as part of normal life.

Unless this dependency is consciously thought about as something that we have all experienced as babies and more importantly will experience again as a normal part of human life, it will continue to be parcelled off as the specialized experience of people who, by the terms of our culture, are useless and need 'special' and paternalist treatment. Dependency and suffering, painful as they are, have to be acknowledged as a part of life itself, and particular groups should not be made to carry their associations for everyone else.

Notes

1   The link between degeneracy and racial ranking has left us with one legacy – the term 'mongolism' (English word) for the chromosomal disorder of Trisomy 21. Dr Down, in the 1860s linked 'idiocy' with the working classes and was worried about the propagation of an enfeebled race. He based his categorization of idiots on observation of their bodies, and recorded visual similarities of eyes and skin colour of Mongolian nationals and some 'idiots' – his perceptions fitted the nineteenth-century theory of 'recapitulation' which held that certain forms of idiocy were the result of arrested development at an earlier stage in the evolution of white males. The 'idiots' of the 'race' of white males could be explained as being simply the living residues of primitive races. Dr Down's Eurocentric theories led him, therefore, to perceive certain idiots as 'mongols' – the observation of arbitrary characteristics seemed to him to be proof of his theory. Down's fallacy should serve as a warning for those who would make deductions from the observation of appearance to that of social policy. For the seminal account of Dr Down's eugenic persuasion see Gould (1983) (see also Gould, 1981: 134–5; Evans, 1986/7, 1988). For references to eugenics as it relates to disability, see Ryan and Thomas (1987: ch. 5); for a historical survey of how mentally ill and learning-disabled people have been pictorially represented, including the Social Darwinism of photographic physiognomy, see Gilman (1982); for the history of intelligence testing and ranking and the biological determinist categorization of people as feeble-minded, see Gould (1981). On the Nazi 'Euthanasia' Programme see Proctor (1988) and Burleigh (1994). [. . .]

2   David Hevey (1992: 44) has argued that the purpose of charity advertising is not to appeal to a general public, for the income generated by this process is negligible compared to that of legacies and other donations. Its central purpose is to appeal to the internal army of volunteers, a kind of mission statement from the leaders. There have not been many empirical investigations of actual viewer-response to disability images; however, one study in 1990 found that posters which generated feelings of guilt, pity,

and sympathy were those which generated the greatest desire to donate (Eayrs and Ellis, 1990; see also Doddington et al., 1994). My own view is that the kind of research which sets out to measure 'the public's attitudes' is problematic for three reasons: first, that it is limited to people's conscious response which may conflict with their unconscious feelings; second, that this conscious response is likely to be modified by what the interviewees think they ought to say, for many people do not want to appear to be prejudiced; and third, that it assumes a one-to-one cause–effect relationship between a single text and attitude-formation and thus neglects both the cumulative effects of certain kinds of images, and how their meaning is a consequence of their articulation with cultural values and discourses and with developments and transformations in social relations – all of which provide a structuring context for the ways in which people may think about disability, which, for example, may be closely linked to the way they think about ageing or the welfare state.

References

Barnes, C. (1992) *Disabling Imagery and the Media: an Exploration of Media Representations of Disabled People*. Belper: British Council of Organisations for Disabled People.

Barthes, R. (1973) *Mythologies*. London: Granada.

Barton, L. (ed.) (1996) *Disability and Society*. Harlow: Addison-Wesley-Longman.

Bogdan, R. (1988) *Freakshow: Presenting Human Oddities for Amusement and Profit*. Chicago: University of Chicago Press.

Burleigh, M. (1994) *Death and Deliverance: 'Euthanasia' in Germany 1900–45*. Cambridge: Cambridge University Press.

Craib, I. (1994) *The Importance of Disappointment*. London: Routledge.

Cumberbatch, G. and Negrine, R. (1992) *Images of Disability on Television*. London: Routledge.

Doddington, K., Jones, R.S.P. and Miller, B.Y. (1994) 'Are attitudes to people with learning disabilities negatively influenced by charity advertising? An experimental analysis', *Disability and Society*, 9(2) pp. 207–222.

Donzolot, P. (1977) *The Policing of Families*. New York: Pantheon.

Douglas, M. (1966) *Purity and Danger*. Harmondsworth: Penguin.

Drake, R. (1996) 'Disability, charities, normalisation and representation', in L. Barton (ed.), *Disability and Society*. Harlow: Addison-Wesley-Longman.

Eayrs, C.B. and Ellis, N. (1990) 'Charity advertising: for or against people with a mental handicap?', *British Journal of Social Psychology*, 29.

Evans, J. (1986/7) 'The imagined referent', *Block*, 12 (winter) pp. 71–82.

Evans, J. (1988) 'The iron cage of visibility', *Ten.8*, 29: 40–51.

Foucault, M. (1980) 'The politics of health in the eighteenth century', in C. Gordon (ed.), *Michel Foucault: Power/Knowledge*. Brighton: Harvester.

Gilman, S.L. (1982) *Seeing the Insane*. New York: Wiley.

Gould, S.J. (1981) *The Mismeasure of Man*. Harmondsworth: Penguin.

Gould, S.J. (1983) *The Panda's Thumb: More Reflections in Natural History*. Harmondsworth: Penguin.

Green, D. (1984) 'Veins of resemblance', *Oxford Art Journal*, 7(2).

Green, D. (1996) 'On Foucault: disciplinary power and photography', in J. Evans (ed.), *The Camerawork Essays*. London: Rivers Oram Press.

Haffter, C. (1968) 'The changeling: history and psychodynamics of attitudes to handicapped children in European folklore', *Journal of the History of Behavioural Studies*, 4.

Hevey, D. (ed.) (1992) *The Creatures Time Forgot: Photography and Disability Imagery*. London: Routledge.

Jordanova, L. (1989) *Sexual Vision*. New York: Harvester.

Longmore, P.K. (1987) 'Screening stereotypes: images of disabled people in television and motion pictures', in A. Gartner and T. Joe (eds), *Images of the Disabled, Disabling Images*. New York: Praeger.

Parkin, D. (1985) 'Entitling evil: Muslims and non-Muslims in coastal Kenya', in D. Parkin (ed.), *The Anthropology of Evil*. Oxford: Basil Blackwell.

Proctor, R. (1988) *Racial Hygiene: Medicine under the Nazis*. London: Harvard University Press.

Ryan, J. and Thomas, F. (1987) *The Politics of Mental Handicap*, rev. edn. London: Free Association Press.

Scott-Parker, S. (1989) 'The aren't in the brief: advertising people with disabilities', discussion paper. London: King's Fund Centre.

Tagg, J. (1988) *The Burden of Representation*. London: Macmillan.

Williamson, J. (1990) 'Hell on wheels', *Guardian*, 10 May.

18

Marketing mass photography **Don Slater**

The pen is the model of media use in the consumer society: it is the cheapest media technology available; every household possesses one; some sort of literacy is a part of compulsory education; 'it' (to stretch a point) can produce an infinite range of language and expression. Yet far from producing a torrent of public discourse, this truly mass medium is mainly reduced to the filling out of official forms, shopping lists and the occasional correspondence: for most of the population the pen can only be used in passive and privatized ways, while its public use is thoroughly mono-polized by a small world of media professionals.

What is true of the pen is equally true of the camera: almost two-thirds of UK households possess at least one camera (93 per cent in the USA) and each year over 80 million films are sold to 27 million people. Yet this enormous productive power is effectively contained as a conventio-nalized, passive, privatized and harmless leisure activity. The mass of photography – snapshooting – is hardly a conscious activity at all: it is an undeliberated moment spliced into the flow of certain ritual events: watching the baby, being at a tourist site, spending Sunday with the grandparents. Where mass photography is a conscious focus of activity – as with the amateur – the focus is on the technology, which is fetishized, not on the procedures and rhetoric of representation, which are standard-ized. A thorough sociology of mass photography is still needed. Bourdieu (1990) is a starting point, but dated and local. However, the broad outlines of an available practice, from which is somehow excluded all but the most rudimentary questioning – or instrumental use – of representation, are easy to distinguish.

In critical contrast, we must implement Raymond Williams's (1974) crucial ground rule that any medium must be analysed not only in terms of its present use (a restriction which encourages technologism) but also

This chapter is taken from Language, Image, Media, edited by H. Davis and P. Walton (Oxford, Blackwell, 1985), pp. 245–263.

in terms of its potential forms: as the practice of many community photographers and photographers in educational institutions has shown, the camera as an *active* mass tool of representation is a vehicle for documenting one's conditions (of living, working and sociality); for creating alternative representations of oneself and one's sex, class, age-group, race, etc; of gaining power (and the power of analysis and visual literacy) over one's image; of presenting arguments and demands; of stimulating action; of experiencing visual pleasure as a producer, not consumer, of images; of relating to, by objectifying, one's personal and political environment.

Yet we are still left – given camera or pen – with a passive medium, a state of the 'art' accomplished without visible constraints or enforcible laws. However, while the power of public photography – advertisements, news photos, record sleeves, etc. – preoccupies both radical theory and media hacks, the impotence of mass photography (on which that power partly depends) is almost entirely ignored. There has been no attempt at an adequate analysis which encompasses the whole complex of relations of economic forces, ideology and power within which is constructed this specific form of photographic practice and practitioner.

For what is at stake here is obviously rather more than the 'reading' of discursive texts (photos). What is at stake are the determinations and structures of *use* of a medium: mass photography is a range of material practices – practices set within developing social relations. Mass photography is integrated into the very fabric of the most intimate social relations (in particular, the family, leisure, personal remembrance and private vanity); is inscribed in institutions (from the photo press and camera clubs to high-street photographers and schools); and is bound up with the material conditions of consumption (relating to class, income, sex, advertising and retailing, the ownership of the means of distributing images). It is also the result of a complex history of competing strategies and rationalities (e.g. the business imperatives and consequent marketing aims of the photographic industry; the same concerns of complementary leisure industries; the defensive manoeuvres of professional photographers). Mass photography is not simply an encounter in discourse.

Available space – and the state of available research – precludes presenting the entire picture here. This chapter abstracts just one element from the web of forces which constructs and constricts the medium – the production and marketing imperatives of the photographic manufacturing industry. The second part of the chapter points out the implications of this analysis for one theoretical tradition – the structuralist-semiotic tradition.

The photographer on the assembly line

In contrast to the television, film and record industries, the monopolization of photography by professionals and the impoverishment of its wider use has not been based on restricting access to the media technology; it has actually been carried out in large part precisely through the high-pressure mass marketing of photographic equipment. It has been restricted in the course of its very proliferation, through its technical form, through its retailing, through the 'training' of consumers through advertising, the photo press and other publicity organs of the photographic manufacturing industry. The central question we must ask is: what is the relation between the proliferation of photography *in this form* and the interests of the business organizations which do the proliferating?

Any economic activity labours under the imperatives of its mode of production, operating strategically within the terms set by a level of technology, a form of economic organization and other relations of production, and a complex of other social relations (most crucially here, the structure of the family and of leisure). Moreover, as part of the very process of operating within these imperatives, economic organizations must both aim at and produce specific forms of consumption. As Marx wrote in the 1859 Introduction:

> It is not only the object that production creates for consumption . . . [It] also gives consumption its precise nature, its character, its finish . . . Hunger is hunger, but the hunger that is satisfied by cooked meat eaten with a knife and fork is a different hunger from that which bolts down raw meat with the aid of hand, nail and tooth. Production thus produces not only the object but also the manner of consumption, not only objectively but also subjectively. (Marx, 1973: 92)

The logic of this relation has, over the past century of capitalism, become somewhat more elaborate, more powerful and more conscious, both through the development of marketing and advertising as highly self-conscious functions with progressively greater directive roles in the economic calculations around production, and through the progressive concentration of capital (a crucial feature in photography). The economic imperatives of the photographic industry compel it to aim at a specific structure of photographic consumption – that is, of *media use* – which will maximize its profitability and stable growth.

Invoking the 'needs of industry' is not to advocate a simple form of economism any more that Marx did (in fact, the entire concept of 'the economic' as a hermetic entity becomes tortuous when we deal with the complex options and ideological calculations on which marketing, a crucial *economic* function, is based). Marx's statement, that production creates the consumer, is merely one moment of a dialectical argument and therefore isolated from the mediations which complete its meaning. Similarly, the premise advanced here, that the structure of photographic production and hence marketing gives us the structure of consumption and media use, does not imply that Kodak's marketing imperatives (or, technologistically, the Instamatic itself) created the snapshooter of today. However, both snapshooter and Instamatic are imbued with and inseparable from concepts of media use behind which Kodak has put its economic might for almost a century. The story of how the industry's own imperatives have been articulated with other social features – the development of the nuclear family, the structure of work and the ideology of leisure, for example – is the longer story from which the present one is abstracted. Again, *pace* Marx, production might not create the consumer concretely, without overwhelming mediation, but there is definitely an abstract specific consumer at which it is aimed, and it is this abstract relationship – of the 'manner' of production to the 'manner' of consumption – whose mechanisms must be explored.

Most generously, the capitalist press has come to our aid in this endeavour. In autumn 1979, two major reports on the marketing of photographic equipment in Britain were published, the first by the Economist Intelligence Unit (1979), from which all figures are taken unless otherwise indicated, the second by Euromonitor, a service of Mintel. Both reports are designed for interested parties: investors and top management (EIU's cover price of £50 is not exactly aimed at the mass market). The information presented is organized in a form conducive to finding opportunities for profitable exploitation. Despite their obvious bias, the figures can reveal much about the aims of the capitalists involved: the structure of the market is represented as it relates to the structure they wish to bring about. The figures should therefore be taken as indications of magnitude rather than as precise measures.

We can start from a very broad picture of the size and state of the market: two-thirds of British households now have at least one camera; on an individual basis, 51.3 per cent of adults own a camera. According to Euromonitor, about 15 million people own a still camera, of whom 12 million actually use it – a small figure in Western terms: for example, in 1977 average expenditure on photography per household was $37 in the UK, $114 in Germany and $73 In France. Whatever is said about the UK can be magnified for other advanced capitalist countries. Photography accounts for 0.45 per cent of all consumer spending excluding food.

EIU's estimate of overall photographic expenditure for 1979 is £400 million: 2,515,000 still cameras were sold, a growth in real volume of 4–5 per cent over the previous year. The most basic, and interesting analytical breakdown of the overall expenditure figure is as follows:

	Expenditure	Percentage of total
Equipment	£115,000,000	29
Film	£93,000,000	23
Developing and processing	£192,000,000	48

These proportions have remained constant throughout the decade (and possibly a lot longer): the point is that it would be exceedingly naïve to retain the commonsense view that the photographic industry simply exists to sell cameras, and that all the rest of its structure follows straightforwardly from this aim, supporting it in a subordinate manner. When, at a conservative estimate, 71 per cent of expenditure goes to film and processing, the centre of power cannot be where we expect it. In fact to push the point further, 'equipment' includes not only accessories – lenses, tripods, etc. – but also cine equipment: still camera sales alone total £84,750,000, only 21 per cent of the total.

To compound the situation, the 'film' segment of our breakdown is tending to monopoly. In 1978, 90 per cent of all films sold were colour films, the vast majority of which were Kodak, with Agfa an extremely poor second. It is obvious that monopolistic film manufacturers – as well as many competing film processing firms – stand to gain from any camera sold. Moreover, Kodak is notable in that on top of selling most of the film, it also participates in much of the revenue from processing through its sale of colour paper and above all chemicals to the trade. The key phrase, then, for film manufacturer and processor alike, is 'throughput': the more films pass through cameras, the more profit all around.

But there is also a qualitative aspect which characterizes the kind of throughput that Kodak et al. want. It has become axiomatic in photography (as well as in hi-fi and most electronics) that, as EIU put it: 'The more specialised photography becomes, the fewer the number involved.' In terms of sale of film, and therefore of processing, this means that it is the great number of snapshooters who buy only a few films per year which accounts for the vast majority of the trade:

Heavy film users (6+ films p.a.) constitute 11 per cent of film buyers, buying 27 per cent of all films sold.
Medium users (3–5 films p.a.) are 39 per cent of film buyers, buying 49 per cent of film.
Light users (1–2 films p.a.) are 50 per cent of buyers, buying 24 per cent of all film.

Moreover it is at the margin that the greatest expansion is possible: convincing the light users to buy only one or two more films per year means doubling their consumption and adding 20 per cent to film revenue.

As market leader, Kodak in any case has little to gain from its competitors and need only engage in the occasional defensive operation, as for example with its vastly unprofitable incursion into Polaroid's instant film market. It is the enormous film profits to be made at the margin, through snapshooters, which defines its imperatives: to expand the photography market as a whole by selling the idea of photography to non-photographers, thus creating large numbers of new film users. Kodak shows an extraordinary historical continuity in this regard. Eastman began in 1880 as a dry plate manufacturer and processor. His development of roll film after 1885 was his technical innovation; his cameras were a *marketing* revolution. Instead of providing film backs for existing cameras, he began in 1888 to produce the cheapest, simplest cameras imaginable to act as vehicles through which he could sell as much film to as many people as possible. He had sold 100,000 of these by 1896 (Holmes, 1974). Originally one bought the camera with the film already loaded; when the 100-frame film was finished, the whole camera was sent back to Kodak for processing and replacement. This end of the operation gave both the continuity and bulk of Eastman's revenues. He rated his cameras as good for 20 film cartridges each.

The development of photographic marketing therefore was and is tied to the expansion of the mass snapshooter market through the sale of cheap vehicles for film. The story of how Kodak constructed mini film monopolies through marketing 126s, 110s and other now forgotten film gauges is an old one. Monopoly was certainly a powerful motive. However another motive was equally decisive for the development of the medium as we know it. The mass marketing of cameras, on which film sales depend, means that selling of photography without the costly creation of 'photographers', which would involve teaching skills, would demand serious interest and would lose that vast part of the population which will not enter the market if the entry fee involves spending time, learning and money and frustration spent in making mistakes. Yet this is precisely the market Kodak and its ilk aim at. Thus Kodak's marketing, from 1888 on, depended on building two features into its technology, simplicity and reliability. 'You push the button and we do the rest.' Kodak's solution to this marketing problem, now forming the basis of the whole industry, was as far as possible to divorce the camera operator from the process of photography. By making the process opaque, one makes the practice transparent, if not invisible: it requires no thought to operate, therefore it can be taken for granted, and conventionally – thoughtlessly, inserted into everyday social usages.

The modern Instamatic or 110 is merely a refinement of the original Kodak idea: fixed focus and fixed speed, a choice between two (or a few more) apertures marked by pictures of sun and clouds, built-in flash becoming standard. These cameras also incorporate Kodak's greatest twentieth-century innovation, the solution to people's problem with getting film into cameras: the cartridge. The final consumer resistance was overcome. Add to this the latitude of modern films and Mr Eastman's dream has come true: utter simplicity and very near total reliability (i.e. the largest number of technically successful pictures). In fact Eastman claimed in the 1890s that the success rate for amateurs with his cameras was 80 per cent.

This camera which allows practice without process or knowledge is both liberating and constricting: it has put the technology into millions of hands, but in its most restricted (and mystified) form. Reducing process to 'point and press' means designing the technology to operate optimally under certain standard conditions, such as three people out of doors smiling at the lens from over five feet away. Trying to avoid a techno-logistic interpretation, one can say that some degree of versatility is possible on an Instamatic, but it requires consciously transcending the design bias and limitations which result from the imperatives of simplicity and reliability. This transcending requires some understanding of process which is kept hidden, and consciousness of the conventions, which are taken for granted. It requires that the act of taking a picture become consciously considered as an act of representation: that the viewfinder be considered not as a window to be looked through but as a 'canvas' to be worked upon. Such an attitude does not encourage exponential increases in firm throughput.

Should it be felt that this argument overrates the role, power or success of Kodak, there are several further points. First, one can add to Kodak's predominance in manufacturing film and processing material, the fact that (according to Euromonitor) 62.2 per cent of all the cameras owned in the UK are Kodak. Add to this figure the Polaroid, Agfa and Boots cameras owned (all of which firms are involved in film processing *and* cameras, like Kodak), and we get to 76.5 per cent of all cameras owned. For comparison: Pentax, Nikon, Olympus and Canon together account for 7.7 per cent of cameras. Kodak, uniting film, processing and camera interests, exemplifies the logic which dominates this sector of the market and largely structures the other sectors. Second, because it is market leader and because it unites the various interests, its role, as their advertising man (quoted in EIU) put it, is to 'find its growth by stimulating the market to expand'. In 1979 Kodak's advertising accounted for 36 per cent of all advertising by photographic manufacturers. Third, on another level, Kodak is simply the exemplar but also the originator of a marketing approach which involves the whole industry: it has set the terms in which the others operate.

If Kodak (along with Polaroid, Agfa, Boots and numerous smaller names) goes for – and gets – photography as a mass, it leaves behind other areas of mass photography which are equally crucial to understanding the use of the medium: the smaller, specialist crumbs of 'amateur' and 'hobbyist' photography which Kodak leaves behind for myriad smaller operations to fight over (see figures 18.1 and 18.2). This market has its own logic.

Briefly, the crucial marketing problem is to achieve a high *rate* of growth (never simply stable sales) within a restricted and specialized market. A small increase is possible through bringing more people into the market (largely through upgrading amateurs). EIU actually advises the industry to form something like the Milk Marketing Board to do just this in the interests of all, but in the absence of this organization, or of a Kodak-style firm whose interests lie in performing its function of expanding the market as a whole, the growth of amateur photography cannot sustain great increase in sales. Other stratagems must be employed.

First, firms must clearly differentiate their markets: their product must compete within a product category which is not interchangeable with any other. A kind of rationalization of the market is enforced on manufacturers in the scramble to retain an identifiable portion of a limited population of consumers, so as not to fall between the force-fields of available purchasing power. A striking example of this logic at work is EIU's prediction of increasingly hard times for the 35mm compact camera: its specific market is being eroded by the greater versatility of 110s and the increased simplicity of automated SLR (single lens reflex) cameras. It falls between two quite clear stools. So one of the important learning and teaching formats may go to the wall, leaving a yawning price gap between cheap 110s and expensive SLRs, forcing everyone to choose (in marketing terms) between being a snapshooter and a committed amateur. Needless to say, this would render unto SLR and 110 manufacturers captive and cleanly differentiated markets, simultaneously exploiting, rigidifying and stimulating existing schisms in media use.

However, if formats and special product groups are becoming more differentiated, within these categories the competition is simply

Leave the others to their snaps while you take a photograph.

You're in the second row of a crowd at an air show, everyone is taking snaps, but all you can see are the backs of heads. How can anyone possibly take a decent photograph in this situation? Well, this photographer noticed that one of the stunt planes looked as if it was bouncing off the man's head in front. However, he was able to set his camera so both the men and the plane were in focus, whilst freezing the plane in the sky. Of course he could only do this because he was using an SLR camera. But what if you haven't an SLR camera? Maybe they seem a bit daunting? Well, Canon have created one especially for the ambitious amateur. It's a camera that's so easy to use you don't need a surname like Einstein or a degree in technology to use it. The EOS 500. It's an advanced SLR camera that as you develop, has the capacity to develop with you. In fact, the only thing Canon didn't include was the imagination. That they're going to leave up to you. It's the perfect introduction into Canon's award winning EOS range of cameras. In fact once you are armed with any EOS camera, as the saying goes, 'the sky's the limit'.

Canon EOS

Table 18.1 *Camera sales 1979 (EIU estimate)*

Format	Volume (000s)	% of total	Value (£m RSP)	% of total
35mmSLR	160	6.4	20	23.6
35mm compact	160	6.4	9	10.6
110	1000	39.8	25	29.5
126	180	7.0	2	2.6
Instant	1000	39.8	25	29.5
Roll film	15	0.6	4	4.4

bewildering. This relates to the second main set of stratagems employed in super-exploiting a restricted market. The paradigm case is the SLR market, the opposite pole to Kodak-style marketing. The SLR market is numerically relatively small, but in value terms is disproportionately lucrative (see table 18.1).

The SLR generates a vast revenue, one-quarter of the total, on an insignificant and specialized fraction of market volume – only 6 per cent. (Euromonitor puts the disparity even higher, at 36 per cent of value.) In addition, these figures only include the camera itself, whereas the biggest growth area in all photography at the moment is in SLR accessories – for example, there are 800 different lenses on the market, and a massive autowind sales drive. On the other hand, the already very small volume base of 6.4 per cent is further narrowed by the fact that Zenith alone (which is in a class on its own by virtue of being outrageously inexpensive but very reliable with no frills) accounts for 75,000 of the 160,000 SLRs sold in 1979, a full 47 per cent of the market.

The central stratagem employed by manufacturers to cope with the situation is the idea of permanent technical revolution. Over the past decade this has primarily taken the form of incorporating more and more electronics into cameras with a view to both increased versatility and increased automation, aiming at cameras which can do all the thinking for their human button-pushers. On the one hand, this follows Kodak logic: develop the market as a whole by simplifying operation and guaranteeing 'good results'. On the other hand its main function is quite different. In Euromonitor's words:

> One need only look at the electronic equipment or electrical appliance market and observe how product development has revitalised sagging sales to realise that any new product begins a complete new cycle as far as consumer acquisition is concerned. With a new product, ownership level drops to nil – nobody has one and everybody wants one.

Through a logic complementary to product differentiation and market rationalization, the introduction of new technology is not meant to signify the entry of just another competing camera, but the replacement of all hitherto existing cameras, which are rendered redundant. The market is increased by being inaugurated anew. The sale of accessories is a version of the same game: your camera is not actually a camera at all until it has an autowinder/telephoto lens/filter, etc. Each time the necessity of a new accessory is 'proven' to the consumer (and they do come in waves), 'ownership level drops to nil' and the small base market is recreated again, at square one.

Here at least are the economic forces which desire that snapshooter technology ends in an ever more invisible medium, while hobbyist technology should be inseparable from the fetishism of technology. In order to grow, SLR must create gaps which did not previously exist, must create products which constitute, and are seen to constitute, totally new categories of desirability. Where the snapshooter should learn to look through the viewfinder as if it were a window, the amateur's sight should not get beyond the gleaming chrome or black body of his or her revolutionary new triumph of technology. A tremendous example of 'correct' desire is provided by the case of the Canon A1, an SLR which was voted camera of the year by the readers of *Practical Photography* two years running. As EIU comments without a glimmer of irony:

> The staggering thing, however, is that this vote was made by readers who had probably had no opportunity to see or handle the camera because of the delays in delivery. Canon's publicity, which is firmly based on highlighting the innovative features of the A1 . . . has thus made a tremendous impression.

To summarize: we have taken two major areas of photographic marketing, snapshooting and amateur photography – the former being the major structuring force in the field, the latter structuring itself through strategies appropriate to the specialized and therefore limited market dynamics which remain. We have restricted ourselves to the main outlines – mere examples really – of the richly textured field of strategies at work. We have related the marketing context and business calculations of the photographic industry to the type of consumption which these must try to produce directly or which they indirectly entail as part of their logic. This 'type of consumption' is the foundation of the use of the medium: broadly speaking, either the transparent, insertable practice without process, or the fetishized commodity without a practice.

One could add that these two areas of photographic consumption emerge in another form within the self-conscious calculations of the industry: EIU also presents a broad market profile of the consumer. It takes the form of a 'consumer ladder' which people enter on the ground floor as snapshooters and which they are then eased up, purchase by purchase, thorough hobbyist to, ultimately, semi-professional. The various rungs of the ladder – the types of consumer – are distinguished by the kind of equipment owned and the frequency of its use. Complementing the picture we have already drawn of the strategies and dynamics at work – the *moving* picture – the EIU 'consumer ladder', again presenting its research in the form most usable to its capitalist readership's aims, gives us a snapshot of the structure of photographic consumption to which the industry works: in its 'ideal types' of consumers and ways of consuming, it represents both the byproducts and the raw material of marketing calculation.

There are some obvious immediate extensions to be made to the analysis presented here, in particular the role and functioning of advertising (and the history of photographic advertising), the dynamics of the retail trade, and the photographic press. Though integrated into the overall marketing logic, an understanding of their specific functioning is crucial.

However, the most critical work is that of contextualizing the present level of analysis within a broader framework, of both substantively and theoretically demonstrating the ways in which the forces and strategies presented here are mediated within the totality of the photographic nexus, of returning this abstracted moment of economic calculation to its concrete history and context.

This is unfortunately not a simple matter of relating economic structures to other (political, ideological, institutional) structural instances as entities with their own specific conditions of existence, which is the current practice. The discourses underlying photography, the genres and conventions in which it takes form, the family rituals and relations which define its use and content, the values it adopts (whether the sexism, fetishism, aestheticism of camera clubs, or the nostalgia, selective amnesia, totemism of family photography), etc. – treating any of these separately, as bearing unique determinants (however unique their functioning), is an act of abstraction equal to that carried out above.

To give an example: the twentieth-century family and the structure of leisure are central to mass photography – they provide the social relations and material practices which structure most of its use. The family and the terrain of leisure are of course completely interlinked, their interweaving being crucial – historically and structurally – to the development of a consumerist capitalism wherein the dynamic space of the family and the stereotyped time of leisure have been forged into the primary, and quite efficient, unit of consumption. For this very reason, the history and dynamics of the photographic industry and that of the family at leisure have to be analysed together, as part of the same process: the social relations which constitute families (and which seem so naturally amenable to certain uses of photography) were themselves determined by the same forces which determined photographic production and marketing in the first place. The specific form of photography inserted into the family is only one instance of an evolving consumerist system colonizing the very structure which was created by the forces which created it – the overall relations of consumption necessitated by the relations of capitalist production. On one level at least this is obvious: understanding mass photography as a practice gains more from looking at the articulation of the camera with other consumption goods (for example, the bicycle in the 1890s, the car in the 1920s, the package holiday in the 1970s) than from starting from the representations it produces.

Similarly central to mass photography is the ideology of empiricism. Locally, this is the discourse of photographic truth and objective record which grounds the reading and use of photography and is instrumental to photography's appropriateness to its current social relations of consumption (for example, family album, holiday slide show, emblem of remembrance, proof of wellbeing). However, to regard empiricism as a free-floating, autonomously developing discourse fortuitously exploitable by the photographic marketing machinery is misleading: positivism as a whole is historically crucial and instrumental to capitalism, painfully constructed by it. It is not an autonomous development within ideology with which the concrete practices of photography must be brought into analytic relation as externals with separate determinants: rather, empiricism grounds the rationality of production as clearly as it emerges within specific forms of consumption. We are dealing with one history, not two. Photographic marketing and the discourse of photographic consumption are simply local achievements within industrial society's secular project.

Semiotics and materialism

The analysis outlined above, contrary to present tendencies, does not 'decode' a single photograph, nor engage the processes of 'reading' directly. Its interest is to set the terms for explaining the *use* of a medium (i.e. terms which involve the active forces of both production and consumption of significations). It does not aim at deriving discourses through which texts are structured and read, and subjects formed, but at pointing towards the material practices and social relations within which discourses, texts and subjects operate and are forged. It also does not redefine material practices as readable discourses. This is to say, it cuts across the assumptions of the structuralist-semiotic tradition which is now the dominant discourse on processes of representation, nearly hegemonic in left cultural theory. It will be necessary to work through several aspects of this tradition in order to proceed further.

Over the past two decades, the structuralist tradition has been the most progressive and fertile strategy for engaging cultural processes. It has now become a barrier to further progress. Though it does not consciously exclude as irrelevant the political economy of media and the social relations within which they are consumed, it has ultimately consigned them to theoretical limbo. The structuralist tradition takes as assumed, as given, precisely what needs to be explained: the relations and practices within which discourses are formed and operated. It would like to specify the transactions and mutual constitution of subject and representation within the processes of signification, but to do this by appealing to discourses which are inexplicable in the terms of its theoretical apparatus. To use a vocabulary it would not recognize, the structuralist tradition aims to analyse 'ideological effect', yet takes as given precisely those discourses whose effect it would like to trace. It is still a formalist theory which refuses all substance, elaborating processes of meaning construction within an abstracted epoch. The historic and dynamic construction of discourses within a force-field of social practices is obscured and ignored in order to focus on the negotiations of meaning carried out within the ambit of the text and the moment of reading. The hallowed terrain of bourgeois criticism remains, while the groundwork of materialist theory is not begun.

A strange process has occurred to reach this state: the structuralist-semiotic tradition has always addressed itself to a very specific and limited question: 'How is meaning produced and sustained within a text?'. This question points to a level of analysis whose objects are the formal and systematic properties of closed systems: it involves decoding the discourses which structure texts; the devices employed and their place within the system of signification; the formation of subjects within and between texts, etc. Though the question was broadened by moving from the productivity of texts to the more global moment of 'reading', the essential limitation of the originating premise remains: this tradition proposes a radically internal analysis of signification, an analysis which – directed entirely at uncovering the structuring of a closed system (whether text or signification as a whole) – finds all the terms necessary to analysis within its theoretical object: signification. Through its roots in structural linguistics, and a mode of analysis which stretches from the more ancient axiomatics such as logic and geometry to more modern equivalents such as ethnomethodology and Kuhnian analysis of paradigms (a tradition Terry Lovell (1980) calls 'conventionalist theories of knowledge'), semiotics has resulted in a metaphor and a procedure in which the encounter and mutual constitution of text and subject within discourse is isolated from any possible determination outside discourse, in order to abstract the formal mechanisms of this process.

If one recognizes the limits of the original question and the original process of abstraction, no danger arises. Semiotics promises ultimately to return the captured moment of reading to its determinations: this has been indefinitely postponed and then utterly forgotten. Semiotics has now taken its limited terrain to be the whole world, thereby foreclosing the possibility of ever breaking out of its limits. The process of reading, the procedures and content of discourse, are released from all the social relations which determine them and are left to formal, self-constituting emptiness.

This abstraction of reading has led to confusions over the explanatory status of semiotics: because it forgets what it has excluded it is likely to take its descriptions for explanation. This is crucially true of the category 'discourse'. Discourse is taken for a kind of 'deep structure', which in certain structuralisms was an explanatory category: that which explains the structure of the text. It is in fact a rather different animal: it is a signifying formation produced within a field of determinations, among which are those included within semiotic theory. The result is that within semiotics, discourses are in fact taken as given (formed outside the semiotic field) yet are used as if they were central explanatory concepts: they structure subjects and texts and their encounter in 'reading'.

This results in one of two sins: functionalism or tautology. Functionalism seems to be the necessary explanatory mode for theories which abstract structure from social process: it admits of thoroughly internal solutions to problems of determination. Until the mid-1970s, structuralism explained the existence of the discourse whose workings and effects it wished to determine in terms of Althusserian functionalism: capitalism produces the necessary conditions of its own existence, including its ideological means of reproduction. The history of their emergence is irrelevant; their logical necessity is crucial. Aside from the obvious circularity involved, the argument allows for a completely unspecified notion of relative autonomy, which eventually becomes full autonomy.

When these assumptions were largely discredited, their place was never filled: semiotics closed ranks against concerns outside its own terms. 'Decoding' became an end in itself, the pursuance of the specific processes of the formation of subjects within discourses becoming both beginning and end of analysis. The 'structuring discourses' and the processes of reading which were the only possible outcome of analysis could be alternatively characterized as the 'cause' and the result of the processes under analysis: everything occurs within these discourses; they are allocated no external determinations but are taken as given. Tautologically, wherever one starts one ends in the same place – the structuring discourse, the stuff of which everything is made.

The problem again is not so much what semiotics says as what it leaves out, namely whatever cannot be absorbed into the field of signification under discussion. For example, Victor Burgin (1980) attempts to get away from the textual object/artifact by asserting the productive role of the 'social subject' at the point of consumption of the image. However, this consumption is once again purely the abstract moment of reading, an empty encounter between subject and text whose content is given by forces not included in the terms of analysis. Moving from this abstract moment to the specific readings of specific photographs, Burgin appeals to the preconscious of contemporary social actors which will contain certain knowledges through which the photographs will be read: 'It is surely reasonable to suppose that the knowledge of events such as these suffused the collective consciousness of Americans in the 1960s' (Burgin, 1983: 236). It is a reasonable assumption. It is an explanation of nothing. Burgin purports to explain the motivation behind a particular reading while simply smuggling in an obvious content as self-evident. The crucial feature, the determinations of the structuring discourse, lie outside the terms of the theory and are simply taken as given, leaving us with a concept similar to that of 'socially available knowledge' in phenomenology. The critical question of how specific knowledges and experiences come to enter the politics of representation, come to be socially constituted, is simply assumed to be answered. What we are looking for is precisely an analysis of those institutions, technologies, power relations, specific practices and their histories which determined the 'suffusion' of the collective consciousness and allowed this reading in the first place.

'Reading', and the processes of signification, thus become a highly abstract social moment. The crime was compounded by hypostatizing the abstraction: not only was the production of discursive formations rendered self-explanatory, but the consumption of texts was construed as an equally internal matter. In the first instance, this was achieved by the assumption of 'objective readings – *the* reading of the text. The uncovering of the internal mechanisms of meaning production in the text promised logically to uncover the *actual* meanings the mechanisms were constructing. Meaning was utterly under the control of the text: the meaning was not an historical achievement but a formal one. Texts were not misread or subverted by readers; populations did not have to be trained to certain ways of reading; institutions and strategies were not involved; the objective reading of the text was simply known to be its achieved, its actual meaning.

This assumption was fractured in the mid-1970s into the 'problem of audience'. The tendency was to theorize the gap between the structured meaning of the text and the actual readings which concrete readers came to in terms of the freed play of the subject on the shifting terrain of meaning. This was the final abstraction of reading, its unhinging. It finally foreclosed the positing of any determinations outside language and discourse: instead of placing and connecting text and audience within their material conditions, their formation within the same movements of strategic historical forces, the relationship between them was bracketed for analysis, reduced to a private encounter. This courted the danger of collapsing text, subject and signification into one anarchic unanalysable morass, for – released from all possible concrete determinations – the other options were even less appealing: in order to find, let alone explain, the actual meaning established within any reading one had either to return to the worst form of empiricist sociology (ask what did individual A actually think that film X meant, then aggregate all the individuals surveyed, and extrapolate) or return to the tyranny of the text.

The fantasy we have come to – of a machinery of signification producing in a social vacuum – can be redescribed from another angle, as the history of complex negotiations between structuralism and Marxism. In rather schematic terms, structuralism and its derivations were taken up by the left as the last in a line of attempted syntheses between Marxist theory and theories of the subject, consciousness, language and ideology. As a sanctuary from the travesties of Marxist economism and base and super-structure mechanistics during the 1960s, a decade in which consciousness and ideology became structurally central in all political movement, embracing structuralism was a matter of urgent practical and political necessity. Under the banner of structuralism and then semiotics, activists and academics could deal with matters of vital urgency and still claim to be Marxist, for theoretical fusion was promised and seemed imminent. However, the negotiations instead instituted a division of theoretical labour which perpetuated a division in theory between the ideological and economic instances as objects of analysis; we still retain a negotiated alliance rather than a theoretical synthesis. The relations between the semiotic and Marxist traditions reveal an artificiality and improvised nature which is only duplicated in the rickety connections drawn between their theoretical objects. Reference to the materiality of the signifier, or reliance on a language full of metaphors of materialism ('the work of the text', 'ideological production', etc.), cannot fill the gap. The division we desperately desired to overcome is not only perpetuated but dignified theoretically: the materialist analysis is not economistic now, and the analysis of signification is not reductive, but only at the cost of total separation.

The real task starts here. It is not to assert the analysis of ideology as against the economic instance, but to analyse how the economic, institutional, ideological and political forces, strategies and dynamics have constructed the social relations within which material cultural practices are carried out. The task is to establish a materialist analysis of the politics of cultural practice. In the case of mass photography this means asserting the centrality of ideological processes within the economic instance (namely 'marketing', the management of consumption and of the social relations of consumption) as much as it means finding the material determinants of signification, the social relations within which they are constructed.

We began with a concrete political problem: mass photography constructed within restrictive rationalities, within exploitative strategies, within social relations grounded in the most insidious drives of a capitalist mode of production, resulting in material practices which – posed against alternative practices – are virtually tragic. Hopefully we can finish with a political direction. Our fight for a democratized medium must certainly engage the discursive textures of our readings – we must reread, recode, converse. But unless this practice and analysis is placed solidly, integrally, within an understanding of the total material circumstances of the use of the medium, we will be indulging in an academic exercise. If our present use of photography is founded on the consumer capitalist form of the family, the site of resistance and reconstitution is within feminism and other movements within politics, in collective practices of photography, and alternative social relations such as community groups, campaigns, community arts, etc. If mass photography is privatized, our obstacle is the monopolization of the means of distribution as much as it is discourses which fetishize the home as castle and private life as sanctuary: our practice is to develop alternative distribution, construct new audiences and reclaim the 'owned' media from hoardings to satellites. If photography is trapped within leisure consumption, our battle is against the structure of work. If photography is read through notions of representation as a reflection of reality, then there is a campaign within ideology to carry out in very concrete strategic forms.

The politics of representation is waged on a broad front. If mass photography is impoverished in that sector which has hypnotized us for a decade – the textual product – the complexity of the forces which forge its use constantly turns us around to face the materiality of practice and, therefore, returns us to politics.

References

Bourdieu, P. (1990, first published 1965) *Photography: a Middlebrow Art*. Cambridge: Polity Press.
Burgin, V. (1980) 'Photography, phantasy, function', *Screen*, 21(1): 43–80; reprinted in V. Burgin (ed.), *Thinking Photography*. London: Macmillan, 1981.

Burgin, V. (1983) 'Seeing sense', in Howard Davies and Paul Walton (eds), *Language, Image, Media*. Oxford: Blackwell.

Economist Intelligence Unit (1979) *Special Report no. 70: The UK Market for Amateur Photography*.

Holmes, E. (1974) *An Age of Cameras*. London: Fountain Press.

Lovell, T. (1980) *Pictures of Reality: aesthetics, politics and pleasure*. London: British Film Institute.

Marx, K. (1973) *Grundrisse*. Harmondsworth: Penguin.

Williams, R. (1974) *Television, Technology and Cultural Form*. London: Fontana.

Looking and subjectivity

The chapters in Part III take the argument forward, from the question of how to conceptualize 'visual culture' to the relation between the viewer and what is viewed. It is concerned with the cultural practices of 'looking' and seeing. It takes as its point of departure the image, which stands at the centre of visual culture, and its capacity to function as a sign or text which constitutes and produces meaning. It understands visual culture as composed of 'systems of representation', using visual 'languages' and modes of representation to set meaning in place. However, it assumes that the meanings of the image – for all images are multi-vocal and are always capable of bearing more than one interpretation – cannot be completed within the text as a self-sufficient entity.

It is always part of, and constructed across, a wider discursive formation. In W. J. T. Mitchell's terms, the picture must be understood as 'a complex interplay between visuality, apparatus, institutions, bodies and figurality' (1994: 16). The power or capacity of the visual sign to convey meanings is only 'virtual' or potential until those meanings have been realized in use. Their realization requires, at the other end of the meaning chain, the cultural practices of looking and interpretation, the subjective capacities of the viewer to make images signify.

A concern with the viewers or audiences of images is not new to media studies and has been approached in a variety of ways, from audience survey analysis in the empirical mass communications research tradition through to more ethnographically based, interpretative and 'reception' forms of cultural analysis. One of the problems which beset the more positivistic end of this spectrum is that 'meaning' tends to be conceptualized in a very reductive way – largely, in effect, as manifest content or message, on the basis of a very simple notion of 'language' as one-way communication. The audience is characterized as a 'population', defined in terms of broad socioeconomic variables; its relation to 'the message' is viewed externally – an encounter between two already fully formed entities – and the meaning of the image for the audience is couched in terms of behavioural effects.

This 'model' may be contrasted with that which has guided the selection of chapter for Part III. Here, the image is understood as a visual sign, constituting meaning through the ways in which, following Saussure's general approach to language, we understand such 'languages' to operate – that is to say, as 'systems of difference'. The viewer is understood as socially positioned, these positionings shaping the parameters within which interpretations are made. Reading of 'seeing' is treated, here, as a social practice. However, in relation to visual culture as a meaning-system, what matters is not simply the external sociological places which 'seeing subjects' occupy, but their subjective capacity to take meaning, to interpret and make sense of what is seen, and how social positions help to shape those subjective capacities. In that sense 'seeing' is regarded as a cultural practice. By 'subjective capacity' and 'cultural practice' we understand how so-called objective social and psychic positionings are formed and become productive of interpretations, are used and 'lived' subjectively, influencing from the inside – not always in manifest or conscious ways – both what and how meaning is taken.

The articulation between viewer and the viewed is thus conceptualized in this body of work – despite its many other differences – as an internal relation. Indeed, the two points in the circuit of articulation privileged here – the viewer and viewed – are seen as mutually constitutive. Each is implicated in the other; neither could exist without the other. The subject is, in part, formed subjectively through what and how its 'sees', how its 'field of vision' is constructed. In the same way, what is seen – the image and its meaning – is understood as not externally fixed, but relative to and implicated in the positions and schemas of interpretation which are brought to bear upon it. Visual discourses already have possible positions of interpretation (from which they 'makes sense') embedded in them, and the subjects bring their own subjective desires and capacities to the 'text' which enable them to take up positions of identification in relation to its meaning. It is this 'little system' (composed, as it were, of two inter-dependent but relatively autonomous moments) which 'produces meaning'. It follows from this argument that 'the meaning' of the image cannot be seen as fixed, stable or uni-vocal across time or cultures. Also, the subject itself is not a completed entity but something which is produced, through complex and unfinished processes which are both social and psychic – a subject-in-process.

Another important distinction arises in the way in which the so-called 'effects' of what is viewed for the viewer is understood. In the bodies of work represented here, 'effects' cannot be reductively limited to the behavioural level. Meanings have all sorts of 'effects', from the construction of knowledge to the subjection of the subject to the meaning offered. If they have an influence on 'behaviour' it is more likely to be indirectly because knowledge is always implicated in power and power implies limits on what can be seen and shown, thought and said. Their broader cultural 'effects' have to be seen in terms of how meaningful discourses construct what is held to be 'normative', which of course regulates conduct, but in ways which cannot be reduced to or empirically measured as a behavioural impulse.

Meanings have a complicated relationship to practices and conduct. Indeed, the term 'discursive', which in these investigations increasingly replaces the narrow notion of 'text', is useful precisely because it blurs and refuses that classical distinction between thought and action, ideas and practices. If meanings 'compel', it is not because they lead automatically to an acting out of their imperatives in behaviour, but because, in the course of forming our subjectivities – of making us 'subjects' of our actions – they 'subject' us to their normative regulation. This kind of 'subjection' is rarely at what one would call the fully manifest of fully intentional level of action and can never be simply an external compulsion because it requires subjective identification. The meanings which images construct 'subject' us largely 'out of awareness' – at the same level as that at which, in the course of using a language, we follow and obey the taken-for-granted rules which make our utterances intelligible, without consciously knowing those rules or deliberately 'intending' to follow them. They are rather the discursive 'conditions of existence' of meaningful action or enunciation.

What is more, many of the image's 'effects' operate, not just 'discursively', but at the symbolic and psychic level of the unconscious. The symbolic power of the image to signify is in no sense restricted to the conscious level and cannot always easily be expressed in words. In fact, this may be one of the ways in which the so-called power of the image differs from that of the linguistic sign. What is often said about the 'power of the image' is indeed that its impact is immediate and powerful even when its precise meaning remains, as it were, vague, suspended – numinous. In noticing this, we register the image's capacity to connote on a much broader symbolic field, to touch levels of experience which seem remote or 'archaic', beyond the purely rational level of awareness, and which disturb by the very way in which they exceed meaning. The cultural practices of looking and seeing, then, which are foregrounded here, themselves rest on complex conditions of existence, some of which have psychic and unconscious dimensions of which the behavioural definition of meaning's 'effects' has only a very reductionist understanding.

Section E on 'Theoretical Perspectives' draws on a variety of contemporary theoretical traditions which differ considerably among themselves. We need to be aware of the different paradigms and assumptions within which these perspectives are working. They tend to operate at different levels of abstraction: some at the societal or ideological level, others at the subjective of the psychic. However, despite these differences, there are some significant similarities. They all speak, not of 'individuals' but of 'subjects'; that is, recognizing that culture comes into play at precisely the point where biological individuals become subjects, and that what lies between the two is not some automatically constituted 'natural' process of socialization but much more complex processes of formation. These constitute 'subjectivity' historically, in different periods, and rarely deliver a completed or normatively secured end-point.

Not all the chapters in Section E deal directly with meaning and visual language, but all of them are relevant to our concerns with the cultural relations of looking and seeing. Moreover, it is interesting to note that most of them use visual metaphors in their theory construction. W. J. T. Mitchell reminds us that there are not only 'pictures in theory' (i.e. theories which are expressed through the use of pictorial metaphors) but also 'theory itself as a form of picturing' (1994: 9). For example, Althusser's concern in Chapter 19 is with ideological forms of power, taking his starting point from an attempt to rethink the Marxist theory of ideology. But his way of doing so is to reconceptualize an ideology as a 'system of representation', to represent the way in which the subject is caught or 'hailed' by an ideology in terms of a 'recognition scene', and to address the mirroring or, as he puts it, the 'speculary' effect as the general condition of the functioning of all ideology.

An extract from Foucault's theory of discourse appeared in Part I, but in terms of the argument, his theories of the subject, discourse and power, and attention to the inscription of knowledge and power in 'the gaze' also belong here. A substantial part of Foucault's work consists of mapping how different discourses and their rules of operation make different 'facts' and different 'subjects' sayable or 'visible' in different historical periods. He is also concerned with those practices of power/knowledge which take the form of 'surveillance' or the power to overlook both individuals and populations. His work on genealogies points to the possibility of writing a set of histories of 'the gaze', a history of different visual or scopic 'regimes of truth'.

✗ Freud and those theorists influenced by psychoanalysis, on the other hand, are concerned with the subjective, psychic and, indeed, unconscious dimensions and 'effects' of both the image itself and the practices of 'looking' for the formation of subjectivity. In his work on fetishism (Chapter 20), we find Freud attempting to demonstrate how the substantiated presence of a foregrounded image or object becomes the repository of profoundly displaced feelings and unresolved emotions which cannot, other than indirectly, find expression. Here, the very figure or 'presence' of the image conceals or stands in for the absent and unconscious operations which confer on it its ambivalent power. Freud himself, and others writing within the tradition of his work, have also done much to explore the erotic components of the compulsion to 'look' – the way 'looking' is so often constructed across desire: a sort of 'eroticization' of looking relations, which Fenichel (Chapter 21) and others refer to as 'scoptophilic'. One question which they address is why 'the look' is so powerfully inscribed by the play of desire, so that no look is ever satisfying, but always excites the drive to look more, to see beyond, as if to gaze enough would be to see what is forbidden, what should not be shown or seen, what the very 'there-ness' of the image masks and denies.

Fantasy, another area of concern to psychoanalysis, is, *par excellence*, discussed by Freud as a 'scenario' – and requires the *mise-en scène*, the 'putting-into-a-scene', of submerged feeling and the scenic or spatial representation of unresolved desires or disturbing emotions. The process of identification, and the relation to 'the other', by which, according to psychoanalytic theory, biological individuals become 'subjects' are, within the framework of this theory, constituted through the metaphors of scenes and looking relations, from the famous 'primal scene' of Freud's; though the Oedipal scene and the 'mirror effect' which, according to Lacan, are the scenes of entry into sexual identity and which establish the 'misrecognitions' on which the subject's relation to significant others and the external world is founded; to castration, which is the critical 'scenario' of separation, for Freud, between the sexual development of men and women, and which is founded on 'what is seen' (the fact that the woman does not bear the penis) or, more accurately, 'what cannot be seen' and what 'she' is seen to lack (and he is seen, by contrast, to possess!).

Psychoanalysis and feminism have been a fruitful point of theoretical intersection, and many of the pieces selected here have been informed by this conjuncture. In her important collection, *Sexuality in the Field of Vision* (1986), in which Chapter 28 was originally published, Jacqueline Rose lays the foundation for many of these subsequent elaborations, especially in relation to cinematic representation, as in the following passage:

Freud often related the question of sexuality to that of visual representation. Describing the child's difficult journey into adult sexual life, he would take as his model little scenarios, or the staging of events, which demonstrated the complexity of an essentially visual space . . . The sexuality lies less in the content of what is seen than in the subjectivity of the viewer, in the relationship between what is looked at and the developing sexual knowledge of the child. The relationship between the viewer and scene is always one of fracture, partial identification, pleasure and distrust. (p. 411)

Homi Bhabha's essay (Chapter 24) on the stereotype in the context of a colonial discourse brings racial and sexual forms of difference together through what he calls a double articulation: 'the body is always simultaneously inscribed in both the economy of pleasure and desire and the economy of discourse, domination and power' (p. 371). And though his work is appropriate to both verbally and visually based discourses, it has a privileged reference to the visual domain because of the inscription of 'race' on the body of the subject through a variety of different 'visible' signifiers. Indeed, both racial and sexual difference differ, in some ways, from other forms of difference because of the centrality of 'vision' – of what can be seen – to the 'truth' and legitimacy of 'differences' which these discourses produce. Ultimately, these differences are made to seem 'real' and therefore 'true' – and unchangeable – because the differences we can 'see' – the skin colour and other ethnic markers in race, the biological differences between men and women's bodies – appear to ground their 'truth' beyond history, in what is naturally so, in Nature. The stereotype itself mirrors this discursive operation in its fixity. However, the central point of Bhabha's work here is to contextualize this attempt to fix difference, and to insist on the colonial stereotype as a 'complex, ambivalent, contradictory mode of representation' (1983: 22). He is also concerned to show, as it were, the visual components of power – a power both 'disciplinary and pleasurable' – and specifically 'the surveillance of colonial power as functioning in relation to the regime of the scopic drive' (this volume, p. 375).

In Sections F and G which complete Part III we look at a number of seminal contributions which take these general theoretical points of departure further through more concrete development and exemplification. The cultural practices of looking and seeing, like all fundamental social practices, are organized around these founding principles of the articulation of difference, especially race and gender/sexuality. A great deal of recent work in cultural studies has shown in detail how these articulating principles structure the field of visual culture. Much of this has consisted of the analysis of how images become sexually and racially marked and produced through the practices of representation. The focus in these sections is complementary but different. Here we are concerned with how the subjective field of vision itself is produced through sexual, racial and gendered difference – and how looking and seeing, as cultural practices, are always constructed 'in the field of sexuality, gender and race'.

References

Bhabha, Homi K. (1983) 'The other question: the stereotype and colonial discourse', *Screen*, 24, 4, pp. 18–36.

Mitchell, W.J.T. (1994) 'The pictorial turn', in *Picture Theory*. Chicago: University of Chicago Press.

Rose, Jacqueline (1986) *Sexuality in the Field of Vision*. London: Verso.

E

Theoretical perspectives

19

Ideology and ideological state apparatuses
(notes towards an investigation)
Louis Althusser

[. . .]

Ideology is a 'representation' of the imaginary relationship of individuals to their real conditions of existence

In order to approach my central thesis on the structure and functioning of ideology, I shall first present two theses, one negative, the other positive. The first concerns the object which is 'represented' in the imaginary form of ideology; the second concerns the materiality of ideology.

THESIS I: Ideology represents the imaginary relationship of individuals to their real conditions of existence.

We commonly call religious ideology, ethical ideology, legal ideology, political ideology, etc. so many 'world outlooks'. Of course, assuming that we do not live one of these ideologies as the truth (e.g. 'believe' in God, Duty, Justice, etc. . . .), we admit that the ideology we are discussing from a critical point of view, examining it as the ethnologist examines the myths of a 'primitive society', that these 'world outlooks' are largely imaginary, i.e. do not 'correspond to reality'.

However, while admitting that they do not correspond to reality, i.e. that they constitute an illusion, we admit that they do make allusion to reality, and that they need only be 'interpreted' to discover the reality of the world behind their imaginary representation of that world (ideology = *illusion/allusion*).

[. . .]

All these interpretations thus take literally the thesis which they presuppose, and on which they depend, i.e. that what is reflected in the

This chapter, originally published in 1969 is taken from *Mapping Ideology*, edited by S. Zizek (London, Verso, 1994), pp. 100–140.

imaginary representation of the world found in an ideology is the conditions of existence of men, i.e. their real world.

Now I can return to a thesis which I have already advanced: it is not their real conditions of existence, their real world, that 'men' 'represent to themselves' in ideology, but above all it is their relation to those conditions of existence which is represented to them there. It is this relation which is at the centre of every ideological, i.e. imaginary, representation of the real world. It is this relation that contains the 'cause' which has to explain the imaginary distortion of the ideological representation of the real world. Or rather, to leave aside the language of causality, it is necessary to advance the thesis that it is the *imaginary nature of this relation* which underlies all the imaginary distortion that we can observe (if we do not live in its truth) in all ideology.

[. . .] [W]hy is the representation given to individuals of their (individual) relation to the social relations which govern their conditions of existence and their collective and individual life necessarily an imaginary relation? And what is the nature of this imaginariness? Posed in this way, the question explodes the solution by a 'clique', by a group of individuals (Priests or Despots) who are the authors of the great ideological mystification, just as it explodes the solution by the alienated character of the real world. [. . .]

THESIS II: Ideology has a material existence.

[. . .]

While discussing the Ideological State Apparatuses and their practices, I said that each of them was the realization of an ideology (the unity of these different regional ideologies – religious, ethical, legal, political, aesthetic, etc. – being assured by their subjection to the ruling ideology). I now return to this thesis: an ideology always exists in an apparatus, and its practice, or practices. This existence is material.

Of course, the material existence of the ideology in an apparatus and its practices does not have the same modality as the material existence of a paving stone or a rifle. But, at the risk of being taken for a Neo-Aristotelian (NB: Marx had a very high regard for Aristotle), I shall say that 'matter is discussed in many senses', or rather that it exists in different modalities, all rooted in the last instance in 'physical' matter.

Having said this, let me move straight on and see what happens to the 'individuals' who live in ideology, i.e. in a determinate (religious, ethical, etc.) representation of the world whose imaginary distortion depends on their imaginary relation to their conditions of existence; in other words, in the last instance, to the relations of production and to class relations (ideology = an imaginary relation to real relations). I shall say that this imaginary relation is itself endowed with a material existence.

[. . .] The individual in question behaves in such and such a way, adopts such and such a practical attitude, and, what is more, participates in certain regular practices which are those of the ideological apparatus on which 'depend' the ideas which he has in all consciousness freely chosen as a subject. If he believes in God, he goes to church to attend Mass, kneels, prays, confesses, does penance (once it was material in the ordinary sense of the term) and naturally repents, and so on. If he believes in Duty, he will have the corresponding attitudes, inscribed in ritual practices 'according to the correct principles'. If he believes in Justice, he will submit unconditionally to the rules of the Law, and may even protest when they are violated, sign petitions, take part in a demonstration, etc.

Throughout this schema we observe that the ideological representation of ideology is itself forced to recognize that every 'subject' endowed with a 'consciousness', and believing in the 'ideas' that his 'consciousness' inspires in him and freely accepts, must '*act* according to his ideas', must therefore inscribe his own ideas as a free subject in the actions of his material practice. If he does not do so, 'that is wicked'.

Indeed, if he does not do what he ought to do as a function of what he believes, it is because he does something else, which, still as a function of the same idealist scheme, implies that he has other ideas in his head as well as those he proclaims, and that he acts according to these other ideas, as a man who is 'inconsistent' ('no one is willingly evil') or cynical, or perverse.

In every case, the ideology of ideology thus recognizes, despite its imaginary distortion, that the 'ideas' of a human subject exist in his actions, or ought to exist in his actions, and if that is not the case, it lends him other ideas corresponding to the actions (however perverse) that he does perform. This ideology talks of actions: I shall talk of actions inserted into *practices*. *And* I shall point out that these practices are governed by the *rituals* in which these practices are inscribed, within the *material existence of an ideological apparatus*, be it only a small part of that apparatus: a small Mass in a small church, a funeral, a minor match at a sports club, a school day, a political party meeting, etc. [. . .]

I shall therefore say that, where only a single subject (such and such an individual) is concerned, the existence of the ideas of his belief is material in that *his ideas are his material actions inserted into material practices governed by material rituals which are themselves defined by the material ideological apparatus from which derive the ideas of that subject.* Naturally, the four inscriptions of the adjective 'material' in my proposition must be affected by different modalities. [. . .]

[. . .] [I]t is clear that certain notions have purely and simply disappeared from our presentation, whereas others on the contrary survive, and new terms appear.

Disappeared: the term *ideas.*
Survive: the term *subject, consciousness, belief, actions.*
Appear: the terms *practices, rituals, ideological apparatus.* [. . .]

Ideas have disappeared as such (in so far as they are endowed with an ideal or spiritual existence), to the precise extent that it has emerged that their existence is inscribed in the actions of practices governed by rituals defined in the last instance by an ideological apparatus. It therefore appears that the subject acts in so far as he is acted by the following system (set out in the order of its real determination): ideology existing in a material ideological apparatus, prescribing material practices governed by a material ritual, which practices exist in the material actions of a subject acting in all consciousness according to his belief. [. . .]

Ideology interpellates individuals as subjects

This thesis is simply a matter of making my last proposition explicit: there is no ideology except by the subject and for subjects. Meaning: there is no ideology except for concrete subjects, and this destination for ideology is made possible only by the subject; meaning: *by the category of the subject* and its functioning.

[. . .] [T]he category of the subject (which may function under other names: e.g. as the soul in Plato, as God, etc.) is the constitutive category of all ideology, whatever its determination (regional or class) and whatever its historical date – since ideology has no history.

I say: the category of the subject is constitutive of all ideology, but at the same time and immediately I add that *the category of the subject is constitutive of all ideology only in so far as all ideology has the function (which defines it) of 'constituting' concrete individuals as subjects*. In the interaction of this double constitution exists the functioning of all ideology [. . .].

As St Paul admirably put it, it is in the 'Logos', meaning in ideology, that we 'live, move and have our being'. It follows that, for you and for me, the category of the subject is a primary 'obviousness' (obviousnesses are always primary): it is clear that you and I are subjects (free, ethical, etc. . . .). Like all obviousnesses, including those that make a word 'name a thing' or 'have a meaning' (therefore including the obviousness of the 'transparency' of language), the 'obviousness' that you and I are subjects – and that that does not cause any problems – is an ideological effect, the elementary ideological effect. It is indeed a peculiarity of ideology that it imposes (without appearing to do so, since these are 'obviousnesses') obviousnesses as obviousnesses, which we cannot *fail to recognize* and before which we have the inevitable and natural reaction of crying out (aloud or in the 'still, small voice of conscience'): 'That's obvious! That's right! That's true!'

At work in this reaction is the ideological *recognition* function which is one of the two functions of ideology as such (its inverse being the function of *misrecognition – méconnaissance*).

To take a highly 'concrete' example: we all have friends who, when they knock on our door and we ask, through the door, the question 'Who's there?', answer (since 'it's obvious') 'It's me'. And we recognize that 'it is him' or 'her'. We open the door, and 'it's true, it really was she who was there'. [. . .]

As a first formulation I shall say: *all ideology hails or interpellates concrete individuals as concrete subjects*, by the functioning of the category of the subject. [. . .]

I shall then suggest that ideology 'acts' or 'functions' in such a way that it 'recruits' subjects among the individuals (it recruits them all), or 'transforms' the individuals into subjects (it transforms them all) by that very precise operation which I have called *interpellation* or hailing, and which can be imagined along the lines of the most commonplace everyday police (or other) hailing: 'Hey, you there!'

Assuming that the theoretical scene I have imagined takes place in the street, the hailed individual will turn round. By this mere one-hundred-and-eighty-degree physical conversion, he becomes a *subject*. Why? Because he has recognized that the hail was 'really' addressed to him, and that 'it was *really him* who was hailed' (and not someone else). [. . .]

I might add: what thus seems to take place outside ideology (to be precise, in the street), in reality takes place in ideology. What really takes place in ideology seems therefore to take place outside it. That is why those who are in ideology believe themselves by definition outside ideology: one of the effects of ideology is the practical *denegation* of the ideological character of ideology by ideology: ideology never says 'I am ideological.' [. . .]

That an individual is always-already a subject, even before he is born, is nevertheless the plain reality, accessible to everyone and not a paradox at all. Freud shows that individuals are always 'abstract' with respect to the subjects they always-already are, simply by noting the ideological ritual that surrounds the expectation of a 'birth', that 'happy event'. Everyone knows how much and in what way an unborn child is expected. Which amounts to saying, very prosaically, if we agree to drop the 'sentiments', i.e. the forms of family ideology (paternal/maternal/conjugal/fraternal) in which the unborn child is expected: it is certain in advance that it will bear its Father's Name, and will therefore have an identity and be irreplaceable. Before its birth, the child is therefore always-already a subject, appointed as a subject in and by the specific familial ideological configuration in which it is 'expected' once it has been conceived. I hardly need add that this familial ideological configuration is, in its uniqueness, highly structured, and that it is in this implacable and more or less 'pathological' (presupposing that any meaning can be assigned to that term) structure that the former subject-to-be will have to 'find; 'its' place, i.e. 'become' the sexual subject (boy or girl) which it already is in advance. It is clear that this ideological constraint and pre-appointment, and all the rituals of rearing and then education in the family, have some relationship with what Freud studied in the forms of the pre-genital and genital 'stages' of sexuality, i.e. in the 'grip' of what Freud registered by its effects as being the unconscious. But let us leave this point, too, on one side. [. . .]

Let us therefore consider the Christian religious ideology. [. . .] The Christian religious ideology says something like this:

It says: I address myself to you, a human individual called Peter (every individual is called by his name, in the passive sense, it is never he who provides his own name), in order to tell you that God exists and that you are answerable to him. [. . .] This is your place in the world! This is what you must do! By these means, if you observe the 'law of love' you will be saved, you, Peter, and will become part of the Glorious Body of Christ! Etc. . . .

Now this is quite a familiar and banal discourse, but at the same time quite a surprising one.

Surprising because if we consider that religious ideology is indeed addressed to individuals, in order to 'transform them into subjects', by interpellating the individual, Peter, in order to make him a subject, free to obey or disobey the appeal, i.e. God's commandments; if it calls these individuals by their names, thus recognizing that they are always-already interpellated as subjects with a personal identity (to the extent that Pascal's Christ says: 'It is for you that I have shed this drop of my blood!'); if it interpellates them in such a way that the subject responds: '*Yes, it really is me!*' if it obtains from them the *recognition* that they really do occupy the place it designates for them as theirs in the world, a fixed residence: 'It really is me, I am here, a worker, a boss or a soldier!' in this vale of tears; if it obtains from them the recognition of a destination (eternal life or damnation) according to the respect or contempt they show to 'God's Commandments', Law become Love – if everything does happen in this way (in the practices of the well-known rituals of baptism, confirmation, communion, confession and extreme unction, etc. . . .), we should note that all this 'procedure' to set up Christian religious subjects is dominated by a strange phenomenon: the fact that there can be such a multitude of possible religious subjects only on the absolute condition that there is a Unique, Absolute *Other Subject*, i.e. God. [. . .]

It then emerges that the interpellation of individuals as subjects presupposes the 'existence' of a Unique and central Other Subject, in whose Name the religious ideology interpellates all individuals as subjects. [. . .]

God thus defines himself as the Subject *par excellence*, he who is through himself and for himself ('I am that I am'), and he who interpellates his subject, the individual subjected to him by his very interpellation, i.e. the individual named Moses. And Moses, interpellated-called by his Name, having recognized that it 'really' was he who was called by God, recognizes that he is a subject, a subject *of* God, a subject subjected to God, *a subject through the Subject and subjected to the Subject*. [. . .]

God is thus the Subject, and Moses and the innumerable subjects of God's people, the Subject's interlocutors–interpellates: his *mirrors*, his *reflections*. [. . .]

We observe that the structure of all ideology, interpellating individuals as subjects in the name of a Unique and Absolute Subject, is *speculary*, i.e. a mirror-structure, and *doubly* speculary: this mirror duplication is constitutive of ideology, and ensures its functioning. Which means that all ideology is *centred*, that the Absolute Subject occupies the unique place of the Centre, and interpellates around it the infinity of individuals into subjects in a double mirror-connection such that it *subjects* the subjects to the Subject, while giving them in the Subject in which each subject can contemplate its own image (present and future) the *guarantee* that this really concerns them and Him, and that since everything takes place in the Family (the Holy Family: the Family is in essence Holy), 'God will *recognize* his own in it', i.e. those who have recognized God, and have recognized themselves in Him, will be saved.

Let me summarize what we have discovered about ideology in general.

The duplicate mirror-structure of ideology ensures simultaneously:

1   the interpellation of 'individuals' as subjects;

2   their subjection to the Subject;

3   the mutual recognition of subjects and Subject, the subjects' recognition of each other, and finally the subject's recognition of himself;

4   the absolute guarantee that everything really is so, and that on condition that the subjects recognize what they are and behave accordingly, everything will be all right: Amen – 'So be it.'

Result: caught in this quadruple system of interpellation as subjects, of subjection to the Subject, of universal recognition and of absolute guarantee, the subjects 'work', they 'work by themselves' in the vast majority of cases, with the exception of the 'bad subjects' who on occasion provoke the intervention of one of the detachments of the (Repressive) State Apparatus. But the vast majority of (good) subjects work all right 'all by themselves', i.e. by ideology (whose concrete forms are realized in the Ideological State Apparatuses). They are inserted into practices governed by the rituals of the ISAs. They 'recognize' the existing state of affairs (*das Bestehende*), that 'it really is true that it is so and not otherwise', and that they must be obedient to God, to their conscience, to the priest, to de Gaulle, to the boss, to the engineer, that thou shalt 'love thy neighbour as thyself', etc. Their concrete, material behaviour is simply the inscription in life of the admirable words of the prayer: '*Amen – So be it.*'

Yes, the subjects 'work by themselves'. [. . .]

20

Fetishism   **Sigmund Freud**

In the last few years I have had an opportunity of studying analytically a number of men whose object–choice was dominated by a fetish. There is no need to expect that these people came to analysis on account of their fetish.'For though no doubt a fetish is recognized by its adherents as an abnormality, it is seldom felt by them as the symptom of an ailment accompanied by suffering.'Usually they are quite satisfied with it, or even praise the way in which it eases their erotic life.'As a rule, therefore, the fetish made its appearance in analysis as a subsidiary finding.'[. . .]

In every instance, the meaning and the purpose of the fetish turned out, in analysis, to be the same. It revealed itself so naturally and seemed to me so compelling that I am prepared to expect the same solution in all cases of fetishism.'When now I announce that the fetish is a substitute for the penis, I shall certainly create disappointment; so I hasten to add that it is not a substitute for any chance penis, but for a particular and quite special penis that had been extremely important in early childhood but had later been lost.'That is to say, it should normally have been given up, but the fetish is precisely designed to preserve it from extinction. To put it more plainly:'the fetish is a substitute for the woman's (the mother's) penis that the little boy once believed in and – for reasons familiar to us – does not want to give up.'

What happened, therefore, was that the boy refused to take cognizance of the fact of his having perceived that a woman does not possess a penis. No, that could not be true: for if a woman had been castrated, then his own possession of a penis was in danger; and against that there rose in rebellion the portion of his narcissism which Nature has, as a precaution, attached to that particular organ. In later life a grown man may perhaps experience a similar panic when the cry goes up that Throne and Altar are in danger, and similar illogical consequences will ensue. If I am not

This chapter, originally published in 1927, is taken from Sigmund Freud's *On Sexuality: Three Essays on the Theory of Sexuality and Other Works*, vol. 7, edited by James Strachey (Harmondsworth, Penguin, Pelican Freud Library, 1977), pp. 351–408.

mistaken,' Laforgue would say in this case that the boy "scotomizes" his perception of the woman's lack of a penis.' A new technical term is justified when it describes a new fact or emphasizes it. This is not so here. The oldest word in our psychoanalytic terminology, 'repression', already relates to this pathological process.' [. . .] [T]he correct German word for the vicissitude of the idea would be, *Verleugnung* (disavowal).[1] [. . .] It is not true that, after the child has made his observation of the woman, he has preserved unaltered his belief that women have a phallus. He has retained that belief, but he has also given it up. In the conflict between the weight of the unwelcome perception and the force of his counter-wish, a compromise has been reached, as is only possible under the dominance of the unconscious laws of thought – the primary processes. Yes, in his mind the woman *has* got a penis, in spite of everything; but this penis is no longer the same as it was before. Something else has taken its place, has been appointed its substitute, as it were, and now inherits the interest which was formerly directed to its predecessor. But this interest suffers an extraordinary increase as well, because the horror of castration has set up a memorial to itself in the creation of this substitute. Furthermore, an aversion, which is never absent in any fetishist, to the real female genitals remains a *stigma indelebile* of the repression that has taken place. We can now see what the fetish achieves and what it is that maintains it. It remains a token of triumph over the threat of castration and a protection against it. [. . .] In later life, the fetishist feels that he enjoys yet another advantage from his substitute for a genital. The meaning of the fetish is not known to other people, so the fetish is not withheld from him: it is easily accessible and he can readily obtain the sexual satisfaction attached to it. What other men have to woo and make exertions for can be had by the fetishist with no trouble at all. [. . .]

'One would expect that the organs or objects chosen as substitutes for the absent female phallus would be such as appear as symbols of the penis in other connections as well.' This may happen often enough, but is certainly not a deciding factor. It seems rather that when the fetish is instituted some process occurs which reminds one of the stopping of memory in traumatic amnesia. As in this latter case, the subject's interest comes to a halt half-way, as it were; it is as though the last impression before the uncanny and traumatic one is retained as a fetish. [. . .]

For me, the explanation of fetishism had another point of theoretical interest as well. [. . .] In the analysis of two young men I learned that each – one when he was two years old and the other when he was ten – had failed to take cognizance of the death of his beloved father – had 'scotomized' it – and yet neither of them had developed a psychosis. [. . .] It turned out that the two young men had no more 'scotomized' their father's death than a fetishist does the castration of women. It was only one current in their mental life that had not recognized their father's death; there was another current which took full account of that fact. The attitude which fitted in with reality existed side by side. In one of my two cases this split had formed the basis of a moderately severe obsessional neurosis. The patient oscillated in every situation in life between two assumptions:

the one, that his father was still alive and was hindering his activities; the other, opposite one, that he was entitled to regard himself as his father's successor. I may thus keep to the expectation that in a psychosis the one current – that which fitted in with reality – would have in fact been absent.

Returning to my description of fetishism, I may say that there are many and weighty additional proofs of the divided attitude of fetishists to the question of the castration of women. In very subtle instances both the disavowal and the affirmation of the castration have found their way into the construction of the fetish itself. This was so in the case of a man whose fetish was an athletic support-belt which could also be worn as bathing drawers. This piece of clothing covered up the genitals entirely and concealed the distinction between them. Analysis showed that it signified that women were castrated and that they were not castrated; and it also allowed of the hypothesis that men were castrated, for all these possibilities could equally well be concealed under the belt – the earliest rudiment of which in his childhood had been the fig-leaf on a statue. A fetish of this sort, doubly derived from contrary ideas, is of course especially durable. In other instances the divided attitude shows itself in what the fetishist does with his fetish, whether in reality or in his imagination. To point out that he reveres his fetish is not the whole story; in many cases he treats it in a way which is obviously equivalent to a representation of castration. This happens particularly if he has developed a strong identification with his father and plays the part of the latter; for it is to him that as a child he ascribed the woman's castration. Affection and hostility in the treatment of the fetish – which run parallel with the disavowal and the acknowledgement of castration – are mixed in unequal proportions in different cases, so that the one or the other is more clearly recognizable. [. . .]

Note

1   It may be remarked that in chapter VIII of the *Outline of Psycho-Analysis* (1938) Freud makes a different distinction between the uses of the two words: 'repression' applies to defence against internal instinctual demands and 'disavowal' to defence against the claims of external reality [original editorial note].

21

The scoptophilic instinct and identification
Otto Fenichel

I

[. . .] When someone gazes intently at an object, we say that he 'devours it with his eyes', and there are many similar phrases. Psychoanalytical writers have been struck by this unconscious significance in one form of looking in particular. Strachey in his paper on reading begins by examining its pathology (the inhibitions of reading and the passion for it) and goes on to show that the participation of the unconscious mind in reading always represents the idea that the sentences, words, or letters read are objects being devoured by the reader.[1] [. . .] Another conclusion which Strachey draws is that the idea of devouring, which in the unconscious underlies that of reading, actually represents a form of sadistic incorporation, with all the qualities which we associate with other ambivalent oral incorporation tendencies. This interpretation throws immediate light upon certain types of libidinal reading. If reading represents an act of incorporation, it explains the passion which so many pregenitally fixated persons have for reading in the water closet. It is an attempt to preserve the equilibrium of the ego; part of one's bodily substance is being lost and so fresh matter must be absorbed through the eyes. Some persons of an oral-erotic disposition are prompted by libidinal impulses to read whenever they are eating, but here the matter is more complicated. We must assume that their oral erotism, when stimulated, requires a twofold satisfaction.

We have other evidence to show that looking has the unconscious significance of devouring. The wolf in Little Red Riding Hood declared, first, that he had such big eyes, the better to see his victim and, next, that he had such a big mouth, the better to eat her up. Probably every psychoanalyst could produce analytical material in support of this equation.

This chapter is taken from *The Collected Papers of Otto Fenichel*, edited by H. Fenichel and D. Rapaport (London, Routledge and Kegan Paul, 1954), pp. 373–397.

In magic the act of looking has various meanings, of which devouring is only one; the lore of magic knows many methods of putting a spell upon a victim by means of a look. By the magic glance one renders him defenseless, generally by paralyzing him or otherwise making him incapable of movement. My readers will recollect that snakes are said to fix with their gaze animals which they wish to devour, so that the victims walk into the snake's jaws of their own accord; anyone who encounters the basilisk's eye is turned to stone, and similarly the 'true' hypnotist (as the attraction of the uncanny prompts people to conceive of him) lays a spell on his victim by fixing upon him an irresistible gaze. In all these cases the eye, or the glance, is a sadistic weapon. Freud[2] and other writers have pointed out that this is because they eye is used to symbolize the penis. But in many cases it is quite clear that the sadism which has its source in the eyes is *oral* in character. Curiously enough, this is sometimes the case precisely when the phallic significance of the eye is unmistakable. The snake fascinates its victim in order to devour it. The most familiar instance of erection symbolism in relation to the eye is to be found in Andersen's story of the Tinder Box, where we read of dogs with eyes as large as saucers, as soupplates, and as the Round Tower at Copenhagen. Now what anyone fears about a dog is, of course, that it may bite or devour him. It is noteworthy that in all such magic procedures as I have mentioned the eye plays a double part. It is not only actively sadistic (the person gazing puts a spell on his victim) but also passively receptive (the person who looks is fascinated by that which he sees).

One particular type of enchantment by the glance of the eye is specially interesting in connection with what I shall say later. In this case the victim is neither paralyzed, transfixed, nor devoured, but is compelled to *imitate* all the movements which the magician makes. Freud once said that fairy tales were 'the descendants of legends, come down in the world', and we may certainly say the same of children's traditional games. There is a well-known game in which the children sing:

> Adam had seven sons,
> Seven sons had Adam.
> They did not eat, they did not drink,
> They looked at each other without a blink,
> And they all went like this . . .

At the last line one of the children makes some sort of fantastic movements and the other have to copy everything that they see him do. Again, in Kipling's story, the gigantic snake Kaa dances its 'hunger-dance' in front of the monkeys and they imitate it until finally they jump into its jaws. Any collection of examples of 'imitative magic' contains instances of this kind. In psychoanalysis we are familiar with the term [. . .] 'magic gesture' which we apply in cases where the purpose of a neurotic symptom is that someone else should copy it. The person who magically compels others to imitate him is, in fact, making use of the expedient of demonstration. If the hypnotist, that uncanny character, can compel the person he gazes at to do anything he chooses, this is certainly only a further elaboration of the original idea that he can compel him to imitate the gestures which they hypnotist himself makes.

To turn now to quite a different field. We take it as a matter of course when we say that a child who has witnessed his parent's sexual activities in a 'primal scene' identifies himself with that which he sees, and we are agreed that this identification has important consequences for his whole life; but we seldom reflect on the relation between looking and identification.

Here is another point. In his book on looking-glass magic[3] Roheim devotes several pages to the enumeration of magical customs and beliefs connected with looking-glasses. Why is a looking-glass so suited to be a magical property? In the first place, it confronts everyone with his own ego in external bodily form, thus obliterating the dividing line between ego and non-ego. And, secondly, it gives the scoptophilic instinct a very special chance; 'looking-glass magic' is another instance in which looking is associated with changes in the relation between ego and non-ego.

Let us sum up our conclusions so far. In the unconscious, to look at an object may mean various things, the most noteworthy of which are as follows: to devour the object looked at, to grow like it (be forced to imitate it), or, conversely, to force it to grow like oneself. What is the connection between these relations?

II

In order to answer this question it will perhaps be a good thing to recall briefly what we know of the scoptophilic instinct in general. As Freud has shown in his *Three Essays on the Theory of Sexuality* (1905), this instinct is a component of the sexual instinct. In adults it serves the purpose of inducing sexual forepleasure and this in a typical way, since all end-pleasure requires contact with the partner, whereas an object which is only seen remains at a distance. Since sight is the sense by which human beings are mainly guided, we must regard it as the chief agent in the production of forepleasure, though, at the same time, we must remember that it is precisely in the realm of sensuality that the so-called lower senses are most prominent. (Whether, when subserving the scoptophilic instinct, the eye is to be regarded as an erotogenic zone, as it is for instance when rubbing the eyes is equivalent to masturbation, is a point which I do not propose to examine here, because it would sidetrack us unnecessarily into the domain of physiology.) At all events the scoptophilic instinct, like other component instincts, is liable to repression and may give rise to fixation. Freud has devoted a special paper to a description of the neurotic symptoms which ensue from the specific forms of repression of this instinct.[4] And today we know that these may result in equally specific neurotic character traits: especially among obsessional neurotics do we find persons suffering from a typical inhibition in looking, who, instead of seeing objects, make contact with the world around them only through concepts and words or by way of the other senses. The original scoptophilic instinct generally betrays itself here in some sort of 'return of the repressed from under repression'.[5] [. . .]

What is the aim of the scoptophilic instinct? I think there can be no possible doubt that it is *to look at* the sexual object. Freud adds: to look at the genitals of the desired person or to watch him or her performing the functions of excretion.[6] We need only take at random any phenomenon from the sphere of the scoptophilic instinct, or watch children who are deriving libidinal gratification from looking, in order to know what accompanies or conditions pleasurable looking: one looks at an object in order *to share in* its experience. This comes out specially clearly in the psychoanalysis of scoptophiliac perverts. Anyone who desires to witness the sexual activities of a man and woman really always desires to share their experience by a process of empathy, generally in a homosexual sense, i.e. by empathy in the experience of the partner of the opposite sex. Exhibitionists, too (who unconsciously are always active scoptophiliacs as well), enter by empathy, during their perverse activities, into what is actually, or what in their magical fantasy they conceive to be, the experience of their objects. Freud arrived at this conclusion long ago,[7] and Landmark has emphasized the universal significance of this fact for object love in general.[8] Very often sadistic impulses enter into the instinctual aim of looking; one wishes *to destroy* something by means of looking at it, or else the act of looking itself has already acquired the significance of a modified form of destruction. Thus, for instance, the compulsion so frequently met with in women to look at the region of a man's genitals is really a modified expression of active castration tendencies. It seems, then, that there are two tendencies which always or often determine the goal of the scoptophilic instinct: (*a*) the impulse to injure the object seen, and (*b*) the desire to share by means of empathy in its experience. Here 'empathy' is a complicated psychological process which cannot immediately be reduced to a short formula. But at any rate it has something to do with the mechanism of *identification*.[9]

III

Now let us consider the position. Every pregenital component of the sexual instinct is in part autoerotic and in part directed toward objects. In so far as pregenital instinctual impulses are directed toward objects, their object relations are primitive and the primitive object relation, the precursor of love and hate, is *incorporation*.[10] Thus incorporation may be associated with any erotogenic zone. Thus there is a strong inherent probability that this holds good of the scoptophilic instinct. The underlying tendency may be formulated as follows: 'I wish what I see to enter into me.' Now this certainly does not *necessarily* mean that the eye itself is thought of as the avenue of introjection. So there are two problems with regard to this process of 'ocular introjection', which takes its place with oral, anal, epidermal, and respiratory introjection; (1) Are the two aims 'I desire to incorporate that which I see' and 'I desire to participate in the experience of that which I see' identical? and (2) Is there such a thing as incorporation through the eye?

All that we know of the relation between empathy, identification, and introjection makes it very probable that we should answer the first question in the affirmative. Empathy is always conditioned by identification and it seems that we have already good grounds for believing that all identification takes place through an act of introjection.[11] [. . .]

It is scarcely possible to doubt that there is such a thing as incorporation through the eye (for we know that incorporation may be associated with any erotogenic zone). The only question is how frequent such fantasies are and what is their significance in the whole course of libidinal development.

When a child is present during a primal scene and identifies himself with his parents, we might suppose that two successive acts have taken place: first, the child *perceives* (and we must, of course, discriminate between perception and introjection, i.e. the fantasy of taking possession of and assimilating oneself to the object – a point to which we shall recur). And, secondly, he *identifies himself* with that which he perceives. But here two separate problems present themselves. In the first place, it is doubtful whether these two acts are in reality so distinct as they are when viewed in the abstract. It is not possible that there is a mode of perception which amounts to identification? Are not the subsequent manifestations of 'ocular introjection' possibly the residue or resumption of a more primitive mode of visual perception, when the objective external world was as yet not so much perceived as taken possession of, by a process akin to identification, and then subjectively elaborated? And in the second place we must ask: with what unconscious fantasies and physical prototypes of mental processes is this identification with the object seen associated?

IV

Let us begin with the first problem. When looking has become libidinized, so that the aim of the person who looks is not perception but sexual gratification, it differs from the ordinary kind of looking. Libidinal looking often takes the form of a fixed gaze, which may be said to be spastic, just as the act of running, when libidinized, is spastic. (Libidinization has the effect of impairing an ego function.)[12]

Now the *magic* glance of which we have already spoken is always supposed to be a 'stare'. (The eye of the basilisk or of the hypnotist.) Moreover, in libidinal looking in general the motor function plays a greater part than in ordinary looking. The process is more active: the world does not approach the eye but the person looking makes an onslaught with his eye upon the world, in order to 'devour' it. But, it may be objected, is it really otherwise in the ordinary, physiological act of seeing? Freud[13] and the exponents of perceptual psychology are agreed that even this process is not so much passive as active and that only the centrifugal impetus of cathectic energy from within the organism enables a sense organ to function, so that it can, as it were, sample the outside world. It is, then, impossible to discover any fundamental antithesis between libidinal and ordinary seeing. Evidently the position is that [what] is characteristic of every act of seeing merely becomes more manifest when the seeing is libidinized. Moreover, the stronger motor element is in evidence not only in libidinal seeing but equally in every mode of 'archaic' seeing, so that the scoptophiliac would seem to have regressed wholly or in part to a more primitive mode of seeing. Bally points out the importance for psychoanalytical theory of investigations in the field of optics, and what he says is briefly this:[14] There is a primitive mode of looking or of visual representation. This original mode of seeing cannot be divorced from motility: there is as yet no sharp distinction between perception and ideation; seeing is a piece of active behavior by means of which one enters into the object seen. When we say that seeing cannot be divorced from motility, we mean, of course (since the control of the motor function depends on the deep-seated sensibility which directs it)[15] that visual perception cannot be separated from kinesthetic perception; in seeing, our whole body undergoes change. The object seen is at first not sharply differentiated from one's own body – and this is true originally of the whole object world by whatever sense it may be perceived; perception and the consequent motor reaction are still one and the same thing. All primitive perception is a taking part in what is perceived. It is only later that perception as a separate process is differentiated both from the behavior with which we react to what we perceive and from thought ('experimental action'), in which use is made of the data acquired by perception. Goldstein has reported that patients suffering from cerebral lesions, who could apparently read well, became incapable of reading if anyone held their heads still. They had accustomed themselves to trace with their heads the forms of the letters that they saw and to read kinesthetically with the help of their own movements, in order to compensate for the defect of a central function. The organic disturbance of a cerebral function had caused these patients to regress to an earlier phase. Thus in libidinal seeing certain characteristics of *primitive* seeing are reproduced; that is to say, the motor and kinesthetic faculties play a greater part than in ordinary seeing. And, since in psychic development a lower phase always persists to a certain extent behind a higher one, *every* act of seeing still retains something of these characteristics.

The first relation of a human being to the object world is invariably that of primary identification,[16] i.e. imitation of the external world as perceived. Here, however, another factor comes in: it is only by means of the co-operation of the motor system that full perception is possible; observation takes place *by way of* identification.

This brings us to the problem already alluded to of the relation of perception to introjection in general. It would certainly be incorrect to regard these two concepts as identical or to define perception as a variety of introjection. One does not become like every object which one has seen. Nevertheless the relation between perception and introjection must be a close one and we can surmise its nature. Perception and secondary identification are two separate products of what was originally a single process. Freud long ago recognized that primitive perception is akin to introjection.[17]

Simmel holds that the oral erotogenic zone, the first organ of incorporation, is also the organ of our earliest perceptions, so that all the organs concerned in subsequent perception derive some of their qualities from this, their original predecessor. He defines the eye and the ear as 'organs of introjection for the elaboration and satisfactory assimilation of optical and acoustic perceptions'.[18] In fantasy also the eye and the ear are conceived of as organs of sex designed for the reception of the object. (We must observe that, all the same, they seem less suitable for such representation than another sense organ, the nose, for in olfactory perception the introjection of minute particles of the objects is actually *real*.)

The fact that libidinal seeing is a partial regression to these archaic forms of seeing explains how it is that, as we have already noted, the aim of the scoptophilic instinct regularly includes elements of sadism and the desire to incorporate the object.

V

Let us now turn to the second question: with what fantasies of 'physical prototypes of mental processes' is incorporation by means of the eye associated? [. . .]

VI

[. . .] Fantasies of 'ocular introjection' must be accorded the same status as the ideas of incorporation associates with the other erotogenic zones. There are still some problems in this connection which demand our consideration.

Long ago Freud recognized, and we regard it as a matter of course, that the eye is a phallic symbol and that, accordingly, to be blinded signifies to be castrated (especially as a punishment for some transgression promoted by the scoptophilic impulse). Can it be that the eye acquires this significance only through identification with a penis which is seen and thereby introjected? This can hardly be so; the *tertia comparationis* – 'the most noble organ' and 'the vulnerable organ' – probably suffice to explain the phallic nature of the eye. But no doubt ideas of incorporation may *reinforce* the symbolism. If the eye stands for the penis, then the eye fixed in a stare stands for the penis in erection.

In our patient's associations there constantly recurred the fairytale of the stone prince in the Arabian Nights. Over and over again in her dreams and fantasies figures of men appeared which had their prototype in this tale. The upper part of their bodies was ordinary and familiar, perhaps that of her father, while the lower part was somehow uncanny, being rigid or like that of an animal. The man with the belly of stone signified to her the man with the belly of a beast – in fact, a centaur; a counterpart was the Little Mermaid from Hans Andersen's story, who had a fish's tail instead of legs; a figure which also played a great part in her fantasy. The purpose of these fantasies was simply to repress or psychically to master her observations of the genitals of adults in childhood. Now the rigidity of the stone prince, his disability, and his immobility were stressed in a very remarkable fashion. They signified something more than erection. We recall the fact that to be turned into stone is, like losing his sight, a very frequent punishment for the scoptophiliac. A person who looks at something terrible is turned into stone (you will remember the story of the head of Medusa).[19] This means that, like the victim who encounters the paralyzing glance of a snake, he is incapable of movement. The head of Medusa and other objects the sight of which is fatal have been conclusively demonstrated to be symbols for the female genital, and so to be turned into stone symbolizes the shock of castration with which such a sight is visited, or even castration itself. Loss of the power of motion signifies loss (not only of life but) of the penis, while a stony immobility signifies (being dead and) castration. When we reflect that the object which turns people into stone is very often a glaring eye (basilisk, snake, hypnotist), it is natural to conclude that such an eye is another symbol for the terrible, devouring, female genital. Now we noted that the oral-sadistic eye, which seeks to devour everything, also has this fixed glare, a fact which accords well with the interpretation just given. Let us recollect further that one of the problems which I suggested at the beginning of this paper was how the eye comes to acquire an oral significance precisely in cases in which there can be no doubt of its phallic character. We begin to realize what is the idea which in the unconscious is the link between the penis and the mouth. It is that of the vagina, which is seen but not comprehended and about which the child is uncertain whether it conceals within it a penis or is a kind of devouring mouth. In the unconscious, contradictions can exist side by side. To be turned into rigid stone symbolizes not only erection but also castration, just as the eye symbolizes not only a penis but a vagina (and a mouth).

The idea of being turned into stone reminds us of the strange immobility of the wolves in the Wolf-Man's dream.[20] Freud interprets this as 'representation through the opposite'; i.e. the immobility stands for the vigorous movement which the child must have witnessed during the primal scene. Now there was one person who, as Freud also has noted, actually was rigid during this scene: the child who witnessed it. So, 'to be turned into stone' by the sight of something means to be fascinated by it. The primary basis of this fantasy must have been the recollection of the physical feeling of actual inability to move and rigidity which comes over a person who suddenly sees something terrifying. This fascination represents the child's helplessness in face of the enormous masses of excitation experienced when he witnesses the primal scene. Further, it has something to do with the adult genitals which he observes – with both erection and absence of the penis – and indicates his identification of his own condition with both of these, and especially his expectation of castration. At all events, in the case of the stone prince, the immobility of the person who looked was displaced onto the object looked at. And a similar displacement takes place in the act of libidinal seeing, when subject is confused with object and the ego with the outside world.

There is, however, a still deeper significance in the mechanisms of introjection or identification here at work.

Why were Lot and his company forbidden to look at Sodom as it perished? Because the sight was the sight of God Himself! But no one can bear the sight of God. Why not? What is the sin in looking? Surely it is that looking implies identification. If a man looks upon God face to face, something of the glory of God passes into him. It is this impious act, the likening of oneself to God, which is forbidden when man is forbidden to look at God. 'Thou shalt not make to thyself any graven image' is a variation of the more general prohibition which forbids us to look at God.

So to be turned into stone means also to be punished for seeking to become that which one has seen and, after the fashion familiar to us in hysterical identification, the idea includes that of sacrilegious identification, translated, however, into terms of the superego. And this identification is achieved by looking at the object: he who looks at that which has been castrated (the head of Medusa) himself undergoes castration. He who looks at the dead is himself struck dead. Therefore the counterpart to the dread of being turned into stone is that of being forced in some uncanny way to look at a stone (dead) man (cf. the 'guest of stone' in *Don Juan*). Again, the eyes of the dead must be closed, because otherwise they would slay with their look those who still live;[21] the underlying idea here is the same, but the sadism of the eyes is once more displaced from the person looking to the object looked at.

When we realize that, from a schematic point of view, the idea of being turned into stone represents the reaction to the witnessing of a primal scene, we can appreciate how many elements are contained in it: erection and castration, the death of the parents, and, above all, identification with that which is seen, identification which is at one and the same time a wish fulfillment and a punishment. What concerns us most in our present context is that, when we are fascinated by some sight, the fixity of our own devouring gaze (of which we have an inner perception) is not only the basis of physical feeling on which is founded the fantasy of being turned into stone but is also, in fantasy, the bridge by which identification occurs. I would add that such an experience of fascination results in more than a fixity of gaze: the whole muscular system becomes rigid (feeling of paralysis), especially the respiratory muscles.

An idea frequently met with in the analysis of patients is that the moon is a 'dead man' (or, in the primal scene, 'a man in vigorous action') whom one is forced to look at by some fascination and yet dare not look at because, if one did, one would die and become rigid oneself. The wan light of the moon does give a very strong impression of fixity and immobility. It is said to lay a spell upon the 'moonstruck' somnambulist;[22] obviously it is here equated with the unwavering eye of the hypnotist who puts a spell on his victim. The movements of the somnambulist, like those of persons in hypnosis, are described as unnaturally stiff and wanting in freedom. He is compelled to follow the direction of the moonbeams, just as a person in hypnosis is compelled to imitate the movements of the hypnotist. The characteristics of the subject's own state of fascination are projected onto the moon; it is as motionless and silent as the watching child, as dead as the child fears that he himself will shortly be. (One of the ideas associated with somnambulism is that the 'moon-struck' person is in imminent danger of his life, that he might, for instance, fall off a roof. This is in accordance with the psychoanalytical observation that the dread of falling is derived from the dread of bursting as a result of the discharge of one's own excessive sexual excitation.) The moon, at which one is compelled to look, is perceived as a face, an eye, which, like the eye of God, sees everything. It too symbolizes those terrible objects of the scoptophilic instinct, identification with which takes place by means of a look and upon which are projected one's peculiar bodily sensations; they are, of course, the parents in the primal scene and, above all, their genitals. Here, as in the case of the head of Medusa, the female (maternal) elements predominate. It is clear, then, that the moon stands for an eye and that one identifies oneself with it by looking at it.

Akin to the idea of being turned into stone is the childish fantasy that a grimace may 'stick' or 'you'll be struck like that'. The uncanny feeling experienced with dead people look as if they were still alive, as if they had 'stuck' in the midst of whatever they happened to be doing, has the same character (cf. the story of the Sleeping Beauty). Here again we often discover the idea of identification accomplished by means of a look.

Thus we arrive at the conclusion that the rigidity of a person turned into stone stands for the fixed gaze and the rigidity of the whole muscular system of a person fascinated by something he sees, and that it signifies erection or (death and) castration. In this train of thought the essential point is that looking is conceived of as a means of identification. If we pursue it, it leads us finally to the problems of the effect of shock and of traumas in general – i.e. the victim's sudden inability to master the outside world, a reaction which is a mode of defense against excessive masses of excitation.

[. . .]

VIII

[. . .] The patient's dread of being painted was really a dread of retribution, and this suggests that certain other well-known facts of ethnology and folklore come into the same category. The fear manifested by primitive or superstitious persons at the thought of having their likeness taken is commonly explained as a dread of magic. The idea is that anyone who possesses a likeness of someone else has him in his power, for everything that he does to the likeness happens to the person himself. This is also the reason for the efforts which such primitive persons make to prevent a stranger's possessing himself of any part of their bodies (e.g. fingernails) or of their excrement. It is clear that they regard a likeness as part of the ego which the other person's eye (or the apparatus he uses) can take away from them, just as his hands can take away excrement. We have the best illustration of this in the idea that, as soon as the likeness begins to exercise its magical influence, the person whom it represents loses part of his personality – e.g. his reflection or his shadow. When a primitive or superstitious person is looked at (has his likeness taken), he feels that something is taken away from him. Once again the eye is conceived of as an organ which robs or bites.

Finally let me remind you that man's mechanical ingenuity has actually created a 'devouring eye', which looks at and incorporates the external world and later projects it outward again. I refer, of course, to the camera. When we analyze the dread so frequently displayed by children (and occasionally by grown-ups too) at the sight of a camera, we invariably find that they think of it as an eye which is going to bite off some part of them. Here the genital significance of the eye is obvious; we have found that the 'devouring eye' always has this significance. One patient had had an acute attack of anxiety as a child, when he was to undergo an X-ray examination. In analyzing this anxiety it had to be admitted that radioscopy really does enable the eye to penetrate into the interior of the body, just as the patient had always wished unconsciously that his own eye might do, while his dread of retaliation made him constantly afraid that such a thing might happen to himself. But the sadism which informed these fantasies was not in fact a feature of the objective X-ray apparatus.

We have seen that being blinded and being turned into stone are the specific punishments of the active scoptophiliac. We can now add that there is a corresponding specific punishment for the exhibitionist: the eye which looks at him will bite off part of him or devour him whole. One often meets with ideas of this sort when analyzing an exaggerated sense of shame. Probably some similar notion of ocular introjection is a regular element in the sense of shame in general.

IX

In conclusion I wish to refer to a problem of medicine, for the solution of which many more works, on quite different lines from this, will doubtless be required.

In psychoanalytical literature the problems of the psychogenesis of myopia have at various times been discussed.[23] The writers in question have taken as their point of departure the effect of myopia and have simply introduced the idea that it served some psychical purpose. What they asked was: what does the patient gain by not being able to see distant objects or by hiding his face behind a pair of spectacles? Put in this way, the question seems to me unjustifiable, and over-simple. We cannot disregard the somatic nature of the symptom. If there is a psychic factor in its genesis, we must look for it elsewhere.

It is a well-known fact that when an organ is constantly used for purposes of erotogenic pleasure, it undergoes certain somatic changes. It happens that Freud was speaking of the eyes of persons in whom the scoptophilic instinct is specially developed, when he said, 'If an organ which serves two purposes overplays its erotogenic role, it is in general to be expected that this will not occur without alterations in its response to stimulation and in innervation'[24] – i.e. of the physiological factors in general. From the point of view of research it is probably more useful, when studying myopia, to consider the somatic changes which take place in the eye in consequence of its being used for libidinal purposes than to regard the incapacity to see at a distance as a symbol of castration. We have an additional reason for thinking that we shall discover somatic-neurotic relations when we read further in Freud: 'Neurotic disturbances of vision are related to psychogenic as, in general, are the actual neuroses to the psychoneuroses; psychogenic visual disturbances can hardly occur without neurotic disturbances, though the latter surely can without the former.'[25]

What has ophthalmic medicine to say on the subject of myopia? We are told that it is caused by an elongation of the axis of the eyeball. This elongation is attributed partly to the external muscles of the eye and partly to general vegetative changes which alter the contour of the eyeball itself. It would seem, than, that incapacity to see distant objects has no psychic significance but is the involuntary, mechanical sequel to processes which either affect the external optic muscles or take place within the eyeballs. But what causes these processes? At all events the vegetative nervous system plays a decisive part in them, and the functioning of that system is, apart from various somatic factors, physically determined. The question is this. We have seen that the constant use of the eye for the libidinal gratification of scoptophilic impulses causes it actively to strain in the direction of objects, in order psychically to incorporate them. It is not possible that this may finally result in a stretching of the eyeball?

We recognize that this is putting the problem very crudely. Of course an exact knowledge of the ways in which such stretching may occur would be necessary to explain why many people in whom the scoptophilic instinct is peculiarly strong are not in the least shortsighted. There is no difficulty about the converse fact, namely, that many shortsighted people (often those in whom the symptom is most pronounced) show no sign of a marked scoptophilic tendency. There is no reason to suppose that every case of myopia is psychogenic. And, while the stretching of the eyeball may sometimes be due to the attempt to incorporate objects at the bidding of scoptophilic impulses, in other cases the origin of the disability is undoubtedly purely somatic.

Notes

1   J. Strachey, 'Some unconscious factors in reading', *International Journal of Psychoanalysis*, 11 (1930).
2   The first reference to this idea occurs in *The Interpretation of Dreams*.
3   G. Roheim, *Spiegelzauber* (Vienna, Int. Psa. Verlag, 1919).
4   S. Freud, 'Psychogenic visual disturbance according to psycho-analytical conceptions', *Collected Papers*, vol. II (London, Hogarth, 1948).

5   O. Fenichel, *Perversionen, Psychosen, Charakterstoerungen* (Vienna, Int. Psa. Verlag, 1931), p. 170.

6   S. Freud, *Three Essays on the Theory of Sexuality*, vol. 7 (Penguin, Harmondsworth, Pelican Freud Library, 1977).

7   Ibid.

8   J. Landmark, 'Ueber den Triebbegriff', *Imago*, 20 (1934).

9   O. Fenichel, 'Identification', in *The Collected Papers of Otto Fenichel*, first series, eds. H. Fenichel and D. Rapaport (London, Routledge and Kegan Paul, 1954).

10 K. Abraham, 'A short study of the development of the libido, viewed in the light of mental disorders', *Selected Papers* (London, Hogarth, 1948).

11 S. Freud, 'Mourning and melancholia', *Collected Papers*, vol. IV.

12 S. Freud, *The Problem of Anxiety* (New York, Psa. Quart. Press and Norton, 1936).

13 S. Freud, 'A note upon the "mystic writing-pad"', *Collected Papers*, vol. V.

14 G. Bally, 'Die Wahrnehmungslehre Jaenschs und ihre Beziehung zu den psycho-analytischen Problemen', *Imago*, 17 (1931).

15 O. Fenichel, 'Organ libidinization accompanying the defence against drivers', in Fenichel and Rapaport (eds) (1954).

16 O. Fenichel, 'Identification', in Fenichel and Rapaport (eds) (1954).

17 Compare in this connection Freud's remarks on the 'purified pleasure-ego' in 'Instincts and their vicissitudes', *Collected Papers*, vol. IV.

18 E. Simmel, 'Praegenitalprimat und intestinale Stufe der Libidoorganisation', author's abstract, *Int. S. Psa.*, 19 (1933).

19 S. Ferenczi, 'On the symbolism of the head of Medusa', *Further Contributions to the Theory and Technique of Psycho-Analysis* (London, Hogarth, 1950).

20 S. Freud, 'From the history of an infantile neurosis', *Collected Papers*, vol. III.

21 Roheim, *Spiegelzauber*.

22 In German the word *mondsuechtig* has the double sense of 'moonstruck' and 'somnambulistic' – Trans. note.

23 S.E. Jelliffe, 'Psychoanalysis and organic disorder: myopia as a paradigm', *International Journal of Psychoanalysis*, 7 (1926).

24 S. Freud, 'Psychogenic visual disturbance according to psycho-analytical conceptions', *Collected Papers*, vol. II.

25 Ibid., p. 112.

The subject   **Kaja Silverman**

[. . .]

The Lacanian model

French psychoanalyst Jacques Lacan has exercised an enormous influence over the direction recently taken by semiotic theory. He has initiated the return of psychoanalysis to Freud's early writing, which for years was neglected in favor of his later works, and in so doing he has deflected therapeutic attention away from the ego to the unconscious. In addition, he has encouraged the re-reading of Freud's writings in relation to the contributions of Saussure and Lévi-Strauss, thereby demonstrating the profound but previously unnoticed affinities between psychoanalysis on the one hand, and linguistic and anthropological semiotics on the other. Finally, Lacan has extended and enriched the Freudian model, further consolidating the theoretical interconnections between subject, signifier, and cultural order. His writings and seminars have provided the inspiration for much interesting work in the area of film theory, and they are increasingly playing the same role in the related field of literary theory.

[. . .] Lacan's prose is notoriously remote, and his presentation deliberately a-systematic. Many of the terms to which he most frequently returns constantly shift meaning. These qualities make it almost impossible to offer definitive statements about the Lacanian argument; indeed, Lacan himself almost never agreed with his commentators. Finally, although Lacan insists that everything he says has its origins in Freud's writings, his followers have been hard pressed to reconcile Lacan's pronouncements on certain key issues, such as the unconscious, with those made by Freud. We will consequently not attempt a comprehensive survey of the Lacanian

This chapter is taken from Kaja Silverman, *The Subject of Semiotics* (Oxford, Oxford University Press, 1983), pp. 126–193.

argument, but will focus instead on those parts of it which have proved most assimilable to a broader psychoanalytic theory, while at the same time extending that theory in the direction of semiotic linguistics and anthropology.

Lacan's theory of the subject reads like a classic narrative – it begins with birth, and then moves in turn through the territorialization of the body, the mirror stage, access to language, and the Oedipus complex. The last two of these events belong to what Lacan calls the symbolic order, and they mark the subject's coming of age within culture. Since each of the stages of this narrative is conceived in terms of some kind of self-loss or lack, we will first attempt to determine exactly what is implied by that notion, particularly in relation to the subject's birth and the zoning of its body. We will then progress with that subject through the mirror stage, the acquisition of language, and the adventures of the Oedipal.

Birth, territorialization, and lack

The concept of lack appears again and again in Lacan's writings and in the transcripts of his seminars, figuring centrally at every moment in the development of the subject. Indeed, one could say of the Lacanian subject that it is almost entirely defined by lack.

This point emerges with particular clarity in *Four Fundamental Concepts of Psycho-Analysis* (Seminar XI) which more than once invokes the story told by Aristophanes in Plato's *Symposium* (1961: 542–44) about the birth of desire:

> . . . in the beginning we were nothing like we are now. For one thing, the race was divided into three . . . besides the two sexes, male and female, which we have at present, there was a third which partook of the nature of both. . . .
>
> And secondly . . . each of these beings was globular in shape, with rounded back and sides, four arms and four legs, and two faces. . . . And such . . . were their strength and energy, and such their arrogance, that they actually tried . . . to scale the heights of heaven and set upon the gods.
>
> At this Zeus took counsel with the other gods as to what was to be done. . . . At last . . . after racking his brains, Zeus offered a solution.
>
> I think I can see my way, he said, to put an end to this disturbance. . . . What I propose to do is to cut them all in half, thus killing two birds with one stone, for each one will be only half as strong, and there'll be twice as many of them. . . .
>
> Now, when the work of bisection was complete it left each half with a desperate yearning for the other, and they ran together and flung their arms around each other's necks, and asked for nothing better than to be rolled into one. So much so, that they began to die. . . . Zeus felt so sorry for them that he devised another scheme. He moved their privates round to the front . . . and made them propagate among themselves. . . . So you see . . . how far back we can trace our innate love for one another, and how this love is always trying to reintegrate our former nature, to make two into one, and to bridge the gulf between one human being and other.

I have quoted this passage at length because it contains a surprisingly large number of critical Lacanian assumptions. One of these assumptions is that the human subject derives from an original whole which was divided in half, and that its existence is dominated by the desire to recover its missing complement. Another of these assumptions is that the division suffered by the subject was sexual in nature – that when it was 'sliced' in half, it lost the sexual androgyny it once had and was reduced to the biological dimension either of a man or a woman. This biological dimension is seen by Lacan, if not by Plato, as absolutely determining the subject's social identity. Finally, Lacan shares with Aristophanes the belief that the only resolution to the loss suffered by the subject as the consequence of sexual division is heterosexual union and procreation. We will examine each of these points in greater detail.

Lacan situates the first loss in the history of the subject at the moment of birth. To be more precise, he dates it from the moment of sexual differentiation within the womb, but it is not realized until the separation of the child from the mother at birth. This lack is sexual in definition; it has to do with the impossibility of being physiologically both male and female. [. . .]

Lacan tells us that the only way the subject can compensate for its fragmentary condition is by fulfilling its biological destiny – by living out in the most complete sense its own 'maleness' or 'femaleness', and by forming new sexual unions with members of the opposite sex. It is by means of such unions that the subject comes closest to recovering its lost wholeness.

[. . .]

According to the Lacanian argument, the sexually differentiating scenarios of the culture into which the subject is later assimilated show it the 'way' to 'sexual fulfillment', the path to personal salvation. The Oedipus complex plays a particularly important role [in this]. [. . .]

What Lacan here suggests is that human 'nature' finds its logical expression and complement in the cultural definitions of 'male' and 'female'. However, at the same time he draws attention to the coerciveness of those definitions, and of the sexually differentiated narratives into which the subject is inserted. [. . .]

The second loss suffered by the Lacanian subject occurs after birth, but prior to the acquisition of language. Although it takes place before the assimilation of the subject into the symbolic order, it can be viewed as the result of a cultural intervention. The loss in question is inflicted by what might be called the 'pre-Oedipal territorialization' of the subject's body – by the preparation of the human body for the sexually differentiated scenarios into which it will later be accommodated.

For a time after its birth, the child does not differentiate between itself and the mother upon whose nurture it relies, or the blanket whose warmth it enjoys, or the pillow whose softness supports its head. Its libidinal flow is directed toward the complete assimilation of everything which is experiences as pleasurable, and there are no recognized boundaries. [. . .]

However, the partitioning of the subject begins almost immediately. The child's body undergoes a process of differentiation, whereby erotogenic zones are inscribed and libido is canalized (i.e. encouraged to follow certain established routes). Specific somatic areas are designated as the appropriate sites of pleasure, and the areas which are so designated are all ones which open onto the external world – most importantly the mouth, the anus, the penis and the vagina. The mother is the usual agent of this inscription, defining the erotic zones through the care she lavishes upon them.

The territorialization of the infant's body provides the means whereby the outpouring of libido can be directed and contained. By indicating the channels through which that libido can move, the mother or nurse performs a social service, assists in the conversion of incoherent energy into coherent drives which can later be culturally regulated. Indeed, by organizing the infant's body in relation to its reproductive potential, the mother or nurse already indicates the form which that cultural regulation will take: the orchestration of the drives around sexual difference.

The drives possess a coherence which needs do not have because they are attached to particular corporal zones – because they in effect represent those zones (mouth, anus, penis, vagina). As a result of this attachment, the drives provide only an indirect expression of the original libidinal flow. Thus very early in its history the subject loses unmediated contact with its own libidinal flows, and succumbs to the domination of its culture's genital economy. [. . .]

[In 'From Love to the Libido' in Lacan, 1978] the erotogenic zones or somatic gaps become the points through which the child attempts to introject into itself those things which give it pleasure, and which it does not yet distinguish from itself. The first such object is generally the breast, and it is of course inserted into the orifice of the mouth. The child perceives the breast as its missing complement, that things the loss of which has resulted in a sense of deficiency or lack [. . .]

There will be many such objects in the life of the subject. Lacan refers to them as 'objets petit a', which is an abbreviation for the more complete formula 'objets petit autre'. This rubric designates objects which are not clearly distinguished from the self and which are not fully grasped as other (autre). The object (a), as we will henceforth refer to it, derives its value from its identification with some missing component of the subject's self, whether that loss is seen as primordial, as the result of a bodily organization, or as the consequence of some other division. [. . .]

The register within which these identifications are sustained – within which the objects (a) acquire their privileged status – is called by Lacan the 'imaginary'.

The imaginary

'Imaginary' is the term used by Lacan to designate that order of the subject's experience which is dominated by identification and duality.

Within the Lacanian scheme it not only precedes the symbolic order, which introduces the subject to language and Oedipal triangulation, but continues to coexist with it afterward. The two registers complement each other, the symbolic establishing the differences which are such an essential part of cultural existence, and the imaginary making it possible to discover correspondences and homologies. The imaginary order is most classically exemplified by the mirror stage.

Lacan tells us that somewhere between the ages of six months and eighteen months the subject arrives at an apprehension of both its self and the other – indeed, of its self *as other*. This discovery is assisted by the child seeing, for the first time, its own reflection in a mirror. That reflection enjoys a coherence which the subject itself lacks – it is an *ideal* image. [. . .]

This self-recognition is, Lacan insists, a mis-recognition; the subject apprehends itself only by means of a fictional construct whose defining characteristics – focus, coordination – it does not share. It must also be stressed that the mirror stage is one of those crises of alienation around which the Lacanian subject is organized, since to know oneself through an external image is to be defined through self-alienation.

The situation here closely resembles that in which the subject identifies with the mother's breast, voice, gaze, or whatever other object is perceived as its missing complement. The mirror image can no more be assimilated than can any of those other privileged objects, yet the subject defines itself entirely in relation to it. As a consequence of the irreducible distance which separates the subject from its ideal reflection, it entertains a profoundly ambivalent relationship to that reflection. It loves the coherent identity which the mirror provides. However, because the image remains external to it, it also hates that image.

This radical oscillation between contrary emotions in respect to the same object characterizes all of the relationships of the imaginary order. As long as the subject remains trapped within that order, it will be unable to mediate between or escape from the binary oppositions which structure all of its perceptions; it will fluctuate between the extremes of love and hate toward objects which will undergo corresponding shifts in value. Moreover, the subject will itself be capable of identifying alternately with diametrically opposed positions (victim/victimizer, exhibitionist/voyeur, slave/master).

[. . .]

The important role played by visual images in the identifications of the imaginary order has made this part of Lacan's model particularly rich in implications for the study of film. Indeed, as we noted earlier, Christian Metz (1975) in *Le Signifiant imaginaire* has defined the cinematic signifier as an imaginary one – as one which induces by means of visual images the same sorts of identifications which occur early in the subject's life, and within which absence plays the same structuring role. However, it would seem important to understand that the images which figure so centrally in the imaginary register exceed any strictly specular definition, and that they can be generated by many other sources. [. . .]

A closely related issue which would seem to warrant some additional clarification is the relationship between the mirror stage and the Oedipus complex, i.e. between pre- and post-symbolic identifications. Lacan suggests that the image which the child discovers in the mirror is ideologically neutral, that it has no social determination. At the same time he tells us that the child's identification with that image takes exactly the same form as subsequent identifications with images which *are* socially determined. During the Oedipus complex, for instance, the male subject identifies with an ideal paternal representation which exceeds him in much the same way as the mirror image exceeds the child, and he entertains the same ambivalent feelings toward that representation. The question we are thus obliged to ask is whether the mirror stage is not in some manner culturally induced.

Careful scrutiny of the account given to us of the mirror stage reveals undeniable traces of cultural intervention, most notably in the term 'ideal' by means of which Lacan qualifies the pronoun 'I'. 'Ideal' is a term which has meaning only within a system of values. It indicates that social norms play an important role in the mirror stage, and that the child's identity is from the very beginning culturally mediated. That mediation may be as simple and direct as the mother's interpretation of the mirror image for the child, or as complex and diffuse as the introduction into the child's environment of various representations (dolls, picture-books, trains, or toy guns) which determine the way in which it will eventually regard itself. As most readers of 'The Mirror Stage' are quick to point out, we cannot interpret the reflection within which the child finds its identity too literally; it must be understood at least to some degree as a cultural construct. [. . .]

As we noted above, there can be no resolution of the emotional extremes of the original narcissistic relationship so long as the subject remains within the imaginary order. That resolution comes only with the subject's access to language and its accommodations within the triangular configuration of the Oedipal paradigm – in other words, with its entry into the symbolic order. [. . .]

Signification

We will begin our discussion of the subject's acquisition of language with a brief account of Lacan's theory of signification. [. . .]

When Lacan refers to the synchronic network he invokes the Saussurean tenet that every signifying element assumes value in relation to all of the other signifying elements with which it is paradigmatically classed. In other words, he reminds us that meaning emerges as the result of the play of differences within a closed system. However, whereas Saussure (1966) indicates that both signifiers and signifieds enjoy paradigmatic relationships, Lacan associates those relationships exclusively with the signifier.

Lacan establishes a corresponding connection between syntagmatic relationships and the signified. He argues that meaning emerges only through the temporal or diachronic unfolding of a signifying chain. Since it does not pre-exist the syntagmatic alignment of signifiers, the signified *is* that syntagmatic alignment. Lacan thus denies the possibility of meaning inhering in any isolated unit, attributing signifying capabilities only to the discursive complex.

Coexisting with the definition of signifier as paradigm and signified as syntagm is another, equally important conceptualization of those terms. Although Lacan repeatedly emphasizes the linguistic status of the signifier – i.e. its formal properties – many passages in his writings project a more inclusive understanding of it – an understanding which encompasses what Saussure would call the signified. He conceives of the relationship between the formal and conceptual dimensions in determinedly abstract ways; he tells us that the concept 'insists' within the form or 'letter'. The Lacanian signifier is thus an elusive blend of idea and form.

'Function and Field of Speech and Language' suggests that what is really at issue in this super-subtle definition is the signifier's liberation from any obligation to represent the world of real objects. [. . .] Within the Lacanian argument the signifier is the mark of the subject's radical alienation from the real – from its organic nature, from actual mothers or fathers, or from any phenomenal experience. Thus the signifier 'father' has no relation whatever to the physical fact of any individual father. Instead, that signifier finds its support in a network of other signifiers, including 'phallus', 'law', 'adequacy', and 'mother', all of which are equally indifferent to the category of the real.

For Lacan, the definitive criterion of a signifier is that it abandon all relation to the real, and take up residence within a closed field of meaning, not that it partake of a given materiality. Language is consequently not the only source of signifiers; dietary rituals, marriage ceremonies, hysteria, conventions of dress, and neuroses all generate signifiers. Indeed, since signification constitutes the matrix within which the subject resides after its entry into the symbolic order, nothing escapes cultural value. In a celebrated passage from 'Function and Field of Speech and Language', Lacan describes the subject as entirely contained within a network of signification:

> Symbols . . . envelop the life of man in a network so total that they join together, before he comes into the world, those who are going to engender him 'by flesh and blood'; so total that they bring to his birth . . . the share of his destiny; so total that they give the words that will make him faithful or renegade, the law of the acts that will follow him right to the very place where he *is* not yet and even beyond his death; and so total that through them his end finds its meaning in the last judgement, where the Word absolves his being or condemns it. (Lacan, 1977a: 68)

At the same time as we indicate the range of signifying materials, it is important to note the privileged position enjoyed by language. For Lacan, as for Barthes, languages mediates all other signifiers. This means that we have access to the signifiers generated by dietary rituals, marriage ceremonies, hysteria, conventions of dress, or neuroses only through linguistic ones. It also means that the subject participates in signification only after the acquisition of language. Prior to that acquisition, the subject engages in representation, but not what Lacan calls the 'non-representative representation' which constitutes signification.

This last distinction is a critical one within the Lacanian argument. It is used to differentiate iconic and indexical signifiers from purely conventional ones – to distinguish, that is, between a mirror image or a photograph, which refers in some way (albeit indirectly) to an actual object, and a word, which has abandoned any such association and refers only to other elements within the same system. A consequence of the non-representational status of language is that the signified is always provisional – that it is never 'resolved back into a pure indication of the real'. [. . .] Lacan is not as explicit as one might like him to be about the subject's entrance into language. However, he does return repeatedly to three points: he tells us that language isolates the subject from the real, confining it forever to the realm of signification; he indicates that the unconscious comes into existence at the moment of the subject's access to language; finally, he insists that the unconscious is organized around an irreducible signifier, otherwise called the 'unary' signifier.

The real from which language excludes the subject consists of both the subject's own 'being' (its libidinal resources or needs) and the phenomenal world. Once the subject has entered the symbolic order its organic needs pass through the 'defiles' or network of signification and are transformed in a way which makes them thereafter impossible to satisfy. The drives offer only a partial and indirect expression of those needs, but language severs the relationship altogether. It is, as we have just observed, *non-representative*. Moreover, since language speaks no more to the reality of objects than it does to that of subjects, it effects as complete a rupture with the phenomenal world.

With the subject's entry into the symbolic order it is reduced to the status of a signifier in the field of the Other. It is defined by a linguistic structure which does not in any way address its being, but which determines its entire cultural existence. Lacan insists that the subject is linguistically coerced not only at the level of the preconscious, as Freud would argue, but at that of the unconscious as well. Within this scheme 'the unconscious is the discourse of the Other'; its desires are those of an already constituted social order, and it is organized by means of the same language as the preconscious.

Lacan conceives of the unconscious not as an inarticulate and chaotic region, but as a signifying network. He observes in 'Agency of the Letter in the Unconscious' that it is 'neither primordial nor instinctual; what it knows about the elementary is no more than the elements of the signifier' (Lacan, 1977a: 170). Within the Lacanian scheme the unconscious is split off not only from the undifferentiated needs which comprise the subject's being, but from the drives, which as we indicated earlier are themselves already the product of a cultural mediation, i.e. of the territorialization of the body. Indeed, the unconscious is as sharply partitioned from the drives as the preconscious/conscious system is from the unconscious. It is thus altogether opposed to the area designated as the 'id' in the late Freudian topography, an area which is virtually synonymous with the drives. It much more closely resembles the unconscious elaborated by *The Interpretation of Dreams*, in that it too can only be defined through its signifying activities.

Within the Lacanian account both the subject's entrance into the symbolic and the formation of the unconscious are effected through a single signifying event. This event involves only to signifiers – what Lacan calls the 'unary' and the 'binary' signifiers. Together they inaugurate a closed system of signification, one which excludes both the phenomenal world and the drives. Lacan pays particular attention to the second of these exclusions, and he illustrates it through the story Freud tells about his grandson in *The Interpretation of Dreams* and *Beyond the Pleasure Principle*. Although we have already had occasion to discuss this story briefly, I will quote the second version of it in full here:

> The child was not at all precocious in his intellectual development. At the age of one and a half he could say only a few comprehensible words; he could also make use of a number of sounds which expressed a meaning intelligible to those around him. He was, however, on good terms with his parents and their one servant-girl, and tributes were paid to his being a 'good boy'. He did not disturb his parents at night, he conscientiously obeyed orders not to touch certain things or go into certain rooms, and above all he never cried when his mother left him for a few hours. At the same time, he was greatly attached to him mother, who had not only fed him herself but had also looked after him without any outside help. This good little boy, however, had an occasional disturbing habit of taking any small objects he could get hold of and throwing them away from him into a corner, under the bed, and so on, so that hunting for his toys and picking them up was often quite a business. As he did this he gave vent to a long-drawn-out 'o-o-o–', accompanied by an expression of interest and satisfaction. His mother and the writer of the present account were agreed in thinking that this was not a mere interjection but represented the German word '*fort*' [gone]. I eventually realized that it was a game that the only use he made of any of his toys was to play 'gone' with them. One day I made an observation which confirmed my view. The child had a wooden reel with a piece of string tied round it. It never occurred to him to pull it along the floor behind him, for instance, and to play at its being a carriage. What he did was to hold the reel by the string and very skillfully throw it over the edge of his curtained cot, so that it disappeared into it, at the same time uttering his expressive 'o-o-o-o'. He then pulled the reel out of the cot again by the string and hailed its reappearance with a joyful '*da*' [there]. This, then, was the complete game – disappearance and return. (Freud, 1953: xviii, pp. 14–15)

There are significant differences between the Lacanian and Freudian approaches to this important episode in the history of an exemplary subject. Whereas Freud describes the child's actions as an attempt to diminish the unpleasure caused by his mother's absences, Lacan stresses instead the self-alienation which those actions dramatize. In other words, Lacan identifies the toy with which the child plays as an object (a), one of those privileged items which the subject perceives as its own missing complement. Lacan thus interprets the story more as a parable about the disappearance of the self than the disappearance of the mother. In 'Tuché and Automation' he asserts that

> This real is not the mother reduced to a little ball by some magical game worthy of the Jivaros – it is a small part of the subject which detaches itself from him while still remaining his, still retained . . . If it is true that the signifier is the first mark of the subject, how can we fail to recognize here – from the very fact that this game is accompanied by one of the first oppositions to appear – that it is in the object to which the opposition is applied in act, the reel, that we must designate the subject. To this object we will later give the name it bears in the Lacanian algebra – the *petit a*. (Lacan, 1978: 62)

What Lacan here suggests is that at this stage in its history the subject does not yet distinguish between itself and an external realm; it is still caught up in the imaginary register, the register of identification and emotional ambivalence. It identifies the toy with itself, just as it identifies parts of the mother or its own mirror image with itself, and it directs toward the toy the same conflicting emotions that crystallize around those other objects. The young subject, here represented by Freud's grandson, stages a drama ideally suited to express these conflicting emotions – a drama of presence and absence, appearance and disappearance.

The notion that what the child thereby acts out are not so much his mother's entrances and departures as his own was unwittingly suggested by Freud himself, in a footnote to the final account of the game:

> One day the child's mother had been away for several hours and on her return was met with the words 'Baby o-o-o-o!' which was at first incomprehensible. It soon turned out, however, that during this long period of solitude the child had found a method of making *himself* disappear. He had discovered his reflection in a full-length mirror which did not quite reach to the ground, so that by crouching down he could make his mirror-image 'gone.' (Freud, 1953: xviii, p. 15)

Not only does a mirror image play a prominent role in this version of the game, but the child manifests in relation to that image precisely the combination of love and hate described by Lacan. The whole of the Lacanian theory of the imaginary register, complete with the mirror stage and the object (a), is thus contained within the simple story about his grandson which Freud tells twice. So, as we shall see, is Lacan's theory of signification.

Like Freud, Lacan reads the *'fort' 'da'* episode as an allegory about the linguistic mastery of the drives. However, whereas Freud connects that mastery with the binding activity which helps to bring the *preconscious* into existence, Lacan associates it with a signifying transaction by means of which the *unconscious* is established. This signifying transaction involves the terms '*fort*' and '*da*', and the play of differences between them which has the effect of eliminating any outside reference.

[. . .]

Within the Lacanian account of subjectivity one other momentous event is linked to these others – to the inauguration of meaning, the loss of the real, the formation of the unconscious, and the entry into the symbolic – and that event is the birth of desire. Desire commences as soon as the drives are split off from the subject, consigned forever to a state of non-representation and non-fulfillment. In short, it begins with the subject's emergence into meaning. Desire has its origins not only in the alienation of the subject from its being, but in the subject's perception of its distinctness from the objects with which it earlier identified. It is thus the product of the divisions by means of which the subject is constituted, divisions which inspire in the subject a profound sense of lack.

Lacan characterizes desire as 'impossible' – impossible both because it derives its energy from the drives, and because it derives its goals from the symbolic. [. . .] Moreover, desire is directed toward ideal representations which remain forever beyond the subject's reach. The first of these representations, as we have already observed, is the mirror image in which the subject initially 'finds' its identity. The identifications which the subject is encouraged to make immediately upon its entry into the symbolic order, and which exercise a kind of retroactive influence over the mirror stage, are calculated to induce in the subject an even more radical sense of inadequacy and lack. It is as a consequence of these identifications – identifications, that is, with maternal and paternal representations – that the subject discovers itself to be 'castrated'.

The Oedipus complex will not only determine the subject's future relations with itself, but those it entertains with others. Desire will therefore always be impossible, whether it pertains to the self or to an other. Indeed, since others will be loved only if they are believed to be capable of completing the subject, desire must be understood as fundamentally narcissistic.

[. . .] Not only does language provide the agency of self-loss, but cultural representations supply the standard by which that loss is perceived. We look within the mirror of those representations – representations which structure every moment of our existence – not only to discover what we are, but what we can never hope to be and (as a consequence) hopelessly desire. [. . .]

What Lacan here suggests is that desire results from the cultural co-optation of the subject's libidinal resources – that the subject supplies the raw materials, but is barred access to the site of production. In short, Lacan indicates that the subject's desires are manufactured for it. The factory – the site of production – is the symbolic. As we shall see, the family plays as central a role there as signification does. Indeed, within the Lacanian argument, language and the Oedipus complex always work in tandem.

The concept of a symbolic register has its origins in the writings of the French anthropologist Claude Lévi-Strauss, although Lacan has considerably enriched it. In *Elementary Structures of Kinship*, Lévi-Strauss (1969) attempts to account for what he takes to be the universal imposition of the incest taboo through the symbolic network which it articulates. Of crucial importance here is the distinction which he makes between nature and culture. In the former, mating is unregulated, whereas in the latter it is subordinated to certain rules. The essence of the incest taboo is its regulatory status, and that status makes it virtually synonymous with culture. Indeed, the simple imposition of the incest taboo transforms a state of nature into a state of culture [. . .].

Thus for Lévi-Strauss the incest taboo is really an exogamy rule, and it has the effect of establishing a grid of structural relationships, not only among members of the family but members of the group. It sets up a system of marital exchange which provides the basis for all of the other systems of exchange upon which culture depends. Women are the privileged commodity within this rudimentary system of exchange [. . .].

The rules of kinship and marriage dictate the positions and possibilities open to all members of the group. Each individual is thus born into an already defined symbolic system, and inserted into a fully articulated familial diagram. Consanguinity is irrelevant, except insofar as its categories overlap with cultural ones. The positions of 'father', 'mother', 'daughter' and 'son' all exceed the individuals who temporarily occupy them. Those positions also determine a wide range of things, such as appropriate responses to other members of the familial diagram, acceptable mates, the names and attitudes with which the subject identifies, the distribution of power, legal and economic status, etc.

Lévi-Strauss concludes his lengthy analysis of primitive marriage rules with a comparison between the ordering capacities of exogamy and language, and he stresses the far greater precision and stability of the latter. Language, even more than kinship rules, ensures that all of the members of a group inhabit the same psychic territory, and regiments the exchanges which take place between them.

Lacan's theory of the subject pushes the analogy much farther. He suggests a close affinity – indeed, a virtual collaboration – between the structuring agency of the family and that of the signifier. In 'Field and Function of Speech and Language' Lacan attributes to the Oedipus complex the same determinative role as that of language in the constitution of the unconscious, subjectivity and the symbolic order [. . .]. Lacan indicates [in this essay] that the Oedipus complex and language do not merely resemble each other, but that they are 'identical'. He supports this claim by pointing out that the incest taboo can only be articulated through the differentiation of certain cultural members from others by means of linguistic categories like 'father' and 'mother', and he indicates that those differentiations bring the subject within the Oedipal matrix even before the moment of 'crisis'. Lacan further consolidates the relationship between the Oedipus complex and language by defining the paternal signifier – what he calls the 'Name-of-the-Father' as the all-important one both in the history of the subject and the organization of the larger symbolic field. In short, he conceptualizes the Oedipus complex as a linguistic transaction.

Lacan describes the family as a set of symbolic relations which always transcend the actual persons who are defined by means of them. 'Mother' and 'father' signify cultural positions, and hence have no necessary correlation to biological realities. Those positions may be occupied by persons who have no 'natural' claim to them. Moreover, even when actual mothers and fathers strive to fulfill their symbolic roles, they can never be equal to the task. This is because 'mother' and 'father' are binary terms within a closed system of signification; each sustains its value and meaning through its relation to the other, and not through any reference to the real.

That value and that meaning can only be realized within discourse, within a syntagmatic chain which includes 'daughter' and/or 'son'. [. . .] Like 'I' or 'you', these familial signifiers are activated only when subjects identify with them. The discourse of the family – a discourse which is absolutely central to the perpetuation of the present, phallocentric symbolic order – needs subjects.

The discourse of the family produces the subjects it needs by aligning them with the symbolic positions of 'father' and 'mother', an operation which is considerably more complex with the Lacanian argument that it is within the Freudian one. That operation begins when the subject confuses its actual parents with their symbolic representations, and concludes at the unhappy moment of a fully realized lack or inadequacy. Some of the more important intervening stages involve the organization of the subject's desires in relation to the mother, the identification of the subject with the ideal image of the parent of the same sex, and the subordination of the subject to the law of the father. Sexual difference provides the informing principle of this discourse, its major structuring opposition.

Lacan gives us a very different account of sexual difference from that provided by Freud, one in which the privileged term is no longer the penis but the *phallus*. 'Phallus' is a word used by Lacan to designate all of those values which are opposed to lack, and he is at pains to emphasize its discursive rather than its anatomical status. However, it must be noted that this signifier, like the one to which it is opposed, sustains two radically different meanings, neither of which at all points maintains its autonomy from the penis. Since those contradictory meanings have not only been the source of enormous confusion to Lacan's listeners and readers but have fostered a radical misapprehension of female subjectivity, we will attempt to place a maximum distance between them.

On the one hand, the phallus is a signifier for those things which have been partitioned off from the subject during the various stages of its constitution, and which will never be restored to it, all of which could be summarized as 'fullness of being'. [. . .] The phallus is thus a signifier for the organic reality or needs which the subject relinquishes in order to achieve meaning, in order to gain access to the symbolic register. It signifies that thing whose loss inaugurates desire.

On the other hand, the phallus is a signifier for the cultural privileges and positive values which define male subjectivity within patriarchal society, but from which the female subject remains isolated. It is thus closely aligned with two other very privileged terms within the Lacanian grammar, 'symbolic father' and 'Name-of-the-Father'. All three are signifiers of paternal power and potency.

The relation of the phallus to the penis, or the symbolic to the actual father, requires a very precise formulation. The first point which should be made about this relation is that it involves an irreducible disequivalence. The penis can never approximate the phallus, just as the actual father can never conform to the epic proportions of the symbolic father. As Lacan observes in 'Function and Field of Speech and Language', 'Even when . . . it is represented by a single person, the paternal function concentrates in itself both imaginary and real relations, always more or less inadequate to the symbolic relation that essentially constitutes it' (Lacan, 1977a: 67).

The inevitable failure of the actual father to correspond to the symbolic father, or the penis to embody the phallus, in no way jeopardizes the existing cultural order. The ideal paternal representation to which those two signifiers refer remains determinedly abstract and diffuse, finding expression less through individual human agents than through the institutional supports with which it is finally synonymous. Those supports include not only the patriarchal family, but the legal, medical, religious, technological, and educational systems, and the dominant political and economic organizations. [. . .]

In spite of these institutional supports, however, we will see that the desire of the son proves indispensable to the maintenance of the current symbolic order. What this means is that the actual father must be identified with the symbolic father, and that the son must believe him to be in possession of the phallus. The mother plays a critical part in this project, since it is her 'lack' which defines the father as potent, and her desire which awakens in the son the impossible wish to supply her with the missing phallus.

[. . .] Despite Lacan's repeated assertions that the penis is not the phallus, it is clear that there is a very intimate and important relation between the two. Lacan suggests that the male subject 'pays' for his symbolic privileges with a currency not available to the female subject – that he 'mortgages' the penis for the phallus. In other words, during his entry into the symbolic order he gains access to those privileges which constitute the phallus, but forfeits direct access to his own sexuality, a forfeiture of which the penis is representative. The problems with the formulation are manifold, and they are further compounded by the assumptions it makes about female subjectivity.

[. . .] [T]he contradictory meanings of 'lack' and 'phallus' always become particularly evident when Lacan speaks about the female subject. His language doubles back upon itself in the form of paradoxes and repetitive tropes, no sooner acknowledging woman's cultural deprivation than nullifying the importance of that observation with assertions about the *jouissance* (ecstatic pleasure) she supposedly enjoys elsewhere.

[. . .] However, we are asked not only to understand the phallus as the signifier *par excellence*, but to conceive of it as having been motivated by the real. It is after all a very specific pound of flesh which the male subject exchanges for his symbolic legacy, one which the female body conspicuously lacks. The inevitable conclusion to which Lacan's argument pushes us is that the phallus somehow mirrors or resembles the penis. The fundamental symmetry between the penis and the phallus within the Lacanian scheme is nowhere more startling evidently than in his seminars on *Hamlet*, where he remarks that 'Claudius's real phallus is always somewhere in the picture' (Lacan, 1977b: 28).

The phallus thus comes to refer not only to the privileges of the symbolic and the fullness of being which can never coexist with those privileges, but to the penis whose sacrifice activates them. The first and third of these meanings – privileges of the symbolic and 'mortgaged' penis – are brought together to define male subjectivity in terms which rigorously exclude woman both at the anatomical and cultural levels, an exclusion which is further overdetermined at the theoretical level by her association with the second of them – fullness of being.

We are now in a position to decode the paradoxes and repetitive tropes cited earlier, and having done so to leave them behind. What woman lacks within the Lacanian scheme is the phallus-as-lost-penis, the 'amputated' or 'castrated' appendage which assures the male subject access to the phallus-as-symbolic-legacy. She thus continues to 'be' the phallus as fullness-of-being long after the male subject has been alienated from the real. This phenomenal plenitude precludes her ever having the phallus, i.e. ever acquiring symbolic power and potency, but it provides her with a *jouissance* denied to man.

In fact, however, both sides of this subjective coin have been stamped within the symbolic treasury; woman as plenitude and woman as lack are merely two alternative cultural projections by means of which man can always be assured of having the phallus – in the first instance through appropriation, and in the second through an oppositional definition. These two equations are also signifying strategies for justifying the exclusion of the female subject from symbolic authority and privilege.

The phallus, like any other signifier, derives its meaning and value entirely from its relation to the other terms in the closed systems and concrete discursive events of which it is a part. It has no more foundation in reality than does any other semantic unit. There is thus a radical impossibility inherent in Lacan's use of the word 'phallus'. It cannot apply simultaneously to the privileges of the symbolic and to a phenomenological plenitude, any more than it can denote both a real pound of flesh and the signifier which usurps it, or anatomical difference and the discourse of sexual difference. All of these dual applications imply a continuity between those very realms which Lacan is otherwise at such pains to keep distinct, thus collapsing the symbolic into the real.

If we are to benefit from Lacan's discovery that the phallus is not the penis but a signifier we must remember the conditions under which it can function as such. Like any other signifier it can be activated only within discourse, and like any other signifier it is defined by those terms with which it is paradigmatically connected, whether through similarity or opposition. The discourse of the family serves constantly to activate the paternal signifier, and one of the most important ways in which it does so is through the evocation of its binary complement, i.e. 'lack'. In short the paternal signifier finds its support in what might be called the 'maternal' signifier. It is only through the mother's desire that the cultural primacy of the phallus can be established and maintained, and that the discourse of the patriarchal family can be perpetuated. Finally, and at the risk of a tautology which is endemic to the symbolic order, it must be stated that the mother will desire the phallus only if her own relation to it is negative, i.e. if she has been defined as lacking.

[. . .] It is preposterous to assume either that woman remains outside of signification, or that her sexuality is any less culturally organized or repressed than that of her male counterpart. If the entry into language is understood as effecting an automatic breach with the real – and the Lacanian argument is very persuasive on this point – then the female subject's linguistic inauguration must be seen as locating her, too, on the side of meaning rather than being. She makes the same 'sacrifice' as does the male subject, a sacrifice which cannot be localized in the way suggested by Lacan. Secondly, while it is unquestionably true that her sexuality is negatively rather than positively defined, it does not for that reason escape structuration. On the contrary, female sexuality would seem to be even more exhaustively and intensively 'spoken' than is male sexuality, to be a site where numerous discourses converge. 'Lack' is inscribed not only at the orifices, but across the entire surface of the female body, and it is precisely at the level of that (constructed) surface that woman is obliged to live a great deal of her cultural existence. [. . .]

References

Freud, Sigmund (1953) *The Standard Edition of the Complete Psychological Works*, vols I–XXIII, trans. James Strachey. London: Hogarth Press.

Lacan, Jacques (1977a) *Ecrits: a selection*, trans. Alan Sheridan. New York: Norton.

Lacan, Jacques (1977b) 'Desire and the Interpretation of Desire in *Hamlet*', trans. James Hulbert, *Yale French Studies*, 55/56.

Lacan, Jacques (1978) *The Four Fundamental Concepts of Psycho-Analysis*, trans. Alan Sheridan, ed. Jacques-Alain Miller. New York: Norton.

Levi-Strauss, Claude (1969) *The Elementary Structures of Kinship*, trans. James Harle Bell, John Richard von Sturmer, Rodney Needham. Boston: Beacon Press.

Metz, Christian (1975) 'The imaginary signifier', trans. Ben Brewster, *Screen*, 16(2): 14–76.

Plato (1961) *The Symposium*, trans. Michael Joyce, in E. Hamilton and H. Cairns (eds), *Collected Dialogues of Plato*. New York: Pantheon.

de Saussure, Ferdinand (1966) *Course in General Linguistics*, trans. Wade Baskin. New York: McGraw-Hill.

Fantasia   **Elizabeth Cowie**

[. . .]

Fantasy in psychoanalysis

(1) Fantasy[1] is the fundamental object of psychoanalysis, it is the central material for the 'talking cure' and for the unconscious: 'the psychoanalyst must endeavour in the course of the treatment to unearth the phantasies which lie behind such products of the unconscious as dreams, symptoms, acting out, repetitive behaviour etc.' (*Language of Psychoanalysis*, 1973, p. 317). Fantasy is an imagined scene in which the subject is a protagonist, and which always represents the fulfilment of a wish albeit that its representation is distorted to a greater or lesser extent by defensive processes. Fantasy has a number of modes: conscious fantasies or day-dreams, unconscious fantasies such as those uncovered by analysis as the structures underlying a manifest content, and primal fantasies. These are not mutually exclusive modes; on the contrary, a day-dream will at the same time involve an unconscious wish underlying its manifest content and the structure of that unconscious wish will be related to the primal fantasies. For this reason Freud saw the model of fantasy as being, Laplanche and Pontalis (1968: 13) suggest, 'the reverie, that form of novelette, both stereotyped and infinitely variable, which the subject composes and relates to himself in a waking state'. The difference between these modes does not involve a difference in the objects of fantasy, nor primarily a distinction between conscious or unconscious, but a difference in their relation to repression, and the workings of censorship.

(2) The word 'fantasy' is defined in the dictionary (*Chambers Twentieth Century English*) as meaning 'an imagined scene', and further listings are

This chapter is taken from *Representing the Woman* (Macmillan, 1997), pp. 127–141.

'fabulous; fancy (now a separate meaning); imagination, mental image; love, whim; caprice; fantasia; pre-occupation with thoughts associated with unattainable desires'. The word derives through Latin from the Greek term meaning to 'make visible'. However, rather than a notion of revelation, making visible what we would not otherwise be able to see – as with a microscope allowing us to see bacteria etc. invisible to the 'naked' eye – fantasy as a term has come to mean the making visible, present, of what isn't there, of what can never *directly* be seen.

In German *phantasie* is the term used to denote the imagination, but not so much in the sense of the faculty of imaginings as in terms of the imaginary world and its contents, the imaginings of fantasies into which the poet – or the neurotic – so willingly withdraws. As Laplanche and Pontalis (1968) note, it is difficult to therefore avoid defining the word in terms of what it is not, the world of reality. The opposition of fantasy and reality, however, cannot be reduced to the conventional opposition between the terms 'fiction' and 'real life'. Freud discovered the importance of fantasy, in particular its importance in the neuroses, when he abandoned his theory of sexual seduction by a parent or other adult as a real event, producing a real trauma with all its consequences in adult life. Notorious as this has become for feminists, the importance of Freud's assertion is nevertheless extremely relevant for feminism. For what Freud came to understand, with regard to the fantasy of rape or seduction by the father so common amongst his women patients, was not that the woman was making something up, pretending, or trying to fake, dupe, us/Freud, but that since the event had not happened, then sexuality in the women could not be thought of as simply the 'effect' of outside events, or the seduction or rape, whether pleasurable or traumatic. Rather sexuality was already there, in play. The fantasy and its attendant traumas were not the *result* of a seduction but of the *wish* for a seduction, implying a sexuality already there motivating the wish. Freud is then concerned to elaborate on *how* it is already there. The consequences of this are important: for feminism, it shows again that women's sexuality is not a simple consequence (again, whether traumatic or pleasurable) of male sexuality, of the seduction as a real event. Furthermore the wish is not simply passive – its object is the father. It also implies its inverse, the wish to seduce or rape the father. The father as sexual object is of course the consequence of the Oedipal scenario, and therefore of a wish to seduce/be seduced by the mother. What Freud shows is that it is irrelevant to consider whether the event was fantasied or real, or whether the woman wishes it to be real, for the fantasy refers not to physical reality but to psychical reality. This psychical reality is not simply the internal world, a psychological domain of the mental: Laplanche and Pontalis (1968: 3) argue that for Freud fantasy 'denotes a nucleus within that domain which is heterogeneous and resistant and which is alone in being truly "real" as compared with the majority of psychical phenomena' and quote Freud 'If we look at unconscious wishes reduced to their most fundamental and truest shape, we shall have to conclude no doubt that psychical reality is a particular form of existence not to be confused with material reality' (Freud, 1900: 620).

This psychical reality of which fantasy is the nucleus has an effect on and for the subject just as much as the material, physical world may have. In analysing fantasy, it is not a criterion that there be any factual basis for the fantasy 'in reality' or that there be a wish for it to 'really happen', rather the criterion is the level of 'reality' the fantasy has for and in the psychical system of the subject. What is refused here, then, is any privileging of material reality as necessarily more important, more serious. A patient recounts that he is an adopted child and relates fantasies in which, while searching for this true mother, he discovers that she is a society woman turned prostitute. Here is the banal theme of the 'family romance', which, of course, might equally well have been composed by a child who had not been adopted.

(3) Freud never sought to divide fantasy into conscious and unconscious, for the nature and work of fantasy is always the same. From the work of Laplanche and Pontalis it is possible, however, to see different modes of fantasy, but these different modes do not correspond to the division conscious/unconscious. A different distinction must be made. They argue, following Freud, for a distinction between original fantasies and other, secondary fantasies, whether conscious or unconscious: 'the unity of the fantasy as a whole depends however on its mixed nature, in which both the structural, original and the imaginary or secondary are found. From this we can see why Freud always held the model fantasy to be the reverie' (Laplanche and Pontalis, 1968: 13). While two modes exist they are generally found in combination in any fantasy, conscious or unconscious. Fantasy again emphasised as a scene. The importance of this idea cannot be overestimated, for it enables the consideration of film as fantasy in the most fundamental sense of this term in psychoanalysis. The same content, the same activation can be revealed in imaginary formations of day-dreams and psychopathological structures as diverse as those described by Freud, such as hysteria, delusional paranoia etc., and public forms of fantasy such as film and the novel. This argument is seen of course in Freud's papers such as 'Creative Writers and Day-dreaming' (1908a), 'Family Romances' (1908b), etc. And these forms are not just conscious re-workings, i.e. censored representations of unconscious, repressed fantasies. For Freud realised that it is conscious fantasy itself which may be repressed and thus become pathogenic. Freud argues for example that fantasy is present at both extremes of the process of dreaming. Laplanche and Pontalis (1968: 12) note that fantasy is:

> On the one hand linked with the ultimate unconscious desire, the 'capitalist' of the dream, and as such it is at the basis of that 'zig-zag' path which is supposed to follow excitation through a succession of psychological systems, leading from the unconscious scenes of fantasies to the preconscious where it collects 'the day's residues'.

But fantasy is also present at the other extreme, in the secondary elaboration of the dream, the *a posteriori* re-working of the dream once we are awake, which seeks to place a minimum of order and coherence onto the raw material handed over by the unconscious mechanisms of displacement and condensation. Imposing a scenario, a façade of coherence and continuity – in a word, a narrative – it will thus also draw on those ready-made scenarios, the subject's day-dreams. But this re-working is not simply a masking, a mistaken distorting and arbitrary revision, for it will draw on the same impetuses for fantasy as the dreams of sleep. Of course, the same fantasy may not be involved in the initial situation of the dream and in its revision by secondary elaboration, but as Laplanche and Pontalis (1968: 13) suggest, the fantasies do seem 'if not to link up, at least to communicate from within and, as it were, to be symbolic of each other'.

The distinction, in fact, is not between conscious and unconscious, between the censored and uncensored, but rather between primal or originally unconscious fantasies, and secondary fantasies which may be unconscious or conscious. Primal fantasy does not imply a simple causality, primacy or origin, of *original content*. Rather it is to be understood as originary in the instituting of a structure of fantasy, a scene of fantasied origins – the origin of the child in its parents' love-making; the origin of sexual difference, and its corollary castration; in the wish to take the father's place and have the mother, or usurp the mother's place and have the father – thus a parental seduction. The primal fantasies are not so much an inherited pre-history, as a pre-structure, which is actualised and transmitted by the parents' fantasies.

> In their content, in their theme [primal scene, castration, seduction . . .] the original fantasies also indicate this postulate of retroactivity: they relate to the origins. Like myths, they claim to provide a representation of, and a solution to, the major enigmas which confront the child. Whatever appears to the subject as something needing an explanation or theory, is dramatised as a moment of emergence, the beginning of a history . . . There is a convergence of theme, of structure, and no doubt also of function: through the indications furnished by the perceptual field, through the scenarios constructed, the varied quest for origins, we are offered in the field of fantasy, the origin of the subject himself. (Laplanche and Pontalis, 1968: 11)

The original fantasy explains the beginnings of the child but thus always pre-exists the child, for to pose a beginning is also to pose a before the beginning; and there is always an already-there for every child, its parents, grandparents, a history. The original fantasy then as structuring rather than a structure, for it is activated by contingent elements. Laplanche and Pontalis make this clear in their discussion of Freud's first reference to primal fantasies in 'A Case of Paranoia Running Counter to the Psychoanalytic Theory of the Disease'. In it Freud describes the case of a woman patient who declared that she had been watched and photographed while lying with her lover. She claimed to have heard a 'noise', the click of a camera. Behind this delirium Freud saw the primal scene: the sound is the noise of the parents making love, thus awakening the child: it is also the wound the child is afraid of making lest it betray her listening. It is difficult to assess the role of this noise in the fantasy. In one sense, says Freud, it is only a provocation, an accidental cause, whose role is solely to activate 'the typical phantasy of overhearing' which is a component of the parental complex, but he then corrects himself by saying 'It is doubtful whether we can rightly call the noise "accidental" . . . Such phantasies are on the contrary an indispensable part of the phantasy of listening.' In fact the sound alleged by the patient was, according to Freud, a projection, the projection of a beat in her clitoris, in the form of a noise. Laplanche and Pontalis (1968: 10) suggest 'It reproduces in actuality the indication of the primal scene, the element which is the starting point for all ulterior elaboration of the phantasy. In other words, *the origin of the fantasy is integrated in the very structure of the original fantasy.*' The primal fantasy then as the instituting of this structuring, as a scene in which the child is also present interchangeably with the other participants as onlooker, as one or other parent, or even, as the person who will discover the child looking on. 'The primal scene, this "foreign" body which is to be internally excluded, is usually brought to the subject, not by the perception of a scene, but by parental desire and its supporting fantasy' (Laplanche and Pontalis, 1968: 8).

(4) What is shown here is the originary structuring of fantasy, but it presupposes a structuring of *wishing* already present in the subject, raising the question of the origin of fantasising as such. This, Laplanche and Pontalis argue, cannot be isolated from the origin of the drive itself. Reinterpreting Freud's concept of *the experience of satisfaction*, they locate this origin in auto-eroticism, which they define not as a stage of evolution but as the moment of a repeated disjunction of sexual desire and non-sexual functions. That is, 'the experience of satisfaction' is separated from the object which satisfies, and the latter is represented as a sign. For the baby, the 'breast' becomes the object of desire – as giving the experience of satisfaction – but it is so not as itself but as signifier of the *lost* object which is the *satisfaction* derived from suckling the breast, but which comes to be desired in *its absence*. This is the emergence of auto-eroticism, for the sexual drive is separated from the non-sexual functions, such as feeding, which are its support and which indicate its aim and object. The feeding still nourishes the child, but the experience of satisfaction in feeding has been split off through the function of representation, and moves into the field of fantasy and by the very fact starts existing as sexuality. It is auto-erotic because the external object has been abandoned, the drive is 'objectless' and satisfaction is derived from 'organ-pleasure' – the motions of sucking, rather than the instinctual act of sucking and obtaining nourishment.

The importance of relating fantasy to auto-eroticism is to show that desire is not purely an upsurging of the drives but comes to exist as sexual through its articulation in fantasy.

(5) As noted earlier, fantasies are wishful; however they are not about a wish to have some determinate object, making it present for the subject. Lacan (1973: 185) writes that:

The phantasy is the support of desire, it is not the object that is the support of desire. The subject sustains himself as desiring in relation to an ever-more complex signifying ensemble. This is apparent enough in the form of the scenario it assumes, in which the subject, more or less recognisable, is somewhere, split, divided, generally double, in his relation to the object, which usually does not show its true face either.

Similarly, Safouan (1984: 65) notes 'instead of being co-opted to an object, desire is first co-opted to a phantasy.'

Fantasy involves, is characterised by, not the achievement of desired objects, but the arranging of, a setting our of, desire: a veritable *mise-en-scène* of desire. For of course, Lacan says, desire is unsatisfiable, much as Freud commented that there is something in the nature of sexuality which is resistant to satisfaction. The fantasy depends not on particular objects, but on their setting out; and the pleasure of fantasy lies in the setting out, not in the having of the objects. Within the day-dream and more especially in fictional stories, the demands of narrative may obscure this, for the typical ending will be a resolution of the problems, the wars, feuds, etc., the achievement of union in marriage of the hero and heroine, etc. Yet inevitably the story will fall prey to diverse diversions, delays, obstacles and other means to postponing the ending. For though we all want the couple to be united, and the obstacles heroically overcome, we don't want the story to end. And marriage is one of the most definitive endings. The pleasure is in how to bring about the consummation, is in the happening and continuing to happen; in how it will come about, and *not* in the moment of *having happened*, when it will fall back into loss, the past. This can extend into producing endings which remain murky, ill-defined, uncertain even. It is thus not modesty which veils the endings of romantic fiction but wise caution. Sternberg's film *Morocco* is perhaps an extreme example in cinema of the refusal to narrate an ending, to consummate the narrative, for it concludes with another repetition of the setting out of a lack to be fulfilled, which has already been played twice over and more, i.e. Dietrich leaving an anguished Adolphe Menjou for an unknowing Gary Cooper. Fantasy as a *mise-en-scène* of desire is more a setting out of lack, of what is absent, than a presentation of a having, a being present. Desire itself coming into existence in the representation of lack, in the production of a fantasy of its becoming present.

It can be seen, then, that fantasy is not the object of desire, but its setting.

In phantasy the subject does not pursue the object or its sign: he appears caught up himself in the sequence of images. He forms no representation of the desired object, but is himself represented as participating in the scene although, in the earliest forms of fantasy, he cannot be assigned any fixed place in it . . . As a result, the subject, although always present in the fantasy, may be so in a de-subjectivised form, that is to say, in the very syntax of the sequence in question. (Laplanche and Pontalis, 1968: 17)

The subject is present or presented through the very form of organisation, composition, of the scene. It is perhaps only the most re-worked, conscious, day-dream which is able to impose the stabilisation of the ego, so that the subject's position is clear and invariable as the 'I' of the story, which the subject as it were 'lives out'. Nevertheless it will be argued later with regard to the fiction film that it is not only in the original fantasies that this de-subjectivisation takes place. Both the day-dream 'thoughtlessly' composed, and the more complex fictional narrative join with the 'original' fantasies in visualising the subject in the scene, and in presenting a varying of subject position so that the subject takes up more than one position and thus is not fixed.

In Freud's analysis of the fantasy in 'A Child is Being Beaten: a Contribution to the Study of the Origin of Sexual Perversions' he shows three phases in this fantasy, each involving a different subject-position. In the first phase, the fantasy is 'my father is beating a child, whom I hate'; thus, 'my father loves me since he is beating the other child' but also 'I am making my father beat the other child to show he loves me' in which the subject erases the other, rival child, from the father's affections. It is thus egoistic, identifying both father/self-love and father/self as beater of the other child. For this to become transposed into 'A child is being beaten' with its third-person syntax, Freud proposed a second phase 'I am being beaten by my father'; while the first phase may be remembered through analysis, this second phase is wholly unconscious and can only be inferred from analysis. However it produces the move from sadism to masochism. (Though the first phase is not yet properly sadistic, or erotic, inasmuch as it is pre-genital.) The implicit incestuous desire of the first phase is subject to repression in the second phase, by a reversal: 'No, my father does not love me (you), for he is beating me (you).' The beating is not only the punishment for the incestuous wish but is also the 'regressive substitute for that relation, and from this latter source it derives the libidinal excitation which is from this time forward attached to it'. Guiltiness and punishment are thus attached to the sexual desire: to be punished is to have had the forbidden sexual relation, for why else would you be punished? In the third phase, the consciously remembered fantasy 'A child is being beaten' once more appears sadistic

> but it is only in form; the satisfaction which is derived from it is masochistic. Its significance lies in the fact that it has taken over the libidinal cathexis of the repressed portion and at the same time the sense of guilt which is attached to the content of that portion. All the many unspecified children who are being beaten by the teacher are, after all, nothing more than substitutes for the child itself. (Freud, 1919: 191)

The fantasy escapes repression by a further distortion, the disguise of the third-person syntax. Out there, there are children being beaten (like I should be, for my forbidden wishes). Apparently sadistic, inasmuch as it represses the parenthesis. The stake, the effectiveness, of this third phase of the fantasy is the interchangeability of the subject and the other children being beaten.

Laplanche and Pontalis give the seduction fantasy as a similar example, which they summarise as 'A father seduces a daughter', emphasising the 'peculiar character of the structure, in that it is a scenario with multiple entries, in which nothing shows whether the subject will be immediately located as *daughter*; it can as well be fixed as *father*, or even in the term *seduces*' (1968: 14).

(6) It is however precisely to the extent that desire is articulated in fantasy that the latter is also thereby the locus of defensive operations – it facilitates and can become the site of the most primitive defensive processes, such as turning around upon the subject's own self, reversal into its opposite, projection and negation. Fantasies provide satisfaction, then, not only by presenting a wish but also be presenting the failure of a wish if the latter has undergone repression. This has been seen in the example of 'A child is being beaten'. Defences are inseparably bound up with the work of fantasy, namely, the *mise-en-scène* of desire, a *mise-en-scène* in which what is prohibited is always present in the actual formation of the wish. (Walsh's film *Pursued* can be cited as a filmic example of this.) It is also interesting to consider here Freud's example in his essay on hysterical fantasies (1908); he cites as an involuntary irruption of fantasy, a day-dream which was produced by one of his women patients. She recounts that on one occasion she had suddenly found herself in tears in the street and that, rapidly considering what it was she was actually crying about, she had got hold of a fantasy to the following effect: in her imagination she had formed a tender attachment to a pianist who was well known in the town (though she was not personally acquainted with him); she had had a child by him (she was in fact childless); and he had then deserted her and her child and left them in poverty. It was at this point in her 'romance'. Freud says, that she burst into tears.

Freud goes not give any analysis of the fantasy himself, but I would like to suggest it as an example of a fantasy subject to defensive processes. Consider the moment of the tears; narratively appropriate, tears of self-pity at her imagined loss. But why has she produced a story to make herself cry, and may not the tears be a response not to the pathos of the story but to its satisfactions? The crying thus acting as a defence, brings the fantasy to an end in the same way Freud speaks of waking oneself up from a dream. This becomes even more plausible if the possibility of multiple subject positions in the story is considered. It commences with a pleasant and typical erotic wish in relation to the pianist, together with its happy consummation. But the fruit of the affair, a child, places the fantasy into an Oedipal context, for the child is the one wished for with the father. A forbidden desire has found expression in the fantasy, that it is forbidden is marked by the punishment immediately meted out – not only that the man deserts her and the child, but more importantly they are left in poverty. More importantly, for it marks that it was not enough punishment for the man to desert her, another hardship must be given to her. But even this is not enough, tears intervene to halt the fantasy. This might suggest that the man's desertion is *not* the punishment, but part of the wish, i.e. for the eviction of the father, so that the child has the mother to herself, and it is *this* wish which provokes the final censorship of tears. (The outline of the day-dream bears an astonishing resemblance to Max Ophuls' *Letter from an Unknown Woman*.) It is in the same essay that Freud presents a series of formulas on the nature of hysterical symptoms, in which he suggests that 'Hysterical symptoms are the realisation of an unconscious phantasy which serves the fulfilment of a wish', and 'Hysterical symptoms are the expression on the one hand of a masculine unconscious sexual phantasy, and on the other hand of a feminine one.' He restates here the innate bisexual disposition of the human made so visible in the analysis of psychoneurotics. But what is thereby emphasised is that this is not a mixing of the masculine and feminine but the juxtaposition, side by side, of both the feminine and masculine as distinct sexual positions of desire.

Fantasy in the realm of the public

Fantasy has, of course, never been simply a private affair. The public circulation of fantasies has many forms, from the publishing of psychoanalytic case studies, to feminist articles such as those in the issue of *Heresies* (1981), or speaking-out in consciousness-raising groups: and anthologies such as *My Secret Garden* (Friday, 1974) which, besides their pseudoscientific claims of extending human knowledge, are also offering forms of circulation of fantasy just as much as do the letters in *Forum, Men Only, Penthouse* etc. But by far the most common form of public circulation of fantasy is what Freud described as 'creative writing' of which film can also claim to be a part. Unlike confessional forms, such as letters, diaries etc., in the novel or the film the subject of the fantasy and the 'author' are differentiated. Fantasy, as a *mise-en-scène* of desire will nevertheless be at work in film, but how, and with what implications? Laplanche and Pontalis have shown how all fantasy involves original fantasies which are limited in thematic, re-worked through the material of the everyday, that-day, experiences:

> The day-dream is a shadow play, utilising its kaleidoscopic material drawn from all quarters of human experience, but also involving the original fantasy, whose *dramatis personae*, the court cards, receive their notation from a family legend which is mutilated, disordered and misunderstood. (Laplanche and Pontalis, 1968: 13)

And Barthes (1973: 47) writes:

> If there is no longer a father, why tell stories? Doesn't every narrative lead back to Oedipus? Isn't storytelling always a way of searching for one's origins, speaking one's conflicts with the law, entering into a dialectic of tenderness and hatred.

This appears reductive, for there cannot now be anything more to say of fantasy in general, whether in film or the novel, which is not merely banal. And this is supported by the realisation of the enormous repetition of cinema: the same stories replayed before the cameras, always the same but differently, which has been the key to cinema's success as a mass form of entertainment. On the other hand there is the rich diversity of cinema, the world on the big screen, the range of genres, narrative devices, cinematographic techniques.

Between the 'limited thematics' of original fantasy and the diverse, often complex webs of modern forms of representation, how to pose the question of fantasy in film? Before considering in detail particular films, I'd like to note certain questions and points, and summarise in relation to these, the important starting point and contribution of Freud's essay 'On Creative Writing and Daydreaming' (1908a).

Freud asks what the role of conscious fantasies, of day-dreams is, and argues that they function for adults as play had done in childhood, with all the same seriousness:

> In spite of all the emotion with which he cathects his world of play, the child distinguishes it quite well from reality; and he likes to link his imagined objects and situations to the tangible and visible things of the real world. This linking is all that differentiates the child's 'play' from 'phantasying'. The creative writer does the same as the child at play. He creates a world of phantasy which he takes very seriously – that is, which he invests with large amounts of emotion – while separating it sharply from reality. (Freud, 1908a: 144)

And behind the play, behind fantasy, is a wish: for the child, to be grown-up, which is acted out in scenarios; for the adult, ambitious and erotic wishes are fantasied (in scenarios). These can be infinitely various and varied, shifting with the new impressions received everyday, changing to fit the new situations and contexts of the subject – the kaleidoscopic material Laplanche and Pontalis refer to. The fantasy, Freud suggests, thus hovers between three times: the present provides a context, the material elements of the fantasy; the past provides the wish, deriving from the earliest experiences; the dreamer then imagines a new situation, in the future, which represents a fulfilment of the wish. Freud's example is of an orphan boy, going for a job interview, imagining not only obtaining the job but being so successful that he is taken into the employer's family, marries the owner's daughter, and succeeds him in running the business. Ambitious and erotic wishes are both fulfilled. But, whether dreams of sleep or consciousness, censorship and secondary revision are central; in various ways, more or less, the fantasies are tailored to, address 'reality' in the sense of Lacan's symbolic, a domain of prohibition, and in the sense of 'reality-testing', actualised social relations. Fantasy then as a privileged terrain on which social reality and the unconscious are engaged in a figuring which intertwines them both.

Day-dreams, fantasies, are normally very private affairs (which is why their rare forms of public circulation are so fascinating) and a certain amount of 'shame' and embarrassment is involved whenever the fantasies are found out, or when we fear being found out in them. A shame not only for being childish (and hence for a denial of reality) as Freud suggests, but also surely because of the cathexis deriving from the archaic, original wishes involved. Despite censoring, the existence of the fantasy as such bears witness to the pressure of a desire itself absent (i.e. not represented as such). Yet, as Freud suggests, a publicly sanctioned form of fantasy does exist – creative writing in which all this is in play. For his argument Freud addresses initially the most despised form of creative writing, popular fiction, where he notes the recurrent feature of an invincible hero 'for whom the writer tries by every means to win our sympathies', and that 'through the revealing characteristic of invulnerability we can immediately recognise His Majesty the Ego, the hero alike of every daydream and of every story' (Freud, 1908a: 150). And the hero always gets the girl, against terrible odds. This remains true even for 'serious' literature, where the hero may die nobly on the scaffold, or indeed be no hero at all. Nevertheless the anti-hero too is a centred-ego, the privileged character and the site of a celebration, however negative. Freud similarly suggests that the psychological novel, where there is no centred hero, 'owes its special nature to the inclination of the modern writer to split up his ego, by self-observation, into many part-egos, and, in consequence, to personify the conflicting currents of his own mental life in several heroes' (1908a: 150). Creative writing is thus seen to be the presenting in a public form of the author's own fantasies – and the same time structure as that of the day-dream can be seen to operate.

Freud's theses, however, while opening up the study of fantasy in public forms of representation, seem to lead back to the author as origin of the fantasy, and as site for any answer to questions about the organisation of fantasy in the text. If fantasies *are* 'personal' in this way, how can they work for a general public, for a mass audience? Firstly, fantasy-scenarios involve original wishes which are universal. Secondly, they are contingent, so that just as we draw on events of the day to produce our own, so we can adopt and adapt the ready-made scenarios of fiction, as if their contingent material has been our own. Nevertheless a paradox exists: the disavowal of reality – 'I know this isn't real, is only an illusion but . . .', with an attendant pleasure in the *realism* of the illusionism, to the extent that it is the most typical aesthetic criteria for good film, i.e. that it be realistic. Notwithstanding the fact that realism, the realistic, are the effects of, are produced by, filmic and literary conventions, it is still held to be axiomatic by critics and audiences alike that some films are realistic – and good – while others are mere fantasy, and only good because particularly qualities redeem them (such as the fine, i.e. realistic, acting in *Now Voyager*, or the 'solidly plausible detail' in *The Reckless Moment*, (see figure 23.1). The vehement demand that we should be able to tell the difference between reality and fantasy even in fiction, bears witness perhaps to the fear involved in apprehending the reality of fantasy. But inasmuch as this wish

Figure 23.1

*The Reckless Moment
(Lucia Harper is
played by Joan
Bennett; Donnelly by
James Mason)*

is located in relation to representation it is condemned to a hopeless circularity: reality is realistic in representation insofar as it conforms to the accepted conventions of representing. 'Realism' in representation can be seen both as a *defence* against fantasy and as a 'hook', involving the spectator in the fantasy structure 'unawares', and thus as fore-pleasure. This making real of what isn't real reaches an extraordinary culmination in cinema, the dream factory *par excellence*. For not only does cinema offer the specularisation of fantasy, but it offers this as a *real* experience, at the level of auditory and visual perceptions.

The fiction will fail as ready-made fantasy then if it is felt to be too 'far-fetched'; the criteria for this are not fixed but depend on the conventions of realism, of verisimilitude, pertaining. That is, the norms of motivation for 'believable' behaviour, the requirements for effects to be shown to have causes and hence the demand for certain forms of narrative conventions. This of course is slightly different from the demand for realism referred to above, which involves a demand for the representation to have a relation to reality as truth, to actuality, as *distinct* from fantasy. But the difference *is* only slight between the conventions of realism in a Vietnam documentary and in *Apocalypse Now*. Thus it is not the content of the contingent as such which makes it 'work' for an audience (though it may be so for any particular spectator), but the presentation of that material, its form.

Conventions are also the means by which the author re-works his or her fantasy for public consumption. For the author (whether the single author of the literary text, or the collective 'authors' of a film) produces a further secondary revision of his or her fantasies which lead us to accept what would otherwise appear as rampant egoism, by altering, softening and disguising the characters of the fiction. This is carried out by drawing on the conventions of the novelistic.

[. . .]

Conventions are thus the means by which the structuring of desire is represented in public forms, inasmuch as, following the arguments of Laplanche and Pontalis (1968) earlier, fantasy *is the mise-en-scène* of desire. What is necessary for any public forms of fantasy, for their collective consumption, is not universal objects of desire, but a setting of desiring in which we can find our place(s). And these places will devolve, as in the original fantasies, on positions of desire: active or passive, feminine or masculine, mother or son, father or daughter. [. . .]

Note

1   The decision in this chapter (apart from in quotations where the term is given as it occurs in the original) to use the spelling 'fantasy' rather than 'phantasy', has been adopted inasmuch as the former spelling is normally used in discussions of film and literature, and the intention here is to show that fantasy in film can be understood to work in the same way as fantasy in the day-dream and in the unconscious. See Laplanche and Pontalis (1968) who make a cogent argument for rejecting this distinction.

References

Barthes, R. (1973) *The Pleasure of the Text*, trans. R. Miller. New York: Hill and Wang, 1974.

Freud, S. (1900) *The Interpretation of Dreams, The Standard Edition of the Complete Psychological Works*, vol. V, trans. James Strachey. London; Hogarth Press, 1953.

Freud, S. (1905) *Three Essays on the Theory of Sexuality, Standard Edition*, vol. VII.

Freud, (1908a) 'Creative Writers and Day-Dreaming', *Standard Edition*, vol. IX.

Freud, S. (1908b) 'Family Romances', *Standard Edition*, vol. IX.

Freud, S. (1908c) 'Hysterical Phantasies and their Relation to Bisexuality', *Standard Edition*, vol. IX.

Freud, S. (1919) 'A Child is Being Beaten: a Contribution to the Study of the Origin of Sexual Perversions', *Standard Edition*, vol. XVII.

Friday, N. (1974) *My Secret Garden*. New York: Pocket Books.

Heresies (1981), vol. 3, no. 4, issue 12.

Lacan, J. (1973) *The Four Fundamental Concepts of Psychoanalysis*, trans. A. Sheridan. London: Hogarth Press, 1977.

Laplanche, J. and Pontalis, J-B. (1968) Fantasy and the origins of sexuality', *The International Journal of Psycho-Analysis*, 49(1).

Laplanche, J. and Pontalis, J-B. (1973) *The Language of Psychoanalysis*, trans. D. Nicholson-Smith. London: Hogarth Press.

Safouan, M. (1984) 'Men and women: a psychoanalytic point of view', *m/f*, p pp. 61–69.

24

The other question: the stereotype and colonial discourse
Homi K. Bhabha

An important feature of colonial discourse is its dependence on the concept of 'fixity' in the ideological construction of otherness. Fixity, as the sign of cultural/historical/racial difference in the discourse of colonialism, is a paradoxical mode of representation: it connotes rigidity and an unchanging order as well as disorder, degeneracy and daemonic repetition. Likewise the stereotype, which is its major discursive strategy, is a form of knowledge and identification that vacillates between what is always 'in place', already known, and something that must be anxiously repeated – as if the essential duplicity of the Asiatic or the bestial sexual license of the African that needs no proof, can never really, in discourse, be proved. It is this process of *ambivalence*, central to the stereotype, that my essay explores as it constructs a theory of colonial discourse. For it is the force of ambivalence that gives the colonial stereotype its currency: ensures its repeatability in changing historical and discursive conjunctures; informs its strategies of individuation and marginalisation; produces that effect of probabilistic truth and predictability which, for the stereotype, must always be in *excess* of what can be empirically proved or logically construed. [. . .]

[. . .] To recognise the stereotype as an ambivalent mode of knowledge and power demands a theoretical and political response that challenges deterministic or functionalist modes of conceiving of the relationship between discourse and politics, and questions dogmatic and moralistic positions on the meaning of oppression and discrimination. My reading of colonial discourse suggests that the point of intervention should shift from the *identification* of images as positive or negative, to an understanding of the *processes of subjectification* made possible (and plausible) through stereotypical discourse. To judge the stereotyped image on the basis of a prior political normativity is to dismiss it, not to displace it, which is only possible by engaging with its *effectivity*; with the repertoire of positions of

This chapter is taken from *Screen*, vol. 24, no. 4 (1983), pp. 18–36.

power and resistance, domination and dependence that constructs the colonial subject (both coloniser and colonised). [. . .] Only then does it become possible to understand the *productive* ambivalence of the object of colonial discourse – that 'otherness' which is at once an object of desire and derision, an articulation of difference contained within the fantasy of origin and identity. What such a reading reveals are the boundaries of colonial discourse and it enables a transgression of these limits from the space of that otherness.

The construction of the colonial subject in discourse, and the exercise of colonial power through discourse, demands an articulation of forms of difference – racial and sexual. Such an articulation becomes crucial if it is held that the body is always simultaneously inscribed in both the economy of pleasure and desire and the economy of discourse, domination and power. [. . .]

II

[Colonial discourse] is an apparatus that turns on the recognition and disavowal of racial/cultural/historical differences. Its predominant strategic function is the creation of a space for a 'subject peoples' through the production of knowledges in terms of which surveillance is exercised and a complex form of pleasure/unpleasure is incited. It seeks authorisation for its strategies by the production of knowledges of coloniser and colonised which are stereotypical but antithetically evaluated. The objective of colonial discourse is to construe the colonised as a population of degenerate types on the basis of racial origin, in order to justify conquest and to establish systems of administration and instruction. Despite the play of power within colonial discourse and the shifting positionalities of its subjects (e.g. effects of class, gender, ideology, different social formations, varied systems of colonisation etc.), I am referring to a form of governmentality that in marking out a 'subject nation', appropriates, directs and dominates its various spheres of activity. Therefore, despite the 'play' in the colonial system which is crucial to its exercise of power, colonial discourse produces the colonised as a fixed reality which is at once an 'other' and yet entirely knowable and visible. It resembles a form of narrative whereby the productivity and circulation of subjects and signs are bound in a reformed and recognisable totality. It employs a system of representation, a regime of truth, that is structurally similar to Realism. And it is in order to intervene within that system of representation that Edward Said proposes a semiotic of 'Orientalist' power, examining the varied European discourses which constitute 'the Orient' as an unified racial, geographical, political and cultural zone of the world. Said's analysis is revealing of, and relevant to, colonial discourse:

> Philosophically, then, the kind of language, thought, and vision that I have been calling orientalism very generally is a form of *radical realism*; anyone employing orientalism, which is the habit for dealing with questions, objects,

qualities and regions deemed Oriental, will designate, name, point to, fix what he is talking or thinking about with a word or phrase, which then is considered either to have acquired, or more simply to be, reality . . . The tense they employ is the timeless eternal; they convey an impression of repetition and strength . . . For all these functions it is frequently enough to use the simple copula *is* (my emphasis).[1]

For Said, the *copula* seems to be the point at which Western Rationalism preserves the boundaries of sense for itself. Of this, too, Said is aware when he hints continually at a polarity or division at the very centre of Orientalism.[2] It is, on the one hand, a topic of learning, discovery, practice; on the other, it is the site of dreams, images, fantasies, myths, obsessions and requirements. It is a static system of 'synchronic essentialism', a knowledge of 'signifiers of stability' such as the lexicographic and the encyclopaedic. However, this site is continually under threat from diachronic forms of history and narrative, signs of instability. And, finally, this line of thinking is given a shape analogical to the dream-work, when Said refers explicitly to a distinction between 'an unconscious positivity' which he terms *latent* Orientalism, and the stated knowledges and views about the Orient which he calls *manifest* Orientalism.

Where the originality of this pioneering theory loses its inventiveness, and for me its usefulness, is with Said's reluctance to engage with the alterity and ambivalence in the articulation of these two economies which threaten to split the very object of Orientalist discourse as a knowledge and the subject positioned therein. He contains this threat by introducing a binarism within the argument which, in initially setting up an opposition these two discursive scenes, finally allows them to be correlated as a congruent system of representation that is unified through a political-ideological *intention* which, in his words, enables Europe to advance securely and *unmetaphorically* upon the Orient. Said identifies the *content* of Orientalism as the unconscious repository of fantasy, imaginative writings and essential ideas; and the *form* of manifest Orientalism as the historically and discursively determined, diachronic aspect. This division/ correlation structure of manifest and latent Orientalism leads to the effectivity of the concept of discourse being undermined by what could be called the polarities of intentionality.

This produces a problem with Said's use of Foucault's concept of power and discourse. The productivity of Foucault's concept of power/ knowledge lies in its refusal of an epistemology which opposes essence/ appearance, ideology/science. '*Pouvoir/Savoir*' places subjects in a relation of power and recognition that is not part of a symmetrical or dialectical relation – self/other, Master/Slave – which can then be subverted by being inverted. Subjects are always disproportionately placed in opposition or domination through the symbolic decentering of multiple power-relations which play the role of support as well as target or adversary. It becomes difficult, then, to conceive of the *historical* enunciations of colonial discourse without them being either functionally overdetermined or strategically elaborated or displaced by the *unconscious* scene of latent Orientalism.

Equally, it is difficult to conceive of the process of subjectification as a placing *within* Orientalist or colonial discourse for the dominated subject without the dominant being strategically placed within it too. There is always, in Said, the suggestion that colonial power and discourse is possessed entirely by the coloniser, which is a historical and theoretical simplification. The terms in which Said's Orientalism is unified – the intentionality and unidirectionality of colonial power – also unify the subject of colonial enunciation.

This is a result of Said's inadequate attention to representation as a concept that articulates the historical and fantasy (as the scene of desire) in the production of the 'political' effects of discourse. He rightly rejects a notion of orientalism as the misrepresentation of an Oriental essence. However, having introduced the concept of 'discourse' he does not face up to the problems it makes for the instrumentalist notion of power/ knowledge that he seems to require. [. . .]

This brings me to my second point – that the closure and coherence attributed to the unconscious pole of colonial discourses and the unprob- lematised notion of the subject, restricts the effectivity of both power and knowledge. It is not possible to see how power functions productively as incitement and interdiction. Nor would it be possible, without the attribution of ambivalence to relations of power/knowledge, to calculate the traumatic impact of the return of the oppressed – those terrifying stereotypes of savagery, cannibalism, lust and anarchy which are the signal points of identification and alienation, scenes of fear and desire, in colonial texts. It is precisely this function of the stereotype as phobia and fetish that, according to Fanon, threatens the closure of the racial/epidermal schema for the colonial subject and opens the royal road to colonial fantasy.

[. . .]

What is this other scene of colonial discourse played out around the 'medium category'? What is this theory of encapsulation or fixation which moves between the recognition of cultural and racial difference and its disavowal, by affixing the unfamiliar to something established, in a form that is repetitious and vacillates between delight and fear? It is not analogous to the Freudian fable of fetishism (and disavowal) that circulates within the discourse of colonial power, requiring the articulation of modes of differentiation – sexual and racial – as well as different modes of discourse – psychoanalytic and historical?

[. . .]

In this spirit I argue for the reading of the stereotype in terms of fetishism. The myth of historical origination – racial purity, cultural priority – produced in relation to the colonial stereotype functions to 'normalise' the multiple beliefs and split subjects that constitute colonial discourse as a consequence of its process of disavowal. The scene of fetishism functions similarly as, at once, a reactivation of the material of original fantasy – the anxiety of castration and sexual difference – as well as a normalisation of that difference and disturbance in terms of the fetish object as the substitute for the mother's penis. Within the apparatus of colonial power, the discourses of sexuality and race relate in a process of *functional overdetermination,* 'because each effect . . . enters into resonance of contradiction with the others and thereby calls for a readjustment or a re-working of the heterogeneous elements that surface at various points'.[3]

There is both a structural and functional justification for reading the racial stereotype of colonial discourse in terms of fetishism.[4] My re-reading of Said establishes the *structural* link. Fetishism, as the disavowal of difference, is that repetitious scene around the problem of castration. The recognition of sexual difference – as the pre-condition for the circulation of the chain of absence and presence in the realm of the Symbolic – is disavowed by the fixation on an object that masks that difference and restores an original presence. The *functional* link between the fixation of the fetish and the stereotype (or the stereotype as fetish) is even more relevant. For fetishism is always a 'play' of vacillation between the archaic affirmation of wholeness/similarity – in Freud's terms: 'All men have penises'; in ours 'All men have the same skin/race/culture' – and the anxiety associated with lack and difference – again, for Freud 'Some do not have penises'; for us 'Some do not have the same skin/race/culture.' Within discourse, the fetish represents the simultaneous play between metaphor as substitution (masking absence and difference) and metonymy (which contiguously registers the perceived lack). The fetish or stereotype gives access to an 'identity' which is predicated as much on mastery and pleasure as it is on anxiety and defence, for it is a form of multiple and contradictory belief in its recognition of difference and disavowal of it. This conflict of pleasure/ unpleasure, mastery/defence, knowledge/disavowal, absence/presence, has a fundamental significance for colonial discourse. For the scene of fetishism is also the scene of the reactivation and repetition of primal fantasy – the subject's desire for a pure origin that is always threatened by its division, for the subject must be gendered to be engendered, to be spoken.

The stereotype, then, as the primary point of subjectification in colonial discourse, for both coloniser and colonised, is the scene of a similar fantasy and defence – the desire for an originality which is again threatened by the differences of race, colour and culture. My contention is splendidly caught in Fanon's title *Black Skin White Masks* where the disavowal of difference turns the colonial subject into a misfit – a grotesque mimicry or 'doubling' that threatens to split the soul and whole, undifferentiated skin of the ego. The stereotype is not a simplification because it is a false representation of a given reality. It is a simplification because it is an arrested, fixated form of representation that, in denying the play of difference (that the negation through the Other permits), constitutes a problem for the *representation* of the subject in significations of psychic and social relations. [. . .]

III

There are two 'primal scenes' in Fanon's *Black Skins White Masks*: two myths of the origin of the marking of the subject within the racist practices and discourses of a colonial culture. On one occasion a white girl fixes Fanon in a look and word as she turns to identify with her mother. It is a scene which echoes endlessly through his essay *The Fact of Blackness*: '*Look*, a Negro . . . Mamma, *see* the Negro! I'm frightened. Frightened. Frightened.' 'What else could it be for me', Fanon concludes, 'but an amputation, and excision, a haemorrhage that spattered my whole body with black blood.'[5] Equally, he stresses the primal moment when the child encounters racial and cultural stereotypes in children's fictions, where white heroes and black demons are proffered as points of ideological and psychical identification. Such dramas are enacted *every day* in colonial societies, says Fanon, employing a theatrical metaphor – the scene – which emphasises the visible – the seen. I want to play on both these senses which refer at once to the site of fantasy and desire and to the sight of subjectification and power.

[. . .]

It is this context that I want to allude briefly to the problematic of seeing/being seen. I suggest that in order to conceive of the colonial subject as the effect of power that is productive – disciplinary and 'pleasurable' – one has to see the *surveillance* of colonial power as functioning in relation to the regime of the *scopic drive*. That is, the drive that represents the pleasure in 'seeing', which has the look as its object of desire, is related both to the myth of origins, the primal scene, and the problematic of fetishism and locates the surveyed object within the 'imaginary' relation. Like voyeurism, surveillance must depend for its effectivity on 'the *active consent* which is its real or mythical correlate (but always real as myth) and establishes in the scopic space the illusion of the object relation'.[6] The ambivalence of this form of 'consent' in objectification – real as mythical – is the *ambivalence* on which the stereotype turns and illustrates that crucial bind of pleasure and power that Foucault asserts but, in my view, fails to explain.

My anatomy of colonial discourse remains incomplete until I locate the stereotype, as an arrested, fetishistic mode of representation within its field of identification, which I have identified in my description of Fanon's primal scenes, as the Lacanian schema of the Imaginary. The Imaginary[7] is the transformation that takes place in the subject at the formative mirror phase, when it assumes a *discrete* image which allows it to postulate a series of equivalences, samenesses, identities, between the objects of the surrounding world. However, this positioning is itself *problematic*, for the subject finds or recognises itself through an image which is simultaneously alienating and hence potentially confrontational. This is the basis of the close relation between the two forms of identification complicit with the Imaginary – narcissism and aggressivity. It is precisely these two forms of 'identification' that constitute the dominant strategy of colonial power exercised in relation to the stereotype which, as a form of multiple and contradictory belief, gives knowledge of difference and simultaneously disavows or masks it. Like the mirror phase 'the fullness' of the stereotype –its image *as* identity – is always threatened by 'lack'.

The construction of colonial discourse is then a complex articulation of the tropes of fetishism – metaphor and metonymy – and the forms of narcissistic and aggressive identification available to the Imaginary. Stereo-typical racial discourse is a four-term strategy. There is a tie-up between the metaphoric or masking function of the fetish and the narcissistic object-choice and an opposing alliance between the metonymic figuring of lack and the aggressive phase of the Imaginary. A repertoire of conflictual positions constitute the subject in colonial discourse. The taking up of any one position, within a specific discursive form, in a particular historical conjuncture, is thus always problematic – the site of both fixity and fantasy. It provides a colonial 'identity' that is played out – like all fantasies of originality and origination – in the face and space of the disruption and threat from the heterogeneity of other positions. As a form of splitting and multiple belief, the 'stereotype' requires, for its successful signification, a continual and repetitive chain of other stereotypes. The process by which the metaphoric 'masking' is inscribed on a lack which must then be concealed gives the stereotype both its fixity and its phantasmatic quality – the *same old* stories of the Negro's animality, the Coolie's inscrutability or the stupidity of the Irish *must* be told (compulsively) again and afresh, and are differently gratifying and terrifying each time.

[. . .]

[. . .] [W]e must acknowledge some significant differences between the general theory of fetishism and its specific uses for an understanding of racist discourse. First, the fetish of colonial discourse – what Fanon calls the epidermal schema – is not, like the sexual fetish, a secret. Skin, as the key signifier of cultural and racial difference in the stereotype, is the most visible of fetishes, recognised as 'common knowledge' in a range of cultural, political, historical discourses, and plays a public part in the racial drama that is enacted every day in colonial societies. Secondly, it may be said that sexual fetish is closely linked to the 'good object'; it is the prop that makes the whole object desirable and lovable, facilitates sexual relations and can even promote a form of happiness. The stereotype can also be seen as that particular 'fixated' form of the colonial subject which *facilitates* colonial relations, and sets up a discursive form of racial and cultural opposition in terms of which colonial power is exercised. If it is claimed that the colonised are most often objects of hate, then we can reply with Freud that 'affection and hostility in the treatment of the fetish – which run parallel with the disavowal and acknowledgement of castration – are mixed in unequal proportions in different cases, so that the one or the other is more clearly recognisable.'[8] [. . .]

[. . .] For our purposes I tend towards [a] reading which then provides a 'visibility' to the exercise of power; gives force to the argument that skin, as a signifier of discrimination, must be produced or processed as visible. As Abbot says, in a very different context,

> whereas repression banishes its object into the unconscious, forgets and attempts to forget the forgetting, discrimination must constantly invite its representations into consciousness, re-inforcing the crucial recognition of difference which they embody and revitalising them for the perception on which its effectivity depends . . . It must sustain itself on the presence of the very difference which is also its object.[9]

[. . .] The role of fetishistic identification, in the construction of discriminatory knowledges that depend on the 'presence of difference', is to provide a process of splitting and multiple-contradictory belief at the point of enunciation and subjectification. It is this crucial splitting of the ego which is represented in Fanon's description of the construction of the colonial subject as effect of stereotypical discourse: the subject primordially fixed and yet triply split between the incongruent knowledges of body, race, ancestors. Assailed by the stereotype, 'the corporeal schema crumbled, its place taken by a racial epidermal scheme . . . It was no longer a question of being aware of my body in the third person but a triple person . . . I was not given one, but two, three places.[10]

This process is best understood in terms of the articulation of multiple belief that Freud proposes in the essay on fetishism. It is a non-repressive form of knowledge that allows for the possibility of simultaneously embracing two contradictory beliefs, one official and one secret, one archaic and one progressive, one that allows the myth of origins, the other that articulates difference and division. Its knowledge 'value' lies in its orientation as a defence towards external reality. [. . .]

It is through this notion of splitting and multiple belief that, I believe, it becomes easier to see the bind of knowledge and fantasy, power and pleasure, that informs the particular regime of visibility deployed in colonial discourse. The visibility of the racial/colonial other is at once a *point* of identity ('Look, a Negro') and at the same time a *problem* for the attempted closure within discourse. For the recognition of difference as 'imaginary' points of identity and origin – such as Black and White – is disturbed by the representation of splitting in the discourse. What I called the play between the metaphoric-narcissistic and metonymic-aggressive moments in colonial discourse – that four-part strategy of the stereotype – crucially recognises the prefiguring of desire at a potentially conflictual, disturbing force in all those regimes of 'originality' that I have brought together. In the objectification of the scopic drive there is always the threatened return of the look; in the identification of the Imaginary relation there is always the alienating other (or mirror) which crucially returns its image to the subject; and in that form of substitution and fixation that is fetishism there is always the trace of loss, absence. To put it succinctly, the recognition and disavowal of 'difference' is always disturbed by the question of its re-presentation or construction. The stereotype is in fact an 'impossible' object. [. . .]

[. . .] Stereotyping is not the setting up of a false image which becomes the scapegoat of discriminatory practices. It is a much more ambivalent text of projection and introjection, metaphoric and metonymic strategies, displacement, overdetermination, guilt, aggressivity; the masking and splitting of 'official' and phantasmatic knowledges to construct the positionalities and oppositionalities of racist discourses.

[. . .] It is recognisably true that the chain of stereotypical signification is curiously mixed and split, polymorphous and perverse, an articulation of multiple belief. The black is both savage (cannibal) and yet the most obedient and dignified of servants (the bearer of food); he is the embodiment of rampant sexuality and yet innocent as a child; he is mystical, primitive, simple-minded and yet the most worldly and accomplished liar, and manipulator of social forces. In each case what is being dramatised is a separation – *between* races, cultures, histories, *within* histories – a separation between *before* and *after* that repeats obsessively the mythical moment of disjunction. Despite the structural similarities with the play of need and desire in primal fantasies, the colonial fantasy does not try to cover up that moment of separation. It is more ambivalent. On the one hand, it proposes a teleology – under certain conditions of colonial domination and control the native is progressively reformable. On the other, however, it effectively displays the 'separation', makes it more visible. It is the visibility of this separation which, in denying the colonised the capacities of self-government, independence, western modes of civility, lends authority to the official version and mission of colonial power. Colonial fantasy is the continual dramatisation of emergence – of difference, freedom – as the beginning of a history which is repetitively denied. Such a denial is the clearly voiced demand of colonial discourse as the legitimation of a form of rule that is facilitated by the racist fetish. [. . .]

Notes

1   Edward Said, *Orientalism* (London, Routledge and Kegan Paul, 1978), p. 72 (emphasis added).

2   Ibid., p. 206.

3   Michael Foucault, 'The confession of the flesh', in *Power/Knowledge* (London, Harvester, 1980), p. 195.

4   See Sigmund Freud, 'Fetishism' (1927) in *On Sexuality*, vol. 7 (Harmondsworth, Pelican Freud Library, 1981), p. 345ff (extracted in Chapter 20 of this volume); Christian Metz, *Psychoanalysis and Cinema: the Imaginary Signifier* (London, Macmillan, 1982), pp. 67–78. See also Steve Neale, 'The same old story: stereotypes and differences', *Screen Education*, 32/33, (1979/80), pp. 33–7.

5   Frantz Fanon, *Black Skin White Masks* (London, Paladin, 1970), p. 79.

6   Metz, *Psychoanalysis and Cinema*, pp. 62–3.

7   For the best account of Lacan's concept of the Imaginary see Jacqueline Rose, 'The imaginary' in Colin MacCabe (ed.), *The Talking Cure* (London, Macmillan, 1981).

8   Freud, 'Fetishism', p. 357.

9   Paul Abbott, 'Authority', *Screen*, 20(2) (summer 1979), pp. 15–16.

10   Fanon, *Black Skins White Masks*, p. 79.

F

Gendering the gaze

25

Visual pleasure and narrative cinema   **Laura Mulvey**

[. . .]

II   Pleasure in looking/fascination with the human form

(A) The cinema offers a number of possible pleasures. One is scopophilia (pleasure in looking). There are circumstances in which looking itself is a source of pleasure, just as, in the reverse formation, there is pleasure in being looked at. Originally, in his *Three Essays on Sexuality*, Freud isolated scopophilia as one of the component instincts of sexuality which exist as drives quite independently of the erotogenic zones. At this point he associated scopophilia with taking other people as objects, subjecting them to a controlling and curious gaze. His particular examples centre on the voyeuristic activities of children, their desire to see and make sure of the private and forbidden (curiosity about other people's genital and bodily functions, about the presence or absence of the penis and, retrospectively, about the primal scene). In this analysis scopophilia is essentially active. (Later, in 'Instincts and their Vicissitudes', Freud developed his theory of scopophilia further, attaching it initially to pre-genital auto-eroticism, after which, by analogy, the pleasure of the look is transferred to others. There is a close working here of the relationship between the active instinct and its further development in a narcissistic form.) Although the instinct is modified by other factors, in particular the constitution of the ego, it continues to exist as the erotic basis for pleasure in looking at another person as object. At the extreme, it can become fixated into a perversion, producing obsessive voyeurs and Peeping Toms whose only sexual satisfaction can come from watching, in an active controlling sense, an objectified other.

This chapter, written in 1973 appeared in *Screen*, vol. 16, no. 3 (1975), pp. 6–18.

At first glance, the cinema would seem to be remote from the undercover world of the surreptitious observation of an unknowing and unwilling victim. What is seen on the screen is so manifestly shown. But the mass of mainstream film, and the conventions within which it has consciously evolved, portray a hermetically sealed world which unwinds magically, indifferent to the presence of the audience, producing for them a sense of separation and playing on their voyeuristic fantasy. Moreover the extreme contrast between the darkness in the auditorium (which also isolates the spectators from one another) and the brilliance of the shifting patterns of light and shade on the screen helps to promote the illusion of voyeuristic separation. Although the film is really being shown, is there to be seen, conditions of screening and narrative conventions give the spectator an illusion of looking in on a private world. Among other things, the position of the spectators in the cinema is blatantly one of repression of their exhibitionism and projection of the repressed desire onto the performer.

(B) The cinema satisfies a primordial wish for pleasurable looking, but it also goes further, developing scopophilia in its narcissistic aspect. The conventions of mainstream film focus attention on the human form. Scale, space, stories are all anthropomorphic. Here, curiosity and the wish to look intermingle with a fascination with likeness and recognition: the human face, the human body, the relationship between the human form and its surroundings, the visible presence of the person in the world. Jacques Lacan has described how the moment when a child recognises its own image in the mirror is crucial for the constitution of the ego. Several aspects of this analysis are relevant here. The mirror phase occurs at a time when children's physical ambitions outstrip their motor capacity, with the result that their recognition of themselves is joyous in that they imagine their mirror image to be more complete, more perfect than they experience in their own body. Recognition is thus overlaid with misrecognition: the image recognised is conceived as the reflected body of the self, but its misrecognition as superior projects this body outside itself as an ideal ego, the alienated subject which, re-introjected as an ego ideal, prepares the way for identification with others in the future. This mirror moment predates language for the child.

Important for this article is the fact that it is an image that constitutes the matrix of the imaginary, of recognition/misrecognition and identification, and hence of the first articulation of the I, of subjectivity. This is a moment when an older fascination with looking (at the mother's face, for an obvious example) collides with the initial inklings of self-awareness. Hence it is the birth of the long love affair/despair between image and self-image which has found such intensity of expression in film and such joyous recognition in the cinema audience. Quite apart from the extraneous similarities between screen and mirror (the framing of the human form in its surroundings, for instance), the cinema has structures of fascination strong enough to allow temporary loss of ego while simultaneously reinforcing it. The sense of forgetting the world as the ego has come to perceive it (I forgot who I am and where I was) is nostalgically reminiscent of that pre-subjective moment of image recognition. While at the same time, the cinema has distinguished itself in the production of ego ideals, through the star system for instance. Stars provide a focus or centre both to screen space and screen story where they act out a complex process of likeness and difference (the glamorous impersonates the ordinary).

(C) Sections A and B have set out two contradictory aspects of the pleasurable structures of looking in the conventional cinematic situation. The first, scopophilic, arises from pleasure in using another person as an object of sexual stimulation through sight. The second, developed through narcissism and the constitution of the ego, comes from identification with the image seen. Thus, in film terms, one implies a separation of the erotic identity of the subject from the object on the screen (active scopophilia), the other demands identification of the ego with the object on the screen through the spectator's fascination with the recognition of his like. The first is a function of the sexual instincts, the second of ego libido. This dichotomy was crucial for Freud. Although he saw the two as interacting and overlaying each other, the tension between instinctual drives and self-preservation polarises in terms of pleasure. But both are formative structures, mechanisms without intrinsic meaning. In themselves they have no signification, unless attached to an idealisation. Both pursue aims in indifference to perceptual reality, and motivate eroticised phantasmagoria that affect the subject's perception of the world to make a mockery of empirical objectivity.

During its history, the cinema seems to have evolved a particular illusion of reality in which this contradiction between libido and ego has found a beautifully complementary fantasy world. In *reality* the fantasy world of the screen is subject to the law which produces it. Sexual instincts and identification processes have a meaning within the symbolic order which articulates desire. Desire, born with language, allows the possibility of transcending the instinctual and the imaginary, but its point of reference continually returns to the traumatic moment of its birth: the castration complex. Hence the look, pleasurable in form, can be threatening in content, and it is woman as representation/image that crystallises this paradox.

III   Woman as image, man as bearer of the look

(A) In a world ordered by sexual imbalance, pleasure in looking has been split between active/male and passive/female. The determining male gaze projects its fantasy onto the female figure, which is styled accordingly. In their traditional exhibitionist role women are simultaneously looked at and displayed, with their appearance coded for strong visual and erotic impact so that they can be said to connote *to-be-looked-at-ness*. Woman displayed as sexual object is the *leitmotif* of erotic spectacle: from pin-ups to strip-tease, from Ziegfeld to Busby Berkeley, she holds the look, and plays to and signifies male desire. Mainstream film neatly combines spectacle and narrative. (Note, however, how in the musical song-and-dance numbers interrupt the flow of the diegesis.) The presence of woman is an indispensable element of spectacle in normal narrative film, yet her visual presence tends to work against the development of a story-line, to freeze the flow of action in moments of erotic contemplation. This alien presence then has to be integrated into cohesion with the narrative. As Budd Boetticher has put it:

> What counts is what the heroine provokes, or rather what she represents. She is the one, or rather the love or fear she inspires in the hero, or else the concern he feels for her, who makes him act the way he does. In herself the woman has not the slightest importance.

(A recent tendency in narrative film has been to dispense with this problem altogether; hence the development of what Molly Haskell has called the 'buddy movie', in which the active homosexual eroticism of the central male figures can carry the story without distraction.) Traditionally, the woman displayed has functioned on two levels: as erotic object for the characters within the screen story, and as erotic object for the spectator within the auditorium, with a shifting tension between the looks on either side of the screen. For instance, the device of the show-girl allows the two looks to be unified technically without any apparent break in the diegesis. A woman performs within the narrative; the gaze of the spectator and that of the male characters in the film are neatly combined without breaking narrative verisimilitude. For a moment the sexual impact of the performing woman takes the film into a no man's land outside its own time and space. Thus Marilyn Monroe's first appearance in *The River of No Return* and Lauren Bacall's songs in *To Have and Have Not*. Similarly, conventional close-ups of legs (Dietrich, for instance) or a face (Garbo) integrate into the narrative a different mode of eroticism. One part of a fragmented body destroys the Renaissance space, the illusion of depth demanded by the narrative; it gives flatness, the quality of a cut-out or icon, rather than verisimilitude, to the screen.

(B) An active/passive heterosexual division of labour has similarly controlled narrative structure. According to the principles of the ruling ideology and the psychical structures that back it up, the male figure cannot bear the burden of sexual objectification. Man is reluctant to gaze at his exhibitionist like. Hence the split between spectacle and narrative supports the man's role as the active one of advancing the story, making things happen. The man controls the film fantasy and also emerges as the representative of power in a further sense: as the bearer of the look of the spectator, transferring it behind the screen to neutralise the extra-diegetic tendencies represented by woman as spectacle. This is made possible through the processes set in motion by structuring the film around a main controlling figure with whom the spectator can identify. As the spectator identifies with the main male protagonist, he projects his look onto that of his like, his screen surrogate, so that the power of the male protagonist as he controls events coincides with the active power of the erotic look, both giving a satisfying sense of omnipotence. A male movie star's glamorous characteristics are thus not those of the erotic object of the gaze, but those of the more perfect, more complete, more powerful ideal ego conceived in the original moment of recognition in front of the mirror. The character in the story can make things happen and control events better than the subject/spectator, just as the image in the mirror was more in control of motor co-ordination.

In contrast to women as icon, the active male figure (the ego ideal of the identification process) demands a three-dimensional space corresponding to that of the mirror recognition, in which the alienated subject internalised his own representation of his imaginary existence. He is a figure in a landscape. Here the function of film is to reproduce as accurately as possible the so-called natural conditions of human perception. Camera technology (as exemplified by deep focus in particular) and camera movements (determined by the action of the protagonist), combined with invisible editing (demanded by realism), all tend to blur the limits of screen space. The male protagonist is free to command the stage, a stage of spatial illusion in which he articulates the look and creates the action. (There are films with a woman as main protagonist, of course. To analyse this phenomenon seriously here would take me too far afield. Pam Cook and Claire Johnston's study of *The Revolt of Mamie Stover* in Phil Hardy (ed.), *Raoul Walsh* (Edinburgh, 1974), shows in a striking case how the strength of this female protagonist is more apparent than real.)

(C1) Sections III A and B have set out a tension between a mode of representation of woman in film and conventions surrounding the diegesis. Each is associated with a look: that of the spectator in direct scopophilic contact with the female form displayed for his enjoyment (connoting male fantasy) and that of the spectator fascinated with the image of his like set in an illusion of natural space, and through him gaining control and possession of the woman within the diegesis. (This tension and the shift from one pole to the other can structure a single text. Thus both in *Only Angels Have Wings* and in *To Have and Have Not*, the film opens with the woman as object of the combined gaze of spectator and all the male protagonists in the film. She is isolated, glamorous, on display, sexualised. But as the narrative progresses she falls in love with the main male protagonist and becomes his property, losing her outward glamorous characteristics, her generalised sexuality, her show-girl connotations; her eroticism is subjected to the male star alone. By means of identification with him, through participation in his power, the spectator can indirectly possess her too.)

But in psychoanalytic terms, the female figure poses a deeper problem. She also connotes something that the look continually circles around but disavows: her lack of a penis, implying a threat of castration and hence unpleasure. Ultimately, the meaning of woman is sexual difference, the visually ascertainable absence of the penis, the material evidence on which is based the castration complex essential for the organisation of entrance to the symbolic order and the law of the father. Thus the woman as icon, displayed for the gaze and enjoyment of men, the active controllers of the look, always threatens to evoke the anxiety it originally signified. The male unconscious has two avenues of escape from this castration anxiety: preoccupation with the re-enactment of the original trauma (investigating the woman, demystifying her mystery), counterbalanced by the devaluation, punishment or saving of the guilty object (an avenue typified by the concerns of the *film noir*); or else complete disavowal of castration by the substitution of a fetish object or turning the represented figure itself into a fetish so that it becomes reassuring rather than dangerous (hence overvaluation, the cult of the female star).

This second avenue, fetishistic scopophilia, builds up the physical beauty of the object, transforming it into something satisfying in itself. The first avenue, voyeurism, on the contrary, has associations with sadism: pleasure lies in ascertaining guilt (immediately associated with castration), asserting control and subjugating the guilty person through punishment or forgiveness. This sadistic side fits in well with narrative. Sadism demands a story, depends on making something happen, forcing a change in another person, a battle of will and strength, victory/defeat, all occurring in a linear time with a beginning and an end. Fetishistic scopophilia, on the other hand, can exist outside linear time as the erotic instinct is focused on the look alone. These contradictions and ambiguities can be illustrated more simply by using works by Hitchcock and Sternberg, both of whom take the look almost as the content or subject matter of many of their films. Hitchcock is the more complex, as he used both mechanisms. Sternberg's work, on the other hand, provides many pure examples of fetishistic scopophilia.

(C2) [. . .] In Hitchcock [. . .] the male hero does see precisely what the audience sees. However, although fascination with an image through scopophilic eroticism can be the subject of the film, it is the role of the hero to portray the contradictions and tensions experienced by the spectator. In *Vertigo* in particular, but also in *Marnie* and *Rear Window*, the look is central to the plot, oscillating between voyeurism and fetishistic fascination. Hitchcock has never concealed his interest in voyeurism, cinematic and non-cinematic. His heroes are exemplary of the symbolic order and the law – a policeman (*Vertigo*), a dominant male possessing money and power (*Marnie*) – but their erotic drives lead them into compromised situations. The power to subject another person to the will sadistically or to the gaze voyeuristically is turned onto the woman as the object of both. Power is backed by a certainty of legal right and the established guilt of the woman (evoking castration, psychoanalytically speaking). True perversion is barely concealed under a shallow mask of ideological correctness – the man is on the right side of the law, the woman on the wrong. Hitchcock's skilful use of identification processes and liberal use of subjective camera from the point of view of the male protagonist draw the spectators deeply into his position, making them share his uneasy gaze. The spectator is absorbed into a voyeuristic situation within the screen scene and diegesis, which parodies his own in the cinema.

In an analysis of *Rear Window*, Douchet takes the film as a metaphor for the cinema. Jeffries is the audience, the events in the apartment block opposite correspond to the screen. As he watches, an erotic dimension is added to his look, a central image to the drama. His girlfriend Lisa had been of little sexual interest to him, more or less a drag, so long as she remained on the spectator side. When she crosses the barrier between his room and the block opposite, their relationship is reborn erotically. He does not merely watch her through his lens, as a distant meaningful image, he also sees her as a guilty intruder exposed by a dangerous man threatening her with punishment, and thus finally giving him the opportunity to save her. Lisa's exhibitionism has already been established by her obsessive interest in dress and style, in being a passive image of visual perfection; Jeffries's voyeurism and activity have also been established through his work as a photo-journalist, a maker of stories and captor of images. However, his enforced inactivity, binding him to his seat as a spectator, puts him squarely in the fantasy position of the cinema audience.

In *Vertigo*, subjective camera predominates. Apart from one flashback from Judy's point of view, the narrative is woven around what Scottie sees or fails to see. The audience follows the growth of his erotic obsession and subsequent despair precisely from his point of view. Scottie's voyeurism is blatant: he falls in love with a woman he follows and spies on without speaking to. Its sadistic side is equally blatant: he has chosen (and freely chosen, for he had been a successful lawyer) to be a policeman, with all the attendant possibilities of pursuit and investigation. As a result, he follows, watches and falls in love with a perfect image of female beauty and mystery. Once he actually confronts her, his erotic drive is to break her down and force her *to tell* by persistent cross-questioning.

In the second part of the film, he re-enacts his obsessive involvement with the image he loved to watch secretly. He reconstructs Judy as Madeleine, forces her to conform in every detail to the actual physical appearance of his fetish. Her exhibitionism, her masochism, make her an ideal passive counterpart to Scottie's active sadistic voyeurism. She knows her part is to perform, and only by playing it through and then replaying it can she keep Scottie's erotic interest. But in the repetition he does break her down and succeeds in exposing her guilt. His curiosity wins through; she is punished.

Thus, in *Vertigo*, erotic involvement with the look boomerangs: the spectator's own fascination is revealed as illicit voyeurism as the narrative content enacts the processes and pleasures that he is himself exercising and enjoying. The Hitchcock hero here is firmly placed within the symbolic order, in narrative terms. He has all the attributes of the patriarchal superego. Hence the spectator, lulled into a false sense of security by the apparent legality of his surrogate, sees through his look and finds himself exposed as complicit, caught in the moral ambiguity of looking. Far from being simply an aside on the perversion of the police, *Vertigo* focuses on the implications of the active/looking, passive/looked-at split in terms of sexual difference and the power of the male symbolic encapsulated in the hero. Marnie, too, performs for Mark Rutland's gaze and masquerades as the perfect to-be-looked-at image. He, too, is on the side of the law until, drawn in by obsession with her guilt, her secret, he longs to see her in the act of committing a crime, make her confess and thus save her. So he, too, becomes complicit as he acts out the implications of his power. He controls money and words; he can have his cake and eat it.

IV Summary

The psychoanalytic background that has been discussed in this article is relevant to the pleasure and unpleasure offered by traditional narrative film. The scopophilic instinct (pleasure in looking at another person as an erotic object) and, in contradistinction, ego libido (forming identification processes) act as formations, mechanisms, which mould this cinema's formal attributes. The actual image of woman as (passive) raw material for the (active) gaze of man takes the argument a step further into the content and structure of representation, adding a further layer of ideological significance demanded by the patriarchal order in its favourite cinematic form – illusionistic narrative film. The argument must return again to the psychoanalytic background: women in representation can signify castration, and activate voyeuristic or fetishistic mechanisms to circumvent this threat. Although none of these interacting layers is intrinsic to film, it is only in the film form that they can reach a perfect and beautiful contradiction, thanks to the possibility in the cinema of shifting the emphasis of the look. The place of the look defines cinema, the possibility of varying it and exposing it. This is what makes cinema quite different in its voyeuristic potential from, say, strip-tease, theatre, shows and so on. Going far beyond highlighting a woman's to-be-looked-at-ness, cinema builds the way she is to be looked at into the spectacle itself. Playing on the tension between film as controlling the dimension of time (editing, narrative) and film as controlling the dimension of space (changes in distance, editing), cinematic codes create a gaze, a world and an object, thereby producing an illusion cut to the measure of desire. It is these cinematic codes and their relationship to formative external structures that must be broken down before mainstream film and the pleasure it provides can be challenged.

To begin with (as an ending), the voyeuristic–scopophilic look that is a crucial part of traditional filmic pleasure can itself be broken down. There are three different looks associated with cinema: that of the camera as it records the pro-filmic event, that of the audience as it watches the final product, and that of the characters at each other within the screen illusion. The conventions of narrative film deny the first two and subordinate them to the third, the conscious aim being always to eliminate intrusive camera presence and prevent a distancing awareness in the audience. Without these two absences (the material existence of the recording process, the critical reading of the spectator), fictional drama cannot achieve reality, obviousness and truth. Nevertheless, as this article has argued, the structure of looking in narrative fiction film contains a contradiction in its own premises: the female image as a castration threat constantly endangers the unity of the diegesis and bursts through the world of illusion as an intrusive, static, one-dimentional fetish. Thus the two looks materially present in time and space are obsessively subordinated to the neurotic needs of the male ego. The camera becomes the mechanism for producing an illusion of Renaissance space, flowing movements compatible with the human eye, an ideology of representation that revolves around the perception of the subject; the camera's look is disavowed in order to create a convincing world in which the spectator's surrogate can perform with verisimilitude. Simultaneously, the look of the audience is denied an intrinsic force: as soon as fetishistic representation of the female image threatens to break the spell of illusion, and the erotic image on the screen appears directly (without mediation) to the spectator, the fact of fetishisation, concealing as it does castration fear, freezes the look, fixates the spectator and prevents him from achieving any distance from the image in front of him.

This complex interaction of looks is specific to film. The first blow against the monolithic accumulation of traditional film conventions (already undertaken by radical film-makers) is to free the look of the camera into its materiality in time and space and the look of the audience into dialectics and passionate detachment. There is no doubt that this destroys the satisfaction, pleasure and privilege of the 'invisible guest', and highlights the way film has depended on voyeuristic active/passive mechanisms. Women, whose image has continually been stolen and used for this end, cannot view the decline of the traditional film form with anything much more than sentimental regret.

26

Desperately seeking difference **Jackie Stacey**

Feminist film criticism has become increasingly concerned with questions of gendered spectatorship and the pleasures of popular cinema. In this context, one focus has been a critical analysis of the pleasures of looking constructed by dominant cinematic forms, which, it has been argued, reproduce 'an active/passive heterosexual division of labour'.[1] But if these pleasures have been organised in accordance with the needs, desires and fears of heterosexual masculinity, then what is the place of *women's* desire towards women within this analysis of narrative cinema? Indeed, is it possible to analyse representations of desire between women within the psychoanalytic framework characteristic of so much feminist film criticism, or are there other frameworks we could turn to instead? [. . .]

Theories of feminine spectatorship: masculinisation, masochism or marginality

Laura Mulvey's 'Visual Pleasure and Narrative Cinema'[2] has been the springboard for much feminist film criticism during the last decade. Using psychoanalytic theory, Mulvey argued that the visual pleasures of Hollywood cinema are based on voyeuristic and fetishistic forms of looking. Because of the ways these looks are structured, the spectator necessarily identifies with the male protagonist in the narrative, and thus with his objectification of the female figure via the male gaze. The construction of woman as spectacle is built into the apparatus of dominant cinema, and the spectator position which is produced by the film narrative is necessarily a masculine one.

Mulvey maintained that visual pleasure in narrative film is built around two contradictory processes: the first involves objectification of the image and the second identification with it. The first process depends upon

This chapter is taken from *The Female Gaze*, edited by Lorraine Gamman and Margaret Marshment (London, The Woman's Press, 1988), pp. 112–200.

'direct scopophilic contact with the female form displayed for [the spectator's] enjoyment'[3] and the spectator's look here is active and feels powerful. This form of pleasure requires the separation of the 'erotic identity of the subject from the object on the screen'.[4] This 'distance' between spectator and screen contributes to the voyeuristic pleasure of looking in on a private world. The second form of pleasure depends upon the opposite process, an identification with the image on the screen 'developed through narcissism and the constitution of the ego'.[5] The process of identification in the cinema, Mulvey argued, like the process of objectification, is structured by the narrative. It offers the spectator the pleasurable identification with the main male protagonist, and through him the power indirectly to possess the female character displayed as sexual object for his pleasure. The look of the male character moves the narrative forward and identification with it thus implies a sense of sharing in the power of his active look.

Two lacunae in Mulvey's argument have subsequently been addressed in film criticism. The first raises the question of the male figure as erotic object,[6] the second that of the feminine subject in the narrative and women's active desire and the sexual aims of women in the audience in relationship to the female protagonist on the screen. As David Rodowick points out:

> her discussion of the female figure is restricted only to its function as masculine object-choice. In this manner, the place of the masculine is discussed as both the subject and object of the gaze: and the feminine is discussed only as an object which structures the masculine look according to its active (voyeuristic) and passive (fetishistic) forms. So where is the place of the feminine subject in this scenario?[7]

There are several possible ways of filling this theoretical gap. One would use a detailed textual analysis to demonstrate that different gendered spectator positions are produced by the film text, contradicting the unified masculine model of spectatorship. This would at least provide some space for an account of the feminine subject in the film text and in the cinema audience. The relationship of spectators to these feminine and masculine positions would then need to be explored further: do women necessarily take up a feminine and men a masculine spectator position?

Alternatively, we could accept a theory of the masculinisation of the spectator at a textual level, but argue that spectators being different subjectivities to the film according to sexual difference,[8] and therefore respond differently to the visual pleasures offered in the text. I want to elaborate these two possibilities briefly, before moving on to discuss a third which offers a more flexible or mobile model of spectatorship and cinematic pleasure.

The first possibility, then, is to argue that the film text can be read and enjoyed from different gendered positions. This problematises the monolithic model of Hollywood cinema as an 'anthropomorphic male machine'[9] producing unified and masculinised spectators. It offers an explanation of women's pleasure in a narrative cinema based on different processes of spectatorship, according to sexual difference. What this 'difference' signifies, however, in terms of cinematic pleasure, is highly contestable.

Raymond Bellour has explored the way the look is organised to create filmic discourse through detailed analyses of the system of enunciation in Hitchcock's work.[10] The mechanisms for eliminating the threat of sexual difference represented by the figure of the woman, he argues, are built into the apparatus of the cinema. Woman's desire only appears on the screen to be punished and controlled by assimilation to the desire of the male character. Bellour insists upon the masochistic nature of the woman spectator's pleasure in Hollywood film: 'I think that a woman can love, accept, and give positive value to these films only from her own masochism, and from a certain sadism that she can exercise in return on the masculine subject, within a system loaded with traps.[11]

Bellour, then, provides an account of the feminine subject and women's spectatorship which offers a different position from the masculine one set up by Mulvey. However, he fixes these positions within a rigid dichotomy which assumes a biologically determined equivalence between male/female and the masculine/feminine, sadistic/masochistic positions he believes to be set up by the cinematic apparatus. The apparatus here is seen as determining, controlling the meaning produced by a film text unproblematically: 'the resulting picture of the classical cinema is even more totalistic and deterministic than Mulvey's. Bellour sees it as a logically consistent, complete and closed system.'[12] The problem is that Bellour's analysis, like those of many structural functionalists, leaves no room for subjectivity. The spectator is presumed to be an already fully constituted subject and is fixed by the text to a predetermined gender identification. There is no space for subjectivity to be seen as a process in which identification and object choice may be shifting, contradictory or precarious.

A second challenge to the model of the masculinised spectator set up by Mulvey's 1975 essay comes from the work of Mary Ann Doane. She draws on Freud's account of asymmetry in the development of masculinity and femininity to argue that women's pleasures are not motivated by fetishistic and voyeuristic drives. [. . .]

Feminist critics have frequently challenged the assumption that fetishism functions for women in the same way that it is supposed to for men. Doane argues that the girl's understanding of the meaning of sexual difference occurs simultaneously with seeing the boy's genitals; the split between seeing and knowing, which enables the boy to disown the difference which is necessary for fetishism, does not occur in girls.

> It is in the distance between the look and the threat that the boy's relation to the knowledge of sexual difference is formulated. The boy, unlike the girl in Freud's description, is capable of a re-vision . . . This gap between the visible and the knowable, the very possibility of disowning what is seen, prepares the ground for fetishism.[13]

This argument is useful in challenging the hegemony of the cinema apparatus and in offering an account of visual pleasure which is neither based on a phallic model, nor on the determinacy of the text. It allows for an account of women's potential resistance to the dominant masculine spectator position. However, it also sets women outside the problematic pleasures of looking in the cinema, as if women do not have to negotiate within patriarchal regimes. As Doane herself has pointed out:

> The feminist theorist is thus confronted with something of a double bind: she can continue to analyse and interpret various instances of the repression of woman, of her radical absence in the discourses of men – a pose which necessitates remaining within that very problematic herself, repeating its terms; or she can attempt to delineate a feminine specificity, always risking a recapitulation of patriarchal constructions and a naturalization of 'woman'.[14]

In fact, this is a very familiar problem in feminist theory: how to argue for a feminine specificity without falling into the trap of biological essentialism. If we do argue that women differ from men in their relation to visual constructions of femininity, then further questions are generated for feminist film theory: do all women have the same relationship to images of themselves? Is there only one feminine spectator position? How do we account for diversity, contradiction or resistance within this category of feminine spectatorship?

This problem arises in relation to all cultural systems in which women have been defined as 'other' within patriarchal discourses: how can we express the extent of women's oppression without denying femininity any room to manoeuvre (Mulvey in 1975), defining women as complete victims of patriarchy (Bellour in 1979), or as totally other to it (Doane in 1982)? Within the theories discussed so far, the female spectator is offered only the three rather frustrating options of masculinisation, masochism or marginality.

Towards a more contradictory model of spectatorship

A different avenue of exploration would require a more complex and contradictory model of the relay of looks on the screen and between the audience and the diegetic characters. 'It might be better, as Barthes suggests, neither to destroy difference nor to valorize it, but to multiply and disperse differences, to move towards a world where differences would not be synonymous with exclusion.[15]

In her 1981 'afterthoughts' on visual pleasure, Mulvey addresses many of the problems raised so far. In an attempt to develop a more 'mobile' position for the female spectator in the cinema, she turns to Freud's theories of the difficulties of attaining heterosexual femininity.[16] Required, unlike men, to relinquish the phallic activity and female object of infancy, women are argued to oscillate between masculine and feminine identifications. To demonstrate this oscillation between positions, Mulvey cites Pearl Chavez's ambivalence in *Duel in the Sun*, the splitting of her desire (to be Jesse's 'lady' or Lewt's tomboy lover), a splitting which also extends to the female spectator. Mulvey's revision is important for two reasons: it displaces the notions of the fixity of spectator positions produced by the text, and it focuses on the gaps and contradictions within patriarchal signification, thus opening up crucial questions of resistance and diversity. However, Mulvey maintains that fantasies of action 'can only find expression . . . through the metaphor of masculinity'. In order to identify with active desire, the female spectator must assume an (uncomfortably) masculine position: 'the female spectator's phantasy of masculinisation is always to some extent at cross purposes with itself, restless in its transvestite clothes.'[17]

Oppressive dichotomies

Psychoanalytic accounts which theorise identification and object choice within a framework of linked binary oppositions (masculinity/femininity: activity/passivity) necessarily masculinise female homosexuality.

[. . .] This insistence upon a gendered dualism of sexual desire maps homosexuality on to an assumed antithesis of masculinity and femininity. Such an assumption precludes a description of homosexual positionality without resorting to the manoeuvres cited by Doane. In arguing for a more complex model of cinematic spectatorship, I am suggesting that we need to separate gender identification from sexuality, too often conflated in the name of sexual difference.

In films where the woman is represented as sexual spectacle for the masculine gaze of the diegetic and the cinematic spectator, an identification with a masculine heterosexual desire is invited. The spectator's response can vary across a wide spectrum between outright acceptance and refusal. It has proved crucial for feminist film theorists to explore these variations. How might a woman's look at another woman, both within the diegesis and between spectator and character, compare with that of the male spectator?

This article considers the pleasures of two narrative films which develop around one woman's obsession with another woman, *All About Eve* and *Desperately Seeking Susan*. I shall argue that these films offer particular pleasures to the women in the audience which cannot simply be reduced to a masculine heterosexual equivalent. In so doing I am not claiming these films as 'lesbian films' but rather using them to examine certain possibilities of pleasure. I want to explore the representation of forms of desire and identification in these films in order to consider their implications for the pleasures of female spectatorship. My focus is on the relations between women on the screen, and between these representations and the women in the audience. Interestingly, the fascinations which structure both narratives are precisely about difference – forms of otherness between women characters which are not merely reducible to sexual difference, so often seen as the sole producer of desire itself.

The inscription of active feminine desire

[. . .] *All About Eve* is particularly well suited to an analysis of these questions, as it is precisely about the pleasures and dangers of spectatorship for women. One of its central themes is the construction and reproduction of feminine identities, and the activity of looking is highlighted as an important part of these processes. The narrative concerns two women, a Broadway star and her most adoring spectator, Eve. In its course, we witness the transformation of Eve Butler (Ann Baxter) from spectator to star herself. The pleasures of spectatorship are emphasised by Eve's loyal attendance at every one of Margot Channing's (Bette Davis) performances. Its dangers are also made explicit as an intense rivalry develops between them. Eve emerges as a greedy and ambitious competitor, and Margot steps down from stardom into marriage, finally enabling her protégée to replace her as 'actress of the year' in a part written originally for Margot.

Eve's journey to stardom could be seen as the feminine equivalent to the masculine Oedipal trajectory [. . .] Freud's later descriptions of the feminine Oedipal journey[18] contradict his previous symmetrical model wherein the girl's first love object is her father, as the boy's is his mother. In his later arguments, Freud also posited the mother as the girl's first love object. Her path to heterosexuality is therefore difficult and complex, since it requires her not only to relinquish her first object, like the boy, but to transform both its gender (female to male) and the aim (active to passive) directed at it. Up to this point, active desire towards another woman is an experience of all women, and its re-enactment in *All About Eve* may constitute one of the pleasures of spectatorship for the female viewer.

Eve is constantly referred to as innocent and childlike in the first half of the film and her transformation involves a process of maturation, of becoming a more confident adult. First she is passionately attached to Margot, but then she shifts her affection to Margot's lover Bill, attempting unsuccessfully to seduce him. Twice in the film she is shown interrupting their intimacy: during their farewell at the airport and then during their fierce argument about Margot's jealousy, shortly before Bill's welcome-home party. Eve's third object of desire, whom she actively pursues, is the married playwright Lloyd Richards, husband to Margot's best friend. In both cases the stability of the older heterosexual couples, Margot and Bill, Karen and Lloyd, is threatened by the presence of the younger woman who completes the Oedipal triangle. Eve is finally punished for her desires by the patriarchal power of the aptly named Addison de Wit, who proves to be one step ahead of her manipulations.

The binary opposition between masculinity and femininity offers a limited framework for the discussion of Eve's fascination with Margot, which is articulated actively through an interplay of desire and identification during the film. In many ways, Margot is Eve's idealised object of desire. She follows Margot from city to city, never missing any of her performances. Her devotion to her favourite Broadway star is stressed at the very start of the film.

| Karen: | But there are hundreds of plays on Broadway . . . |
| Eve: | Not with Margot Channing in them! |

Margot is moved by Eve's representation of her 'tragic' past, and flattered by her adoration, so she decides to 'adopt' her.

| Margot | (Voice-over): We moved Eve's few pitiful possessions into my apartment . . . Eve became my sister, mother, lawyer, friend, psychiatrist and cop. The honeymoon was on! |

Eve acts upon her desire to become more like her ideal. She begins to wear Margot's cast-off clothes, appearing in Margot's bedroom one morning in her old black suit. Birdie, Margot's personal assistant, responds suspiciously to Eve's behaviour.

Margot:	She thinks only of me.
Birdie:	She things only *about* you – like she's studying you – like you was a book, or a play, or a set of blueprints – how you walk, talk, eat, think, sleep.
Margot:	I'm sure that's very flattering, Birdie, and I'm sure there's nothing wrong with it.

The construction of Bette Davis as the desirable feminine ideal in this narrative has a double significance here. As well as being a 'great star' for Eve, she is clearly the same for the cinema audience. The film offers the fictional fulfilment of the spectator's dreams as well as Eve's to be a star like Bette Davis, like Margot. Thus the identifications and desires of Eve, to some extent, narrativise a traditional pleasure of female spectatorship.

Margot is not only a star, she is also an extremely powerful woman who intimidates most of the male characters in the film. Her quick wit and disdain for conventional politeness, together with her flair for drama offstage as much as on, make her an attractive figure for Eve, an 'idealistic dreamy-eyed kid', as Bill describes her. It is this *difference* between the two women which motivates Eve, but which Eve also threatens. In trying to 'become as much like her ideal as possible', Eve almost replaces Margot in both her public and her private lives. She places a call to Bill on Margot's behalf, and captures his attention when he is on his way upstairs to see Margot before his coming-home party. Margot begins to feel dispensable.

| Margot: | I could die right now and nobody would be confused. My inventory is all in shape and the merchandise all put away. |

Yet even dressed in Margot's costume, having taken her role in the evening's performance, Eve cannot supplant her in the eyes of Bill, who rejects her attempt at seduction. The difference between the two women is repeatedly stressed and complete identification proves impossible.

All About Eve offers some unusual pleasures for a Hollywood film, since the active desire of a female character is articulated through looking at the female star. It is by watching Margot perform on the stage that Eve becomes intoxicated with her idol. The significance of active looking in the articulation of feminine desire is foregrounded at various points in the narrative. In one scene, we see Eve's devoted spectatorship in progress during one of Margot's performances. Eve watches Margot from the wings of the stage, and Margot bows to the applause of her audience. In the next scene the roles are reversed, and Margot discovers Eve on the empty stage bowing to an imaginary audience. Eve is holding up Margot's costume to sample the pleasures of stardom for herself. The process is then echoed in the closing scene of the film with Eve, now a Broadway star herself, and the newly introduced Phoebe, an adoring schoolgirl fan. The final shot shows Phoebe, having covertly donned Eve's bejewelled evening cloak, holding Eve's award and gazing at her reflection in the mirror. The reflected image, infinitely multiplied in the triptych of the glass, creates a spectacle of stardom that is the film's final shot, suggesting a perpetual regeneration of intra-feminine fascinations through the pleasure of looking.

The desire to be desperate

Like *All About Eve*, *Desperately Seeking Susan* concerns a woman's obsession with another woman. But instead of being punished for acting upon her desires, like Eve, Roberta (Rosanna Arquette) acts upon them, if in a rather more haphazard way, and eventually her initiatives are rewarded with the realisation of her desires. Despite her classic feminine behaviour, forgetful, clumsy, unpunctual and indecisive, she succeeds in her quest to find Susan (Madonna).

Even at the very beginning of the film, when suburban housewife Roberta is represented at her most dependent and childlike, her actions propel the narrative movement. Having developed her own fantasy narrative about Susan by reading the personal advertisements, Roberta acts upon her desire to be 'desperate' and becomes entangled in Susan's life. She anonymously attends the romantic reunion of Susan and Jim, and then pursues Susan through the streets of Manhattan. When she loses sight of her quarry in a second-hand shop, she purchases the jacket which Susan has just exchanged. The key found in its pocket provides an excuse for direct contact, and Roberta uses the personals to initiate another meeting.

Not only is the narrative propelled structurally by Roberta's desire, but almost all the spectator sees of Susan at the beginning of the film is revealed through Roberta's fantasy. The narrativisation of her desires positions her as the central figure for spectator identification: through her desire to seek, and see, Susan. Thus, in the opening scenes, Susan is introduced by name when Roberta reads the personals aloud from under the dryer in the beauty salon. Immediately following Roberta's declaration 'I wish I was desperate', there is a cut to the first shot of Susan.

The cuts from the Glasses' party to Susan's arrival in New York City work to the same effect. Repelled by her husband's TV commercial for his bathroom wares, Roberta leaves her guests and moves towards the window, as the ad's voice-over promises 'At Gary's Oasis, all your fantasies can come true.' Confronted with her own image in the reflection, she pushes it away by opening the window and looking out longingly on to Manhattan's skyline. The ensuing series of cuts between Roberta and the bridge across the river to the city link her desiring gaze to Susan's arrival there via the same bridge.

At certain points within *Desperately Seeking Susan*, Roberta explicitly becomes the bearer of the look. The best illustration of this transgression of traditional gender positionalities occurs in the scene in which she first catches sight of Susan. The shot sequence begins with Jim seeing Susan and is immediately followed with Roberta seeing her. It is, however, Roberta's point of view which is offered for the spectator's identification. Her look is specified by the use of the pay-slot telescope through which Roberta, and the spectator, see Susan.

In accordance with classic narrative cinema, the object of fascination in *Desperately Seeking Susan* is a woman – typically, a woman coded as a sexual spectacle. As a star Madonna's image is saturated in sexuality. In many ways she represents the 1980s 'assertive style' of heterosexual spectacle, inviting masculine consumption. This is certainly emphasised by shots of Susan which reference classic pornographic poses and camera angles; for example, the shot of Susan lying on Roberta's bed reading her diary, which shows Susan lying on her back, wearing only a vest and a pair of shorts over her suspenders and lacy tights. (Although one could argue that the very next shot, from Susan's point of view, showing Gary upside down, subverts the conventional pornographic codes.) My aim is not to deny these meanings in *Desperately Seeking Susan* in order to claim it as a 'progressive text', but to point to cinematic pleasures which may be available to the spectator *in addition* to those previously analysed by feminist film theory. Indeed, I believe such a project can only attempt to work within the highly contradictory constructions of femininity in mainstream films.

Susan is represented as puzzling and enigmatic to the protagonist, and to the spectator. The desire propelling the narrative is partly a desire to become more like her, but also a desire to know her, and to solve the riddle of her femininity. The protagonist begins to fulfil this desire by following the stranger, gathering clues about her identity and her life, such as her jacket, which, in turn, produces three other clues, a key, a photograph and a telephone number. The construction of her femininity as a riddle is emphasised by the series of intrigues and misunderstandings surrounding Susan's identity. The film partly relies on typical devices drawn from the mystery genre in construction the protagonist's, and thus the spectator's, knowledge of Susan through a series of clues and coincidences. Thus, in some ways, Susan is positioned as the classic feminine enigma; she is, however, investigated by another woman.

One line of analysis might simply see Roberta as taking up the position of the masculine protagonist in expressing a desire to be 'desperate', which, after all, can be seen as identifying with Jim's position in relation to Susan, that of active desiring masculinity. Further legitimation for this reading could be seen in Jim's response to Roberta's advertisement to Susan in the personals. He automatically assumes it has been placed there by another man, perhaps a rival. How can we understand the construction of the female protagonist as the agent and articulator of desire for another woman in the narrative within existing psychoanalytic theories of sexual difference? The limitations of a dichotomy which offers only two significant categories for understanding the complex interplay of gender, sexual aim and object choice, are clearly demonstrated here.

Difference and desire between women

The difference which produces the narrative desire in *Desperately Seeking Susan* is not sexual difference, but the difference between two women in the film. It is the difference between suburban marriage and street credibility. Two sequences contrast the characters, using smoking as a signifier of difference. The first occurs in Battery Park, where Roberta behaves awkwardly in the unfamiliar territory of public space. She is shown sitting on a park bench, knees tightly clenched, looking around nervously for Susan. Jim asks her for a light, to which she timidly replies that she does not smoke. The ensuing cut shows Susan, signalled by Jim's shout of recognition. Susan is sitting on the boat rail, striking a match on the bottom of her raised boot to light a cigarette.

Smoking is again used to emphasise difference in a subsequent sequence. This time, Roberta, having by now lost her memory and believing she may be Susan, lights a cigarette from Susan's box. Predictably, she chokes on the smoke, with the unfamiliarity of an adolescent novice. The next cut shows us Susan, in prison for attempting to skip her cab fare, taking a light from the prison matron and blowing the smoke defiantly straight back into her face. The contrast in their smoking ability is only one signifier of the characters' very different femininities. Roberta is represented as young, inexperienced and asexual, while Susan's behaviour and appearance are coded as sexually confident and provocative. Rhyming sequences are used to emphasise their differences even after Roberta has taken on her new identity as Susan. She ends up in the same prison cell, but her childlike acquiescence to authority contrasts with Susan's defiance of the law.

Susan transgresses conventional forms of feminine behaviour by appropriating public space for herself. She turns the public lavatory into her own private bathroom, drying her armpits with the hand blower, and changing her clothes in front of the mirror above the washbasins as if in her own bedroom. In the streets, Susan challenges the patronising offer of a free newspaper from a passer-by by dropping the whole pile at his feet and taking only the top copy for herself. In contrast to Susan's supreme public confidence, Roberta is only capable in her own middle-class privacy. Arriving home after her day of city adventures, she manages to synchronise with a televised cooking show, catching up on its dinner preparations with confident dexterity in her familiar domestic environment.

As soon as Roberta becomes entangled in Susan's world, her respectable sexuality is thrown into question. First she is assumed to be having an affair, then she is arrested for suspected prostitution, and finally Gary asks her if she is a lesbian. When the two photographs of Roberta, one as a bride and one as a suspected prostitute, are laid down side by side at the police station, her apparent transformation from virgin to whore shocks her husband. The ironic effect of these largely misplaced accusations about Roberta's sexuality works partly in relation to Susan, who is represented as the epitome of opposition to acceptable bourgeois feminine sexuality. She avoids commitment, dependency or permanence in her relationships with men, and happily takes their money, while maintaining an intimate friendship with the woman who works at the Magic Box.

Roberta's desire is finally rewarded when she meets Susan in an almost farcical chase scene at that club during the chaotic film finale. Gary finds Roberta, Des finds 'Susan' (Roberta), Jim finds Susan, the villain finds the jewels (the earrings which Susan innocently pocketed earlier in the film), Susan and Roberta catch the villain, and Susan and Roberta find each other . . . The last shot of the film is a front-page photograph of the two women hand in hand, triumphantly waving their reward cheque in return for the recovery of the priceless Nefertiti earrings. In the end, both women find what they were searching for throughout the narrative: Roberta has found Susan, and Susan has found enough money to finance many future escapades.

Roberta's desire to become more like her ideal – a more pleasingly co-ordinated, complete and attractive feminine image[19] – is offered temporary narrative fulfilment. However, the pleasures of this feminine desire cannot be collapsed into simple identification, since difference and otherness are continuously played upon, even when Roberta 'becomes' her idealised object. Both *Desperately Seeking Susan* and *All About Eve* tempt the woman spectator with the fictional fulfilment of becoming an ideal feminine other, while denying complete transformation by insisting upon differences between women. the rigid distinction between *either* desire *or* identification, so characteristic of psychoanalytic film theory, fails to address the construction of desires which involve a specific interplay of both processes.

Notes

1   Laura Mulvey, 'Visual pleasure and narrative cinema', *Screen*, 16, 3 (autumn 1975), pp. 11–12 [extracted in Chapter 25 of this volume].
2   Ibid.
3   Ibid., p. 13
4   Ibid., p. 10
5   Ibid.
6   There have been several attempts to fill this theoretical gap and provide analyses of masculinity as sexual spectacle: see Richard Dyer, 'Don't look now: the male pin-up',

Screen, 23, 3/4 (1982); Steve Neale, 'Masculinity as spectacle', *Screen*, 24, 6 (1983); and Andy Medhurst, 'Can chaps be pin-ups?', *Ten.8*, 17 (1985).

7   David Rodowick, 'The difficulty of difference', *Wide Angle*, 5, 1 (1982), p. 8.

8   Mary Ann Doane, 'Film and the masquerade: theorising the female spectator', *Screen*, 23, 3/4 (September/October 1982).

9   Constance Penley, 'Feminism, film theory and the bachelor machines', *m/f*, 10 (1985).

10 According to Raymond Bellour, the term *enunciator* 'marks both the person who possesses the right to speak within the film, and the source [instance] towards which the series of representations is logically chanelled back', Raymond Bellour, 'Hitchcock the enunciator', *Camera Obscura*, 2 (1977), p. 2.

11 Raymond Bellour, 'Psychosis, neurosis, perversion', *Camera Obscura*, 3/4 (1979), p. 97.

12 Janet Bergstrom, 'Enunciation and sexual difference', *Camera Obscura*, 3/4 (1979), p. 57. See also Janet Bergstrom, 'Alternation, segmentation, hypnosis: an interview with Raymond Bellour', *Camera Obscura*, 3/4 (1979).

13 Doane, 'Film and the masquerade', p. 80.

14 Mary Ann Doane, Patricia Mellencamp and Linda Williams, 'Feminist film criticism: an introduction' in *Re-Vision*, p. 9.

15 Ibid., p. 14.

16 Laura Mulvey, 'Afterthoughts on "Visual Pleasure and Narrative Cinema" inspired by *Duel in the Sun*', *Framework*, 15/16/17 (1981), pp. 12–15.

17 Ibid., p. 15.

18 See, for example, Sigmund Freud, 'Some physical consequences of the anatomical distinction between the sexes' (1925), in *On Sexuality*, vol. 7 (Harmondsworth, Penguin, Pelican Freud Library, 1977).

19 See Jacques Lacan, 'The mirror stage as formative of the function of the I as revealed in the psychoanalytic experience', in *Ecrits: a Selection*, trans. Alan Sheridan (London, Tavistock, 1977), pp. 1–7.

27

White privilege and looking relations: race and gender in feminist film theory
Jane Gaines

[. . .]

What I want to do here is to show how a theory of the text and its spectator, based on the psychoanalytic concept of sexual difference, is unequipped to deal with a film which is about racial difference and sexuality. The Diana Ross star-vehicle *Mahogany* (directed by Berry Gordy, 1975) immediately suggests a psychoanalytic approach because the narrative is organised around the connections between voyeurism and photographic acts, and because it exemplifies the classical cinema which has been so fully theorised in Lacanian terms. But as I will argue, the psychoanalytic model works to block out considerations which assume a different configuration, so that, for instance, the Freudian–Lacanian scenario can eclipse the scenario of race–gender relations in Afro-American history, since the two accounts of sexuality are fundamentally incongruous. The danger here is that when we use a psychoanalytic model to explain black family relations, we force an erroneous universalisation and inadvertently reaffirm white middle-class norms.

By taking gender as its starting point in the analysis of oppression, feminist theory helps to reinforce white middle-class values, and to the extent that it works to keep women from seeing other structures of oppression, it functions ideologically. [. . .]

[. . .] In retrospect, we understand that the apparent intransigence of the theory of cinema as patriarchal discourse, as it developed out of such essays by British Marxist feminists as Claire Johnston's 'Women's Cinema as Counter-Cinema' and Laura Mulvey's 'Visual Pleasure and Narrative Cinema'[1], is the legacy of the Althusserian theory of the subject. While it is clear from the point of view of Marxist feminism that the psychoanalytic version of the construction of the subject was a welcome supplement to

This chapter is taken from *Screen*, vol. 29, no. 4 (1988), pp. 12–27.

classical Marxism, what was gained with a theory of the social individual was at the cost of losing the theory of social antagonism.

[. . .]

Within film and television studies in the US, the last three years have seen a break with the theory of representation which, it appears, had gripped us for so long. The new feminist strategies which engage with, modify or abandon the stubborn notion that we are simultaneously positioned in language and ideology, are too numerous to detail. In the US, as in Britain, one of the most influential challenges to this theory posed the question of our reconstitution at different historical moments. How could the formative moment of one's entry into language be the one condition overriding all other determining conditions of social existence? This question would become especially pertinent as theoretical interest shifted from the text which produced subjects to the subjects who produced texts; the 'real historical subject' became the escape route through which theorists abandoned a text weighted down with impossible expectations.

I

In the US, lesbian feminists raised the first objections to the way in which film theory explained the operation of the classic realist text in terms of tensions between masculinity and femininity. The understanding of spectatorial pleasure in classical cinema as inherently male drew an especially sharp response from critics who argued that this theory cancelled the lesbian spectator whose viewing pleasure could never be construed as anything like male voyeurism. Positing a lesbian spectator would significantly change the trajectory of the gaze. It might even lead us to see how the eroticised star body might be not just the object, but what I would term the visual objective of another female gaze within the film's diegesis – a gaze with which the viewer might identify; following this argument, Marilyn Monroe and Jane Russell in *Gentlemen Prefer Blondes* are 'only for each other's eyes'.[2] [. . .]

In Marxist feminist analysis, the factors of race and sexual preference have remained loose ends; as categories of oppression they fit somewhat awkwardly into a model based on class relations in capitalist society. Although some gay historians see a relationship between the rise of capitalism and the creation of the social homosexual, only with a very generous notion of sexual hierarchies – such as the one Gayle Rubin has suggested – can sexual oppression (as distinct from gender oppression) be located within a framework based on class.[3] Race has folded into Marxist models more neatly than sexual preference, but the orthodox formulation which understands racial conflict as class struggle, is still unsatisfactory to Marxist feminists who want to know exactly how gender intersects with race. The oppression of *women* of colour remains incompletely grasped by the classical Marxist paradigm.

Just as the Marxist model based on class has obscured the function of gender, the feminist model based on the male/female division under patriarchy has obscured the function of race. The dominant feminist paradigm actually encourages us not to think in terms of any oppression other than male dominance and female subordination. Thus it is that feminists and lesbians, says Barbara Smith, seem 'blinded to the implications of any womanhood that is not white womanhood'.[4] For purposes of analysis, black feminists agree that class is as significant as race; however, if these feminists hesitate to emphasise gender as a factor, it is in deference to the way black women describe their experience, for it is clear that Afro-American women have historically formulated identity and political allegiance in terms of race rather than gender or class.[5] Feminism, however, seems not to have heard the statements of women of colour who say that they experience oppression first in relation to race rather then gender, and that for them exploitation can be personified by a white female.[6] Even more difficult for feminist theory to digest is black female identification with the black male. On this point, black feminists diverge from white feminists, in repeatedly reminding us that they do not necessarily see the black male as patriarchal antagonist, but feel instead that their racial oppression is 'shared' with men.[7] In the most comprehensive analysis of all, black lesbian feminists have described race, class and gender oppression as an 'interlocking' synthesis in the lives of black women.[8]

The point here is not to rank the structures of oppression in a way that implies the need for black women to choose between solidarity with men or solidarity with women, between race or gender as the basis for a political strategy. At issue is the question of the fundamental antagonism which has been so relevant for Marxist feminist theory. Where we have foregrounded one antagonism in our analysis, we have misunderstood another, and this is most dramatically illustrated in applying the notion of patriarchy. Feminists have not been absolutely certain what they mean by patriarchy: alternately it has referred to either father-right or domination of women; but what is consistent about the use of the concept is the rigidity of the structure it describes.[9] Patriarchy is incompatible with Marxism where it is used trans-historically without qualification, and where it becomes the source from which all other oppressions are tributary, as in the radical feminist theory of patriarchal order, which sees oppression in all forms and through all ages as derived from the male/female division.[10] This deterministic model, which Sheila Rowbotham says functions like a 'feminist base-superstructure', has the disadvantage of leaving us with no sense of movement, or no idea of how women have acted to change their condition, especially in comparison with the fluidity of the Marxist conception of class.[11]

The radical feminist notion of absolute patriarchy has also one-sidedly portrayed the oppression of women through an analogy with slavery, and since this theory has identified woman as man's savage or repressed Other it competes with theories of racial difference which understand the black as the 'unassimilable Other'.[12] Finally, the notion of patriarchy is most obtuse when it disregards the position white women occupy over black men as well as black women.[13] In order to rectify this tendency in feminism, black feminists refer to 'racial patriarchy', which is based on an analysis of the white patriarch/master in US history, and his dominance over the black male as well as the black female.[14]

II

I want now to reconsider the connotations of sexual looking, with refer-ence to a film in which racial difference structures a hierarchy of access to the female image. In *Mahogany*, her follow-up to *Lady Sings the Blues*, Diana Ross plays an aspiring fashion designer who dreams of pulling herself up and out of her Chicago South Side neighbourhood by means of a high-powered career. During the day, Tracy Chambers is assistant to the modelling supervisor for a large department store. At night she attends design school, where the instructor reprimands her for sketching a cocktail dress instead of completing the assignment, the first suggestion of the exotic irrelevance of her fantasy career. She loses her job, but the famous fashion photographer Sean McEvoy (Anthony Perkins) discovers her as a model and whisks her off to Rome. There, Tracy finally realises her ambition to become a designer, when a wealthy Italian admirer gives her a business of her own. After the grand show unveiling her first collection of clothes, she returns to Chicago and is reunited with community organiser Brian Walker (Billy Dee Williams), whose political career is a counterpoint to Tracy's modelling career.

With its long fashion photography montage sequences temporarily interrupting the narrative, *Mahogany* invites a reading based on the alternation between narrative and woman-as-spectacle as theorised by Laura Mulvey in 'Visual Pleasure and Narrative Cinema'. To the allure of pure spectacle these sequences add the fascination of masquerade and transformation. Effected with wigs and make-up colours, the transformations are a ply on and against 'darkness'; Diana Ross is a high-tech Egyptian queen, a pale mediaeval princess, a turbaned Asiatic, a body-painted blue nymph. As her body colour is powdered over or washed out in bright light, and as her long-haired wigs blow around her face, she becomes suddenly 'white'.

Contemporary motion pictures never seem to exhaust the narrative possibilities associated with the camera-as-deadly-weapon metaphor; *Mahogany* adds to this the sadomasochistic connotations of high fashion photography with reference to the mid-seventies work of Guy Bourdin and Helmut Newton, linked to the tradition of 'attraction by shock'.[15] The montage sequences chronicling Tracy's career, from perfume ads to high fashion magazine covers, equate the photographic act with humiliation and violation. Camera zoom and freeze-frame effects translate directly into aggression, as in the sequence in which Sean pushes Tracy into a fountain and her dripping image solidifies into an Italian Revlon advertisement. Finally, the motif of stopping-the-action-as-aggression is equated with the supreme violation: attempted murder. Pressing his favourite model to her expressive limits, Sean drives her off an expressway ramp. Since this brutality escalates after the scene in which he fails with Tracy in bed, the film represents her punishment as a direct consequence of his impotence (figure 27.1).

With its classic castration threat scenario, its connection between voyeurism and sadism, and its reference to fetishisation – as seen in Sean's photographic shrine to the models he has abused – *Mahogany* is the perfect complement to a psychoanalytic analysis of classical Hollywood's visual

pleasure. The film further provides material for such an analysis by producing its own 'proof' that there is only an incremental difference between
voyeurism (fashion photography) and sadism (murder). The black and
white photographic blow-ups of Tracy salvaged from the death car seem
undeniable evidence of the fine line between looking and killing, or, held at
another angle, between advertising imagery and pornography.

This, then, is to suggest the kind of evidence in the film which would
support an analysis of it as patriarchal discourse, in its use of the female
image as fetish to assuage castration anxiety, and through its rich offering
of views to please the male spectator. There's even an inescapable suggestion of voyeurism as pathology, since the gaze is that of the actor whose
star persona is fatally haunted by the protagonist of *Psycho*. To explain the
ideological function of the film in terms of the construction of male
pleasure, however, is to 'aid and abet' the film's other ideological project.
In following the line of analysis I have outlined, one is apt to step into
an ideological signifying trap set up by the chain of meanings that lead
away from seeing the film in terms of racial conflict. Because there are so
many connotative paths – photographer exploits model, madman assaults
woman, voyeur attempts murder – we may not immediately see white man
as aggressor against black woman. Other strategies encourage the viewer
to forget or not notice racial issues. For instance, the narrative removes
Tracy from racially polarised Chicago to Rome, where the brown Afro-
American woman with Caucasian features is added to the collection of a
photographer who names his subjects after prized objects or their qualities.

Losing her black community identity, Tracy becomes Mahogany, acquiring the darkness, richness and value the name connotes; that is, her blackness becomes commodified.

Mahogany functions ideologically for black viewers in the traditional Marxist sense, that is, in the way the film obscures the class nature of social antagonisms. This has certain implications for working-class black viewers, who would gain most from seeing the relationship between race, gender and class oppression. Further, *Mahogany* has the same trouble with representing black femaleness that the wider culture has had historically; a black female is either all woman and tinted black, or mostly black and scarcely woman. These two expectations correspond with the two worlds and two struggles which structure the film: the struggle over the sexual objectification of Tracy's body in the face of commercial exploitation, and the struggle of the black community in the face of class exploitation. But the film identifies this antagonism as the hostility between fashion and politics, embodied respectively by Tracy and Brian, and it is through them that it organises conflict and, eventually, reconciliation. Intensifying this conflict between characters, the film contrasts 'politics' and 'fashion' in one daring homage to the aesthetic of 'attraction by shock'; Sean arranges his models symmetrically on the back stairwell of a run-down Chicago apartment building and uses the confused tenants and street people as props. Flamboyant excess, the residue of capital, is juxtaposed with a kind of dumbfounded poverty. For a moment, the scene figures the synthesis of gender, class and race, but the political glimpse is fleeting. Forced together as a consequence of the avant-garde's socially irresponsible quest for a new outrage, the political antagonisms are suspended – temporarily immobilised as the subjects pose.

The connection between gender, class and race oppression is also denied as the ghetto photography session's analogy between commercial exploitation and race/class exploitation merely registers on the screen as visual incongruity. visual discrepancy, which, as I have argued, is used for aesthetic effect, also makes it difficult to grasp the confluence of race, class and gender oppression in the image of Tracy Chambers. The character's class background magically becomes decor in the film – it neither radicalises her nor drags her down; instead it sets her off. Diana Ross is alternately weighted down by the glamour iconography of commercial modelling or stripped to a black body. But the *haute couture* iconography ultimately dominates the film. Since race is decorative and class does not reveal itself to the eye, Tracy can only be seen as exploited in terms of her role as a model.

If the film plays down race, it does not do so just to accommodate white audiences. In worshipping the success of the black cult star and combining this with Diana Ross's own dream-come-true – a chance to design all of the costumes in her own film – *Mahogany* hawks the philosophy of black enterprise and social aspiration. Here it does not matter where you come from, what you should be asking yourself, in the words of the theme song, is 'Where are you going, do you know?' Race, then, should be seen as any other obstacle – to be transcended through diligent work and dedication to a goal. Supporting the film's self-help philosophy is the related story of Diana Ross's 'discovery' as a skinny teenager singing in a

Baptist Church in Detroit. With *Mahogany*, Motown president and founder Berry Gordy (who fired Tony Richardson and took over the film's direction) helps Diana Ross to make something of herself again, just as he helped so many aspiring recording artists, by coaching them in money management and social decorum in his talent school.[16]

The phenomenon of Motown Industries is less a comment on the popularity of the self-help philosophy than a verification of the discrepancy between the opportunity formula and the social existence of black Americans. Ironically, black capitalism's one bid success thrives on the impossibility of black enterprise: soul entertainment as compensation and release sells because capitalism cannot deliver well-being to all.[17] Black music and performance, despite the homogenisation of the original forms, represents a utopian aspiration for black Americans, as well as for white suburbanites. Simon Frith describes the need supplied by rock fantasy: 'Black music had a radical, rebellious edge: it carried a sense of possibility denied in the labor market; it suggested a comradeship, a sensuality, a grace and joy and energy lacking in work . . . the power of rock fantasy rests, precisely on utopianism.'[18] [. . .]

One of the original tenets of contemporary feminist film theory – that the (male) spectator possesses the female indirectly through the eyes of the male protagonist (his screen surrogate) – is problematised here by the less privileged black male gaze. Racial hierarchies of access to the female image also relate to other scenarios which are unknown by psychoanalytic categories. Considering the racial categories which psychoanalysis does not recognise, then, we see that the white male photographer monopolises the classic patriarchal look controlling the view of the female body (figure 27.2), and that the black male protagonist's look is either repudiated or frustrated. The sumptuous image of Diana Ross is made available to the spectator via the white male character (Sean) but *not* through the look of the black male character (Brian). In the sequence in which Tracy and Brian first meet outside her apartment building, his 'look' is renounced. In each of the three shots of Tracy from Brian's point of view, she turns from him, walking out of his sight and away from the sound of his voice as he shouts at her through a megaphone. The relationship between the male and female protagonists is negotiated around Brian's bullhorn, emblem of his charismatic black leadership, through which he tries to reach both the black woman and his constituents. Both visual and audio control is thus denied the black male, and the failure of his voice is consistently associated with Tracy's publicity image in the white world. The discovery of Brian's aides of the Mahogany advertisement for Revlon in *Newsweek* coincides with the report that the Gallup polls show the black candidate trailing in the election. Later, the film cuts from the *Harper's Bazaar* cover featuring Mahogany to Brian's limping campaign where the sound of his voice magnified through a microphone is intermittently drowned out by a passing train as he makes his futile pitch to white factory workers. The manifest goal of the film, the reconciliation of the black heterosexual couple, is thwarted by the commercial appropriation of her image, but, in addition, its highly mediated form threatens the black political struggle.

Figure 27.2

Racial hierarchies of access to the female image: white males monopolise the classic patriarchal look

III

[. . .]

IV

[. . .] [O]ne of the most difficult questions raised by Afro-American history and literature has to do with interracial heterosexuality and sexual 'looking' *Mahogany* suggests that, since a black male character is not allowed the position of control occupied by a white male character, race could be a factor in the construction of cinematic language. More work on looking and racial taboos might determine whether or not mainstream cinema can offer the male spectator the pleasure of looking at a white female character via the gaze of a black male character. Framing the question of male privilege and viewing pleasure as the 'right to look' may help us to rethink film theory along more materialist lines, considering, for instance, how some groups have historically had the licence to 'look' openly while other groups have 'looked' illicitly. [. . .]

Notes

1   Claire Johnston, 'Women's cinema as counter-cinema', in Claire Johnston (ed.), *Notes on Women's Cinema* (London, Society for Education in Film and Television, 1973); Laura Mulvey, 'Visual pleasure and narrative cinema', *Screen*, 16, 3 (1975) [extracted in Chapter 25 of this volume].

2   Lucie Arbuthnot and Gail Seneca, 'Pre-text and text in *Gentlemen Prefer Blondes' Film Reader 5* (winter 1981), pp. 13–23.

3   Gayle Rubin, 'Thinking sex: notes for a radical theory of the politics of sexuality', in Carol Vance (ed.), *Pleasure and Danger* (Boston and London, Routledge and Kegan Paul, 1984), p. 307.

4   Barbara Smith 'Towards a black feminist criticism', in Elaine Showalter (ed.), *The New Feminist Criticism* (New York, Pantheon, 1985), p. 169.

5   Bonnie Thornton Dill, 'Race, class, and gender: prospects for an all-inclusive sisterhood', *Feminist Studies*, 9, 1 (spring 1983), p. 134; for a slightly different version of this essay see '"On the hem of life": race, class, and the prospects for sisterhood', in Amy Swerdlow and Hanna Lessinger (eds), *Class, Race, and Sex: the Dynamics of Control* (Boston, Hall, 1983); Margaret Simons, 'Racism and feminism: a schism in the sisterhood', *Feminist Studies*, 5, 2 (summer 1979), p. 392.

6   Adrienne Rich, in *On Lies, Secrets, and Silence* (New York, Norton, 1979), pp. 302–3, notes that while blacks link their experience of racism with the white woman, this is still patriarchal racism working through her. It is possible, she says, that 'a black first grader, or that child's mother, or a black patient in a hospital, or a family on welfare, may experience racism most directly in the person of a white woman, who stands for those service professions through which white male supremacist society controls the mother, the child, the family, and all of us. It is *her* racism, yes, but a racism learned in the same patriarchal school which taught her that women are unimportant or unequal, not to be trusted with power, where she learned to mistrust and hear her own impulses for rebellion; to become an instrument.'

7   Gloria Joseph, 'The incompatible menage à trois: marxism, feminism and racism', in Lydia Sargent (ed.), *Women and Revolution* (Boston, South End Press, 1981), p. 96; The Combahee River Collective, 'Combahee River Collective Statement', in Barbara Smith (ed.), *Home Girls* (New York, Kitchen Table Press, 1983), p. 275, compares their alliance with black men with the negative identification white women have with white men: 'Our situation as Black people necessitates that we have solidarity around the fact of race, which white women of course do not need to have with white men, unless it is their negative solidarity as racial oppressors. We struggle together with Black men against racism, while we struggle with Black men about sexism.'

8   Combahee River Collective 'Statement', p. 272.

9   Michèle Barrett, *Women's Oppression Today* (London, Verso, 1981), p. 15.

10   For a comparison between radical feminism, liberal feminism, Marxist and socialist feminism, see Alison Jaggar, *Feminist Politics and Human Nature* (Sussex, Harvester 1983).

11   Sheila Rowbotham, 'The trouble with patriarchy', in Raphael Samuel (ed.), *People's History and Socialist Theory* (London and Boston, Routledge and Kegan Paul, 1981), p. 365.

12   Frantz Fanon, *Black Skin, White Masks*, trans. Charles Lam Markmann (Paris, 1952; repr. New York, Grove Press, 1967) p. 161.

13   Simons, 'Racism and feminism', p. 387.

14   Barbara Omolade, 'Hearts of darkness', in Ann Snitow, Christine Stansell, and Sharon Thompson (eds), *Powers of Desire* (New York, Monthly Review Press, 1983), p. 352.

15   Nancy Hall-Duncan, *The History of Fashion Photography* (New York, Alpine Books, 1979), p. 196.

16   Stephen Birmingham, *Certain People* (Boston and Toronto, Little, Brown, 1977), pp. 262–3.

17   Manning Marable, in *How Capitalism Underdeveloped Black America* (Boston, South End Press, 1983), p. 157, lists Motown Industries as the largest grossing black-owned corporation in the US which did 64.8 million dollars in business in 1979.

18   Simon Frith, *Sound Effects* (New York, Pantheon, 1981), p. 264.

28

Sexuality in the field of vision   **Jacqueline Rose**

Freud often related the question of sexuality to that of visual representation. Describing the child's difficult journey into adult sexual life, he would take as his model little scenarios, or the staging of events, which demonstrated the complexity of an essentially visual space, moments in which perception *founders* (the boy child refuses to believe the anatomical difference that he sees)[1] or in which pleasure in looking tips over into the register of *excess* (witness to a sexual act in which he reads his own destiny, the child tries to interrupt by calling attention to his presence).[2] Each time the stress falls on a problem of seeing. The sexuality lies less in the content of what is seen than in the subjectivity of the viewer, in the relationship between what is looked at and the developing sexual knowledge of the child. The relationship between viewer and scene is always one of fracture, partial identification, pleasure and distrust. As if Freud found the aptest analogy for the problem of our identity as human subjects in failures of vision or in the violence which can be done to an image as it offers itself to view. For Freud, with an emphasis that has been picked up and placed at the centre of the work of Jacques Lacan, our sexual identities as male or female, our confidence in language as true or false, and our security in the image we judge as perfect or flawed, are fantasies. And these archaic moments of disturbed visual representation, these troubled scenes, which expressed and unsettled our groping knowledge in the past, can now be used as theoretical prototypes to unsettle our certainties once again. Hence one of the chief drives of an art which today addresses the presence of the sexual in representation – to expose the fixed nature of sexual identity as a fantasy and, in the same gesture, to trouble, break up, or rupture the visual field before our eyes.

This chapter, is from *Sexuality in the Field of Vision* (London, Verso, 1986).

The encounter between psychoanalysis and artistic practice is therefore *staged*, but only in so far as that staging has *already taken place*. It is an encounter which draws its strength from that repetition, working like a memory trace of something we have been through before. It gives back to repetition its proper meaning and status: not lack of originality or something merely derived (the commonest reproach to the work of art), nor the more recent practice of appropriating artistic and photographic images in order to undermine their previous status; but repetition as insistence, that is, as the constant pressure of something hidden but not forgotten – something that can only come into focus now by blurring the field of representation where our normal forms of self-recognition take place. . . .

Artists engaged in sexual representation (representation *as* sexual) come in at precisely this point, calling up the sexual component of the image, drawing out an emphasis that exists *in potentia* in the various instances they inherit and of which they form a part.[3] Their move is not therefore one of (moral) corrective. They draw on the tendencies they also seek to displace, and clearly belong, for example, within the context of that postmodernism which demands that reference, in its problematised form, re-enter the frame. But the emphasis on sexuality produces specific effects. First, it adds to the concept of cultural artefact or stereotype the political imperative of feminism which holds the image accountable for the reproduction of norms. Secondly, to this feminist demand for scrutiny of the image, it adds the idea of a sexuality which goes beyond the issue of content to take in the parameters of visual form (not just what we see but how we see – visual space as more than the domain of simple recognition). The image therefore submits to the sexual reference, but only in so far as reference itself is questioned by the work of the image. And the aesthetics of pure form are implicated in the less pure pleasures of looking, but these in turn are part of an aesthetically extraneous political space. The arena is simultaneously that of aesthetics and sexuality, and art and sexual politics. The link between sexuality and the image produces a particular dialogue which cannot be covered adequately by the familiar opposition between the formal operations of the image and a politics exerted from outside.

The engagement with the image therefore belongs to a political intention. It is an intention which has also inflected the psychoanalytic and literary theories on which such artists draw. The model is not one of applying psychoanalysis to the work of art (what application could there finally be which does not reduce one field to the other or inhibit by interpretation the potential meaning of both?). Psychoanalysis offers a specific account of sexual difference but its value (and also its difficulty) for feminism lies in the place assigned to the woman in that differentiation. In his essay on Leonardo, Freud himself says that once the boy child sees what it is to be a woman, he will 'tremble for his masculinity' henceforth.[4] If meaning oscillates when a castrato comes onto the scene, our sense must be that it is in the normal image of the man that our certainties are invested and, by implication, in that of the woman that they constantly threaten collapse.

A feminism concerned with the question of looking can therefore turn this theory around and stress the particular and limiting opposition of male and female which any image seen to be flawless is serving to hold in place. More simply, we know that women are meant to *look* perfect, presenting a seamless image to the world so that the man, in that confrontation with difference, can avoid any apprehension of lack. The position of woman as fantasy therefore depends on a particular economy of vision (the importance of 'images of women' might take on its fullest meaning from this).[5] Perhaps this is also why only a project which comes via feminism can demand so unequivocally of the image that it renounce all pretensions to a narcissistic perfection of form.

At the extreme edge of this investigation, we might argue that the fantasy of absolute sexual difference, in its present guise, could be upheld only from the point when painting restricted the human body to the eye.[6] That would be to give the history of the image in Western culture a particularly heavy weight to bear. For, even if the visual image has indeed been one of the chief vehicles through which such a restriction has been enforced, it could only operate like a law which always produces the terms of its own violation. It is often forgotten that psychoanalysis describes the psychic law to which we are subject, but only in terms of its *failing*. This is important for a feminist (or any radical) practice which has often felt it necessary to claim for itself a wholly other psychic and representational domain. Therefore, if the visual image in its aesthetically acclaimed form serves to maintain a particular and oppressive mode of sexual recognition, it does so only partially and at a cost. Our previous history is not the petrified block of a singular visual space since, looked at obliquely, it can always be seen to contain its moments of unease.[7] We can surely relinquish the monolithic view of that history, if doing so allows us a form of resistance which can be articulated *on this side of* (rather than beyond) the world against which it protests.

Among Leonardo's early sketches, Freud discovers the heads of laughing women, images of exuberance which then fall out of the great canon of his art. Like Leonardo's picture of the sexual act, these images appear to unsettle Freud as if their pleasure somehow correlated with the discomfort of the sexual drawing (the sexual drawing through its failure, the heads of laughing women for their excess). These images, not well known in Leonardo's canon, now have the status of fragments, but they indicate a truth about the tradition which excludes them, revealing the presence of something strangely insistent to which these artists return. 'Teste di femmine, che ridono'[8] – laughter is not the emphasis here, but the urgent engagement with the question of sexuality persists now, as it did them. It can no more be seen as the beginning, than it should be the end, of the matter.

Notes

1   Sigmund Freud, (1925) 'Some physical consequences of the anatomical distinction between the sexes, *The Standard Edition of the Complete Psychological Works*, vol. XXIV (London, Hogarth Press, 1955–74), 252, 335–6.

2   Sigmund Freud, *From the History of an Infantile Neurosis* (1918), *The Standard Edition of the Complete Psychological Works*, vol. XVII (London, Hogarth Press, 1955–74), 29–47; 80–1.

3   For a discussion of some of these issues in relation to feminist art, see Mary Kelly, 'Reviewing modernist criticism', *Screen*, 22, 3 (autumn 1981).

4   'Leonardo da Vinci and a memory of his childhood' (1910), *Standard Edition*, vol. II: 95, 186–7.

5   The status of the woman as fantasy in relation to the desire of the man was a central concern of Lacan's later writing; see *Encore*, especially 'God and the jouissance of woman' and 'A love letter' in *Feminine Sexuality: Jacques Lacan and the École Freudienne*, ed. Juliet Mitchell and Jacqueline Rose (London, Macmillan, 1982).

6   Norman Bryson describes post-Albertian perspective in terms of such a restriction in *Vision and Painting: the Logic of the Gaze* (London, Macmillan, 1983).

7   See Lacan on death in Holbein's 'The Ambassadors', *The Four Fundamental Concepts of Psycho-Analysis*, trans. Alan Sheridan, ed. Jacques-Alain Miller (New York, Norton, 1978) pp. 85–90.

8   'Leonardo da Vinci and a memory of his childhood', *Standard Edition*, vol. II, 203. An exhibition entitled 'The Revolutionary Power of Women's Laughter', including works by Barbara Kruger and Mary Kelly, was held at Protetch McNeil, New York, January 1983.

G

'Seeing' racial difference

29

The fact of blackness   **Frantz Fanon**

'Dirty nigger!' Or simply, 'Look, a Negro!'

I came into the world imbued with the will to find a meaning in things, my spirit filled with the desire to attain to the source of the world, and then I found that I was an object in the midst of other objects.

Sealed into that crushing objecthood, I turned beseechingly to others. Their attention was a liberation, running over my body suddenly abraded into nonbeing, endowing me once more with an agility that I had thought lost, and by taking me out of the world, restoring me to it. But just as I reached the other side, I stumbled, and the movements, the attitudes, the glances of the other fixed me there, in the sense in which a chemical solution is fixed by a dye. I was indignant; I demanded an explanation. Nothing happened. I burst apart. Now the fragments have been put together again by another self.

As long as the black man is among his own, he will have no occasion, except in minor internal conflicts, to experience his being through others. There is of course the moment of 'being for others', of which Hegel speaks, but every ontology is made unattainable in a colonized and civilized society. It would seem that this fact has not been given sufficient attention by those who have discussed the question. In the *Weltanschauung* of a colonized people there is an impurity, a flaw that outlaws any ontological explanation. Someone may object that this is the case with every individual, but such an objection merely conceals a basic problem. Ontology – one it is finally admitted as leaving existence by the wayside – does not permit us to understand the being of the black man. For not only must the black man be black; he must be black in relation to the white man. Some critics will take it on themselves to remind us that this proposition has a converse. I say that this is false. The black man has no ontological resistance in the eyes of the white man. Overnight the

This chapter, originally published in 1967, is taken from Frantz Fanon, *Black Skin, White Masks* (New York, Grove Press, 1986), pp. 109–140.

Negro has been given two frames of reference within which he has had to place himself. His metaphysics, or, less pretentiously, his customs and the sources on which they were based, were wiped out because they were in conflict with a civilization that he did not know and that imposed itself on him.

The black man among his own in the twentieth century does not know at what moment his inferiority comes into being through the other. Of course I have talked about the black problem with friends, or, more rarely, with American Negroes. Together we protested, we asserted the equality of all men in the world. In the Antilles there was also that little gulf that exists among the almost-white, the mulatto, and the nigger. But I was satisfied with an intellectual understanding of these differences. It was not really dramatic. And then. . . .

And then the occasion arose when I had to meet the white man's eyes. An unfamiliar weight burdened me. The real world challenged my claims. In the white world the man of color encounters difficulties in the development of his bodily schema. Consciousness of the body is solely a negating activity. It is a third-person consciousness. The body is surrounded by an atmosphere of certain uncertainty. I know that if I want to smoke, I shall have to reach out my right arm and take the pack of cigarettes lying at the other end of the table. The matches, however, are in the drawer on the left, and I shall have to lean back slightly. And all these movements are made not out of habit but out of implicit knowledge. A slow composition of my *self* as a body in the middle of a spatial and temporal world – such seems to be the schema. It does not impose itself on me; it is, rather, a definitive structuring of the self and of the world – definitive because it creates a real dialectic between my body and the world.

For several years certain laboratories have been trying to produce a serum for 'denegrification'; with all the earnestness in the world, laboratories have sterilized their test tubes, checked their scales, and embarked on researches that might make it possible for the miserable Negro to whiten himself and thus to throw off the burden of that corporeal malediction. Below the corporeal schema I had sketched a historico-racial schema. The elements that I used had been provided for me not by 'residual sensations and perceptions primarily of a tactile, vestibular, kinesthetic, and visual character',[1] but by the other, the white man, who had woven me out of a thousand details, anecdotes, stories. I thought that what I had in hand was to construct a physiological self, to balance space, to localize sensations, and here I was called on for more.

'Look, a Negro!' It was an external stimulus that flicked over me as I passed by. I made a tight smile.

'Look, a Negro!' It was true. It amused me.

'Look, a Negro!' The circle was drawing a bit tighter. I made no secret of my amusement.

'Mama, see the Negro! I'm frightened!' Frightened! Frightened! Now they were beginning to be afraid of me. I made up my mind to laugh myself to tears, but laughter had become impossible.

I could no longer laugh, because I already knew that there were legends, stories, history, and above all *historicity*, which I had learned about from Jaspers. Then, assailed at various points, the corporeal schema crumbled, its place taken by a racial epidermal schema. In the train it was no longer a question of being aware of my body in the third person but in a triple person. In the train I was given not one but two, three places. I had already stopped being amused. It was not that I was finding febrile coordinates in the world. I existed triply: I occupied space. I moved towards the other – and the evanescent other, hostile but not opaque, transparent, not there, disappeared. Nausea. . . .

I was responsible at the same time for my body, for my race, for my ancestors. I subjected myself to an objective examination, I discovered my blackness, my ethnic characteristics; and I was battered down by tom-toms, cannibalism, intellectual deficiency, fetichism, racial defects, slave-ships, and above all else, above all: 'Sho' good eatin'.'

On that day, completely dislocated, unable to be abroad with the other, the white man, who unmercifully imprisoned me, I took myself far off from my own presence, far indeed, and made myself an object. What else could it be for me but an amputation, an excision, a hemorrhage that spattered my whole body with black blood? But I did not want this revision, this thematization. All I wanted was to be a man among other men. I wanted to come lithe and young into a world that was ours and to help to build it together.

[. . .]

'Look at the nigger! . . . Mama, a Negro! . . . Hell, he's getting mad. . . . Take no notice, sir, he does not know that you are as civilized as we. . . .'

My body was given back to me sprawled out, distorted, recolored, clad in mourning in that white winter day. The Negro is an animal, the Negro is bad, the Negro is mean, the Negro is ugly; look, a nigger, it's cold, the nigger is shivering, the nigger is shivering because he is cold, the little boy is trembling because he is afraid of the nigger, the nigger is shivering with cold, that cold that goes through your bones, the handsome little boy is trembling because he thinks that the nigger is quivering with rage, the little white boy throws himself into his mother's arms: Mama, the nigger's going to eat me up.

All round me the white man, above the sky tears at its navel, the earth rasps under my feet, and there is a white song, a white song. All this whiteness that burns me. . . .

[. . .]

In *Anti-Semite and Jew*, Sartre says: 'They [the Jews] have allowed themselves to be poisoned by the stereotype that others have of them, and they live in fear that their acts will correspond to this stereotype. . . . We may say that their conduct is perpetually overdetermined from the inside.'[2]

All the same, the Jew can be unknown in his Jewishness. He is not wholly what he is. One hopes, one waits. His actions, his behavior are the final determinant. He is a white man, and, apart from some rather debatable characteristics, he can sometimes go unnoticed. He belongs to the race of those who since the beginning of time have never known cannibalism. What an idea, to eat one's father! Simple enough, one has only not to be a nigger. Granted, the Jews are harassed – what am I thinking of? They are hunted down, exterminated, cremated. But these are little family quarrels. The Jew is disliked from the moment he is tracked down. But in my case everything takes on a *new* guise. I am given no chance. I am overdetermined from without. I am the slave not of the 'idea' that others have of me but of my own appearance.

I move slowly in the world, accustomed now to seek no longer for upheaval. I progress by crawling. And already I am being dissected under white eyes, the only real eyes. I am *fixed*. Having adjusted their microtomes, they objectively cut away slices of my reality. I am laid bare. I feel, I see in those white faces that it is not a new man who has come in, but a new kind of man, a new genus. Why, it's a Negro! [. . .]

Notes

1   Jean Lhermitte, *L'Image de notre corps* (Paris, Nouvelle Revue critique, 1939), p. 17.
2   J.-P. Sartre, *Anti-Semite and Jew* (New York, Schocken, 1948), p. 95.

Alexander von Humboldt and the reinvention of America
Mary Louise Pratt

[. . .]

You are interested in botany? So is my wife.

Napoleon's (only) words to Alexander von Humboldt, (1805)

It was an intricate social fabric and a critical historical juncture into which Alexander von Humboldt and Aimé Bonpland set foot when they arrived in South America in 1799. For the five eventful years that followed, they participated in that moment as they made their way around what they liked to call the New Continent. Their historic journey, and the monument of print it produced, laid down the lines for the ideological reinvention of South America that took place on both sides of the Atlantic during the momentous first decades of the nineteenth century. For thirty years, while popular uprisings, foreign invasions, and wars of independence convulsed Spanish America, Alexander von Humboldt's vast writings on his equinoctial travels flowed in a steady stream from Paris, reaching thirty volumes in as many years. At a time when loosening travel restrictions began sending European travelers to South America by the dozen, Humboldt remained the single most influential interlocutor in the process of reimagining and redefinition that coincided with Spanish America's independence from Spain. Humboldt was, and still is, considered 'the most creative explorer of his time'; his American travels were regarded as 'a model journey of exploration and a supreme geographical achievement.[1] [. . .]

[. . .]

This Chapter is taken from Mary Louise Pratt, *Imperial Eyes* (London, Routledge, 1992), pp. 111–143.

The two partners sailed (in a vessel called the *Pizarro*, no less) to Venezuela in 1799. They spent over a year there traveling up and down the Orinoco, across the great plains (the *llanos*), up mountains, down rivers, through jungles, from village to village, hacienda to hacienda, mission to mission, measuring, collecting, experimenting, sketching, writing it all down. On the Orinoco they were able to witness and report in detail on the preparation of curare poison, a subject on which there was great curiosity in Europe. By personally traveling the interior waterway that joins the Orinoco and the Amazon, Humboldt and Bonpland definitively confirmed its existence for European doubters. (Non-doubters had been using it for decades as a mail route.) It was here too that local inhabitants demonstrated to them the wonders of the electric eel. Laden with immense collections of specimens and plants, they moved on to Havana early in 1802, but almost immediately heard that a French expedition round the world was expected to stop in Peru. Hoping to join it, they returned to South America. The *System of Nature* continued to unify the planet: Humboldt and Bonpland decided to travel to Peru by land rather than by sea, in order to pass through Bogotá and share notes with the Linnaean naturalist José Celestino Mutis. They spent two months with him and his collections. Crossing the Cordillera, they arrived in Quito, where they spent another six months. Their stay was marked by the feat which more than any other captured the public imagination in Europe when word of it reached the papers a few months later: the attempt to scale the Andean peak Chimborazo, then believed to be the highest mountain in the world. Dressed in a frock coat and button boots and accompanied by a small party, Humboldt came within 400 metres of the 6,300-meter summit before turning back because of cold and want of oxygen. In late 1802 his expedition reached Lima, already aware that the French rendezvous would not materialize. Instead they sailed for Mexico, where they spent another year, mainly researching in a wealth of Mexican archives, libraries, and botanical gardens never before open to non-Spaniards. They made a brief visit to the United States, where Humboldt was befriended by Thomas Jefferson. In August of 1804 they returned to Paris to a hero's welcome from a public which, off and on, had followed their feats through their letters, and in between, had imagined them both dead.

Like La Condamine, and perhaps following his example, Humboldt set out immediately to capitalize on his travels in the interlocking Parisian worlds of high society, science, and officialdom. Within weeks of his return, he set up a botanical exhibition at the Jardin des Plantes. While Bonpland faded into the background, and eventually disappeared back into the contact zone, Humboldt became a continental celebrity. The hunger for firsthand information on South America was widespread and intense, and Humboldt had made himself a walking encyclopedia. He gave lectures, organized meetings, wrote letters by the hundred, visited dignitaries, held forth tirelessly (and, for some, tiresomely) in salons. Meanwhile, he set teams of annotators and illustrators to work converting his collections and his notes into books.

Books! Humboldt's authorial ambitions were on the same epic scale as his travels. During the course of his American journey, he had often busied himself sketching out plans for the vast monument of print his voyage would produce. Spanish America, in Northern Europe, was a virtual *carte blanche* which Humboldt seemed determined to fill completely with his writings, drawings, and maps. He took to unprecedented lengths the encyclopedic impulse which in the case of the French expedition to Egypt would produce the twenty-four-volume *Description de l'Egypte*. For one present-day admirer, Humboldt's textual ambitions amounted to 'an incredible, almost maniacal addiction to papers, registers and annotations . . . a cultural hypochondria.'[2] Nothing could be more distant from the mansized aspirations of the sentimental storytellers than the thirty-volume *Travels to the Equinoctial Regions of the New Continent in 1799, 1800, 1801, 1802, 1803, and 1804*, all published in Paris and in French, and much of it attributed jointly to Humboldt and Bonpland. [. . .] In all, the *Travels* includes sixteen volumes of botany and plant geography, two of zoology, two of astronomical and barometric measurements, seven of geographical and geopolitical description (including the famed *Political Essay on the Kingdom of New Spain*), and three of travel narrative *per se*. An experimenter with form, Humboldt specialized not only in print but graphics as well, at great expense to himself. His visual innovations set new standards for the use of charts, graphs, and tables. In his non-specialized works the engravings of archeological and natural phenomena are still breathtaking (see figures 30.1–30.4).

It was through his non-specialized writings rather than his scientific treatises that Humboldt sought, and won, his broadest impact on the public imaginations of Europe and Euroamerica. [. . .] These above all were the books that continental and Spanish American reading publics were reading, reviewing, excerpting, and discussing in the 1810s and 1820s. Travel writings in the immediate sense, these non-specialized works are also bold discursive experiments in which, as I will argue, Humboldt sought to reinvent popular imaginings of America, and through America, of the planet itself. Even as he undertook to recreate South America in connection with its new opening to Northern Europe, Humboldt sought simultaneously to reframe bourgeois subjectivity, heading off its sundering of objectivist and subjectivist strategies, science and sentiment, information and experience. Along with others of his time, he proposed to Europeans a new kind of planetary consciousness. [. . .]

'Wild and gigantic nature'

As the titles of his writings suggest, Alexander von Humboldt reinvented South America first and foremost as nature. Not the accessible, collectable, recognizable, categorizable nature of the Linnaeans, however, but a dramatic, extraordinary nature, a spectacle capable of overwhelming human knowledge and understanding. Not a nature that sits waiting to be known and possessed, but a nature in motion, powered by life forces many of which are invisible to the human eye; a nature that dwarfs humans, commands their being, arouses their passions, defies their powers of perception. No wonder portraits so often depict Humboldt engulfed and miniaturized either by nature or by the own library describing it.

MARY LOUISE PRATT   **423**

Figure 30.1

*Natural bridges of
Icononzo* (from
Humboldt's *Views of
the Cordilleras and
Monuments of the
Indigenous Peoples
of America*, trans.
Helen Maria Williams,
London, Longman,
1814)

Natural Bridges of Icononzo.

Pub.d by Longman, Hurst, Rees, Orme & Brown. Aug.t 1, 1814.

Figure 30.2

Statue of an Aztec priestess (from Humboldt's Views of the Cordilleras and Monuments of the Indigenous Peoples of America, trans. Helen Maria Williams, London, Longman, 1814)

Statue of an Aztech Priestess.

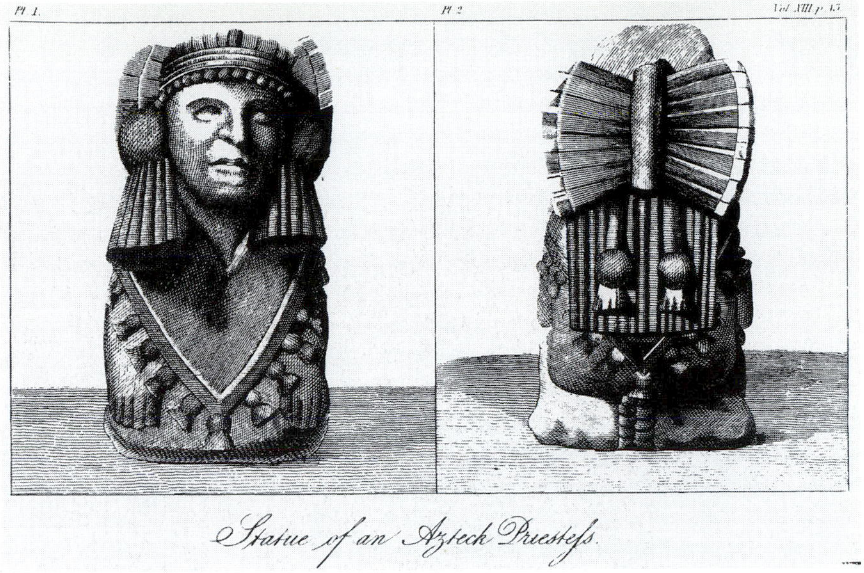

Figure 30.3

Aztec hieroglyphic manuscript found by Humboldt in the Vatican (from Humboldt's Views of the Cordilleras and Monuments of the Indigenous Peoples of America, trans. Helen Maria Williams, London, Longman, 1814)

So engulfed and miniaturized was the human in Humboldt's cosmic conception that narrative ceased to be a viable mode of representation for him. He deliberately avoided it. His first non-specialized writings on the Americas took the form of descriptive and analytical essays prepared as lectures. *Views of Nature*, which first appeared in 1808 in German as *Ansichten der Natur* and in French as *Tableaux de la nature*, began as a series of widely acclaimed public lectures given in Berlin in 1806. It was followed by the lavishly illustrated *Views of the Cordilleras and Monuments of the Indigenous Peoples of America* in 1810. The 'view' or tableau was the form Humboldt chose for his experiments in what he called 'the esthetic mode of treating subjects of natural history'. His were innovative attempts to correct what he saw as the failings of travel writing in his time: on the one hand, a trivializing preoccupation with what he called 'the merely personal', and, on the other, an accumulation of scientific detail that was spiritually and esthetically deadening. Humboldt's solution in his *Views* was to fuse the specificity of science with the esthetics of the sublime. The vividness of esthetic description, he was convinced, would be complemented and

intensified by science's revelations of the 'occult forces' that made Nature work. The result, in the words of one literary historian, 'introduced into German literature an entirely new type of nature discourse'.[3]

Humboldt's discursive experimentation is well illustrated by the famous opening essay in *Views of Nature*, titled 'On Steppes and Deserts'. It departs, as many of the 'views' do, from the perspective of a hypothetical traveler, the vestige of a narrative persona. In this instance, the abstract (yet thoroughly European, and male) persona turns his eyes away from the cultivated coastal zone of Venezuela toward the *llanos* or great plains of the interior. In the following excerpt, notice the interweaving of visual and emotive language with classificatory and technical language, and the deliberate orchestration of the reader's response:

Figure 30.4

Frontispiece of Humboldt's Atlas of America *(the allegory depicts a defeated Aztec warrior prince being consoled by Athena, goddess of wisdom, and Hermes, god of trade. At the bottom lies a smashed statue. In the background stands a mountain modelled on Chimborazo and the pyramid of Chulula in Ecuador in Mexico. The caption reads 'Humanity, Knowledge, Economy')*

At the foot of the lofty granitic range which, in the early ages of our planet, resisted the irruption of the waters on the formation of the Caribbean Gulf, extends a vast and boundless plain. When the traveller turns from the Alpine valleys of Caracas, and the island-studded lake of Tacarigua, whose waters reflect the forms of the neighboring bananas, – when he leaves the fields verdant with the light and tender green of the Tahitian sugar cane, or the somber shade of the cacao groves, – his eye rests in the south on Steppes, whose seeming elevations disappear in the distant horizon.

From the rich luxuriance of organic life the astonished traveller suddenly finds himself on the drear margin of a treeless waste.[4]

Having produced his reader's desolation, Humboldt sets about alleviating it, filling the wasteland (stretched before us, like the naked stony crust of some desolate planet) with dense and powerful meaning. Displaying his own brand of planetary consciousness, he compares the Venezuelan *llanos* to the heaths of Northern Europe, the interior plains of Africa, the steppes of central Asia. Pages of analytical, often statistical, description ensue, but in a language that is also filled with drama, struggle, and a certain sensuality. In the following rather lengthy excerpt, for instance, Humboldt undertakes to explain why South America is less hot and dry than lands at similar latitudes elsewhere. The passage is not narrative; not a single animate being appears. Yet the prose is so action-packed as to promote exhaustion. Readers should imagine it being delivered as a lecture (my italics):

The narrowness of this extensively indented continent in the northern part of the tropics, where the fluid basis on which the atmosphere rests, occasions the ascent of a less warm current of air; its *wide* extensions towards both the *icy* poles; a *broad* ocean *swept* by cool tropical winds; the flatness of the eastern shores; currents of cold sea-water from the antarctic region, which, at first following a direction from south-west to north-east, *strike* the coast of Chili below the parallel of 35° south lat., and *advance* as far north on the coasts of Peru as Cape Parina, where they *suddenly diverge* toward the west; the numerous mountains *abounding* in springs, whose snow-crowned summits *soar* above the strata of clouds, and cause the *descent* of currents of air down their declivities; the *abundance* of rivers of *enormous* breadth, which after many windings invariably seek the *most distant* coast; Steppes, *devoid* of sand, and therefore less readily acquiring heat; *impenetrable* forests, which, protecting the earth from the sun's rays, or radiating heat from the surface of their leaves, cover the *richly-watered* plains of the Equator and *exhale* into the interior of the country, *most remote* from mountains and the Ocean, *prodigious* quantities of moisture, partly absorbed and partly generated. . . . On these *alone* depend the *luxuriance* and *exuberant* vegetation and that *richness* of foliage which are so peculiarly characteristic of the New Continent.[5]

Here is a prose that fatigues not by flatness or tedium, as the Linnaeans sometimes did, but by a dramatic and arhythmic ebb and flow that would have been intensified by oral delivery. An 'ascent' of 'less warm' air flashes to 'wide extensions' at 'icy poles'; a 'broad ocean' to a continent's 'flat shores'; cold water, like an unwelcome invader of the tropics, strikes, advances, suddenly turns; mountains abound, soar; rivers are enormous, abundant, aggressively seeking coasts; forests are impenetrable, and humming with invisible activity as they protect, radiate, cover, exhale, absorb, generate. One thinks of a camera that is continually both moving and shifting focus – except that the visual actually plays almost no role in the description. Humboldt invokes here not a system of nature anchored in the visible, but an endless expansion and contraction of invisible forces. In this respect his discourse contrasts markedly with that of his Linnaean predecessors. Humboldt drew the contrast himself in a letter written the night before he left on his American journey. While he would be collecting plants and fossils and making astronomical observations, he wrote a friend in Salzburg, 'none of this is the main purpose of my expedition. My eyes will always be directed to the combination of forces, to the influence of the inanimate creation on the animate world of animals and plants, to this harmony.[6] Certainly Humboldt was looking for what he found in the new continent, and found what he was looking for. His goal as a scientist became his goal as a writer. In the preface to *Views of Nature* he declares his aim is to reproduce 'the enjoyment which a sensitive mind receives from the immediate contemplation of nature . . . heightened by an insight into the connection of the occult forces'. Without such insight, 'the wonderful luxuriance of nature' reduces simply to 'an accumulation of separate images', lacking 'the harmony and effect of a picture'.[7]

As all his commentators have noted, Humboldt's emphasis on harmonies and occult forces aligns him with the spiritualist esthetics of Romanticism. It also aligns him with industrialism and the machine age, however, and with the developments in the sciences that were producing and being produced by that age. (Indeed, there was perhaps no clearer intersection of 'inanimate creation' and 'the animate world of plants and animals' than the mining industry in which Humboldt had worked for many years and which was one of Europe's main objects of interest in the Americas.) Other writers have discussed Humboldt's work in relation to European scientific debates of his time. I am approaching his writings from an entirely different angle, looking at their ideological dimensions and their relations to the literature of travel.

In contrast with [other contemporary] ego-centered sentimental narratives [. . .] may of which he had certainly read, Humboldt sought to pry affect away from autobiography and narcissism and fuse it with science. His goal, he says in the preface to *Views of Nature*, is to reproduce in the reader 'Nature's ancient communion with the spiritual life of man'. The equatorial world is a privileged site for such an exercise: 'Nowhere', says Humboldt, 'does she [Nature] more deeply impress us with a sense of her greatness, nowhere does she speak to us more forcibly.'[8]

Though sharing the basic structure of the scientific anti-conquest, then, Humboldt's brand of planetary consciousness makes claims for science and for 'Man' considerably more grandiose than those of the plant classifiers who preceded him. Compared with the humble, discipular herborizer, Humboldt assumes a godlike, omniscient stance over both the planet and his reader. For of course it is most immediately he rather than Nature who undertakes to 'impress', to 'speak to us forcibly'. Virtuoso-like, he plays on elaborate sensibilities he presupposed in his audience. The main sensory images above, for example, are unpredictable blasts of cold – the last thing a northerner expects or desires in the imagined torrid zone. (How fitting for that frigid current running up the Pacific to bear Humboldt's name.)

[. . .] In contrast with strictly scientific writing, the authority of the discourse here plainly does not lie in a totalizing descriptive project that lives outside the text. Here, the totalizing project lives *in* the text, orchestrated by the infinitely expansive mind and soul of the speaker. What is shared with scientific travel writing, however, is the erasure of the human. The description just quoted presents a landscape imbued with social fantasies – of harmony, industry, liberty, unalienated *joie de vivre* – all projected onto the non-human world. Traces of human history, unidentified, are there: the horse and oxen arrived through a force no less occult than the invading Spanish. But the human inhabitants of the *llanos* are absent. The only 'person' mentioned in these 'melancholy and sacred solitudes' is the hypothetical and invisible European traveler himself.

Views of Nature was a very popular book, and one that seems to have mattered a great deal to Humboldt. Long after he abandoned his *Personal Narrative*, he revised and expanded *Views of Nature* twice, in 1826 and again in 1849. He was right to care about it. From Humboldt's

Views of Nature and its sequel *Views of the Cordilleras*, European and South American reading publics selected the basic repertoire of images that came to signify 'South America' during the momentous transition period of 1810–50. Three images in particular, all canonized by Humboldt's *Views*, combined to form the standard metonymic representation of the 'new continent': superabundant tropical forests (the Amazon and the Orinoco), snow-capped mountains (the Andean Cordillera and the volcanos of Mexico), and vast interior plains (the Venezuelan *llanos* and the Argentine pampas). Humboldt singled out this canonical triad himself in the last edition of *View of Nature*, which he introduced as 'a series of papers which originated in the presence of the noblest objects of nature – on the Ocean, – in the forests of the Orinoco, – in the savannahs of Venezuela, – and in the solitudes of the Peruvian and Mexican mountains'.[9]

In point of fact, it took a highly selective reception of Humboldt's writings to reduce South America to pure nature and the iconic triad of mountains, plain, and jungle. I will be referring below to some of the other ways in which Humboldt wrote and thought about South America, notably archeological and demographic ones. But it was unquestionably the image of primal nature elaborated in his scientific works and his *Views* that became codified in the European imaginary as the new ideology of the 'new continent'. Why? For one thing, the ideology, like the continent, was precisely not new. Nineteenth-century Europeans *re*invented America as Nature in part because that is how sixteenth- and seventeenth-century Europeans had invented America for themselves in the first place, and for many of the same reasons. Though deeply rooted in eighteenth-century constructions of Nature and Man, Humboldt's seeing-man is also a self-conscious double of the first European inventors of America, Columbus, Vespucci, Raleigh, and the others. They, too, wrote America as a primal world of nature, an unclaimed and timeless space occupied by plants and creatures (some of them human), but not organized by societies and economies; a world whose only history was the one about to begin. Their writings too portrayed America in a discourse of accumulation, abundance, and innocence. Humboldt's rhapsodic invocation of a flourishing primal world echoes such writings as Columbus' famous letter to the Spanish monarchs in 1493:

> All these islands are very beautiful, and distinguished by a diversity of scenery; they are filled with a great variety of trees of immense height, and which I believe to retain their foliage in all seasons; for when I saw them they were as verdant and luxuriant, as they usually are in Spain in the Month of May. . . . There are besides in the same island of Juana seven or eight kinds of palm trees, which, like all the other trees, herbs, and fruits, considerably surpass ours in height and beauty. The pines also are very handsome, and there are very extensive fields and meadows, a variety of birds, different kinds of honey, and many sorts of metals, but no iron.[10]

In Humboldt's writings, Columbus turns up from time to time in person. In *Views of Nature*, for example, the essay on the Cataracts of the Orinoco replays Columbus' famous encounter with the Orinoco River on his third voyage to America.

[. . .]

The point is not to argue that Humboldt's representations were somehow implausible or lacking in verisimilitude. I do want to argue, however, that they were not inevitable, that their contours were conditioned by a particular historical and ideological juncture, and by particular relations of power and privilege. South America didn't *have* to be invented or reinvented as primal nature. Despite the emphasis on primal nature, in all their explorations, Humboldt and Bonpland never once stepped beyond the boundaries of the Spanish colonial infrastructure – they couldn't, for they relied entirely on the networks of villages, missions, outposts, haciendas, roadways, and colonial labor systems to sustain themselves and their project, for food, shelter, and the labor pool to guide them and transport their immense equipage. Even the canonical images of interior plains, snow-capped mountains, and dense jungles did not lie outside the history of humankind, or even the history of Euroimperialism. The inhabitants of the Venezuelan *llanos* and the Argentine pampas, however removed from colonial centers, were about to be recruited as soldiers in the wars of independence. The jungle had been penetrated by the colonial mission system, whose influence extended far beyond the microcosmic social orders of its outposts. The Andean Cordillera (Humboldt's 'mountain solitudes') was also the living place for most of the inhabitants of Peru, among whom pre-Columbian lifeways and colonial resistance continued to be powerful everyday realities. Historically, it was also the great mother lode of colonial mineral wealth. Humboldt's ecological depiction of Mount Chimborazo (see figure 30.5) contrasts intriguingly with indigenous Andean representations of another famous peak, the Cerro de Potosi, where the Virgin of Copacabana presided over the biggest silver mine in the world (see figure 30.6).

[. . .]

[. . .] What hand did Humboldt's American interlocutors have directly and otherwise, in the European reinvention of their continent? To what extent was Humboldt a transculturator, transporting to Europe knowledges American in origin; producing European knowledges infiltrated by non-European ones? To what extent, within relations of colonial subordination, did Americans inscribe themselves on him, as well as he on America?

Such questions are difficult to answer from within bourgeois, author-centered ways of knowing texts – which is why it is important to ask them, not just of Humboldt but of all travel writing. Every travel account has this heteroglossic dimension; its knowledge comes not just out of a traveler's sensibility and powers of observation, but out of interaction and experience usually directed and managed by 'travelees', who are working from their own understandings of their world and of what the Europeans are and ought to be doing. For instance, Humboldt prided himself on being the first person to bring guano to Europe as a fertilizer, a 'discovery' that eventually led to the guano boom which by the end of the century caused a war between Peru and Chile and brought the latter's economy into total dependence on British bankers. Of course, Humboldt's discovery consisted

Figure 30.5

Pictorial representation of nature in the Andes (1805) after a drawing made by Humboldt in 1803 following his ascent of Mount Chimborazo (the written labels identify different botanical species found at the varying altitudes)

of coastal Peruvians telling him of the substance and its fertilizing properties. Who knows what their assumptions and expectations were? The conventions of travel and exploration writing (production and reception) constitute the European subject as a self-sufficient, monadic source of knowledge. That configuration virtually guarantees that the interactional history of the representation will turn up only as traces, or through the 'travelee's' own forms of representation, such as autoethnographic materials of the sort mentioned at points throughout this book.

[. . .]

In some sectors of creole culture, then, a glorified American nature and a glorified American antiquity already existed as ideological constructs, sources of Americanist identification and pride fueling the growing sense of separateness from Europe. In a perfect example of the mirror dance of colonial meaning-making, Humboldt transculturated to Europe knowledges produced by Americans in a process of defining themselves as separate from Europe. Following independence, Euroamerican elites would reimport that knowledge *as European knowledge* whose authority would legitimate Euroamerican rule.

Romantic interlude

The perspective I have been proposing on Humboldt's writings often provokes an impatient response among literary critics. What is the point, I am

Figure 30.6

Drawing by an indigenous Andean artist of the Cerro de Potosí, site of the largest silver mine in the Americas, dated 1588

asked, of all this historical–colonial–ideological explanatory apparatus, when it is perfectly obvious that Humboldt in his writings is simply *being* a romantic, simply *doing* Romanticism? As a Romantic, the German kind, how else would he write about South America? One need read no farther than the preface to *Views of Nature*, which ends with a quotation from Schiller's *Bride of Messina* about how nature is perfect till man deforms it with care. Before he had even set foot outside Prussia was Humboldt not the only scientist Schiller offered to publish in his journal? Though Schiller might not have seen it this way (he apparently disliked Humboldt), might one not argue, for example, that Humboldt in his American *Views* simply carries out the program of Schiller's *Aesthetic Education of Man* (1795)? Is it not the Romantics who call for the 'cultivation of the sensibilities'? Is Humboldt not, for example, trying to 'culture' his reader in the way Schiller prescribes: 'providing the receptive faculty with the most multifarious contacts with the world'?[11] Why does one need Columbus, Spanish colonialism, independence struggles, slave revolts, or even America to understand Humboldt's way of writing? What is already known about Romanticism provides a perfectly satisfying account without stepping beyond the borders of either Europe or Literature.

As some readers will have anticipated, it is that very satisfaction and those very borders I would call into question through Humboldt's American writings. To the extent that Humboldt 'is' a Romantic, Romanticism 'is' Humboldt; to the extent that something called Romanticism constitutes or 'explains' Humboldt's writing on America, those writings constitute and 'explain' that something. To argue that the former simply 'reflects' the latter is to privilege the Literary and the European in a way which must be opened to question. The perspective of this book would call for rethinking 'Romanticism' (and 'Literature', and 'Europe') in the light of writers like Humboldt and historical processes like changing contact with the Americas. 'Romanticism', then, provides an occasion to rethink habits of imagining 'Europe' and 'literature' as *sui generis* entities that invent themselves from within then project outward onto the rest of the world. One can glimpse what it is like to imagine 'Europe' as also constructing itself from the outside in, out of materials infiltrated, donated, absorbed, appropriated, and imposed from contact zones all over the planet.

To the degree that 'Romanticism' shapes the new discourses on America, Egypt, southern Africa, Polynesia, or Italy, *they* shape *it*. (Romantics are certainly known for stationing themselves round Europe's peripheries – the Hellespont, the Alps, the Pyrenees, Italy, Russia, Egypt.) Romanticism *consists*, among other things, of shifts in relations between Europe and other parts of the world – notably the Americas, which are, precisely, liberating themselves from Europe. If one unhooks Humboldt from Schiller and locates him in another 'Romantic' line – George Forster and Bernardin de St Pierre (two of Humboldt's personal idols), Volney, Chateaubriand, Stedman, Buffon, Le Vaillant, Captain Cook, and the Diderot of the 'Supplement to the Voyage of Bougainville' – one might be tempted to argue that Romanticism originated in the contact zones of America, North Africa, and the South Seas. [. . .]

Notes

1   Hanno Beck, 'The geography of Alexander von Humboldt', in Wolfgang-Hagen Hein (ed.), *Alexander von Humboldt: Life and Work*, trans. John Cumming (Ingelheim am Rhein, C. H. Boehringer Sohn, 1987) (German original 1985), pp. 221, 227.

2   Oscar Rodríguez Ortiz (ed.), *Imágenes de Humboldt* (Caracas, Monte Avila, 1983), p. 10.

3   Robert van Dusen, 'The literary ambitions and achievements of Alexander von Humboldt', *European University Papers* (Bern, Herbert Lang, 1971), p. 45.

4   Alexander von Humboldt, *Views of Nature*, trans. E.C. Otte and Henry G. Bohn (London, Henry G. Bohn, 1850), p. 3.

5   Ibid., pp. 7–8.

6   Quoted in *Alexander von Humboldt: Leben und Werken*, ed. Wolfgang-Hagen Hein (Ingeleheim am Rhein, C. H. Bochringer Sohn, 1985), trans. John Cumming (1987), p. 56.

7   Humboldt, *Views of Nature*, p. ix.

8   Ibid., p. 154.

9   Ibid., p. ix.

10   Christopher Columbus, Letter of March 14, 1493, in *Four Voyages to the New World: Letters and Selected Documents*, ed. and trans. R. H. Major (New York, Corinth Books, 1961), pp. 4–5.

11   Quoted by John Brenkman in *Culture and Domination* (Ithaca, Cornell University Press, 1988), p. 64.

Reading racial fetishism:
the photographs of Robert Mapplethorpe
Kobena Mercer

[. . .]

Imaging the black man's sex

[. . .] Mapplethorpe first made his name in the world of art photography with his portraits of patrons and protagonists in the post-Warhol New York avant-garde milieu of the 1970s. In turn he has become something of a star himself, as the discourse of journalists, critics, curators and collectors has woven a mystique around his persona, creating a public image of the artist as author of 'prints of darkness'.[1] As he has extended his repertoire across flowers, bodies and faces, the conservatism of Mapplethorpe's aesthetic has become all too apparent: a reworking of the old modernist tactic of 'shock the bourgeoisie' (and make them pay), given a new aura by his characteristic signature, the pursuit of perfection in photographic technique. The vaguely transgressive quality of his subject matter – gay S/M ritual, lady bodybuilders, black men – is given heightened allure by his evident mastery of photographic technology.

In as much as the image-making technology of the camera is based on the mechanical reproduction of unilinear perspective, photographs primarly represent a 'look'. I therefore want to talk about Mapplethorpe's *Black Males* not as the product of the personal intentions of the individual behind the lens, but as a cultural artifact that says something about certain ways in which white people 'look' at black people and how, in this way of looking, black male sexuality is perceived as something different, excessive, Other.[2] Certainly this particular work must be set in the context of Mapplethorpe's oeuvre as a whole: through his cool and deadly gaze each found object – 'flowers, S/M, blacks'[3] – is brought under the clinical

This chapter, originally published in 1986, is taken from Kobena Mercer, *Welcome to the Jungle* (London, Routledge, 1994), pp. 174–219.

precision of his master vision, his complete control of photo-technique, and thus aestheticized to the abject status of thinghood. However, once we consider the author of these images as no more than the 'projection, in terms more or less psychological, of our way of handling texts',[4] then what is interesting about work such as *The Black Book* is the way the text facilitates the imaginary projection of certain racial and sexual fantasies about the black male body. Whatever his personal motivations or creative pretensions, Mapplethorpe's camera-eye opens an aperture onto aspects of stereotypes – a fixed way of seeing that freezes the flux of experience – which govern the circulation of images of black men across a range of surfaces from newspapers, television and cinema to advertising, sport and pornography.

Approached as a textual system, both *Black Males* (1983) and *The Black Book* (1986) catalogue a series of perspectives, vantage points and 'takes' on the black male body. The first thing to notice – so obvious it goes without saying – is that all the men are *nude*. Each of the camera's points of view lead to a unitary vanishing point: an erotic/aesthetic objectification of black male bodies into the idealized form of a homogenous type thoroughly saturated with a totality of sexual predicates. We look through a sequence of individual, personally named, Afro-American men, but what we *see* is only their *sex* as the essential sum total of the meanings signified around blackness and maleness. It is as if, according to Mapplethorpe's line of sight: Black + Male = Erotic/Aesthetic Object. Regardless of the sexual preferences of the spectator, the connotation is that the 'essence' of black male identity lies in the domain of sexuality. Whereas the photographs of gay male S/M rituals invoke a subcultural sexuality that consists of *doing* something, black men are confined and defined in their very *being* as sexual and nothing but sexual, hence hypersexual. In pictures like 'Man in a Polyester Suit', apart from his hands, it is the penis and the penis alone that identifies the model in the picture as a black man.

This ontological reduction is accomplished through the specific visual codes brought to bear on the construction of pictorial space. Sculpted and shaped through the conventions of the fine art nude, the image of the black male body presents the spectator with a source of erotic pleasure in the act of looking. As a generic code established across fine art traditions in Western art history, the conventional subject of the nude is the (white) female body. Substituting the socially inferior black male subject, Mapplethorpe nevertheless draws on the codes of the genre to frame his way of seeing black male bodies as abstract, beautiful 'things' (see figures 31.1, 31.3 and 31.4). The aesthetic, and thus erotic, objectification is totalizing in effect, as all references to a social, historical or political context are ruled out of the frame. This visual codification abstracts and essentializes the black man's body into the realm of a transcendental aesthetic ideal. In this sense, the text reveals more about the desires of the hidden and visible white male subject behind the camera, and what 'he' wants-to-see, than it does about the anonymous black men whose beautiful bodies we see depicted.

Within the dominant tradition of the female nude, patriarchal power relations are symbolized by the binary relation in which, to put it crudely, men assume the active role of the looking subject while women are passive objects to be looked at. Laura Mulvey's contribution to feminist film theory revealed the normative power and privilege of the male gaze in dominant systems of visual representation.[5] The image of the female nude can thus be understood not so much as a representation of (hetero)sexual desire, but as a form of objectification which articulates masculine hegemony and dominance over the very apparatus of representation itself. Paintings abound with self-serving scenarios of phallocentric fantasy in which male artists paint themselves painting naked women, which, like depiction of feminine narcissism, constructs a mirror image of what the male subject wants-to-see. The fetishistic logic of mimetic representation, which makes present for the subject what is absent in the real, can thus be characterized in terms of a masculine fantasy of mastery and control over the 'objects' depicted and represented in the visual field, the fantasy of an omnipotent eye/I who sees but who is never seen.

In Mapplethorpe's case, however, the fact that both subject and object of the gaze are male sets up a tension between the active role of looking and the passive role of being looked at. This *frisson* of (homo)sexual sameness transfers erotic investment in the fantasy of mastery from gender to racial difference. Traces of this metaphorical transfer underline the highly charged libidinal investment of Mapplethorpe's gaze as it bears down on the most visible signifier of racial difference – black skin. In his analysis of the male pinup, Richard Dyer (1982) suggests that when male subjects assume the passive, 'feminized' position of being looked at, the threat or risk to traditional definitions of masculinity is counteracted by the role of certain codes and conventions, such as taught, rigid or straining bodily posture, character types and narrativized plots, all of which aim to stabilize the gender-based dichotomy of seeing/being seen.[6] Here, Mapplethorpe appropriates elements of commonplace racial stereotypes in order to regulate, organize, prop up and *fix* the process of erotic/aesthetic objectification in which the black man's flesh becomes burdened with the task of symbolizing the transgressive fantasies and desires of the white gay male subject. The glossy, shining, fetishized surface of black skin thus serves and services a white male desire to look and to enjoy the fantasy of mastery precisely through the scopic intensity that the pictures solicit.

As Homi Bhabha has suggested, 'an important feature of colonial discourse is its dependence on the concept of "fixity" in the ideological construction of otherness'.[7] Mass-media stereotypes of black men – as criminals, athletes, entertainers – bear witness to the contemporary repetition of such *colonial fantasy*, in that the rigid and limited grid of representations through which black male subjects become publicly visible continues to reproduce certain *idées fixes*, ideological fictions and psychic fixations, about the nature of black sexuality and the 'otherness' it is constructed to embody. As an artist, Mapplethorpe engineers a fantasy of absolute authority over the image of the black male body by appropriating the function of the stereotype to stabilize the erotic objectification of racial otherness and thereby affirm his own identity as the sovereign I/eye empowered with mastery over the abject thinghood of the Other: as if the pictures implied, Eye have the power to turn you, base and worthless creature, into a work of art. Like Medusa's look, each camera angle and photographic shot turns black male flesh to stone, fixed and frozen in space and time: enslaved as an icon in the representational space of the white male imaginary, historically at the centre of colonial fantasy.

There are two important aspects of fetishization at play here. The erasure of any social interference in the spectator's erotic enjoyment of the image not only reifies bodies but effaces the material process involved in the production of the image, thus masking the social relations of racial power entailed by the unequal and potentially exploitative exchange between the well-known, author-named artist and the unknown, interchangeable, black models. In the same way that labor is said to be 'alienated' in commodity fetishism, something similar is put into operation in the way that the proper name of each black model is taken from a person and given to a thing, as the title or caption of the photograph, an art object which is property of the artist, the owner and author of the look. And as items of exchange-value, Mapplethorpe prints fetch exorbitant prices on the international market in art photography.

The fantasmatic emphasis on mastery also underpins the specifically sexual fetishization of the Other that is evident in the visual isolation effect whereby it is only ever *one* black man who appears in the field of vision at any one time. As an imprint of a narcissistic, ego-centred, sexualizing fantasy, this is a crucial component in the process of erotic objectification, not only because it forecloses the possible representation of a collective or contextualized black male body, but because the solo frame is the precondition for a voyeuristic fantasy of unmediated and unilateral control over the other, which is the function it performs precisely in gay and straight pornography. Aestheticized as a trap for the gaze, providing pabulum on which the appetite of the imperial eye may feed, each image thus nourishes the racialized and sexualized fantasy of appropriating the Other's body as virgin territory to be penetrated and possessed by an all-powerful desire, 'to probe and explore an alien body'.[8]

Superimposing two ways of seeing – the nude which eroticizes the act of looking, and the stereotype which imposes fixity – we see in Mapplethorpe's gaze a reinscription of the fundamental *ambivalence* of colonial fantasy, oscillating between sexual idealization of the racial other an anxiety in defence of the identity of the white male ego. Stuart Hall (1982) has underlined this splitting in the 'imperial eye' by suggesting that for every threatening image of the black subject as a marauding native, menacing savage or rebellious slave, there is the comforting image of the black as docile servant, amusing clown and happy entertainer.[9] Commenting on this bifurcation in racial representations, Hall describes it as the expression of 'both a nostalgia for an innocence lost forever to the civilized, and the threat of civilization being over-run or undermined by the recurrence of savagery, which is always lurking just below the surface; or by an untutored sexuality threatening to 'break out'.[10] In Mapplethorpe, we may discern three discrete camera codes through which this fundamental ambivalence is reinscribed through the process of a sexual and racial fantasy which aestheticizes the stereotype into a work of art.

The first of these, which is most self-consciously acknowledged, could be called the *sculptural* code, as it is a subset of the generic fine art nude. As Phillip pretends to put the shot, the idealized physique of a classical Greek male statue is superimposed on that most commonplace of stereotypes, the black man as sports hero, mythologically endowed with a 'naturally' muscular physique and an essential capacity for strength, grace and machinelike perfection: well hard. As a major public arena, sport is a key site of white male ambivalence, fear and fantasy. The spectacle of black bodies triumphant in rituals of masculine competition reinforces the fixed idea that black men are 'all brawn and no brains', and yet, because the white man is beaten at his own game – football, boxing, cricket, athletics – the Other is idolized to the point of envy. This schism is played out daily in the popular tabloid press. On the front page headlines black males become highly visible as a threat to white society, as muggers, rapists, terrorists and guerrillas: their bodies become the imago of a savage and unstoppable capacity for destruction and violence. But turn to the back pages, the sports pages, and the black man's body is heroized and lionized; any hint of antagonism is contained by the paternalistic infantilization of Frank Bruno and Daley Thompson to the status of national mascots and adopted pets – they're not Other, they're OK because they're 'our boys'. The national shame of Englands' demise and defeat in Test Cricket at the hands of the West Indies is accompanied by the slavish admiration of Viv Richards's awesome physique – the high-speed West Indian batsman is both a threat and a winner. The ambivalence cuts deep into the recess of the white male imaginary – recall those newsreel images of Hitler's reluctant handshake with Jesse Owens at the 1936 Olympics.

If Mapplethorpe's gaze is momentarily lost in admiration, it reasserts control by also 'feminizing' the black male body into a passive, decorative *objet d'art*. When Phillip is placed on a pedestal he literally becomes putty in the hands of the white male artist – like others in this code, his body becomes raw material, mere plastic matter, to be molded, sculpted and shaped into the aesthetic idealism of inert abstraction, as we see in the picture of Derrik Cross (see figure 13.3): with the tilt of the pelvis, the black man's bum becomes a Brancusi. Commenting on the differences between moving and motionless pictures, Christian Metz suggests an association linking photography, silence and death as photographs invoke a residual death effect such that, 'the person who has been photographed is dead . . . dead for having been seen.'[11] Under the intense scrutiny of Mapplethorpe's cool, detached gaze it is as if each black model is made to die, if only to reincarnate their alienated essence as idealized, aesthetic objects. We are not invited to imagine what their lives, histories or experiences are like, as they are silenced as subjects in their own right, and in a sense sacrificed on the pedestal of an aesthetic ideal in order to affirm the omnipotence of the master subject, whose gaze has the power of light and death.

In counterpoint there is a supplementary code of *portraiture* which 'humanizes' the hard phallic lines of pure abstraction and focuses on the face – the 'window of the soul' – to introduce an element of realism into the scene. But any connotation of humanist expression is denied by the direct look which does not so much assert the existence of an autonomous subjectivity, but rather, like the remote, aloof, expressions of fashion models in glossy magazines, emphasizes instead maximum distance between the spectator and the unattainable object of desire. Look, but don't touch. The models' direct look to camera does not challenge the gaze of the white male artist, although it plays on the active/passive tension of seeing/being seen, because any potential disruption is contained by the subtextual work of the stereotype. Thus in one portrait the 'primitive' nature of the Negro is invoked by the profile: the face becomes an afterimage of a stereotypically 'African' tribal mask, high cheekbones and matted dreadlocks further connote wildness, danger, exotica. In another, the chiseled contours of a shaved head, honed by rivulets of sweat, summon up the criminal mug shot from the forensic files of police photography. This also recalls the anthropometric uses of photography in the colonial scene, measuring the cranium of the colonized so as to show, by the documentary evidence of photography, the inherent 'inferiority' of the Other.[12] This is overlaid with deeper ambivalence in the portrait of Terrel, whose grotesque grimace calls up the happy/sad mask of the nigger minstrel: humanized by racial pathos, the Sambo stereotype haunts the scene, evoking the black man's supposedly childlike dependency on ole Massa, which in turn fixes his social, legal and existential 'emasculation' at the hands of the white master.

Finally, two codes together – of *cropping* and *lighting* – interpenetrate the flesh and mortify it into a racial sex fetish, a juju doll from the dark side of the white man's imaginary. The body-whole is fragmented into microscopic details – chest, arms, torso, buttocks, penis – inviting a scopophilic dissection of the parts that make up the whole. Indeed, like a talisman, each part is invested with the power to evoke the 'mystique' of black male sexuality with more perfection than any empirically unified whole. The camera cuts away, like a knife, allowing the spectator to inspect the 'goods'. In such fetishistic attention to detail, tiny scars and blemishes on the surface of black skin serve only to heighten the technical perfectionism of the photographic print. The cropping and fragmentation of bodies – often decapitated, so to speak – is a salient feature of pornography, and has been seen from certain feminist positions as a form of male violence, a literal inscription of a sadistic impulse in the male gaze, whose pleasure thus consists of cutting up women's bodies into visual bits and pieces. Whether or not this view is tenable,[13] the effect of the technique here is to suggest aggression in the act of looking, but not as racial violence or racism-as-hate; on the contrary, aggression as the frustration of the ego who finds the object of his desire out of reach, inaccessible. The cropping is analogous to striptease in this sense, as the exposure of successive body parts distances the erotogenic object, making it untouchable so as to tantalize the drive to look, which reaches its aim in the denouement by

Figure 31.1
Robert
Mapplethorpe, Jimmy
Freeman, 1982 (The
Estate of Robert
Mapplethorpe)

Figure 31.2
Robert
Mapplethorpe,
Roedel Middleton,
1986 (The Estate of
Robert
Mapplethorpe)

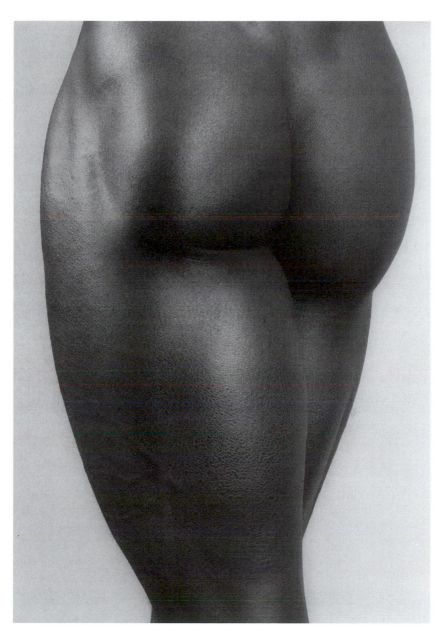

Figure 31.3

Robert
Mapplethorpe,
Derrik Cross, 1983
(The Estate of Robert
Mapplethorpe)

which the woman's sex is unveiled. Except here the unveiling that reduces the woman from angel to whore is substituted by the unconcealing of the black man's private parts, with the penis as the forbidden totem of colonial fantasy.

As each fragment seduces the eye into ever more intense fascination, we glimpse the dilation of a libidinal way of looking that spreads itself across the surface of black skin. Harsh contrasts of shadow and light draw the eye to focus and fix attention on the texture of the black man's skin. According to Bhabha, unlike the sexual fetish *per se*, whose meanings are usually hidden as a hermeneutic secret, skin color functions as '*the most visible of fetishes*'.[14] Whether it is devalorized in the signifying chain of 'negrophobia' or hypervalorized as a desirable attribute in 'negrophilia', the fetish of skin color in the codes of racial discourse constitutes the most visible element in the articulation of what Stuart Hall calls 'the ethnic signifier'.[15] The shining surface of black skin serves several functions in its representation: it suggests the physical exertion of powerful bodies, as black boxers always glisten like bronze in the illuminated square of the boxing ring; or, in pornography, it suggests intense sexual activity 'just before' the photograph was taken, a metonymic stimulus to arouse spectatorial participation in the imagined *mise-en-scène*. In Mapplethorpe's pictures the specular brilliance of black skin is bound in a double articulation as a fixing agent for the fetishistic structure of the photographs. There is a subtle slippage between representer and represented, as the shiny, polished, sheen of black skin becomes consubstantial with the luxurious allure of the high-quality photographic print. As Victor Burgin has remarked, sexual fetishism dovetails with commodity fetishism to inflate the economic value of the print in art photography as much as in fashion photography, the 'glossies'.[16] Here, black skin and print surface are bound together to enhance the pleasure of the white spectator as much as the profitability of these art-world commodities exchanged among the artist and his dealers, collectors and curators.

In everyday discourse *fetishism* probably connotes deviant or 'kinky' sexuality, and calls up images of leather and rubberwear as signs of sexual perversity. This is not a fortuitous example, as leather fashion has a sensuous appeal as a kind of 'second skin'. When one considers that such clothes are invariably black, rather than any other color, such fashion–fetishism suggests a desire to simulate or imitate black skin. On the other hand, Freud's theorization of fetishism as a clinical phenomenon of sexual pathology and perversion is problematic in many ways, but the central notion of the fetish as a metaphorical substitute for the absent phallus enables understanding of the psychic structure of disavowal, and the splitting of levels of conscious and unconscious belief, that is relevant to the ambiguous axis upon which negrophilia and negrophobia intertwine.

[. . .]

We have been looking at some pictures to talk about a certain way in which white peoples' 'looking' at black people involves a *racial fetishism*. The question of ambivalence underscored by Mapplethorpe's recuperation of commonplace stereotypes within a restaging of the classical male nude concerns the strange and uncharted landscape of the Western imaginary,

Figure 31.4

Robert Mapplethorpe, Thomas, 1986 (The Estate of Robert Mapplethorpe)

and more specifically, the political unconscious of white masculinity. However, in the current context, where the interventions of black feminists have prioritized issues at the interface of race, gender and sexuality, a new wave of black cultural practitioners are setting out to untangle our own ambivalences and to explore the diversity of sexual desires and identities within black communities. Refusing to think of ourselves as Other, such artists as Joan Riley and Jackie Kay in literature; Maureen Blackwood and Martina Attille of Sankofa Collective in filmmaking; visual artists shown in Lubaina Himid's *Thin Black Line* exhibition at the ICA in 1985, have all engaged questions of sex and race in representation in challenging ways.[17] Yet these initiatives have so far found little critical and theoretical support in debates about sexual representation.

In a conjuncture where progressive intellectual alliances among feminists, advocates of sexual politics, and critical theory in film and media studies have gained momentum in the academic world, the subject of race is still a structured absence from both public debate and course curricula. What worries me is the way a certain kind of psychoanalysis has come to function as a 'master discourse' in this situation, yet the ethnocentrism of classical Freudian theory remains unquestioned. While the concept of fetishism is suggestive precisely because it connects the economic and sexual contraflow of ideological investments, it is also problematic, for its roots in European thought lie in the colonizing discourses of missionaries and anthropologists on 'primitive religions'.[18] Moreover, the occlusion of race in the 1970s theorization of sexual difference is by the same token the instance of its heterosexism as well as its Eurocentrism. The Greek tragedy of Oedipus, as the grand narrative upon which desire-as-lack or 'castration' is based, is culture-bound despite the universalistic claims staked out for it. Other cultures may be patriarchal, but does that mean they produce an Oedipal sexuality?

The feminist appropriation of Lacanian psychoanalysis to theorize cultural struggles over the image has been profoundly enabling, but questions now being raised by cultural struggles over the meaning of 'race' suggest that universalist pretensions can be disenabling, for they preempt the development of pluralist perspectives on the intersections of multiple differences in popular culture. With regard to the psychoanalytic theory of fetishism, Metz confesses that 'it has helped me . . . (but) I have also used the theory of fetishism as a fetish.'[19] If psychoanalysis continues to offer insight into cultural practices such as photography because it is 'the founding myth of our emotional modernity', then perhaps the unanswered questions of race may render visible some of the many blind spots that characterize our intellectual postmodernity. [. . .]

Notes

1   Dick Tracings, *Time Out*, 3 November 1983.
2   References are primarily to Robert Mapplethorpe, *Black Males* (Amsterdam, Gallerie Jurka, 1983) (with an introduction by Edmund White); *Robert Mapplethorpe, 1970–*

    1983 (London, Institute of Contemporary Arts, 1983) (introduction by Allan Hollinghurst); and Robert Mapplethorpe, *The Black Book* (Munich, Schirmer/Mosel, 1986).

3   Hollinghurst, *Robert Mapplethorpe*, p. 13.

4   Michel Foucault, 'What is an author?', *Language Counter-memory, Practice*, ed. Donald Bouchard (Oxford, Basil Blackwell, 1977), p. 127.

5   Laura Mulvey 'Visual pleasure and narrative cinema', *Screen*, 16, 3 (autumn 1975) [extracted in Chapter 25 of this volume].

6   Richard Dyer (1982) 'Don't look now – the male pin-up', *Screen*, 23, 3–4, Sept/Oct. also the art historical perspective offered in Margaret Walters, *The Nude Male* (London, Paddington Press, 1978).

7   Homi K. Bhabha, 'The other question: the stereotype and colonial discourse', *Screen*, 24, 4 (1983), pp. 18–36 [extracted in Chapter 24 of this volume].

8   Edmund White, in Mapplethorpe, *Black Males*, p. v.

9   Stuart Hall, 'The whites of their eyes: racist ideologies and the media', in George Bridges and Rosalind Brunt (eds), *Silver Linings: Some Strategies for the Eighties* London, Lawrence and Wishart, 1981).

10   Ibid., p. 41.

11   Christian Metz, 'Photography and fetish', *October*, 34 (fall 1985), p. 85.

12   Anthropometric uses of photography are discussed in David Green, 'Classified subjects', *Ten.8*, 14 (1984); and 'Veins of resemblance: eugenics and photography', in *Photography/Politics: Two*, eds P. Holland, J. Spence and S. Watney (London, Photography Workshop/Comedia, 1986); and with reference to photography as surveillance, in Frank Mort, 'The domain of the sexual', and John Tagg, 'Power and photography', *Screen Education*, 32 (autumn 1980).

13   Rosalind Coward, 'Sexual violence and sexuality', *Feminist Review*, 11 (summer 1982), pp. 17–22.

14   Bhabha, 'The other question', p. 30.

15   Stuart Hall, 'Pluralism, race and class in Caribbean society', in *Race and Class in Post-Colonial Society* (New York, UNESCO).

16   Victor Burgin, 'Photography, fantasy, fiction', *Screen*, 21, 1 (spring 1980), p. 54.

17   See Joan Riley, *The Unbelonging* (London, The Women's Press, 1985); and poetry by Jackie Kay in *Feminist Review*, 18 (1984), and *A Dangerous Knowing* (London, Sheba Feminist Publishers, 1985). Related issues are raised by Martina Attille and Maureen Blackwood, 'Black Women and representation', in Charlotte Brundson (ed.), *Films for Women* (London, British Film Institute, 1986).

18   See Jean Baudrillard, 'Fetishism and ideology', *For a Critique of the Political Economy of the Sign* (St Louis, Telos Press, 1981 [1977]). An important genealogy of the concept of fetishism is provided by William Pietz, 'The problem of the fetish', parts 1, 2 and 3, in *Res*, 9 (spring 1985), pp. 5–17; 13 (spring, 1987), pp. 23–45; and 16 (autumn 1988), pp. 105–123.

19   Metz, 'Photography and fetish', p. 89.

Dark continents: epistemologies of racial and sexual
difference in psychoanalysis and the cinema
Mary Ann Doane

I The dark continent as trope

Freud's use of the term 'dark continent' to signify female sexuality is a
recurrent theme in feminist theory. The phrase transforms female sexuality
into an unexplored territory, an enigmatic, unknowable place concealed
from the theoretical gaze and hence the epistemological power of the
psychoanalyst. Femininity confounds knowledge while male sexuality is its
stable guarantee. Yet, the more pertinent question may not be 'What is the
dark continent?,' but 'Where is it?' The fact that Freud himself borrowed the
phrase from Victorian colonialist texts in which it was used to designate
Africa is often forgotten. As Patrick Brantlinger points out, 'Africa grew
"dark" as Victorian explorers, missionaries, and scientists flooded it with
light, because the light was refracted through an imperialist ideology
that urged the abolition of "savage customs" in the name of civilization.'[1]
The term is the historical trace of Freud's link to the nineteenth century
colonialist imagination. In its textual travels from the colonialist image of
Africa to Freud's description of female sexuality as enigma to feminist
theorists' critique of psychoanalysis (particularly in Luce Irigaray's
Speculum of the Other Woman), the phrase has been largely stripped of its
historicity. Something of Freud's link to this colonist imagination has been
lost as well. For although Freud did not recapitulate 'an imperialist ideology
that urged the abolition of "savage customs" in the name of civilization', the
binary opposition between the savage and the civilized in their relation to
sexuality was a formative element of his thinking, one often dismissed in
Lacanian influenced accounts as a 'pre-Freudian' aspect of the Freudian text.

[. . .]

The dark continent trope indicates the existence of an intricate
historical articulation of the categories of racial difference and sexual

This chapter is taken
from Mary Ann
Doane *Femmes
Fatales* (New York,
Routledge, 1991),
pp. 215–248.

difference. In it, there is an extraordinary condensation of motifs linking the white woman and the colonialist's notion of 'blackness'. Just as Africa was considered to be the continent without a history, European femininity represented a pure presence and timelessness (whose psychical history was held, by Freud, to be largely inaccessible). The trope, however, reduces and oversimplifies the extremely complex relations between racial and sexual difference articulated by the colonialist enterprise. For that enterprise required as a crucially significant element the presence of the black woman (who is relegated to non-existence by the trope). The colonialist discourses of photography, poetry, and the essay frequently equated the African woman and the African continent – the conquest of the former signified the successful appropriation of the latter. Within the context of a collection of photographs taken in Africa between 1840 and 1918, and with specific reference to a photograph entitled 'Girl of Beggiuk tribe', Nicolas Monti writes:

> In a very peculiar way eroticism became a medium for establishing contact, for penetrating the secret of nature, the reality and the 'otherness' of the continent. The seduction and conquest of the African woman became a metaphor for the conquest of Africa itself. A powerful erotic symbolism linked a woman's femininity so strongly to the attraction of the land that they became one single idea, and to both were attributed the same irresistible, deadly charm.[2]

Indeed, the photographic terms of the visibility of the dark continent dictated the incessant visualization of native eroticism.[3] Within a photographic discourse which brought the dark continent home to Europeans, the exotic and the erotic were welded together, situating the African woman as the signifier of an excessive, incommensurable sexuality. These images were later invoked to blame black women for the victimization inflicted upon them by white males.

As Sander L. Gilman had demonstrated, the female Hottentot became, for Europeans the exemplary representative of this hyperbolic sexuality. Medical dissections and treatises established her sexuality as a form of pathology associated with 'enlarged buttocks' and 'distended labia'. Gilman also describes the nineteenth century's cultural investment in constituting a close affinity between the female Hottentot and the white prostitute who is, similarly, the object of a certain medical pathology. The prostitute's physical anomalies as delineated by 'scientific' investigation as well as aesthetic representation are often strikingly comparable to those of the Hottentot, so much so that 'the perception of the prostitute in the late nineteenth century . . . merged with the perception of the black.'[4] In Manet's portrait, *Nana*, certain physical features such as enlarged buttocks and 'Darwin's ear' indicate that 'even Nana's seeming beauty is but a sign of the black hidden within. All her external stigmata point to the pathology within the sexualized female.'[5] And in Zola's novel, Nana dies of smallpox and in death 'begins to revert to the blackness of the earth, to assume the horrible grotesque countenance perceived as belonging to the world of the black, the world of the "primitive", the world of disease,'[6] Yet, this special kinship between the white woman and the black woman is a quite limited one. The white woman, in her unknowability and sexual excessiveness, does indeed have a close representational affiliation with blackness. On the other hand, the 'civilized' white woman, exemplar of culture, racial purity, and refinement, is situated as the polar opposite of the Hottentot. Nevertheless, what the representational affinity seems to indicate is a strong fear that white women are always on the verge of 'slipping back' into a blackness comparable to prostitution. The white woman would be the weak point in the system, the signifier of the always too tenuous hold of civilization.

Whether in the colonialist discourse of photography, the medical discourse delineated by Gilman, or the aesthetic languages of the nineteenth century, the hyperbolic sexualization of blackness is presented within a visual framework; it is a function of 'seeing' as an epistemological guarantee – Nana's 'blackness' emerges to the surface so that it can be seen and hence verified. It is not surprising, therefore, that the cinema as an institution would embrace the colonialist project and reinscribe its terms within its uniquely optical narrative logic. The privileged genre for this inscription is the travel narrative or adventure film of the 1930s, within which Merian C. Cooper's 1933 *King Kong* would be an exemplary instance. The eroticism of *King Kong* is a result of its titillating conjunction of blonde white femininity and the immense sexual power suggested by King Kong – undoubtedly linked to fears of black masculinity and its alleged uncontainability. Here, in the Hollywood cinema, as in Freud's trope of the dark continent, the term which undergoes erasure, becomes invisible, is the black woman. The representational violence inscribed within Hollywood's colonialist project would be most predictable within the adventure/horror genre of the 1930s. But it is particularly interesting to note the presence of such violence within the genre most closely associated with the white woman – the maternal melodrama. In Josef von Sternberg's 1932 *Blonde Venus*, Marlene Dietrich does cross over the line separating respectable femininity from prostitution (whiteness from blackness in the nineteenth century imagination). Yet, within the maternal melodrama, the figure of the prostitute is not the target of an unambiguous censure but of a sympathy manifested in the textual organization of pathos. Revised sexual mores connected with the emergence of the 'New Woman' in the 1920s required a more flexible understanding of white female sexuality which weakened the polarization between the respectable Victorian lady and the prostitute. Marlene Dietrich is, in fact, recuperated by the nuclear family at the end of the film. Yet, the near collapse of the moral opposition between types of white femininity also threatened to collapse certain racial distinctions as well, Nana's 'blackness within' is predicated upon her role as a prostitute (the nineteenth century locus of excessive female sexuality). If the white woman's excessive sexuality cannot be contained within that subclass, the status of the upper-class white woman as guarantee of racial purity is seriously threatened.

[. . .] Why have racial differences been insistently infused with sexual desires and prohibitions? Is psychoanalysis simply complicit in this operation or is it potentially useful in its analysis? Here, I single out the work of

Freud and Frantz Fanon as instances of a psychoanalytic engagement with these questions. The pivotal position of the white woman in a racist economy – a position which often relegates the black woman to a realm outside of femininity – is *enacted* in psychoanalysis in Freud's appeal to the dark continent metaphor as well as in Fanon's analysis of rape and its relation to female subjectivity. It is also enacted in the cinema, in films as diverse as D. W. Griffith's *Birth of a Nation* (1915) and Douglas Sirk's *Imitation of Life* (1959) [. . .]. But Fanon also provides a psychoanalysis of the surface and of visibility which is potentially useful in the analysis of the cinema's racial politics. For *Birth of a Nation*, instrumental in the historical development of the classical system of narrative, directly confronts the issue of visibility and its relation to racial politics by transforming the visible aspects of racial identity – blackness and whiteness – into signs whose theatricality is marked. [. . .]

II Psychoanalysis and race: the case of Fanon

Feminist neglect of or disregard for *where* the dark continent is located is symptomatic of a problem recently brought to the foreground in critical discourse. A psychoanalytically informed feminist theory is accused of hierarchizing sexual difference over racial difference and of being ill-equipped to deal with issues of racial oppression.[7] The allegation is not simply that psychoanalytic feminist theory has *neglected* the analysis of racial difference but that there is an active tension between them. If certain races (associated with the 'primitive') are constituted as outside or beyond the territory of the psychoanalytic endeavor – insofar as they lack repression or neurosis (perhaps even the unconscious) – the solution cannot be simply to take this system which posits their exclusion and apply it to them. The trope of the dark continent, through its territorialization of the trope of knowledge, indicates a difficulty here which is both theoretical and historical, to the extent that Freud's project is linked to the colonial imagination and its structuring binarism. Psychoanalysis, unshaken in its premises, cannot be *applied* to issues of racial difference but must be radically destabilized by them.

The work of Frantz Fanon (particularly *Black Skin, White Masks*)[8] constitutes one of the few attempts to activate psychoanalysis in the examination and indictment of the relation between colonizer and colonized – a relation subtended by racism. For Fanon, a psychoanalytical understanding of racism hinges on a close analysis of the realm of sexuality. This is particularly true of black–white relations since blacks are persistently attributed with a hypersexuality. Why is it sexuality which forms a major arena for the articulation of racism? From a psychoanalytic point of view, sexuality is the realm where fear and desire find their most intimate connection, where notions of otherness and the exotic/erotic are often conflated. Whether heterosexual or homosexual, sexuality is generally thought to be indissociable from the effects of polarization and differentiation, often linking them to structures of power and domination.

Fanon's Sartrean influenced *Black Skin, White Masks* organizes its investigation of colonialism and racism to a large extent through a tracing of the various permutations in the relations between black men and white women, black women and white men, and white men and black men (the excluded relation is that between white women and black women – a relation to which I will return later). [. . .]

III Vision, the body, and the cinema

Fanon, although he focuses upon black *male* subjectivity in this respect, produces an extremely insightful analysis of the representational power of racism and of its intersection with the psychical. And because this analysis circulates around questions of vision, visibility, and representability, there is a sense in which it is strongly applicable to black women, who are the objects of a double surveillance linked to race and gender. Yet Fanon, like Sartre, transforms the problematic of racial vision into an affair between men. In 'Black Orpheus', his introduction to an anthology of poetry by blacks espousing negritude,[9] Sartre discusses the seeing/being seen nexus from the white man's point of view.

> Here, in this anthology, are black men standing, black men who examine us; and I want you to feel, as I, the sensation of being seen. For the white man has enjoyed for three thousand years the privilege of seeing without being seen. It was a seeing pure and uncomplicated; the light of his eyes drew all things from their primeval darkness. The whiteness of his skin was a further aspect of vision, a light condensed. The white man, white because he was man, white like the day, white as truth is white, white like virtue, lighted like a torch of creation; he unfolded the essence, secret and white, of existence. Today, these black men have fixed their gaze upon us and our own gaze is thrown back in our eyes. . . .[10]

The transgressiveness of the notion of the black man 'looking back', actively appropriating the gaze, is underlined by its resistance to the biblical myth used to rationalize slavery and colonization, the story of Ham who after 'looking upon his father's nakedness' was cursed with descendants who would be both dark skinned and slaves.[11] In Sartre's account, 'the sensation of being seen' is alien to the white man – his own privileged vision makes him effectively invisible. Fanon's emphasis in his analysis of the black psyche is on a form of constant visibility – a disabling overvisibility – which is a function of skin color.

Skin becomes the locus of an alienation more acute to the extent that it is inescapable – *at first sight*, racial identity is ineluctably established and the Manichaean polarity of black/white with all its metaphysical implications is activated. As the site of various barriers as well as transactions between inside and outside, skin is a primary signifier of psychical intensity. In his psychoanalysis of surface (which often confounds the concept of the unconscious), Fanon foregrounds the corporeal prison of acute visibility inhabited by the black. Homi Bhabha, in an analysis of Fanon, maintains that

> The fetish of colonial discourse – what Fanon calls the epidermal schema – is not, like the sexual fetish, a secret. Skin, as the key signifier of cultural and racial difference in the stereotype, is the most visible of fetishes, recognized as common knowledge in a range of cultural, political, historical discourses, and plays a public part in the racial drama that is enacted every day in colonial societies.[12]

At one point Fanon begins to write of the 'internalization' of inferiority on the part of the black, but reconsiders and decides that the term 'epidermalization' is more appropriate. Wherever the black goes, his or her identity is immediately given as a function of the most visible organ – the skin. Fanon persistently returns to the imperative call – 'Look, a Negro!' – uttered by a little white boy in a state of fascination and terror. The call is a somewhat perverse version of the Althusserian process of interpellation or hailing. Although it addresses and at the same time refuses to address the black directly (the second person pronoun is not used), the exclamation fixes the black person, producing a subjectivity which is fully aligned with a process of reification. As Fanon puts it, 'I am overdetermined from without. I am the slave not of the "idea" that others have of me but of my own appearance.'[13]

Whiteness hence relegates blackness to a certain corporeal schema or, more accurately, to corporeality itself. The black *is* the body, *is* the biological. Fanon explains in detail how the black is subject to a hyper-awareness of the body which attends his/her overvisibility. The specificity of the black male's situation becomes apparent in its comparison with that of the Jew. Strongly influenced by Sartre's *Anti-Semite and Jew*, Fanon compares the punishment usually meted out to the Jew (murder or sterilization) to that associated with the black (castration).

> The penis, the symbol of manhood, is annihilated, which is to say that it is denied. The difference between the two attitudes is apparent. The Jew is attacked in his religious identity, in his history, in his race, in his relations with his ancestors and with his paternity; when one sterilizes a Jew, one cuts off the source; every time a Jew is persecuted, it is the whole race that is persecuted in his person. But it is in his corporeality that the Negro is attacked. It is as a concrete personality that he is lynched. It is as an actual being that he is a threat. The Jewish menace is replaced by the fear of the sexual potency of the Negro.[14]

The collapsing together of the concrete, the corporeal, and sexuality indicates that the fate of the black is that of a body locked into its own non-generalizability. Such a contingently defined threat would need to be countered repeatedly in a constantly renewed racism.

Yet, it is clearly the black *male* body which is at issue here and which poses the greatest threat to white male subjectivity. Fanon invokes Lacan's theory of the mirror stage in order to illuminate the articulation of image, identity, body and racial otherness. Although Fanon begins the discussion by pointing out that the black man is the 'real Other' for the white man and is perceived entirely on the level of the body image as 'the not-self', 'the unidentifiable, the unassimilable',[15] his analysis transforms itself into a discussion of the black's identification of himself as white (e.g. young Antilleans claiming in school compositions that they like vacations because they give them 'rosy cheeks').[16] But earlier, he hints at a more extensive interpretation of the mirror stage in its interracial dimension. Referring to the 'influence exerted on the body by the appearance of another body', Fanon claims, 'the Negro, because of his body, impedes the closing of the postural schema of the white man.'[17] In Lacanian psychoanalysis, the significance of the mirror phase lies in its provision of an illusory yet strong identity based on a body image. The image of a completely whole and unified body which props up the ego also provides the basis of the psychical terror associated with castration anxiety. To the extent that the black 'impedes the closing of the postural schema of the white man', to the extent that he poses the possibility of *another* body, his position would appear analogous to that of the woman in psychoanalysis, who embodies the threat of castration. Yet, the woman's threat is configured as a physical lack of absence while the black male's threat is posited as that of an *overpresence*, a monstrous penis. This overpresence is not unrelated to the hypervisibility associated with skin color (the penis being, in the Freudian account, not only the most visible of sexual organs but also metaphorically linked with the eye).[18] The *obviousness* of racial difference appears as the symptom of this surface politics of the psyche. This drama of the white male ego, which undoubtedly plays itself out differently in different historical epochs according to their varying distributions of bodies, can contribute to an explanation of the intense sexualization of racism in the colonialist and post-colonialist period.

The symbolic network which welds visibility, skin color, identity, image, and ego to castration anxiety gives a clue to the reasons for the disappearance of the black woman in Fanon's account, to the limitations of his knowledge about her. For within this schema, she is figuratively invisible, penis-less. This is true for Fanon even in the context of his discussion of the cinema, where one might anticipate the conjunction of spectacle and female sexuality. Fanon is concerned not so much with the spectacle on the screen as with the spectacle in the audience, the deeply troubling aspect of crossover identification. The black spectator has no access to the 'seeing pure and uncomplicated' of Sartre's white man. Identificatory procedures are instead testimony to the effectivity of the cultural imperialism of Hollywood. In another context, Kwame Njrumah has delineated what Brantlinger calls the 'special impact of the American mass media on the African situation'.[19]

> The cinema stories of fabulous Hollywood are loaded. One has only to listen to the cheers of an African audience as Hollywood's heroes slaughter red Indians or Asiatics to understand the effectiveness of this weapon. For, in the

developing continents, where the colonialist heritage has left a vast majority still illiterate, even the smallest child gets the message. . . . Here, truly, is the ideological under-belly of those political murders which so often use local people as their instruments.[20]

Fanon is also deeply concerned with the phenomenon of black identification with whites in their exploitative relation to the Other – particularly when the black is forced to realize that he *is* the Other. His privileged example is the reception of *Tarzan*, which takes on a different affective valence in different viewing contexts.

> Attend showings of a Tarzan film in the Antilles and in Europe. In the Antilles, the young Negro identifies himself *de facto* with Tarzan against the Negroes. This is much more difficult for him in a European theater, for the rest of the audience, which is white, automatically identifies him with the savages on the screen. It is a conclusive experience.[21]

Fanon's 'white mask' would be most fully in place in the cinema theater up until the moment of unmasking accomplished by the gaze of others. Fanon is extremely sensitive to the psychical impact of the representational field of race relations – children's stories, comic books, films. But because the oppressiveness of black cultural identity is so intimately connected to the anguish and anxiety of the visible, of the epidermal schema, the cinema would potentially be a prime site for the corroboration of such an identity. Its corroboration, however, takes place not on the screen (or not only on the screen) but in the theater itself. 'I cannot go to a film without seeing myself. I wait for me. The people in the theater are watching me, examining me, waiting for me. A Negro groom is going to appear. My heart makes my head swim.'[22] The space of the theater becomes a space of identificatory anxiety, a space where the gaze is disengaged from its 'proper' object, the screen, and redirected, effecting a confusion of the concept of spectacle. [. . .]

Notes

1   Patrick Brantlinger, 'Victorians and Africans: the genealogy of the myth of the dark continent', *Critical Inquiry*, 12, 1 (autumn 1985), p. 166.

2   Nicolas Monti (ed.), *Africa Then: Photographs 1840–1918* (New York, Knopf, 1987), p. 56.

3   See also Malek Alloula, *The Colonial Harem*, trans. Myrna Godzich and Wlad Godzich (Minneapolis, University of Minnesota Press, 1986).

4   Sander, L. Gilman, 'Black bodies, white bodies: toward an iconography of female sexuality in late nineteenth-century art, medicine, and literature', *Critical Inquiry*, 12 1 (autumn 1985), p. 229.

5   Ibid., p. 232.

6   Ibid., p. 235.

7   See, for instance, Jane Gaines, 'White privilege and looking relations: race and gender in feminist film theory', *Screen* 29, 4 (1988), pp. 12–27 [extracted in Chapter 27 of this volume].

8 Frantz Fanon, *Black Skin, White Masks*, trans. Charles Lam Markmann (New York, Grove Press, 1967) [extracted in Chapter 29 of this volume].

9 In *Black Skin, White Masks* (pp. 132–40), Fanon is highly critical of the argument about negritude Sartre presents in this introduction.

10 Jean-Paul Sartre, *Black Orpheus*, trans. S. W. Allen (Paris, Présence Africaine, 1963), pp. 7–8.

11 Winthrop D. Jordan, *White over Black: American Attitudes towards the Negro 1550–1812* (Baltimore, Penguin, 1969), pp. 17–19.

12 Homi K. Bhabha, 'The other questions: difference, discrimination and the discourse of colonialism', in Francis Barker, Peter Hulme, Margaret Iversen and Diana Loxley (eds), *Literature, Politics, and Theory: Papers from the Essex Conference, 1976–84*, (London, Methuen, 1986), pp. 165–6.

13 Fanon, *Black Skin, White Masks*, p. 116.

14 Ibid., pp. 163–4.

15 Ibid., p. 161

16 Ibid., p. 162.

17 Ibid., p. 160.

18 Sigmund Freud, 'The "uncanny",' *On Creativity and the Unconscious*, ed. Benjamin Nelson (New York, Harper and Row, 1958), pp. 122–61.

19 Brantlinger, 'Victorians and Africans', p. 199.

20 Ibid.

21 Fanon, *Black Skin, White Masks*, p. 152–3n.

22 Ibid., p. 140.

White   **Richard Dyer**

[. . .] Trying to think about the representation of whiteness as an ethnic category in mainstream film is difficult, partly because white power secures its dominance by seeming not to be anything in particular, but also because, when whiteness *qua* whiteness does come into focus, it is often revealed as emptiness, absence, denial or even a kind of death.

It is, all the same, important to try to make some headway with grasping whiteness as a culturally constructed category. 'Images of' studies have looked at groups defined as oppressed, marginal or subordinate – women, the working class, ethnic and other minorities (e.g. lesbians and gay men, disabled people, the elderly). The impulse for such work lies in the sense that how such groups are represented is part of the process of their oppression, marginalisation or subordination. The range and fertility of such work has put those groups themselves centre-stage in both analytical and campaigning activity, and highlighted the issue of representation as politics. It has, however, had one serious drawback, long recognised in debates about women's studies. Looking, with such passion and single-mindedness, at non-dominant groups has had the effect of reproducing the sense of the oddness, differentness, exceptionality of these groups, the feeling that they are departures from the norm. Meanwhile the norm has carried on as if it is the natural, inevitable, ordinary way of being human.

Some efforts are now being made to rectify this, to see that the norm too is constructed, although only with masculinity has anything approaching a proliferation of texts begun. Perhaps it is worth signalling here, before proceeding, two of the pitfalls in the path of such work, two convolutions that especially characterise male writing about masculinity – guilt and me too-ism. Let me state that, while writing here as a white person about whiteness, I do not mean either to display the expiation of my guilt about being white, nor to hint that it is also awful to be white (because it is an

This chapter is taken from *Screen*, vol. 29, no. 4 (1988), pp. 44–65.

inadequate, limiting definition of being human, because feeling guilty is such a burden). Studies of dominance by the dominant should not deny the place of the writer in relation to what s/he is writing about it, but nor should they be the green light for self-recrimination or trying to get in on the act.

Power in contemporary society habitually passes itself off as embodied in the normal as opposed to the superior.[1] This is common to all forms of power, but it works in a peculiarly seductive way with whiteness, because of the way it seems rooted, in common-sense thought, in things other than ethnic difference. The very terms we use to describe the major ethnic divide presented by Western society, 'black' and 'white', are imported from and naturalised by other discourses. Thus it is said (even in liberal text books) that there are inevitable associations of white with light and therefore safety, and black with dark and therefore danger, and that this explains racism (whereas one might well argue about the safety of the cover of darkness and the danger of exposure to the light); again, and with more justice, people point to the Judaeo-Christian use of white and black to symbolise good and evil, as carried still in such expressions as 'a black mark', 'white magic', 'to blacken the character' and so on.[2] I'd like to look at another aspect of commonsensical conflations of black and white as natural and ethnic categories by considering ideas of what colour is.

I was taught the scientific difference between black and white at primary school. It seemed a fascinating paradox. Black, which, because you had to add it to paper to make a picture, I had always thought of as a colour, was, it turned out, nothingness, the absence of all colour; whereas white, which looked just like empty space (or blank paper), was, apparently, all the colours there were put together. No doubt such explanations of colour have long been outmoded; what interests me is how they manage to touch on the construction of the ethnic categories of black and white in dominant representation. In the realm of categories, black is always marked as a colour (as the term 'coloured' egregiously acknowledges), and is always particularising; whereas white is not anything really, not an identity, not a particularising; whereas white is not anything really, not an identity, not a particularising quality, because it is everything – white is no colour because it is all colours.

This property of whiteness, to be everything and nothing, is the source of its representational power. On the one hand, as one of the people in the video *Being White*[3] observes, white domination is reproduced by the way that white people 'colonise the definition of normal'. Paul Gilroy similarly spells out the political consequences, in the British context, of the way that whiteness both disappears behind and is subsumed into other identities. He discusses the way that the language of 'the nation' aims to be unifying, permitting even socialists an appeal in terms of 'we' and 'our' 'beyond the margins of sectional interest', but goes on to observe that: 'there is a problem in these plural forms: who do they include, or, more precisely for our purposes, do they help to reproduce blackness and Englishness as mutually exclusive categories? . . . why are contemporary appeals to "the people" in danger of transmitting themselves as appeals to the white people?'[4] On the other hand, if the invisibility of whiteness colonises the definition of other norms – class, gender, heterosexuality, nationality and so on – it also masks whiteness as itself a category. White domination is then hard to grasp in terms of the characteristics and practices of white people. No one would deny that, at the very least, there are advantages to being white in Western societies, but it is only avowed racists who have a theory which attributes this to inherent qualities of white people. Otherwise, whiteness is presented more as a case of historical accident, rather than a characteristic cultural/historical construction, achieved through white domination.

The colourless multi-colouredness of whiteness secures white power by making it hard, especially for white people and their media, to 'see' whiteness. This, of course, also makes it hard to analyse. It is the way that black people are marked as black (are not just 'people') in representation that has made it relatively easy to analyse their representation, whereas white people – not there as a category and everywhere everything as a fact – are difficult, if not impossible, to analyse *qua* white. The subject seems to fall apart in your hands as soon as you begin. Any instance of white representation is always immediately something more specific – *Brief Encounter* is not about white people, it is about English middle-class people; *The Godfather* is not about white people, it is about Italian-American people; but *The Color Purple* is about black people, before it is about poor, southern US people.

This problem clearly faced the makers of *Being White*, a pioneering attempt to confront the notion of white identity. The opening vox pop sequence vividly illustrates the problem. Asked how they would define themselves, the white interviewees refer easily to gender, age, nationality or looks but never to ethnicity. Asked if they think of themselves as white, most say that they don't, though one or two speak of being 'proud' or 'comfortable' to be white. In an attempt to get some white people to explore what being white means, the video people's inability to see whiteness appears intractable. Sub-categories of whiteness (Irishness, Jewishness, Britishness) take over, so that the particularity of whiteness itself begins to disappear; then gradually, it seems almost inexorably, the participants settle in to talking with confidence about what they know: stereotypes of black people.

Yet perhaps this slide towards talking about blackness gives us a clue as to where we might begin to see whiteness – where its difference from blackness is inescapable and at issue. I shall look here at examples of mainstream cinema whose narratives are marked by the fact of ethnic difference. Other approaches likely to yield interesting results include: the study of the characterisation of whites in Third World or diaspora cinema; images of the white race in avowedly racist and fascist cinema; the use of the 'commutation test',[5] the imaginary substitution of black for white performers in films such as *Brief Encounter*, say or *Ordinary People* (if these are unimaginable played by black actors, what does this tell us about the characteristics of whiteness?) or, related to this, consideration of what ideas of whiteness are implied by such widespread observations as that Sidney Poitier or Diana Ross, say, are to all intents and purposes 'white'. What all these approaches share, however, is reference to that which is not white, as if only non-whiteness can give whiteness any substance. The reverse is not the case – studies of images of blacks, Native Americans, Jews and other ethnic minorities do not need the comparative element that seems at this stage indispensable for the study of whites.

The representation of white *qua* white beings to come into focus – in mainstream cinema, for a white spectator – in films in which non-white characters play a significant role. I want to look at three very different examples here – *Jezebel* (USA, Warner Brothers, 1938), *Simba* (GB, Rank Studios, 1955) and *Night of the Living Dead* (USA, 1969). Each is characteristic of the particular genre and period to which it belongs. *Jezebel* is a large-budget Hollywood feature film (said to have been intended to rival *Gone with the Wind*) built around a female star, Bette Davis; its spectacular pleasures are those of costume and decor, of gracious living, and its emotional pleasures those of tears. *Simba* is a film made as part of Rank's bid to produce films that might successfully challenge Hollywood at the box office, built around a male star, Dirk Bogarde; its spectacular pleasures are those of the travelogue, its emotional ones excitement and also the gratification of seeing 'issues' (here, the Mau-Mau in Kenya) being dealt with. *Night of the Living Dead* is a cheap, independently produced horror film with no stars; its spectacular and emotional pleasures are those of shock, disgust and suspense, along with the evident political or social symbolism that has aided its cult reputation.

The differences between the three films are important and will inform the ways in which they represent whiteness. There is some point in trying to see this continuity across three, nonetheless significantly different, films. There is no doubt that part of the strength and resilience of stereotypes of non-dominant groups resides in their variation and flexibility – stereotypes are seldom found in a pure form and this is part of the process by which they are naturalised, kept alive.[6] Yet the strength of white representation, as I've suggested, is the apparent absence altogether of the typical, the sense that being white is coterminous with the endless plenitude of human diversity. If we are to see the historical, cultural and political limitations (to put it mildly) of white world domination, it is important to see similarities, typicalities, within the seemingly infinite variety of white representation.

All three films share a perspective that associates whiteness with order, rationality, rigidity, qualities brought out by the contrast with black disorder, irrationality and looseness. It is their take on this which differs. *Simba* operates with a clear black–white binarism, holding out the possibility that black people can learn white values but fearing that white people will be engulfed by blackness. *Jezebel* is far more ambivalent, associating blackness with the defiance of its female protagonist – whom it does not know whether to condemn or adore. *Night* takes the hint of critique of whiteness in *Jezebel* and takes it to its logical conclusion, where whiteness represents not only rigidity but death.

What these films also share, which helps to sharpen further the sense of whiteness in them, is a situation in which white domination is contested, openly in the text of *Simba* and explicitly acknowledged in *Jezebel*. The narrative of *Simba* is set in motion by the Mau-Mau challenge to British occupation, which also occasions set pieces of debate on the issues of white rule and black responses to it; the imminent decline of slavery is only once or twice referred to directly in *Jezebel*, but the film can assume the audience knows that slavery was soon ostensibly to disappear from the southern states. Both films are suffused with the sense of white rule being at an end, a source of definite sorrow in *Simba*, but in *Jezebel* producing that mixture of disapproval and nostalgia characteristic of the white representation of the ante-bellum South. *Night* makes no direct reference to the state of ethnic play but, as I shall argue below, it does make implicit reference to the black uprisings that were part of the historical context of its making, and which many believed would alter irrevocably the nature of power relations between black and white people in the USA.

The presence of black people in all three films allows one to see whiteness as whiteness, and in this way relates to the existential psychology that is at the origins of the interest in 'otherness' as an explanatory concept in the representation of ethnicity.[7] Existential psychology, principally in the work of Jean-Paul Sartre, had proposed a model of human growth whereby the individual self becomes aware of itself as a self by perceiving its difference from others. It was other writers who suggested that this process, supposedly at once individual and universal, was in fact socially specific – Simone de Beauvoir arguing that it has to do with the construction of the male ego, Frantz Fanon relating it to the colonial encounter of white and black. What I want to stress here is less this somewhat metaphysical dimension,[8] more the material basis for the shifts and anxieties in the representation of whiteness suggested by *Simba*, *Jezebel* and *Night*.

The three films relate to situations in which whites hold power in society, but are materially dependent upon black people. All three films suggest an awareness of this dependency – weakly in *Simba*, strongly but still implicitly in *Jezebel*, inescapably in *Night*. It is this actual dependency of white on black in a context of continued white power and privilege that throws the legitimacy of white domination into question. What is called for is a demonstration of the virtues of whiteness that would justify continued domination, but this is a problem if whiteness is also invisible, everything and nothing. It is from this that the films' fascinations derive. I shall discuss them here in the order in which they most clearly attempt to hang on to some justification of whiteness, starting, then, with *Simba* and ending with *Night*. [Only one of the three examples is used in this extract.]

Simba

Simba is a characteristic product of the British cinema between about 1945 and 1965 – an entertainment film 'dealing with' a serious issue.[9] It is a colonial adventure film, offering the standard narrative pleasures of adventure with a tale of personal growth. The hero, Alan (Bogarde), arrives in

Kenya from England to visit his brother on his farm, finds he has been killed by the Mau-Mau and stays to sort things out (keep the farm going, find out who killed his brother, quell the Mau-Mau). Because the Mau-Mau were a real administrative and ideological problem for British imperialism at the time of the film's making, *Simba* also has to construct a serious discursive context for these pleasures (essentially a moral one, to do with the proper way to treat native peoples; toughness versus niceness). It does this partly through debates and discussions, partly through characters clearly representing what the film takes to be the range of possible angles on the subject (the bigoted whites, the liberal whites, the British-educated black man, the despotic black chief) but above all through the figure of the hero, whose adventures and personal growth are occasioned, even made possible, through the process of engaging with the late colonial situation. The way this situation is structured by the film and the way Alan/Bogarde rises to the occasion display the qualities of whiteness.

Simba is founded on the 'Manicheism delirium' identified by Frantz Fanon as characteristic of the colonialist sensibility;[10] it takes what Paul Gilroy refers to as an 'absolutist view of black and white cultures, as fixed, mutually impermeable expressions of racial and national identity, [which] is a ubiquitous theme in racial "common sense"'.[11] The film is organised around a rigid binarism, with white standing for modernity, reason, order, stability, and black standing for backwardness, irrationality, chaos and violence. This binarism is reproduced in every detail of the film's *mise-en-scène*. A sequence of two succeeding scenes illustrates this clearly – a meeting of the white settlers to discuss the emergency, followed by a meeting of the Mau-Mau (see figure 33.1). The whites' meeting takes place in early evening, in a fully lit room; characters that speak are shot with standard high key lighting so that they are fully visible; everyone sits in rows and although there is disagreement, some of it hot-tempered and emotional, it is expressed in grammatical discourse in a language the British viewer can understand; moreover, the meeting consists of nothing but speech. The black meeting, on the other hand, takes place at dead of night, out of doors, with all characters in shadow; even the Mau-Mau leader is lit with extreme sub-Expressionist lighting that dramatises and distorts his face; grouping is in the form of a broken, uneven circle; what speech there is is ritualised, not reasoned, and remains untranslated (and probably in no authentic language anyway), and most vocal sounds are whooping, gabbling and shrieking; the heart of the meeting is in any case not speech, but daubing with blood and entrails and scarring the body. The return to whiteness after this sequence is once again a return to daylight, a dissolve to the straight lines of European fencing and vegetable plots.

The emphasis on the visible and bounded in this *mise-en-scène* (maintained throughout the film) has to do with the importance of fixity in the stereotyping of others – clear boundaries are characteristic of things white (lines, grids, not speaking till someone else has finished and so on), and also what keeps whites clearly distinct from blacks. The importance of the process of boundary establishment and maintenance has long been

Figure 33.1

*Binarism in Simba's
mise-en-scène: white
culture (above) and
black culture (below)*

recognised in discussions of stereotyping and representation.[12] This process is functional for dominant groups, but through it the capacity to set boundaries becomes a characteristic attribute of such groups, endlessly reproduced in ritual, costume, language and, in cinema, *mise-en-scène*. Thus, whites and men (especially) become characterised by 'boundariness'.[13]

Simba's binarism is in the broadest sense racist, but not in the narrower sense of operating with a notion of intrinsic and unalterable biological bases for differences between peoples.[14] It is informed rather by a kind of evolutionism, the idea of a path of progress already followed by whites, but in principle open to all human beings – hence the elements in the binarism of modernity versus backwardness. Such evolutionism raises the possibility of blacks becoming like whites, and it is the belief in this possibility that underpins the views of the liberal characters in the film, Mary (Virginia McKenna) and Dr Hughes (Joseph Tomelty), the latter pleading with his fellow settlers at the meeting to 'reason', not with the Mau-Mau but with the other Africans, who are not beyond the reach of rational discussion. The possibility is further embodied in the character of Peter Karanja (Earl Cameron), the son of the local chief (Orlando Martins), who has trained to be a doctor and is now running a surgery in the village. The film is at great pains to establish that Peter is indeed reasonable, rational, humane, liberal. It is always made quite clear to the viewer that this is so and the representatives of liberalism always believe in him; it is the whites who do not trust him, and one of Alan's moral lessons is in learning to respect Peter's worth. It seems then that part of the film is ready to take the liberal evolutionist position. Yet it is also significant that the spokespeople for liberalism (niceness and reason) are socially subordinate; a woman and an Irish doctor (played for comic eccentricity most of the time), and that liberalism fails, with its representatives (Mary, Peter and now won-over Alan) left at the end of the film crouched in the flames of Alan's farm, rescued from the Mau-Mau in the nick of time by the arrival of the white militia, and Peter dying from wounds inflicted on him by the Mau-Mau (represented as a black mob). Although with its head, as it were, the film endorses the possibility of a black person becoming 'white', this is in fact deeply disturbing, setting in motion the anxiety attendant on any loosening of the fixed visibility of the colonised other. This anxiety is established from the start of the film and is the foundation of its narrative.

As is customary in colonial adventure films, *Simba* opens with a panoramic shot of the land, accompanied here by birdsong and the sound of an African man singing. While not especially lush or breathtaking, it is peaceful and attractive. A cry of pain interrupts this mood and we see the man who has been singing stop, get off his bicycle and walk towards its source to find a white man lying covered in blood on the ground. The black man kneels by his side, apparently about to help him, but then, to the sound of a drum-roll on the soundtrack, draws his machete and plunges it (off screen) into the wounded man. He then walks back to his bike and rides off. Here is encapsulated the fear that ensues if you can't see black men behaving as black men should, the deceptiveness of a black man in Western clothes riding a bike. This theme is then reiterated throughout the film. Which of the servants can be trusted? How can you tell who is Mau-Mau and who not? Why should Alan trust Peter?

This opening sequence is presented in one long take, using panning. As the man rides off, the sound of a plane is heard, the camera pans up and there is the first cut of the film, to a plane flying through the clouds. There follows (with credits over) a series of aerial shots of the African landscape, in one of which a plane's shadow is seen, and ending with shots of white settlement and then the plane coming to land. Here is another aspect of the film's binarism. The credit sequence uses the dynamics of editing following the more settled feel of the pre-credit long take; it uses aerial shots moving through space, rather than pans with their fixed vantage point; it emphasises the view from above, not that from the ground, and the modernity of air travel after the primitivism of the machete. It also brings the hero to Africa (as we realise when we see Bogarde step off in the first post-credit shot), brings the solution to the problems of deceptive, unfixed appearances set up by the pre-credit sequence.

Simba's binarism both establishes the differences between black and white and creates the conditions for the film's narrative pleasures – the disturbance of the equilibrium of clear-cut binarism, the resultant conflict that the hero has to resolve. His ability to resolve it is part of his whiteness, just as whiteness is identified in the dynamism of the credit sequence (which in turn relates to the generic expectations of adventure) and in the narrative of personal growth that any colonial text with pretensions also has. The Empire provided a narrative space for the realisation of manhood, both as action and maturation.[15] The colonial landscape is expansive, enabling the hero to roam and giving us the entertainment of action; it is unexplored, giving him the task of discovery and us the pleasures of mystery; it is uncivilised, needing taming, providing the spectacle of power; it is difficult and dangerous, testing his machismo, providing us with suspense. In other words, the colonial landscape provides the occasion for the realisation of white male virtues, which are not qualities of being but of doing – acting, discovering, taming, conquering. At the same time, colonialism, as a social, political and economic system, even in fictions, also carries with it challenges of responsibility, of the establishment and maintenance of order, of the application of reason and authority to situations. These, too, are qualities of white manhood that are realised in the process of the colonial text, and very explicitly in *Simba*. When Alan arrives at Nairobi, he is met by Mary, a woman to whom he had proposed when she was visiting England; she had turned him down, telling him, as he recalls on the drive to his brother's farm, that he had 'no sense of responsibility'. Now he realises that she was right; in the course of the film he will learn to be responsible in the process of dealing with the Mau-Mau, and this display of growth will win him Mary.

But this is a late colonial text, characterised by a recognition that the Empire is at an end, and not unaware of some kinds of liberal critique of colonialism. So *Simba* takes a turn that is far more fully explored by, say,

Black Narcissus (1947) or the Granada TV adaptation of *The Jewel in the Crown* (1982). Here, maturity involves the melancholy recognition of failure. This is explicitly stated, by Sister Clodagh in *Black Narcissus*, to be built into the geographical conditions in which the nuns seek to establish their civilising mission ('I couldn't stop the wind from blowing'); it is endlessly repeated by the nice whites in *The Jewel in the Crown* ('There's nothing I can do!') and symbolised in the lace shawl with butterflies 'caught in the net' that keeps being brought out by the characters. I have already suggested the ways in which liberalism is marginalised and shown to fail in *Simba*. More than this, the hero also fails to realise the generically promised adventure experiences: he is unable to keep his late brother's farm going, nor does he succeed in fighting off a man stealing guns from his house; he fails to catch the fleeing leader of the Mau-Mau, and is unable to prevent them from destroying his house and shooting Peter. The film ends with his property in flames and – a touch common to British social conscience films – with a shot of a young black boy who symbolises the only possible hope for the future.

The repeated failure of narrative achievement goes along with a sense of white helplessness in the face of the Mau-Mau (the true black threat), most notably in the transition between the two meeting scenes discussed above. Alan has left the meeting in anger because one of the settlers has criticised the way his brother had dealt with the Africans (too soft); Mary joins him, to comfort him. At the end of their conversation, there is a two-shot of them, with Mary saying of the situation, 'it's like a flood, we're caught in it.' This is accompanied by the sound of drums and is immediately followed by a slow dissolve to black people walking through the night towards the Mau-Mau meeting. The drums and the dissolve enact Mary's words, that the whites are helpless in the face of the forces of blackness.

Simba is, then, an endorsement of the moral superiority of white values of reason, order and boundedness, yet suggests a loss of belief in their efficacy. This is a familiar trope of conservatism. At moments, though, there are glimpses of something else, achieved inadvertently perhaps through the casting of Dirk Bogarde. It becomes explicit in the scene between Mary and Alan just mentioned, when Alan says to Mary, 'I was suddenly afraid of what I was feeling', referring to the anger and hatred that the whole situation is bringing out in him and, as Mary says, everyone else. The implication is that the situation evokes in whites the kind of irrational violence supposedly specific to blacks. Of course, being white means being able to repress it and this is what we seem to see in Alan throughout the film. Such repression constitutes the stoic glory of the imperial hero, but there is something about Bogarde in the part that makes it seem less than admirable or desirable. Whether this is suggested by his acting style, still and controlled, yet with fiercely grinding jaws, rigidly clenched hands and very occasional sudden outbursts of shouting, or by the way Rank was grooming him against the grain of his earlier, sexier image (including its gay overtones),[16] it suggests a notion of whiteness as repression. [. . .]

Notes

1 Cf. Herbert Marcuse, *One Dimensional Man* (Boston, Beacon Press, 1964).

2 Cf. Winthrop Jordan, *White over Black* (Harmondsworth, Penguin, 1969); Peter Fryer, *Staying Power* (London Pluto, 1984).

3 Made by Tony Dowmunt, Maris Clark, Rooney Martin and Kobena Mercer for Albany Video, London.

4 Paul Gilroy, *There Ain't No Black in the Union Jack* (London, Hutchinson, 1987), pp. 55-6. See also the arguments about feminism and ethnicity in Hazel Carby, 'White woman listen! Black feminism and the boundaries of sisterhood', in Centre for Contemporary Cultural Studies, *The Empire Strikes Back* (London, Hutchinson, 1982), pp. 212–23.

5 John O. Thompson, 'Screen acting and the commutation test', *Screen*, 29, 2 (summer 1978), pp. 55–70.

6 See T. E. Perkins, 'Rethinking stereotypes', in Michele Barrett et al. (eds), *Ideology and Cultural Practice* (New York, Croom Helm), pp. 135–59; Steve Neale, 'The same old story', *Screen Education*, 80, 32–3 (autumn/winter 1979) pp. 33–8. For a practical example, see the British Film Institute study pack, *The Dumb Blonde Stereotype*.

7 See Frantz Fanon, *Black Skin, White Masks* (London, Pluto, 1986, extracted in Chapter 29 of this volume); Edward Saïd. *Orientalism* (London, Routledge and Kegan Paul, 1978); Homi K. Bhabha, 'The other question: the stereotype and colonial discourse', *Screen*, 24, 4 (November/December 1983), pp. 18–36 [extracted in Chapter 24 of this volume].

8 See Benita Parry, 'Problems in current theories of colonial discourse', *Oxford Literary Review*, 9, 1–2 (1987), pp. 27–58.

9 See John Hill, *Sex Class and Realism* (London, British Film Institute, 1986), chs 4 and 5.

10 Fanon, *Black Skin, White Masks*, p. 183.

11 Gilroy, *Ain't No Black*, p. 61; see Errol Lawrence, 'In the abundance of water the pool is thirsty: sociology and black pathology', in Centre for Contemporary Cultural Studies, *The Empire Strikes Back*, pp. 95–142.

12 For example, Homi Bhabha, 'The other question'; Richard Dyer, 'Stereotyping', in Richard Dyer (ed.), *Gays and Film* (London, British Film Institute, 1977), pp. 27–39; Sandor L. Gilman, *Difference and Pathology* (Ithaca, Cornell University Press, 1985).

13 Cf. Nancy Chodorow, *The Reproduction of Mothering* (Berkeley, University of California Press, 1978).

14 Michael Banton, *The Idea of Race* (London, Tavistock, 1977); this restrictive definition of racism has been disputed by, *inter alia*, Stuart Hall, 'Race, articulation and societies structured in dominance', in UNESCO, *Sociological Theories: Race and Colonialism*, (Paris, UNESCO, 1980).

15 Cf. Stuart Hall, 'The whites of their eyes: racist ideologies and the media' in George Bridges and Rosalind Brunt (eds), *Silver Linings: Some Strategies for the Eighties* (London, Lawrence and Wishart, 1981), pp. 28–52.

16 See Andy Medhurst, 'Dirk Bogarde', in Charles Barr, *All Our Yesterdays* (London, British Film Institute, 1986), pp. 346–54.

Index

Note: Illustrations are indicated by page references in *italics*.

Barnes, C., 275
Barnes, Thomas, 258, *260*
Barthes, Roland, 4, 13, 16, 33–40, 42–3, 108, 186, 364, 393
  on anchorage and relay, 48
  on myth, 14, 51–8, 275
Barton, I., 274
Baudelaire, Charles, 52, 115, 224
Baudrillard, Jean, 19, 109, 110, 119, 229
Bazin, André, 213
Beato, Felice, 197
beauty, cult of, 76
de Beauvoir, Simone, 461
Being White (video), 458
Bellour, Raymond, 392, 393
Belsey, Catherine, 136
Benjamin, Walter, 2, 5, 6, 14, 16–17, 43, 72–9, 181, 240
Bentham, Jeremy, 63, 67, 69, 251, 260–1
Berenson, Bernard, 24
Berger, John, 108, 113, 147
Bhabha, Homi, 313–14, 370–8, 437, 444, 453
the Bible, 99–100
birth, 342–3
Birth of a Nation (film), 451
black male body, 435–47, 453–4
Black Narcissus (film), 466
blackness, 417–20, 449–50, 452–3, 458
Blackwood, Maureen, 446
Blake, William, 100
Blonde Venus (film), 450
body
  black male, 435–47, 453–4
  political technology of the, 250
  territorialization of the, 342–3
Boetticher, Budd, 384
Bogdan, R., 277
Boice, Bruce, 215, 221
Bonpland, Aimé, 421–2
Bourdieu, Pierre, 129, 130, 133–4, 162–80, 289
Bourne, Samuel, 197
Brantlinger, Patrick, 448, 454–5
Brecht, Bertolt, 42

Brody, Neville, 100
Broodthaers, Marcel, 240
Brushfield, T.N., 257
Bryson, Norman, 11, 12, 23–31
Buck Morss, Susan, *5*
Buen, Daniel, 240
Burger, Peter, 136, 228, 229, 240
Burgin, Victor, 12, 13, 14, 18, 41–50, 136, 144, 145, 226, 240, 303, 444

career, 201
cartoons, 38
castration, 313, 324, 334
castration anxiety, 325, 373, 385–6, 454
Cavell, Stanley, 201
charity practice and ethos, 278–83
Charlesworth, Sarah, 226
Chavez, Pearl, 394
chiasmus, 47
Children's Homes, photography in, 258–60
China, photography in, 88–91, 92
Chung Kuo (film), 88–90
Cimabue, John, 24, 27, *28*
cinema, 177–8
  see also film
class, 134, 142, 154, 158, 403, 404, 407
class ethos, 178
Cocteau, Jean, 85
colonial discourse, 313–14, 370–8, 437, 453
Columbus, Christopher, 429–30
comic strips, 38
commissions, photographic, 202
commodity fetishism, 18
connotation, 14, 36, 39, 40
conscious fantasy, 356, 358, 359
  see also day-dreams
consumption
  of photographic images, 93
  production of, 19, 291–2
context, and meaning, 184
contrast, photographic, 43, 44, 45
Cook, Pam, 385
Cooper, Merian C., 450